PEARSON

Kenneth A. Koenigshofer, Ph.D.

Mind Design

The Adaptive Organization of Human Nature, Minds, and Behavior

Pearson Learning Solutions, 501 Boylston Street, Suite 900, Boston, MA 02116
A Pearson Education Company
www.pearsoned.com

Printed in the United States of America

1 2 3 4 5 6 7 8 9 10 V036 16 15 14 13 12 11

000200010270567666

CT/TB

ISBN 10: 1-256-33652-1
ISBN 13: 978-1-256-33652-5

To my wife CC, our children Gena and John, my son Paul, my granddaughter Kiona, and to my siblings Eric, Mindy, John, and George (Oso)—special thanks to my brother John for all the stimulating and enlightening discussions we have shared over the years.

—

In loving memory of our parents
George Andrew Koenigshofer ("Brownie")
And
Della Lucille (Dodrill) Koenigshofer ("Sis")

—

And of my friend,
Huynh Thi Pham Drost,
who fought ALS for 14 years with
her characteristic courage, humor, and grace

CONTENTS

CHAPTER ONE

The Majesty of Nature

In this book, I hope to inform the reader about a new direction for psychology, which I hope will lead to more useful and accurate conceptualizations of mind and behavior, not only for psychologists and social scientists but for the general public as well. It is my view that psychology has been without a clear organizing principle throughout much of its 130 year history as a separate discipline, once it emerged out of philosophy and sensory physiology in the 1880's. Furthermore, and perhaps, even more significantly, most of the human population at large, in everyday life, continues to rely upon superstition, outdated and inaccurate pop psychology, traditional misinformation, "old wives' tales," and other unreliable sources as the basis for its "folk psychology," the "common sense" set of assumptions and beliefs about human nature, the mind, and human behavior that most people accept (mostly unconsciously, or at least uncritically) as they live their lives and interact with one another, whether as individuals or as nations. Just as centuries ago people were afflicted with widespread mistaken beliefs about the physical world (for example, that the earth was flat and the stationary center of the universe, that disease was caused by demons or imbalances in body "humors," that the stars were only a few thousand miles away, that the sun needed human blood to continue to shine), most people today are in a kind of "Dark Ages" with respect to their knowledge and beliefs about human nature, human motivation and emotions, thought and perception, and the purposes, organization, and nature of their own minds and behavior in general.

We are entering a new age of human understanding. We are just beginning to apply the methods and the conceptual framework of the natural sciences to an understanding of ourselves and our fellow human beings. Scientific thinking has followed an interesting path, first being applied to those aspects of the universe most distant from us, the stars and planets, marked by the development of scientific astronomy and physics, with the thinking and discoveries of such intellectual pioneers as Newton, Galileo,

1

Copernicus, and Tycho Brahe. Later, discoveries by other pioneers such as Vesalius (human anatomy), Schwann (cell theory), and Harvey (circulation of the blood) began to change thinking about anatomy and the physical processes of life, processes much closer to us psychologically than the purely physical forces controlling the inanimate objects of astronomy and physics. Understanding living things as natural phenomena, subject to the same laws of the physical world, led to the demise of 19th century *vitalism* (the belief that a non-physical "vital force" set living things apart from non-living matter), a crucial step in the emergence of a scientific biology, highlighted by the development in the mid-1800's of the cornerstone of modern biology, Darwin's theory of evolution by natural selection.

Just as the development of scientific ideas in astronomy and physics has slowly changed our understanding of our place in the physical universe, modern biology continues to change our views about the nature of life, and thus of ourselves. But with the advent of scientific psychology, scientific thinking is now penetrating even closer to our core. Scientific thinking and scientific methods are no longer confined to the external world of inanimate objects, or even to the physical processes of our bodies, but now this continuing process of revelation about how the natural world works has reached into our minds and our own human nature. And just as scientific views in physics, astronomy and biology have radically changed our views of our world and of ourselves over the past few hundred years, discoveries in psychology and neuroscience will radically and deeply change our understanding of ourselves and our place in the universe. However, until psychology finds its unifying principle, its fundamental and universal laws, it will not have its full impact. Without a unifying principle to guide the formulation of its laws, it will continue to struggle to find its place, and it will fail to fundamentally change the way we think about ourselves, about our minds and our actions.

Psychology needs a new paradigm. It is my firm conviction that this paradigm is to be found in biology. To put it another way, psychology, which is typically defined by psychologists as the scientific study of mind and behavior, is really studying the organism, or at least a part of it. Mind and behavior are really biological processes, firmly rooted in the physical operations of a biological organ, the brain. The brain, like other organs, must be subject to the same laws of biology that apply to other organs of the body. Simply because its operations are more complex, or because its operations are of an information processing nature, or because its functions include such things as language, emotions, perceptions, thoughts, or the production of social behavior and other complex, goal-directed movement, none of this precludes the fact that the brain is a physical entity subject to the same laws of biology that govern biological processes in general. Minds and behavior are functions of organisms and like any other biological process must be thought of in broadly biological terms. The minds and behavior of organisms must have biological origins, biological functions or "purposes," and must follow biological laws, particularly the most fundamental law, which unified all of biology, the law of evolution by natural selection.

It is no wonder that this idea has not yet penetrated deeply into the field of psychology, much less into social science and the human population at large. The approach is still at the fringe, far from the core understanding of most psychologists. According to a study conducted by the American Psychological Association in 2004, only 3% of psychologists specialize in biological psychology, physiological psychology, or neuroscience, and only a handful specialize in the new field of evolutionary psychology. Psychology is still dominated by its original paradigm, termed the Standard Social Science Model (SSSM) by UC Santa Barbara evolutionary psychologists, John Tooby (of the UCSB Anthropology Department) and Leda Cosmides (UCSB Psychology Department; see Cosmides and Tooby, 1987). This founding paradigm is called the Standard Social Science Model because it is the standard set of assumptions and beliefs about the human mind, human nature, and human behavior which shaped the thinking of those who founded the social sciences and psychology in the mid to late 1800's. Among the major assumptions of the SSSM, derived from Aristotle and later from the group of philosophers known as the British Empiricists, is the conviction that "learning is everything" and that biological influences, such as brain processes and particularly innate factors such as genetics and genetic evolution, are not important to an understanding of human nature, the human mind and behavior. In fact, as Harvard psychologist Steven Pinker (2002) has pointed out, the standard view goes so far as to deny the existence of any innate human nature. In the SSSM, experience is everything, while genes and genetic evolution are considered mostly irrelevant, or at best, a distant second in the causation of human mental processes and behavior. But I believe that this is completely reversed.

In fact, genetic information and the genetic evolution of each species (which is the ultimate source of genetic information) are the prime causes of the mental and behavioral organization of its members. Experience is important, but it is secondary, supplementary, and entirely dependent upon the genetically evolved circuit "design" of the brain of the species having the experiences. Experience doesn't operate in a vacuum. It only operates on the brain, and the brain comes equipped from birth with species-typical brain circuitry which dictates how and when, in the course of development, any experience will influence behavior and the mind. The specific kinds of experience, and the ways in which any experience can affect the mind or behavior, is strictly dictated by the genetic organization of the brain of that species, especially the genetically evolved organization of its species-typical learning circuitry, upon which its specific abilities for specific forms of learning depend.

The new field of epigenetics is making exciting discoveries about how experiences during one's individual lifetime can influence the expression of genes affecting many aspects of the organism's functioning, including the effects of stressful experiences on susceptibility to diseases such as cancer. But epigenetics just serves to emphasize the more general principle that experience always only affects the organism in interaction, to a determining degree, with genes and thus with the genetic evolution of the species, the ultimate source of the species-typical information in the DNA of every individual.

Learning and experience during the lifetimes of individual human beings are important to an understanding of differences among individuals and cultures, but can't explain the universals of human nature, the human mind, and human behavior, or how these compare to the natures, minds, and behavior of other species. Furthermore, these differences among individual human beings and among human cultures, though they appear to be large and significant from one perspective, are really quite small and limited from another. Certainly there are cultural differences among different human populations, and these are important and of interest in themselves, but these differences are really very minor, despite appearances to the contrary, when examined in the illuminating light of cross-species comparisons. One of the great contributions of a sub-field of psychology called comparative psychology was the elucidation of the patterns of behavior and the mental processes of other animals. This provided a landscape against which to see more clearly what we have in common with other animal species and how we differ from other animals with regard to our behavior and mental organization. Though there are many behavioral and mental similarities among many animal species and humans, an observation which is to be expected when we apply Darwin's idea of the *continuity of species* to psychology, there are, of course, great differences as well. Humans have an innate human nature. Gorillas have an innate gorilla nature. Wolves have an innate wolf nature, and the Brazilian Boa Constrictor has an innate Boa nature. And this psychological nature of each species is a consequence of its evolved brain circuit "design."

In humans, though there are some differences in food preferences, in religion, in rituals, in the details of political, economic and social organization and so forth, the range of differences is really relatively small, constrained by universal biological factors and universal features of human nature. Take evolved human nature, manifested materially in the physical, evolved circuit "design" of the human brain, put it into different environments, with different climatic and ecological features, and various learned cultural practices will inevitably develop. Those learned behaviors that work will be retained and those that don't work are eventually abandoned, resulting in cultural evolution, as distinct from genetic evolution, although both are best understood as forms of biological evolution. Particularly in the face of geographical and cultural insulation from other human groups, cultural differences will arise, but still only within quite narrow limits dictated by our evolved biological nature as a species. The myth that cultural variation is large and almost unlimited, a myth in part created and perpetuated for too long by the cultural anthropology of Margaret Mead and Franz Boas and their followers, has been exposed as false and should be put to rest for good (Shankman, 2000; Freeman, 1983; McCall, 2001; see Wikipedia, "Derek Freeman").

Humans around the world are in fact very similar, regardless of cultural differences in the details. According to the famous linguist Noam Chomsky, we all have language with structure that is universal to all human languages. This is what Chomsky termed the "universal grammar." We all have the same basic human emotions. We all have powerful disposition to love our children, especially when they are young. In every culture, young children look so cute because our evolved brain circuitry makes them look so cute precisely at that time when they are completely dependent on parents for care, motivating us to nurture them, and indirectly, thereby, to perpetuate our genes. Notice how children get less and less cute as they get older and less needful of parental caregiving. Instead they begin to develop facial and body forms which function to produce feelings of sexual attraction in others as they approach the period in life of their maximum reproductive potential. And, unfortunately, once that period passes, we become less and less sexually attractive as we age, since any genetic advantages of maintaining our sexual attractiveness have already passed. Changes in appearance with age, corresponding to the adaptive requirements of life at various ages, occur in every culture in the same sequence and at similar ages. We all have romantic and erotic emotions, sexual jealousy, preferences for some sexual partners over others, feelings of attraction to faces and to bodies with features indicative of health and high reproductive potential (although we don't subjectively experience our attractions as such), feelings of disgust or fear or aggression to things in our environments harmful to our chances of perpetuating our genes (again, we don't *experience* the feelings this way), and many other human universals which appear in every normal member of our species, regardless of culture or experience. Whether we live in a culture that prefers potatoes or rice, raw fish, barbecued beef or even grilled insects, mangoes and papaya, lychee, or apples and cherries, pho' or pig blood, no human group eats feces or rocks, and all prefer fats, sugars, salt, and protein sources. Whether we live in the jungles of New Guinea isolated from modern cultures or in modern Hong Kong, Los Angeles or Kuala Lumpur, we all show the same basic facial expressions in response to the same emotional situations, and we can read the basic facial expressions of other humans even if they come from the most remote of human cultures. Babies born blind smile at the same age as do sighted babies even though they could not have learned by imitation since they can't see to imitate. A cry face in L.A. is no different at all from a cry face in Sumatra. Take any human group, with any culture, compare it to any other human group with any other culture, and the differences will be minor compared to the similarities and to the much more substantial differences in mind and behavior that will be found between humans and even our closest non-human primate relatives.

This is not unique to humans. For any species, even ours with its variety of cultures, differences within the species are always small compared to differences between species in the organization of mind and behavior. Each species has its own genetically evolved nature built into the evolved circuit "design" of its brain. It is this evolved brain circuitry, this innate "wiring diagram," which is the primary source of the organization of mental processes and behavior. In fact, as we will see in later chapters, learning and culture themselves are really genetically evolved capacities of the brain "designed" to accommodate conditions of the environment which are too short-term, local, unstable, or too rapidly fluctuating to be accommodated by specific, genetically evolved, brain circuit "design."

Note here that when I speak of brain circuit "design," I put the word "design" in quotation marks. I do this for a specific reason. The word "design" may be interpreted by some as teleological, or may even be interpreted to imply the existence of a supernatural, conscious, and purposeful "designer." This raises an important issue in science, especially in psychological science, regarding its relationship to religion.

There is an unfortunate history of antagonism between science and religion. This is understandable, but at the same time, unnecessary. Science and religion, and some branches of philosophy, are interested in many of the same questions about human nature, the human mind, and human behavior which have intrigued human beings for millennia. Each of these fields also makes various claims about these topics of common interest. However, what distinguishes psychological science from philosophy and religion, if not topics of interest, is the method used by each for distinguishing what is true from what isn't true. Science relies upon careful and systematic observation, often under controlled conditions, to discriminate truthful claims from erroneous ones. However, religion uses faith as its method of determining what is true and what isn't and philosophers use philosophical methods such as logical analysis as primary means for determining truth.

Science makes one additional commitment. Science attempts to explain things in the natural world using natural causes only. The goal of science, including psychological science, is to understand as much of nature as possible using natural causes and natural laws alone, without resorting to supernatural explanations or causes. Science doesn't reject supernatural causes and supernatural beings because scientists know with absolute certainty that such things don't exist—in fact, they may exist, and I, for one, hope they do. But the goal of science is to discover natural laws and then to push those natural laws as far as possible to explain as much as possible about nature, without resort to supernatural causes or explanations. God or other supernatural beings and supernatural causes (meaning "above nature," superseding natural law) may in fact exist, but scientists refrain from using such explanations or references to God or other supernatural forces simply because such explanations violate the central goal of science, to explain nature using laws of nature and natural causes alone. Consistent with this goal, then, brain circuit "design" and the title "Mind Design" should not be taken to necessarily imply ultimate purpose or a supernatural designer. On the other hand, for all that scientists really know at this point in the history of science, functional organization or "design" in biological systems might very well have supernatural origins, or, alternatively, might simply be the result of what Richard Dawkins has called "the blind watchmaker" (the natural processes of evolution by natural selection, the working assumption in this book).

Some readers, particularly those with strong religious convictions, are likely to find this last proposition offensive or threatening. This may generate anger or anxiety or immediate rejection since we are "programmed" to respond to perceived threat with "fight or flight," even if, as in this case, the threat is only a psychological one. I once was told by the new acting chair of the psychology department at a university where I taught for years that it was "not appropriate" for me to teach evolution in a general psychology course. And once I even received an anonymous death threat from a student for teaching evolution in my classes and "corrupting the minds" of my students. However, let me try to soften the blow. Think of this. Is it not possible that evolution and God might simultaneously exist? Is it not possible that God could be the source of the processes in nature that make genetic evolution inevitable? We have no idea where the first matter came from. We don't know the answer to the question, "Why does anything at all exist, why isn't there just nothing?" These are deep and perhaps forever impenetrable mysteries about the nature of existence. In light of our ultimate ignorance about origins of things, we must remain open minded to all possibilities. There is no inherent logical contradiction between belief in evolution and belief in God. Here's what I mean.

If you can believe in some laws of nature, for example, laws of physics such as the law of gravitation or Newton's laws of motion, and find no contradiction with your belief in God because you assume that these laws of physics must have been created by God, then why is it not possible to believe in other laws of nature, the laws of biology, particularly the single law that unifies all of our understanding of the biological world, the law of evolution by natural selection? If religious authorities don't condemn those who believe in laws of physics, why condemn those who believe in laws of biology. If God can be the source of the laws of physics, then God can be the source of the laws of biology, including the law of evolution by natural selection. And if this law applies to biology in general, as the modern evolutionary synthesis in biology proposes, then it should apply to brains, just as much as it applies to any other organ or organ system of the body.

Thus, the central proposition of this book is that the origin of the functional organization, the "design," of brains, minds and behavior is evolution by natural selection.

However, on the question of whether God or completely natural causes are the origin of evolutionary processes, I remain neutral. In either case, the elegance of "design" in biological systems, most notably in brains, minds, and behavior, provides dramatic testimony to the majesty of nature, whatever its origins.*

---

*Note: Even if nature turns out to be the work of a supernatural being, this would not change the fact of evolution as the process by which life forms acquire their organization, just as the law of gravitation would not cease to exist if the universe has a supernatural origin. The laws of physics and the laws of life would remain the same, no matter what their source.

CHAPTER TWO

Brains, Minds, and Other Natural Matter: The Astonishing Hypothesis

"... the prospect we face is that a detailed neurophysiological conception of ourselves might simply displace our mentalistic self-conceptions in much the same way that oxidation theory (and modern chemistry in general) simply displaced the older phlogiston theory of matter transformation. ... These more primitive habits can also be displaced, and we may look forward to framing ... a much more adequate and powerful theory of human psychology."

Paul M. Churchland
Scientific Realism and the Plasticity of the Mind

I took my first course in physiological psychology in 1967 while I was an undergraduate at the University of California at Riverside. A few months earlier I had just left the United States Naval Academy at Annapolis after deciding that I was not cut out for the military life. While at the Academy, between thousands of push-ups, eating my meals at attention, struggling with calculus, and learning about what to do to save a sinking ship, I managed to get a hold of a book about the human mind at the Academy library. I was fascinated, especially by the brain and its relationship to consciousness. When I left Annapolis in December of 1966, I had decided that I would pursue a major in psychology.

My first term at the University of California at Riverside as a psych major was uneventful. I took whatever courses I could get—a couple of social psychology courses and one about the American novel. I didn't like any of them very much. One of the two psychology professors I had that first term, Dr. Ray Rhine, was later to tell me, as I entered his office one day while he was tossing out hundreds of social psychology journals that had been filling his bookshelves for a decade, "It's all bullshit." I put two and two together and surmised that he didn't like social psychology back then any more than I did (but in my case the judgment was based on just two courses; it seemed to have taken him a while longer. Incidentally, there actually *was* some good research in social psychology back then: Milgram's studies on obedience, Zimbardo's Prison Study, the work on diffusion of responsibility, and Asch's study on conformity, and it is important to note that social psychology has come a long way since those early days). Sure enough, I later learned that I had witnessed the apex of his mid-career turn-about. He completely abandoned the social psychology of that time, which had been his route to a tenured university professorship, and decided to go to Africa to work with the famous animal behaviorist, Jane Goodall, who by that time had published several works on landmark discoveries she had made about chimpanzee behavior in the wild. Ray became a comparative psychologist, thereafter publishing many scientific papers on chimpanzee social behavior based on his repeated trips to Goodall's camp in the jungles of Tanzania.

I was like Ray. After just two social psychology courses, I wanted more substance to psychology. Later, when I took physiological psychology in 1967, I found exactly what I had been looking for. Something I could sink my teeth into, an approach to the mind that had substance.

Psychophysical Monism

The professor who taught the Physiological Psychology course at UC Riverside was Dr. Marvin Nachman, who among other things, had the "cutest wife in the psychology department," according to my cell biology professor that term, Dr. Crellin Pauling, son of the world renowned Nobel prize winning chemist, Linus Pauling, the only person to have ever won two unshared Nobels. The course in physiological psychology transformed me, and after that term with Marv I knew where my professional life would go thereafter. The brain was the new frontier. Study of the brain gave the mind its substance, its place in the material world. In fact, the single idea from Marv's course that struck me to the core was the proposition that the mind consisted of the physical activities of the brain, that and nothing more. Mind was just the product of a physical organ. Just as the function of the liver was to produce bile, the function of the brain was to produce mind, consciousness, and behavior.

I don't know exactly why this hadn't occurred to me before, but once it sunk in, the idea stunned me. The day in class that I heard it for the first time, I happened to go to a supermarket later that afternoon, where I found myself perusing the meat counter. Thinking about this astounding proposition that mind was just brain function, I picked up a cow brain, waiting there in cellophane to become someone's brain tacos (a delicacy, not far away in Mexico), and I unceremoniously threw it up and down in my hands, feeling its mass, its physicality, and then marveling at the thought that when it was alive and functioning, it produced a mind—a cow mind, but mind nevertheless. I am sure that other shoppers witnessing this odd event could little guess that what they were seeing was a human mind contemplating its own material basis. Playing catch with this cow brain was my way of trying to grasp this profound assertion, a doctrine known variously among philosophers of mind and psychological scientists as *physicalism, identity theory,* or *psychophysical monism*—I prefer the later term, which translated literally means that *the psychological* (mental events such as thoughts, feelings, memories, perceptions, beliefs) *and the physical* (physical events in an entirely material brain) *are one* and the same thing (see Jacobson, 1993, p. 133). *Mind is material,* a proposition that Francis Crick, of the famous Watson and Crick DNA duo, called "the astonishing hypothesis." Mind out of matter—an "astonishing" twist, indeed, in the wondrous manifestations of nature.

Mind-Brain Dualism

Psychophysical monism is diametrically opposed to the more commonly held belief that mind is separate from body and brain, that it is non-material, an ethereal entity or process akin to an immaterial spirit, which somehow animates the physical body, though not physical itself. According to this position, there are two fundamental kinds of substance in the universe, the mental and the physical, and these two "substances" are entirely independent of one another. This view, known as *mind-body dualism* (a more modern designation might be *mind-brain dualism*), was first formally proposed by the French philosopher, Rene Descartes, in the 1600's, although it has probably been the common sense belief of most people since ancient times. The view is still common in the "folk psychology" of most people even today and is often tied closely to their religious beliefs in an afterlife. After all, if consciousness is material, dependent upon material processes in a physical brain, then how could consciousness survive the physical death of body and brain? And here, things get a bit sticky.

The Problem of the Soul

The idea that our minds, and thus ourselves, end at death is disconcerting, to say the least. By contrast, the belief that we, that is, our consciousness, our minds, continue after we die, not only gives us comfort with regard to our own fate, but gives us hope that we will be reunited with our lost loved ones. This is an important idea and I hope that it is actually the case, but how can we reconcile these dualistic beliefs with what science tells us. It seems like an unsolvable dilemma.

One way around this conundrum might be to hypothesize that the mind we possess while we are alive in this "earthly realm" is distinct from "the soul," which, according to religious views, *is* immaterial. At this point, I have to admit that I have had personal experience that leads me to believe that there is something after death, some kind of consciousness that *does* seem to persist after the death of the brain, but the observations upon which this hunch is based are from my own personal, subjective experience and therefore can't be scientifically verified (science requires objective, "publicly" observable evidence for its claims). Although two others were with me at the time of this event and remember it exactly as I do, and although I tape recorded our recollections of the experience within minutes of this event (which took place the morning after my dear mother passed away), science requires repeatability of observations in order for observations to be acceptable as scientific evidence. My personal experience will not, and should not, be accepted as scientific evidence of the "soul," but it is sufficient reason for me to keep an open mind to the possibilities and to recognize that what we know about such things is still very limited.

One day in the distant future, physicists may unexpectedly discover new properties of matter and energy that make a materially-based consciousness after death a scientific possibility, but until then, the immaterial eternal "soul" must remain the exclusive domain of religion, and thus a matter of faith, not evidence—at least for the time being.

But the mind that we utilize in everyday interactions with our physical world is a different matter (in both meanings of the word). Brain matter is yielding more and more of its mysteries to the penetrating eye of science. Neuroscience is pushing its way into our heads, setting the stage for a scientific revolution that will forever alter the way we see ourselves, and eventually affect every aspect of human experience and human culture, just as the Copernican and Darwinian revolutions did. We are entering what cognitive neuroscientist Nancy Kanwisher (2009) of MIT calls "the neuro-century," an age in which discoveries in neuroscience will shake to the core our most cherished beliefs about human nature, mind, and human behavior.

Physicalism

Psychophysical monism is a corollary of the larger philosophical position known as *materialism*, the view that all that exists in the universe is material, that is, matter and energy in one form or another. Among philosophers, the term *physicalism* has gained favor more recently over the older term materialism because physicalism takes account of "far more sophisticated notions of physicality than matter" (see Wikipedia), for example quantum phenomena, wave-particle relationships, and other physical forces, such as gravity, which are physical but not material in a strict sense. Psychophysical monism just takes materialism/physicalism and explicitly applies it to the mind. Thus, the mind is part of the universe, the universe is entirely physical, and therefore, the mind must also be physical. And there is plenty of evidence to back up this reasoning.

If mind is physical, dependent upon physical events in a material brain, then several propositions should be true, but they come down to one central testable hypothesis. If the mind is physical then there should be a reliable correspondence between physical events in the brain and psychological events in the mind. This general proposition leads to several sub-hypotheses. First, physical manipulations of the brain, such as stimulating it, or damaging parts of it, should regularly produce identifiable changes in mind and behavior. Second, mental states should be associated with observable changes in the brain, for example, reliable changes in the brain's electrical or metabolic activities. Third, in cross-species comparisons, differences in brain structure and functioning across species should be associated with differences among the minds of different animal species. Fourth, inherited differences in brain structure and function within a species, such as humans, should produce individual differences in mental functions which are, at least in part, due to genetic differences. Fifth, various physical manipulations of specific circumscribed parts of the brain, including modifications of its electrical and magnetic properties, should reliably produce distinct and specific effects on the mind. Incidentally, this prediction will only be true if different parts of the mind are to be found in the activities of circumscribed regions of the brain, rather than particular mental activities being whole-brain functions. Finally, because the brain's activities are not only electrical but also chemical, chemical manipulations of the brain by drugs should alter the mind. Nowadays, the accuracy of this last prediction is common knowledge. Less well known is the abundance of evidence in support of the others.

Observations supporting the "astonishing hypothesis" that mind is physical

In 1870 two Prussian physiologists, Doctors Gustav Fritsch and Eduard Hitzig, showed that they could stimulate specific movements in dogs by electrical stimulation of specific parts of the dogs' cerebral cortices, regions in the posterior frontal lobes which would eventually come to be known as the *motor cortex*. Later, when drafted as physicians into the Prussian army for one war or another, they carried their brain stimulating device along with them into the battlefield, and when happening upon soldiers down with open head wounds, they stimulated the exposed human brains and confirmed in humans what they had observed in dogs. Stimulate specific parts of the human brain, and just like in dogs, specific movements of the body followed. Was the "will" to move really just a pattern of electrical pulses coming from specific groups of *neurons* (nerve cells) in the material brain? It is starting to look like it.

In the past few years, neuroscientists have shown that humans who are paralyzed because of spinal cord injury or disease can control a mechanical arm or a computer mouse just by thinking about it. If the brain of a paralyzed person is hooked up to a kind

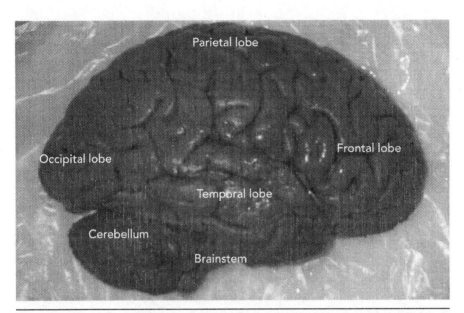

FIGURE 2-1. Photo of right side of human brain showing massive cerebral cortex. Note the convolutions (folds) that characterize human cortex. Both photos by Ken Koenigshofer, PhD.

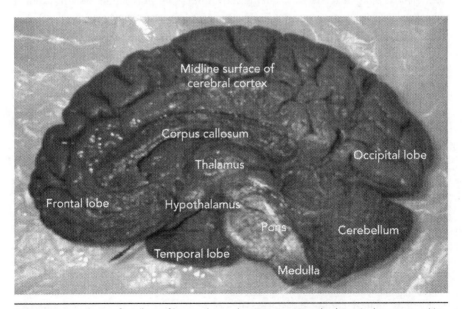

FIGURE 2-2. Photo of midline of human brain showing cortex and subcortical structures. Limbic structures (amygdala and hippocampus), not shown, are buried within temporal lobe cortex. Olfactory bulb (smell) is seen projecting from bottom near temporal lobe.

of brainwave (EEG) machine that recognizes the specific electrical activity of the brain, corresponding to the thought to move this way or that, then the machine can use that signal in the brain, corresponding to the thought, to stimulate a motorized mechanical arm, or the computer mouse, to carry out the specific movement being imagined by the paralyzed person. For example, experiments with a system called *BrainGate*, which relies upon electrodes implanted into the brain of the patient to collect and recognize the brain's electrical activity, permits paralyzed patients to move a computer mouse by thought alone with such precision that one paralyzed patient could even draw circles and other shapes on the computer screen simply by thinking about the movements necessary to draw them. Monkeys with similar devices implanted in their brains can precisely control the movements of a mechanical arm just by thought and are thereby able to use the robotic arm to successfully reach for and grasp objects just by thinking about it. Thus, a thought is shown to be equivalent to a specific pattern of electrical activity in a particular place (or places) in the human brain—the "will" to move is a particular set of physical events in the material brain. This is not only evidence for *psychophysical monism*, but involves a type of explanation known in philosophy as *neuroreductionism*, wherein complex mental events are explained by reducing them to patterns of physical, neurological activity in the brain. Much of neuroscience is based on the conviction that we can learn a great deal about the mind by breaking down complex mental activities into smaller units, perhaps ultimately down to the interactions of groups of brain cells wired together in complex, physical, circuit designs.

Brain injury also gives powerful evidence of the brain-mind equivalency. If mental functions are really physical events in a material brain, then damage to the brain should disrupt specific mental processes. In the 1860's the neurosurgeon, Paul Broca, discovered that damage to specific parts of the frontal and temporal lobes of the human cerebral cortex severely impairs language abilities. Subsequent research and clinical experience, in the hundred some years that have followed, confirms the general finding that damage to left frontal cortex, particularly in a region now known as *Broca's area*, disrupts language expression, whereas damage to a left temporal cortical region, subsequently called *Wernicke's area* after its discoverer, disrupts language comprehension. Peculiarly, damage to Wernicke's area also results in what is sometimes called "word salad." Persons with this brain damage can still clearly articulate but all that comes out is senseless speech, strings of well-pronounced words put together into grammatically correct, but meaningless sentences. Modern studies with *functional magnetic resonance imaging (fMRI)* show many additional brain areas involved in human language, indicating networks more complex than imagined by the pioneers, but the results still confirm, in general, the original observations of Broca and Wernicke (Gazzaniga, Ivry, and Mangun, 1998). Damage to specific regions of the human brain disrupts our most prized human mental capacity, our use of language.

In 1952, a Canadian neurosurgeon named Wilder Penfield stimulated the temporal cortex of a conscious patient under local anesthesia. The patient responded that she heard music, a full orchestra playing a tune that she even hummed for Penfield as she lay on the operating table with her skull laid open under local anesthesia. When Penfield stopped the electrical stimulation of her temporal cortex, his patient reported that the music abruptly stopped. Each time that Penfield resumed the stimulation after a pause, she reported that the same music immediately began again, starting over from the beginning, akin to a tape recording. Penfield had discovered that detailed memories could be elicited from electrical stimulation of the *temporal lobe* in conscious human patients (Penfield, 1952). Thus, it seems that even our memories are physical processes in our brains which can be turned on by application of a few electrical pulses to specific neural circuits. Not only are mental activities apparently physical events in the brain, but specific mental events are often localized within very specific regions of brain matter, a principle in neuroscience known as the *localization of function*.

Localization of function is now well documented in much of the brain, especially in *subcortical brain structures* (those located beneath the *cerebral cortex*, the overlying six-cell-layered structure found only in mammals, including us—see Figure 2-2 above, and images of cerebral cortex and cross sections showing subcortical structures, Wikipedia, "Diencephalon," "Brain," and "Human Brain"). For example, in animals electrical stimulation of various clumps of nerve cells (called *nuclei*) in a brain structure called the *hypothalamus*, just above the roof of your mouth, causes feeding, drinking, fear responses, signs of rage, or sexual behavior dependent upon which specific hypothalamic nucleus is activated (see Valenstein, 1973). In humans, similar effects are produced by this same procedure. Such localized brain stimulation is not done as some diabolical test to settle the dispute between dualists and psychophysical monists, but is, instead, a standard procedure by neurosurgeons during brain surgery to map structures before any brain tissue is ablated for therapeutic reasons. This is necessary because there are slight variations in brain organization from person to person just as there are individual differences in facial anatomy. Everyone has a human face, but no two human faces are identical, and the same is true of human brains (identical twins of course being an exception). In such neurosurgical procedures patients are kept conscious, under local anesthesia only, so they can verbally report the subjective effects of the stimulation to their brains, real time. Human patients undergoing these procedures report feeling hungry, thirsty, or fearful (often not being able to identify the source of their fear; understandable because the real source is electrical activation of their *fear circuits* by a jolt of voltage via an implanted electrode in their brain). Sometimes, if the electrical spark is just at the right place in the hypothalamus, the patient experiences sexual feelings. One case reported by a team of neurosurgeons in Japan is particularly interesting. A woman undergoing this procedure began to make comments to the doctor stimulating her hypothalamus about how handsome he was, about his beautiful eyes, and so on, and by the time the stimulation of her hypothalamus had ended she had made sexually suggestive comments to the doctor and concluded by asking him to marry her. Thus, even romantic yearnings seem to be rooted in the electrical activity of specific groups of neurons, in this case, located in a specific region of the hypothalamus. This brings to mind that wonderful scene in Woody Allen's science fiction spoof, *Sleeper*, when Woody's character steps in the "Orgasmitron" and comes out, hair standing on end, after apparently having had the best sexual experience of his life, all stimulated by the machine electrically activating his brain. Apparently, the woman patient in Japan had a similar experience during her brain surgery, stimulated by the surgeon's electrode in her hypothalamus.

Something very similar has been demonstrated in animals. Rats implanted with electrodes in a subcortical region known as the MFB (*medial forebrain bundle*; a bundle of nerve fibers in the vicinity of the hypothalamus) will press a small rat-sized lever furiously, for hours, even days, on end, until they literally drop from exhaustion, for no other reward than electrical pulses to this brain region, activated by each lever press (see Olds and Milner, 1954). The intense nature of the pleasurable experience for the animal is revealed by the fact that male rats engaging in this "self-stimulation" of their brains show penile erection and repeatedly ejaculate (the rat version of Woody Allen's "Orgasmitron") while pressing the lever which delivers brain stimulation to the MFB. The intensity of the "high" they get is revealed by the fact that rats so trained will readily cross an electrified grid to get to the lever that triggers this stimulation to their brains, even though starving rats will not cross this same grid to get to food, and will die of starvation first, because the pain from the shock grid is so intense. Judging from this, the pleasure from the stimulation of the MFB must be awfully darn good. This behavior is reminiscent of the lengths to which heroin or crystal meth addicts will go just to get their "highs." The same circuitry seems to be involved in natural pleasures such as sex and in addiction to the "pleasure drugs."

These observations also confirm what neuroscientists already know about the "pleasure drugs" and how they work. Just like electrical pulses delivered via an implanted electrode, drugs such as heroin, cocaine, and meth-amphetamine all work by intensely stimulating particular brain circuits that are involved in our psychological experience of pleasure. The brain is not only built for pain to protect us, but for pleasure to lead us to enthusiastically repeat activities that are good for us and good for the species (eating, drinking, and sex, to name a few). Of course, drug addiction isn't good for us, but these ancient brain circuits existed long before the development of our knowledge of chemistry made such drugs a part of our cultural environment, making drug addiction possible (cocaine is found naturally in leaves of the Coca plant, but only in small non-addictive doses, and has been used by South American indigenous peoples for over a thousand years: see Wikipedia, "Cocaine," http://en.wikipedia.org/wiki/Cocaine#Coca_leaf, retrieved May 29, 2010). Thus, pleasure circuits, evolved to make us repeat adaptive behaviors, become "short-circuited" by the modern "pleasure drugs," thereby becoming active when they shouldn't be.

A dramatic illustration of how physical damage to the brain can produce striking effects on psychological functioning, as predicted by the hypothesis of mind-brain equivalency, is the extraordinary 1950's case of Henry Molaison (better known as H.M. in the medical literature). H.M. had severe epileptic seizures that could not be controlled by any of the drug treatments available at the time.

Seizures often originate from an "epileptic locus," a specific region of brain damage that periodically undergoes uncontrollable neural firing leading to the seizure activity. Some seizures are more localized in the brain than others. These *petit mal* seizures produce specific alterations in consciousness called an *epileptic aura*. Generalized, *grand mal* seizures produce loss of consciousness and repetitive spastic movements, especially of the limbs. But the aura of a petit mal seizure is a specific sensation, such as a smell, a specific memory, or a particular feeling, which is reliably generated in the mind of the person as the seizure activity begins and activates the neural tissue in the region of the epileptic locus. The specific psychological character of the aura depends on the specific location of the epileptic locus in the brain. Thus, by getting reports from patients about the nature of the epileptic aura they experience at the onset of one of their seizures, neurosurgeons can get a good idea of where the brain damage, leading to the seizures, is localized. In the case of H.M., seizures were originating from the *medial temporal lobes*, which contain the cortex that Penfield had stimulated in his patient, as well as a number of structures beneath this cortex, including the seahorse-shaped, *hippocampus*, and a walnut-sized brain nucleus known as the *amygdala* (see Figure 2-2; the hippocampus and amygdala are buried beneath temporal lobe cortex).

In 1953, when the neurosurgeon, William Scoville, made the decision to remove much of the medial temporal lobes of H.M. in hopes of controlling his seizures, the functions of the hippocampus were not yet known. Hence, after the surgery, there came a big surprise with the inadvertent discovery of the functions of this mysterious chunk of *paleocortex* (paleocortex or "old" cortex is 3 layered cortex found in the brains of all vertebrates, as distinct from *neocortex*, the cerebral cortex, which has six layers and is found only in the mammals). After H.M.'s surgery, at first, all seemed fine. H.M. still retained language, his reasoning was intact, he had no sensory, perceptual, or movement deficits, and no disturbances of mood or emotions. But soon it became apparent that he had one major disability after his brain surgery. He could no longer form lasting memories about anything that occurred subsequent to the removal of both of his hippocampi. All of his old memories for events prior to the surgery were fine, and he could remember new facts and events for a few minutes even after his brain damage, but what he couldn't do any longer was to form any new lasting memories for facts and events, even though he could learn and retain new motor skills, such as how to do a new jigsaw puzzle or play a computer game, as well and as quickly as anyone. H.M. had not lost memory per se, instead he had lost the ability to *consolidate* or "fix" new memories for facts and events into permanent memory storage (as was the case for Drew Barrymore's character in "Fifty First Dates"). Up until his recent death at 82, H.M. still believed that the year was 1953, that Eisenhower was president, that his wife was still living, and that he was still a young man with a full head of thick, black hair (he had actually become bald decades before). Imagine the shock he experienced every time he would look at himself in a mirror. "Oh, my God, what's happened to me?" Of course, once he stepped away from the mirror, he would quickly forget what he had just seen and return to his 1953 world, where he remained perpetually the young man of his intact 1950's memory (Gazzaniga, Ivry, and Mangun, 1998, p. 262–264). H.M. was a man stuck in time, and in the fifties at that (maybe a better time in some ways at least—before the assassination of John Kennedy, before widespread drug abuse, before 9/11, and nuclear prolifera- tion, but also before things like an effective polio vaccine).

The case of H.M. provided crucial evidence leading to the theory that *short-term working memory*, lasting only a matter of minutes, and *procedural memory* (memory for how to do things) are distinct from the long-term memory of facts and events (called *declarative memory* by modern psychologists), and furthermore that each is dependent upon different brain systems. H.M. shows us that even our personal sense of who we are, knowledge acquired from our experiences throughout our lives, is completely reliant upon the physical processes in particular places in our material brains. Other research soon confirmed even more surprising ways in which *our brains are us*.

Neuroscience of the Self

The Russian, A. R. Luria, founder of clinical neuropsychology in the late 1950's pub- lished "Higher Cortical Functions in Man" in 1966 which examined the effects of spe- cific brain damage on human consciousness. Luria (1966) found extraordinarily precise changes in the minds of human patients depending upon the specific location of their brain lesion. One striking example shows that even highly abstracted mental functions, related to our sense of self, appear to have specific representation within our brain tis- sue. Damage to *right parietal cortex*, located about midway on the right surface of the brain, produces an odd disorder known as *unilateral neglect* in which the patient no longer understands the left half of space, including the left side of their own body. The left half of space, including the left half of one's own body, is simply ignored, neglected.

One patient with the neglect syndrome complained vehemently about something following her wherever she went, even to the bathroom and even to bed at night. She told her doctors that she was extremely annoyed and wanted them to get rid of the intruder, which, as it happened, was the left side of her own body. These patients entirely ignore the left side of their bodies, dressing, washing, combing the hair, and so on, only on the right side. They even deny injury to the left side of their bodies as if the injured body part belonged, not to them, but to someone else (Deutssch and Deutsch, 1973, p. 239–240).

Things get even stranger with damage to one of the limbic structures beneath the temporal lobe neocortex. People with damage to the connections of the *amygdala*, a structure beneath the cortex of the temporal lobe, just below your ear, near the upper tip of the aforementioned hippocampus, show alterations of the personal mind that are even more bizarre. After this specific brain damage, such patients begin to have the peculiar delusion that their family members, their homes, even their pets, are all zombie-like imposters which look like the real thing, but which are really just sham imitations of the real versions, which have somehow vanished. One patient with this strange disorder, known as the *Capgras syndrome*, even thought of himself, on occasion, as an imposter of himself, distinguishing in his speech between himself and the "real David." Such persons are not schizophrenic or suffering from some new form of multiple personality disorder (now known among psychologists as *dissociative identify disorder*). The delusion is so specific that damage to the connections to the amygdala *from the visual system* result in the delusion occurring only when the patient *sees* the family member or when they see themselves in a mirror. If the patient *hears* the same family member on the phone, without seeing them, the patient immediately recognizes the family member normally, as the real thing, without any question at all about their true identity. This thoroughly convincing Capgras delusion occurs only when the person is using vision, but not when they are using hearing. The explanation for this specificity is in the specificity of the brain damage involved. With the auditory connections to the amygdala intact, there is no Capgras delusion with auditory input. The peculiar delusion is specific to visual inputs when the damage is restricted to the visual pathways to the amygdala. This dramatically illustrates a very important principle. Localized damage to specific brain pathways results in very specific pathological alterations of consciousness. This is exactly what we would expect, if consciousness is really physical processes in an entirely physical brain, just as the doctrine of psychophysical monism so boldly claims (V. S. Ramachandran, PBS Nova, *Mysteries of the Mind*; Hirstein and Ramachandran, 1997).

Other research in the 60's and 70's gives even more surprising evidence that our personal identity is in the brain. Sperry and Gazzaniga at Cal Tech tested patients whose brains had been severed into two distinct halves when their corpus callosums had been surgically cut to treat severe epilepsy. The *corpus callosum* is a broad sheet of neural fibers (*axons*) that interconnects the two halves of the brain, permitting integration of the functions of the two hemispheres, each of which, it turns out, is specialized for quite different types of information processing.

The *left hemisphere* is logical, analytic, quantitative, linear, sequential, rational, and, in 90% of the population, it is the *dominant hemisphere* in the sense that it is where most language processing occurs (both Broca's and Wernicke's areas are "lateralized" to the left hemisphere, at least in right handers; for lefties, language tends to be more equally represented in both hemispheres, and in fact, perhaps because of this, the brains of left handers are bigger on the right side than in right handers, and lefties are less likely than right handers to lose language function if they have a stroke in the left hemisphere).

Interestingly, swearing and singing, both emotionally tinged activities are localized in the right half of the human brain, not the left, leading to a quite unexpected peculiarity in those with left hemisphere damage. Though people lose the ability to speak with damage to the left frontal lobe, they can still sing and swear perfectly well. The *right hemisphere* is more involved in emotional processing than the left, and so emotional verbalizations such as singing and swearing remain completely normal in people who have lost even the rudiments of normal speech.

In addition to emotional processing, some researchers have found that the right hemisphere also specializes in holistic, intuitive, imaginative, non-linear processing which may be involved in creativity and even mystical experiences, wherein the distinction between self and the rest of the universe is lost, resulting in a deep and profound sense of unity with the cosmos. It is interesting to consider that holistic and holy seem to be derived from the same root, perhaps giving us insight into the ancient meaning of holy, a state of consciousness in which one deeply feels the unity of all of existence, as one's sense of a separate self vanishes. Neuroanatomist, Dr. Jill Bolte Taylor, experienced this first hand when she had a massive stroke in her left hemisphere one morning several years ago. During the acute phase of the stroke, she found that she had lost her language abilities, much of her memory of facts, and, to her surprise, she lost the perception of herself as a separate entity. Instead, she experienced *right hemisphere consciousness*, a state of perfect, beautiful, euphoric harmony with all of existence in an eternal present, in which the distinction between her self and the rest of the universe didn't exist. She experienced what she calls "the deep inner peace circuitry of our right hemisphere." See her tell her story at http://www.ted.com/talks/view/id/229. It is interesting to speculate that perhaps the story of the Garden of Eden is an allegory telling us about our two natures, centered in our two cerebral hemispheres. Perhaps this story tells us that knowledge of self and analytical knowledge of the world, *left hemisphere consciousness*, was gained at a cost, the loss of right hemisphere consciousness and the sense of blissful unity with all of existence which may have characterized human consciousness prior to the "Fall from Grace," the "expulsion from the Garden," and prior to the ascendancy of left brain awareness, with its focus on detail, linear, analytic logic, and language.

Michael Gazzaniga's research with human *split-brain patients* revealed something else startling about human consciousness and its connections to physical activities inside the brain. He found that split-brain patients appeared to have *two separate minds in the same head*. Gazzaniga tested split-brain patients in an apparatus that projected pictures of things either to the right or left of center in the visual field, and then asked split-brain patients to identify what they saw. If the picture was projected to the right visual field, the patient had no trouble saying what he had seen, but if the picture was projected to the left visual field, patients claimed that they had seen nothing. This is because of how the eyes are wired to the brain, and illustrates the highly precise way in which conscious experience is linked to specific brain circuitry.

The inner half of each retina sends nerve fibers (*axons*) from each eye to the opposite (*contralateral*) side of the brain, and the outer half of each retina projects to the same (*ispsilateral*) side of the brain. Thus, images in the left visual field go to the brain's right hemisphere, and those in the right visual field project to the left brain, where language is localized in most people.

Thus, when a picture of an apple, or a pencil, or a key or some other object is projected to the right visual field, the patient identifies it just like a normal person would. However, when the picture is presented in the left visual field, the left hemisphere, the talking part of the brain, answers that it has seen *nothing*. *And it is telling the truth*, because the image was sent from the eyes to the right side of the brain only, which has little or no ability for speech. When the person with a severed corpus callosum is asked what "he" saw, of course, it is the left, talking side of the brain which answers, and it says accurately and truthfully for itself, "I didn't see anything."

But here's what's truly extraordinary. Gazzaniga discovered that if the patient, who had just said that he had seen nothing, was then asked to use his left hand to feel under a cloth among a number of objects, and to pick out the one "he" had just seen, the patient's left hand, controlled by the right side of his brain, would accurately pick out the object just seen, even while the patient's left-brain continued to insist that "he" had seen nothing at all. The person's right-brain, and the mind there, had perceived the image, and demonstrated so by using its hand (the left hand) to select the correct object under the cloth by touch, while the person's left-brain and its mind, where speech is localized, continued to honestly and vehemently insist that it had not seen anything. Thus, two separate minds were housed in the very same head (Gazzaniga and Ivry, 1998, p. 329–331). If the mind were in fact a non-material entity or process, separate and independent of brain activity as the doctrine of mind-body dualism states, then how could the mind be split with a neurosurgeon's knife?

This split in the mind is demonstrated even in the daily lives of these patients, at least in the first few weeks post-surgery, before they learn compensatory strategies. One female split-brain patient reported to her doctors that she was having difficulties dressing in the morning because when trying to select what to wear, one hand would reach for one dress in her closet and the other hand would reach for a different dress. In the face of these opposing actions by her two hands, she stood there unable to "make up her mind" and remained unable to dress herself. But things get even more bizarre.

Reportedly, a male split brain patient, a few weeks after his return home from the hospital, got in an argument with his wife. In "his" rage, his left hand, controlled by his more emotional right hemisphere, grabbed her throat and began to strangle her. Then, "his" right hand, controlled by the more rational, logical left-brain, grabbed the right hand at his wife's throat, and after a struggle, pulled the right hand away from his wife's bruised neck. The emotional right side of the patient's brain, in its rage, apparently wanted to harm the wife, maybe even kill her, but the more rational left side of "his" brain perhaps reasoned, "Hold on, if you kill her, you are going to jail and I am going with you," so the logical left brain/mind succeeded, using its right hand, in overpowering the emotional right hemisphere which was about to commit a crime that "both" would surely regret later.

Of course, in normal people none of these effects occur because information is continually integrated and shared by the two halves of the brain across an intact corpus callosum. But the lesson remains. Split brain makes split consciousness. And this makes for very good evidence for psychophysical monism. Mind is the physical activity of physical neural structures in a material brain.

Seeing Ideas: Evidence for Psychophysical Monism from Brain Imaging

More recently, functional magnetic resonance imaging (fMRI) confirms the specificity of some of the brain's circuitry for even the most complex functions of the mind. fMRI studies have identified specific brain areas that "light up" when a person engages in one mental activity or another. Much of the recent progress in neuroscience is due to advances in imaging technology. At the 2009 convention of the Association for Psychological Science in San Francisco, Dr. Nancy Kanwisher of the Massachusetts Institute of Technology (MIT) noted that functional magnetic resonance imaging now permits 10-plus images per second of the blood flow changes in the functioning brain, making possible real time movies of brain activity as people engage in various mental tasks. This new fMRI technology is revealing surprising details about the specific design of our brain circuitry and our "mind design."

One example is the *Fusiform Facial Area (FFA)* in the Fusiform gyrus of the human *cerebral cortex* (a *gyrus* is a "hill" on the "hill-and-valley" convoluted surface of the cerebral cortex, found only in the mammals, and thus of more recent evolutionary origin than the deeper subcortical regions of the brain). Numerous studies suggest that the FFA evolved for the specific task of recognizing human faces. The effects of injury to this area of cortex confirm this interpretation. For example, Wada and Yamomoto (2001) studied a stroke patient with damage to the FFA and found he had lost all face recognition, but retained completely normal object recognition, showing that the deficits following damage to the FFA are specific to facial recognition and not visual recognition in general. People who have this area of the cortex damaged can no longer identify individual faces, including those of their own children, their parents, or other close relatives, even though they retain absolutely normal vision in all other respects. They can't even recognize their own face when shown photos of themselves, or when they look in a mirror (although they intellectually understand that the image in the mirror must be them). V. S. Ramachandran, of the Departments of Psychology and Neuroscience at UC San Diego, has hypothesized that the Capgras syndrome, described above, is due to the disconnection of the FFA from the amygdala. Because the FFA and the amygdala are themselves undamaged, people with Capgras syndrome still feel emotion and still recognize faces but because of a disconnection of neural fibers between FFA and the amygdala, the emotional component of the recognition of familiar faces is missing, giving the impression to the person with the Capgras syndrome that something isn't quite right and the delusion that familiar people in their lives are somehow not the real thing, but just imposters (V. S. Ramachandran, PBS Nova, *Mysteries of the Mind*; Hirstein and Ramachandran, 1997, 437–444).

The existence of a brain area which appears to be specifically dedicated to facial recognition is understandable because the identification of individual human beings is essential to successful social interactions and a foundation for social organization in our species. It also provides evidence for one of the major claims of this book, that *humans are social creatures, not because of learning and culture, but because of our genetic evolution as a social species.*

Another discovery in neuroscience reinforces this point. In 1992, Italian neuroscientists discovered *mirror neurons* (di Pellegrino, et. al., 1992), which fire electrical signals not only when the individual performs a specific goal-directed hand movement but also when the individual observes the same movement being performed by another (Fadiga, et. al., 2005). Mirror neurons may be the neurophysiological foundation of our ability to imitate (an important basis for cultural transmission of learned behaviors over generations) and of our ability to understand the ideas and intentions of others—important for successful cooperation among members of a social group, a requirement for the adaptive benefits of living in social groups in our evolutionary past (see Pinel,

2009, p. 194–195). Mirror neurons may be essential to a child's formation of a *theory of mind*, whereby it comes to understand the intentions and other mental states of other people, also essential for complex social interactions (McGovern, 2007). Observations like these are opening up the study of the neurological and evolutionary bases of our social nature as a species in a new field known as social neuroscience or social cognitive neuroscience (see Carlson, 2010, p. 482).

I will discuss more about this later, in the chapter on our social nature. Suffice it to say, at this point, that much of our mind design, including our emotional makeup as a species, is derived from the fact that we are an evolved *social* species. We are social by our species' genes and thus our genetic evolution, not by nurture. Being a social creature requires a whole set of brain specializations—specific design features of the human brain that account for a large chunk of our mind design, our human nature.

Functional MRI studies have also revealed atypical activity of specific brain areas in the pathological perceptual, cognitive, and emotional functioning of schizophrenics, in depression, and in autism. V. S. Ramachandran (2006) has proposed pathology in mirror neurons as a potential cause of autism and perhaps other pathological conditions of the mind and behavior. And the areas of brain involved in these disorders, just like the areas involved in normal functioning of the mind, though often widely distributed in the brain, are nevertheless highly specific, confirming a highly orderly relationship between specific mental events in our minds and very specific physical events in our brains. Furthermore, new research is starting to untangle the genetics involved, debunking many of the myths about psychological disorders and their causes.

Take *schizophrenia* for example. There was time when people with *hallucinations* (false sensory experiences, such as hearing voices), *delusions* (bizarre, irrational beliefs held firmly in spite of overwhelming contradictory evidence, such as the belief that people can hear your thoughts), emotional outbursts unrelated to reality, and loss of contact with reality, as evidenced by bizarre speech and behavior, were thought to be possessed by demons or to be witches. In the Middle Ages, such persons were tortured, burned at the stake, or had holes bored into their heads (a process known as *trephining*) with crude instruments, without anesthesia, to allow the evil spirits, thought to be possessing them, a route of escape. In more modern times, it was not that long ago that even experts believed that schizophrenia was caused by bad parenting, childhood traumatic events, or other factors of nurture, even though Freud himself, the founder of psychiatry, rejected this notion. But today, we know the causes are genetic and neurological, most likely combined with yet unknown environmental triggers, perhaps even exposure to a yet unidentified brain virus early in life.

Researchers are moving toward an understanding of the molecular level causes in schizophrenia. They are seeking DNA polymorphisms related to schizophrenia and are having some notable successes. A gene called DISC 1 and another known as DISC 2

(DISC, Disrupted in Schizophrenia) are associated with increased incidence of mental disorders including schizophrenia, *bipolar affective disorder* (manic-depression) and major depression. The DISC 1 gene is expressed in brain development, especially in the hippocampus and the cerebral cortex, resulting in the failure of these structures to develop sufficient *dendritic branching*, producing volume reduction in both brain areas (dendrites are the receivers of nerve cells and normally branch extensively during brain development forming complex circuitry upon which normal brain function depends). In animals, the same gene is associated with decreased sociability and decreased synaptic transmission in the cortex because of fewer dendrites there, than in normals. DISC1 may be a real candidate for the genetic basis of schizophrenia.

Tyrone Cannon of UCLA (Cannon, 2009) examined the effects of these genes on brain anatomy and physiology. Schizophrenics have less gray matter in an area critical for higher mental functions, the *prefrontal cortex* (at the very front of your head). They have reduced volume in the hippocampal formations essential for memory, and more dense packing of neuron cell bodies in many areas of the cerebral cortex. There is also reduced volume of cortex in the brains of schizophrenics due to reduced connections between cortical neurons, as evidenced by "highly impoverished *dendritic spines* (connection points between neurons) and dendritic complexity." What this surprising finding means is that there are not fewer cells in the cortical areas of schizophrenics, but less "scaffolding" for neuronal interactions, resulting in disrupted cellular connectivity, which would certainly result in impaired information processing in an affected brain. It is no wonder that schizophrenics have an impaired mind. Impoverished circuits result in pathological information processing and impaired consciousness, just as we would expect if mind and brain activity are one and the same. The prefrontal cortex, involved in many "executive functions" of the brain such as planning ahead and anticipating consequences of one's actions, shows hyperactivity compensating for other brain damage in some schizophrenics (perhaps in John Nash whose case was depicted in "A Beautiful Mind"). However, in very severe schizophrenics this is absent. Given the pathological state of neurological structure and function, it is no wonder that schizophrenics have minds that just don't work right.

More data from healthy brains shows the high degree of specificity of brain design for the efficient solution of many different kinds of information processing problems. In addition to the highly circumscribed region of the human cerebral cortex specialized for facial recognition (the Fusiform Face Area, FFA, discussed above), there are many other examples of highly specialized brain topography. For example, fMRI studies have led to the discovery of what neuroscientists call the *Parahippocampal Place Area* (PHPA), a brain area specialized for storage and recognition of images of places in the environment. The PHPA is probably related to our capacity to spatially navigate our environments. Think about how you find your way around your neighborhood, your way to work and home again, or to your aunt Minnie's house. Could you do it without images of familiar places along the way?

Nancy Kanwisher (2009) of MIT states that the data supporting this kind of brain specialization is overwhelming. For example, Downing, et. al. (2001) discovered an *Extrastriate Body Area* (EBA) specialized for perception of parts of the body. Pitcher et. al. (2009) used *Transcranial Magnetic Stimulation* (TMS), which temporarily inactivates specific brain regions, to investigate the EBA and other nearby cortical regions. TMS to the EBA disrupts perception of the body only, while TMS to the occipital face area (OFA) disrupts perception of faces only, and to the Lateral occipital area, objects only, showing that these areas are *not* involved in pattern recognition in general, but instead participate in highly specialized processing related to highly specific categories of inputs—more examples of the *localization of function* within the brain and of the precise relationships between brain function and mind.

Of major significance, especially to the case for psychophysical monism, additional research shows that when humans are asked to *mentally visualize* faces or places, the respective areas of brain (face area or place area) are selectively activated in fMRI images, showing that activation in these brain regions corresponds to *specific conscious experiences,* and is not passively driven by stimulus characteristics of the image.

Similar effects have been shown in studies with animals using sophisticated brain-wave (EEG, *electroencephalogram*) analyses. Recording computer averaged components of the EEG called *evoked potentials (EPs),* researchers were able to precisely predict beforehand whether monkeys would make a correct choice or an incorrect choice in a two-choice visual task. The shape of the electrical response (the EP) coming from the monkey's brain is determined by the spatial and temporal distribution of neural signals within the fabric of its brain circuitry, and this reflects the information processing its brain is doing—and perhaps what it is thinking about. Monkeys were trained to select one of two upside-down cups in order to receive a reward. A visual cue telling them the correct choice was presented on each trial and then a few minutes later they had to reach for the correct cup, but sometimes they made mistakes. By recording the evoked potentials from the monkeys' brains during the task, researchers found that the shape of the evoked potential on the computer screen depended upon the choice the monkey made. Based on the shape of the evoked potentials recorded from the monkey's brain while the monkey thought about its choice, the researchers could "read the minds" of the monkeys and could tell what choice the monkey was thinking about and what choice it was going to make before it put its choice into action (see Gazzaniga, et. al., 1998, p. 388–407). The mental states of the monkey were physical states of its brain as reflected in the shape of the evoked potentials recorded on each trial. Like the findings with fMRI in humans, these results, using an electrical measure of brain activity in monkeys, are exactly the kind of thing we should expect if mind is indeed a physical property of brain function.

Genes and specialized brain regions

Genes are made of DNA, *deoxyribonucleic acid*, the structure of which was first formally described by James Watson and Francis Crick in a landmark paper in 1953 (Watson and Crick, 1953). A double helix, in which the two strands wrap around one another like two snakes, forms the basic molecular skeleton. Rumor has it that after months of puzzling about the structure, Watson had a dream about two snakes coiled together and that this gave him the key clue that allowed him and Crick to be the first to publish the structure of the DNA-double helix (see Watson, 1968). DNA codes hereditary information in the sequences of smaller molecules within it called nucleotide bases. Different base sequences code for different amino acids and it is sequences of amino acids that form the protein building blocks of bodies and brains. (See more about DNA and how it works at: http://nobelprize.org/educational_games/medicine/dna_double_ helix/readmore.html).

If genes (*transcriptional units*—a term for *gene* favored now by some molecular geneticists) make a difference in a trait, that is, if the trait is inherited, then having more genes, more DNA, in common should make two individuals more alike on the trait. If genes don't matter for that particular trait, because the trait is not genetically based, then having more DNA in common *won't* make two individuals more alike on the trait. This fact gives researchers an opportunity to evaluate the relative contributions of *nature* (genes) and *nurture* (learning, culture, and the environment in which one develops) in the organization of any given human trait.

Identical twins (called *monozygotic* because they come from the same fertilized egg) have 100% of their genes (their DNA) in common, but non-identical twins (*dizygotic* because they come from two different fertilized eggs) have only 50% of their genes (and DNA) in common. Comparisons of identical and non-identical twin pairs take advantage of a sort of experiment of nature. We can see whether having more DNA in common, 100% vs. just 50%, makes a difference in how similar twin pairs are on various traits, and thereby determine if a trait is genetic.

Existing data on *concordance rates* (degrees of similarity) in *monozygotic (MZ)* and *dizygotic (DZ)* twin pairs indicates that the specialization of the brain areas for facial and place recognition is genetically based. Polk and colleagues (2007) found higher concordance in MZ compared to DZ for faces and places, but not for written words and chairs. The latter two are recent developments in the evolutionary/genetic history of our species and therefore shouldn't have had time for genetic accommodation into our species DNA, consistent with the reported results. A written-letter-specific brain region may exist, but it is not genetic, since experience with written letters is essential to its development.

Deprivation experiments can also give evidence of the relative roles of genes and experience in the determination of psychological traits. Sugita et.al. (2008) found that macaque monkeys raised with human caregivers who wore masks, to deprive the monkeys of visual experience with faces, showed normal ability to discriminate individual human or monkey faces on their very first try, supporting the hypothesis that face recognition systems (the FFA) in the primate brain are *not* dependent upon learning, but instead are genetically evolved brain mechanisms. However, experience thereafter narrowed the range of faces (something called "perceptual narrowing" by psychological scientists) that could be individually discriminated (either monkey or human faces, depending upon the specific experience), a phenomenon similar to the narrowing with experience of the range of *phonemes* (basic sounds of a language, such as "p" or "sh" in English) that can be discriminated during language development (the phonemes of all languages can be discriminated early on, but become narrowed to one's own language with increasing language-specific experience. This is why adult Japanese speakers, for example, have notorious difficulty discriminating certain English phonemes whereas Japanese infants do not).

Evidence also exists for a specialized brain area for the concept of number. For example, in the brains of cats, single cells that respond to specific numbers of objects, regardless of the nature of the object, have been found (see Gross, Bender, and Rocha-Miranda, 1969, 1972). Recognition of number is presumably important to survival. For example, a mother cat has to be able to quickly ascertain that one of her kittens has wandered off or a group of lions in a territorial dispute with a neighboring group must be aware of relative numbers to quickly calculate the chances of victory or defeat and whether an attack or a strategic retreat is in order. Brain circuit "designs" evolve to help solve adaptive problems thus enhancing chances of survival and reproduction.

Related to the hypothesis that we are a social species by our genetic makeup and that we have brain areas specialized for social processing, Rebecca Saxe has found a specialized area in the brain specifically for "thinking about other people's thoughts," a brain area which seems to be very selective and which may be damaged in autism, a disorder characterized by impaired social functioning. This discovery also lends strong support to a central claim of this book, mentioned above, that we are a social species as a consequence of our genetic evolution, and that this evolutionary history has resulted in a large set of brain systems specialized for the processing of social information required for complex social interactions with other people. Having brain circuits that are specifically dedicated to thinking about the thoughts of other people is just such a mechanism. All of our social interactions involve complex information processing and computation by our brains, including imagining what others are thinking, what their intentions are, and how to influence what they are thinking and feeling, particularly with regard to what they are thinking and feeling about us and what their intentions are toward us. Apparently these kinds of computations are impossible if these "mind-reading" circuits in the brain, specifically "designed" for these computations, are absent or dysfunctional. For autistics, impairment of such a "mind module" in the brain would make social inter-action very difficult.

What about brain areas innately organized for language? Kanwisher (2009) believes that this issue is far from settled, in spite of the predominant view that there are innate, specialized areas of the brain specifically evolved for language. Although the adult human brain clearly has language regions such as Wernicke's and Broca's areas and a host of other regions involved in language, what isn't clear is the relative roles of genet-ics and experience in the formation of these language circuits.

The famous Harvard *behaviorist*, B. F. Skinner, argued in the 1950's that language was acquired and could be explained by the laws of two simple and general forms of associative learning, called *classical and operant conditioning*. The equally famous lin-guist Noam Chomsky countered Skinner and proposed instead that language acqui-sition in humans depended upon a genetically organized *Language Acquisition Device* (LAD), unique to the human species, which utilized different and specialized forms of learning specific to language acquisition. He used as evidence two observations: first, the extraordinary ease with which all normal human children acquire language without formal instruction, and, second, universal features, regardless of language or culture, of the deep grammar of all human languages ("the universal grammar"). In essence, Chomsky was saying that language is acquired too easily, in spite of its complexity, and therefore must be primarily built-in. Exposure to the language of one's own culture sim-ply tweaks genetically organized language circuitry (the LAD) by filling in the details of English, Spanish, Tagalog, Farsi, or whatever language you grow up with. More recently, Harvard's Steven Pinker (1994) has reiterated this *nativist* position in his book, *The Language Instinct,* in which he argues that language in humans is as much an instinct as flying in birds or swimming in fish.

However, research with other species raises some interesting challenges to the view that the brain structures for human language are unique to our species, and therefore based mostly in our DNA. Studies by Sue-Savage Rumbaugh, at Georgia State Univer-sity, with an extraordinary bonobo chimpanzee named Kanzi, show that other species besides us are capable of acquiring sophisticated use of human language. Kanzi was born in captivity to a bonobo mother that was being studied to test the limits of chim-panzee language capacity. Kanzi regularly came along while researchers attempted to teach his mother a form of human language. Although the older chimp did not learn, Kanzi did, even though Kanzi had received no formal training. As is the case with young human children, language exposure was enough for Kanzi to learn to understand human speech, so that today Kanzi demonstrates the ability to understand even grammatically complex sentences in spoken English and has been taught to use a keyboard of symbols connected to a voice synthesizer to "speak" (Savage-Rumbaugh, et. al., 1998). Though neither common chimpanzees nor bonobo chimps have the vocal anatomy to make the sounds of human speech, Kanzi's ability to easily comprehend human speech in conversation, even when sentences are grammatically complex, provides evidence that circuits in this animal brain are sufficient for human language comprehension (for example, when Kanzi was asked to "get the pine needles that are in the refrigerator," Kanzi ignored the pine needles in full view right next to him and instead went to the refrigerator and retrieved the pine needles that he had placed there earlier, even though they, of course, were out of sight). Certainly there is no genetically based "Language Acquisition Device" in the brain of bonobos since there would be no reason for "learning circuitry" dedicated to human language acquisition to have evolved in the bonobo brain in the first place. Thus, language exposure at an early critical age apparently modifies brain circuitry, evolved for other adaptive functions in the bonobo, making this non-linguistic circuitry become capable of linguistic processing. And if this is true for the bonobo brain, it may be true for the human brain as well.

Early language exposure in human infants and children may tweak the design of circuits in the human brain evolved for more general functions, such as the analysis and perception of complex auditory inputs, not necessarily linguistic in form, into language circuitry. Thus, early language exposure might interact with genetic design more general in character to produce functional language acquisition circuitry, such as Broca's and Wernicke's areas in the left frontal lobe. On this view, a Language Acquisition Device is not derived primarily from genetic evolution of our species. Instead, language exposure early in life, when much of the brain circuit design has not yet been fixed, changes non-linguistic auditory processing areas into language circuits, which fully mature later in life. Evidence for this view comes from research at UC San Diego which shows that "language areas" in the human brain initially respond to non-linguistic auditory inputs in human infants, and only later does the specificity for language inputs develop, perhaps another example of "perceptual narrowing." Note here that experience is modifying brain structure, and that the specific experience involved, language, is a *culturally transmitted behavior* (that is, a behavior that is learned and passed on to succeeding generations, not by genes, but by non-genetic modes of transmission such as imitation). A few years ago at a conference at UCLA I discussed these ideas with Sue Savage-Rumbaugh. I suggested that what might be happening in human language acquisition is the cultural transmission of experience-induced neurological changes in human brain circuitry. In other words, our exposure to language early in life modifies our neural structures on the microscopic level and these neurological changes, induced by early language exposure, are then passed on, generation to generation, by *cultural transmission* (imitation, teaching and learning, and other non-genetic modes of transmission). I suggested to Sue that this amounted to "culturally transmitted neurological change." She said she fully agreed (Savage-Rumbaugh, 1996; personal communication).

This line of thinking opens up the possibility that there may be many other specific, culturally transmitted experiences that we have in our lives which may alter our brain circuit design, and thus the way we process information, generation after generation. Is it possible that culturally transmitted neurological change is common in the human brain? I call this general proposition the hypothesis of culturally transmitted neurological change (CTNC) and suggest a specific case of it, the culturally transmitted language acquisition device (CTLAD) as an alternative to Chomsky's LAD theory of human language acquisition. Note that both theories recognize language processing and verbal thinking as physical events in specific circuits in a physical brain and both give an important role to genetics, but CTLAD emphasizes the idea that the language experience itself makes circuits initially non-linguistic into circuits specially dedicated to language. (see video of some of Kanzi's abilities at http://www.greatapetrust.org/video/av17c.htm and at http://www.youtube.com/watch?v=a8nDJaH-fVE).

In spite of overwhelming evidence for specialization of brain circuit design, what about the existence of more general information processing circuitry in the brain? Kanwisher (2009) speculates that the very specialized brain areas (face, body, object/category specializations) are "rare" in the human brain. She states that "There is plenty of room for extensive general-purpose cognitive machinery in the brain." This view is controversial among many evolutionary psychologists who reject the idea of general-purpose brain mechanisms. This will come up again in later chapters as I discuss what neuroscientists refer to as "domain-specific" and "domain-general" mechanisms in the brain.

More evidence that mind is physical from individual differences in intelligence

In normal functioning of the brain, more evidence for psychophysical monism comes from brain imaging research related to human intelligence. Using *PET scans* (*positron emission tomography*), Haier showed that the brains of high IQ people use less energy when solving a mental task than the brains of lower IQ people solving the same task. Based on these observations, Haier argues for an *efficiency model of IQ*. He hypothesizes that individual differences in intelligence may be associated with differences among brains in *information processing efficiency*, particularly in a parietal-frontal network which Haier and a colleague have identified as especially important in general intelligence (see "Brain Network Related to Intelligence Identified," *Science Daily*, September 19, 2007.

Also see Haier, Jung, Yeo, Head, and Alkire, 2004; see Colom, Jung, & Haier, 2006). If information processing consists of sets of physical activities in a physical brain, consistent with the doctrine of psychophysical monism, then differences in brain efficiency must be the result of variations among people in the physical properties of their brains. What physical differences among individual human brains might account for variation in information processing efficiency among them? Though this is a complex question, two possibilities immediately come to mind.

First, differences in circuit "design" may be part of the story (see Jung & Haier, 2007). Brains are electrochemical organs in which information is coded and processed in patterns of electrical activity pushed through complex circuits composed of enormous numbers of *neurons* (nerve cells), hooked up with one another in complex, but specific, pathways. In order to process information to solve any particular problem, the information, coded in electrical voltages called *neuron potentials*, must move through brain circuitry from some initial state, corresponding to where the mind is at the beginning of the task, to a terminal state, corresponding to where the mind is at the solution of the task.

You can think of it as a kind of race, wherein neural activity speeds from one place (and in one form) in the brain, call it Point A, to another place in the brain, call it Point B (transforming the neural activity and the information it carries into another form). In some brains, the route from Point A, the initial brain state, to Point B, the terminal brain state at problem solution, involves circuits that are not designed so well, with a lot of dead ends, unnecessary zigs and zags, wrong turns, and so on, so that, although the final destination is eventually reached, it has taken a lot of time and has expended a lot of metabolic energy. The route has been circuitous and inefficient. Thus, a circuit design that is less than optimal can still function, but it functions with lower efficiency, taking longer and requiring greater energy expenditure to accomplish its tasks. It is always at a disadvantage, though not to a degree that cannot be overcome and compensated for by extra effort and extra expenditure of time. A brain operating with less efficiency can still achieve greatness with persistence and determination.

For other brains, those characterized by high IQ, circuit design is more optimal, with fewer dead ends and wrong turns, so that neural activity moves from Point A to Point B efficiently, without wasted time or excessive energy expenditure. Mental tasks are carried out quickly, with relatively few errors, and with less effort. For such brains, intellectual prowess comes easily, and the chances of intellectual greatness, of genius, for persons with the most efficient circuit designs, is almost inevitable, given an environment that provides the opportunity.

From an early age, we can observe differences among children related to their brain circuit "designs". Take reading, as just one example. Reading to children from an early age is very important to the development of their reading skills. However, even with equal experience, there can be enormous differences among children in the development of their reading ability. Some children are still struggling to read in first or second or even third grade, while others, many fewer, start reading as early as 3 years of age, with little instruction other than having been read to from early on. Such children tend to excel in other intellectual tasks as well, and these exceptional children typically excel intellectually throughout their lives. We admire genius. But much of it is just the luck of the draw, the genetic draw, the result of the brain circuit design one inherits (more about inheritance of IQ and other mental characteristics in a later chapter). Inheritance of circuitry that is well designed, streamlined for efficient information processing, may be the key.

It is interesting to note that in brain development, we all started out with too many neurons. Prior to birth the human brain has many more neurons that it will ever need, or have, later in life. As brain development proceeds after birth, excess neurons and non-functional circuitry are eliminated by a process known as *programmed cell death*. In what has been called "neural Darwinism" by Gerald Edelman formerly at UC Santa Cruz, neurons compete for functional connections. Those neurons that succeed are preserved, but those that fail to form functional connections die off (see: Edelman, 1992; also see video of Gerald Edelman speaking on his thalamo-cortical re-entrant theory of the neural basis of consciousness at http://video.google.com/videoplay? docid=7437432153763631391#). Thus, a good deal of what we call brain development after birth is actually a "sculpting" process that weeds out non-functioning neurons and neural circuits. It seems likely that the degree of completion of this process may vary among individuals, probably as a function of genetic differences, producing some brains with circuit designs streamlined for efficient information processing and other brains less so. Differences in intelligence among people may have roots in individual differences in these early developmental processes which refine brain circuit design beginning just before and shortly after birth. Indeed, a gene has been found that influences these processes of neural "sculpting" or "pruning," and there are likely to be others.

Perhaps, in savant syndromes where individuals are mentally disabled in many ways, while retaining exceptional specialized abilities such as extraordinary mental arithmetic calculations, specific knowledge of calendars for centuries past and future, or astounding musical abilities, this neural "sculpting" has remained incomplete, cluttering the more essential circuits, for more essential things, with neurons and connections which were never "pruned" away, leaving intact circuitry that can do the extraordinary, but which has great difficulty doing the ordinary. Such exceptional people with *autistic savant syndrome* may astound us by their ability to tell us the date of the third Thursday in April 2198, but they may be unable to answer a simple question about the meaning of a common proverb or to do the basic tasks required to care for themselves.

Haier's work also suggests an efficiency model of *learning*. He has found evidence that learning results in increased information processing efficiency, as it proceeds (Haier, et. al. 1992, 2004). After experience performing a task, the brain utilizes progressively less and less metabolic energy to perform the same task. Not only is high IQ associated with processing efficiency, but learning is as well. It is very intriguing that we can actually, somehow, consciously feel this change. As we learn some complex task we can mentally *feel* it getting easier and easier, the subjective mental effort becomes detectably and progressively less and less as we learn. By contrast, prior to practice, we can *feel* the greater mental effort, we can feel our minds being blocked as they struggle for a solution. Think about what it feels like to work on an algebra problem or a calculus problem that you don't know how to do (I am not talking about emotions like frustration here, but the feeling of blocked mental effort independent of any emotions that this may elicit). Then compare that feeling to what you feel when you have already mastered the problem-type and can whiz right through it, and through problems of a similar kind later. You can *feel* the change in the efficiency of information processing by your brain's modified pathways after practice, and the resultant learning. Are we actually feeling the effects of the growth of new neural pathways and perhaps the "pruning" away of those neural connections less effective in the problem solution? A fascinating prospect. But feeling our own brain activity is just what psychophysical monism is all about! The brain activity itself *is* the feeling, and in fact, as I will show in a later chapter, all of our experience, even our perception of the external world, is generated in our brain activity in our particular species-specific circuit design, which gives our experience its uniquely human quality.

Synapses and synaptic transmission

Besides streamlined circuit design, a second possibility that may account for individual differences among people in the brain's efficiency, and thus perhaps differences in IQ, has to do with what are called *synapses*. There was a time in the history of neurology when the cells of the brain were thought to be all physically interconnected to one another in one big continuous net or web-like reticulum. But the advent of better microscopes and better tissue staining techniques revealed, over a century ago, that neurons are not directly physically interconnected, but instead have small gaps between them.

Neurons have three major parts. First, a cell body, or *soma*, containing the cell nucleus, mitochondria (the energy factories found in almost all cells), and other organelles with various metabolic functions. Next is the *axon*, which extends like a long hose out from the cell body and carries the nerve impulse, a large positive voltage of about 120 millivolts, from its origins at one end of the axon, closest to the cell body, to its terminal end, the *axon ending*. And finally, like the branches and twigs of a tree, the *dendrites*, the "receivers" of the neuron; these receive the coded neural messages coming into the neuron from other neurons. The gap between any two neurons is actually a gap between the *axon ending* of one neuron and the dendrite or soma of another. This gap is the *synaptic gap*.

This synaptic gap presents a problem. How is it, early neurophysiologists wondered, that information gets across the gap? One idea was that the electrical signal, the nerve impulse, coming down the axon, simply jumped this tiny space, like the spark in a spark plug in your car's engine. Although the idea had appeal for its simplicity, later research by neurophysiologists showed that the gap was actually bridged chemically at most synapses in the nervous system. It turned out that when the nerve impulse, technically called the *action potential*, travels down the axon to the ending of the axon, the arrival of this electrical pulse there triggers the axon ending to release chemicals which float across the synaptic space, activating the dendrite of the next neuron in line. This whole set of structures, including the axon ending of the sending neuron, the dendrite of the receiving neuron, and the gap between them, is called the synapse. The chemical that bridges the gap is called a *neurotransmitter*. And the whole process whereby neurons communicate in this way is called *synaptic transmission*.

Hebbian cell assemblies and the world in the mind

Now, neuroscientists have long suspected that learning involves modifications at the synapse. In 1949 the Canadian physiological psychologist, Donald Hebb proposed in his classic work, *The Organization of Behavior* (Hebb, 1949), that *"neurons that fire together, wire together."* The idea was that when two sets of neurons are active nearly simultaneously then physical changes ("some growth process or metabolic change") in the synaptic connections between them will occur, so that in the future the connections between them will be strengthened and thus more easily activated. Thus, events that occur together in the world become associated, so that in the future when one event occurs out there in the external world, activating the brain circuitry that represents that event (its "cell assembly," as Hebb called it), then the "cell assembly" representing the second event will be activated in the brain shortly thereafter, as a result. This learned association between *neural representations* ("cell assemblies") in the brain results in a beneficial outcome for the organism. Activation of the first "cell assembly" by an event in the world leads to activation of the second "cell assembly," leading the mind to perceive the association between the corresponding events in the world, and thus to *expect* the second event whenever the first occurs. In this way, the brain is able to build up a mental model of the world by experience, a model which includes information about the *predictive relationships* between events and objects in the world of one's experience. Thus, properties of our minds that allow us to understand the world, to make predictions and have expectations about the objects and events in it, and about the relations among them, are derived from physical changes at synapses which occur as we experience the world and its regularities. Learning is the result of physical changes in synaptic connections between neurons in our brains.

Consider this. Is it likely that the physical processes involved in synaptic change, growth processes or metabolic changes, as Hebb proposed, are equally efficient in all human brains, or, alternatively, are such processes likely to be variable from brain to brain? Does synaptic change occur with equal ease in all human beings, or do physical changes at synapses, as a result of experience, occur more readily in the brains of some people, than in the brains of others?

One of the fundamental observations that biologists have made about living things is that *all things biological show variation among individuals in the population.* No two blades of grass are identical, no two roses, no two bird beaks even in the same species, no two human livers, no two webbed duck feet, no two kangaroo digestive systems, no two human faces, and no two human brains or the processes within them are exactly the same. Individual differences, among members of the same species, in *every* biological trait is the rule. The processes of synaptic modification with experience, most likely the physical mechanism of learning in the brain as Hebb proposed, are *not* likely to be an exception to this powerful rule. Thus, it is highly probable that human brains vary substantially in the ease with which synaptic change occurs within them. Some brains are just born to efficient synaptic change, resulting in rapid and easy learning, whereas others have inherited properties that make synaptic modification with experience much more difficult, slower, and much less efficient, requiring not only more time, but more expenditure of metabolic energy, and involving more errors along the way.

What are these synaptic changes? Do new synapses grow when we learn and remember something? Or is there some kind of structural change in existing synapses that takes place when we learn and form a new memory? Research indicates that both are possibilities. Some neuroscientists have been able to actually observe growth of new "dendritic spines" using electron microscopy, confirming Hebb's speculations of some 60 years ago. These spines are microscopic bumps on dendrites that are thought by many researchers to be synaptic junctions. Some neuroscientists have found increases in the numbers of dendritic spines after learning, suggesting the growth of new synaptic connections in the brain areas involved in the learning, as the learning progresses. Other neuroscientists have observed modifications in existing synapses, as well as the growth of new ones. During learning, the synaptic gap between neurons may actually shrink, by growth processes in existing dendritic spines, changing their morphology. This results in an increase in conductance of neural messages at specific synapses involved in learning a particular piece of information, and storing that new information in memory. This is exactly the kind of modification of the "cell assembly" that was imagined by Hebb, when the neural representation of an object or an event is changed as the result of learning something new about it. Imagine how much more a brain can learn if it is equipped with neurophysiological and metabolic properties that facilitate rapid and efficient synaptic change within its pathways, compared to brains less well endowed. Over a lifetime, the differences in intellectual functioning and in intellectual achievement would mount year after year.

A slew of recent studies provide exciting new insights into the molecular mechanisms involved in the strengthening of the connections between specific neurons when a memory is formed. A protein kinase (a kind of enzyme) known as PKM-zeta found in synapses in the brains of animal species ranging from fruit flies to mammals has been shown to be necessary and sufficient for the maintenance of physical changes at the brain's synapses that occur when specific memories are formed. Injections into the brain of a drug known as ZIP, which specifically interferes with PKM-zeta, destroys the memories of specific learned experiences (see http://www.nature.com/news/2007/070813/full/news070813-10.html). Current research by neuroscientists Yadin Dudai and Reut Shema of the Weizmann Institute and Todd Sacktor and Andre Fenton at the State University of New York Medical Center in Brooklyn indicates that the PKM-zeta molecules help form the physical changes at synapses involved in formation of long-term memories (see Shema, et.al., 2007). PKM-zeta changes some facets of the structure of synaptic contacts between the neurons that code a long-term memory and these structural changes must be maintained or the memory will be lost. Injections of ZIP even a month later into specific regions of the taste sensory cortex or the hippocampus can erase memories of specific learned events such as learned disgust to a taste that previously made rats sick and spatial memories respectively. A single application of ZIP to the taste cortex of rats trained to avoid a specific taste erased the memory of the taste aversion even if the drug was injected as much as a month after the memory had been formed. PKM-zeta seems to act as a molecular level "machine" that keeps a memory up and running. By interfering with it, it is possible to disrupt long-term memories. Short-term memories are unaffected. By varying dose and time of injection of ZIP following a learning experience researchers have found that the role of PKM-zeta in memory seems to start about 72 hours after a memory is first formed, indicating that it is not involved in short-term memory. ZIP "is a molecular version of jamming the operation of the machine," says neuroscientist Dudai. "When the machine stops, the memories stop as well." In other words, long-term memory is not a one-time inscription on the nerve network, but an ongoing process which the brain must continuously fuel and maintain. It seems that persistent phosphorylation by PKM-zeta in the neocortex is necessary to store these long-term memories. These findings raise the possibility of developing future, drug-based approaches for boosting and stabilizing memory. Researchers are hopeful that drugs that enhance PKM-zeta will be developed to improve learning and memory formation and reduce forgetting in people as well as be useful in the treatment of memory loss in Alzheimer's Disease. PKM-zeta also seems to be involved in other processes that affect learning and memory including the metabolic pathways for formation of post-synaptic receptor sites (these are where molecules of neurotransmitter attach to a receiving neuron leading it to produce an electrical response, a post-synaptic potential). The researchers note that PKM-zeta is involved with pathways involving neurotransmitter receptor expression as well as with cytoskeletal modulation in order to enhance synaptic connection strength, but much more detail is needed in order to understand how these types of changes relate specifically to long-term memory.

Research into genes involved in these molecular mechanisms in memory is already underway. It is easy to imagine how genetically based individual differences in these molecular mechanisms of memory formation might impact human intelligence. Inheritance of more efficient operation of these neurophysiological processes would make memory formation easier, faster, and probably more permanent, increasing the amount of information that could be learned and retained per unit of time.

In addition to inherited differences in brain circuit design, and in readiness of the brain for synaptic modification with experience, other possibilities to explain brain-based differences in human intelligence also exist. For example, differences in neurotransmitter activity or other neurochemical processes might also be involved in individual differences in human intelligence.

Psychophysical Monism: Brain chemistry and the mind

As discussed above, information processing by the brain involves communication between neurons, and among populations of neurons, via synaptic transmission. This involves the release of neurotransmitter molecules from a sender cell (technically, the *pre-synaptic neuron*) into the synaptic gap. The molecules of transmitter diffuse across the gap and attach to receptor sites on the dendrites of the receiving neuron on the other side of the synaptic gap (actually these receptor sites are proteins with specific shapes embedded into the cell membrane of the post-synaptic neuron, and so are often called *post-synaptic receptor sites*). This *lock-and-key interaction* between molecules of transmitter of specific molecular shape and receptor sites also of specific molecular shape causes a voltage change in the receiving neuron (this voltage shift is called a *post-synaptic potential, PSP* for short). And there you have it. A message has been transmitted across the synaptic gap from one neuron to another. Multiply this by billions upon billions of synapses and you have some pretty complex information processing taking place leading to thoughts, feelings, memories, perceptions and ultimately action.

Research has shown that *different neurotransmitters are localized to different brain pathways, which themselves are involved in specific forms of information processing related to different psychological and behavioral functions.* In other words, different parts of the mind have their own corresponding neurochemical pathways in the brain, utilizing different neurotransmitters. Imagine that any particular human brain will have its own unique set of strengths and weaknesses, in terms of the operations of its various neural pathways. Thus, inherited variations among brains in the efficiency of their synaptic transmission in any particular set of neural pathways would have an enormous effect on how well each brain processes information related to particular psychological activities. So, for example, one brain may have exceptionally favorable genetics related to one transmitter system that processes information related to spatial tasks such as drawing, reading maps, or mentally manipulating objects in three dimensional space, as might be required in some fields of engineering or architecture. Another brain with other inherited properties related to a different neurotransmitter system, involved in another kind of information processing, might produce a person with exceptional verbal abilities such as articulate speech and ability to write with ease and effectiveness. Others may inherit properties of synaptic transmission in neurotransmitter systems related to musical abilities, or the processing of social information, and so on. It is likely that people inherit different degrees of functioning in different brain systems, at least in part, because of genetic differences in neurotransmitter function, which depend upon different metabolic pathways, probably dependent upon specific genes involved in brain development.

Personality and brain chemistry

Not only differences in human intelligence, but also differences in emotional functioning and personality may be related to inherited neurochemical differences in the brains of people. For example, brain pathways involved in the feeling of pleasure, and even of happiness, utilize the neurotransmitter *dopamine*. These dopamine "pleasure circuits," located in the deeper and more primitive parts of the brain beneath the cortex, are intimately involved in our subjective experiences of pleasure, from sex and love to food and the positive emotion associated with viewing a beautiful sunset or the rewarding experience of a sense of personal achievement (see Chapter 9). People who are depressed have lost the ability to feel pleasure or happiness because of a disorder of their dopamine "pleasure circuits" (and perhaps circuits utilizing *serotonin*, another transmitter widely distributed throughout the brain). In essence their "pleasure circuitry" is depleted or dried up of its dopamine and perhaps serotonin transmitters. This dysfunctional "pleasure circuitry" produces a pathological state of the brain, in which positive feeling is neurophysiologically impossible. Such people are neurochemically disabled.

The pleasure circuits have simply ceased functioning. With "broken" pleasure circuitry, not surprisingly, all that is left over is severe depression of mood.

The drugs used to treat depression give further evidence for the hypothesis that minds are equivalent to the physical operations of material brains. Drugs used to treat depression range from *MAO Inhibitors*, which block the destruction of *monoamine transmitters* (those with a monoamine chemical structure) including dopamine and serotonin, to the *Tricyclics* which block *dopamine and norepinephrine reuptake* following their release. Both types of drug increase levels of dopamine and increase neural activity in dopamine brain circuits, including the dopamine "pleasure circuits." Similar effects, by the way, are produced by *amphetamine* and *cocaine*, and account for the powerfully addicting properties of these "pleasure drugs." Newer anti-depressants called *Specific Serotonin Reuptake Inhibitors (SSRIs)* such as Prozac seem to work by blocking the reuptake of serotonin neurotransmitter, elevating activity in serotonin mood circuits. Many scientific studies show that the mood disorders, including severe clinical depression (*unipolar mood disorder*) and manic-depression (*bipolar mood disorder*), have a substantial genetic component in their causation. Many people get depressed simply because they got a raw deal in the genetic shuffle. Their DNA has the "wrong" information encoded into it. They have simply inherited "bad" brain chemistry, specifically faulty dopamine and serotonin brain chemistry, which predisposes them to experience the world as bleak, punishing, and pointless. It is no wonder that depressives are at high risk for suicide, especially when in the depths of an intense depressive episode. They, that is, their brains, have lost the neurophysiological capacity for any sort of pleasure or positive feeling, something that each of us depends upon moment to moment in order to relate to the world, and to behave in response to it, in an adaptive and productive way.

If pathological conditions of mood and personality can be the result of inherited differences in neurotransmitter function and synaptic transmission, then why not the normal range of personality differences in the general human population? What about those incurable optimists? Are they so optimistic because they happened to inherit genes that sustain high levels of dopamine in their pleasure circuitry even in the face of events that would put many others into an emotional funk? What about those who are typically timid? Or those who are often violent and aggressive? The chronically anxious or those with seemingly limitless courage? And what about all those people in between these extremes? The evidence that genes play a significant role in individual differences in personality traits in the normal human population is strong. Twin studies in humans comparing *identical twins (monozygotic, MZ)*, which remember share 100% of their genes in common, with *non-identical twins (dizygotic, DZ)*, which share only 50% of their genes in common, consistently show that genes do make a difference, and a big one. The *concordance rates* (degrees of similarity) for personality traits in identical twins are significantly higher than those in non-identical twins in study after study

(Carlson, 2011). *Adoption studies* add confirmation of the role of genes in personality. Children adopted out at an early age show personality characteristics later in life much more similar to their biological parents, whom they have never met, than to their adoptive parents who have raised them most of their lives (Carlson, 2011). Furthermore, identical twins become *more* similar in their personality traits as they age, even though their individual experiences increasingly diverge as the years go by (Carlson, 2010). This observation is exactly the opposite of what would be predicted if experience and the environment were more important in the determination of personality than are the genes. How one is raised seems to have less influence on personality than the genes one inherits.

What does this imply for the idea that learning and experience are the sources of personality? After all, Sigmund Freud, the Viennese neurologist who invented *psychoanalysis* and psychiatry, believed that personality was profoundly shaped by experience, especially early childhood experience. John Watson, the founder of *behaviorism* in psychology, the doctrine that psychology should study observable behavior only and thus eliminate the mind from its purview, would have argued, as did later behaviorists such as Harvard's B. F. Skinner, that personality was just a *learned* habitual way of responding in social situations. Though learning, as well as genetics, is certainly involved in personality, physical processes in the brain like those discussed earlier are the basis of learning, including the learning that influences personality, reconfirming the doctrine of psychophysical monism, the idea that mental processes, even learning and personality, are really physical processes in an entirely material brain.

Thoughts are physical because they produce specific chemical effects in the brain

Learned patterns of thinking, not just learned experiences, can also play a role in personality and in psychopathology. The psychologist, Albert Ellis, argued that negative thinking was at the root of depression, anxiety, and other self-destructive emotions and some readers may recall Norman Vincent Peale's "The Power of Positive Thinking," in which positive thinking was touted as the secret to happiness and success, even when pitted against all odds. What brain mechanisms might be involved in the effect of thoughts or habitual ways of thinking on emotion?

A fascinating experiment on pain perception offers some important insights into this question. Researchers recruited dental patients at a university dental school for an experiment to test the effect of *placebo* (an inert substance without any real effects) on their perception of tooth pain stimulated by an instrument which delivered electric shock of increasing intensity to one of their teeth (Levine, et.al., 1978). In this experiment, the placebo substance injected was "physiological saline" (salt water with the same makeup as body fluid). Three groups of subjects received injections prior to initiation of the painful stimulation. One group was given an injection of a potent morphine-like anesthetic. The second group received an injection of placebo (inert physiological saline) without any real pain-killing properties, but this group was lied to and told that they were getting a potent pain-killing drug. The final group was given an injection of the same inert placebo but was not told anything about what they were receiving or what its effects might be. Then the torture began.

Researchers measured subjects' pain thresholds by recording the voltage level to the teeth which first caused the patient to flinch in pain. As expected, subjects getting the real anesthetic reported pain at a significantly higher voltage level than the other groups. This showed that the real anesthetic actually was decreasing pain perception, increasing the pain threshold of those receiving it, as expected from administration of a real anesthetic.

However, the second group, which had gotten an injection of placebo only, but who were misled into thinking that they were getting the real thing, had elevated pain thresholds as well, even though they had not received any true anesthesia. This is an experimental demonstration of the well-known *placebo effect*, an effect produced just *by expectation, by belief.*

As expected, the third group, which had gotten placebo without any expectation that they were getting a pain-killer, flinched in pain at much lower voltages than either of the other two groups. Both this group and the second group had gotten placebo. The only difference between this group and the second group was the absence of any *expectations* or *belief* that the injection being administered to them was an analgesic (a pain-killer). So, we can see the effects of belief, belief alone in this experiment was enough to produce significant analgesic effects in subjects who were led to believe that they were getting an analgesic drug, when all they really got, without their knowledge, was injection of a placebo, inert "physiological saline." The placebo effect, which shows the influence of belief on the mind, was well known prior to this experiment, but what was really surprising and profoundly important was the outcome of the next stage of the experiment.

In this next phase, the experiment was repeated with new subjects but this time an additional placebo group was added, a group that got placebo, and which was led to believe that they were getting a powerful pain-killer, just as in the first experiment, however this additional group was pre-injected with a drug called *Naloxone* (brand name, Narcan). All other groups, in this second experiment, were pre-injected with inert physiological saline, as a control.

Naloxone is a powerful *opiate blocking drug*, which plugs up synapses (more specifically, the post-synaptic receptor sites) in a particular circuit in the deep brainstem where opiate drugs like morphine and heroin have their pain-killing effects. In the first experiment, people in this placebo group *without pre-injection of Naloxone,* had experienced *placebo analgesia,* a measurable decrease in pain sensitivity created by nothing more than the *belief* that they had been given a real pain killer, when in fact, they hadn't been injected with anything but inert physiological saline.

However, in this new experiment, the group pre-injected with Naloxone, and then given placebo along with the belief that they had received a powerful pain-killing drug, *did not* experience any placebo analgesia, even though they had the same false belief that had been effective in suppressing pain in the placebo group which was *not* pre-injected with Naloxone. In other words, pre-injection with Naloxone blocks *placebo analgesia.* Naloxone, a drug, prevents the psychological effects (pain suppression) of a specific *belief.*

Why is this significant? Because it shows that a *belief, a mental state,* is having specific chemical effects in the brain, and that these physical effects are so specific that they can be blocked by a specific molecule, with a specific molecular shape, the Naloxone drug molecule. How could a belief, or any other mental state, have physical effects inside the brain, unless the mental state is really a physical state of the brain?

The details of how Naloxone works to produce this outcome will show how amazing this really is.

Naloxone is a drug used in hospitals and by EMT's in the field to treat heroin, morphine, or other opiate overdose. It is a powerful blocker of *opiate* drugs. Someone who is unconscious, not breathing, and a few moments from death from too much opiate drug, will be brought back from the brink of death in a moment by a single injection of this powerful drug. An addict, full of heroin or morphine, who is injected with a single dose of Naloxone, will be hurled into withdrawal symptoms instantly. Though the addict's body and blood are brimming with the narcotic drug, the Naloxone prevents the drug from having any of its normal effects at all. It does this by physically blocking the receptor sites in specific neural circuits where the morphine or heroin would normally work. I have seen a heroin addict sitting in his car in a fast-food parking lot, slumped over, moments from death, receive an injection of Naloxone from an EMT called to the scene by some concerned citizen, and then almost instantly the addict springs up, as if from the dead, cursing the EMT for ruining his "high," forget about saving his life.

The way Naloxone works in the brain is striking. At the synapse, recall that the dendrites on a receiving neuron (technically, the *post-synaptic neuron*) have microscopic *receptor sites* which receive molecules of neurotransmitter from the sending neuron (the *pre-synaptic neuron*). These receptor sites are chemically "tuned" by their molecular structures to receive only molecules of specific shape. It just so happens that molecules of Naloxone have molecular shape nearly identical to the shapes of opiate drug molecules such as heroin and morphine.

In certain regions of the brain, the neurotransmitter at the synapses of those circuits is a naturally occurring brain opiate called *endorphin*, a contraction of "endogenous morphine," discovered by Rabi Samantov and Solomon Snyder in the 1970's. It is at endorphin receptor sites where heroin and morphine and other opiate drugs act by occupying those receptor sites and activating the corresponding brain circuitry. But Naloxone blocks these receptor sites (and so is technically called an *opiate receptor blocker*), plugging them up like gum in a keyhole, preventing the activation of the endorphin circuitry. Some of the endorphin circuitry is involved in regulation of mood, other endorphin circuitry regulates alertness, attention, and wakefulness. Still other endorphin circuits suppress pain perception when activated. Experiments have shown that pain is still suppressed even if these pain-killing circuits are activated by electrical shocks delivered directly to this area of the brainstem via implanted electrodes. Morphine and heroin suppress pain by chemically stimulating these same circuits. Collectively these molecular effects on synapses in specific brain circuits account for the psychological effects of heroin, morphine, and other opiate drugs because these drugs, by virtue of the similarity in their molecular shapes to the molecular shape of endorphin, occupy and activate the endorphin receptor sites and thus stimulate the corresponding circuitry (in this case, pain suppression circuitry).

It is the last effect in this list, suppression of pain by opiate drugs, which concerns us here, because it helps us understand how Naloxone can suppress placebo analgesia in the experiment on dental pain. It does so by blocking the endorphin receptor sites, and thus blocking the pain suppression circuitry of the brain. Not only will opiate drugs be incapable of activating the pain suppression circuitry in the presence of Naloxone, but the *belief* that one is getting a pain-killer (placebo analgesia) will also be ineffective in the suppression of pain in the presence of Naloxone.

Remember that in the experiment on dental pain, human subjects given an injection of an inert placebo (physiological saline) experienced pain suppression, when one of their teeth is given electric shocks of increasing intensity, but this pain killing effect occurs only if the subjects are also told that they are getting a real pain-killing drug. In other words, the belief, that one is getting a pain killer (when one really isn't), actually reduces pain perception, even though no real pharmaceutical is actually involved.

But what is the mechanism of the psychological effect (reduced pain perception) produced by this psychological cause (the mistaken belief that you got a pain killer)? The addition of the Naloxone group to the original experiment shows how this all works.

In these experiments, pain is suppressed by injection of a real anesthetic, *or* by injection of physiological saline (placebo) coupled with the inaccurate *belief* that one is getting the real pain-killer. Injection of placebo in subjects that were not told anything about what they were being injected with was ineffective. Diagrammed, the first experiment looks like this:

Group 1	injection of real pain-killing opiate	pain is suppressed
Group 2	injection of placebo, but told it is pain-killer	pain is suppressed
Group 3	injection of placebo, but not told anything	pain is not suppressed

This demonstrated that belief alone can work to suppress pain.

In the second experiment, remember we add a fourth group that is pre-injected with Naloxone, given an injection of placebo and told that it is a pain-killer. In this case, pain is not suppressed, even though it is suppressed without the pre-injection of Naloxone.

This second experiment looks like this.

Group 1	physiol saline—injection of real pain-killing opiate—pain is suppressed
Group 2	physiol saline—injection of placebo, but told it is pain-killer—pain is suppressed
Group 3	physiol saline—injection of placebo, but not told anything—pain is not suppressed
Group 4	Naloxone—injection of placebo, but told it is a pain-killer—pain is not suppressed.

This shows that the opiate receptor blocker, Naloxone, prevents the pain-killing effects of the *belief* that one is getting a pain-killer. Additional experiments show that pre-injections with other drugs, in place of Naloxone, have no effects at all on the pain-killing effects of the combination of placebo and the belief that one is getting a potent pain-killer. The effect is specific to the opiate receptor blocker, Naloxone.

In other words, belief that you are getting a pain killer reduces your pain, *unless* you are pre-treated with the opiate receptor blocking drug, Naloxone. This is an extraordinary experimental demonstration that placebo analgesia, the reduction in pain intensity resulting from the mistaken belief that you are getting a real pain-killer, is dependent upon activation of endorphin synapses in the brain. Thus, the subjects' *expectation or belief* that pain should be reduced actually does neurophysiologically reduce pain by causing the release of brain endorphin, which then activates endorphin-dependent pain-killing circuitry, suppressing pain, *unless* Naloxone molecules have blocked the endorphin receptor sites first. In that case, the belief is ineffectual in reducing pain. Thus, a belief is experimentally shown to have specific physical (chemical) effects in the brain, and that these effects occur at specific sites in the brain. Unless the belief, a specific mental state, is, itself, a specific physical state of the brain, it would be very difficult to understand how the belief could produce such specific physical effects in the brain, effects so specific that they can be blocked by the drug, Naloxone, a specific opiate receptor site blocker.

The general principle here is profound. What we have is extraordinary, experimental evidence that beliefs and other mental states are physical states of the brain, and that these physical brain states that constitute a belief can have very specific effects on the activity of other brain areas. It is of interest here to note that *acupuncture*, known to produce analgesia, is also apparently dependent upon endorphins and endorphin-based pain-killing circuits in the brainstem, since Naloxone has been experimentally demonstrated to reverse the analgesia produced by acupuncture.

In sum, mental states, beliefs and expectations, are, demonstrably, physical states of the brain which can have physical effects on other brain circuits, altering their function by modifying synaptic transmission at specific synapses, in localized brain areas. The causal chain is this: psychological event (belief or expectation), itself a physical neural state of the brain, leads to a chemical brain event (release of endorphin transmitter), which produces another neural event (stimulation of pain-suppression circuits in the brainstem), causing another psychological effect (consciously perceived reduction in pain). The *belief*, that pain should be less, causes release of endorphin transmitter in the brain, which activates pain-suppression circuits in the deep brainstem, simulating the effects of an opiate pain-killer such as morphine. This is not only impressive evidence for psychophysical monism, but provides a new understanding of the effects of beliefs and expectancies on our brains and on our psychology.

Is religion really the "opiate of the masses"?

And this understanding of the effects of beliefs on the physical activities of the brain leads to other questions. For example, does religious belief produce specific effects on the activity of the brain, or how about prayer? The evidence suggests that religious belief does affect functioning of specific regions of the human brain. Michael Inzlicht (2009) from the University of Toronto recently reported that belief in God leads to reduced activity in an anxiety and stress center in the brain known as the *Lower Anterior Cingulate Cortex* (LACC). He reports that the more a person believes in God, the lower the amplitude of their electrical activity in the LACC and the fewer errors they make on anxiety sensitive tasks such as the Stroop test. Inzlicht suggests that meaning systems of other sorts, not just religion (for example, firm belief in science) "may have similar palliative effects" on the brain. Firm belief in positive outcomes in one's life, what we often refer to as self-confidence, might also work to change brain function.

Does positive thinking alter brain chemistry?

Remember the "power of positive thinking?" If the specific belief that you are getting a pain killing drug causes the release of endorphin transmitter which then physically activates pain killing circuits in the brain, causing a reduction in pain perception, then what might a "positive thought" do to your brain chemistry?

In his *rational-emotive therapy* from the 1960's, Albert Ellis emphasized that thoughts determine your emotions. To paraphrase him, "It is not what happens to you that matters, it is how you *think* about what happens to you that determines how you feel about the event and how you feel about life and about yourself." In other words, thoughts determine your emotions and your mood. When we are down, we are sometimes given the wisdom of the ages and told to "think positively," to "look on the bright side," or "look at the upside." Or when you lose a lover or a job or something else that you value highly, others may try to console you by saying such things as "it wasn't meant to be," "something better will come along," "you were too good for them, anyway," and so on. Why do these things work to make us feel better at all, when we have experienced a loss or a disappointment? What is the mechanism in the brain?

The experiment described above on placebo analgesia and Naloxone suggests how this works. If a belief that we are getting a pain killer can induce release of a specific neurotransmitter which activates specific pain-killing circuitry in the brain, then another category of beliefs, or thoughts, "positive thinking," may act to elevate mood by triggering the release of other specific transmitters, in this case, most likely dopamine and perhaps serotonin, activating the "pleasure circuits" discussed earlier, thus elevating one's mood (another possibility is that endorphins are released which in turn activate dopamine or serotonin pleasure circuits via interconnections between endorphin and monoamine systems in the brain). The "power of positive thinking" may be no more than the causal relationship between optimistic expectations and a resulting release and elevation of *monoamine neurotransmitters* (dopamine, norepinephrine, and serotonin) in the brain, elevating neural activity in the brain's "pleasure circuits," making you feel more positive affect (i.e. making you feel good, or at least, better).

Some additional support for this hypothesis comes from the observation that when someone experiences an elevated positive mood state, when one is "feeling really good," then one also experiences higher levels of motivation. One feels more motivated to do things, to get work done, to see friends, to pursue one's long term dreams and goals. By contrast, one of the distinguishing features of severe depression is a profound lack of motivation, accompanied by negative thoughts and dismal expectations about oneself and one's future. And, following the line of the arguments presented above, there is evidence showing the expected ties with brain chemistry. Research shows that depletion of the monoamine transmitters in the brain by a drug such as AMPT (alpha-methyl-para-tyrosine for you officiandos of organic chemistry) not only causes depression of mood and loss of motivation in humans but profound lethargy in animals (who may also be emotionally depressed but can't tell us so). Thus, once again, thoughts, feelings, and other mental states are shown to be physical states of the material brain, just as psychophysical monists (physicalists) claim.

Self-esteem (or lack thereof) can change brain chemistry

Incidentally, this line of thinking gives us insight into the nature of self-esteem and its effects on mood and anxiety. Low self-esteem produces low mood. Why? Self-esteem is a form of perception, self-perception, with an evaluative component included. Self-esteem, or lack thereof, is based on one's perception of one's attributes, and one's evaluation of those attributes. These are beliefs! When someone has low self-esteem they attribute negative characteristics to themselves (belief). Seeing oneself this way, lowers ones expectations, making ones future seem bleak, a future in which one may predominantly imagine deprivation, failure, loss, and other negative outcomes. These kinds of expectations or beliefs then trigger the "power of negative thinking," probably triggering reduction in dopamine and other monoamines, reducing activity in the brain's "pleasure circuits," producing negative mood and a reduction in levels of motivation. But for this story to be true, the brain must somehow have ways of distinguishing the hedonic value (positive or negative) of its own thoughts and beliefs. How could this be?

It turns out that one of the most fascinating findings to date from fMRI studies of the brain in action is that when one thinks of something, the same brain areas are activated as when that same event actually occurs in the real world (see above). So, for example, when someone in an fMRI machine experiences pain to her own body, particular areas of her brain are seen to become more active. When she observes someone else experiencing the pain, the same brain regions are active again, even though she herself is not experiencing the pain to her own body, and similar effects are produced in her brain if she just *thinks* about pain. This has been interpreted to show that empathy for another occurs when our own brain state closely matches the brain state of another whom we empathize with. Another example is that when we move a part of our body in a specific way, an arm, let's say, then again a specific region of brain is seen in the fMRI to become active. The fMRI also reveals that when the person just *imagines* moving their arm in that same particular way, then the same brain region becomes active, even though no movement occurs, and the activated brain area shows nearly the same fMRI image (Kanwisher, 2009). Now, it is likely that there are subtle differences in brain activation between the imagined movement and the real movement that current fMRI technology can't yet detect, as good as it is, but still the lesson is that very similar brain areas are involved in the actual experience of something and the thought of that experience in imagination.

So, here's the point. Our brains are likely wired such that certain events in the world trigger a neural representation of the event ("a cell assembly," in Hebb's terminology) which automatically activates pleasure, or pain, or fear circuits in the brain as a result of its evolved brain circuit "design," part of our evolved human nature. So, for example, seeing a beautiful woman scantily dressed will likely trigger activation of pleasure circuits in a man's brain. Or alternatively, getting smacked around by an assailant who attacks you unexpectedly will automatically trigger the fear, anger, and pain circuits in the brain, or merely the sight of a large spider or snake will trigger fear circuits and revulsion circuits. However, not only will these actual events automatically trigger activation of the pleasure or pain, or fear and anger circuits, but just the *thoughts* of these events in imagination will also result in the activation of the same brain circuits producing either positive moods, such as happiness or pleasure, negative feelings such as anxiety or anger, simply as a result of what's knocking around in one's imagination. This is common knowledge that one's own psychology works this way, but the idea that the mechanism whereby thoughts affect mood involves activation of specific brain areas is something that most people don't think about.

One's self-concept, and the associated self-esteem, create in one's imagination sets of expectations, beliefs, and even specific visual images about one's future successes or failures, satisfactions or disappointments, victories or defeats, one's set of chronic expectations about oneself projected into future time. If the net of these expectations involve imagined positive outcomes, then there will be a chronic preponderance of dopamine release and consequent activation of pleasure circuits, and such a person, with high self-esteem, will experience consistently positive mood, high levels of motivation, and be optimistic about their future, even if some of these thoughts and projections about the future are not immediately consciously experienced, but are instead "in the background" of the flow of one's thoughts ("the stream of consciousness," as the early 20th century American psychologist, William James, called it).

The effects of negative self-esteem on the brain, of course, would be the reverse. All of this takes on even more importance when one realizes that chronic activation of fear and anxiety circuitry has been shown by researchers to trigger a whole set of hormonal events that impact the immune system reducing resistance to diseases such as cancer and heart disease. This line of thinking leads to the expectation that low self-esteem may be related to earlier death from disease (McDonald, et.al., 2009), although self-esteem that is too high may lead to high-risk-taking behavior that may increase death rates as a result of increased probability of life-threatening accidents. Perhaps, levels of self-esteem about in the middle are the most beneficial. This suggests promising lines of research for health psychologists, but in addition gives further illustration of the proposition that mental states are really physical states of the brain, and in this case, these brain states can even affect health.

Steve Cole of UCLA has shown that social factors can determine expression of genes in humans related to our ability to resist diseases such as cancer and heart disease (Cole, 2009). Stress produces a hormonal signal that affects "signal-transduction pathways" that then affect gene expression (for example, more specifically, the environment acts on NF-B which acts on promoter sequence which then acts on expression of genes). Cole has found that one's subjective experience of the world, "whether you see the world as safe and engaging or as a threatening and lonely," affects the body's immune response, especially in older people. According to Cole, gene expression drives the threat of cancer, heart disease, and neurodegenerative effects. Cole says, "Stress is the fertilizer for late-life disease." Furthermore, Cole has found that "social isolation" makes people more vulnerable to viral infection because the adverse emotions associated with social isolation interfere with the ability to turn on the genes needed to fight the virus. Many *gene transcription control pathways* are subject to environmental influences via what is known among neuroscientists as the *norepinephrine (NE) sympathetic stress system* and the *beta-adrenergic receptor*. Depression, in part exacerbated by social isolation, increases the death rate, cutting 4–5 years off of the lifespan in some genotypes. However, it is interesting to note, as an example of the complex interactions between genes, environment, brain function and the immune system, other genotypes are immune to these effects. Good genes can buffer against bad environments, but environments, especially those that generate stress can affect gene expression with surprisingly adverse health consequences (Cole, 2009).

Psychoactive Drugs give more evidence for Psychophysical Monism

One of the most obvious lines of evidence supporting psychophysical monism is the action of psychoactive drugs. How could caffeine affect the mood of coffee drinkers if the molecules of the drug weren't acting on the brain to produce the effects on mood? Alternatively, placebo effects might be taking place in coffee drinkers, stimulated by their expectations that the cup of java should elevate their mood. But as we have seen, even placebo effects are demonstrably dependent themselves upon alterations in the physical operations of the material brain. How can marijuana change time perception and produce the munchies if THC (*tetrahydocannabinol*), the active chemical in pot, were not acting directly on the brain to modify its physical activity and if the "munchies" and time perception were not physical states of brain tissue? How could LSD (*lysergic acid diethylamide*) create vivid visual hallucinations or produce religious experiences as reported by some (for example, Timothy Leary, the deposed Harvard psychologist who became the drug guru of the 60's, who founded the League of Spiritual

Development—note the abbreviation—to promote the spiritual transformation he believed the drug caused), if the visual experience and even the religious mysticism were not patterns of physical, neural activity inside our heads? Why did *mescaline and peyote* cactus so regularly produce religious experience in their users that ancient peoples, such as the Mayans, Aztecs, and various American Indian societies, made these drugs sacraments used in their spiritual ceremonies, unless these drugs consist of molecules that modify synaptic transmission in brain pathways in specific ways to produce these modifications of consciousness?

In each case, just as in the case of the opiate drugs discussed earlier, these psychoactive drugs consist of molecules of specific shape which act on synaptic transmission in specific ways, in particular brain pathways, with particular information processing and psychological functions. How could drugs, material things, affect consciousness at all unless consciousnesses, itself, were a physical process in a material brain? If the mind were non-material, then it would be immune to the effects of material things like drugs. By contrast, if the mind is physical, then material things like drugs, or brain damage, or brain stimulation, will change it. The evidence for psychophysical monism seems overwhelming. Even the everyday observation that a good crack on the head can cause you to lose consciousness gives support to the proposition that mind is material, that conscious awareness is critically dependent upon physical brain activity, perhaps even that conscious mental states *are* exactly the same thing as the physical activities of an entirely material brain.

Recent studies are even beginning to localize the brain areas that appear to be involved in mystical experiences. I will have more to say about this research later in this book, but suffice it to say for now that a new field called *neuro-theology* is just beginning to find brain correlates of our religious experience. Several lines of evidence point to the temporal and parietal lobes and the limbic system as "God spots" in the human brain.

Thus, even our religious experiences appear to be physical brain activity localized to specific circuits inside our heads, just as the doctrine of psychophysical monism predicts.

If mind is physical brain activity, how did this come about? Peggy La Cerra (2003) hypothesizes that the mind evolved as a means to ensure that the energetic costs and risks of behavior do not exceed its adaptive benefits. This view is consistent with the evolutionary perspective of this book to be developed in the chapters to come.

In the next chapter, we examine how matter might make mind, or, in the words of Edelman and Tononi (2000), "how matter becomes imagination."

To see video of new developments in video games controlled by thought alone, via brain waves detected by electrodes on the scalp, go to: http://video.google.com/videosearch?hl=en&source=hp&rlz=1W1ADBR_en&q=Emotivsystems&um=1&ie=UTF-8&ei=kNOhSr2pCIr0sgOTt4iNDw&sa=X&oi=video_result_group&ct=title&resnum=4#

CHAPTER THREE

Plastic Brains and the "Right Stuff": The Astonishing Hypothesis, Part II

I n the previous chapter, I presented a broad array of research evidence for the "astonishing hypothesis" that mind is physical, the product of the interactions of billions of neurons arranged into the circuitry of an entirely material brain. But how could this be? How could mind be physical? The characteristics of mental events seem to be so different from the properties of material things. For example, how much does an idea weigh? What color is a memory? If you drop an emotion on the floor will it make a thud? How much space is needed to contain a thought? Does a big idea take up more space than smaller ideas? I was able to "play catch" with a cow brain in the supermarket, but I couldn't play catch with any idea or an emotion or a perception.

These questions seem absurd because they try to ascribe common sense views of what matter is like, to mental states, to states of the mind. Of course, the traits we attribute to material objects in our everyday world such as weight, size, color, texture, and so on, do not apply in any obvious way to thoughts, perceptions, feelings and the other contents of our minds. But these ordinary properties of matter are a limited set of the possible properties that material systems can exhibit. Our everyday experience of material things in our daily lives confines our thinking about the properties that matter may exhibit. Mental events may still be physical, that is, they may be merely physical events in an entirely material brain, however the physical properties of *mental events* might just be of a *kind* that is very unfamiliar to us, but still of a material nature, nevertheless. For example, an idea may in fact occupy space, a particular space in the complex web of circuitry in a brain. So might an emotion and a memory. In fact, much of what was discussed in the previous chapter gives many examples of just this. Ideas and other mental states might even have weight or mass, if we added up the mass of all the neurons active in any particular mental state, such as a particular perception, or thought, or emotion. If we did this, we would find that the mass of the specific neurons and their connections, active in each mental state, would differ from one particular mental state to another. And different mental states must occupy different material spaces within the physical dimensions of the brain. Different mental functions occupy different locations in the material of the brain; they involve activation of different populations of neurons, over the course of different time periods, and in different temporal sequences.

You might object that these neural events are not the same thing as the mental state itself. But, according to the interpretation of psychophysical monism known as *identity theory*, the neural activity *is* the idea, or the emotion, or the memory. These subjective mental states are just neural activity experienced from the inside. The electrical and chemical events we can observe in the brain of another person are just the same thing, but observed from the outside. This is not the same as saying that the neural activity causes the mental state. Instead, the neural activity *is* the mental state. The subjective experience of having an idea, a thought, a perception, an emotion, or recalling a vivid memory, and so on, are just what neural activity in the circuit design of our species "feels" like. Subjective mental states are in the neural activity, not caused by it. This seems peculiar, because surely there must be someone or something *having* the feeling from the neural activity; there must be a "ghost in the machine" doing the experiencing, but according to psychophysical monism, there is no ghost in the machine, the operations of the machine is the ghost. The complex and ever changing pattern of neural activity, in the specific circuit configurations characteristic of our species, *is* the human mind. On this view, the conscious mind is an inevitable property of matter, just as long as the matter is organized in the right way (in this case, the matter is neurons, and by being organized in the right way, I mean that the billions of neurons are hooked up together into the requisite circuit design necessary to produce consciousness). Just as a light bulb gives off light when its structure is activated by electrons flowing through it, the brain "gives off" mental states when its structure is activated by neuron potentials (voltages produced by the movement of electrically charged particles, called *ions*, across neuron cell membranes) flowing through it. An automobile engine generates torque, but though you can't see or feel the torque, but only its effects, you don't doubt that the engine's power is physical.

Neurophilosopher Paul Churchland (1988, 1989) of UC San Diego, has proposed that any thought, any feeling, any perception, or any other mental state is represented in the brain by (and, may, in fact, *be*) specific spatial-temporal patterns of neural activity in large populations of neurons (this same idea was first suggested by the neuroscientist, E. Roy John, back in the 1960's).

Spatial-temporal patterns are patterns that occur in both space and time. According to Churchland, patterns of neural activity which *are* perhaps our mental activities occur in the material space of the 100 billion neurons of the brain over very specific periods of time. Population responses (in the form of electrical voltages) of huge numbers of neurons over brief periods of time create our subjective experiences, our subjective mental states. High speed images of brain activity using modern brain imaging techniques reveal exactly this. In time lapse film, it is possible to actually see the waves of neural activity, coded by different colors in computer generated images, wash across the surface of the brain, over the course of a few milliseconds, when a human in a scanner views a scene, hears a sound, has a thought, or feels a specific emotion (Kanwisher, 2009). And of course, these spatial-temporal patterns of neuronal activity differ depending upon the specific mental state that the person in the scanner is experiencing.

Furthermore, complicating the issue, we are taught a lot of contradictory beliefs about the nature of mind in our "folk psychology." Some people believe that having emotions makes human beings unique among the animals, or even that emotions are not in the brain at all, but somewhere else, like the heart, or perhaps that they are disembodied, ethereal states, part of the immaterial soul. But these are myths. Culture has transmitted these false beliefs over many, many generations, some of these myths originating as far back as the Middle Ages, or even before. Emotions are in the brain, not in the heart, just like any other mental function, and many species of animal have emotions, even complex emotions such as sadness, anxiety, joy, and love. Jane Goodall (1971), Diane Fossey, George Schaller, Konrad Lorenz and other researchers have observed behavior unmistakably indicative of such complex emotions in many mammal species such as chimpanzees, gorillas, lions and elephants, but you need look no further than your pet dog to see it first hand for yourself. Other animals besides us certainly experience complex emotion as part of the daily normal operations of their minds and brains.

Another myth is that complex thinking is unique to humans. This is also completely false. Not only do comparative psychologists and behavioral biologists regularly observe highly intelligent behavior of animals in their natural habitats (for example Jane Goodall was the first to observe chimpanzees make and use tools in the wild; Goodall, 1971), but experimental work in the labs of psychologists show that many mammal species, and even birds, especially crows, are capable of complex thinking processes including generalizing, forming abstract categories, and making logical inferences (see Wasserman, 1993).

Edward Wasserman from the University of Iowa notes that philosophers from the Enlightenment period in Europe such as Rene Descartes and John Locke are to blame for many of these misconceptions that have been passed over generations to the present. Both Descartes and Locke believed that animals did not have minds because they couldn't speak and that this, they claimed, was because they had no thought processes and no consciousness. But Wasserman has shown that by carefully employing the methods of classical and operant conditioning (to be discussed in a later chapter), it is possible to give animals the means to reveal their mental processes, even though they can't speak.

Wasserman (1993) specializes in *comparative cognition* which means that he explores the thought processes of various animal species looking for similarities and differences in mental processes across species. And what he finds is that other animal species have many of the same thinking processes that we do, confirming the idea, first proposed by Darwin, that there should be continuity across species not only in anatomical and physiological traits, but also in mental capacities. When it comes to mental faculties, the differences between us and other species are differences in degree, not in kind.

Mind out of matter: Emergent Properties, Plastic Brains, and "the right stuff"

Still it may seem to be just common sense that mental events such as ideas, feelings, perceptions, and memories couldn't be physical because they just are so different from material things such as rocks, chairs, planets, houses, TV sets, tinker toys, a spoon of salt, or a block of wood. But common sense has been wrong before. Prior to Copernicus and Galileo it was just common sense that the Earth was stationary and that the sun, the moon, the stars, and the planets moved around the fixed (and flat) Earth. This was self evident because anyone could observe the movements of these heavenly bodies in the sky and observe the fixed position of the Earth right beneath our noses. The proposition that the Earth was hurtling through space spinning on its axis at high speed seemed ridiculous, otherwise why wouldn't we be thrown off into outer space by this high speed spin? Common sense was wrong about the basics of astronomy and physics, and it is wrong again when it comes to understanding the nature of our own minds.

But how *can* the properties of mental events be so different from the properties of material things we are familiar with in the everyday world, if mental events really are material events in a material brain? In truth, we don't know yet, but for a start at getting some understanding of what might be going on, we need to turn to chemistry and physics for some help.

Physicists and chemists have long observed peculiar features of material systems in nature that arise when matter is combined. In nature, combinations of material elements often produce new substances with properties that are completely unexpected, and seemingly inexplicable, based on the properties of the elements out of which the whole is composed. Such unexpected properties which emerge from the combination of simpler material elements are called *emergent properties.*

A couple of simple examples will illustrate the idea. Think of table salt, sodium chloride, NaCl. As its chemical formula reveals, table salt is composed of one atom of sodium, a poisonous metal, and one atom of chlorine, a poisonous gas, and yet, when combined a completely new set of properties emerges. The properties of table salt are nothing like the properties of the elements out of which it is composed. Table salt is a crystal, it's not a poisonous gas, like chlorine, nor is it a poisonous metal, like sodium, in fact it is one of the salts in living systems upon which their proper functioning depends. Poisonous gas and poisonous metal put together make table salt. Table salt has emergent properties.

Take another example, water. Two atoms of hydrogen, a highly explosive gas, and one atom of oxygen, another explosive gas, combine them and you get a liquid that we drink, upon which all life depends, certainly not explosive, in fact, we use it to put out fires. The properties of water are nothing like the properties of the elements out of which water is composed. Again, we have an example of emergent properties which arise when matter is put in combination with other matter. Of course, these are just two examples, but because of their familiarity perhaps, they are most striking. These examples suggest that it is a regular property of matter in the universe that when it is combined with other matter, quite unexpected properties arise from the combination.

Now, extend this idea to brain structure. It is estimated by neuroscientists that a single human brain is made up of 100 billion neurons, each neuron, itself, a complex cell in its own right. Now, if we can get such unexpected and seemingly inexplicable emergent properties from the combination of two or three atoms, as observed in the case of table salt or water, imagine how much more complex and unexpected the emergent properties might be when we combine *100 billion* material elements, neurons, (themselves, each much more complex that just "simple" atoms) into the incredibly complex circuits of a human brain. What emergent properties *aren't* possible from this combination of 100 billion complex material elements? Mind may, in fact, be an emergent property of the physical operations of 100 billion neurons (Koenigshofer, 1994b), a claim which we might call *emergent psychophysical monism*.

This version of psychophysical monism has a number of implications and raises a number of important questions? First, does the material matter? If neurons are made of organic materials like proteins and fats, or alternatively if they happened to be made of some other material such as silicon, does it really matter just as long as the functional properties of the information processing units are the same in each case?

I once had the opportunity to speak with the famous UC Berkeley philosopher of mind, John Searle, at a conference on consciousness at the Claremont Colleges in southern California where he appeared as a featured speaker on the nature of mind (Searle, 1992). Searle is a recognized authority in the academic community, worldwide, on questions about the nature of mind and consciousness. He didn't end up at UC Berkeley for nothing. So I wanted to pose a puzzle to him to try to tease out his beliefs about the mind-brain issue, about whether he believed that mind was a completely material process or something else. To do this, I posed the following question to this world famous Berkeley philosopher (what I call "the plastic brain question," a question I encourage you to ponder as well):

"Dr. Searle, suppose that we could construct plastic neurons which had identical functional properties to real biological neurons. Then suppose that we could hook together these plastic neurons, functionally identical to real biological neurons, into circuits that were identical in their structure and function to the circuits in a real human brain, and further suppose that we equip this plastic brain with plastic sensory organs with identical functional properties to real sensory organs and that these plastic sensory organs feed signals to the plastic brain functionally identical to those neural signals received by a real human brain. Given these assumptions, would the plastic brain be conscious?"

Now, I know that Searle doesn't really know, anymore than any of the rest of us. But, still, he has spent his academic life reading, writing, and thinking about the nature of consciousness and, along with a handful of other academics scattered around the world, he forms a collective wisdom on the subject as good as any that exists. So naturally I was interested in what he would have to say.

But before I give you Dr. Searle's answer, ponder this question yourself. What do you think? Would the plastic brain be conscious? Here's what Searle had to say.

Searle was up on a stage in front of hundreds of neuroscientists, other *philosophers of mind*, graduate students in these fields, and other professors and researchers, when I posed this question to him. On the stage with him was a woman colleague of his, perhaps one of his advanced graduate students or perhaps a post-doctoral fellow, but likely an expert herself, in any case. In response to my question, Searle said without hesitation, "Yes, given these assumptions, such a plastic brain would be conscious." But at the exact moment that he spoke these words, the woman on the stage beside him, clearly shocked, said, "No, it wouldn't be conscious." The two looked at each other in some momentary surprise and then had a brief discussion on the stage about their disagreement. Then the woman philosopher seemed to back off and accept Searle's answer, but you could see that she was quite uncomfortable with the thought that the plastic brain would have a conscious mind.

How about you? Does it make you uncomfortable to think that a plastic brain could have a mind? To think that the particular material involved in making a conscious mind isn't important, that the material doesn't even have to be organic material, just as long as the material has the "right" functional properties combined into the right organization? Whatever your reaction, something is revealed to you about your own biases, your own prejudices, regarding the nature of minds and their relationship to physical processes in brains.

First, a plastic brain with a conscious mind challenges the belief that the mind is non-material, as Descartes and other mind-body dualists assert, and that it need have divine origins. If consciousness could exist in the plastic brain, then we certainly would not give God the credit since the plastic brain is imagined in this thought experiment to be a product of human engineering. This may be one source of many people's resistance to the idea that consciousness might be possible in machines made by humans. Would mind in the plastic brain seem more feasible if we imagined, for the sake of argument, that the plastic brain was created by God?

Secondly, if a plastic brain with the right functional properties can have a conscious mind, then this would demonstrate that *inorganic material* can have mind if it is organized in the right way. In this case, no special status is given to organic matter over non-organic matter with regard to its ability to provide the necessary and sufficient conditions for consciousness to emerge.

Third, this means that *the matter doesn't matter*. That is, matter, regardless of whether it is living or not, organic or inorganic, can make mind, just as long as the matter has the necessary and sufficient functional properties (presumably, information processing properties) for consciousness to emerge out of the properties of the constituent material elements. Whether these are organic neurons, or inorganic plastic neurons that have signaling properties identical to those of real neurons, doesn't matter. This would mean that not only is mind physical, but that it can be manifested in a variety of physical materials just as long as the required functional organization exists within those materials. In the mind-body issue, this approach is sometimes called *functionalism* by philosophers of mind (don't get this confused with functionalism in psychology, which was an approach to psychology in the late 1800's and early 1900's formulated by the American psychologist, William James, who proposed that psychology should focus on discovery of the adaptive functions of the mind).

Now, as it happened on our planet, it seems that, to date, the requisite material organization is found in nature only in living brains, composed of neurons, themselves composed of organic materials such as fats and proteins. But if the line of reasoning developed here is correct, then there is the possibility that consciousness might be found on some other planet manifesting itself in materials quite different from the material brains we know here on Earth. If life developed on other planets, not based on carbon, as is the case on Earth, but on some other element, then perhaps extraterrestrial information processing systems (i.e. brains) made of materials we consider inorganic, or materials that we don't even know of, might achieve the functional organization sufficient for conscious minds to emerge from them. In short, we might someday discover (or they may discover us) forms of life that are conscious but which are made of material other than the carbon based organic molecules that life on Earth is based upon.

Furthermore, there is the possibility of such "brains" made of inorganic materials here on our planet. Artificial Intelligence, AI, is far from producing conscious information processing machines any time in the foreseeable future, but could silicon based information processing systems made by humans one day achieve the requisite functional organization that would permit a conscious mind to emerge from a man-made machine? This is what emergent psychophysical monism implies, at least in principle—the possibility that machines with conscious minds might one day be created. This seems very farfetched at the present. It is the stuff of science fiction movies such as Spielberg's "AI." Certainly the technology is very far off, but in principle, conscious machines may not be science fiction at all, but a real possibility given enough time for our computing technologies and knowledge of neuroscience to develop sufficiently. Though this could take 100 years, 1,000, or 10,000 years or more, doesn't matter to the arguments here. What matters is that such a thing might be possible in principle, because if so, the implications for our understanding of the nature of the mind are staggering. Researchers at IBM are engaged in research today to try to understand and eventually duplicate the complex circuitry in the cerebral cortex. The cerebral cortex of mammals has what are called *cortical columns* of neurons which are thought to be information processing units in the cortex. In mice, each column has about 1,000 neurons, but in humans, each neocortical column has about 10,000 neurons. For a talk about research at IBM to create artificial microcircuits that simulate the activity of the brain's neocortical columns, see: http://video.google.com/videoplay? docid=7437432153763631391#docid=3112558958535505740 (Henry Markham, "The Emergence of Intelligence in the Neocortical Microcircuit," IBM Research's Almaden Institute Conference on Cognitive Computing, 2009; retrieved May 30, 2010). The theory discussed in this talk is "dendritic object theory," which hypothesizes that perceptual objects may be created over dendritic fields in neocortical columns, simulations of which may be near. According to researcher Henry Markham, with enough money, a mouse brain could be simulated now using current technology. Intelligence and perhaps even consciousness in machines may be closer than we think (for a short and less technical summary of this research, see: http://video.google.com/videoplay? docid=7437432153763631391#docid=608576559611531440; retrieved May 30, 2010).

These are challenging ideas, perhaps shocking or even offensive to some. Without a doubt, your beliefs about the human mind have been culturally transmitted to you probably since early in your childhood. What are those beliefs? Can mind exist only in humans? Only in "higher animals" or only in living organisms? Only in organic matter? How about in plants, which don't even have nervous systems or brains at all? Is consciousness possible only in living brains, and therefore impossible, in principle, in non-living things like plastic or silicon brains or sophisticated computers (the more technically feasible alternative), no matter how they are put together?

Berkeley philosopher, John Searle, doesn't think so. He revealed in his response to my "plastic brain" problem that he doesn't think that the kind of matter matters. But, at least some neuroscientists do think that the material matters. At a conference of the American Psychological Association in Los Angeles a couple of years ago, I had the pleasure of hearing the eminent, comparative neuroscientist Edward Wasserman, mentioned above, whose experimental work in *comparative cognition* I greatly respect, talk about some of his recent work. To my surprise however he spoke of consciousness in animal and human brains as requiring "the right stuff." When I asked him if what he meant by the "right stuff" was living material, he said "yes, only living material can produce consciousness." Since then, he and I have communicated about this issue and he confirms his conviction that consciousness "can only arise from the biological activities of living organisms" (Edward Wasserman, personal communication, August 2009). Thus, Wasserman differs from Searle on the question about whether the plastic brain, in principle, would be consciousness (and by implication about whether highly complex computers in the future might someday be conscious—recall the cyborg in the original "Terminator" movie, played by Arnold Schwarzenegger, or the Science Officer in the first "Alien" film, both machines that exhibited consciousness). Wasserman believes that the plastic brain would not be conscious. However, he emphasized that he still believes that mind is *equal* to brain function, and that brain function is entirely physical. So, although, Wasserman believes that consciousness can occur only in the brains of living organisms, and not in machines no matter how they are put together, he still is a psychophysical monist or physicalist. For him, mind is still physical, although, in his view, a conscious mind is only possible in living brains composed of *organic* material.

I asked Wasserman whether his position wasn't similar to *vitalism*, a doctrine from 19th century biology, now rejected by modern biologists, which states that all living cells and tissues differ from non-living material because they contain in them a "vital force" that distinguishes them from non-living material. Modern biology long ago replaced vitalism with a completely mechanistic, materialistic view of living matter.

Wasserman stated that his position was not vitalism, because he did not believe that any non-physical processes or forces were at work in the biological activities of living organisms, including those that produce consciousness. But he does believe that the kind of "matter matters," though he admits "I don't know how, but I take that to be a basic truth. Of course, the saying goes: 'never say never': but, I'll continue to hold to the line that no artificial intelligence can ever be produced that approximates the 'real deal.' "

Thus, Wasserman believes that biological processes in living organisms, though entirely physical, are nevertheless different in some crucial way from the physical processes in inorganic matter, though he admits he doesn't know *how* they're different. If he is right, then one of the most pressing tasks for neuroscience is to identify the special properties of living tissue that make living biological neurons in a biological brain the only information processing system that can ever be capable of consciousness.

But is this really the case? If consciousness is an emergent property of the physical functioning of information processing units, neurons in brains, arranged in specific circuits, then at what level of organization do the crucial properties required for consciousness emerge? If conscious minds emerge as a result of complex information processing activities in physical circuits of a specific physical design, then perhaps it can emerge from such activities, even if these activities are carried out by non-organic materials as discussed above. In chemistry, organic compounds are those that contain carbon atoms in their molecules. Inorganic molecules lack carbon. When I pressed Wasserman asking what properties unique to organic material were crucial to the production of consciousness, he said he didn't know, but proposed the following "thought experiment" (a method made famous by the well known theoretical physicist, Albert Einstein) to make his point:

"Imagine that we land on Mars, dig down, and find a subterranean liquid. It's orderless and colorless. It boils at 212 degrees F and it freezes at 32 degrees F. Chemical analysis reveals that it is not composed of hydrogen and oxygen, but of two unknown elements: X2Y. Would you drink it?"

What's Wasserman's point? In his own words, "we routinely distinguish between organic and inorganic matter. We also distinguish among the 104 elements. Why? Are those elements not fundamentally different? What I'm driving at here is simply the fact that those different elements really are different; you can't reproduce them with other stuff (what other stuff would you use?). If that's correct, then why do you believe that you can create artificial nervous systems out of different stuff?"

This is certainly a challenging question. But let's consider it, because from this discussion we can get a clearer understanding of what properties of matter may be necessary for the conscious mind to emerge from completely physical processes, as the doctrine of psychophysical monism claims.

My response to Wasserman's insightful "Martian water thought experiment" was the following: "Of course, the 104 elements are different from one another, but this is a consequence of different numbers of subatomic particles, properties of which presumably don't differ from element to element. Thus the properties of the various elements must be emergent. Differences between the 104 elements would be reducible to these differences in subatomic particles unless the critical differences between them are emergent. So, I guess what you are saying is that these emergent properties at the atomic level are unique to each particular combination of subatomic particles. Granted. Then, at the molecular level, molecules with carbon atoms will certainly have different properties than those without. Agreed. Now to your question about why I believe it would be possible to create an artificial nervous system that is conscious out of other stuff. If consciousness is an emergent property of matter, the question then becomes, "at what level of material organization do the critical properties required for consciousness appear?" If consciousness emerges from processes above the atomic or the molecular levels, which I think it does, then perhaps the particular molecules or atoms *don't* matter. I am certain that consciousness is not a property of a single neuron nor of a single organic molecule. Instead, I am guessing that it must be an emergent property of the interactions of neurons put together in some particular, requisite arrangement. Now, the real question is what properties of neurons are required for them to participate in the requisite organization needed to produce consciousness, and whether these properties are in any way uniquely dependent upon organic molecules. What would be the crucial properties of neurons that are required? Would it be the lipid and protein semi-permeable membrane, specific ion channels, or the production of voltages across the cell membrane by ionic movement, receptor sites, transmitters, etc.? [All of these are properties of real, biological neurons]. Or is it possible that it is the higher level signaling and information processing properties of neurons that are the critical feature that permits consciousness to emerge when neurons are put together in the right way? If so, then, if these signal processing features can be accomplished in silicon, then the silicon circuitry, put together in the right way, should have the emergent property of consciousness, just as long as the crucial properties of neurons making consciousness possible are higher level emergent properties such as their electrical signaling properties and not lower level properties such as the specific combination of subatomic particles in their material composition. So, what it comes down to is at what level of physical organization in nervous systems do the "magic" properties emerge that permit neurons arranged in the right way to make a conscious brain. If, as I suspect, the "magic" properties occur at a level pretty far above the atomic level and even the molecular level, then the atomic or molecular properties, including organic/inorganic distinction, shouldn't come into play at all (i.e. the matter doesn't matter, but its organization does). About that stuff on Mars? An elegant thought experiment, Ed. I get your point, and it is a good one. Matter matters. But it only matters if the critical properties are unique to that particular matter. Would I drink it? Probably not, without giving it to a rat first (the crucial and fastest experiment to test the safety). But supposing no rats are free for this purpose, I would consider the following. First, it does have some critical properties of water. But are those the properties that make water have its specific physiological effects? Probably not, at least there's not enough evidence to say. But it is possible that elements X and Y in the specific combination you suggest could have the critical properties making it safe even though it may not have *all* the properties of water. Just because elements X and Y aren't hydrogen and oxygen, and although they don't have all the properties of water when combined 2:1, doesn't mean that they couldn't have some of the properties of water (after all, the freezing and boiling points of the two compounds are the same and both are odorless and colorless), including the critical properties that give water its physiological effects. I guess that for both water and consciousness the critical question remains. What are the necessary and sufficient properties of the constituent elements that are required to produce the emergent properties of each? For consciousness, what are these properties in neurons and at what level of organization of neuronal structure and function do these critical properties occur. I still don't think that the crucial properties of neurons occur at the atomic or even molecular level. Are you saying that the crucial properties of neurons that make them capable of producing consciousness when combined in the "right way" occur at these levels?"

Wasserman's answer was brief and to the point. He said, "I really don't know, Ken, but if you wouldn't drink the Martian water, then you shouldn't "drink" the view of philosophers that the matter doesn't matter."

At this point, Ed Wasserman and I agreed to disagree. Of course, neither of us really knows the answers to these questions, and neither does anybody else at this stage in our scientific understanding of how brains work to produce the mind. But this discussion helps to point out a key question in psychophysical monism: does the *matter* matter (does the kind of matter, organic or inorganic, make a difference) or is the kind of matter irrelevant just as long as the matter is organized in the "right way"? Is consciousness in the lower level atomic or molecular properties of the material or is it in the way the matter is put together, the way the information processing circuits are designed? If the latter is true, as counter to common sense as it seems (just like a round Earth moving around the sun at thousands of miles per hour defied common sense), then someday a machine may be built that has a mind, a mind just as real as the minds of you and me. It is important to emphasize again that whatever his beliefs about the nature of the matter involved, Wasserman still argues that material events in a material brain are the basis of consciousness. In short, he believes that mind equals brain activity. By the way, a few months later, Ed Wasserman sent me an article that he had just published on these issues (Wasserman, 2009). I like to think that our conversations played some role in inspiring his article, but I didn't ask him.

What are the implications of physical explanations of the mind for religion? In my mind, not many. Many people believe in the divine nature of living matter and of our minds and may reject these views based on this belief, but I see no conflict at all between acceptance of physical explanations of the mind and belief in God. Simultaneous belief in both creation and psychophysical monism is logically possible. God could have created the human brain to produce consciousness by completely physical processes subject to the natural laws of biology, chemistry and physics. An all powerful God would certainly be capable of such an astounding accomplishment. Of course, this is not a scientific view, because questions about God are still in the realm of religion, but it is important to recognize that a religious view is not logically inconsistent with a scientific explanation of the origins and nature of conscious minds. As Einstein once said of physics, it is a study of the mind of God, a study of how the creator may have used the laws of nature to accomplish the divine work.

Now, some readers may recognize a major omission from this chapter. I have not yet defined two of the central issues, mind and consciousness. Up until now, I have relied upon the reader's common sense understanding of these terms. I have purposely delayed the discussion of a more formal definition to allow the presentation of the background discussion in the pages above. Now, let's consider the problem of definition of these elusive terms.

When I refer to the *mind*, I mean the collection of information processing events that occur in the brain of a human being or animal, including those that involve subjective mental states and those that don't. Some of the information processing events involve conscious awareness and others do not.

Consciousness is very difficult to define. It is one of those concepts that language falls short of fully describing. In everyday meaning, consciousness refers to being awake or aware and responsive to the environment. In some ways, consciousness is easier to define by contrast. Consciousness is that state which a human is in, when not asleep or in a coma. Consciousness is what we lose when we are completely anesthetized by a general anesthetic, as in surgery. I remember once being put under general anesthesia to have my wisdom teeth removed. The striking thing about it was that as I waited in the dental chair, I was conscious, aware and responsive, but within a few moments of an injection of a general anesthetic I lost consciousness and in that state of unconsciousness I was aware of absolutely nothing. When I awoke it was as if I had been dead. The 45 minutes that I was not conscious was completely lost to me. It was as if that chunk of time, to me at least, had never existed. I had lost what philosophers call phenomenal consciousness (P-consciousness), simply the experience of the world, the moving, colored shapes, sounds, smells, tastes, and feelings of experience. These subjective mental experiences are known as *qualia*. The philosopher David Chalmers identifies the "hard problem of consciousness" as how to explain P-consciousness "in terms of its neurological basis." Although explaining the neurological basis of consciousness is in its infancy, something akin perhaps to the Dark Ages of physics and chemistry, the glaring fact verified by my experience in the dental chair is that the conscious mind is physical, for how else could my conscious mind be put to an end, at least temporarily, by an injection of a drug?

I conclude this section with a brief discussion of my position on the mind-brain question and on "the hard problem of consciousness." Like Wasserman and Searle, I believe that mind is equal to brain function, or at least, an emergent property of physical events in an entirely physical brain. If mind is an emergent property of the physical activities of the brain, then these emergent properties of brain function must themselves also be physical (*emergent psychophysical monism*).

However, like Searle (when he and I spoke at that conference on consciousness in Claremont, CA), I disagree with Wasserman on the question of what kind of material is needed to produce consciousness. Wasserman believes that conscious minds can only exist in the biological processes of living brains. In short, Wasserman believes that the kind of material, organic matter, is crucial. Matter matters. However, like Searle, I don't think the particular matter is as important as the organization of the matter. Matter doesn't matter, but functional organization of the matter does. On our planet, thus far, the only matter that has achieved the requisite functional organization leading to the emergence of conscious minds is organic matter. But organic material alone is not enough. Even organic matter has to be assembled in just the right way for consciousness to emerge out of it (how it gets the requisite organization is discussed more extensively in Chapter 6 on the evolutionary origins of life).

Not all organic matter has achieved the necessary and sufficient functional organization for consciousness. Plants are complex multi-cellular organisms, but they don't have nervous systems and therefore we can readily eliminate them from the list of organisms on earth that have conscious minds. Bugs have nervous systems, and even rudimentary brain-like ganglia, but I doubt if bugs have conscious minds either. I don't think that their neural tissue has the requisite organization for conscious mental states to emerge. Roaches may run around in seemingly purposeful ways, flies may fly toward sources of nourishment and avoid being swatted with surprisingly great skill, but these sophisticated adaptive behaviors may be mindless, automatic responses, though impressively complex, similar to the seemingly purposeful behaviors of a supermarket door as you approach it or a modern day robot equipped with internal information processing circuitry allowing it a degree of seemingly purposeful self-guidance and goal-direction, without any consciousness at all.

Emergence of a conscious mind most likely requires circuit designs found only in some birds and mammals, and perhaps in that pinnacle of the cephalopods, the octopus. But where to draw the line between species that have conscious minds and those that don't is, at the present, a dangerous game. We just don't know enough yet about what properties of a nervous system are needed to make a conscious mind. Nevertheless, consciousness must require that a species have a brain of a certain requisite size and degree of complexity, and I believe it must also have a specific type of circuit design for consciousness to emerge from its physical operations.

What that circuit design might be is still unknown. However, over 40 years ago, neuroanatomist, Vernon Mountcastle, proposed that consciousness might depend upon recurrent circuits that feed back onto themselves in the cerebral cortex. The eminent neurophysiologist, Sir John Eccles, also emphasizes an essential role of the cerebral cortex in consciousness. More recently, neuroscientist Rodolfo Llinas of New York University School of Medicine hypothesizes that consciousness arises from "recurrent thalamo-cortical resonance" which is manifested as brain waves in the 35–50 Hertz frequency range between thalamus and cortex. Francis Crick proposed other specific brain features crucially dependent on the neural tissue of the pre-frontal cortex (see

Crick, 1994). Others have hypothesized that connections between brainstem, thalamus, and the overlying cortex are essential, while "globalist" theorists suggest that a "global" interaction between widely dispersed regions of cortex is critical to consciousness, but none of the existing theories has gained widespread acceptance among neuroscientists and psychological scientists and all these require cerebral cortex, a brain structure found only in mammals, and so all fail to account for forms of consciousness that might exist in non-mammalian species. The "hard problem of consciousness" remains just that.

It is my view that consciousness occurs as electrochemical neural activity moves through the neural circuitry of the brains of select animal species and that this circuitry has specific organization that gives it information processing properties which lead to the emergence of conscious awareness, sentience, and subjective qualia. Since there are many instances of brain damage that do not result in loss of consciousness, but only selective modification of its character, or in some cases no detectable modification at all, the crucial circuit design must be localized to selective brain regions, and therefore conscious mental activities must not be equally dependent upon all brain tissue. Consciousness is apparently localized in the brain, to at least some degree. Finding brain structures that are essential to consciousness and then examining in detail their microcircuitry and other physiological and anatomical features that may be unique to them is one way to try to tease out the neuroanatomy and neurophysiology of conscious minds.

For example, the *Ascending Reticular Activating System* (ARAS), a cigar-shaped structure in the core of the brainstem with axons that rise to most regions of the cortex in mammals, seems to be critical. Its destruction in a single lesion results in permanent coma in animals, and it may be one of the areas damaged in persons suffering from profound loss of consciousness in coma, after head injury from traffic accidents and other sources of head trauma. In addition, the *centromedian nucleus,* part of the *intralaminar* area of the *thalamus* seems to be essential, but perhaps not sufficient, for consciousness (Carlson, 2011). Bilateral removal of this nucleus, located near the center of the brain, appears to abolish consciousness and produces other symptoms that mimic brain death. These structures should be the focus of continuing study and may yield new clues about the essential features of brains required for consciousness, especially as methods in electrophysiology, brain imaging, computer modeling, electron microscopy and other research technologies continue to improve.

Because selective brain damage can result in the selective loss of the conscious experience of particular qualia, our everyday consciousness may be a collection of specific forms or types of consciousness localized to different brain regions. For example, damage to the visual cortex results in a syndrome known as *blindsight,* characterized by a selective loss of the conscious experience of *visual qualia* (no color, no shape, no visual imagery at all), but with retention of the ability to respond to visual stimuli even though the person has no conscious awareness of them (Carlson, 2011). For example, a man with blindsight who has been studied extensively by neuroscientists can point to the location of a light in a room or duck to avoid obstacles overhead even though he reports no conscious visual experience (no visual qualia) at all. This unconscious vision may depend upon sub-cortical brain areas involved in vision such as the *lateral geniculate nucleus* (LGN), the visual part of the thalamus near the center of the brain. It has been suggested that this may be the type of "vision" that reptiles such as lizards have—the ability to detect, localize, and even identify and respond to inputs to the eyes without any conscious awareness of them. Thus, the visual system of lizards would be similar to a sophisticated version of a bank of photocells on a supermarket door which allows it to detect and respond to the presence of an approaching shopper without any consciousness being involved.

The visual systems of primates, including humans, rely upon several different neural pathways. A *dorsal stream* carries neurally encoded information from the retina of the eye via the thalamus to the parietal cortex on the surface of the brain midway between your forehead and your crown. This is often called the "where" pathway because it allows us to tell where something is in 3 dimensional space just by looking at it. This spatial localizer of the visual system is extraordinarily accurate. Think of merging onto the freeway or hitting a fast ball. This not only requires exceedingly accurate assessment of precise location but also keeping track of the moment to moment changes in position of the objects in motion. These complex functions are carried out with little awareness on your part. Another pathway, the *ventral stream*, follows a similar path from retina to thalamus but ends in the lower temporal lobe of the cortex near your ears. This *inferotemporal cortex* (IT cortex) allows us to visually identify and recognize visual inputs and so is often referred to as the "what" pathway. Damage to the IT cortex causes a peculiar syndrome known as *visual agnosia* in which the person can still see clearly, as indicated by their ability to perfectly describe every detail of a visual input such as the image of a bicycle or a chair, yet the visual agnostic has no idea what they are looking at and can't visually identify even common objects. Another pathway is involved in motion perception. Damage here causes *motion blindness* which selectively involves loss of the ability to see motion while all other visual functions remain normal (Carlson, 2011). Persons with this disorder have difficulty crossing the street because when they look and see an oncoming car, they don't see it moving, instead they see a series of "still shots" of the car in a sequence of stationary positions. At one moment the oncoming car is seen as motionless in the distance, a few moments later it is seen as motionless right in front of them, and then moments later as a stationary car up the road past them. When they try to pour liquid into a cup, they repeatedly over fill it because they report that they don't see it filling but as a series of periodic still images with progressively more liquid inside, the last image of the cup overflowing inevitably coming too late. They report that liquid poured from a pitcher appears to be a frozen, solid arch, without motion of the liquid. Thus, different components of our conscious experience seem dependent upon quite distinct neural pathways, yet consciousness also seems to be a global property of the brain which can be interrupted by damage in brain structures such as the ARAS and the centromedian nucleus of the thalamus discussed earlier.

It is also possible that consciousness across the animal kingdom isn't an all-or-none phenomenon in nature, but instead may exist in degrees or levels of consciousness which vary in some systematic way across species. Perhaps there is a kind of rudimentary conscious awareness in sea turtles, a more advanced form in cephalopods, even though they are invertebrates, suggesting that consciousness might have evolved multiple times in the history of life on Earth, and then in birds, mammals, primates, and humans progressively more advanced forms of conscious mind. Perhaps consciousness occurs in degrees, being "fuzzy" or "hazy" in animals with rudimentary elements of the requisite nervous system organization and much more "acute," or in other ways more developed, in the "higher animals" and humans.

One thing is certain, minds, in both their conscious and unconscious components, will differ significantly from species to species, but, at the same time, will also show varying degrees of similarity—a continuity across species in mind "design," as Darwin implied when he hypothesized a continuity of species in anatomy and physiology, based upon his hypothesis that all species on our planet arose from ancient common ancestry. Molecular genetics reveals that we even have some genes in common with bananas!! And we share over 98% of our genes with our nearest living relatives, the chimpanzees. Common genes mean similar brain designs, and that most certainly means similar mind designs. Just like we see similarities in our anatomy and physiology between ourselves and other animals, it is evident that there are many similarities between our behavior and the behavior of chimpanzees, and among the other primates and mammals and birds in general, and undoubtedly there are many similarities in our *minds*, as well. Research by Ed Wasserman and other comparative cognitive psychologists shows the extraordinary degrees of similarity between our minds and those of other species, but still each species has its own brain design (see The University of Wisconsin's Mammalian Brain Collections at http://www.brainmuseum.org/), and consequently its own species-typical "mind design," the details of which are dictated by the demands of the environmental niche that the species had to adapt to in order to survive and reproduce.

Though consciousness remains a mystery, and the "hard problem" of how it is produced by physical processes in material brains is far from being settled, the conviction that mind is the result of entirely physical processes remains at the center of scientific attempts to understand the nature of mind. Though research and theory in neuroscience continue to seek answers, we don't need to solve the hard problem before progress can be made. Ways to test for consciousness in machines and in animals have been devised and have yielded important information even though they don't tell us what consciousness is or what its neurological basis might be.

In 1950, Alan Turing proposed what has come to be known as the *Turing Test* to determine whether a "machine can think." In this test, a human judge engages in a conversation via computer keyboard with a human and a machine both in remote locations to prevent visual cues from interfering. If the human judge cannot detect the difference between the two based on this natural language conversation, then the machine is said to have passed the test, and in operational terms, the machine is said to be "intelligent."

John Searle, the UC Berkeley philosopher of mind discussed above with regard to my "plastic brain" example, has argued that the Turing Test can't reveal whether a machine is conscious (Searle, 1992). To make his point, he devised the now famous *Chinese Room* thought- experiment. Imagine a non-Chinese speaker locked in a room with a large number of rule books and Chinese symbols, and imagine that questions in Chinese symbols are fed through a slot to this person locked in the room. This person then uses the rule books to look up the symbols and the correct responses to the questions and feeds these responses in Chinese back out the slot. Based simply on the input-output operations, the "Chinese room" gives the appearance of understanding Chinese, but the person inside the room doesn't understand any Chinese at all. Searle's point is that "intelligent" behavior by a machine doesn't necessarily demonstrate any consciousness or understanding by the machine. However, it is interesting to note that the same argument might be made about people. Intelligent behavior doesn't prove that another human being is conscious either. In philosophy, this is known as the *other minds problem*, the realization that we really can't know the consciousness of anyone or anything outside of ourselves, and so, though we reasonably assume that other people are conscious just as we are, there really is no way to verify that they aren't just zombies pretending to be conscious.

What consciousness is and whether it is present in machines, animals, or even other humans is not only an example of a "hard problem" but may ultimately be an unsolvable one. Nevertheless, other interesting and important questions about the mind and its design await us. One approach with great promise is to view the mind in terms of information and its processing.

An idea that will be developed in later chapters is that minds are collections of information processing mechanisms each "designed" to solve information processing problems consistently present in the environment of each species over its evolutionary history. To understand the mind of any animal, including the human mind, we will have to understand the nature of the information processing problems that confronted each species as it developed over the history of life on our planet. In my view, this approach to an understanding of the mind, both its conscious and unconscious components, against the background of *emergent psychophysical monism,* promises the best hope for a long overdue revolution in our understanding of human nature, minds and behavior.

In this book, I try to engender ways of thinking about the mind and behavior that the reader may not have considered before. Toward this lofty goal, now and then it becomes necessary to challenge some of the usual assumptions about these phenomena in order to put them to the test. The hope is that by doing so, a deeper understanding will follow.

One of the major assumptions in our common sense "folk psychology" is that human actions are the consequence of our free will. In the next chapter, we give this idea a road test to see how it holds up under more vigorous scrutiny. Is free will really free?

CHAPTER FOUR

Why We Do What We Do:
From Reflex to Reflection; Volition and Free Will

"Odd, how our view of human destiny changes over the course of a lifetime. In youth we believe . . . that life is all choice. . . The distinct possibility that choice itself may be an illusion is something we disregard . . . But at some point all that changes. . . The man I have become, the life I've lived, what are these but dominoes that fall not as I would have them but simply as they must?"

Richard Russo,
Bridge of Sighs

"If the concept of consciousness were to 'fall to science,' what would happen to our sense of moral agency and free will?"

Daniel Dennet,
Consciousness Explained

"Effort of attention is . . . the essential phenomenon of will."

William James (1890, p. 562)

Like many people in 1950's America, I grew up in a Christian home, first Catholic after my father's religious upbringing, and then Baptist and Lutheran, following my mother's religious training as a child in Omaha, Nebraska. The religious ideas I was brought up with in these two Christian traditions included the ideas of heaven and hell, and the roles of deeds and faith in getting entry to the former and avoiding the fires of the latter. Central to this logic was the concept of free will, the idea that I had free choice in what I did and in what I believed, and that accordingly I would be rewarded or punished for eternity based on what I decided during my life. It was especially the

Baptist and Lutheran ministers and Sunday School teachers, who explained all this to me, who seemed to be saying that even people from some distant primitive place, who had never even heard of a Bible, would be damned if they didn't believe in the Savior. Even then, as a child, this struck me as peculiarly unfair, especially of an all-knowing, all-powerful God. How could this wise and divinely fair Being want to punish someone, especially *forever*, for something that he or she had no control over, such as the ideas and books to which they had been exposed? How could some poor soul living in Timbuktu be held morally responsible for not following Christian teachings if they had never even heard of them? Weren't they being held accountable for things beyond their knowledge and control and outside the limits of their own free choice? Weren't their beliefs and actions caused by factors that were simply outside of themselves?

Thus, as it happened, was my first introduction to the problem of *free will* and its relationship to personal moral responsibility. Today, as a psychologist interested in the nature and causes of behavior, I find that the problem of free will is still just as contentious as it ever was. At least in part, because the concept of *free will* is so central to religious ideas in our culture, discussions about it can generate very heated emotions. Perhaps this is why the concept of free will is almost sacrosanct for many people, a realm that ordinary mortals should not venture to investigate. Any suggestion that free will may not be as free, as it logically should be, if people are to be held morally responsible when their fates for eternity may hang in the balance, may be seen by some as verging on blasphemy, or at least a second-guessing of the divine plan that smacks of arrogance by a mere mortal, biological psychologist or not. But, in this book, I intend to stimulate ways of thinking that may be foreign to the reader, not to convince or convert as much as to open gates to the exploration of new paths. So, based on faith in the power of the human mind to understand itself more deeply today than it did yesterday and more deeply tomorrow than today, we shall push on into this treacherous, philosophical wilderness, all the while cognizant of the perils that lie ahead.

Unquestionably, one of the most cherished beliefs that human beings hold about themselves is that they have free will. For many people, this is the explanation of human behavior, the answer to the question, "What causes human behavior?" As my story above illustrates, religious doctrines in their various forms in our culture have contributed immensely to this belief. But religious beliefs are only one category of cultural influence that affects our sense of free will and its role in the causation of behavior. Our secular literature, movies, the school system, our legal system, parental practices, and so on, all contribute to our culturally transmitted beliefs about free will. We are inundated with the idea from childhood. When we do something and then ask ourselves why we acted the way we did, we usually attribute the cause of our actions to our own inner agency, our own feelings, thoughts, values and personal choices. Certainly, parents seem to see it that way, and they let us know as children that we are responsible for our behavior.

A sizeable chunk of our notions of personal identity, our concept of who we are, and who others are, is closely tied to our belief in our undisputed and absolute free will. We often define ourselves and our personal uniqueness by the choices that we have made and the things we have done in our lives. Much of what we think of as being distinctively human, feeling pride, self-respect, or alternatively, shame, or guilt, requires the belief that what we have done, and what we will do, is the consequence of our own doing. We even see free will as one of the key ingredients that separates us from the rest of the animal kingdom.

But what if this belief in free will weren't really true? What if free choice weren't really possible and free will was just a very convincing illusion? What if we are just very sophisticated robots made of organic parts whose behavior is mechanistically determined by our structure and other causes that are beyond our knowledge and control? Some philosophers and psychologists maintain that this is, in fact, the case. This view is known as *determinism*.

Hard determinism is the view that all events in the universe, including psychological and behavioral events, are the result of an unbroken chain of prior causes. On this view, therefore, human behavior cannot be the result of free will or free choice, because the will and the choices made by the will are determined by prior causes outside the person. Though our own personal volition may induce us to do one thing or another, the volition itself is also caused by outside forces beyond personal control, and often beyond one's personal knowledge. Free will is simply impossible.

Soft determinism also called *self-determinism* or *compatibilism* acknowledges that we are determined but claims that determinism is compatible with free will. On this view, free will means being able to do what one wants to do without outside interference or coercion. However, soft determinists acknowledge that what one wants is, itself, determined by genetics, culture, upbringing, and other outside forces. In a sense, according to soft determinists, we have free will as long as our actions are not forced upon us by others, even though our choices are limited by our circumstances. Soft determinism is similar to the idea that we have free will, but that this free will is partial because it is constrained by forces outside our control.

As discussed in earlier chapters, scientists tend to believe in materialism or physicalism, the proposition that everything in the universe is physical. In part because of this, most also tend to be hard determinists. We will give determinism a run for its money later, in the next chapter. For now, let's look at the origins of the idea of free will. What can account for the feeling of free will if we accept the proposition that all events have prior causes, including our own choices?

Some might say that free will in humans emanates from God and God's plan for human beings. Certainly my religious upbringing was based on an assumption of absolute free will. Although, in an attempt to keep an open mind, we might grant that this religious view of absolute *free will* might ultimately turn out to be the real story, in this book, I attempt a scientific approach, and recall from Chapter 1 that scientific explanations attempt to push laws of nature as far as possible to explain things, including human psychology, without resort to supernatural origins and causes. Thus, in this book, we are going to have to look for naturalistic explanations for the human belief in free will.

I have already mentioned cultural factors such as religion as a source of our belief in free will, but the idea of free will, I suspect, probably has roots much older than the major religions of the world and probably older even than the dawn of complex cultures (as distinct from complex social groups pre-existing complex cultures). The idea that we have free will is so compelling that it is an unquestioned central proposition in most people's common sense (their folk psychology), it is incorporated into human legal systems worldwide, and it forms the center of many philosophical systems, some with very ancient roots. In the Biblical account of the expulsion of Adam and Eve from the Garden of Eden, it is Eve's free will in disobeying God that causes the fall from grace and the origin of sin, death, and separation from God.

Anywhere you go in the world, all people, regardless of culture, seem to experience a sense or feeling of volition when they consider various courses of action and then commit to one option or another. *Human psychological universals* such as this usually mean that common genetics (the genetics typical of our species), common environmental forces, or common experiences across cultures, are at work. From the biologist's perspective, such cultural universals usually suggest that something characteristic of our biology is going on, perhaps something inherent in our brain organization as members of the human species. Are there universals in human brain organization that account for our feeling of free will? To help us tease out what brains might have to do to produce something like a "will" we will have to use an analogy.

Willful Bots

A few years ago, there was a television program called "Robot Wars." Contestants, mostly electrical engineering students and others of this ilk, built their own "bots" which then competed in "life or death" battles, by ramming, hammering, blasting, and generally beating the heck out of one another's metallic, armored, motorized frames, until one of the two bots was finally completely disabled. Bots were controlled by their creators via remote control devices, so the intelligence and the "will" behind the bots' purposeful, goal-directed movements were, of course, human.

These robots are rudimentary compared to robotics coming out of Japanese and European labs these days. Scientists at Essex University have created a robotic fish that swims with movements that look just like the real thing, including mechanisms that allow it to swim around obstacles and to turn in the tank once it bumps against the glass without any aberrations in its vertical fish-like swimming posture. It moves just like the real thing, and these movements are not controlled from outside the bot-fish. This aquatic bot utilizes sensors and an autonomous navigational system that permit it to swim around a tank on its own with movements indistinguishable from those of real biological fish. If it had a skin and scales it would be hard to tell it from the real biological deal (http://www.youtube.com/watch?v=eO9oseiCTdk, retrieved April 19, 2011).

Vietnamese-Canadian engineer, Le Trung, as well as a few Japanese engineering companies, are creating robotic androids that look human, walk, climb stairs, and that even respond to spoken commands and questions. Trung's robotic humanoid, Aiko, can recognize different colors, objects, and even solve mathematical equations presented visually to "her" after which "she" verbally answers with replies such as, "It looks like orange juice," "It looks like a sandwich," "The answer is 4.5776." "She" gives the time and the weather for any location verbally requested of her and then tells you what to wear and cautions you to be careful driving if the weather is wet or snowy. Aiko tells her name when asked, can read out loud, in English and Japanese, printed pages shown to "her," and also answers questions about a large variety of topics including who Michael Jackson was, how to make sushi, and "her" likes and dislikes. Aiko will sometimes refuse requests that "she" doesn't "like" and will tell you why. Aiko has over 13,000 knowledge items built-in to "her" robotic brain. "She" learns new information when she doesn't know something. Aiko even learns the faces of new people "she" meets, stores this information, and is able to recognize them when "she" sees them again. Aiko processes 250 faces/second as "she" searches for a recognizable match in "her" bot-memory. When "she" sees a familiar face, "she" matches the face with the correct name of the person and "she" speaks the person's name as it is retrieved from "her" memory. If you watch the video of "her," with some improvements in Aiko's mouth movements during speech, the experience of conversing with Aiko might be (http://www.youtube.com/watch?v=yHFZVwQ53bk&feature=related) (http://www.youtube.com/watch?v=iCR2PFrLkwA&feature=related) recognizably similar to a conversation you might have with a real human. This mechanical problem has been addressed by other robotic researchers who have produced androids with silicon skin and with facial and eye movements that make the android a pretty convincing simulation of a real, biological human being (see "My Date with a Robot," *Scientific American Mind*, June/July 2006 and the following website http://www.youtube.com/watch?v=MY8-sJS0W1I&NR=1 retrieved June 3, 2011), although the robotics has a way to go.

Aiko's creator, Trung, claims that conversation with Aiko is much like a conversation with a human 10 year old, but he plans to give Aiko a much larger data base that will make "her" behavior even more human-like. Meanwhile, Aiko continues to undergo improvements by Trung. "She" now responds to touch and even verbally reports feeling pain in response to tactile stimuli that are too intense, such as a firm grip of "her" arm by her creator. "She" even objects verbally and pushes the arm away of anyone touching her attractive body in inappropriate places, but in spite of these accomplishments, it is clear that this work has a long way to go. Aiko's movements are jerky and lack fluidity, and look, well, robot-like. Interestingly, this is similar to how humans move when the cerebellum, a large structure on the upper surface of the brainstem, is damaged due to disease or accident (see Figures 2-1 and 2-2), a testimony to the complex information processing that fluidity of movement requires in artificial systems or biological brains.

Honda Motor Company has developed an autonomous robot called Asimov that walks, climbs stairs, kicks soccer balls, and so on with movements that look like their counterparts in humans (http://www.youtube.com/watch?v=Wiw-jbjnyzc&NR=1). The ambulation of Asimov, designed to mimic the walking of humans, does so astonishing well. Asimov is not controlled from outside, but generates its movements internally like Aiko, but with much greater fluidity more closely approximating natural biological movement.

What is striking about Aiko, Asimov, and other examples of this kind of advanced robotics is that so much of the behavior looks self-generated, self-guided, and purposeful, and yet it is just robotics. Of course, none of these machines is conscious and none really has a will of its own. Particularly in the robotic fish, the impression of purposeful, self-generated action is unmistakable. If we didn't know that these were machines that had been programmed by human beings, we might be fooled into thinking that they were willful, conscious, agents. But we do know that they are "just" machines, and we also know that machines can't be willful or anything else that involves anything like conscious awareness—at least, for now. However, computing technology is still in its infancy, and so is robotics. As Daniel Dennet points out in his book, "Consciousness Explained," if we can't imagine an artificial computing system that is conscious and self-interested, perhaps even with a will of its own, this doesn't mean that it couldn't exist in principle. According to Dennet, the problem may be that we simply aren't imagining a system with enough complexity. AI (artificial intelligence) systems which can learn from "experience," compute information about external states of the world, and about themselves and their own internal operations, to reach their goals, may completely change our views about what is possible in AI in the future, and about the nature of our own minds and behavior. It is worth noting that recently in a televised and much publicized episode of the game show "Jeopardy," an IBM created computing machine, given the name "Watson," was pitted against two of the most successful and celebrated human champions in the show's history. Though the outcome was at times up for grabs, ultimately, the machine won (see the PBS NOVA program, "The Smartest Machine on Earth," 2011, NOVA6221, WGBH).

What is surprising is that so much progress has been made, even though computer technology, robotics, and AI are barely half a century old. Where was physics in its first 50 years? Not very far. Newton's laws of motion and even the idea of gravity were still many centuries off, and Einstein's Relativity, Quantum Mechanics, and String Theory were still hundreds of years further in the future. Something like the self-conscious, humanoid, human-created Replicants of "Blade Runner" may not be as far-fetched, or perhaps as far off, as they once seemed when the film, starring Harrison Ford and Rutger Hauer, was made. But still, because this AI research work is in its early stages, it is hard to predict what may, or may not, follow.

Many AI researchers are beginning to believe that the next generation of AI will be too complex and difficult to program. Machines will have to be equipped with self-organizing properties that can take full advantage of the ability to learn and change on their own. Bill Joy of Sun Microsystems believes that design of a conscious, willful machine won't come about by our design but by allowing the AI machines to "design" themselves through learning and a selection process, "the way nature does it," to give them the information processing properties they need to successfully deal with their environments. Creation of simulated environments for these next generation AI machines along with super fast processing capabilities may make truly intelligent machines possible in this century, according to Joy. These developments may be coming faster than even Bill Joy predicts. Recall in the last chapter that one researcher, Henry Markham, at IBM is predicting an artificial, silicon-based human brain in just 10 years (see video at: http://video.google.com/videoplay?docid=7437432153763631391#docid =608576559611531440for a short video clip from the Wall Street Journal about this research; and also see IBM work at http://video.google.com/videoplay?docid= 7437432153763631391#docid=3112558958535505740; retrieved May 30, 2010).

The nuts and bolts of free will

But in this chapter we are not so much interested in where AI and robotics are headed as we are in exploring what human free will might consist of and why our sense of an internal, self-determining free will is so powerful and convincing. Is it actually the reality, in spite of claims by hard determinists that free will is logically impossible? The use of bots and bot-brains here is just to provide us a model to help us think through what properties of the human mind, such as free will, might really consist of. Is it "soul stuff" or just organic hardware and software? What properties would have to be present in a biological or AI system for that system to be able to generate anything even approximating what we think of as *free will*?

This is not an easy problem. Pinning down the specifications precisely enough to examine what *free will* might be made of requires more than just our common sense intuitions. To help, let's extend the robot analogy a bit further.

Imagine that we have much more sophisticated robotics and AI available to us sometime in the future. What properties would a bot need in order to generate its own actions, make its own decisions, and determine its own goals? What would it need in order for us to attribute to it free choice, a "will" of its own, and perhaps even moral responsibility? And, in what sense, if any, would it be said to be acting freely, in a non-deterministic way?

Having a *will* implies goals and "desires," otherwise what's the point of having one? Will is only evidenced by goal-directed behavior. Without goals, there is no need for will, free or otherwise. When we *will* something, when we choose one course of action or another, it is to move us toward some goal or to fulfill some desire, or to avoid some undesired state of the world, such as being eaten by a predator or losing our job. Imagine a bot, or an organism, without goals, desires, or even preferences. Behavior would be random, without any guiding principle, without direction. Certainly an organism put together this way wouldn't make it out there in the big, bad world. Organisms possess two fundamental categories of behavior: 1) automatic behaviors such as *reflexes* (the human eye blink, the knee jerk reflex, salivation) or *fixed action patterns* such as the stereotyped attack behaviors of the stickleback fish or web-construction in spiders, and 2) volitional behaviors such as raising one's hand to answer a question in class, driving a car, or bringing flowers to your spouse. Both types of behavior have goal, function, or "purpose." When advanced AI is designed, the behaviors are usually designed to mimic human or animal behavior whether in a fish-bot or humanoid and this always involves some "purpose," a goal. In the fish-bot, the goal is self-directed swimming. The fish-bot's swimming is similar to that observed in real biological fish in an aquarium. So we can say that the fish-bot at Essex University has a general goal, something like coordinated swimming and avoidance of obstacles, but it doesn't have additional goals arranged in a sort of goal hierarchy like a real biological fish has, including goals such as predator avoidance, mating, feeding, territoriality, and so forth. But just program the fish-bot with such goals and put them in a hierarchy of "importance," such that, say, predator avoidance is at the top of the list, feeding next, then mating, and the fish-bot's behavior gets much more complicated and starts to look a lot more like the behavior of a real organism.

But fish goals are far from human goals, although the similarities are there. After all, we don't like predators either, and mating, feeding, and territoriality are goals that humans also have. And humans have additional goals, many having to do with our innate social nature as a species, a nature derived from our evolutionary roots, and related to the fact that we live in complex human social groups involving formation and maintenance of alliances, control and accumulation of material resources, and status or position in the social hierarchy. Notice these three social goals are much more abstract and have reality only in relation to other members of one's kind. Further, these kinds of goals can't easily be accomplished by automatic behaviors, but seem to require much more flexible behavioral control. How can our robot analogy apply here?

Well, we are going to have to make our "bots" social critters—let's call them *socio-bots*. Imagine a humanoid robot put in a group of other humanoid bots. Imagine that each is programmed with this set of three social goals, mentioned above, along with the information processing mechanisms needed to comprehend what these goals mean, and the information processing capacity to evaluate how one is doing with regard to these goals. Just like in the human case, such things involve *computations* that will have to be performed by our hypothetical bot brains, just like such computations are accomplished in our brains. Given the appropriate computational machinery in our hypothetical bot-brains, we would find that a little "bot" society would emerge, with bots engaging in social behavior, that is, behavioral interactions with other bots, other members of their kind, while computing information about status, alliances, and control of resources within the group. When this is done, the behavior of humanoid robots, our sociobots, starts to look more human. But because such goals are social, that is, involve interactions with other members of one's kind, the information processing mechanisms involved are certainly more complex than those needed for feeding or predator avoidance (if it looks and smells like food, consume it; if it looks big and scary, go the other way as fast as you can), and might need to be specially "designed" specifically for this kind of "social processing." Evolutionary psychologists believe that in human brains there are specially evolved circuits for the processing of just this sort of complex social information.

To feed and mate, you just have to be able to recognize food and mates, each of which has concrete identifiable properties that can be represented by a visual system or by an olfactory system, equipped with mate and food detecting circuits. Arrange circuitry so that when a visual system or olfactory system detects these forms in the environment, a triggering mechanism activates the required behavioral patterns, feeding behaviors or sexual behaviors. The Green Sea turtles I frequently see here in Hawaii, where I am now writing this chapter, show this sort of relatively simple behavioral organization as they ply the warm, shallow coastal waters grazing on algae growing on black lava rock.

But the social goals we are hypothesizing here for our social humanoid bots involve much more complex information processing. How can you represent and recognize a social ally or an enemy without recognition and memory of specific individuals and memory of prior encounters with them? How can you detect status of others within your group, or your own status, for that matter, without information processing machinery for evaluating these variables? It is not an information processing problem as simple as recognition of food or mates. Much more complex and abstract computations are necessary, involving comparisons among, and memory of, individuals of one's own kind and interpretation of the social meanings of prior encounters with them. As we somehow add these goals, and the requisite computational hardware, to the bot brains of our hypothetical group of humanoid sociobots, the machine approximations to human motivation, human behavior, and the human mind will come closer to the real thing.

To have such goals requires the machinery to reach them. Avoiding a predator that is moments from being upon you, or seeking out a mate, whose form or odor in your vicinity triggers a sequence of subroutines that result in copulation, is one thing. But how do you formulate a set of behaviors that is going to increase your status in the group, win an ally, or neutralize an enemy? Automatic responses aren't fluid enough. Planning ahead and volition will be required.

Social goals, social processing, and brain circuits for anticipation of future

These social goals require an ability to organize behavior in the present to accomplish states of one's physical or social environment that are in the future, and often in a distant future (I propose the term *prosponse*, instead of response, to refer to behaviors directed, not to current stimuli, but to anticipated future states of the social or physical environment; Koenigshofer, 1992). Not only is the information processing problem much more computationally complex, but it must involve ways of anticipating two important elements of the future—1) there must be a way to represent one's own possible future behavioral options, and 2) a way to represent the likely outcomes or effects of those potential behavioral options, particularly on others of one's kind, at least when considered within the social context. To do this, the information processing machinery must project one into future so that one can "observe" and evaluate future behavioral options with regard to the goals at hand before putting any particular behavior into action in the real physical world. Something like "movies" in the head would do the job nicely. And this seems to be just what we humans do. We "see" ourselves in future action and "see" and evaluate the likely outcomes of those actions. This may be the reason that consciousness evolved, to permit informed volition (Lee Pierson and Monroe Trout, 2005, "What is Consciousness For?" date retrieved 10-20-09 http://cogprints.org/4482/1/whatisconsciousnessfor.pdf) particularly as required in a complex social animal like us and our primate relatives. Adaptive advantages of such capacity is certainly large enough to have produced strong selection pressure to produce brain circuitry for conscious "viewing" of one's self in action and the probable outcomes of that action in one's "mind's eye," a phrase which reveals our intuitive recognition of the visual-like nature of much of our consciousness.

How does the human brain pull it off?

We know from fMRI studies in humans that the *limbic system* of the deeper and older "reptilian" brain (so-called because it is found in reptiles as well as in the mammals), acting in conjunction with the evolutionarily newer cerebral cortex, is involved in evaluative functions. For example, the *anterior cingulate cortex* (ACC), a narrow of strip of the cerebral cortex, becomes active whenever there are mismatches between a goal and the perceived current state of real world conditions. There is accumulating evidence that the ACC acts as an interface between the brain's limbic functions (drives and goals) and the overlying cerebral cortex (Winterer, et al, 2002), including the *visual and motor cortical areas* which generate the visual imagery, the "pictures in the head," that permit us to imagine our future potential behaviors and their probable outcomes, prior to committing to action. The cortex might generate the "movies," and put them up for review by the limbic system and *prefrontal cortex* via the ACC. This visual-like mental review of future behavioral options and their projected outcomes (all of this, information processing functions of our brains), followed by selection of a "course of action," is, I hypothesize, at the core of what we mean by "volition," our "will."

The emergence of complex social goals in homo sapiens, with the accompanying increase in computational requirements for the brain may have been the crucial impetus for the development of brain circuit design that became better and better at *future prediction*, as a way of selecting among behavioral options, in service of future social goals (and other future goals, it turns out, as well). In other words, in our primitive past, the need to anticipate and to manipulate the future mental and behavioral states of others of our kind for our own social advantage may have been the largest contributing cause in making homo sapiens a supercharged, thinking species. And, it appears, that much of this highly developed penchant for thinking involved a progressively sophisticated capacity to *visualize* ourselves in future action, along with the probable effects of those actions on others and on the physical environment—"movies" in the head, staring the "self" in future time, solving problems, avoiding calamities, reaching goals. What could be more interesting, and more *useful*, than "seeing" ourselves in action and "viewing" the likely future results of those actions on our goals and desires? Seeing others (actors) do this sort of thing in Hollywood films may be one reason why we find films so interesting (and entertaining)—maybe a sort of mental rehearsal for us for situations we may encounter some time in our own future.

One way for nature to do this kind of representation is to take advantage of existing information processing systems and co-opt them for the new purposes, the new goals. As the late Harvard paleobiologist Stephen J. Gould put it, "Structures evolved as adaptations for one function often get co-opted for a different role in a descendant lineage. In the classic case, feathers evolved for thermoregulation in small running dinosaurs get co-opted later for flight in birds" (Gould, 1997). In our case, however, we are not talking about body structures such as feathers, but about brain structures. Brain areas, evolved first for *sensory* processing, get co-opted for the production of mental images and their mental manipulation as a means of producing mental reviews of one's self in future action, giving the brain the capacity for choice among the imagined options.

Let's illustrate the idea by using robots and bot-brains again. Some AI robots have bot-vision based on photocells and circuit boards. For object recognition, bot-brains form and utilize what amounts to vision-like electronic representations of the objects "seen" allowing the bot to "recognize" objects. I will have more to say about this kind of representational trick in a later chapter covering *connectionist systems, artificial neural networks,* and *parallel distributed processing, or PDP* for short—all innovations in modern Artificial Intelligence research. For the time being, assume that we could modify the artificial visual system of our newly social, humanoid robots so that image-like electronic representations within the circuitry of the system could be stored from past experience. This could be done by alterations of existing circuit connections or by formation of new ones (remember the formation of *Hebbian cell assemblies* from Chapter 2). Further imagine that these image-like electronic representations from the bot's "memory" could be modified in relevant ways into novel image-like electronic representations (dare we say imagined?) of future behavioral states and their projected likely effects, related to some problem solution. This hypothetical information processing operation could be used to give the bot-brain the capacity to "invent" new image-like representations to "see" if they might work to solve some novel problem at hand. Sounds too farfetched? Well, I would agree that the computations involved would be extremely complex, but given that they are computations nevertheless, and given the right circuitry, the bot-brain could do the requisite information processing if given enough computational power and the required computational steps. In other words, we are dealing with a computational problem, one which, in principle, can be solved in a physical information processing system, given the "right" circuit design and the required computing power.

Whether existing computing technology is up to the task, or even if AI a thousand years hence is still not capable of these computations, is not the point. What counts here is that the operations taking place in an information processing system that might be capable of generating "autonomous" choices, from within the system, *are physical* operations, and thus, in principle, could be accomplished in a machine, *or* by completely physical processes in a biological organ, a material brain, one like ours. The argument I am making is that our "will" really is comprised of a particular set of physical information processing operations or computations, and thus is a material thing, taking place in a material system, 3 pounds of convoluted "wet ware" crammed into the bony case between our ears. On this view, the "will" is not "soul stuff," but material stuff.

To put it in somewhat more familiar human terms, visual-like mental images of oneself in action stored from past experience could be "mentally" modified (by information processing operations in the brain) to "show" (image-ined; imagined) novel behaviors and their probable effects in the world to the "mind's eye". Such projections into future time could be based on memories (stored representations) from past experience of similar behaviors and their experienced effects in the past. In other words, the bot-brain in one of our future sociobots would have electronically coded image-like representations, "bot-brain-images," of itself engaged in various movements in various situations along with "images" of their subsequent effects in the world. It would have information processing operations that permitted the electronic manipulation of these into representations of new movements in new situations, and based on past experience, it would infer probabilistic "guesses" about likely effects of the associated novel actions, based on "memories" of past similar behaviors in similar situations and their "remembered" effects on particular goals. Simply put, the bot-brain could "view" possible future actions it might engage in, and then "view" the probable effects of those "imagined" behavioral options. Then, the bot-brain could "choose," (again, an information processing operation or set of operations), could exert "volition," and select a behavioral option (involving an evaluative function among imaged alternatives perhaps) that was computed to have the greatest likelihood of successfully reaching the goal or solving the problem at hand. In short, the bot-brain could "plan ahead" and implement the plan most likely to succeed (most likely to lead to the most favorable outcome) as assessed by the computations carried out in its bot-brain circuitry. Not only would the bot be exhibiting something like "willful" choices, it would also be acting "intelligently" (which gives us a clue about the nature of what we call "intelligence").

Further, imagine that relevant stored representations from the past would be reactivated by association depending upon the nature of the goal-seeking problem currently at hand (similar to a strategy used by the IBM computer, Watson, that recently beat two Jeopardy champions at their own game—a search function based on networks of associated information stored in the computer's circuitry; see PBS, NOVA, "The Smartest Machine on Earth," 2011). Thus, an array of potential problem solutions would "automatically" present themselves for "review" (itself a computational process) and might be retained as possibly useful, or discarded as probable dead ends (another kind of selection process that could be accomplished completely computationally in a bot-brain), a kind of "choice-making" operation. It is even possible to imagine that when given a particularly difficult problem, a search engine something like an internal Google could actively ply through stored images and activate ones that might be useful in the goal-reaching, problem solution. Additionally, learning, such as that already exhibited by AI researchers in existing PDP ("connectionist") artificial neural network machines like those developed by Terry Sejenowski and colleagues at UC San Diego's Cognitive Science Department, could be utilized by the bot-brain to improve response selection ("choice"), computationally measured against programmed goals and based on comparisons with stored representations of past response-outcome scenarios, combined with feedback about current successes and failures. (By the way, add the "motive" for play in baby-bots to get them to practice interacting with the world and to "image" (imagine) various manipulations of the environment and to test them out in play, and you have a mechanism for baby-bots to build a knowledge base for later real world action; this suggests one adaptive function of play in human children, and in other young animals, a kind of action-based hypothesis testing).

For my money, this is pretty darn close to what the human brain does when it "chooses" one thing or another. In us, the feeling of a will, of volition, may arise from the operation of similar information processing operations taking place in our biological brains. So, for example, imagine that you see a box of delicious-looking éclairs in the market. Your human, species-specific, bio-programmed goal of seeking sugars and fats, a left over in human brain circuit design from the days when these were scarce commodities in the ancient environment in which we evolved, takes over and draws you to them, and you "picture" yourself biting into the éclair and enjoying the delicious, sweet taste; but then images of yourself not being able to get into your clothes, or mentally "seeing" a belly bulge beginning to develop, or visual-like mental images of being scolded by your doctor or your spouse for being overweight, pop into mind, and so you "decide" that your goal of keeping your weight under control will take precedence. You put the éclairs back on the grocery store shelf. The act of "volition" in "freely" choosing to do one thing and not another is based in visual-like mental imaging of potential behaviors and their projected outcomes before a final commitment to action in the world. Or suppose that you work at an auto manufacturing plant and that you are dissatisfied with your future prospects, so you begin to consider options and you "see" in your "mind's eye" yourself as a lawyer, or a pro-athlete, or as the head of your own company making clean, efficient hydrogen cars. You image yourself in these mental "pictures" receiving the adulation of your clients whom you have successfully defended along with hefty fees for your services or, alternatively, the praise of environmentalists everywhere; you image "in your mind's eye" a big house on the ocean, and a life, happy ever after. You "decide" to go back to college and complete your engineering degree (and you get mental images of these events as well, perhaps "seeing" yourself sitting in a classroom with equations all over the board or cheering crowds as your degree is handed to you on stage; these images of the possible outcomes of your selected behavior focus your attention on these goals and help to reinforce them as well as provide a guidance system keeping behavior on track over the long haul; perhaps in the words of William James, by sustained "effort of attention").

In a bot-brain, imagine that somewhat analogous goals were "programmed," built in to the circuitry of the bot-brain, just as humans end up with goals in their brains derived from their biology (i.e. the evolution of their human brain) and from their experience. In the bot-brain, imagine that specific circuitry has been put in place that compares current energy stores of the bot-battery with a set-point voltage, and when there is a mismatch with the set point of battery energy, the mismatch triggers activity in particular circuits and causes corrective action, guided by an information processing "review" by the bot-brain of possible actions and their likely outcomes based on stored representations of effects of past bot-behaviors in the bot's past experience in similar situations. From the array of alternatives, an intelligent bot would select the appropriate action, and engage the program that would put into effect the appropriate bot move-ments, guided by bot-vision, to accomplish the goal of recharging its batteries, perhaps from the nearest electrical outlet. Now, certainly other scenarios for the bot could be imagined, taping into other pre-programmed goals of greater complexity, but the point has been made that bots could "make choices," they could exhibit "volition," based on scanning operations in their bot-brains that would calculate the relative hedonic (or "adaptive") values of various response alternatives and then "select," via mathematically coded criteria, one option or another based on these evaluative computations.

Once again, is this not very similar to what humans do when "making choices," when exhibiting their *will*? Though we don't consciously experience the "evaluative" processing in our brains in mathematical terms, and we are "blind" to much of the other aspects of all these computational activities taking place in our brains, the underlying processing nevertheless could be completely quantitative, perhaps coded by numbers of, or frequencies of, neural firings in specific "behavioral-option-evaluation circuits" somewhere in the brain. This is not just an imaginary brain design that I am dreaming up, but one which really appears to exist in the brain's mesolimbic *dopamine reward sys-tem*, beginning in the *ventral tegmental area* of the midbrain and projecting forward into the forebrain's amygdala, hippocampus, and the *nucleus accumbens* (Carlson, 2011), all located beneath the neocortex (*dopamine* is one of the *neurotransmitters*, the brain chemicals in *synaptic transmission*, and it is found in the so-called "pleasure circuits" of the brainstem of vertebrates, including humans). Interestingly, the nucleus accumbens projects (sends connections) into the basal ganglia involved in movement control and in learning. Other projections of the *ventral tegmental area* go to the prefrontal cortex (known to be involved in planning ahead), the limbic cortex, and the hippocampus, a structure known to be involved in memory (Carlson, 2011, p. 356).

As discussed in a previous chapter, researchers have shown that just *imagining* pleas-ant or unpleasant things can activate the same reward and anxiety circuits activated by real events in the actual physical world. In short, the evidence suggests that the human brain has neural circuits for pleasure and for fear and anxiety and that these circuits can be activated by the imaging circuitry that underlies our "mind's eye." Thus, there is, in place, a brain system for evaluating the anticipated effects of various imagined potential behaviors, as part of a larger brain system for volitional action, perhaps made up of pre-frontal cortex, visual-motor cortex, the ACC, and several other limbic structures including the mesolimbic reward system and brainstem punishment/pain circuitry. Our model of the "will" is gaining steam.

Free will as a set of information processing operations

If all of this really could be accomplished by mathematically coded computations in a bot-brain, or in a human brain, then for us, our "will" may be a specific set of physical information processing operations in our brains, and perhaps, the subjective feeling of volition may be a non-essential, non-causal artifact of these computational events taking place within the 3 pounds of tissue between our ears. The idea that the conscious experience of our "will" or any other conscious sensation is not really causal in our behavior, but a non-causal artifact of our neural processes, is known as *epiphenomenalism*. Conscious experiences, on this view, are epiphenomena—conscious experiences that have no real causal role in behavior, even though we feel as if the conscious experiences are the cause of our actions. I will have more to say about some experimental evidence related to this peculiar idea in the next chapter.

Now, further imagine that all this information processing could occur in the bot-brain in milliseconds, an order of temporal magnitude within the capabilities of existing microchips, and certainly within the capabilities of biological brains. For our hypothetical humanoid "sociobot" of the future, such processing might well produce, within its bot-brain circuitry, electronically coded visual-like "images" of its potential behavioral alternatives and their likely outcomes, put to evaluative test via computational bot-brain operations similar in function to those of a biological brain (specifically, most likely the brain's limbic system). This is not to say that the bot would need to be conscious of such electronic representations and the computational operations upon them. We aren't. We are only aware of the final outcome of the computations, the feelings. Consciousness in our sociobot might not even be necessary just as long as the electronically coded representations in the bot-brain had the critical information in them to permit a review of behavioral options (another set of complex computations) prior to selection of a physical action (more information processing operations). As discussed above, this would permit the bot to have an internal, electronically coded, "review" of its options, evaluated against "expected" outcomes in relation to future goals, prior to response selection in a choice situation. Doesn't this sound like the very thing that humans do when "making a choice"? Given these information processing properties, would not our bot have a "will" and demonstrate this capacity for volition in its "planned" "choices" and actions? And, wouldn't this "will" seem to be free, or at least internally, volitionally, self-generated?

Now, recall that the bot-brains in our hypothetical future *sociobots* can learn (just like existing artificial neural networks; see later chapters). Expose them to the "ideas" (electronically encoded representations) and "values" (electronically encoded) of the sociobots that they "grow up" with. Let's assume that our *sociobots* as social critters, just like human beings, have a built-in disposition (a pre-programmed information process-ing "bias" or "motive") to learn the practices, ideas, and values of their own sociobot group. This learning, remember, could occur by the modification of connections in existing circuits or the creation of new connections and new circuits in the bot-brain memory stores. As our sociobots acquire "sociobot culture," they acquire a whole set of learned, culturally transmitted, ideas, values, and belief, just like humans do. All these are encoded into their bot-brains in electronically coded representations (remember Hebb's cell assemblies; see Hebb, 1949), which affect information processing as the "cultured" sociobot "considers" various behavioral options in the future, whenever it is confronted with a set of behavioral options, a "choice." When it would engage in these information processing activities in order to select behaviors that were likely to lead to successful problem solution or reaching its goal, it would look like it was exerting its "will," in this case a "will" in part shaped by its social and cultural experiences, just like in the human case.

By the way, give the bot-brain built-in circuit design that makes it "care" about how other sociobots evaluate its sociobot owner, because if other bots "value" any bot too negatively they might "unplug" it, or at least won't share resources with it or defend it against bot-predators (if we think of the case which likely existed for prehistoric humans), and we have a way to make sociobots conform to group norms. Computa-tional mechanisms for *bot-guilt* and *bot-social anxiety* would serve to keep the sociobots "in line" with the values of their group, a mechanism for group cohesion that would tend to benefit all members of the group and thus be functionally valuable—that is, adaptive (probably a clue to why humans have an apparently innate capacity for guilt, social anxiety, obedience to authority, and conformity as part of our universal human nature).

Imaging, image manipulation, and the IBOES routine in human brains

Whether or not these information processing wonders might one day actually be real-ized in a bot-brain remains to be seen (remember Dan Dennet's claim that if we can't imagine such things in machines, we just aren't imaging enough information processing complexity), but we *do* know that these imaging tricks exist in the human brain. Just think about your own thinking processes (a recursive process called *meta-cognition* by psychologists) and you will notice that a lot of what we experience as thinking occurs in visual images, as I have argued above. Furthermore, experiments show that these visual imaging operations actually do occur in our brains, as our intuition tells us, and they include the ability to "mentally" (computationally) manipulate the imagined visual images, just as I propose in model of the "will" described above. In a series of elegant experiments, Stanford University's Roger Shepard (Shepard and Metzler, 1971) has demonstrated that we can perform various mental operations on our internal visual images, such as mentally rotating them in space in real time (just one type of information processing operation we know our astounding brains are capable of). Furthermore, Shepard and Metzler showed that the greater the number of degrees that a figure had to be mentally rotated in order to solve a problem, the longer it took subjects to mentally accomplish the rotation to reach a solution. This suggests that mental images are physically encoded computational states of the brain and that their manipulation, also material computational events in the brain, occurs in a time frame similar to what real rotations of the physical object would require in the actual physical world. This is probably an adaptively useful feature of the brain's mental imaging capacities because it allows our minds to make accurate assessments of the actual time course of real physical manipulations of objects in real physical space, something that a brain would need to know in order to successfully plan future movements effectively. Shepard and Metzler's findings disproved an earlier hypothesis that processing of mental images required the brain to break down images into mathematical propositions, and instead supported the view that the brain maintains and manipulates mental images as topological and topographic wholes. Later, Kosslyn and colleagues (1995) used brain imaging methods to show that the mental images of objects are mapped and mentally manipulated as wholes in the brain's visual cortex. Furthermore, Kosslyn showed that there was considerable overlap in the mapping in the visual cortex of imagined objects and the mapping involved in perception of the same real objects, suggesting that circuits originally evolved for perception of objects in the world have been co-opted in evolution for the production of mental images and the manipulation of imagined objects and events, just as I have proposed as part of my model above. Kosslyn and colleagues (1995) concluded that the brain is optimally organized to handle the kind of mathematics that constantly computes a series of topologically-based images, again consistent with my model. Other research lends further support to my model of how our brains produce a sense of volition and will. Many studies demonstrate that mental images of one's *imagined* actions retain many of the properties of the execution of the corresponding real movements. Jean Decety and Marc Jeannerod (1996) found that when volunteers were asked to walk mentally through gates of various apparent widths at various apparent distances as depicted in a 3-D display in a virtual reality helmet, mental walking time was found to increase with increasing apparent gate distance and decreasing gate width. These researchers propose that there is a functional equivalence between neural states in the brain for physical action and imagined action (motor imagery). Other research- ers have demonstrated that similar cortical circuits are activated in musical imagery and musical performance in pianists (Meister, et al., 2004). Thus, research findings show- ing a high degree of similarity in brain events in imagined action and actual physical execution of action are accumulating. These findings give further empirical evidence for the model of volition, the *will*, which I have proposed above. And, as I have sug- gested earlier, this is a relationship which would facilitate effective movement plan- ning, making possible more accurate and adaptively useful selection of a response from an array of possible choices, in an act of "will" that is reliant upon mental imaging of potential actions and their likely outcomes in the world. Further confirmation comes from a large number of brain imaging studies which demonstrate that mental images of movements are associated with the specific activation of neural circuits used in the early stage of motor control (motor programming). These circuits include the *supple- mentary motor area* of the cortex, the *primary motor cortex*, the *inferior parietal cortex*, the *basal ganglia* beneath the cortex, and the *cerebellum* which sits on the back of the brain stem. All of these studies confirm the hypothesis that the same neural circuits that are involved in preparation of movement by the brain are involved in mental imagery (Decety, et al., 1994; Roth, et al., 1996; Jeannerod, 2001; Decety, et al., 1993). And just as I have proposed above, the Swedish physiologist Hesslow suggests that mental imagery includes an anticipatory component such that an imagined action can elicit mental images of what *would* have occurred if the action had actually been carried out (Hesslow, 2002). Mental images of movement cause heart rate and breathing changes that correspond to the amount of imagined effort involved in the imagined movement (Decety, et al., 1993). In addition, we clearly perform all sorts of other manipulations on our mental imagery—just introspect and observe what kinds of image manipula- tions your mind engages in when thinking about what you are going to do tomorrow, or what you plan to do a year or more from now, when you manipulate mental images of objects to make the imagined objects into imagined tools to solve a particular prob- lem, or when you are deciding to do this thing or that thing, moment to moment. As evidenced by our own introspection and by studies discussed above, visual-like mental images can be manipulated in ways similar to the way we manipulate actual objects in the real world.

To illustrate this visual nature of our thinking to my students, I briefly pull a "fast one" on them in class. Before beginning my lecture, I ask for the class's attention and then I tell them that I have a flat tire on my car in the college parking lot, and that if anyone can loan me their car jack to change my tire, I will give them an A for the day.

Almost immediately after this rather mischievous deception, I ask them to think about what went through their minds. Most of them report visual images related to solution to the problem, such as "seeing" in their "mind's eye" the trunk of their car open and they are mentally searching for their car jack in the image. Others report "seeing" themselves searching the parking lot to find their car, so that they can look for the jack, and so on. Once, one student even told me that he saw himself searching his trunk, then the floor in his car's back seat, and then not finding his jack, got an image of it in his garage, thus realizing that he didn't have it with him.

There are several interesting features about these mental images. First, they are highly visual in nature (not auditory, not olfactory, not kinesthetic, etc), including spatial extent in three dimensions, and they have color, and movement highly similar to the visual images that one receives when one's visual system is activated by external light striking the retina of the eye. This is undoubtedly explained by research using fMRI brain imaging, like that discussed above, showing that when human subjects are asked to imagine various objects, or engage in other kinds of visualization, it is visual areas of the cortex (and the motor cortex) that become active, involving many of the same regions of the brain activated when we actually are looking at an object in the outside world. Thoughts involving visual images are apparently taking place in the broadly visual and motor areas of cortex, suggesting that, as I expect, circuits that were originally sensory/perceptual in nature have been co-opted and expanded into the new visual imaging functions which permit us to anticipate future and thus to potentially manipulate it, a hallmark of an intelligent species. Recent fMRI studies even show that different areas of cortex involved in visual and motor functions are activated by different kinds of visualization operations. In experiments by William L. Thompson, Scott D. Slotnick, Marie S. Burrage, and Stephen M. Kosslyn (2009), visualization of the static spatial location of letters and numbers leads to greater activation near the *occipito-parietal sulcus, medial posterior cingulate, and precuneus,* whereas mental rotation of these stimuli causes activation in *superior portions of the parietal lobe and in the post-central gyrus.* Interestingly, these cortical areas activated in the mental rotation task are regions of brain involved in visual-spatial perception and in movement and are associated with what's known as the *"dorsal stream"* of the visual system sometimes referred to as both the *"where" stream*—as in spatial vision—and the *"how" stream*—as in vision for action. (Mishkin and Ungerleider, 1982; Goodale and Milner, 1992—respectively).

Secondly, the movements in our "mind's eye" are often of one's "self," either "seeing" oneself, or just one's point of view (POV), similar to a Hollywood movie, moving around in an imagined environmental space related to the problem solution, in this case, through the parking lot and then making searching movements through one's car, looking for the car jack. This is important, because our sense of *free will* involves a sense that it is *our* free will, *our* causal agency that is involved in the choice-making.

"Seeing" ourselves in action or "seeing" these mental images from *our own* point of view undoubtedly reinforces at least two things: first, the sensation that the images belong to *me*, to a self, which my brain identifies as *mine*, reinforces the subjective experience that we are a separate self which we differentiate from the rest of the world (more about this later); second, "seeing" one's self in action or viewing mental images from one's POV, manipulating them, and then using these to select behavioral alternatives, when making choices, reinforces the concept that it is *me, my* self, as an individuated entity, that is *causing* the behaviors selected by imaging them and mentally reviewing their projected probable effects before the selected behavior is put into physical action. These components of our mental imagery, all information processing events in our brains, go a long way in giving us the feeling of decision-making, volition, "choice," and free will.

Third, when we "move" through our mental images we often focus attention on parts of the visual-like images that are most relevant to the problem solution. This observation shows that attention in mental images is similar to how attention operates when we deal with visual images derived from actual external visual inputs, reinforcing the sense of a *self, my self*, actively involved in these information processing operations. We experience these shifts of mental attention as we witness shifts of our mental POV.

Fourth, when I ask my students if they initially "willed" these images as part of their attempt to solve the problem, somewhat surprisingly, the answer is unanimously a firm "No." The relevant images often "pop" into mind without any volition necessary to bring the appropriate images forth. This shows that a lot of the requisite information processing involved is not conscious and, furthermore, that, by association, stored visual images (in memory), relevant to solution of the problem at hand, are searched and retrieved "automatically," without volition and without our conscious awareness of the processes involved. We seem to be "pre-programmed" to solve problems by use of visual imagery in this way. This can't be a learned ability; it must be genetically built-in to the design of our neural machinery (just like it was built into the IBM computing system, "Watson," that beat two of the most celebrated human Jeopardy champions; see above; PBS NOVA, 2011). However, sometimes, when a problem solution is less concrete and less evident, "we," that sense of an individuated self, may actively seek appropriate images in our "mind's eye" by an active search (which we even sometimes experience as mentally effortful, the essence of the "will" according to William James; see quote at the head of this chapter), and we may even invent the images required for problem solution, if we don't find them, by manipulating images we *do* have stored in visual memory in ways relevant to the problem at hand. And, of course, we *sense* this information processing as occurring within us, within our own particular subjective experience, our own mind. For example, though a purple and yellow striped unicorn with a red and white candy cane horn doesn't exist, and though we probably haven't ever seen a drawing or painting of one just like this, still we can manipulate the images we do have stored in memory of candy canes, unicorns, and color sensations to create the image of this particular imaginary critter in our "mind's eye." I am fairly certain that this is the kind of process that inventor's might use to create things like the first flint spear, the first light bulb, the heliocentric model of the solar system, or atomic theory, and so on.

That these are certainly physical information processing operations in our material brains would lead me to suspect that the more unusual and the more complex the images that we must mentally assemble, the more time and the more metabolic energy will be consumed by doing so. Undoubtedly, this is why contemplation of very difficult and abstract problem solutions such as the original formulation of concepts such as quarks, the theory of relativity, black holes, prions, the invention of calculus, ionic mechanisms in neuron potentials, and the like must involve a lot of time and metabolic energy expenditure, which we experience as "mental effort," in William James' terms, "the effort of attention," "the essential phenomenon of will." Contrast this "effort" with the much smaller "effort" required to think of very familiar things such as trees, birds, your dog, or the ideas of "eating breakfast" or "starting the car." These ideas are probably represented in our brains by assemblages of neurons very similar to Hebb's cell assemblies (see Chapter 2). Those that are simpler and more familiar depend upon synaptic connections fewer in number, and because of the more frequently repeated exposure to the familiar ideas they represent in the world, the connections are probably already at "full strength," and so such ideas require less mental effort, less "effort of attention" (William James, again). In fact, Pierson and Trout (2005) make the observation that as a task (such as driving our automobile) becomes more familiar with practice, we must expend less and less conscious "effort of attention" to the task; consciousness plays less and less a role in directing the behavior. The same is true not only of more familiar and practiced behaviors, but it is also true of more familiar ideas. The more familiar the idea, the less mental effort involved, and likely the less time and metabolic expenditure required to "use" the ideas. Pierson and Trout also note that too much "mental" effort is often experienced as unpleasant, as my six year old son, working on a homework task he finds too difficult, frequently informs me and my wife (he whines, "But it is too hard!" and sometimes even cries because he finds the mental effort so unpleasant; how many students can relate to this feeling?). Pierson and Trout speculate that this sensation of excess mental effort as unpleasant may be an adaptation that motivates us to conserve our information processing resources whenever possible, a built-in mental laziness to help conserve calories that otherwise might be burned too readily on processing activities not of immediate adaptive usefulness (another example of the prime principle espoused in this book—that the mind is organized by natural selection, and this assures that most of its operations adhere to the *Law of Adaptation* (Koenigshofer, 1994b), organisms tend to behave in ways—and have minds—that promote survival and reproduction of their genes). *Sensing* these information processing operations as occurring *within our own minds* helps reinforce the sense of an individuated self, as does of course, observations of our own bodies and their physical extents in three-dimensional space. And seeing and feeling parts of our body move after we consciously sense the volition, "our will" to move, reinforces our perception that it is our volition which is acting as a cause of any behaviors which follow, reinforcing our perception of free will as the cause of our own behavior.

Finally, the mental images in our "mind's eye" are future oriented and they are often novel, at least in the manipulative detail. Not that these students hadn't seen their cars before, or the college parking lot where they park, or their car trunk, etc. In fact, they have seen all of these before. These images are stored in their visual memories, and accessing these images, related to the problem solution, as noted above, often occurs seemingly automatically, without conscious awareness. But what is truly novel in these mental images results from the highly skillful manipulation of the mental images that we accomplish in order to solve the problem at hand. When confronted with a problem or a *choice*, we visualize ourselves in action related to the problem solution, as in an internal movie, "movies in the head" (philosopher Daniel Dennet speaks of the "Cartesian *Theater*"). For example, in this case, students mentally image themselves opening the trunk, then perhaps "see" themselves moving books or papers or rags that they might "see" there, in the way, as they mentally search their trunk, and then they "picture" themselves looking for the jack there, and then, if they don't "see" it there in their "mind's eye," then they might "see" themselves lift the cover over the spare tire compartment to "see" if their jack is there, or they might "see" themselves "looking" on the floor behind their front seats, etc. (note all the use of visual terms to describe our thinking processes). In other words, the search for the jack, in this case, the problem at hand, proceeds in fairly detailed and fairly realistic visual-like mental images of one's self in motion, engaging in movements needed to solve the problem at hand, and accompanied by feedback about the envisioned effect of these movements. And remember, as discussed above, the neural activity involved in these imaging functions seems to be primarily in the same visual and motor areas of the cerebral cortex which are also utilized in visual perception and early stage movement control (Roth, et al., 1996; Jeannerod, 2001; Hesslow, 2002).

We are capable of self-generated visual-like images in our mind/brains showing us ourselves in action, and then other images, as part of the process, give us feedback about the consequences of each imagined action we mentally review (perhaps involving activity in prefrontal cortex, and the ACC, the anterior cingulate cortex and other limbic structures as discussed above), guiding us on our way to our goal or problem solution.

In summary, this process by a biological brain or by a "bot brain" can be conceptualized as consisting of four processing steps or stages carried out by the brain: 1) image an array of potential behaviors (IB, image behaviors), 2) image the probable outcomes of each behavioral alternative (IO, image outcomes), 3) evaluate each imaged behavioral option in terms of projected likely effects (EB, evaluate behaviors), 4) then select the behavioral option most likely to lead to the goal (SB, select behavior). For a short hand we can call this information processing routine IBIOEBSB, and shorter still IBOES—generate images of behavioral options, their projected outcomes, evaluate options, select behavior (i.e. image behaviors, outcomes, evaluate, select = IBOES) to be put it into action in the real world. It is my bet that this would look like volition from the outside, and that it would feel like volition in the brain doing the IBOES routine, and it might even be subjectively experienced as *free will*.

From reflex to reflection

There are enormous benefits of this "mental trial and error" for organisms that have the brain design to engage in the IBOES information processing routine. First, instead of simple, relatively inflexible reflex responses to stimuli in the immediately present environment, the organism can extend itself into future time, mentally reviewing an array of relevant potential future behaviors, and their probable outcomes, measured against the organism's goals. Much greater flexibility of response (or to use my term, *prosponse*—future oriented behavior) is the result, permitting the organism equipped with brain design for IBOES to adapt to a wider range of environmental conditions, even when those conditions are rapidly fluctuating and relatively unstable over evolutionary time, or even short periods of time such as "a day in the life." Reflexes, on the other hand, are only useful in response to immediately present instances of long-term stable conditions of the environment which have been present over evolutionary time scales, time scales long enough for natural selection to "design" them (or more correctly, to "design" the neural circuits that embody the reflexes).

Furthermore, such "mental trial and error" has payoffs in temporal and caloric efficiency. Actual action in the physical world requires time and often a hefty caloric expenditure. Movement of muscles and bones occurs in real time and burns a lot of metabolic energy. For example, in the absence of IBOES brain circuitry, my students would have to walk from the classroom all the way up the hill to the parking lot, find their cars, open car doors, the trunk, etc. to physically search for the jack, and then, after all the expenditure of time and energy, may find that the jack wasn't in their car after all. All the time and energy had been expended for nothing. However, by using visual-like images in their "mind's eye" to do a "virtual" search in which they "see" themselves looking in various places for the jack, and perhaps "mentally finding it, they conserve time and calories, compared to what would be required of an animal whose only option, because of its brain design, was to expend the time and calories doing a "real" trial and error search in actual physical action.

There is another adaptive advantage of the "movies in the head" provided by the information processing operations in IBOES, and this one is hard to overestimate. The search in "the mind's eye" (corresponding to neural activity in specific circuits in the brain) before committing to physical behavior can eliminate costly errors before the fact, saving not only time and energy, but minimizing physical risk to the organism to boot. Potentially dangerous future behaviors can be given "a dry run" in mental images, and identified by imaging their potentially harmful outcomes, permitting them to be mentally "weeded out" before any action in the physical world, and before any danger is actually encountered in the external world. (Note the implicit meaning of the word "actually;" it discriminates between what happens in our minds and what happens in *actuality*, in the external, physical world; thus existence of the word itself is an implicit acknowledgement of how our brains work; our brains conjure up and compare mental images of objects and events and various mental manipulations of them to safely and efficiently select behaviors that are most likely to lead to adaptive outcomes, before actually committing to an action physically employed in the external physical world).

Survival benefits of the IBOES information processing circuit design must have been enormous, compared to alternative brain designs which lacked capacity for IBOES. For a somewhat simple example, imagine one of our arboreal primate ancestors moving through 40 foot tall trees in a jungle canopy. It is engaged in the selection of limbs and branches to jump to next, as it navigates its way toward its destination in the canopy. While selecting its path it must anticipate whether a branch is too far out of reach and whether it can support its body weight. The primate must rapidly perform mental calculations to assess any potential danger of falling. Because it can test out various alternative courses of action by a mental review of the projected effects of each option (in this case, selecting one branch vs. another), it can eliminate most potential errors, preventing potentially fatal falls, and it can do so within the safety of its "mind's eye" before actually committing to any particular alternative in its physical movement.

The payoffs are enormous for the organism. The time and energy conserved would be enough by themselves to justify this brain/mind design, but the additional survival advantage of being able to eliminate potentially harmful "choices" beforehand makes brain design for IBOES so highly favored by nature that it might even be considered inevitable, given sufficient evolutionary time. Without IBOES the animal cannot vicariously test alternatives beforehand, but can only learn to improve the adaptive effectiveness of its behaviors by actually committing to physical action first, and then "seeing what happens" after the fact—not a very efficient or safe way to avoid harmful and even potentially fatal mistakes. Think of the powerful survival advantage of this ability to *image* various behavioral solutions to problems presented by one's social and physical environments and to test them out before the fact—before the act. Furthermore, a continuous update from feedback about an ongoing behavior can be used to adjust action in "mid-flight" making corrections "on the go" permitting the organism to even more effectively hone in on the goal and/or to avoid potential catastrophes.

Not only is the ability to image solutions to problems safe, and time and energy efficient (in terms of caloric expenditure), but it permits novel solutions to problems by what appears to be "insight." Think of the term, "insight", loosely "inner vision," emphasizing that our language "reflects" (there's another one) the visual nature of much of our thinking and decision-making. Insight is the use of visual-like mental images, in which we "see" ourselves in action, manipulating things, including other members of our species, in our physical and social environments, to solve the problems that our environments present to us. In other words, in the more complex animal brains such as ours, behavior is no longer controlled primarily by *reflex* as in bugs, jellyfish, clams, fish, frogs, turtles and lizards, but by "*reflection*," the presentation and review of mental images of oneself in action, the probable consequences of those projected actions, followed by selection of behavioral options guided by internal goals (the IBOES computational routine).

In short, the evolution of behavioral control mechanisms in animals has transformed (via natural selection of brain circuit "design") over evolutionary time *from reflex to reflection.* That's what big, complex brains did for life on earth. And there has resulted an explosion of intelligence in animal and human brains as a consequence. The *intelligence explosion* in animal forms on earth was born.

So much of our thinking is of this sort that we frequently think of abstract concepts using concrete, "visible" objects or events as analogies to represent the abstract ideas and to make them easier to manipulate. For example, to reason about the implications of the constant velocity of light, Einstein, in his formulation of the Special Theory of Relativity, used visual images of two trains speeding toward one another at the velocity of light and imagined (image-ined) what would happen to a beam of light on one of the trains as it approached the other. Watson and Crick used mental images of two snakes coiling around one another to imagine the double-helix structure of DNA. Poets and novelists frequently make use of analogies and metaphors often highly visual in nature. Are our brains, like our hypothetical sociobot-brains, visual-imaging-thought-making machines? Are these functions the primary source of what we call intelligence and volition? Of our perception of our own "will"?

These abilities are not uniquely human, suggesting their origins in our ancient ancestry. The use of mental images appears to occur in at least some other mammals such as chimpanzees, probably to help them anticipate future states of the environment and to imagine novel solutions to problems and the steps needed to actualize those imagined goals and solutions. Chimpanzees can learn to fish for termites by trial and error (Goodall, 1971), but to think up the behavior in the first place, so that it develops as a skill after guided practice toward the imagined goal of getting the termites by the fishing behaviors, suggests that the chimp has at least *some* ability to mentally image ("imagine") future states of the environment and the steps to get there—in short, chimps, our closest living relatives, "think," and they think visually, like we do (see PBS DVD/video, The Human Spark, 2009). For chimps, just as for human ancestors such as Homo Erectus and Homo Habilis, having hands that are adept at manipulating physical objects in the environment must have facilitated the kind of brain evolution that leads to the ability to image (to "imagine") future states of the environment that can be brought about by one's own planned, intentional, action. By one's own *will*. And in the absence of knowledge of all the causes acting on one's behavior, this sense of causal agency from within one's self, must feel like it is free, perhaps even to the chimpanzee, although they have no way to put that feeling into words. However, if we could ask a chimp why it did this thing or that, and if it had the language to think about it and to tell us, it would probably report a sense of free will, a sense of inner personal causal agency, just as humans do.

German psychologist, Wolfgang Kohler, describes in his 1917 book, "The Mentality of Apes," how chimpanzees show *insight* when solving the problem of how to reach bunches of tasty bananas hung just out of reach by Kohler and his fellow researchers. Kohler observed that after initial failures of behavioral trial and error, chimps typically would walk away, perhaps out of frustration, but then after looking back and forth between the hanging bananas and various objects such as boxes and sticks in their cages, chimps suddenly begin to use the boxes or sticks as tools to get the food, in some experiments even putting together sticks that were individually too short by themselves to reach the fruit (Kohler, 1917).

As revealed by fMRI studies (discussed in Chapter Two and above), *imagining* objects, which might not even be physically present, activates the same visual regions of the brain as do visual "images" from the retina of the eye (Kanwisher, 2009). A major step in the evolution of intelligence must have occurred when visual images could be generated internally, without the external stimulus energy being present in the environment, and when these images could be voluntary manipulated in the "mind's eye" in order to formulate a plan to achieve some imagined state of the world—just as Kohler's chimps apparently did when they had a flash of "insight" that permitted them to suddenly discover a way to reach the fruit, and then put that imaged (imagined) solution into action. Did the flash of insight in Kohler's chimps result from mental manipulation of visual-like images in the chimp's "mind's eye" just as happens in the human case? I think it is very probable, although we can't know for sure because we can't climb into the mind of the chimpanzee. But the chimp or monkey brain shows patterns of activity in visual association areas just as in the human case when the experimental task at hand involves "thought" (Banich and Compton, 2011; Carlson, 2011).

The mental processing that occurs in chimps or in us that permits such outcomes has the *feel* of free will, of internal causal agency. But once formulated, we can subject our plan to another level of internal control, we can, with additional processing, "decide" to postpone the action or perhaps even abort it all together, based upon additional processing, additional visualizations of actions and projected outcomes (additional "reflection;" again note the use in everyday language of a visual term to describe part of the human thinking process).

Furthermore, the brain is learning all the while as these processes are going on. A problem and its successful solution, which are novel the first time they are experienced, become familiar and practiced with additional future encounters with the same or similar problems and solutions. As repeated exposure to the same problem and its successful solution occur, control of the required behavior requires less "effort of attention," less conscious control, less IBOES, and it becomes more and more automated, more unconscious, freeing some of the brain's finite information processing capacity for other tasks and probably conserving energy as neural control becomes less conscious. I am going to make the prediction that conscious processing requires more overall metabolic energy than does unconscious processing so that after conscious, willful, effort of attention directed to solution of a novel problem has done its work, and as the same problem class is repeatedly encountered and problem solved, practice leads to the progressive *automatization* of behavioral control by unconscious processing, which, I hypothesize, is more efficient in terms of caloric expenditure by the brain than is conscious processing and "effort of will." Thus, in animals with the capacity for *reflection*, problems once novel, after repeated experience as they become familiar, come to be handled by the brain with reflex-like efficiency (Haier, et.al., 1992). Thus, the more energy-demanding conscious, willful, reflective processing involving IBOES functions will only be utilized when more caloric efficient, reflex-like processing is inadequate because of the novelty of the problem at hand. Therefore, in animals (or future bots) with IBOES capacities, we can expect a dynamic interplay between reflex, reflection, and learned reflex-like responding (probably involving the cerebellum, known to be involved in the formation of learned motor programs with practice). Still, the survival advantage of an explosion in response flexibility created by the evolution of *reflection* as a means of behavioral control is impossible to overestimate.

Now, none of these examples is about solving a social problem such as "how to win friends and influence people," though it may be this type of social problem that ignited much of the development of our exceptional abilities to image future states of things, especially the behavior and minds of others (an ability evolutionary psychologists attribute to the so-called *Theory of Mind Module*—TOM—in the brain, a circuit including *medial prefrontal cortex*, the anterior pole of the *temporal cortex*, and the *amygdala*; see figure 2-2). But the examples here do illustrate how an ability that may have arisen to permit us to imagine the mental states and future behaviors of others in our social group, in order to manipulate them for our own social ends, could be generalized to solutions of all kinds of problems of behavioral control, problem solving, decision-making, and even inventiveness (a hypothesis that may contradict the claim by evolutionary psychologists that the TOM is *domain-specific* and characterized by *information encapsulation*, but more about these issues in later chapters).

When Leonardo DaVinci thought of the first prototype helicopter he used visual-like mental images as evidenced by his drawings in his journals, just as Watson and Crick used visual imagery when figuring out the structure of DNA, or Copernicus when coming up with the theory of a sun-centered solar system. In each case, the visual-like mental images each experienced contributed to solution of the problem at hand. And, I suspect, in each case, contributed to the sense that their free will, their own free causal agency, was the cause of these inventions. Mental "reflection," as a way to organize our behavior, has inherent within it the perception of a "self" actively engaged in the business of freely made choices, especially when long-term strategies for planned actions in more and more distant futures are involved. Remember your "day dreams," your visualizations of your future when you were younger? Some of those visualizations may have played a determining role in where and who you are today. In the control of human behavior, the role of *imagined futures* is almost impossible to overestimate as behavioral control shifted over the course of brain evolution from reflex to reflection.

The use of internal, visual-like, neurally encoded "mental" images to "see" possible future behavioral options and their probable outcomes, to "envision" novel states of physical objects which don't yet exist, and after mental review of such images, to put a course of action to work in the physical world, to realize a future state or goal—perhaps this is the information processing at the root of what we experience as volition, and by extension our own free will, and it may help explain what consciousness might be for. Imagine if you could *not* image future behaviors and their probable outcomes, and neither could you image future states of physical objects in the environment so that you might "envision" manipulating them into tools and other useful inventions, how would you organize your behavior, how would you make any choices other than those which were ill informed and haphazard, or simply reflex? What sense of a free will would you retain then? I venture to say that without these processes of "reflection," imaging by the brain of future behavioral options and their probable outcomes, there wouldn't be much of a sense of free will left at all.

We are primates, and life in the trees required that our tree-living ancestors have especially good 3-D vision; otherwise, our arboreal ancestors would have been miscalculating and missing branches as they moved through the trees, ending up on the ground more than would have been much good for them. Our primate heritage demanded good visual systems, and our social life demanded co-opting of the visual system to put visual-like mental images to new uses—the anticipation of increasingly distant futures in the formation of behavioral plans, projected sequences of actions to reach complex and temporally distant goals. The seeds of an intelligence explosion in animal evolution were sown.

Now, all of these functional properties of the human brain are information process-ing events. If, as I argued in Chapters 2 and 3, these events are material events, then information processing machinery that could accomplish these *imaging tricks* should be found not only in the human brain, but in some animal brains as well, and maybe one day in intelligent machines. The evolutionary journey *from reflex to reflection* would not have taken a direct route to the human species. There is continuity in animal life on earth. There are not only similarities in anatomy and physiology among species, but in the psychological adaptations they possess as well. The continuity of species leads to the expectation that many other animal species, particularly our closest primate rela-tives, possess to varying degrees the ability to reflect, to image behavioral options and their likely future outcomes, and then to select a behavior more likely to accomplish their goals—perhaps this would be most likely in the social primates in the context of their social interactions. Jane Goodall (1971) observed that chimps in the jungles of Tanzania seemed to have a sense of when it was safe to beg meat from a dominant male who had made a kill, perhaps by reading the mind and mood of the dominant animal by using visual-like images of the likely response from him.

However, there are extraordinary examples of behavior in many other species that suggest mental reflection in the planning of behavior. Dolphins in the wild have been observed to encircle a school of fish and then cooperatively herd them toward the shal-low waters of the shoreline, then flop their bodies up and down in the water in unison to create waves that strand the fish on the shore. Once this is accomplished, the dol-phins wiggle up onto the beach and feast on the stranded fish. Lions hunt in groups. They have been observed in the wild to organize ambushes, wherein one or two of the group hide in tall grass or behind rocks while two or three of the others circle around behind a group of gazelle or wildebeest and herd them toward the lions in hiding, who then make an easy kill as the unsuspecting prey passes close by. Then, all members of the lion hunting party share the spoils. Killer whales have been observed in the Arctic Ocean while hunting sea lions. In one spectacular case, documented on film, a sea lion had perched itself on a large chunk of ice, a mini-ice berg, for safety from two killer whales on the hunt. Though the surface of the ice chunk was smooth and level, it was large enough to prevent the whales from reaching the sea lion. The killer whales, ani-mals noted for their intelligence, circled the large chunk of floating ice for several min-utes, often popping their heads up out of the water to see the sea lion on top of the ice, just out of reach. Being unable to reach the sea lion, the two killer whales suddenly retreated, submerging themselves. Then a few moments later both reappeared and in perfect unison simultaneously rose up and then splashed down into the water right next to the mini-ice berg, setting up a large wave which abruptly and powerfully tilted the chunk of ice, causing the sea lion to slide off, right into their waiting jaws. In each case, highly social mammals demonstrated sophisticated intelligence in organizing a cooperative hunting effort which must have involved planning of the sort that in us involves the manipulation of mental images in the "mind's eye" to achieve an imaged (imagined) goal. Primates like us and chimpanzees are not the only animals capable of sophisticated planning which appears to involve mental imaging, but other mammals appear to have this same capacity.

How could something so sophisticated have evolved by natural selection? In animals, the neural hardware and functional properties creating small steps in the direction of these full blown capacities would have varied among individual members of ancestral species. By chance, some individuals would have had closer approximations to the requisite variations than others, giving them slight advantage in the struggle for existence, and providing a mechanism for the slow accumulation (or relatively abrupt big leaps which can come about as a result of relatively small mutations in DNA switches—see Chapter 6) of just these kinds of favorable changes in mind design, over enormous expanses of deep time. Given enough time, natural selection could do the job.

This is exactly the kind of "design" process, one by selection for reproduction/replication of favorable variations, suggested by Bill Joy at Sun Microsystems for the future generation of intelligent bots. The only difference is that the bot-brain design process would be vastly speeded up, according to Joy, by a much quicker selection process which would take place within human designed microcircuits equipped with the capacity for self-organization—what Dr. Aubrey De Grey, of the Singularity Institute for Artificial Intelligence (SIAI) and the Methuselam Foundation, refers to as "recursively self-improving systems," systems which improve by repetition of a set of self-referential rules of evaluation and self-correction. This is a process of "creation" must faster than "mother nature's" *natural* selection. See videos at these websites regarding "singularity" and "friendly" AI: (http://www.youtube.com/watch?v=0A9pGhwQbS0) (http://www.youtube.com/watch?v=9PWXrnsSrf0&NR=1; retrieved June 4, 2011).

With regard to future bot-brains, nanotube (molecular 3-D computing) circuits with self-organizing features are soon to be commercially available. But, according to inventor and computer scientist, Ray Kurzweil, speaking at the Singularity Summit at Stanford University in 2006, even conventional two-dimensional chips by 2020 are expected to have computing capacity sufficient to emulate all regions of the human brain and will cost just $1,000. And this technology is calculated to be a billion times more powerful in less than 30 years after that, says Kurzweil. Furthermore, he notes that fMRI image resolution is doubling every year, so that even now the operations of single neuronal connections are visible to neuroscientists in real time. This will permit rapid progress in *reverse engineering* the brain, so that what is learned about the brain at an ever accelerating pace can be used in the design of what Kurzweil calls "strong AI systems," those capable of matching or exceeding the abilities of the human brain. How could this be possible?

A few tens of thousands of bytes of information in our DNA is all that separates us from the other primates. The amount of information in DNA that is responsible for human brain design is, according to Kurzweil, quite manageable for human technological attempts to duplicate the brain design of humans. This is because the DNA information for human brain design represents general *rules* for construction of brains by recursive self-organizing principles with a little randomness thrown in, and in interaction with environmental inputs (for example, it is known that during brain development of mammals in the embryo and fetus, the cerebral cortex is built, layer by layer, deepest layer first, by the repetition of cell divisions of progenitor cells, the number of such divisions being controlled by a protein, beta-catenin, the amount of which determines the number of cell divisions and thus the size and complexity of the cortex in different mammals species; see Carlson, 2011, p. 66–67). Kurzweil states that the brain is a "self-organizing probabilistic fractal" so that its duplication may be accomplished by iterations of a relatively small number of organizational principles exploiting regularities in the system. Our knowledge of the brain will increase exponentially just as computing power in AI systems continues to do. Thus, we may see "spiritual machines" with human-like computing abilities, (http://www.youtube.com/watch?v=9PWXrnsSrf0&NR=1, retrieved June 4, 2011), including perhaps the co-opting of bot visual systems into the kind of anticipatory, visual-planning circuitry which permits projection of "self" into future states of the world and internal ("mental") imaging of one's "self" in action in future time. "Reflection" via recursive circuitry that processes information about its own information processing operations, specifically those related to selection of options for action, may become possible in future bot-brains sooner than we think. In other words, with this kind of computational hardware and software, willful bots may be possible. We had better be sure that they like us or something like the human vs. robot wars of the original *Terminator* film could turn out to be more than mere science fiction. Such an outcome is not just my wild imagination or that of the screenwriters of "The Terminator" films. One of the stated goals of the founders of the Singularity Institute for Artificial Intelligence is to prevent "dangerous AI" from creating such globally disastrous outcomes by promoting what they call "friendly AI," AI designs aimed at making sure that the AI machines don't have the capacity to do us harm as they "evolve."

But, I don't want to get too far afield here. We are considering the concept of free will as a causative factor in human behavior and what it is about us (or sophisticated next generation humanoid sociobots) that might be required to conjure up the feeling of free will.

What else would humans or robots need to have, in addition to the abilities described thus far for "reflection" using visual-like imagery, in order for us to say that a free will is present? With the capacity in us and in our imagined sociobots to "view" in visual-like "mental" images the available behavioral options along with the probable outcomes of each of those options, and then to evaluate the options with respect to internal, neurally encoded, (mental) goals, in our case derived from our biological and social nature, prior to selection of one behavior or another, haven't we accounted for the subjective feeling that we have a will and that it is the freely acting cause of our actions? Belgian neuroscientist, M. Boly, and colleagues identify specific fMRI activity in the brain in response to spatial and motor imaging tasks as evidence of conscious volition, a *will* (Boly, et.al., 2007, pp. 979–992). Thus, I think we are close, but there are other factors to consider which add the convincing touches to our sense that we, as humans, possess a free will.

Booting up with words, categories, and natural logic

For one thing, humans have language and this gives us capacity for another kind of thinking involving another medium, not visual symbols, but verbal symbols—those arbitrary symbols we call "words." And this equips us with the ability to form new goals, goals about things more abstract to which we can aspire, such as political ideals, accumulation of wealth, abstract moral principles, self-actualization, the pursuit of excellence, and the like. We can use not only visualization of future, but we can engage in internal "talk" to ourselves, internal self-conversations to formulate plans to achieve goals and thereby evaluate various courses of action. These verbal-like processes that we "hear" in self-generated auditory-like verbal representations in our brains are subject to internal manipulations by linguistic and, more or less, logical rules.

How such logical rules get into our brains in the first place is still controversial. Learning is one option, but research shows that even very young infants have what appears to be an innate, internal understanding (non-verbal of course at this age) of cause and effect and of other ways in which the physical world works, suggesting innate properties of our "mind design" already present at birth (Gopnik et al, 1999; see A. Gopnik, "How Babies Think," Scientific American July 2010, retrieved April 14, 2011 at http://www.alisongopnik.com/Papers_Alison/sciam-Gopnik.pdf).

Specific logical rules exist for many kinds of thought. According to evolutionary psychologists, John Tooby and Leda Cosmides (1995), "There are specialized systems for grammar induction [knowledge], face recognition [hardware/ algorithm], for dead reckoning [algorithm], for construing objects [knowledge] and for recognizing emotions from the face[algorithm/hardware]. There are mechanisms [hardware] to detect animacy [knowledge], eye direction [algorithm] and cheating[knowledge]. There is a 'theory of mind' module [knowledge] . . . a variety of social inference modules [knowledge] and a multitude of other elegant machines [hardware]" in our minds.

Just like our brains are designed by our DNA to see color, as a code for wavelength and other properties of reflective surfaces in the world, our brains are also designed (wired) to "see" cause and effect and to understand and use logical rules, some of which are highly specific to specific adaptive problems such as language acquisition, reading of emotions in the faces of others, and navigating our way around the environment.

One set of these logical rules is related to the disposition built into our brains to group things, to put them into categories. Then, we use logical programs such as *induction and deduction* derived from *categorization* to draw "logical" conclusions such as, if all men are mortal, Louie is a man, then Louie is mortal. The disposition to categorize things, to lump them into groups based upon their similarities, is probably an evolved property of how our brains, and the brains of a lot of other animals, are put together. The famous behaviorist psychologist, B. F. Skinner, was one of the first to show that even pigeons form and use categories, but of course, they do so without the capacity for language. Language makes possible much more abstract categories, based on more abstract similarities. This permits humans to form not only categories, but abstract categories that we refer to as concepts. Thus, our abilities for abstract conceptual thought emerge (see chapter 10).

The ability to *generalize* and to form categories probably evolved in animals as diverse as pigeons and humans, and all those in between, based in the principle, a fact of the physical world, that things that are similar in their properties tend to have similar adaptive consequences, and therefore, from an adaptive standpoint, should be lumped together into categories of "natural kinds," that can be safely treated (behaved to) in the same way. The evolution of a brain design like this would come about as a result of the survival advantage that animal brains organized in this way would produce (Shepard, 1987b). We have a built-in disposition in our mind design to form *categories*, to learn about the properties of instances of any particular group of similar things, and then to ascribe these properties to all members of the category that we encounter in the present and in the future. Then we use these attribute-rich categories, stored in our minds either in images, words, or both, to *make inferences and predictions* about new instances of the category when we encounter them in the world again, in the future. And the use of categories can help us anticipate the future effects of encounters with new instances of a category and therefore help us organize our behavior in response to an anticipated future (recall this is what I have called "prosponse") to better meet the challenges that our environments present to us.

Grouping things into categories has another use; it probably increases information processing efficiency, and permits us to make useful inferences rather automatically. At other times, we use "effort of attention" to willfully reason our way through a difficult problem to a solution, adding to our sense of free will as a cause of our actions.

These design features of the brain which predispose us to categorize things, it turns out, duplicate the real properties of the external, physical world, producing a synchrony between brain design and the world the brain is designed to deal with. The brain's design has to reflect the organization of the external world, otherwise the brain wouldn't do us much good. The genes involved in brain design must accommodate adaptively significant features of the world, such as the fact that things that are similar in the world have similar adaptive consequences, by incorporating representations of these features into the hard wired organization of the brain's circuit "design." And this comes about by a selection process, similar to that suggested for bot-brain design by Bill Joy at Sun Microsystems, but organic brains get their functional organization as a result of evolution by natural selection. Brain design unfolds by the simple fact that individuals with "bad" (maladaptive) brain design die off, and those with better brain design survive another day to reproduce and pass on the favorable information in their genes, the genetic information that made their brain design more useful in dealing with the challenges the world presents to the organism.

Thus, there arises a close, but not perfect, correspondence between mind design and the actual characteristics of the external world. Our mind design represents the *adaptively important* features of the world, but not all the features of the world. For example, things that have adaptive significance (i.e. lions, ripe fruit, poisonous insects, germ filled feces—things that bear on human survival in particular ways) are represented by brains while things without adaptive significance are not represented, causing us to ignore, or be entirely unaware of many other properties such as the color of air (what color? Air doesn't have color—exactly the point) or the smell of rocks (same argument; rocks don't have smells, precisely because they don't contain harmful bacteria that might make us sick if we come into contact with them, nor do they contain nutrients useful to us like fruit does; so rocks "have" no smell; or more accurately, our brains do not create a smell to represent any of the properties of rocks, because rocks aren't important to our survival in the way that fruit, cooking meat, or germ-filled feces are; see chapter 8).

Further, the real world does have regularities even in abstract properties. The fact that things in the world, that are similar in various ways, tend to have similar adaptive consequences (for example, each instance of a lion is likely to be dangerous; each instance of ripe fruit is likely to be nutritious), itself leads to the evolution of brain designs that are capable of forming abstracted categories and generalizing from the properties of particular instances of the category to new instances for purposes of prediction, and expectancy, for "foretelling" future. With words, with language, we co-opt these processes of categorization, generalization, and inference, originally based on similarities in more concrete sensory properties of things, to apply these mental operations to verbal categories, making possible more abstract categories, concepts, and inferences about abstractions such as justice, morality, electron shells, harmonic motion, chemical bonding, and the like. We can "talk" to ourselves in subvocal, auditory-like mental "images" of words about such abstract concepts, verbally manipulate them, and, by mentally "talking" ourselves through the likely outcomes of this or that idea, we can select mentally how to bring about political or moral goals, to form or evaluate schemas of how the world works, make predictions from our theories or those of others, imagine ourselves achieving abstract goals of excellence and personal achievement, often socially defined, or we may simply consider what to cook for dinner tonight ("Hmm, should I make fish or pot stickers?"). In the midst of this mental talking to ourselves, we perceive these information processing events as coming from within our own minds, our own localized subjective experience, and any behaviors that follow we therefore perceive as emanating from our own internal causal agency, our own free will.

Assuming that mental states are really states of our brain (see Chapters 2 and 3), in summary, when we are confronted with options, we all experience something of our own mental operations, as the information processing in our brains develops towards a "choice." We *sense* the internal locus of our conscious mental states as our brain activity proceeds (this is an example of what psychologists call meta-cognition, an awareness of our own mental functioning). As we consider options and their likely outcomes, as discussed above, we experience visual images and/or we "talk to ourselves" as we formulate a "choice." Then we generate, seemingly as a consequence, a "voluntary" response. We use visual imagery or talking to ourselves, or both, to do a kind of *mental trial and error*, wherein we "consider" (verbally or in images or both) this action or that, and then our brains quickly engage in mental calculations assessing the probabilities of one outcome or another and the relative values of each outcome, in terms of our goals (the end product of these evaluative computations is our subjectively experienced emotions; good feelings indicate something good for us and our genes, bad feelings indicate something that will decrease the chances of the survival and reproduction of our genes—emotions, you see, have biological function, to "inform" us about the computed adaptive implications of this thing or that thing). These computations of probabilities take place largely unconsciously, but can be brought to consciousness to some degree, by conscious shifts of our attention to them (which also add to our perception of an internal will). Much of this valuing system is genetically programmed into us in what we experience as "biological drives," such as hunger, thirst, fear, aggression, sex, and so on (colorfully summarized by some biologists and psychologists as the four F's, feeding, fighting, fleeing and mating) and in the emotions (as described briefly above). And then other "values," abstract and social, are acquired along the way by our cultural, social, and personal experiences. Then, on the basis of these computations, our brains select a behavioral option to put into physical action; we "make a choice." Because this response selection so quickly follows our conscious experience of these various mental events, which we subjectively sense as localized within our *own* minds, these mental events are perceived to be the cause of the response, and we *feel* them, not only as causal, but as "ours."

This process and the resulting experience of volition, and of its internal locus within our own minds, is, I will venture to guess, as I have suggested above, a human universal resulting from how our brains operate, how our neural hardware processes information about future, *regardless of what culture we live in*, and this undoubtedly plays a critical role in our perception that we have a *will* and that it operates freely to cause our actions.

Certainly our religious upbringing and other cultural beliefs we learn play a part in our construction of stories or schemas about free will as the cause of our actions. But these cultural influences are not causes, instead they are results. Cultural beliefs about free will are likely derived from, and are culturally transmitted ideas that simply reinforce our perceptions of volition, perceptions that actually originate primarily as a consequence of the human brain/mind "design" that produces the information processing operations of IBOES described above.

When our brains process information preliminary to selection of a behavioral option, ultimately, this information is pushed through brain systems involved in movement control, and many of these systems are "forward-looking." For behavior to be most useful, in complex animals like us, the brain must anticipate future. In fact, all of our brain's neuro-cognitive hardware is designed ultimately for more and more effective movement control, and this entails more and more successful prediction of future states of the world. The elaborate information processing that the brain needs to do to accomplish a more or less accurate assessment of the future is in large part what gives us the feeling of volition. We sense this future-prediction-function in our own visual-like mental images of future potential behaviors with their probable outcomes, evaluated by our brains against our values and desires, and in their verbally encoded mental counterparts. Our brains then select a behavioral option out of those that we (our brains) have "reviewed" in mental imagery or verbally. All of these experienced mental events (really brain events; see Chapters 2 and 3) contribute to the sense of personal agency we feel as we organize our behavior moment to moment, as our brains select some options and reject others—a feeling that we label as our "will."

Given these properties of how our brains evaluate options prior to movement, it is no wonder that we feel as if we have a "will," and that it is acting freely. It just seems to be common sense, and in the above sense, it is. But wouldn't a sociobot with the same information processing properties in its bot-brain arguably be exhibiting what also appeared to be a will, operating of its "own" accord, to cause its self-generated behavior? Whatever the answer to this question is, it seems clear that our brains are sophisticated computing machines made of 100 billion complex, information process-ing cells, hooked up into unimaginably complex circuit "designs" which generate our conscious experience—including our feeling of volition, of a freely acting will. Thus, it appears that our sense of will, of volition, is perhaps not founded in "soul stuff" at all, but instead in the nature of the evolved information processing operations of our brains.

In the next chapter we consider other factors in our perception of free will, focusing upon the question of how free our "will" can actually be, and whether the "will" is really the cause of our behavior or simply a non-causal epiphenomenon.

CHAPTER FIVE

Building the Self, Degrees of Determinism, and Moral Responsibility

"A self is also an abstract object, a theorist's fiction."

Daniel Dennet,
The Self as Center of Narrative Gravity, 1992

The reader may have noticed that much of the formulation in Chapter 4 describes information processing operations with regard to a "self." We are not only reflective creatures, but being reflective requires that we be self-reflective as well, especially in order for anything approximating free will to emerge in us. To have the sensation of free will, we must have a concept of self, of an "I," acting as a causal agent in control of our behavior. Having a sense of internal control of our actions requires that we have a concept of an "internal" source for our actions as opposed to an "external" source for our actions, versus no sense at all about the source of one's action. For example, I doubt if spiders have any sense of a "self" much less a concept of "free will." The spider just does what it does and doesn't "think" or "reflect" about it, and probably doesn't even have any consciousness at all about its own behavior, nor, perhaps, about anything else. I suspect that pretty much the same would be true of a jellyfish, a lizard, a frog, a Hawaiian green sea turtle, or a crawfish. But when it comes to mammals and at least some species of birds, particularly that group known as the corvids (including crows), we can't be as sure.

For example, European Magpies, a *corvid* speices, have demonstrated self-awareness in *mirror tests*, as have bottlenose dolphins, elephants, and great ape species, including chimpanzees, orangutans, gorillas, and bonobos (http://en.wikipedia.org/wiki/Mirror_test). Notable animals who do not pass the mirror test are dogs, cats, and human infants less than 18 months of age. In the *mirror test* researchers seek to determine if an animal can recognize its own image in a mirror. To do this, the animal is anesthetized and a mark with an odorless dye is placed on its head or face or other body part that would be visible in a mirror. Then later, when awake, the animal is presented with its own image in a mirror and researchers look for behavioral signs of recognition such as touching the spot on its own head or face or repositioning its body or head to get a better view, while looking at the image in the mirror, instead of touching the image on the surface of the mirror (which presumably indicates that the animal treats the image as not of itself but of something else, another animal, but not itself).

The usefulness of this comparative data is that it immediately suggests that having self-awareness has something to do with a species' brain organization, and furthermore, that having a sense of self is not unique to humans. The hypothesis that having a sense of self is dependent upon brain organization is reinforced by the observation that human infants up to 18 months of age fail the mirror test, but pass it thereafter, suggesting an effect of brain maturation (by two years of age, the brain is 75% of adult brain size, whereas at six month of age it is only 50% of the adult size and at birth only 25%). Most of the growth in brain size in the developing infant is due *not* to more neurons (the human brain at birth has more brain cells than it will have at any other time in life; see Chapter 2), but to massive development of *dendritic branching*—the growth and maturation of the brain's circuitry. Circuits that are not yet functional before 18 months of age, but which do become functional thereafter, make self-awareness possible. This provides evidence that there must be specific circuitry in the brain required for self-awareness, and further that such circuits must be in place and functional before a sense of self can emerge. The fact that some species do show self-awareness, and others never do, also reinforces the hypothesis that self-awareness is dependent upon certain features of the circuit design in the brains of these species. There are two possibilities with regard to the nature of these circuits. Either these circuits have been "designed" specifically *for* self-awareness (an example of *domain-specific* circuitry, to be discussed in a later chapter) or the self-awareness arises as a secondary effect when circuits initially evolved for one purpose get "co-opted" into a new function, in this case the self-awareness function (co-option of traits in evolution into new functions was first proposed by Steven J. Gould and Richard Lewontin, 1979, and is related to their concept of "exaptation").

I suspect that the former, the domain-specific hypothesis of the self, is more probable, especially in species which have evolved complex social organizations in which status within the group is an important feature of social life for that species. In such cases, self-awareness would pay off in terms of biological success because awareness of self and of others as individuated entities, distinct from the self, would facilitate the kind of social manipulation of others that permits achievement of one's own ends (an idea discussed in the previous chapter). However, I will also make an argument below that the concept of self may also arise from more domain-*general* (less specific, less specialized, more general) cognitive processes, and may even arise initially as a "spandrel" (a by-product of other characteristics which evolved as adaptations) but one that takes on significant functional importance for human beings, especially with regard to human conceptions of free will. In other words, on this later view, a self-concept may arise first as an accidental by-product of other features of our brain/mind "design," but once a self-concept forms in individuals it serves valuable adaptive functions which cause natural selection to reinforce the information processing adaptations that make a self-concept possible in the first place in the brains of some species.

Still, there is a third alternative, a mixture of both. There is a strong likelihood that the circuits involved in self-awareness, particularly its specific idiosyncratic content for each individual (specific ideas and beliefs about oneself), acquire their organization from a complex mixture of genetics and learning. Certainly in humans, an adult self-concept gets populated with content as a result of experiences of the individual. For example, children as they grow hear things about themselves. "Oh, isn't she cute." "My goodness, what a smart little boy." "You are such a bad boy." And later, "You got 732 on the verbal section of the SAT." "You have a credit score of 650." And, the like. But even before consciously verbal inputs are impinging on the growing sense of self-awareness, the developing *self*, as a concept in the mind of the individual, is being built by much more primitive and fundamental inputs.

From the very beginning of our lives and from every moment thereafter, when we observe the world around us we do so from a specific *point of view* (POV) which has localization in three-dimensional space (recall the imaging functions of our brains discussed in the previous chapter). For example, right now, I am sitting on the lanai of a condo in Kona, Hawaii, looking out over grassy hills toward the ocean, and the view I have, *my* POV, is localized in this particular area of three-dimensional space, it is localized here (actually it even has specific Google map coordinates), not in Pittsburgh, on Mars, or a mile from here. This POV localizes "me" in my mental 3-dimensional space. Research shows that we have not only a sense of 3 dimensional space but of ourselves in it, and there are specific areas of the brain that this orientation of ourselves in 3-D space is dependent upon.

Furthermore, beginning as early as we are capable of forming visual images, we see our own body parts uniquely *from* this subjective point of view (POV) and via *classical conditioning* (a simple version of classical conditioning is the principle that stimuli paired together in time become associated—as, for example, in the case of Pavlov's dogs learning to associate a bell with food) we associate these limbs, shoulders, legs, feet, and other body parts with the POV we have come to recognize as "ours."

Further, we experience sensations (visual, auditory, tastes, etc.) of various sorts, again and again, while we "observe" the world from our own localized POV, and we also experience other sensations within our body parts localized in space along with our own POV. Consequently we associate these myriad sensations with our POV, as part of a "me." Inevitably, at a very young age, we begin to discriminate between our POV, and its coincident sensations and associated body parts, and other bodies and non-living objects in our environments localized "outside," external to our POV.

Shortly after birth, we are capable of orienting toward our mother's breast as we feel hunger and the movements toward the breast are accompanied by kinesthetic and other muscle and joint sensations associated with the movement, and these too add to the collection of things associated with our POV. At some point in development after birth, the random flailing about of our limbs lessens and we become capable of reaching for objects. Each time we reach for and grasp objects that we see in our POV, the reaching action is accompanied by desires, and other mental states, that we also experience from our own mental POV. And there is not just desire there, but other emotion as well. Just take an object away from an infant who has reached for it and listen to the cries of frustration and protest. All these feelings and sensations and views of one's own body parts in motion at the behest of one's subjective feeling states are associated by classical conditioning more and more firmly with our own POV, always localized at a particular place in 3-D space. When I watch a sunset from the shore in Hawaii, I don't feel my *self* to be somewhere in Iowa nor do I see my body parts in Greenland, or even up the beach somewhere. My body and my POV are co-localized. Furthermore, we see ourselves, including our faces, in mirrors or puddles of water and other reflective surfaces and incorporate these co-localized images into our growing model of self.

Later, as language capacities begin to develop, we learn that we have a name. And the effects of words begin to shape our perception of our self, and then words we hear from others will continue to place us, more and more precisely, in an abstract dynamic *social space*, with socially defined properties or traits, ebbing and flowing throughout our lives. We drive a particular car and live in a particular neighborhood and have a particular career with its associated roles, and status, or lack thereof. Our self gets firmly established as an indisputable psychological reality and the classically conditioned association between our felt mental states such as desires, plans, and intentions, and our behavior makes it our own "common sense" that we are the cause of our own behavior. Our society and its institutions, secular and religious, then reinforce the idea of self and free will convincing all of us that these ideas and feelings are unquestionably real and accurately reflect the way things really are. But, we can see that much of this self is a social construction, created by feedback, mostly in words, that we get from others about who we are. Much of *who* each of us is, our self-concept, is a social construction dependent upon the values, beliefs, and evaluations of the social group in which we live, yet somehow it feels much more objectively real and absolute.

Thus, further adding to the story of "me" are more things I am told about this self, this POV, more things that this self, my POV experiences. For example, it goes to school and to church, and has friends, gets a bank account, a family and so on and all these things get woven into a story, a personal narrative, with the POV at, what the philosopher Dan Dennet calls, the "center of Narrative Gravity." This self-model, the "I" or the "me" is a self-representation which is taking place in the brain. Pains, hungers, desires, discomforts, all of which seem to be localized in the same vicinity of these body parts and this POV, are followed by relevant actions in response to these subjective feelings, and so the "I" comes to feel, to perceive, that the personal narrative, the "me", includes the concept of "me" as a *causal agent* of what I have come to call "my" behavior. Especially when my brain does mental computations involving imaging of this self in future action to mentally "see" the likely outcomes of those future possible actions, as discussed extensively in the previous chapter, then the "I" gets an irresistibly strong sense of this self as freely choosing, since the "I" can "see" a number of options, none of which feels determined, because the subjective "I" doesn't know all the causes that set up this particular set of options that have been presented to it. Thus, the options and "my" "choice" seem free of outside causes. In this way, the feeling of free will may emerge, and it does so, convincingly. Now, the subjective "I" *does* engage in the act of making a choice from the options that the "I" can imagine as being available to my "self," my POV, but generally the "I" doesn't sense how limited, how constrained, the imagined choices really are, because "I" am not aware of that of which I am not aware, and further, I am not aware that I am not aware. So, I happily *feel* free and I generalize this feeling to others and I make the default assumption, probably unconsciously, that they must be making *free* choices just as I imagine that I do. Then, on top of it all, cultural ideas from philosophy and religion, most likely developed as consequences of these events, take this feeling of free will at face value and create culturally transmitted ideas and institutions to support the perception of personal free will even more, so that belief in free will snowballs and becomes a ubiquitous belief in the culture, a belief that is utterly irresistible. It is literally "common sense." And it has a biological reality behind it. The "me" is housed in a body with specific limited extent in space, with particular organs which are proprietary, and it is localized to particular coordinates that cannot be occupied simultaneously by any other physical entity.

The initial stages of this whole process are, most certainly, universal to all normal human beings, regardless of culture, because all human beings (and all sentient animals) have POVs localized in space, because their brains, the source of the POV, are physical entities localized in particular places in three-dimensional physical space. However, once the stage occurs wherein language enters the picture, then cultural variation becomes a factor. The personal narrative, the representation of self, is subject to the varieties of cultural experience and the varieties of socially constructed concepts and values that cultures weave. Thus, the strength and particular nuances of the sense of self and associated feelings of free will are likely to vary from culture to culture, but the *sense of a self* is universal to all normal human beings (although in some religious traditions the goal may be to become self-less or to escape the confines of experiencing the world from the standpoint of a separate, individuated self; but typically this doesn't come naturally, but instead requires years of arduous self-discipline and spiritual training).

Surprisingly, questions about the transcendence of the self have yielded unexpected insights into the brain mechanisms that might be involved in the perception of an individuated self. The question of where is "the self" (or the sensation of self) is fundamental in much of ancient Eastern (Asian) religious thought. One could conclude that in some spiritual traditions the "enlightened state" eliminates the "self sensation" and awareness takes on a quality of stark, absolute and direct engagement with the present (this is known as "Suchness," "Beingness" in some esoteric spiritual teachings)—this is "when the perceiver and the perceived become One" (John Edward Koenigshofer, personal communication October 5, 2009). In a sense, some of the individuated POV is lost, and the person feels an unusual expansiveness. Interestingly, this is the opposite of what Da Bubba Free John, the late avatar of a large spiritual following in the West, referred to as personal "contraction" of awareness into the restrictive confines of the individuated self, instead of the expansiveness of self-transcendence. It is of interest that the term *ecstasy* literally means to escape the confines, the localized POV, of the self in the achievement of more universal, less localized, consciousness. It is also interesting that many people find this experience highly rewarding, and apparently have experienced it so throughout history, considering the persistence over millennia of the ancient methods of achieving such altered states of consciousness and the pursuit of these altered states by millions of people over thousands of years throughout the world.

Here is where we get some insights into possible brain mechanisms involved in the sense of self. Recent studies in *neurotheology* (the study of the brain correlates of spiritual experiences) reveal that during meditation and related spiritual states the areas of the brain known to be involved in perception of space (regions of the parietal lobe of the neocortex) and one's place in it seem to shut down. In other words, one's localized POV gets shut off leading to a sense of "expansiveness" in one's subjective experience of oneself in 3D space. It is also important to recall the experience of the neuroanatomist, Dr. Jill Bolte Taylor, who lost her sense of self as a separate individuated entity as a result of a stroke in her left hemisphere (http://www.ted.com/talks/view/id/229, retrieved November 1, 2009), suggesting a specific localization of the sense of an individuated self in the cortex of that hemisphere. While this hemisphere was "shut down" she experienced a euphoric state of expansive oneness with the universe in which a sense of self as separate from the rest of the universe vanished.

It is interesting to speculate in what ways the culturally transmitted variations in concepts of self, and the self as freely acting causal agent, might have influenced the economic, historical, and political development of various countries. Fatalistic cultures (with belief in ideas such as "karma" or "fate" as causal in human affairs, for example) might be expected to be less imperialistic, less geographically exploratory, less interested in "conquering" nature and developing science and technology, less inclined toward rapid, capitalistic economic development, and less inclined to develop democratic forms of government. It would be interesting to see if there were correlations between the firmness and degree of ubiquity of beliefs in free will and objective measures of such political, economic, and historical variables in various societies. With just a little "tongue in cheek," we might call this an "effect of belief in free will" theory of history.

What's good enough for me is good enough for you: the default assumption of free will

We have seen, in the last chapter, how the sensation of volition, of *will*, may arise from the character of those information processing operations of our brain which are involved in future-oriented, reflective behavioral control. Imaging future potential behaviors, their projected outcomes, evaluating them measured against our goals, and then selecting a course of action (IBOES), coupled with perception of an individuated self, as described above, and our awareness of these mental states in our subjective POV, manufactures our perception of a self in action, capable of volition, of free will. But there may be other reasons for our perception of "free will" as the cause of our behavior—it provides us with a ready-made explanation for the behavior of *others*.

We seem to use the conscious mental experiences that lead us to the assumption of our own free *will* to imagine what must be taking place in the minds of others when they do what they do. In other words, we seem to generalize from our own internal experience of our own mental operations to make inferences about what others must experience in their minds when they formulate an action from among their available behavioral alternatives. Not only do we typically think of ourselves as having free will, but we regularly make the *same attribution about others*. We ascribe the actions of other people to their internal psychological states such as their free choice, or at least to personal psychological traits such as their personality, their moral character, their will, or other internal psychological causes. And we treat these internal causes of action within others as if they are freely made. If we didn't, how could we blame anyone, admire anyone, or punish anyone? The default assumption of *free will* is at the core.

When making assessments about the behavior of others, the brain engages in more or less automatic and mostly unconscious information processing, which is almost always accompanied by value judgments about the psychological traits the observer attributes to the other. This causes a mix of either mostly positive or mostly negative emotions toward the person which, among other things, provides us a set of general expectations about who the person is, how we should react to them, and what the person might say or do next. And therein lays the social usefulness of the concept of *free will*. It is *an information processing short cut* by our brains.

In our everyday interactions with other people, these information processing functions by our brains are operating continuously. We seem almost pre-programmed to make attributions about the internal mental states taking place in the minds of other people—their feelings, their motives, their intentions, their *will*—probably based, at least in part, on generalizations from our own mental experience, and then we use these personal attributions as default assumptions about the causes of the behavior of others. But are our attributions of free will, as a default assumption in our understanding of the behavior of other people, simple generalization from our own inner experience, or does this disposition in us reflect the design features of specialized brain circuitry specifically dedicated to processing information about the mental states of others of our kind?

A mind-reading module in the brain

This "mind reading" has been identified by psychologists as an important component in the complex web of information processing that our brains must do in order for us to interact successfully with other members of our species. Think about this a moment. Interacting with other people isn't a trivial information processing task for the brain by any means. Complex and rapidly changing cues of voice, face, posture, expressive body movement, memory of past social encounters with the individual, judgments about their likely intent, assessments of whether trust or suspicion is warranted, about their honesty or dishonesty, whether they are friend or foe, their relative status within the group, assessments of what they might be thinking about you, what they want from you and what you want from them, what they might have really meant when they said . . . , and so on. As discussed in Chapter Two and earlier in this chapter, recent research suggests that there is a specialized *brain module* that engages in this sort of "mind reading" about the mental states of others. Many researchers believe that damage to this *theory of mind (TOM) module* may be one of the major contributing factors in autism (Ramachandran and Oberman, 2006; McGovern, 2007). Without the ability to "read" the internal mental states of others (perhaps by generalizing from one's own mental states, a *domain-general* explanation, or by virtue of a specialized TOM module, a *domain-specific* explanation) and to ascribe their actions to those internal mental states, children and adults with autism are missing essential information in their brains vital to social processing, and are therefore left unable to engage in normal social interaction. Without ability to understand the internal mental states of others as causes of their behavior, the person with autism is left with a specifically social disability, a devastating gap in their social cognition. This suggests that what seems to be a natural tendency in us to attribute behavior to specific internal mental states, our own and those of others, may be the result of specifically evolved circuitry in our brains. In fact, some researchers have suggested that the TOM module may be localized in the *orbito-frontal cortex* in the forward region of the neocortex, but autistic-like symptoms can also be produced by damage in the amygdala, located beneath the cortex of the temporal lobe (Baron-Cohen, 1994; Baron-Cohen, et. al, 1998, 2000; Stone, et. al, 1998). Perhaps the orbital-frontal cortex and the amygdala are both part of a specially evolved brain circuit that leads us to perceive the causes of human behavior as internally generated willful acts (as opposed to acts caused by forces outside the person, which might be the real cause of one's actions). [For an indication of the complexity of the causation of behavior, focusing on schizophrenia and William's syndrome, see a lecture at the M.I.N.D. Institute at the University of California, Davis, see http://www.uctv.tv/search-details.aspx?showID=14662, retrieved June 5, 2011.]

Religious teachings and other cultural beliefs about free will may have first arisen as *consequences* of this kind of brain "design," which might just be standard equipment for every normal, healthy member of our species.

Why would such a brain circuit "design" with these particular information processing operations evolve in the human brain? These circuits may function to facilitate our social interactions, the bread and butter of human life, and thus help assure our success as a highly social species. Attributing behavior to *free will* may just be an essential information processing short cut, a computational strategy to increase information processing efficiency in social situations in the brain of a species (us) which is highly social by its genetically evolved nature. Imagine if we *were* aware of all of the multitudinous, real, external causes acting on people in the determination of their behavior, how would we know how to respond to them in our moment to moment, real-time, interactions with them? The information processing needed might cripple our social interactions. It would be much more efficient for the brain to use a *default assumption of "free will,"* as cause of the behavior of others, as part of the complex computations it must perform to pull off successful real-time social interactions. Natural selection may have built the *free will default assumption* into human brain circuit "design" in the interests of information processing efficiency.

This suggests that the feeling of free will, in us and in others, may originate from an information processing adaptation, a trick evolved into the brain's circuitry to provide an information processing short cut, making possible smooth, effective, real-time social interaction. Perhaps one of the pieces of information missing in the computations performed by the brains of those with severe autism is the default assumption of free will as the cause of the behavior of other people, and without this information processing short cut in place, their brains are overwhelmed with information processing overload, crippling social interaction.

We even make attributions about internal mental states to explain the behavior of people, and groups of people, whom we have never even met. For example, I have heard some say that the poor don't deserve health care or welfare checks from the government because they are lazy, irresponsible, and just don't want to work. Of course, these judgments are hypotheses about the personal psychological makeup of "the poor," a whole category of people, who could *not* have been individually known by the person making these attributions. Such prejudices may emanate, in part, from our disposition to engage in "mind reading" which may include a default assumption (let's call it *the default assumption of free will*) that the behavior of others is caused by their internal mental states, personal traits, and freely made choices, rather than by external causes. Such default assumptions, perhaps built-in to our "theory of mind module," or the result of generalizations we make from our own experience of our own mental operations, were probably very useful in facilitating human social interactions in our distant prehistoric past and likely still serve similar function in the present. Belief in free will in others, and in ourselves, simplifies things by providing an efficient and ready-made way to understand behavior, making it easier and quicker for us to gauge how we should respond to others. The *default assumption of free will* in ourselves and others may serve an important social information processing function, useful to us as a species, beginning long ago in our prehistoric origins as a social creature. If we had to take into account all the forces acting on a person that influence their behavior, our brains might encounter the problem of *combinatorial explosion*, an overload of possibilities that would computationally cripple our brains. The result might be what John Barth's character, Jacob Horner experiences in the novel, *The End of the Road*—a psychological paralysis that Barth coined as "cosmopsis."

Part of what contributes to our belief in free will may be the design of our brain circuitry, a circuit design that causes us to explain the behavior of ourselves and others in terms of an internal causal agency, a will, to avoid combinatorial explosion and the resulting "cosmopsis." One important function of the belief in free will may be to grease the wheels of human social interaction by increasing efficiency of the information processing required.

Ready, set, go, or not—the makings of "free won't"

Is the will actually a causal agent, is the feeling of intention or will *actually* causing behavior, as it subjectively seems to be doing? Psychologist Benjamin Libet in the 1980's did some interesting experiments showing that the sensation, the feeling of volition, actually *follows* the critical neural events which physically cause an action, by about half a second (Libet, 1983). It had been well known for years among neuroscientists that a distinct brain wave, known as the *readiness potential (RP)*, is observed to build in the brain over a period of a few hundred milliseconds (thousandths of a second) prior to any actual physical movement. Research shows that the RP has two components, an earlier electrical component, RP1, generated from the *supplementary (pre-motor) motor area (SMA)* of cortex in the frontal lobe, and a later component, RP2, generated from the *primary motor cortex* of the anterior parietal lobe. Libet wondered whether either component of the RP corresponded to the subjective experience of volition. But, the startling finding was that the RP starts about 0.35 seconds *before* the reported feeling that "now he or she feels the desire to make a movement." Thus, the subjective conscious feeling of wanting to move, what we experience as the "will," occurs *after* the readiness potential, which reliably precedes "voluntary" movement. Therefore the initiation of voluntary movement can't be caused by the perceived "will." The "will" is just a little too late! Causes only act forward in time, not backwards. Libet (1983) therefore concluded that *free will* couldn't exist, because the neural events taking place that actually caused "voluntary" movements are unconscious, and they precede the subjective sensation of the "will" or any conscious "decision" to act, thus making it impossible for the "will" to be the cause of the movement. According to Libet, we have no *free will* in the initiation of our movements.

However, Libet did observe that we can consciously *abort* a movement at the very last moment, something fondly known among neuroscientists as *"free won't."* But, of course, even "free won't" must be a neurological event in the brain, as suggested by research at the Max Plank Institute in Germany which has identified the *fronto-median cortex* as the center of a brain network for self-initiated inhibition of intended actions (Brass and Haggard, 2007).

Though, Libet's work has been criticized by the philosopher Dan Dennett, other studies generally confirm Libet's results. One study in particular is especially convincing. Ammon and Gandevia (1990) from the Department of Clinical Neurology at Prince Henry Hospital in Australia asked subjects to decide not only when to move but also which hand to move. Then the experimenters used *transcranial magnetic stimulation (TMS)* to try to influence subjects' choices about which hand to move. Right-handers chose to move their right hands 60% of the time without TMS. However, when researchers used TMS to stimulate an area of the right frontal lobe involved in movement planning (right brain controls the left hand), subjects "chose" to move their *left* hands 80% of the time. In spite of the fact that the "choice" was thus heavily influenced by the stimulation to their brains provided by the TMS, the subjects nevertheless reported no diminution in their sense of free will as the cause of their action. Their *feeling* of *free will* was maintained even though their "choice" was determined by events stimulated in their brains by TMS administered by the researchers prior to the "choice" made. Surprisingly, the fact that their choices were determined by physical forces external to their "will" went unnoticed by the subjects, and their firm perception of free will as the cause of their action remained intact.

Thus, the sensation of a freely chosen, willful decision looks like it could be some sort of non-causal artifact, not itself directly a cause of behavior, because the feeling follows the actual neural events which physically cause the movement. Keep in mind, that this does not provide any evidence of dualism, since the unconscious information processing involved in volition itself must be based in other neural activity in other places in the brain, probably in circuitry in the prefrontal cortex known by neuroscientists to be involved in planning ahead and in the anticipation of future outcomes (remember the discussion above about our ability to image future behaviors and their projected outcomes), as well as in the limbic system, a major source of basic biological drives, our emotions, and our desires. This evidence suggests that free will may be an epiphenomenon, a subjective conscious experience without causal effects on behavior.

It is very important to understand that this doesn't mean that the person isn't "choosing" by processes of visual-like mental imaging described in the previous chapter, since these imaging processes precede the subjectively perceived choice-point that Libet's work deals with. In Libets's experiment a simple choice situation related to a simple sensory discrimination task was used. In this simple and immediate kind of "choice" task presumably little, if any, future projection and planning of the kind the IBOES routine (described in the previous chapter) accomplishes would be involved. It could very well be that the readiness potential (RP) precedes the felt "will to move" but the RP itself must follow all of the consciously experienced imagistic representations and processing which I have extensively described in Chapter 4, and the RP itself must be the causal result of all of that prior processing which I propose as the basis of our perception of personal volition and free will. But if the *feeling* of free will is a non-causal epiphenomenon might it still have "purpose" or adaptive function nevertheless? As I have argued above, that purpose, that adaptive function of the feeling of free will, so common to our subjective experience, may be that it serves as a default assumption in the information processing operations of the *theory of mind module*, in service of the efficiency of the information processing required for successful social interaction.

As testimony to how natural it is to us to attribute the causes of behavior to free will, some people even ascribe free will to the behavior of animals, no matter how simple their nervous systems, and in ancient times, even some inanimate objects were believed to have free will—for example the sun, in the Aztec mind, *willed* that Aztec warriors of 15th century Mexico should deliver captives to Aztec priests who cut out the hearts of the living victims to appease the sun, and to garner favor with it, in order to prevent it from willing disaster upon them.

The fundamental attribution error and determinism

When it comes to attributions of free will, clearly the Aztecs over did it, but maybe we are overdoing it too. Let's take another look at determinism.

Recently, some of my fellow professors demonized former Defense Secretary (under Presidents John F. Kennedy and Lyndon Johnson), Robert McNamara, upon his death, for his role in escalating America's involvement in the Vietnam War. McNamara, according to some of my history and sociology colleagues, was despicable and bereft of morality. His low moral character was pinpointed as the reason for his decisions during his tenure in office. Feelings against him ran so high that one of my colleagues (a now retired sociologist and gerontologist) even celebrated his death, presumably because of her judgment that McNamara was personally responsible for the deaths and maiming of tens of thousands of Americans and Vietnamese. I am certain that many other people hold similar beliefs about the man. But such thinking is natural and should be expected, if we accept my hypothesis that by our own brain "design" we are predisposed to see the causes of behavior as originating from within the person. We might even call this disposition, the *"free will instinct."* But should McNamara really be demonized and held personally responsible, as if he were acting completely freely? To be morally culpable would he not have to be acting and making decisions of his own free will and choosing for his own personal gain or for some other unworthy reason? Did he really act completely freely, of his own free will? Let's consider.

He did not create the historical, economic, social and political conditions that led to the war, nor did he originate many of the beliefs of his day about the cold war that influenced and even "informed" his decisions. In some sense, was he not acting within a set of constraints set by the social and political forces of his time, the political and military policies of the Presidents he worked under, and even perhaps by the limiting factors of his own personal experiences, such as his training and service as a member of Cal Berkeley's Army ROTC while a Cal student, followed by his active duty in World War II as a Captain assigned to the Army Air Forces Office of Statistical Control? We can imagine that exposure to military thinking and values may have determined the course of much of his thinking and decision making during his tenure as Defense Secretary. Quite conceivably McNamara was also powerfully determined by the stated policy of John F. Kennedy to "prevent the steady erosion of the Free World through limited wars," (Wikipedia, http://en.wikipedia.org/wiki/Robert_McNamara) thus preventing an ultimate confrontation involving nuclear war between the Free World and the Communists in China and the Soviet Union. These are powerful determining causes, and they are external to the person of Robert McNamara.

Nevertheless, in defense of free will, we can imagine that McNamara could have done differently, or that someone else in his position might have done differently, had the appropriate moral character guided what one might claim was his unmitigated free will. The fact that he didn't do differently is one reason that many people may believe that he should be condemned. But why didn't he end the war instead of escalating? As illustrated by the reactions of some of my fellow professors, many people feel that some fatal flaw in his moral character led him to continue the war even when he knew that the United States couldn't win. This kind of attribution is exactly what we would expect if we human beings have a powerful inner disposition in our brains to perceive the causes of the behavior of others as internal to them, as properties or characteristics of the person, their personality, their character, instead of arising as a result of external causes.

Some perceive him as a war criminal, and criminals are presumed to act by free choice, aren't they, otherwise how could they be culpable? The causes of McNamara's behavior were assumed to be his internal mental traits, such as his moral character, under his voluntary and free control, rather than external circumstances. However, some accounts of his actions emphasize beliefs of the time that withdrawal from Vietnam would have triggered the "domino effect" leading to a communist take-over of Southeast Asia, to the detriment of the United States. Was McNamara evil, was he morally flawed, did he act out of free will and free choice, or was he just misinformed by his beliefs, subject to the policies of his president, determined by his past experience, and by factors perhaps even from his childhood, which shaped his personality, his beliefs, and his values?

Let me be clear. I am not trying to defend or to condemn Robert McNamara, nor to give a history lesson, but only to use his case to illustrate two distinct ways of thinking about the causes of human behavior—attributing it either to internal, personal causes such as moral character and free will or, alternatively, to external causes such as "the times," and other social, cultural, and personal experiences (and even biological causes) outside the person.

Back in the mid-1960's, two social psychologists, Edward Jones and Keith Davis, identified what they called *correspondence bias*. Later, Lee Ross at Stanford University coined the term *fundamental attribution error*. Both terms refer to the observation that when people explain the behavior of others they typically overemphasize the role of internal, personal psychological traits of the person and underestimate the causal role of external, situational factors. In the case of "the poor," the causes for their poverty are ascribed to their alleged internal, personal psychological characteristics such as slothfulness or lack of character, when, in fact, the causes of their poverty may be external social factors such as deteriorating neighborhoods, crime, a culture of self-defeating attitudes, and inadequate opportunities for work and quality schooling. In the case of McNamara, he may have acted in ways that many people in his situation would have acted, given the times and the fears about the cold war which dominated the period. In both cases, according to the *fundamental attribution error* hypothesis, causation of the behavior in question was not so much a matter of the person's will or free choice, as it was external factors of which the person had little or no knowledge or control. In other words, behavior was determined by antecedent causes outside the person.

Yet, someone with both feet firmly planted in the *free will* camp could argue in retrospect that if McNamara had possessed a firmer grip on a moral compass he might have concluded that immediate withdrawal of all U.S. troops and an end to the war was the morally right thing to do, no matter what the consequences for the country and for Western democracies in general might be. However, someone from the not-so-free-will camp, might counter that factors in McNamara's past may have predisposed him to believe in the truthfulness of the cold war fears prominent at the time which predicted that a communist victory in Vietnam would have surely been the first step in future world domination by communist China and the Soviet Union. With this belief in mind, he may have concluded that his first moral responsibility was to the people of the United States requiring him to continue a war that he knew the United States would ultimately lose.

But suppose that the cause of his actions really could be tied to lack of moral character in the man. Would this hypothesized lack of morality have been a consequence of his free choice? Or would it more likely have been the result of something like inadequate moral training in his childhood, or perhaps the influence of other experiences in his life over which he had no control?

Free will in diminishing portions approximating zero

This whole line of reasoning behind the *fundamental attribution error* is troubling to many people because the suggestion of external causes of behavior appears to weaken concepts of personal and moral responsibility that human beings seem to rely upon to guide principled behavior. By acknowledging that factors external to the person determine behavior, there is the danger that people will feel a reduced personal responsibility. The belief that mitigating circumstances can somehow excuse behavior and exonerate one from moral responsibility may itself end up becoming a factor (a "self-fulfilling prophecy") in the causal web controlling people's actions, with potentially undesirable side effects. If I believe that my behavior is the result of outside forces over which I have little control, am I not more likely to engage in criminal and other socially irresponsible acts to the detriment of society? If I am not the cause of my own behavior, then doesn't this give me license to do anything and not feel morally responsible for my actions?

The so-called "Twinkie defense" used by Dan White's attorneys to get only a 5 year sentence for their client after he murdered San Francisco Supervisor Harvey Milk and San Francisco Mayor George Moscone is an example of what many people fear. White's attorneys argued that a sugar rush from too many sweets consumed by White exacerbated a pre-existing depression in their client which played a determining role in his actions, thus making him not fully morally responsible. The potential dangers inherent in such reasoning are evident. With this diminished capacity argument, White was convicted of voluntary manslaughter, and escaped the murder charge although neither he nor his attorneys denied that he had shot both Milk and Moscone with the intent to kill them. The jury judged that White was not fully morally responsible because his free will had been compromised by depression and a sugar rush from junk food (for those who may not know, "Twinkies" are a sugar-rich junk food). Is free will only free within limits imposed by external circumstances beyond an individual's control? Can there be such a thing as free will in degrees? Does the concept of *free will* imply that it must be *absolutely* free, without degrees of determination from outside forces?

Clearly, our concepts of morality are intimately aligned with the idea of free will, as the McNamara and White cases illustrate. We see ourselves and others as morally and legally responsible because we believe that human actions are the result of freely made choices (as discussed above, an idea central to religious views justifying eternal damnation when the wrong choices are made). To the extent that choices are perceived to result from forces outside the person, the moral culpability of the individual seems lessened.

Our entire system of law and much of our religious doctrine, including punishment for violations of law, and concepts of guilt and retribution, are based on the assumption of individual free will, although the legal theory of diminished capacity is based on the proposition that free will is not absolute and it recognizes existence of degrees of free will and thus degrees of moral responsibility. Is the legal system to be commended for an enlightened understanding of the complex internal and external causes of human action, or should it be condemned for opening a Pandora's box of legal and moral loopholes undermining the moral fiber and personal character of human beings and weakening the social stability of our institutions? Or, perhaps both?

Without the belief that human beings are rational agents that exercise control over their own actions and decisions, how can the concept of individual responsibility for one's actions, upon which perhaps our social order depends, be sustained? Perhaps, the idea of free will is a central belief in human common sense, in our "folk psychology," for very good, pragmatic reasons. Not only does belief in free will serve as an information processing short cut in our social interactions, as discussed earlier in this chapter, but social order may depend upon *belief* in free will and personal responsibility, even though many factors outside the individual's knowledge and control may, in objective fact, be acting to compel them to do what they do (and the particular effects of experiences of individuals on them is itself determined by their genetics and the nature of human nature, and the laws that govern it, determined by the evolutionary history of our species).

When we evaluate the behavior and intentions of others we not only use impressions about and observations of their behavior, but underlying our emotional evaluation of others and their actions is the default assumption of free will. If we did not assume that others act as they do as a result of their own free will, how could we condemn anyone, ascribe blame to them, or praise and admire them, unless we believe that they are who they are, and that they do what they do, because of their own free choice, their own internal causal agency?

Sigmund Freud, the founder of *Psychoanalysis* in the early 1900's, believed that much of our behavior was caused by unconscious forces, acting to control our actions beneath the level of our awareness, and thus outside our personal control. For Freud, free will was certainly not absolute, but, instead, he saw it as severely limited because so much of our behavior was caused not by rational, conscious choices, but by unconscious desires and conflicts, about which we have limited knowledge and no free choice. The *id*, according to Freud, is a store of unconscious desires for sex and aggression. These often unconscious desires, combined with unconscious conflicts between these desires and our culturally determined morality (Freud's *superego*), were the real causes of our choices and our actions. In Freud's view, it could be argued that free will didn't exist at all, adding more ammunition to the no-free-will camp. Human action, in Freud's world, resulted from unconscious psychodynamics and early childhood experiences, not free choice.

In 1971, the Harvard psychologist and ardent behaviorist, B. F. Skinner published "Beyond Freedom and Dignity." Skinner, like most behaviorists, was a firm believer in the role of the immediate environment as the cause of the behavior of animals and humans. According to Skinner, what we do is determined, not by free will or by unconscious mental forces, but instead by learned associations and by rewards and punishments dished out by the people and events in our experience. In Skinner's view, *classical conditioning*, the kind of learning whereby we recognize predictive contingencies between stimuli in the environment, and *operant conditioning*, the process whereby we learn about the rewarding and punishing consequences of our behaviors, are what really determine human and animal behavior. Skinner saw the concepts of free will and dignity (moral autonomy) as outmoded ideas that hindered the development of more scientific approaches to the understanding and control of human behavior. With these concepts out of the way, he believed the path would be cleared for psychologists to consciously apply principles of conditioning in order to create a better society. In his science fiction novel, "Walden Two," Skinner outlines how principles of operant conditioning could be used to "engineer" human behavior toward a utopian society. People, according to Skinner, do not have free will. Instead, their choices are determined by events in their past and present environments over which they have had little if any control. Therefore, the concept of personal dignity, which Skinner defined as the process whereby people are given credit for their actions or alternatively blamed for them, is mistaken, because it relies upon the false belief in an inner, personal, causality of behavior. It wouldn't be an exaggeration to say that Skinner believed that the sum total of what any person should be given credit for, or blamed for, approaches zero. People are who they are, and they do what they do, as a result of the rewards and punishments, and other events beyond their control, that they have experienced during their lifetimes in their physical and social environments. You are what your experiences have made you.

Skinner and Freud can certainly be considered determinists. Recall that *hard determinism* is the position that *every* event in the universe, including human psychological events such as thinking, feelings, choices, and actions, is the result of an unbroken chain of prior causes. No event occurs without prior cause. Therefore, human choices can't really be freely selected alternatives since the choice itself is caused, and the person who "makes" the choice is, him/herself, the result of an unbroken chain of prior causes over which the person has had little or no control and only limited knowledge. If early childhood experiences are formative, how much of those early experiences do you have conscious recollection and understanding of? How many did you have any control over? I would guess approximately none!

Skinner's position is consistent with *social determinism*, the view that individual human behavior is the product of social factors such as the social institutions, traditions, and mores of one's culture. On this view, free will is actually only an illusion because our choices are not free at all, but instead are caused by our social and cultural experiences and by the opportunities that our culture and society present or withhold. We, our minds and our behavior, are made by our socio-cultural experience, according to social determinism.

In the extreme form of this view, culture and experience are *everything* in the determination of behavior. Biology is ignored completely, or, at best, is acknowledged in passing, but is believed to be of no real importance. This view emanates from the conviction that the human mind is somehow "blank" at birth, devoid of any innate dispositions of any significance, other than perhaps a few basic reflexes. Beyond some knee-jerk stimulus-response reactions, nothing else is built-in to the human nervous system. Somehow, on this view, genetics can influence our bodies in determining ways, but apparently the brain was somehow missed by the genes, other than for a few reflexes and the purported design of a brain that is little more than a general purpose learning machine, which determines behavior exclusively through experience—individual, social, and cultural. These beliefs in the supremacy of learning to the exclusion of genetics, and that the brain is little more than a receptacle for experience, are so pervasive in the social sciences and humanities, such as sociology, political science, economics, and history, that evolutionary psychologists, John Tooby and Leda Cosmides at UC, Santa Barbara, have designated these beliefs, the *Standard Social Science Model* (SSSM) (Cosmides and Tooby, 1992). It is their position that the SSSM is "radically defective," because the set of assumptions upon which is based are so biologically naïve, a view I share.

Biological Determinism, Nature-Nurture, and Bio-socio-cultural Determinism

Another form of determinism, a counter weight to the SSSM, emphasizes the causal role of biological factors in the determination of mind and behavior. *Biological determinism* usually refers to genetic determinism; however, I use the term *biological determinism* in this book to refer to biological factors in general, not exclusively genetic causes. As described in a previous chapter, according to psychophysical monism, or physicalism, mental events are biological events in the brain. Because these events are physical, they are subject to the physical laws of nature, and are the result of a causal chain of anteced- ent events, just like any other event or state of things in the world. And this causal chain is ancient, extending deep into our evolutionary past, and reaches forward, without interruption, all the way up to the present day.

These two types of determinism, biological and social/cultural, are often referred to in a long standing debate in philosophy and the behavioral sciences known as the nature-nurture issue, about which I will have much more to say in a later chapter on the biological nature of learning. Suffice it to say, at this point, that the *nature-nurture issue* involves the question of whether genes or learning/experience make the larger contri- bution in determining mind and behavior. The philosopher John Locke (1632–1704) believed the human mind at birth was a *tabula rasa* ("blank slate") written upon "by the hand of experience," an idea uncritically accepted approximately two hundred years later as the founding principle of the Standard Social Science Model which became incorporated almost "unconsciously" into the nascent social and behavioral sciences as they were being founded in the second half of the nineteenth century. By contrast the philosophers, Jean-Jacques Rousseau (1712–1778) and Thomas Hobbs (1588–1679) believed in innate human nature—good, or evil and brutish, respectively. Modern views on the question recognize an interaction between both nature and nurture, but what remains at issue is the relative contribution of genetic and evolutionary causes (nature) compared to learning and experience (nurture) in the determination of mind and behavior. In this debate, determinism is not at issue. What is in dispute is the kind of determinism. In a later chapter of this book, I discuss how the nature-nurture ques- tion really has different answers depending upon the species and the specific behavior under consideration, resulting in what I call a *nature-nurture continuum* of causes in the organization of minds and behavior (see the chapter in this book on learning).

The idea that the mind is entirely physical and the result of laws of the natural world may make some readers uncomfortable, and maybe even hostile (as I mentioned in the first chapter, I have even had a death threat delivered to me for teaching psychophysi- cal monism, determinism and evolution and "corrupting the minds of the youth"; the threat I received didn't make any distinction among them, to my dismay as a professor. If they are going to threaten me, at least learn the concepts!).

Why are these ideas so disturbing to so many people? One reason is that these views imply a kind of biological determinism which, like other forms of determinism, leaves little or no elbow room for the concept of free will. Like other forms of determinism, this version threatens our sense of self, as an independent, rational, causal force capable of making free choices which make us morally responsible for our behavior and which also allows us to take credit for our successes. It challenges our sense of who we are, counters our common sense intuitions, and questions the fundamental assumptions upon which our basic institutions such as the law and religion are founded, and, not surprisingly, many people don't like that very much.

Whenever people's cherished views of the world are challenged they tend to get upset. Psychologist Michael Inzlicht of the University of Toronto hypothesizes that people are fearful of a chaotic universe and therefore take comfort in a sense of orderliness (Inzlicht, 2009). For this reason, fundamental change, even at the intellectual level, can cause stress and fear which can trigger defensive aggression and hostility.

Remember what happened to Copernicus, Galileo, and other early astronomers whose ideas threatened the established order, provided by the predominant belief system of their time, which included misconceptions about the Earth's place in the universe, and, by extension, the place of humanity in the scheme of things. By teaching that the Earth was not the center of the universe, these early astronomers challenged the idea that humans were at the center of everything. This upset a lot of people in power who ended up making Galileo recant these teachings or face burning at the stake. Modern scientific psychology (not the popular "psychology" of Dr. Phil) has the potential to call into question many of the cherished beliefs that we hold about ourselves and our minds. It is no surprise, then, that the closer the psychological threat comes, the more vehement the emotional response that wells up inside people. What are we, who are we, if our behavior, our emotions, our minds are just patterns of electrical potentials popping off in the neurons inside our heads? What are we to make of research reports that reveal that the neural events that cause our behavior precede our conscious "will" thereby eliminating it as a true cause of our behavior, relegating it to a mere illusory artifact? Do we really have the power of choice if all of our mental states are actually physical states in our material brains, and if these physical states are the end result of a complex fabric of genetic, experiential, cultural, and ultimately neurological causes (even culturally transmitted beliefs are represented in the synaptic connections in our brains) about which we have little direct knowledge and over which we have little, if any, control?

Hierarchical Causation and Supervening Biological Determinism

It seems clear that a hierarchical web of complex, interacting causes, past and present, outside of personal control produces the emergent mental states (thoughts, feelings, choices, beliefs and so on) which we end up attributing our actions to, along with our feeling that free will is at the root.

It is my view, that in this hierarchy of causation, biological causes (evolutionary, genetic, and physiological) set the parameters within which human behavior can vary.

We can't sprout wings and fly, but neither can we perceive the world or feel about the things in it in ways other than those permitted by our brain organization as a member of the human species with a particular, species-specific, evolved neurological organization. Perhaps theoretical physics will never adequately explain paradoxes such as "wavicles" or the relationship between gravity and electromagnetic phenomena because of limits on what our brains can conceive. Our brains are designed for survival on this planet, not especially for unlocking the deepest secrets of the universe; perhaps totalitarian governments will always ultimately fail because they are incompatible with our innate human nature; perhaps, we shall never be able to truly understand the nature of our own consciousness because our brain design limits us from conceiving properties of matter which to us will always be inconceivable; thus, in each case we can only strive toward better and better approximations to the limits of what our brain design permits. Though not ultimate truth, the closer and closer approximations nevertheless do make for important progress, ultimately a greater understanding of the forces acting on the universe, and thus upon us. With increases in knowledge, we can become conscious of more of the forces acting upon us, and sometimes this can lead to greater self-determination, and a measure of greater *relative* free will as a consequence.

Next, nested beneath the species-wide genetic, evolutionary, and neurophysiological parameters constraining every human being, cultural and individual variation occurs, and it is in this relatively narrow range of options, limited by our biological nature, that specific institutional, cultural, and historical causes operate. Typically, people think of cultures as being highly variable, creating large degrees of variation in human behavior. But, in fact, these culturally based variations are really quite small when compared to differences in behavior between humans, regardless of culture, and other species, even those closely related to our own species. This comparative perspective is important, but it is typically ignored by most social scientists and experts in the humanities because they are usually unaware of such comparative, cross-species contrasts, or consider them irrelevant to their interests. This can lead to a kind of *species blindness*, causing social scientists to take human nature for granted or to make it invisible, causing them to exaggerate the magnitude of the effects of culture on human behavior compared to the "invisible" effects of our species' genetics and evolutionary history.

Then further, nested within that still narrower range of behavioral options set by institutional, cultural, and historical causes, individual experience, beginning early in childhood and continuing throughout the life span, creates even more variation in the behavior of individual people, but always only within the range of possibilities "permitted" by the levels of causation above (biological, social, and cultural). Individual differences in personal experience within any cultural context add this additional variation in individual behavior, but again the range of variation (with the exception of pathological variations) is relatively narrow, when examined from a comparative, cross-species perspective. Pathology of genes and/or experience can lead to pathological behavior outside the typical range. A Hitler, a Jeffrey Dahmer, or a Saddam Hussein command interest, even fascination, from many people precisely because their behavior is so far outside the range that is typical of most of the human species.

This is because of our "curiosity instinct." We, as a species, are attracted by the unusual. This fascination with the atypical occurs, in large part, because of brain design of intelligent animal species that causes such animals to seek information, and novelty—the unknown is information-rich precisely because it isn't known. Information-seeking, what we call a "curiosity drive," is a biological adaptation built-in to brain/mind designs because it motivates animals and humans, mostly without their awareness, to gather a complex system of knowledge that can be drawn upon if needed in the future when the organism encounters new environmental situations that require a novel adaptive response. Curiosity is a cardinal feature of the brain design of the mammals (including especially us), and probably the corvid birds such as crows and parrots, and probably some invertebrates that are noted for their intelligence, such as cuttlefish and the octopus.

But aside from our attraction to behavioral pathology (most students love to study about mental disorders), these extreme deviations from the norm are perfectly understandable. They simply arise from pathological genes and/or experiences, and the resulting pathological choices that follow. Hitler had something wrong with him. So did Dahlmer, Charles Manson, and Saddam Hussein. These people had defective brains. Those with typical healthy experiences and genetic endowment do not become cruel, sadistic killers. Something in the emotional parts of their brains was haywire.

However, firm believers in free will, in spite of all the causes and constraints acting on a person to determine the available choices, might claim that there is still a tipping point, perhaps no more than a moment of indeterminacy, where one can freely choose to do something other than what all the causes constraining free will seem to inevitably dictate. Where, at what point, does an uncaused decision intervene and change the course of a causal chain that extends link by link inextricably to the person and their actions? We have seen in the first part of this chapter that *soft determinism* defines free will as making choices that are not forced upon one by others. Perhaps this is the only sense in which we can have a will that is free. Considering all the places in the world where political and economic oppression constrain people's choices, perhaps that kind of free will is all we need to worry about.

For reasons that I will explain in the following chapters, I conceive of social and cultural events themselves, as ultimately biological in nature. Social and cultural causes arise from features of species-typical, human brain design that dictate that we are, by our genes, a social species, equipped with certain, specific social "instincts" and, further, that we are specialized for efficient cultural transmission of learned behaviors across generations, as one of our primary means of adaptation to the environment. Though my view of human behavior emphasizes the biological character of its causes, this approach is not a one-cause explanation since, as I have explained above, I am proposing a hierarchy of nested causes, which I will argue in later chapters are all best understood as biological in their deeper nature and function. I call this view of the causation of human behavior *supervening biological determinism*. On this view, genetic and physiological causes, interacting with causes derived from social, cultural and individual experience, all of which are constrained by biological factors and all of which have biological origins and functions, determine human action. This concept is similar to the biological/social/cultural determinism I mentioned above, except that *supervening biological determinism* sees even the social and cultural causes of human action as fundamentally biological phenomena. Some inkling of the reasons why I make this claim (to be developed more fully in later chapters) can be understood when one takes on the comparative perspectives of ethology, evolutionary biology, and comparative psychology. Each of these sees human behavior in a broader comparative context, in which we can see that human behavior, including its social and cultural features, is just the way that one species (us) deals with the challenges presented to it by its environment, and these forms of human behavioral adaptation have their counterparts in other species. We are not as unique as we think we are. In other words, being social, and then becoming a species that is as good at cultural transmission of learned behaviors as we are, is just a form of biological adaptation in our species, just as much as flying in birds or swimming in fish are adaptations for those animals. How successful would humans be as a species if we had not evolved brain organization specialized for living in groups (many species are non-social species by virtue of the evolved organization of their brains) and for cultural transmission? Where would we be today without the invention and transmission over generations of human innovations such as agriculture, written language, mathematics, medicine, law, and myriad other culturally transmitted learned behaviors? We are a social and cultural species for biological reasons. These traits evolved because living in groups and cultural transmission of learned behavior over generations produced powerful advantages for survival and reproduction, and these behavioral traits still serve these biological purposes for our species. The adaptive function and biological origins of sociality and culture are not diminished by the fact that the human mind has also produced some cultural products such as art and literature which are emergent from these adaptations and so do not impact biological fitness. The origins of our sociality and our propensity for culturally transmitting learned behavior are biological nevertheless. For example, think of all the culturally transmitted behaviors, invented by humans who lived in prior generations, upon which we depend to solve basic biological problems such as obtaining food, water, shelter, and so forth. Agriculture, plumbing, and construction practices, for example, are solutions

to biological problems which profoundly affect biological fitness as do most all culturally transmitted behaviors. Cultural transmission is our specialty as a species.

But even from the more traditional approach to the role of social, cultural, and other
experiential influences on human behavior, it is clear that most such causes are well
beyond our knowledge and control, just as Freud, Skinner, and Locke believed. Do we
choose our parents? Where we grew up? The parenting styles and skills of our father
and mother? The people, ideas and beliefs that we were exposed to? The breadth of
experience that we had as children? Where we went to high school? The teachers we
had? What ideas were taught to us by those teachers? Whether we were athletic, outgo-
ing or shy, academically adept, popular or a loner? Do we choose our religion and if so,
as a result of what influences from our culture, our parents, our friends, and the time in
history in which we live?

Social cultural determinism is just as deterministic as biological determinism

It is interesting that many people who reject the idea that much of what we do is determined by biological causes are the same people who are perfectly willing to accept that
we are determined by our personal and cultural experiences, as if the things we experience in our lifetimes are somehow less deterministic than the biological causes of our
mental states and our behavior. Perhaps, it is the belief that biological causes are more
permanent and that they are more impervious to change (after all, how can we change
our genes?), while social and cultural causes seem less deterministic because we imagine that they *are* subject to change, making the deterministic influences of our experiences seem less fixed and so less threatening. Maybe this explains why many people
who recoil at the thought of biological determinism are quite comfortable with the
belief that human behavior is determined by experience, history, and culture. It may
also be that social determinists believe that social and cultural factors are less deterministic of human action because somehow these social and cultural causes are more
subject to modification by free will. But this view fails completely if free will is no more
than an illusion.

Research over the past 50 years has clearly shown that both biology and experience
determine who we are and what we do. Biology sets the range of variation in our behavior that is possible for our species, our own specific culture restricts us further, and
then our own individual experiences (or lack thereof) add more constraints on what
we do, what choices we can imagine, and which features of physical and social reality
act to limit what we can actually achieve. Certainly, when we are confronted with a
choice, we can process information from our environment and following such processing by our brains, we can decide to do this behavior or that, based on our values and our

beliefs, but think about where these have come from—from within or from without? How many of them did we consciously choose and were those choices that we did make entirely free or the result of other influences in our lives that were not of our own making or even knowledge? Did we choose to be exposed to one set of values and beliefs and choose not to be exposed to another? Did we choose those who influenced us as we grew up? Were the people we met, the examples they set, or the lessons we learned from them, the beliefs and values we acquired from them, the result of our own choosing or just happenstance? Does the child growing up in an impoverished ghetto, and in a family, rife with violence, deceit, and desperation, have the same chance of becoming a successful contributing member of society as one raised by educated, successful, family-oriented parents in Beverly Hills, Silicon Valley, or Hyannis Port (JFK's home town)? Where, at one point in the causal chain that makes us who we are and what we do, does free will enter the picture? Is there somewhere a personal first cause, a choice free of other prior causes in the events and conditions of the environment in which we exist? Since all events, including psychological events must be caused, there seems to be no such thing as a choice or an action free of influences outside of us.

For example, if you happened to be born to parents who resided in Thailand because their parents also had resided in Thailand, and this is because their parents were born and grew up in Thailand, you would likely be a Buddhist, and if you were a male, you would spend a couple of years of your adolescence in an orange robe wandering the country as a young Buddhist monk. You wouldn't have become a surfer or a Catholic or a mall rat or fan of extreme fighting, or an admirer of NFL or NBA stars, nor would you wear brand name designer clothes or have chosen to go to college to get an MBA so you could work on Wall Street. And if you grew up in Los Angeles or Bussey, Iowa, it is very unlikely that you would have spent a couple of years of your young adulthood as a Buddhist monk accepting handouts of rice to sustain you as part of a spiritual quest.

The old cherished concept of absolute free will operating in our world leading to something even approximating absolute free choice appears to be an idyllic illusion, a Platonic ideal, not found in the real world. The relative or partial free will of soft determinism seems closer to the truth. This suggests a kind of biological/social/cultural determinism in which who we are and what we do is determined to a large degree by biological causes such as the toss of the genetic dice and the physical states of our biological brains, as well as by our personal and socio-cultural experiences during our lifetimes.

Memes and Genes and the "grace of God"

Units of learned behavior, "moving" from one individual to another and across generations, by imitation, teaching and learning, books, film, the internet, and other forms of cultural transmission, are known as *memes*, a term originated by British evolutionary biologist, Richard Dawkins. Humans are not only subject to the influence of their genes, but also their minds and behaviors are influenced by memes "jumping" into them (their brains), as stealthily as a parasite infecting its host. Genes and memes, neither of which we control, buffet us around like leaves on a windy day.

It seems difficult to see how we do anything other than what we are caused to do by forces originating outside ourselves. I make the choices I do because of emotion and sometimes reasoned choice, but the choices I can imagine and the ones I select are determined by things such as my past experiences, the values of my parents, and my society, the circumstances and opportunities that happen to present themselves at the time, and so on. There seems to be very little evidence that anything like free will plays much of a role in anything that we do, except when I exert volition following the execution of a IBOES routine, utilizing visual-like images in my "mind's eye" to select from the behavioral alternatives that I can imagine. Determination and self-discipline are real things, and can have real effects on our behavior and in our lives (as will be discussed below), but even the choice to have the determination to achieve some goal is learned (and perhaps, at least to a degree, a personality trait with genetic roots), and must depend on the opportunity for the critical learning experience, and the acquisition of the requisite memes, to generate the attitude of determination that can make a long-term difference in behavior and in a life. Not only the genetic makeup of our species and our own unique genetic makeup determine our behavior, but in addition we are determined by the memes of our society and culture and the time in history during which we live.

We may have the illusion of free will, and that illusion may be powerful, but if you look at all the causes that operate on us, it seems that the idea of absolute free will has little to offer other than personal comfort in the belief that we deserve the good things that happen to us, an idea which I don't believe much either. It all seems to be external cause and chance. Still, the feeling of free will is so compelling. But, this is probably due to our direct personal subjective experience of imaging response alternatives and their projected outcomes when we plan our long term behaviors. Perhaps this accounts, in part, for the persistence of our perceptions of free will even in the face of all the evidence against absolute free will. The powerful perception of free will arises from the images we experience in our minds when we are considering behavioral options, and from circuit design that may "make" us understand behavior using the default assumption of free will because it greases the wheels of social interaction and prevents an information processing overload from combinatorial explosion (a multitude of causes, and causes of causes, such as discussed above). But there is more.

Some evolutionary psychologists have argued that the illusion of free will arises from the exceedingly large number and complexity of the causes that determine our minds and behavior (see Barkow, et. al. 1992). The illusion of free will arises and is so compelling because we simply cannot be knowledgeable of all of the causes outside of ourselves that determine what we think, choose, feel, and do. Perhaps an understanding of this might induce those more fortunate to be more willing to share with those who have not gotten the same breaks, genetic, cultural, and experiential. I am reminded of the wisdom in the quote "There, but for the grace of God, go I," but in this case it may be the luck of the draw rather than grace, but the *moral* message remains.

If it isn't free will, then what is it?

Here in Kona, Hawaii, where I am writing this now, each year in October, there is an extraordinary athletic contest, the Iron Man Triathlon World Championships. Nearly two thousand athletes from all over the world converge on this small resort town on the west coast of the Big Island to compete. There are professional athletes as well as amateurs, but all who compete must have qualified in their age category (or disability category; some athletes are paraplegics) during the year at preliminary Iron Man competitions around the world. What makes the event so extraordinary is the sheer magnitude of the athletic stamina required. The Triathlon in Kona starts at 7 a.m. with a 2.4 mile swim from the Kona pier out into the ocean for 1.2 miles and back. Nearly two thousand swimmers fill the warm, Hawaiian waters, and once they swim out over a mile, they swim back to the small beach beside the pier, they clamber up the steps, exhausted, and run (and sometimes stumble) to a changing tent on the pier, get out of swim suits and into biking gear. Then they run to their bicycles and peddle 112 miles up the coast highway through old black lava fields in temperatures over 100 degrees to the Kohala Coast town of Hawi. With strength and endurance tested to its fullest, Iron Man hopefuls then follow the same highway, and after 4 or 5 or more hours of grueling, gut-splitting cycling, they arrive back at the Kona pier where they jump, or fall, off their bicycles, run to the change tents on the pier and get into their running shoes to immediately start off on a 26 mile marathon run to Keauhou's Kahaluu Bay then up a long steep hill to Kuakini Highway to the Alternative Energy Labs out in the lava fields again, and back along miles of highway to Kahaluu Bay and then finally a couple of links back and forth along Alii Drive before the final stretch to the finish in front of the Kona pier where the race began 8 to 18 hours before. This year, 2009, the winning man, in his thirties from Australia, finished this brutally demanding course, the 2.4 mile swim, 112 mile bike ride, and the 26 mile run, in just over 8 hours and 20 minutes, crossing the finish line in Kona in front of the entry to the pier at about 3:20 p.m. after passing the American who had been leading most of the triathlon since the swim. The first place woman, also Australian, finished this incredible race about an hour later. But, by midnight, the official cutoff for the race, there were perhaps 100 athletes still out on the dark course, still struggling to finish. Many didn't make it, but almost 1,600 did cross the finish line, including a dozen or so athletes, men and women, in their 60's and 70's, before the midnight deadline, earning them the title of "Iron Man." About 10:00 pm I saw one athlete come out of the darkness of the course on oceanfront Alii Drive into the bright lights beginning the last 150 yards from the finish line, a man in his late 40's bent over, barely moving, inches from crawling, struggling to make the finish line before his body gave out completely and collapsed in a heap. The crowd, lining the course in this last stretch to the finish line, seeing this man in extreme pain and exhaustion, began to cheer in unison, perhaps two thousand late-night Iron Man onlookers, shouting their encouragement to this crumpled figure to give his last ounce of strength to make it to the finish. His body listed to one side and he almost went down but, to the wild cheering of the Iron Man fans there from all over the world, he tried to lift his head above his stooped body to see the finish line and he pushed himself onward somehow, until he stumbled across the finish and then collapsed. From the speakers above the finish line the voice of the announcer boomed the man's name, his age, and his country, and then said, "You are an Iron Man."

I tell this story because it illustrates something about what we commonly refer to as the human *will*, especially that expression of human will that we commonly refer to as determination. This story demonstrates that the determination to reach a goal does make a difference. Volition, the mental act of visualizing a goal and the steps to reach it, and then the strength of desire to put those steps into action even against great odds, is a causal force in the complex interacting array of causes of human action. As such, the act of volition is just as real as any of the external causes acting on human behavior. The arguments for determinism are compelling, perhaps even overwhelming, and yet volition of the magnitude demonstrated in the Iron Man competition, and other human feats of great determination such as scaling Mt. Everest, putting men on the moon, or devoting one's life to help the impoverished, can't be ignored if we are to truly understand human "mind design." The will to achieve a goal imagined by a human brain, visualized for years, driving the person to the self-discipline to make the sacrifices to train day after day or to make other sacrifices of other goals and desires, year after year, for no other purpose than to reach the goal of becoming an "Iron Man," or a "saint," shows that there is something powerful in the human brain, something originating within human brain design itself, not in external causes, that is a significant and, in some sense, a determining causal factor in human action.

This human *will*, the act of volition, to the point of sustained determination is real, but it is also *in* the human brain, a property of particular brain circuits, molded in part by socially based and culturally transmitted beliefs, values, and concepts. Research indicates these circuits are localized in the unusually large prefrontal cortex of human beings. Though these parts of the frontal lobe are found in other mammals, they are far more developed in us than in any other species and are much more structurally complex—remember from Chapter 3 that each neocortical column in the mouse cortex has 1,000 neurons, but the neocortical columns in the human cortex contain about 10,000 neurons and there are about 1 million such columns (see the talk by Henry Markham, "The Emergence of Intelligence in the Neocortical Microcircuit," given at the IBM Researcher's Almaden Institute Conference on Cognitive Computing in 2009, at http://video.google.com/videoplay?docid=7437432153763631391#docid=3112558958535505740 , Retrieved May 30, 2010). The emotion and the cognitive planning involved in this volition, of the human kind, are brain states. For example, the choice to pursue the training with the required diligence to make it to the Iron Man competition on the Big Island of Hawaii and to finish, if not to win, is an extraordinary example of how the human brain can plan and organize long sequences of behavior to achieve future goals. By visual-like mental imaging of the achievement of goals and the associated rewards, in this case social, emotional, and symbolic and thus dependent upon language and culture, and the steps needed to reach those goals, the human brain shows its capacity for willful, goal-directed action of an order not found elsewhere in the animal kingdom.

But is this volition uncaused, and in this sense, absolutely free? No. It can't be, as real and as compelling as it is. Would an impoverished young man in the slums of Manila surviving by fishing for garbage in the municipal dump, competing with thousands of others there for scraps of food, have the same chances of having the time or strength to condition his body for an opportunity to compete in Hawaii's Iron Man competition? Would the winners and even other competitors be able to condition themselves were they not already in social and economic circumstances that permitted them to do so? Yet, for every Iron Man athlete, there must be hundreds of thousands or maybe even millions of people who have the same social and economic opportunities to condition their bodies to this state of near perfection, but they don't. And, in fact, in exceptional cases, great poverty like that described above, can be overcome given the determination, in combination with the right opportunities, as shown by the life of the great Philippine boxer, Manny Pacquiao, who rose from great poverty to find his way to a rundown boxing gym in his home country, which opened the door to the discovery of his talent by the American trainer, Freddie Roach, who helped make Manny one of the greatest boxers of all time. So our admiration for those who accomplish great things is justified, though their will to accomplishment and the sacrifices made toward the goal are only part of the causal chain involved. Would Manny Pacquiao, with all of his determination, become the phenomenal success he has become if he had never had the good fortune to find boxing and those already in boxing, such as Freddie Roach, who could give him the opportunity to bring his natural talents to such a high level of skill?

There has to be opportunity, the option presented, combined with the selection of that option, to train, to compete, to pursue the goal to its achievement. It is within this constrained range of options where choice can make the difference. Free will is not free, but it is will, volition, and involves a choice, an ongoing decision to seek a goal and to do what is necessary to achieve that visual-like mentally imaged, and perhaps verbally imaged, future state of the world and of one's life. The large prefrontal lobe of the cerebral cortex of the human brain makes such long-term goals and their pursuit possible. It is the acquisition of symbolic and abstract goals, by social and cultural experience mediated by language, another result of human brain design, in interaction with values acquired from the same origins, within the genetic and evolutionary opportunities and constraints imposed upon our biology as a species, which makes such human pursuits possible. And the goals themselves, when social in nature, are in part the result of our emotional makeup as a genetically evolved social species.

The complexity of the causation involved is staggering. The multitude of causes and their interactions is probably supra-astronomical in number. But one thing we can say for sure is that humans, as a result of our species brain design, have the capacity to plan, to select from options for action, and to pursue courses of action that result from a host of internal factors as well as a multitude of external factors.

Whether we perceive the causes of behavior as internal or external depends on which causes we focus upon, and so whether we are free-will-ists or determinists of one variety or another may depend on where in the causal web of human behavior we focus our attention. Both sets of causes, internal and external, operate to shape our behavior, and sometimes we see the internal causes and conclude that behavior is the result of free will, and then at other times, our attention is drawn to the external causes of behavior and we then conclude that we are determined. In a sense, both are true, two sides of the same coin. And yet, neither is true in any absolute sense. We are simultaneously free and determined, or rather free within rather narrowly defined determinants, biological, social, cultural, historical, and personal. We have limited free will, free will in degrees. The more options we become aware of, and the more options presented to us, our freedom is increased by some small amount. The more aware we become of the factors operating on us to affect our actions, our feelings, our thoughts, the more free we become. It is in this way, that this book can help make the reader become freer of constraints, at least those where knowledge of them makes them less influential, by making their influence subject to conscious review, perhaps revealing choices not previously "seen" in one's "mind's eye."

Free will in an absolute sense is not possible because of the multitude of causes outside our control and our awareness acting upon us. Free choice is a matter of gradation. But the will to do great things does make, in many cases, the determining difference in what is possible in a human life, notwithstanding the roles of chance and opportunity.

The Twilight Zone of Free Will and Volition and the Person as Information Processor

When I was a kid, I liked to watch the Rod Serling TV series, The Twilight Zone. I remember an episode in which a lone individual wakes to find himself locked inside a room with nothing but a few objects such as a table and chair, a few books, a clock, but little else. Human choice is like being locked in such a room, with a few choices available, but even the choices that are available are constrained by circumstances over which we have little if any control. Volition, internally generated action, is possible, but it is different from anything like absolute free will. Knowledge can expand the size of the room (the available choices), although walls at some distance will always be there, even if they are often transparent and beyond our abilities to perceive them.

What I am getting at here is that it certainly seems as if *free will* isn't really free in the ordinary sense that it can be a first cause, but instead, this *will*, volition, is highly constrained by all the other biological and experiential causes (including social, cultural, and individual) originating prior to and independent of the individual. Yet, although volition, will, is not a *first* cause, it is nevertheless still *a cause*, in a complex tapestry of other causes. Though not free, not immune to other causes, volition is a cause that can have life-changing effects, and it is self-generated, arising from the information processing functions within our brains. By evolution, the neurological systems for movement in our brain "design" are forward looking, future oriented, because of the survival advantages of behavior that is *reflective*, rather than just reflexive. It is out of the forward-looking, reflective components of our neural systems for movement control that our volition is made.

Look at it this way. Inputs from the environment are constantly impinging upon the person from the sensory organs. This information comes into the person, the self, that is, the self's brain, and then an output is generated in the form of some behavior. But the output is not identical to the input. The input is transformed by the person, that is, the information processing mechanisms in the person's brain. Inputs come in, then they are processed by the person's brain in various ways, before an output is computed. The person makes a difference. The person, really an information processing entity, and the information processing properties of the person's particular brain circuitry (formed by that person's species-wide and individual genetics, and their cultural and personal experiences, including all their upbringing, their childhood and adult experiences, their cultural experiences, etc.), transforms the inputs coming into the person in particular ways, ways unique in detail to that person (although mostly the same, at least in general, because of species-wide similarities among people) to determine the behavioral outputs from that person. The same inputs coming into another person would be transformed differently, at least in the details, producing a different output, a different behavior. So, the *feeling* that the outputs, the behaviors, coming out of the person are *due to the person* is an accurate reflection of the reality in some sense. The outputs are *not* just a function of the inputs to the person—the person, herself, actually transforms the inputs, via information processing, before outputs (behaviors) are generated.

However, the person, the information processing entity upon which all these inputs impinge, is, him or herself, the result of myriad external causes. But might the person play an active causal role in making themselves who they are, by the decisions they make. Well, yes . . . and no. The decisions change the person, and so are contributing factors to who, what kind of information transformer, the person is, but the causal impacts of these internal forces created by personal decisions are not acting in isolation, not independently of all the other external factors that have made the person the kind of information transformer they are. So it starts to look, as worked through earlier, that something like some graded amount of free will is possible—volition with constraints. Behavior is determined by individual choices coming out of the person, but the person himself is the result of a complex mix of external and internal (self-generated) causes ("choices," determination, "effort of attention"). An added factor is the emotions, which are generally more automatic and which result from processing in other brain systems (the limbic structures). These are less subject to volition, and interact with the biological, social, cultural, and personal factors influencing them. All these factors interact dynamically to cause the outputs coming out of the person, that is, the person's brain. A weave of causation so complex, it is no wonder that the topic of free will has engendered so many conflicting and controversial philosophical positions.

The person feels that their volition is free because what *makes* the person, the information processing features of the person's brain, is mostly invisible to the person, to their brain, especially on a day to day basis, giving the overwhelming impression to the person that the outputs coming out of them are caused by them. And, in fact, they are—they are the immediate cause of the behavioral events because those behaviors are the output resulting from inputs transformed by the information processing taking place in the person's brain. We are aware of some of the information processing that is the immediate cause of our actions, but we are generally denied the awareness that we, the perceived agency of our behavior, were made largely, if not entirely, by forces outside ourselves.

Complicating things further, recall from Chapter 2 that beliefs can have causal effects on the brain's chemistry, and certainly on the brain's information processing properties. Belief in free will, in the power of one's own determination to produce causal effects in the world, can itself have causal effects on behavior. Belief in your own ability to change things in your world, or in the world at large, has affects your motivational levels. Belief in the efficacy of your own actions encourages you to initiate action and to follow through. Knowledge that belief in free will and in the power of choice and commitment can be powerful causal agents in how our brain processes the inputs to it gives us an added piece of freedom. By choosing to believe in these ideas, the belief itself becomes causal. Belief in the thing makes it so. Thus, people who have the belief that they can do anything if they "put their mind to it," a belief that the 2009 winner of the Iron Man women's championship espoused in her victory speech, can, and usually do, get more done, and achieve greater heights of accomplishment and success. Persons in this way can help create themselves. The beliefs they incorporate change the way their brain processes the information coming into them, and thus changes the behaviors coming out. Disbelief in free will causes measurable changes in specific brain activity (the RP, "readiness potential" in the EEG) in the motor association cortex related to the planning and execution of voluntary movements (Rigoni et.al., 2011). But the interaction between one's beliefs and the causes/origins of these beliefs is a classic chicken and egg circularity, adding to the difficulty in understanding the complex interactions between internal and external causation of human action.

Let's use an analogy. Imagine a machine, a loom, completely made of wooden parts, that weaves tapestries by the movements of its parts, powered by a stream and water wheel adjacent to the wooden building that houses the loom. Imagine too that the parts can be assembled in different ways to produce different movements which produce different outputs, that is, different weaving movements (behaviors in our analogy), resulting in different designs in the tapestries the machine makes (outcomes or effects of behaviors). Of course, though there can be variation in detail in the structure of the machine, overall, the range of variations is constrained by the weaving functions to be performed and by the structure designed to perform those weaving functions. The parts of the loom can't be arranged in such a way that the resulting movements can't do weaving and end up making haphazard and useless, non-functional movements, or movements that do something else besides weaving such as milking a cow or sweeping the floor. Each person is analogous to a slightly different version of the machine, with its parts arranged in slightly different ways, so that the loom will create tapestries of slightly different pattern from case to case. The loom is made by forces and causes external to it, and beyond its control, just as a person is. So, though the immediate causation of the movements of the loom are in the loom itself, emanating from its structure, still the structure of this machine is the ultimate cause of the movements that it makes and thus the ultimate cause of the tapestry ("the life") it weaves. And that structure is not caused by the machine itself, but is the result of something outside the machine which has determined the details of the machine's particular structure. And so it is with persons. But it is genes and experiences that are the external forces that have made the person. Choices come out of the person, just as movements come out of the loom, and the choices are of the person, just as the movements of the loom are of the loom, but the movements of the loom and the choices and resultant movements of the person are the result of the structures of each of these "machines," and these structures originate from outside forces/causes. Choices are information processing events and so emanate from the information processor, but the processor hasn't designed itself, at least not in any absolute way, even by its decisions. The choices themselves are partially determined because the options available are constrained. But what about those who say they are "self made." Is this really so? Yes and no. A series of choices or, in some instances, a single choice can set in motion a course of events that can change a life, many of which follow, without being anticipated or intended at the choice-point by the chooser. Thus, because much of what follows couldn't be anticipated and therefore couldn't be intended, what results from the chooser's choices is not under the control of the chooser but instead is a consequence of external causes and happenstance. In other words, though choices are possible within constraints, and although choices can have an effect on events to follow, often the chooser has no idea what ramifications will follow his or her choices. Choices are causes in a myriad of other causes acting on behavior and its consequences. Choices are made on the basis of best guesses about future, based on the information processing events in the brain of the chooser. In the overall scheme of things, capacities for "choice" proved to give adaptive advantage, in the long run, over thousands upon thousands of generations in brain evolution, over alternative brain "designs" without the capacities for "choice," such as they are, that exist in our brains.

The information processing features that make a perception of volition a part of the operations of a brain are not likely to be found in just any brain. We shouldn't expect that sensations of free will and volition are going to be found in flies, clams, roaches, jellyfish or lizards, since I am pretty confident that, in these animals, consciousness does not exist (see Chapters 2 and 3). The brains are just too simple and the kinds of lives these animals lead, dictated by the environmental problems they encounter, aren't conducive to the genetic development of conscious awareness. Awareness isn't needed. Running under a refrigerator when the lights come on in a kitchen (or under a rock, more likely before humans came on the scene) looks purposeful and conscious ("Yikes, they're home, run for cover or you're gonna get stepped on"), but the same could be accomplished by a robot "bug" with the right circuit design. In fact, engineers have accomplished these kinds of behaviors in robots decades ago with batteries, some photocells, circuit boards, and some wire. I am quite sure that these robots are not conscious, nor do they have free will or any sensations of volition, and neither are such things likely to be found in simple animals with relatively simple nervous systems. And as already discussed, in order to make an inner perception of free will possible, there must also be present in a brain the neural processing that generates a perception of self. Not only is a lot of neural tissue required, but it must contain highly specialized circuit "designs" to accomplish such sophisticated and functionally specific information processing feats as volition and a sense of self.

Metaphysical (ontological) free will, pragmatic free will,
and an intersection with Existentialism

Is free will really dead? Has the idea run its course in human history? Is it no more than another superstition like belief in witchcraft or astrology? Should we now abandon the belief, as Skinner argued? Should we strive to overcome this fiction once and for all? Would the world be a better place without this concept that is so subjectively convincing and which resides at the center of our psyches? Well, in a word, No! The implications of the belief are just too large.

As noted above, a collective belief in free will may be essential to the successful operation of human social groups, and as discussed in Chapter Two, beliefs can have powerful effects on the brain, and thus of course, on action. Without widespread belief in free will, the concept of personal responsibility for one's own actions loses its power, and there is danger that people may behave less well if they are freed from a sense of personal responsibility because they believe their actions have been determined by outside forces. Belief in absolute free will, though *metaphysically* untenable, may, nevertheless be our only alternative if we are to retain stable social order and preserve our aspirations to higher personal and collective achievements. Belief in free will may have essential adaptive utility.

For example, psychologists K. D. Vohs and J. W. Schooler reported in a 2008 paper in *Psychological Science* that experiments with college students show that when they are introduced to the concept of *determinism* they are more likely to cheat on a test. And in 2009, psychologists Roy F. Baumeister, E. J. Masicampo, and C. Nathan DeWall (2009) reported that disbelief in free will causes reduction in helpful behavior and increases aggression toward others. If we can generalize from these results, belief in determinism, in place of the common sense belief in free will and personal responsibility, could have widespread deteriorating effects on the stability of social organization in human groups. It is a paradox that modern scientific thinking leads to the weakening of ideas that our social fabric seems to depend upon. Some psychologists and philosophers such as Edmund Burke have suggested that one of the essential benefits provided to human societies by organized religion is its emphasis on personal free will, moral responsibility, and punishment and retribution in the afterlife for transgressions in this life against one's fellow human beings. Psychologist Azim Shariff of the University of British Columbia speculates that religion may have provided a solution to the group coordination problem in large human groups in our evolutionary past. In large groups, people can free load, cheat, or defect, without others knowing, leading to group collapse. Religion may provide a cultural solution to such large group problems by increasing pro-social behavior (giving, sharing, cooperation) and conformity with group interests because the concept of an all-seeing, punishing God helps keep people "in-line" consistent with the interests of the group. According to Shariff, "Mean Gods, make good people" (Shariff and Norenzayan, 2007; Norenzayan and Shariff, 2008; Shariff et.al, 2008a, 2008b, 2008c; Shariff, Norenzayan, and Henrich, in press; http:// www2.psych.ubc.ca/~henrich/pdfs/ShariffNorHenReligionChapter_final%20sep26. pdf, retrieved June 5, 2011). Belief in free will and personal responsibility as causal agents in human behavior should not be underestimated. These beliefs are essential ingredients in the formula for human social stability and much of the human success story.

But there are also important beneficial effects of the belief in free will on the individual, independent of any effects of this belief on the stability of the social order. In the 1950's and 60's Ohio State psychologist, Julian Rotter, and a group of his graduate students, developed the concept of *locus of control* (LOC). LOC refers to the extent to which people believe that they can control events that affect them. Those with an *internal locus of control* tend to believe that they have control over their own lives and believe in their abilities to effect change, while those who believe that the forces which act upon them are external to them and mostly beyond their control are said to have an *external locus of control*. Clearly, belief in free will is associated with an internal LOC because one believes in oneself as casual agent, while belief in determinism is associated with an external LOC. This is particularly interesting because decades of research, since, has shown that an external LOC, and by implication belief in determinism, is correlated with lower achievement motivation, increased stress and increased risk for clinical depression. Multiply these effects by the tens or hundreds of thousands or even by millions and it is easy to imagine that whole groups of people, perhaps whole nations, may suffer from an epidemic of deterministic, fatalistic belief. By contrast, one can imagine that value systems which emphasize personal control (free will?) and responsibility may be more likely to heal a society suffering from a viral-like epidemic of fatalistic and pessimistic memes (recall from Chapter 2 how beliefs can affect the brain chemistry that influences mood and motivation). Perhaps there are important lessons here for the modern world. Is America or segments of its population afflicted with beliefs that sap their sense of free will? And if so, what effects on the psyches (brain/minds) and on the behavior of these people might follow? Are there subpopulations of people, in America, and worldwide, infected with too much determinism and not enough determination?

In his theory of personality development, psychologist Albert Bandura emphasized the importance of a related concept, *self-efficacy*, the belief in one's ability to succeed in particular situations. Those with high self-efficacy tend to believe that their lives are controlled by their own actions and decisions, whereas those with low self-efficacy tend to report feeling that things are much less under their own control—in other words, they feel more determined by forces external to themselves. As is the case in "locus of control," degree of self-efficacy is related to the concepts of free will and determinism.

Belief in free will should be associated with higher levels of self-efficacy belief, and this seems to result in advantageous health outcomes for the person. Research has shown that those with high levels of belief in their own self-efficacy are more likely to engage in healthy behaviors such as exercise, weight control, cessation of smoking, wearing seat belts, using condoms, and so on, and are more likely to persist in the face of obstacles and setbacks that might otherwise undermine motivation. Given these results, it is not much of a stretch to conclude, as common sense might lead us to expect, that those with belief in free will, an internal locus of control, and high self-efficacy are more likely to have higher levels of motivation, higher levels of self-esteem, better health, and be at less risk for stress, anxiety, and depression. Belief in free will, even if it doesn't truly exist in any absolute metaphysical sense, appears to have multiple benefits for the individual.

Perhaps, as a practical matter, the ideas of Austrian neurologist and psychiatrist, Viktor Frankl, may have something very important to offer here. Frankl, like many existential philosophers, emphasized the role of personal choice and personal responsibility in the course of one's life. On his view, human beings are ultimately alone and the basic challenge for each individual is to overcome meaninglessness by creating one's own values and meaning, a major stroke of volition and self-efficacy. Each individual is fully responsible for her/his own decisions and can blame no one but themselves for their outcomes. This belief is a powerful one, and, when believed in firmly, it most probably has an important causal role in the mix of causes that mold human actions (the belief affects neural activity in the brain related to initiation of voluntary movements; see Rigoni, et al., 2011). Frankl founded a form of psychotherapy, *logotherapy*, which is based on the principle that the highest need of human beings is the creation of personal meaning in one's life (logos is Greek for meaning).

The British biologist and philosopher, Richard Dawkins, suggests that certain fictions are useful to humans because we live in what he calls the "middle world," a world at a scale at which the very small and the very large don't affect us in the ordinary course of our existence (see http://www.ted.com/talks/richard_dawkins_on_our_queer_universe.html; retrieved 9-5-10). For example, in terms of the physics of things, solid objects, including our own bodies, are actually made up of mostly empty space because of the great relative distances between the nucleus and electrons that make up atoms out of which everything is composed, yet because we live in the "middle world" of biological organisms, this fact about the very small scale nature of matter is irrelevant and so we evolved perceptual systems that disregard the facts of atomic structure and that represent solid objects, even though solidity is a fiction. Color sensations are another example. Color is a fiction created by our brains to represent wavelength and other properties of reflected light and the surfaces that do the reflecting. Color doesn't exist in the external world, neither does luminosity, both are creations of our brains designed to represent features of radiant energy important to our survival. The world is really dark and colorless; though light exists, it is really as dark and colorless as radio waves or gamma rays; like light, these are also forms of electromagnetic energy, all that differs is the wavelengths (see chapter 8). Our consciousness of things is a neurologically constructed model, a model that has biological utility. Along these lines, it is conceivable that concepts such as free will are adaptively useful illusions that function for the efficient operation of our everyday social interactions, and, as discussed above, for beneficial effects of the belief on the individual, even though logically such concepts make little ontological sense in any absolute way.

This leads to an important conceptual distinction. With all the myriad, antecedent causes acting to determine human choices and behavior, belief in anything like absolute free will is untenable. Thus, it seems to me that we can safely reject, on logical grounds, what we might call *metaphysical or ontological free will*, the belief that human choices are first causes, themselves freely made in the sense that they are uncaused by external forces. All the arguments presented above contradict the belief in an absolute free will or anything approaching it, and instead make the doctrine of determinism, that all things are caused, even human choices, seem indisputable.

Yet, we have a convincing sense of our own personal efficacy; we tend to make default attributions about the causes of our own behavior and the behavior of others in terms of internal psychological factors such as free will and moral responsibility, perhaps as a result of an evolved "mind reading module" in our brains which has helped grease the wheels of social interaction since our beginnings; and, as we have seen above, belief in free will has stabilizing effects on social order in human groups, and also provides numerous psychological and health benefits to the individual. Furthermore, there are *real* effects of personal choices and sustained effort toward imagined goals such as becoming an "Iron Man" or devoting one's life to the welfare and care of the less fortunate. For all these reasons, even though *metaphysical free will* apparently can't logically exist, what we might call *pragmatic free will* is an essential belief for human beings, and belief in this form of free will is a real causal force in the determination of human action.

In this regard, I believe Skinner was wrong. We cannot make do without widespread belief in the concept of free will and moral autonomy. We can think of metaphysical and pragmatic free will as two sides of a coin existing simultaneously in two worlds, in two realities. In the imaginations of some philosophers and theologians, absolute metaphysical free will exists and forms a foundation for absolute moral responsibility while for others absolute metaphysical or ontological free will is an illusion; still, in the human social world, belief in free will permits our brains to accomplish efficient, short-cut, economical ways of processing social information beneficial to, and consistent with, our social nature as a species. Though metaphysical free will is unsupportable, belief in free will, for pragmatic reasons, for the benefits it provides individuals and society, is far too valuable to discard. Rules of the human social game require the assumption of free will, and to play the game, it seems we have *no choice* but to play by the rule of free will and to insist that others do as well, or face the consequences imposed by the group for the sake of the common good.

Free will may be a neurological construction within our brains, just like colors or smells. Such psychological things don't really exist in the external, objective, physical world, but they do exist in the mind because they serve adaptive function, they promote survival and reproduction, and the mind is "designed" for adaptation as a result of the creative forces of natural selection operating over the evolutionary history of the human brain.

Believe in free will and moral responsibility—make a society founded upon these beliefs, if not for metaphysical reasons of free will, then for the utility of pragmatic free will. The social game requires all play by this rule, regardless of its *ontological* status. Though there are costs, there are also benefits that accrue from belief in the power of our own will, our focused determination, to effect change and to direct our behavioral accomplishments to stunning heights, beyond the capacities of any other species. One of the characteristics that distinguishes us from the rest of the animal kingdom is not free will, not even volition, since other animals also exhibit volition, but the ability to formulate symbolic goals such as becoming an "Iron Man" or a "Mother Theresa" and the emotional and cognitive makeup to maintain focus on the steps to achieve such distant, abstract, socially defined goals. No other species has the capabilities required for such action. In this regard, we really are different from other species, as our history and the material manifestations of our human cultures attest.

The tough discrimination for a humane society to make is where to draw the line between the larger social good and compassion for the individual who violates the interests of the common good when seemingly overwhelming, determining factors are at play. Is a Bernie Madoff more morally culpable than a Charles Manson? It seems that in both cases our legal system functioned well. It removed both from the society, helped to protect social stability, and prevented both from doing additional harm to other members of their species. This is all we should expect of the law. Now, I know some of my fellow professors will cringe at the phrase, social stability, because setting it up as a value important to human survival may seem to leave no room for legitimate social change. However, in the cultural evolution of human groups, new memes, sometimes destructive of an existing social order, may emerge, necessitating the weeding out of an older social order that has served the common good less effectively or has been counter to it. The French and American revolutions and recent revolutions in several countries in the Middle East and northern Africa, including Egypt and Libya, are examples (Wikipedia, http://en.wikipedia.org/wiki/2011_Egyptian_revolution; retrieved June 5, 2011). So, I am not arguing against the need at times for revolutions, political, economic, and scientific. Human progress requires them.

One final reason for belief in pragmatic free will is suggested by the philosopher, Thomas Nagel (1971, p. 397; after Daniel Dennet, Consciousness Explained, 1991, p. 424) when he writes, "It may be impossible for us to abandon certain ways of conceiving and representing ourselves, no matter how little support they get from scientific research." We, our brains, might just be made that way.

The Neuroscience World View (NSWV) and the Weinberg Problem

University of Pennsylvania neuroscientist Martha Farah argues that "cognitive neuroscience with its powerful new tools for monitoring and manipulating the human mind and with its physical, mechanistic view of human nature" will radically change conceptions about the nature of human life in this century, what she calls the "neuro-century," because of the astounding discoveries in neuroscience that are already on the way (see Farah's talk at http://www.psychologicalscience.org/observer/getArticle. cfm?id=2592; retrieved June 5, 2011). For example, some developments which portend things to come in this century are brain-based lie detection, drugs to selectively erase traumatic memories, the use of Transmagnetic stimulation of the brain to enhance alertness in soldiers, products such as EmotivSystems and BrainGate that permit specific movements of a computer mouse or an artificial arm by paralyzed people just by thought alone, anti-androgen pharmaceuticals to eliminate sex drive in sex offenders, and other drugs to enhance learning and memory, Oxytocin to enhance trust, non-lethal neuro-weaponry to temporarily confuse and disable enemy soldiers, specific serotonin reuptake inhibiting drugs to treat impulsiveness in violent and sexual offenders, and so on.

Farah believes that along with the neuro-century comes the *Neuroscience World View* (NSWV). Neuroscience implies that a person equals their brain, and so the person becomes a material thing, destroying dualism ("the ghost in the machine"). As neuroscience reveals the physical basis of personality, love, etc. the need for the "ghost" vanishes, affecting religion and challenging ideas of moral and legal responsibility, as I have described above. If pathological brain structure and function in schizophrenia is responsible for pathology of mind and behavior, as discussed in Chapter Two, and if the brain pathology is, at least in part, the result of the genetic draw, then what about other behavior such as criminality? Is it possible that criminality may have, at least in part, genetic and/or neurological causes? And if so, what does this do to our conceptions of free will and personal responsibility, cornerstones of our legal system? If someone does something bad, are they responsible or is it a breakdown in the machine? Farah states, "retribution for crime doesn't make sense in the neuroscience world view. Behavior should be incentivized, not punished." She comes to this conclusion in large part because of the implication of the NSWV that bad behavior is not the result of free choice, because so many other causes external to the individual are operating. The NSWV implies determinism.

But the NSWV also presents other major challenges. As I mention above, when people are introduced to the idea of determinism, they are more likely to cheat, to be more aggressive and less pro-social, suggesting that the NSWV has the potential to erode moral standards and social cooperation (see the "Brain Series," http://www.charlierose.com/view/collection/10702).

Farah points out that for some the problem is how to assimilate the NSWV without becoming nihilistic. For example, Steven Weinberg has written: "The more the universe seems comprehensible, the more it seems pointless." In other words, if the universe is the result of mindless, random processes combined with the operation of laws of nature that are not part of a divine plan of some sort, then why are we here, what is the meaning of life, and does it matter what we do? In my view, there are at least three possible answers to what I will call *the Weinberg problem*.

First, in some sense, such revelations may be interpreted as liberating. As the existentialists such as Nietzsche claimed, the absence of a divine plan gives human beings the opportunity and the responsibility to create meaning and values, given the constraints on our minds and behavior set by the nature of our species. As will be discussed in later chapters, I believe that human beings have an innate human nature that sets limits on what we can become. Our choices are not infinite, but must conform to our innate nature, otherwise choices which are counter to our innate nature are doomed to ultimately fail. We are not infinitely malleable. But we can design our own destiny within limits by increases in our knowledge, understanding, and wisdom about the natural world and our place within it. Though we may be much more determined than we like to think, we need not be helpless or fatalistic. We have wiggle room.

Given the realities of our existence, of the nature of suffering in the world, of our nature as an innately social species whose members are mutually interdependent, we are given the responsibility and the opportunity to create human social institutions that will reflect humanistic values that can maximize the greatest good for the greatest number. An enlightened interpretation of this goal includes respect and care for the earth and its other inhabitants in recognition of the benefits of biodiversity to human existence. Science will play a large role in providing us an ever increasing data base of reliable information about nature and ourselves to better inform human choices, as determined, as they may be, by biological and social constraints alluded to above. According to Farah, *neuroliteracy* is needed for the coming neurocentury (judges, educators, law makers, etc. must be educated about the discoveries and implications of continuing research in the brain sciences). Democratic development and regulation of neurotechnology is essential (if funding is mostly from private sources, then only for profit research and applications are likely). Instead of being a threat, neurotechnology can be used for the benefit of humanity in spite of the challenges that the NSWV presents to us. Perhaps we are on the verge of an enlightened scientific humanism.

A second answer to the Weinberg problem is a theistic one, belief in God, or at least in the possibility that some supernatural being is behind it all, and that natural laws are simply the mechanisms used by God to put into effect the divine purpose. This is not a scientific solution, but we shouldn't necessarily expect one, since the Weinberg problem is a problem of meaning and values, and thus, by definition, outside the purview of science. But science can inform us about nature and our place in it and thus give us new insights which can complement the role of theism.

A third possible answer to the Weinberg problem is that meaning comes from human relationships. This is not a prescription for a meaningful life dreamed up by some touchy-feely therapist, but instead reflects the realization that we are a species that is social by its nature, by the information in our species-wide DNA that designs our brains and minds. The meaning that relationships with other human beings gives us, such as relationships with our children, our spouses or lovers, our friends, and our colleagues, is built-in to our brain circuit "design," particularly in limbic system structures involved in subjective pleasure sensations related to the positive emotions like love, affection, happiness, belonging and joy. To discover this source of a "meaning-full" life, we need not make effortful cognitive rationalizations or other complex ruminations to discover it; we just engage in social interaction and relationship, then let the social instincts inherent in our human brain circuit design provide us with the flow of emotional rewards and consequent meaning which we experience without any need of analysis. We, that is, our mind/brains, are designed to feel meaning when we are in healthy relationship with other members of our species, simply because of the way our brain circuitry has been put together over our deep history as a species on this planet.

Humans are embedded in the same complex web of natural causes that control the destinies of everything, living and non-living, on this planet. The sooner we realize that we are not free and in control, in any absolute sense, our new wisdom as a species will permit us to use the concept of free will to human advantage and to discard remnants of the idea which have not served us well. Though free will is literally and logically impossible in any absolute sense, something that feels like it does occur, and belief in free will, independent of the accuracy of the belief, has benefits to the individual and to society, but at times, it also can have drawbacks and adverse consequences. We need to use it as a tool, not as an absolute and irrefutable truth, to better our lot as creatures adrift in the vastness of the universe. Perhaps the old wise and powerful dictum, the golden rule, "Do unto others, as you would have them do unto you," no matter how "corny" it may sound to some, will finally be understood as being as close to any kind of moral certainty as we will ever get. To my mind, it is the one true principle that all should and must live by, for the common good of all creatures on the earth. In this light, no God of violence can be a true God. Violence against others must surely be blasphemy of the highest order.

In the next chapter, we examine the processes that have shaped life since it first appeared in its most primitive forms on the earth over a billion years ago. Those same forces which determined the form and function of bodies also "designed" the form and function of brains. Just as bodies of animals of divergent species show fundamental similarities, rooted in common ancestry, the brains of each animal species, including our own, show deeply rooted continuity, yet diversity and specialization. And from brains come minds and behavior.

CHAPTER SIX

Origins: Entropy, Life, and Psychology's First Fundamental Law

"Another curious aspect of the theory of evolution is that everybody thinks he understands it"

Jacques Monod
(after Richard Dawkins, *The Selfish Gene*, p. 18)

"In the distant future I see open fields for far more important researches. Psychology will be based on a new foundation, that of the necessary acquirement of each mental power and capacity by gradation. Light will be thrown on the origin of man and his history."

Charles Darwin,
The Origin of Species by Means of Natural Selection, 1859

In prior chapters we have examined how physical processes in a material brain might generate mind, and how conscious minds have developed over deep time shifting control of behavior from simple reflexes and *fixed action patterns* to behavior informed by reflection—mental images of one's self in future action, leading to volition and, in humans, to the perception of intention and "free" will.

But to really understand the nature of human nature, minds, and behavior, we must answer deeper, more fundamental questions. Why do organisms move at all? What is the origin of behavior in the first place? Why aren't living things more stationary like mountains, or rocks, or soil? How is movement of an organism different from movement of inanimate objects such as the planets, a billiard ball, or the "reactions" of chemicals? Why did capacity for movement develop so extensively in animals while plants remain "planted"? Why do the movements of animals take the particular forms that they do? What functions are served by movements of organisms and by the underlying mental processing we call mind? What are the processes that shape, or "design," minds and an organism's behavior? To answer such questions, we must look back in time, back to the origins of life on earth.

Ultimately, life is chemical. It is the presence of certain molecules with certain particular properties that permit us to identify something as living. One of the key properties that some scientists have identified as characteristic of life is the ability of living organisms to reduce or reverse *entropy*, molecular disorder—that is, organisms are characterized by the ability to organize matter and energy into more complex forms (note that organism and organize come from the same root word). On the molecular level, living systems are engines that take in energy from the exterior world and use it to order, to structure, matter into more complex forms, against entropy—the tendency for all states of matter, in the absence of energy input, to tend toward greater and greater disorder or randomness. The ability to order, to structure matter and energy into more complex forms against the forces of entropy is one of the hallmarks of life. The chemical reactions which accomplish these ordering or structuring processes collectively are known as *metabolism*. But how did organisms acquire these properties?

Richard Dawkins (1989; 2006), in his book "The Selfish Gene," gives a marvelously clever and credible account of how the first glimmerings of life might have gotten their start from the inorganic materials present on the primitive earth. His story begins with the formation of the first atoms and molecules, long before living matter, and even before organic evolution existed.

Cosmologists believe that the universe began with the *Big Bang*, a massive explosion of a compaction of formative matter of unimaginable density. In Dawkins' view, soon after this initial explosion, simple atoms were formed throughout the expanding universe flung out in all directions at incredible speed. Some of these congealed into larger atoms with greater structural stability. Many of these atoms then linked up together in chemical reactions to form the first simple molecules. Dawkins observes a general principle operating even in the beginning—in the presence of external energy, "atoms tend to fall into stable patterns" and once there, they tend to stay that way. Thus, the "things" that we observe in the universe such as stars, rocks, mountains, diamonds, rain drops, ocean waves, galaxies, and other things that we recognize as objects, of one sort or another, are really just examples of how atoms tend to fall into stable arrangements in the presence of energy.

From these primordial origins, stars, galaxies, and planets were formed. Out of the enormous numbers of celestial objects in the vastness of the nascent universe, some planets such as the earth happened, by statistical probability, to develop conditions conducive to formation of water and other critical molecules. At this early stage, prior to the emergence of life, Dawkins believes that a kind of naturally occurring "selection" for structural stability operated on huge populations of molecules floating around in the primitive earth's atmosphere and oceans. On his view, molecules which possessed chemical properties that made them more stable tended to be preserved, while less stable molecular arrangements, by definition, were eliminated. Stability of molecular structure was thus favored by this early form of "selection," even before the emergence of any molecular structures that might be called living. In this way, from early atoms and molecules "selected" for stability, the materials for life were in place. But something else, some additional organizing force, was needed.

Dawkins notes that early selection for molecules of greater and greater stability still couldn't lead to life. Just throwing a bunch of atoms together isn't going to produce molecular structures of any great complexity, certainly not those which characterize complex multicellular organisms. As an example of this complexity, Dawkins makes the fascinating observation that the human body consists of a thousand million million million million atoms arranged in a highly specific structural order. He notes that the chances of this highly ordered configuration occurring spontaneously, even assuming early and ongoing selection for molecular stability, are infinitesimally small—so small, Dawkins claims, that the spontaneous formation of complex life from the random assemblage of atomic material would take so long that, by comparison, the "entire age of the universe would seem like an eye-blink." And therein lies the problem. Random processes alone can't do the job. Even with "selection" processes for molecular stability, an otherwise random molecular walk could never produce the complex arrangements of matter that are characteristic of even the simplest of living creatures. Something else, long ago, was needed to supply the astonishing molecular order required for the emergence of life.

To many people, this need for an organizing force in the origin of the universe, and particularly in the origins of life itself, is not an unfamiliar idea. Just think about the Bible. In Genesis, we read that in the act of creation God brought about *order* out of the chaos of the formless void. Is it merely accident that modern science and the Biblical account of the origins of the universe, and of life, converge so nicely?

Well, one of the themes of this book is that religion and science need not be in conflict with one another. Some of the imagined conflict arises from misunderstanding and from fear, the fear that scientific explanations will displace religious ones. But this may be a good thing, when the religious explanations are shown to have been clearly wrong (such as the belief that the earth was the center of the universe). Correcting misconceptions about nature and replacing them with scientific explanations about how things really are (the earth is just one planet of a medium sized star in one of the arms of the Milky Way galaxy) need not displace religion, but merely reveal more accurate detail about the way things really are in the universe, and perhaps at the same time, as Einstein speculated, tell us something about "the mind of God."

Our dominant religious traditions in the West suggest that the required ordering force needed for the origin of life was the non-random, purposeful, organizing influence of a divine will, an act of creation by God. In fact, the first primordial matter may ultimately require such an explanation unless that matter, from which the universe emerged at the Big Bang, had somehow always existed, or unless the so-called "cosmological singularity," the moment of creation, involved the spontaneous emergence of something out of nothing—an event one cosmologist, at least, claims to have been a mathematical inevitability given Einstein's theory of General Relativity (http://www.infidels.org/library/modern/greg_scorzo/kalam.html).

But, regardless of whether God did it, or even whether God exists, remember that the goal of science is to try to explain as much of nature as possible by laws of nature alone, without resort to supernatural causes (causes above and beyond natural law; albeit, that at the singularity, no laws of physics yet existed). Science attempts to push natural laws as far as possible, to explain as much as possible about nature (including the origins of things) by the laws of nature alone.

The genius of Darwin was that he discovered a law of nature that constrained otherwise random processes into a mechanism that could order matter into the unlikely, complex forms needed for the evolution of life. According to Dawkins, "This is where Darwin's theory, in its most general form, comes to the rescue. Darwin's theory takes over from where the story of the slow building up of molecules leaves off." And by doing so, Darwin's theory hands us a plausible, naturalistic explanation for the origins of living organisms and their functional "designs," including, eventually, "designs" of brains, behavior, and even minds, found in the more complex species with the more complex nervous systems.

As mentioned in an earlier chapter, experiments by Urey and Miller in the 1950's showed that if you put into a flask several simple molecules thought to have been present in the earth's early atmosphere and its oceans—water, carbon dioxide, methane, and ammonia—heat up the mixture to simulate the influence of volcanic activity in the sea, and add an additional source of energy such as periodic bursts of voltage to simulate lightning, after a few weeks you get amino acids, the building blocks of proteins, the molecular material out of which all organisms on the earth are made. Sometimes variations on this experiment using an energy source such as ultraviolet light (a natural electromagnetic frequency released onto the earth from the sun) can even produce purines and pyrimidines, building blocks of DNA, the coding molecule that forms the genes of all living things (Miller and Urey, 1959). However, some scientists now believe that a more likely scenario is that the organic building blocks of life arose in hydrothermal vents under the sea, perhaps like those discovered near the junction of tectonic plates at the Mid-Atlantic Ridge between Bermuda and the Canary Islands. In these vents, sea water about 90 degrees centigrade reacts with rock called peridotite producing chemical conditions for the synthesis of organic compounds from inorganic materials, a condition needed for the evolution of life. Such vents are thought to have been plentiful in the primitive earth's oceans (Bradley, 2009).

Now, Dawkins' story of how life originated gets to the real heart of things. He makes the guess that some primitive molecules in the seas and atmosphere of the early Earth became capable of replicating themselves. He imagines that a soup of smaller component molecules provided the source of the material out of which bigger, more complex molecules were formed as the smaller molecules linked together into long chains through chemical reactions. If the smaller, component molecules that made up these larger molecular strings had a tendency to hook up with other constituent molecules of like kind (or with their molecular complements), then strings of these which duplicated the original molecule (or which made a complement of it) would be formed, and then, when the original molecule and its copy split apart, two identical (or complementary) molecules would result—a kind of molecular Xerox machine. Dawkins calls such molecules, with this ability for self-copying, "replicators."

These "replicators," once formed, would duplicate themselves again and again. Furthermore, each copy would copy itself, and so on, until there would have been ever increasing numbers of these self-replicating molecules filling the environments of the early Earth. However, this molecular version of a copy machine would differ from the Xerox version in one important way. Sometimes the molecular copying process would produce copying errors resulting in molecular copies that were slight *variations* from the original. Thus the "molecular soup" in the early Earth's air and oceans would have had an abundance of such replicator molecules, ever increasing in number, and in variation from one another.

This is highly significant. At this point, two of the vital components in Darwin's theory of evolution would be in place—reproduction or replication, and individual variation among members of the population, in this case, a population of self-replicating molecules floating about aimlessly in a cauldron of primitive seas.

Those replicator molecules which, simply by chance, had a more stable structural arrangement of atoms, and which replicated themselves the fastest, would have been "favored" in a "struggle" for continued existence. Those with greater stability and faster replication would automatically increase in numbers, and those lacking these properties to the same degree would decline in frequency in the population. This situation provided the third component of evolution, "competition" among the individual variants in a population. Over time, those replicator molecules with properties that made them more stable and long-lasting, and faster at replicating themselves, would increase in number. Other "replicator" variants, less favorably endowed, would have been at a "competitive disadvantage" and these would have "survived" for shorter periods and would have reproduced fewer copies of themselves, decreasing in number as a result.

Variant forms of self-replicating molecules would undergo differential rates of "survival" and "reproduction." As a consequence, automatically and inevitably, over time, without any need of intention or plan or conscious design, the "better adapted" replicator molecules would be preserved, in ever increasing numbers, and the less well "adapted" would eventually vanish. Then, all that would remain would be better and better adapted replicator molecules. With this "selection" of the more favorable forms, for "survival" and replication, and the elimination of the less favorable variants, evolution by natural selection was born—even before life existed.

Note that evolution follows automatically from these ingredients: 1) *reproduction* or self-replication, 2) individual *variation* among members of a population of self-replicators, and 3) *competition* among variants of the self-replicators in the population. (Isn't it interesting that these three things are easily recognized as central components of everyday human life on many levels and in many arenas? Now, we can see why these three—reproduction, variation among individuals, and competition—are general properties of any life form on earth, including us.) Also note that the winning formula in the competition is determined by the environment. Self-replicating entities which just happen to have "traits" that make them "survive" and "reproduce" in greater numbers, in a particular environment with its particular features, are the winners in *that environment*. In a different environment, other traits would give competitive advantage, and would be "favored." Evolution ends up working like a kind of matching process wherein features of self-replicating entities (in this case, self-replicating molecules) that match, or fit the environment where those entities exist, get preserved automatically, and features that don't match the environment so well get weeded out. Over time, as a result, more and more members of the population end up with the traits of the successful variants, those traits that are the best fit, the best match to that particular environment. The unsuccessful versions are weeded out and eventually disappear. *That's evolution.* Evolution is not really a thing, but the name of a process that inevitably follows whenever the above described conditions in nature are present—self-replicating entities, variation of features among them, and an environment in which self-replicating entities with some features replicate more frequently than those with other features less well fit to the environment. This last condition is known as "differential rates of reproduction" among self-replicating entities (from "replicator" molecules through advanced forms of life) and is recognized by modern biologists as the engine of evolutionary change. If you and I are both reproducing, but you reproduce with greater frequency than I do, then your traits will persist into the future with greater frequency, but my traits will gradually disappear and ultimately will be replaced by yours. That's evolution. In this story, survival is only important because it provides opportunity for reproduction.

As Dawkins notes, this "competition" need not involve any awareness or intention on the part of the "competitors." The variant "designs" within the population of self-replicators reproduce at different rates just because some variants, by chance, have traits that increase their chances of self-replication. In the Dawkins' example, these molecules will be either preserved or eliminated, selected or not, by the environment. This selection is most certainly blind and senseless, that is, without awareness, intention, or purpose within those evolving, and yet the process of evolution still works. The competition among self-replicating entities, and the results of this "competition," the evolution of favorable traits over time, occurs in a completely automatic or mechanistic way, without the need of any ultimate goal—yet a "creative" process results anyway. Over time, self-replicating entities that are better and better fit, or matched, to continued existence in the environment in which they find themselves, are manufactured, again and again, with some variations "favored" over others, improving the match or fit to the environment, as the process continues over time. Creation of self-replicating entities better and better matched to their environment inevitably follows from this blind and automatic process—what Darwin called "natural selection." The process is not only natural, but inevitable, and it is creative, though blind and without any ultimate goal.

Of course, as Dawkins points out, not only was this competition (and the resulting molecular evolution) unknown to the replicator molecules, but it would be equally unknown to the complex plants and animals that would eventually be created eons later by its operation. Always, it was simply an automatic process, without any intention or purpose required. It just happened in a mechanical kind of way, simply as a result of the laws of chemistry and physics once the first self-replicating molecules were formed. Biological systems, and biological laws, didn't even exist when the early self-replicating molecules were busily vying for molecular stability sufficient for greater frequency of self-replication; at this early stage there was nothing like life, just self-replicating molecules containing carbon, and thus, using today's terminology, called organic, but still not yet life.

Thus, at this point in the story, we have gone from the first primordial atoms, to the first small molecules, then to molecules with the capacity for self-replication, accompanied by occasional copying errors which produced self-replicating molecular variants in the molecular soup of the primitive Earth. These various versions of the original "replicator" molecules then "competed" with one another leading to greater numbers of "replicator" molecules with ever improving stability and means for their own self-replication, and, at the same time, the weeding out of those molecular variants that were less fit to "survival" and "reproduction" in the conditions that existed on earth in the beginning. Presto, evolution—but, at this point, just the evolution of organic molecules, not even a rudimentary form that can yet be called "living."

Any copying errors that resulted in greater molecular stability in the "replicator," *or* which produced ways to *reduce* the molecular stability of rival replicators or their ability to reproduce themselves, would have been preserved in the population by higher rates of replication of these more favorably endowed replicator molecules. In Dawkins' account, mindless competition among such "replicators" would have eventually taken more direct forms, including molecular sabotaging of rival molecules by production of "poisons" that could break down the chemical structure of the rivals, freeing their smaller, constituent molecules to be used by the "attacker" for its own further replication.

Defenses would have improved too. Some replicators may eventually have exploited variations in their molecular codes to produce enveloping shields against the destructive influences of rival molecules. Perhaps these early protective barriers were made of fatty acids. These molecules have been shown to form spontaneously, given chemicals thought to have been present in the oceans, atmosphere, and land environments of the primordial earth (http://www.scientificamerican.com/article.cfm?id=origin-of-life-on-earth; retrieved November 10, 2009), or perhaps such barriers were made from surface-layer proteins acting like "chain-mail" (as found in present-day archaea) providing both chemical and physical protection to the replicator molecule inside (http://en.wikipedia.org/wiki/Archaea#Cell_wall_and_flagella; retrieved 11/12/09).

Such protective, molecular barriers to "attack" may have resulted in the first cell membranes and the formation of the first prototype "cells" perhaps some 3 billion years ago (probably early prokaryotes—cells without a cell nucleus or other membrane-bound organelles—or something quite similar). Such prototype cell membranes would have enclosed the replicator molecules and some of the sea water in which they were suspended (even today sea water and cellular fluids show surprising similarity in chemical makeup). Thus, the replicator molecules evolved ways, by selection processes described above, to enclose themselves in relative "safety," helping to insure their "victory" in the "struggle" for continued existence—and all of this could be accomplished without need of intention or purpose or knowledge, on the part of the replicators. All that was needed to do the job was the fact that some replicators, because of their properties, had higher rates of "survival" and self-replication (reproduction) than others with slightly different properties. The resultant differential rates of "survival" and "reproduction" did the trick needed to produce and preserve "good" (adaptive) "designs" and to eliminate "bad" (maladaptive) "designs." Over the eons, ongoing competition among these prototype "cells," and their replicators hidden inside, spawned increasingly complex molecular contraptions (enzymes, organelles, and so on), serving improved stability and ever more efficient copying of the replicator molecules housed within.

From Fish to Philosophers

These prototype cells became the first "survival machines" (Dawkins, 2006), devices inescapably "designed" to slavishly serve their masters, the replicator molecules tucked away safely inside them. Like the first replicator molecules themselves, these primordial

"survival machines" attain their ever improving "designs" as a result of the same processes that act on the replicator molecules they support and protect. Inevitably, "survival machines" are working for the replicators inside them. It could be no other way.
The "survival machines," no matter how complex they become, arise as extensions of
the replicator molecules within them. The same conditions that produce molecules
better and better at replicating themselves end up making "survival machines" better
and better at survival, and thus at reproducing the replicators they carry within them.
As Dawkins notes, today, all the organisms we see around us are the "survival machines"
and the replicator molecules within them, we know as "genes." All came about as a result
of three conditions in nature: self-replication, errors in replication that produce variation in the population of self-replicating entities, and selection, the differential rates of
"survival" and replication among individuals in the population of competing entities
(whether molecules, organisms, or even machines—remember the story line of the
first "Terminator" movie?).

As described above, these are the components of Darwin's theory of evolution by
natural selection. In the presence of these three conditions of nature, those "competitors," which happen to have characteristics that make them a better fit or match to
the environment in which they find themselves, will inevitably "survive" and replicate
themselves (reproduce) in greater numbers, and those with traits that make them less
well adapted (fit or matched to the environment) will tend to survive and reproduce
less and less frequently. Thus, over time (generations), "survival machines" (first, primordial cells, and then much later, multicellular organisms of great complexity) with
traits that better match the environment will come to be the dominant forms (in terms
of numbers) and those less well fit will tend to be weeded out and gradually disappear.

In this sense, natural selection acts like a filter, filtering out variations in the population that don't work, leaving only those that do work to replicate their traits again and
again, over time, toward better and better adapted "design." Adaptive "design" is thus
inescapable. It is inevitable. "Survival machines" that work better to preserve the self-
replicating molecules within them will reproduce themselves in greater numbers compared to those less well suited to the task. And, significant to the major theme of this
book, these processes which "designed" bodies, also "designed" brains, and the minds
that they produce. "Mind design" is just as inevitable as body "design" in nature. And
the underlying principle of the "design" is fitness, or match, to features of the environment that affect the chances of survival and reproduction of genes.

Notice that Darwin didn't invent evolution. His genius was that he recognized it,
and that he recognized the mechanism, natural selection, by which it worked to create organisms with splendidly effective adaptive "design." As a result of the automatic
processes of natural selection, "survival machines" have become better and better at
preserving the genes within them over the eons. As Dawkins has noted, "genes are

the immortals." The genes in each of us today have survived and have been replicated countless times over millions of generations up to the present day. In the genes of each of us are the genes of our most ancient ancestors, not just the first humans, but back further to our first vertebrate relatives, the bony fish, and in the case of some of our genes, even back further to the first self-replicating molecules at the very beginning. We will see later that these facts help explain many *similarities among the brains, minds, and behavior of creatures ranging from fish to philosophers.*

Given the three conditions described above, those "survival machines" that, by chance, happened to possess better ways of surviving and reproducing themselves, and thus the replicator molecules within them, increased in number over time, while the less effective survival machines were weeded out—once again, this is Darwin's powerful idea of natural selection, the process which acted on random variation to produce adaptive "design." Relentless competition drove ever increasing complexity and sophistication of these new life forms. "Survival machines" got bigger and better at doing the job for which they were "designed" by selection, the protection, nurture and reproduction of the replicator molecules within them (Dawkins, 2006). Given enormous amounts of time these processes produced innovation after innovation, preserving and building upon each randomly generated success, as natural selection filtered out the failures and inescapably "perfected" newer forms.

About 2.4 billion years ago, the first photosynthesizing prokaryotes (bacteria and archaea) began to release free oxygen into the Earth's atmosphere, a by-product of their conversion of carbon dioxide, water, and sunlight into sugars for energy to run their metabolism. The resulting oxygenation of the atmosphere set the stage for the evolution of oxygen breathing animals which was to follow eons later. Evidence of the first eukaryotic cells, those with a nucleus and membrane-bound *organelles*, dates them from about 1.85–2.1 billion years ago. It is enlightening, with regard to how complexity builds upon itself, that at least some organelles, most notably mitochondria (energy factories for cells) and chloroplasts (which contain chlorophyll for photosynthesis), probably originated from formerly autonomous bacteria which became incorporated, early on, into the eukaryotic cell in symbiotic relationship. Once these bacteria were enclosed in the eukaryote's cell membrane, mutual benefits preserved and improved the symbiosis modifying the welcome "invaders" into permanent fixtures within the eukaryotic "survival machines," like a group of specialized servants catering to the needs of the replicators in the cell's nucleus.

Primitive cells joined others and formed protective colonies. About 1.7 billion years ago, defensive strategies and competition among eukaryotes led to evolution of the first multicellular organisms, perhaps slug-like creatures composed of aggregations of amoeba, or single-celled organisms who reproduced daughter cells that did not separate, but remained together in one organism and which could later differentiate into specialized tissues.

The first fossilized animals were jelly-fish-like species about 580 million years ago, although multicellular forms which didn't fossilize probably existed earlier. Early sponge-like animals may have existed as early as 600 million years ago and flatworms, the first animals with rudimentary brains, appeared about 550 million years ago.

Later multicellular life forms became enclosed in protective cellular barriers, which in animal lines eventually became an exoskeleton, as in insects, or a skin. And in many species, millions of years later, these barriers would be covered by additional layers of protection ranging from feathers and fur to scales and even rigid protective shells.

The first *vertebrates* (animals with backbones) were the bony fish, emerging about 525 million years ago during the *Cambrian explosion* (a period of seemingly rapid appearance of most of the complex animals, although interpretation of the evidence for the "explosion" is still somewhat controversial even among paleontologists). During the next 70 or 80 million years, the rate of origination and extinction of species greatly accelerated. Evidence in the fossil record of the earliest land plants and the first land *invertebrate* animals (those without backbones, including the insects) dates back to about 476 and 490 million years ago respectively.

The first *land vertebrates*, early reptile-like amphibians, with legs and lungs, did not evolve from ocean forms for about another 120 million years (350 million years ago) to occupy land already inhabited by insects, mosses, ferns and other plants. The first *amniotes* followed about 10–30 million years later; these were exclusively land based small lizard-like vertebrates which reproduced using land-adapted eggs enclosed in protective coverings, (amniotic membranes inside shells or much later in the body of the mother) which permitted the eggs to survive away from bodies of water (the necessary fluid was carried by the egg or inside the mother). This allowed the primitive amniotes to spread out away from water into drier environments. The amniotes included ancestors of modern reptiles, birds, turtles, and mammals, which diversified as they radiated into different environments with diverse ecological niches, eventually becoming the dominant form of land-based vertebrate. Within another ten million years, the amniotes (characterized by amniotic fluid surrounding the egg either in shells or inside the female's body) split into two distinct amniotic lines, the synapsids, which include the mammals, and the sauropsids, including reptiles, dinosaurs, and birds.

The first true *mammals* arose approximately 200 million years ago in the late Triassic age, following the Permian-Triassic mass extinction, and these animals, with milk-giving mammary glands and which give birth to live young, diverged into *marsupials* (animals with pouches like modern kangaroos) and *placentals* roughly 125 million years ago. Mammals flourished and began to increase in size and diversity after the extinction of the dinosaurs 60 million years later. Within another few million years or so, modern families of mammals began to appear, eventually including the rodents, shrews, large carnivores, hoofed ungulates, bats, whales, and the primates, including tarsiers, monkeys, apes, ancestral human lines, and finally modern human beings (http://en.wikipedia.org/wiki/Evolutionary_history_of_life; retrieved 11/10/09), all "survival machines," protecting, nourishing, and reproducing the genes within them (Dawkins, 2006).

It is important to note, at this point, that humans did not evolve from monkeys, chimpanzees or gorillas, as the common misunderstanding of human evolution supposes. Instead, monkeys, modern apes, and human ancestral lines diverged millions of years ago from a common now extinct primate ancestor.

About 65 million years ago, the first primates diverged from a founding group of small, nocturnal, arboreal, insect-eating mammals called Euarchonta. Within the next 25 million years, the founding group of primates diverged further into prosimians (lemurs, lorises, tarsiers, and other primitive primates) and the simians (monkeys and apes).

Human and chimpanzee ancestral lines *diverged from a common ape-like ancestor* and followed different evolutionary paths beginning about 6–7 million years ago. The first hominid human ancestors did not appear for another 4–5 million years, and by that time had been separated for millions of years from the ancestors of the modern great apes—chimpanzees, bonobos, orangutans, and gorillas.

Homo erectus, a species resembling modern humans but with a brain only three-quarters the size of the brain of modern humans, migrated all over Eurasia from Africa, used stone tools, and dates from about 1.8 million years ago. About 500,000 years ago, the common ancestor of modern humans and the Neanderthals lived. Genetically modern humans, homo sapiens, are found in Africa beginning only about 200,000 years ago. Interestingly, the last Neanderthals became extinct only 25,000 years ago and thus co-existed with our own species for roughly 175,000 years.

The replicator molecules, inside each cell of these and every organism—plant, animal, bacteria, or virus, and eventually human—have indeed come a long way. As Richard Dawkins notes, today we call these replicator molecules *genes*. The colonies of cells inside the skin have become specialized tissues and organs performing varied specialized survival functions for the collection of interacting cells that make up the organism. As Dawkins observes, today's complex multicellular organisms, including you and me, are the new "survival machines" on the block, which live and reproduce to serve the continued existence of "the immortal genes," the descendants of the first "replicator" molecules that populated the Earth's primordial seas at least 3.7 billion years ago (Dawkins, 2006).

The Diversity of Species and the Mechanics of Change

But none of this history reveals how the big leaps in evolution took place, how one species becomes another.

Early on, Darwin observed diversification among species of finches on his voyage on the HMS Beagle, a British ship given the task of mapping the coast of parts of South America. As the ship's naturalist, Darwin collected specimens along the way, many of them previously unknown to Europeans. Darwin observed finches on different islands in the Galapagos chain and noted that although they were obviously related to one another, they were, nevertheless, distinct species.

One feature that distinguished these species of small bird from one another was the size and shape of their beaks. Some were long and narrow, others were short and stout and other species showed other variations in beak size and shape. Darwin recognized that the shape and size of the beak of each species was related to the food getting requirements of the birds on each island. On islands where food was to be found deep inside large flowers, long slender beaks characterized the finches there. On islands nearby in the same chain where insects lived inside the bark of trees, finches there had stronger woodpecker-like beaks, and so on. Darwin recognized that different environments created different demands on inhabitants favoring different characteristics, leading to evolution of related but distinct lines, and ultimately new species. In other words, different environments created different rules of competition, and thus created different winners. When a population composed of members of the same species became geographically separated and thus exposed to different environmental conditions, then different traits would be naturally selected for, and evolution would follow a different path with different results, that is, different "designs." Darwin eventually concluded that this process was slow, occurring over very long periods of time in small gradations, and that it was this process that resulted in the evolution of new species from an original ancestral species.

There is plenty of evidence for this kind of evolution in the fossil record and even among living species. In fact, recently biologists have found that changes in beak characteristics can be observed in just a few generations in the Galapagos (Weiner, 1994). More generally, insect populations and populations of bacteria readily evolve resistance to the poisons designed by humans to kill them. This is evolution in action and it is directly observable. Mice living in the deserts of Arizona have undergone evolutionary change in the color of their fur depending on whether they live on the sand or on black volcanic rock in the same desert (Michael Nachman, University of Arizona, "What Darwin Never Knew," NOVA, PBS, 2009). Moths in England evolved a darker wing color when the trees in the forests they inhabited became darkened by industrial pollution, because those moths that happened to have the darker wing color were better hidden from predator birds. Again, remember, all these adaptive changes took place without will, purpose, or knowledge in the evolving populations—differential rates of survival and reproduction in response to particular environmental conditions was sufficient to do these tricks of nature, producing "survival machines" better fit for the environments in which the genes inside found themselves. Today, the evidence for evolution is so overwhelming, so rich, and so varied that "Darwin's great idea" is considered by modern biologists to be a fact, no longer just a theory. There may be some uncertainty about the details of its mechanisms, but none about the fact of evolution itself. Evolution is a fact as certainly as the fact that the Earth is not flat, but round (Dawkins, 2009).

Those who find this claim to be offensive or disturbing on religious grounds should not. Evolution could simply be just one of the ways in which God accomplishes the creation (although science, by the rules of the scientific game, must necessarily remain neutral on this issue—unlike Dawkins who is vehemently anti-religion, as he makes clear in his recent book, *The God Delusion*).

One of the areas of science from which comes perhaps the most convincing evidence for evolution is modern molecular and evolutionary genetics, which, as it happens, has recently revealed an answer to one of the greatest challenges to evolutionary thinking: How could evolution produce big leaps or changes leading to the development of entirely new species?

Microevolution, the occurrence of small gradual changes in a feature of a species, can be directly observed (i.e. the moths in England, changes in beak size in Galapagos finches, or the development of resistance to antibiotics in bacteria are examples), but how can one account for macroevolution, the big leaps from one species or group of species to another—say, from fish to four-limbed amphibian or from scaly reptile to feathered bird. In Darwin's time, no one yet knew about genes, and certainly no one knew what we know today about DNA.

Ground breaking insights have recently been uncovered, in large part as the result of the mapping of the human genome (the detailed code of DNA in the genes and chromosomes).

Here, we must make a digression to be sure the reader is up to speed on some basics of molecular genetics required to understand what will follow. Molecular genetics, among other things, studies the molecule that codes hereditary information. That molecule is DNA, short for deoxyribonucleic acid. The molecular code in DNA uses sequences of smaller constituent molecules, nucleotides, strung together like the beads of a necklace. There are four types of these nucleotides distinguished by other smaller molecules within them called bases. The letters, A, T, G, and C are a short-hand for these four bases and the nucleotides that contain them. Just these four letters can be arranged in sequences to make an infinite number of genetic "words." Just as the Morse Code, sequences of only two coding elements, dots and dashes, in various combinations, can code the information in an infinite number of books, sequences of the four nucleotide bases, A, T, G, and C, can code all the hereditary information needed to direct the making and growth of an organism, a "survival machine" of any degree of complexity.

But DNA changes; mutations occur and create variation. Remember that the copying process in the replicator molecules is not perfect like a photocopier, but "errors" occasionally occur. An A, for instance, might replace a T or a G for a C. Such small changes in the DNA can cause big changes in characteristics. For example, just four changes in the DNA "letters change a light colored "pocket mouse" into a dark one, an example of evolution in action. The colobus monkey can see color because of a single mutation, making it possible for the animal to distinguish leaves ready to eat from those less nutritious ("What Darwin Never Knew," NOVA, PBS, 2009).

One of the expectations at the outset of the Human Genome Project (the mapping and sequencing of the human genome had its inception in the late 1980's and was completed in 2003) was that complex species like us should have many more protein-making genes than simpler species. But as the HG Project proceeded, researchers got an unexpected shock. Humans have only about 23,000 protein-coding genes, less than an ear of corn, and about the same number as a chicken or a lowly nematode worm. Furthermore, many of our key genes are the same as those in other species. To show how far genetic similarities go, we even share some genes in common with bananas. How then do species become so different from one another, and, more specifically how did we become so different from other species?

Clues to this puzzle are beginning to emerge. Genes and their mutations are only part of the evolutionary story. There must be something more to account for the big jumps in characteristics that can result in new species, and in the emergence of humans with our unusual mental and behavioral capacities for things like science and technology, literature, art, and religion.

Some biologists have suggested that the key to understanding how big leaps in evolution can occur is to be found in the embryo (PBS, NOVA, "What Darwin Never Knew"). A few days after conception the embryos of many species, including us, look about the same. It is only after the embryos grow that they start to differ from one another in significant ways. Biologists are beginning to recognize that the embryo is the "platform" for genetic diversity. How does this happen?

Molecular geneticists have discovered that during embryological development special genes called "body plan genes" determine where the head will be, what kind of limbs develop and where they will form, where the eyes will go, and so on. Another set of genes determines the patterning of coloring of the animal. Presumably other sets determine development of other features, including brain development.

Providing striking support for Darwin's idea that all species have arisen ultimately from common ancestry (Darwin referred to evolution as "descent with modification"), incredibly these "body plan genes" are identical across a large variety of species. Molecular geneticists are thus beginning to recognize that it is not the number and type of genes that's important to an understanding of differences between species, but instead it is how those genes are *used* that ends up generating the great diversity of life.

For example, the males of one species of fruit fly do a courtship dance to attract females for sex (thus, ultimately the behavior serves reproduction of fly genes; if this reminds you of human antics to attract mates, you are not alone). This dance involves display of dark spots on the wings of the male. The female is attracted to the dark spots on the dancing male's wings. But the males of some species of fruit fly don't have wing spots and they don't do much dancing during courtship either. This courtship dancing behavior is not learned, but genetic, and so are the wing spots. So, naturally, molecular geneticists wanted to know what was different in the DNA of fruit fly species with, and without, the wing spots and the courtship dancing. They identified a "paint-brush gene" responsible for the spots (and presumably the dancing behavior), but surprisingly the gene is found in both species, yet only one of the species has spots and does the dancing; the other does not. Thus the big difference between these species in spots (anatomy) and behavior (brain circuit design) is not in this protein-making "paint-brush" gene, but in how the gene is used. One species uses it to make the spots and to make brain circuitry for the dancing behavior, but the other species doesn't use it for making spots or courtship dancing. To understand why, molecular geneticists have discovered that we have to look to the "junk DNA," the "dark matter of the genome," to find the answer.

Research subsequent to the HG Project shows that this "junk DNA" comprises an astonishing 98% of the DNA of a species, and it doesn't code for proteins, the building blocks of living things. Molecular geneticists do not yet know what most of this 98% of the DNA does, but some of it is composed of what has come to be known as DNA "switches." It appears that it is this non-coding DNA, not the genes, but these "switches" that cause the difference in traits between species, such as having or not having the wing spots and the courtship dancing. Research has shown that in the fly species without spots and without the dancing, a DNA "switch" is broken. Though the genes are there for making wing spots and the brain circuitry for courtship dancing it never gets turned on in the embryo of the spotless species.

The DNA switches themselves aren't genes, they don't make protein. Instead, they turn protein-making genes on or off, choreographing the timing of genes, when they come on, how long they stay on, and when they turn off, thereby controlling development of the organism. A change in characteristics can occur just by "switches" in the DNA changing from on to off or by alterations in the timing of the on and off. The on-switch may get "broken" in a mutation, as in the spotless fly species, and so genes that once came on, no longer do. Big leaps in evolution can occur as a result. For example, manatees, whales, and snakes have "legs-genes" that are repressed; the "switch" for legs is turned off, so that these species don't develop legs, even though leg remnants are found in the embryo and even in the skeletal structures of the adults of these species.

The DNA switches can help answer some otherwise perplexing questions, such as how one species evolves into another. Whales have the bones for legs and arms, even fingers, and the remnants of a pelvis, so, according to evolutionary biologists, the whale must have evolved from earlier land forms. The ancestors of whales lost their legs by mutation, perhaps in DNA switches, an adaptive mutation, making them more stream-lined when moving through a water environment. Mutation of the DNA switch controlling growth of legs, turning it off, would cause legs to be suppressed, causing species that were ancestors of whales to lose their legs on the way to becoming whales.

Other big changes in the characteristics of a species could be accomplished by similar mutations in "switches" controlling a variety of protein-making genes, and thus a variety of characteristics, even brain circuit "design" and thus the underlying psychology, and behavior, typical of any particular animal species. If big changes in the "designs" of bodies from one species to another can occur by mutations in DNA "switches," then big changes in brains, minds, and behavior may also similarly arise over the course of evolution.

Another important question in this story is "What controls the DNA "switches"? Body-plan genes are turned on at different times and to differing degrees in the embryos of different species. These body-plan genes then turn off and on the protein-making genes, thereby controlling them and thus controlling development. For example, ocean living stickleback fish have a pair of fin-like spikes that protect them by making it hard for predators to eat them, but freshwater stickleback, which have evolved from the ocean variety, don't have these spikes. Researchers have found that the genes for the spikes are identical in the two stickleback varieties. What does differ between them, however, is a section of DNA which makes up the DNA "switch" for the development of the spikes. This switch is "broken" in the freshwater form so that it isn't turned on and therefore the spikes don't develop. But, there are traces of bones for the spikes still there in the freshwater variety. Importantly, these bone remnants are asymmetrical in size, with the bone remnants on the left being slightly larger. Significantly, in manatees, the same asymmetry is found. The remnants of legs in the manatee are also larger on the left than on the right. This suggests the possibility that the same DNA switch in different species is responsible for loss of limbs, another astonishing example of Darwin's continuity of species, and it is observable at the level of DNA. But, this also provides a glimpse of the mechanisms at the level of DNA that might be involved in generating the big evolutionary leaps. And if these processes apply to big changes in bodies, it will likely turn out that they also apply to big changes in brains, and thus may help explain some of the mysteries of human brain evolution which have made our minds so different from the minds of other species in thought, in language, in complex social institutions, and in capacities for invention. For example, there is only a 2% difference between our protein-coding genes and those in chimpanzees, yet our brains are three times the size of the chimpanzee brain. Might this difference in brain size be the result of mutation in DNA switches which are involved in the timing and control of brain growth and development? As we shall see later in this chapter, recent research on brain development suggests that this indeed may be an important key to an understanding of the differences in brain development among species such as us and the great apes.

In the Galapagos finches, modern researchers find that differences in the developing embryos of different species account for the observed differences after birth in beak size and shape, which make each beak specialized for different food sources available on the different islands. What genes are involved in making the beaks different? A group of genes involved in the shape of the face has been examined by researchers. In all of the species of finch, the same genes were responsible for the beaks; what differed was the timing of the gene action—when they are turned on, for how long, and when they were turned off, resulting in beaks of different shapes and sizes. Switches turn on and off the genes that actually make the beak (the protein-coding genes, "stuff genes") and thus determine shape of the face, including beak size and shape. This might explain the big changes that led to the emergence of new species of finch, differentiated by different size and shape of beak (i.e. different faces), each specialized for getting the different kinds of food found on each island where each species lives today.

Molecular geneticists have found that it is the "body plan genes" which control the DNA switches. This helps solve the problem of how different forms occur—how creatures that started out looking the same, such as the original population of Galapagos finches, end up looking so different as they differentiate into new species.

Microevolution has plenty of evidence, but how did the big changes occur—what accounts for macroevolution? For example, how could a fish develop legs and become a land creature (or how did humans acquire such a large and complex brain)? The switches and body plan genes (and their analogues in brain evolution and development) may indeed be the answer.

Paleontologists have evidence that the first creature with legs appeared about 365 million years ago. Neil Shubin at the University of Chicago found the fossil of a transitional form, a creature between a fish and a legged critter, which has been dated at about 375 million years ago. Shubin called this creature *techtolic*, a flat snouted fish with upward looking eyes and arm-like fins, characteristics of a creature that crawled up on land. Significantly, it had the bone structure of every modern day land animal. Why would it develop this ability to push itself up out of the water? What would be the adaptive advantage? Shubin thinks that it could drag itself to safety from predators confined to the sea.

A living relative of the techtolic is the modern day paddle fish, which is more primitive because it doesn't have the leg-like limbs of the extinct variety. But in spite of this difference, the two species should still have similar genes.

Segments of DNA known as HOX genes, at the top of the DNA command structure, give orders to entire networks of the DNA switches and protein-making genes determining the form of any creature. Research shows that HOX genes had a key role in the fins of the paddlefish. Notably, in all four-limbed animals, fish or otherwise, it is exactly the same set of HOX genes that controls the development of the upper limb bones. Exactly the same genes control our forearm bones, and then another set, the same in all limbed creatures, makes the fingers and toes. This means that the genes needed to make legs and arms were already present in vertebrates, even before Shubin's techtolic fish. Pre-historic fish had these same genes, but they had always made fins; all that was needed was mutation in the timing of the DNA "switches." To many evolutionary biologists, it now appears that the jump from fish to four-limbed creatures occurred because of mutation in HOX genes.

An enormously important general principle that emerges from these observations is that old genes can be refigured to make very new things just by modifications in the HOX genes which then act on the switches, which in turn act on the "stuff genes," the protein-making segments of the DNA. When the leap from fish to four legged creatures is explained in this way, the leap doesn't look as big as it once did. The big changes that make one species become another may be relatively small steps at the level of the DNA.

After limbs are formed in the first four-limbed creatures, these limbs undergo further specialization to perform a variety of functions in a large variety of four-limbed creatures, from fins or wings to feet, hands, and hooves, all because of changes in an ancient set of genes—the "stuff" genes, the "switches," and the HOX genes which give the orders to the "switches." Together, along with mutation and natural selection, mutations in these sets of genes have produced the great variety of life forms on the Earth (PBS, NOVA, "What Darwin Never Knew").

Brain Evolution and DNA

But what about the biggest question of all—What makes humans so different? What makes our minds so distinctively human? Among other things, we think about what others think about us. We punish others for transgressions of abstract laws. We have concepts such as the laws of motion, gravity, justice, political equality. We have music, language, science, agriculture, medicine, mathematics, complex economic and political systems, and more. But things like gill slits in the human embryo show that we are still descended from fish and we are close relatives with the other primates. More than 98% of our DNA is identical to chimp DNA, so where are the differences that make us so distinct from the other primates? Part of the answer may originate in the unique form of the human hand (PBS, NOVA, "What Darwin Never Knew").

The human hand has a structure that makes it capable of two highly adaptive ways of grasping and manipulating objects—the "precision grip" and the "power grip." The former, allowing precise manipulation of objects, important in our ability to make and use tools, depends upon our capacity to touch our fingers to our thumb. One particular piece of DNA found in both humans and chimpanzees shows 13 nucleotide (the "letters" in the DNA code) differences. When molecular geneticists inserted this DNA segment into mouse DNA to see what it coded, they were amazed to find that it caused changes in the mouse thumb and big toe. They had discovered that this section of DNA in both chimps and humans is a DNA "switch," which when turned "on" produces the structure of the hand that makes the precision grip possible. In humans, this DNA switch is turned on. But in chimps, with a 13 nucleotide difference in this same section of DNA, the switch for the development of the precision grip is not turned on. Thus, while humans develop a hand structure for the precision grip, chimpanzees don't. Though chimpanzees in the wild make and use tools (Goodall, 1971), their tool making and tool use are rudimentary compared to that in humans. The precision grip in humans gave us the manipulative dexterity to create and use much more sophisticated tools—but motor dexterity alone isn't enough.

As is sometimes the case, changes in one trait are accompanied thereafter by changes in other traits. This is because evolution of a trait sometimes helps create the conditions for selection, and thus *coevolution,* of other traits. In this case, a hand adept at making tools would have favored evolution of a *brain* better and better at *conceiving* tools and other things that one might create with such dexterous hands. Evolution of the human hand may thus have been one of the primary factors that set the stage for the evolution of increased imaginative intelligence in our species. So, researchers now speculate that the 13 letter difference in the DNA switch, which controls development of the precision grip, was not only the cause of changes in the hand, but also likely responsible for significant changes in the brain, as humans and chimpanzees diverged from their common ancestry. As mentioned earlier, the human brain is three times the size of the chimp brain, perhaps in part because of differences in the hands of humans and apes. But there are other surprises coming out of genetics which may ultimately explain why human brain evolution took such a sharp turn away from that of our closest living relatives, chimpanzees and other apes (PBS, NOVA, "What Darwin Never Knew").

Research in molecular genetics has unexpectedly revealed that human DNA contains a damaged muscle gene (missing a couple of nucleotides) that looks like it should cause some disease in humans, but it doesn't. This same gene is not "damaged" (not missing a couple of critical nucleotides) in chimpanzees. The affected muscle is a jaw muscle for chewing, so humans chew with much less force than chimps do. But this turns out to be an evolutionary opportunity for humans. The "damaged" gene which grows smaller jaw muscles allows development of a larger brain case in the skull of humans because a more powerful jaw, like that found in apes, causes the skull plates in apes to fuse into a solid bony brain case much sooner after birth, at an earlier age, than in humans. This delayed fusion of the skull plates in us permits the human brain to expand much more after birth, after head and brain size are no longer limited by the limited size of the birth canal (Steadman, in "What Darwin Never Knew," NOVA, PBS), compared to the great apes. But simply having the opportunity for a bigger brain doesn't guarantee that one will develop. There must be other things going on in human DNA that trigger the more extensive brain growth that occurs in our species.

What does it take besides extra space to stimulate a brain to enlarge during its development? Clues from disease caused by a genetic defect may help provide an answer. Microcephaly is a severe disorder of development in which human head and brain size remain abnormally small, about half normal size, producing profound mental impairment. Studies of this disorder reveal a section of DNA that controls when brain cells stop multiplying and dividing, thus determining brain growth, and when a developing brain has become "big enough." In humans with microcepahly, this section of DNA is mutant, showing 21 different mutations, possibly leading to the stunted head and brain growth which characterize human microcephaly. Could this segment of DNA help to explain the difference in brain growth between humans and other species? When this DNA segment in normal humans is compared to the same DNA segment in normal chimpanzees, the comparison reveals a large series of mutations making this section of DNA very different in humans compared to chimps (Walsh, in "What Darwin Never Knew," NOVA, PBS). The differences in this segment of DNA between chimpanzees and humans might help explain why the brain continues to grow longer in humans and why it becomes so much bigger than the brain of chimpanzees, helping to explain why our cognitive capacities are so different from those of our closest living relative.

Other research seems to narrow down the critical differences in DNA between us and other species even further. 15 million nucleotide letters differ between chimpanzees and humans. Researchers are trying to discover which of these 15 million nucleotide differences are important in why humans are so different from other species.

One way to do this is to find places in the genome where chimpanzee DNA is about the same in chimp and other animals, but different between chimpanzees and humans. When Katie Pollard of the University of California, San Francisco, examined such differences between human and chimp DNA, she found that most of these differences are not in genes, but in the DNA "switches" that turn on and off nearby "stuff" genes that make proteins. She found that more than half of these are located near genes involved in brain development. One particular piece of DNA stood out, a piece of DNA known to be active in development of the cerebral cortex in the embryo. In chimpanzee and chicken, this DNA is different by only two letters (two nucleotides), but in human and chimpanzee this piece of DNA is different in 18 nucleotide "letters," "a massive mutation" in DNA switches critical in turning on and off the development of the *cerebral cortex*, the surface layers of the brains of mammals responsible for much of the higher level processing important in intelligence. Small differences in DNA "switches" of just a few letters can cause huge differences in characteristics, the big leaps between species—in this case, between the chimpanzee brain and the human brain ("What Darwin Never Knew," NOVA, PBS). Mutations in DNA "switches" causing the protein-making genes involved in production of the cerebral cortex to remain turned on longer in humans than in chimps could produce big changes in brain anatomy giving humans a big advantage in computing power and intelligence compared to the great apes. Recent research suggests just such a story.

More clues are being discovered about how the human brain might have evolved to be so different from that of our closest primate relatives, and how this evolution might have come about as a result of relatively small changes at the level of DNA. To understand what is going on, once again, we must look to the embryo.

Brain development begins with a thin sheet of proto-neural tissue derived from the embryo's ectoderm layer. This tissue folds into a thin tube, known as *the neural tube*, and eventually, via repetitive cell division, develops into a complex brain consisting of at least a hundred billion cells. How does this cell division take place?

The cells which line the inside of the neural tube, known as *the ventricular zone*, are known as *progenitor cells*, and these give rise to the cells of the central nervous system (the brain and the spinal cord). This process involves two types of cell division, *symmetrical division*, in which progenitor cells divide to form other progenitor cells, and *asymmetrical cell division* in which progenitor cells divide producing one new progenitor cell and one new neuron (brain cell). In the first stage of brain development, symmetrical division produces large numbers of progenitor cells. Then, seven weeks after conception, a chemical signal sent to progenitor cells causes them to begin asymmetrical division and the production of neurons. This period of asymmetrical cell division which produces neurons lasts about 3 months in the developing embryo (Carlson, 2011).

The outer layers of the brain of mammals consists of the cerebral cortex, approximately 3 millimeters thick in humans, larger in humans, when adjusted for body size, than in any other species, and responsible for cognition, intelligence, and other "higher" mental functions in the mammals. During embryological development, the cerebral cortex develops from the inside out. Cells first produced by the progenitor cells of the ventricular zone migrate out a short distance to form the first, and deepest, of six cellular layers that characterize the cortex in all mammals. The next layer of cells, newly produced by the progenitor cells of the ventricular zone, then migrates a little further, passing through the earlier and deeper layer, and so on, until all six layers of the cortex have been formed. Each successive layer has had to pass through all the layers below that had been formed earlier. This process of cell development in the cerebral cortex ends when a chemical signal binds with receptors that activate "killer genes" that cause the progenitor cells to die. Once neurons in the cortex have been produced and have migrated to their final destinations (at one point, a billion newly formed neurons each day, are literally crawling, like amoeba, following a chemical trail along fibers of support cells in the brain called *radial glia*), they begin to form connections with other neurons in a process of circuit formation (Carlson, 2011). Circuits of incredible complexity are formed, including thousands of pathways interconnecting various brain regions together, often in highly orderly ways. In fact, the surface of the body ends up being "mapped" onto the surface of the somatosensory cortex, and the surface of the light-sensitive retina of the eye is "mapped," point-for-point, onto the surface of the visual cortex. This high degree of orderliness in circuit organization is found throughout the brain.

As mentioned earlier the human brain is three times the size of the chimpanzee brain. It is ten times larger than the brain of a rhesus macaque monkey. These size differences may come about as a result of a relatively simple process involving the progenitor cells of the ventricular zone and the time during which they are "permitted" to undergo cell division.

The ultimate size of the brain is determined by the size of the ventricular zone of the neural tube during embryological development, which in turn is determined during the period of symmetrical division of the progenitor cells located there. Each symmetrical division doubles the number of progenitor cells and doubles the size of the brain. In human embryos, the stage of symmetrical division lasts about two days longer than it does in the macaque monkey embryo, which provides enough time for three more divisions in the human, enough to account for the difference in brain size between humans and macaques. The period of asymmetrical division also lasts longer in humans, accounting for the fact that the human cortex is 15% thicker than it is in the macaque monkey (Carlson, 2011). Thus, a few small changes in DNA, perhaps in DNA "switches," which delay the termination of symmetrical and asymmetrical divisions of progenitor cells during embryological brain development could be the cause of the increased size of the human brain. Note that this conclusion is consistent with the findings by UC San Francisco's Katie Pollard, discussed above. Thus, a few simple mutations controlling the timing of brain development may explain how small differences in DNA between us and our closest primate relatives may produce the big differences in our brains (Carlson, 2011, p. 63–67).

Insight into some of the details of the processes involved in the control of brain size has been provided by an extraordinary experiment by Chenn and Walsh (2002). The protein, *beta-catenin*, is involved in control of cell division and tissue growth. It also appears to be involved in regulation of symmetrical cell division of progenitor cells in development of the cerebral cortex in mammals. These researchers used genetic engineering methods to increase the production of beta-catenin in mouse fetuses. The result was an enormous increase in the number of progenitor cells which then had the predictable effect of increasing brain size in the mice. Heads of the mice got bigger too, to accommodate the larger brains produced by the increased amounts of beta-catenin. The cerebral cortex grew so much that it developed convolutions (folds) normally found only in the brains of larger, more complex mammals (see convolutions of the human cortex in Figure 2-2). A follow-up study by Woodhead, et. al. (2006) found that interfering with signaling by beta-catenin during brain development resulted in a smaller cerebral cortex. Thus, it is possible that relatively small mutations in human DNA over the course of evolution may have resulted in our characteristically large brains and highly developed cerebral cortex by modifying the production of beta-catenin or other molecules with which this protein interacts (Carlson, 2011, p. 67).

Though these findings help explain our much larger brains and our more developed cerebral cortex, processes similar in principle, may eventually explain key differences, likely to be discovered in the future, between our microscopic circuit design and that of our primate relatives, accounting in more detail, for the key differences between our minds and theirs.

Not only the anatomy and physiology of an organism determine its fit or match to the environment, but, as research like Katie Pollard's and Chenn and Walsh's suggests, so does the information processing by an animal's brain. There can be no doubt that the same processes of evolution by natural selection that produce the anatomy and physiology of an organism also produce the characteristics of the minds and behavior of each animal species, as research, like that discussed above, demonstrates. The "design" of complex "survival machines" in service of the genes inside, certainly includes not only the evolution of bodies, but also of brains, and the minds and behavior that follow. This realization has recently led to what has been called "the second Darwinian revolution," the application of evolutionary thinking to an understanding of minds and behavior (Cosmides and Tooby, 1987). If the first "Darwinian revolution" was the realization of how bodies of species originated, the "second Darwinian" revolution is the application of evolutionary principles to an understanding of psychology—a theme which is the main focus of this book. Research by Pollard, Chenn and Walsh, and others is beginning to reveal the details of evolution at the level of DNA that may account for each species' "mind design." Research findings like these are just beginning to shed light on how minds and behavior may have evolved. In doing so, we are beginning to see the beginnings of a new psychology, one based, as Darwin predicted, "on a new foundation."

Behavior, Minds, Entropy, and Evolution

Now, it is probably self-evident that behavior doesn't fossilize, and neither do minds. So, the study of evolution of life by evolutionary biologists and paleontologists has naturally focused on anatomical changes. But, as noted above, the same processes that shaped the anatomy and physiology of life forms on Earth have shaped the minds and behavior of animals over deep time. Minds and behavior are just as much a part of "survival machines" as are their anatomical and physiological gadgetry. Though we can only speculate about the specifics of mind and behavior over the course of evolution, we can look back for evidence about early behavior to gain insight about our own behavior and our own "mind design" and about the nature and origins of minds and behavior in general. Why do organisms behave at all? Why do minds and behavior take the forms that they do? The prior discussion of evolution should give you plenty of clues.

Behavior has been around for a long time, even the single-celled bacteria and archaea have flagella (long whip-like tails, attached to an organic motor comprised of about 20 proteins, powered by an electrochemical gradient) that move them about. These single-celled creatures respond to various forms of stimuli including chemical, light, and magnetic gradients (although this later occurs even in dead bacteria and so is passive, as opposed to responses to the first two). Responses to chemical stimuli (chemotaxis) help bacteria find food and avoid harm, causing them to swim toward concentrations of energy-rich molecules (glucose, for example) and away from poisons such as phenol. Phototaxis is the movement of photosynthesizing bacteria toward light resulting in more efficient photosynthesis—the conversion of light, carbon dioxide, and water into sugar as fuel to run the photosynthesizing organism's chemical machinery.

Even at this single-celled level of life we see hints of the functions of behavior and of differences between the movement of living things and the movements of inanimate objects such as rocks in a landslide or the planets rotating on their axes or revolving around the sun. To understand why such differences exist, let's do a "thought experiment" using a familiar and more complex form of life.

Imagine that you have a pet dog at home and that you also have a rock, let's say, about the size of a basketball. Now, imagine for purposes of this thought experiment, that for some reason, you lock both the dog and the rock in your empty garage for a couple of months. When you come back and open the garage, what will be the condition of each? Will the rock be in about the same condition as it was when you left it a couple of months earlier? How about the dog? Obviously, the latter will have changed a great deal. It will be a dead dog, and much of its structure will already have started to disintegrate, to unstructure, to disorganize, on both a molecular and visible level.

However, in stark contrast, the rock will be in essentially the same condition as it was when you left it. Rocks do a lot better in empty locked garages than dogs do. Why? In short, the difference has to do with the molecular stability of non-living matter such as rocks, stars, or water compared to the molecular stability of organisms.

Organisms are put together on the molecular level with such a degree of complexity that their molecular organization is relatively tenuous and easily disrupted unless certain conditions are met. Rocks and other everyday inanimate objects, on the other hand, have very stable molecular bonds and simpler, more stable molecular organizations.

Recall from the beginning of this chapter that one of fundamental laws of physics is that the entropy, or disorder, of material systems without an energy input tends to increase over time, approaching maximum disorder at equilibrium. This is known in physics as the Second Law of Thermodynamics. Also recall that one of the characteristic features of life is that living things organize matter into more complex forms, thus counteracting the physical forces of entropy, at least for a while, while alive. In a sense, the molecular organizing forces in living things are in a continuous "struggle" against the tendency for all things in the universe to fall ultimately toward states of maximum disorder, disorganization, maximum entropy, or randomness. This structuring of matter in living systems against entropy is accomplished by chemical reactions within the organism. As mentioned above, these chemical reactions of life are collectively known as metabolism. Also recall that molecules tend to fall into stable patterns, but only in the presence of energy. The chemical reactions of metabolism are *endothermic reactions*, meaning that to run they require an energy input from energy sources outside of themselves. The chemical machinery of life needs to be plugged into an external energy source or it won't run. In the evolution of life, the first "survival machines" had to develop mechanisms for extracting energy from the environment to put it to use in running the uphill battle against the Second Law. In short, this is why all living things must either photosynthesize glucose from sunlight, carbon dioxide, and water, (excepting extremophiles that get energy from minerals such as iron in rocks) or they must eat organisms that do (or eat animals that eat the plant eaters—prey animals which themselves are smaller or "weaker" carnivores). The food chain is a chain of energy suppliers, from sunlight to sugar (glucose) to meat (proteins) converted by digestion back into sugar, running the uphill battle in all multicellular organisms against the disorganizing forces of the inevitable fall towards entropy.

Rocks and other such stable inanimate objects aren't immune to entropy either, they are disorganizing too, but at a much slower rate so that we typically don't notice. Certainly the amount of molecular disorder that occurs in the rock locked in the garage for a couple of months, or even for a couple of thousand years, isn't going to be visible to us. But, the dog, composed of an incredibly complex array of proteins and lipids and other such organic molecules, falls downhill toward entropy with surprising rapidity in the absence of the energy input required to run its anti-entropy metabolic machinery. Once the dog's metabolic pathways run out of the energy supplied by its own muscles as it "starves," the organizing effects of its metabolic chemistry cease, and the fall toward entropy is unchecked. Death is the name we give to the end of the anti-entropic organizing forces of metabolism (aging is the progressive decline in the efficiency of the anti-entropic metabolic processes, as the Second Law progressively chips away even at these ordering processes themselves). The dog now passively disorganizes, deteriorates, aided by microorganisms which use what remains of it as their entry into the food chain.

One of the things that distinguishes the rock from the dog is that the rock doesn't do anything to combat the Second Law and the fall toward maximum entropy, yet it can remain structurally stable for extended periods of time without any additional energy, once the heat and pressure that formed it, millions of years ago, are gone. But the dog, like other living matter, is so structurally improbable, such a high order above and counter to entropy, that to overcome the Second Law of Thermodynamics, a continuous supply of energy is required. This energy supply in the form of food for the dog is needed to sustain the continuous push toward molecular organization against entropy. Thus plants photosynthesize and animals eat—both evolved mechanisms that provide the energy to run the chemical reactions of life sustaining the "survival machines" that carry, nurture, and replicate the genes within them.

These chemical and thermodynamic facts are the ultimate source of a whole complex category of behaviors in animals including not just the act of eating, that is, the movements to get energy sources, vegetable or animal, into the mouth and then grind and tear them into pieces that can be swallowed, but all the food-getting behaviors of animals that allow them to get something close enough to consume. In carnivorous animals, these behaviors range from single-celled non-photosynthesizing organisms "consuming" other microbes to the stalking and hunting behaviors in multicellular insectivores and carnivores, which in many species involves social behavior in the form of coordinated, cooperative movements of a group of conspecifics, such as a pack of wolves or wild dogs, or a pride of lions. In herbivores, food-getting behaviors typically include gathering grasses, fruits, roots, and nuts and other concentrated packets of nutrients found in plant materials, but in some species involves filtering small nutrient particles from water, a strategy that filter-feeders such as sponges, krill, whale sharks, and baleen whales engage in, a way of feeding which doesn't require much in the way of goal-directed movement (especially in the sponges).

An enormous proportion of available time and much of the complexity of human behavior is devoted to getting food, ranging from hunting and gathering to the domestication of animals and the invention of agriculture, and eventually complex systems of transport and exchange of nutrient sources (among other things) as part of what we humans call our economy. From "termite-fishing" in chimpanzees using specially prepared sticks, to otters cracking shells on stones cradled on their bellies, to humans inventing and using irrigation, fertilizers, pesticides, harvesters, hunting rifles, growth hormones for cattle, food stamps, UNICEF, and supermarkets, much of the tool use in us and in other species was invented and is used to get food into bodies of "survival machines" to energize their metabolism. An enormous proportion of the activities of animals is derived from and devoted to solution of this energy problem, the problem of how to get external sources of energy into the organism to run the chemical reactions that slow the fall toward entropy.

Much of brain "design" is likewise devoted to organization of energy-getting behavior. The taste buds and taste cortex, brain and sensory systems for smell, as well as color-sensitive receptors in our eyes and the brain mechanisms for color vision, help us to find and select food sources rich in energy and nutrients. Specifically "designed" brain circuitry such as that in the hypothalamus makes us feel hungry and then full and controls our specific appetites for foods rich in specific nutrients that will run metabolism. Similar brain circuits regulate our body fat, an energy source for "lean times." Squirrels burying nuts in preparation for scare food supplies in the winter must have brain circuitry specifically evolved for exceptional spatial memory so that the nuts buried months earlier can be found when needed. Humans have put their large cerebral cortex to similar uses inventing refrigeration, canning, grain silos, and even astronomy to better control the distribution of food sources over time to deal with times of scarcity.

But capturing sufficient amounts of energy and putting it to use is only one of the problems that organisms have to solve. The chemical reactions of metabolism typically require that the molecules interacting in the metabolic pathways of the body be dissolved in water. If not suspended in sufficient amounts of water, the anti-entropic chemical reactions of metabolism can't take place. We may "die of thirst." Entropy quickly follows to dissolve the structure of the organism. So brain evolution has equipped animals and humans with circuits "designed" for water regulation—producing behaviors as diverse as the search for water, and drinking, in all animals, to the invention, engineering and construction of plumbing, aqueducts, and dams, to the organization of water companies and research efforts to desalinate sea water in humans.

Furthermore, the molecular ordering, achieved by metabolic chemical reactions in living systems, not only requires energy and water inputs, but in addition, the chemical reactions of metabolism, for most multicellular organisms, can only occur within a fairly narrow temperature range. So, in addition to an *energy problem* and a *water problem*, organisms must somehow solve the *temperature problem*; they must somehow avoid, or, in other fashion, deal with extremes of temperature (once again, however, extremophiles, organisms that thrive in extreme conditions such as undersea volcanic vents, are an exception). Temperature regulation is one solution for animals, or going dormant in the winter is a solution for some plant species. The temperature regulation can be physiological such as in homeotherms, animals that maintain a constant internal temperature, as well as behavioral, as when a lizard moves from the shade onto a rock in full sun to heat itself, in service of the temperature requirements of its metabolic chemistry. Penguins huddle in groups against the arctic cold, sea lions sun themselves on warm sand, a dog moves into the shade on a hot day, and humans invented clothing,

blankets, camp fires, construction of shelters such as houses, heating and air conditioning systems, as well as all the other technologies to produce these things more efficiently—obsidian knives for skinning animals for their fur, bone and then steel needles,
the cotton gin, spinning wheels, the garment industry, hammers and nails, saws and
lumbering, drilling and storing natural gas or heating oil and then pipes to distribute it
to run gas or oil heaters, gas and heating oil companies, with stock holders and boards
of directors, and tens of thousands of employees, and eventually public utilities—
all derived from the *temperature problem* which arises from the specific chemistry of
metabolism, common to all species.

Then, additionally, organisms use molecules that exist as gases in the atmosphere,
oxygen in the case of animals and carbon dioxide (CO_2) in the case of plants, in their
metabolic reactions, so there arises, then, the problem of gas exchange between ambi-
ent air and organism and the evolution of mechanisms in the organism such as lungs
or gills and brain mechanisms to regulate the rate and volume of breaths to solve the
biological problem of gas exchange under varying environmental conditions and activity levels of the organism. Part of these brain systems involve brain circuits in the hypothalamus which control the sympathetic nerves to produce an anticipatory increase in
breathing rate and volume (and heart rate) when threat or danger are perceived.

In the molecular evolution described by Dawkins (2006), there must have been basic
chemical reasons for why life developed out of the molecular organization of carbon-
based proteins and lipids rather than out of the molecular organization of iron-based,
hydrogen-based, or silicon-based compounds, or other sorts of molecules. Carbon can
give up or take 4 electrons in chemical bonding, but so can silicon, so other factors
may have caused failure of other early "experiments" of nature with non-carbon-based
"life" forms. For example, a metabolism involving oxygen in a silicon-based life form
would entail the problem of how to get rid of silicon dioxide (counterpart to CO_2),
a solid waste product of cellular respiration; expelling sand would be much more difficult for an organism than expelling carbon dioxide. Chemical bonds of silicon are not
as strong as they are in carbon. Silicon-based molecules don't achieve the variety and
structural complexity that carbon-based molecules do. Furthermore, perhaps water
would not work as a solvent in silicon-based systems, and on planet Earth there may be
no other alternative readily available (http://www.physicsforums.com/archive/index.
php/t-156166.html; retrieved 11/13/09).

The stability of rocks is based on atomic structure quite different from the less
enduring stability of carbon-based molecules that form the building blocks of living
matter. Rocks and minerals don't require continuous inputs of energy or other things
to counter the forces of the Second Law, but compounds with molecular complexity
sufficient for anything approximating the characteristics of living organisms could
achieve sufficient stability, particularly in complex forms of life, only with continuous

inputs of energy and sufficient supplies of water. As a consequence, derived from the earliest molecular evolution of carbon compounds, life was destined to reach forms of incredible molecular, and then cellular complexity, but only under the strictest of conditions (extremophiles set the upper limits of the range of conditions required). As a consequence, living things like the dog locked in the garage have problems that must be solved (an energy problem, a water problem, a temperature problem, a gas-exchange problem, and so on) to permit, at least temporarily, the organism to overcome the disorganizing forces pulling at them, toward entropy. But inanimate objects like rocks don't, for the simple reason that the inanimate objects in our world are for the most part much more structurally stable by virtue of their chemistry, thus they never "needed" to develop anti-entropy mechanisms such as those that characterize life.

Now with these thoughts in mind, we can ask the fundamental question that drove much of Darwin's thinking. Why do organisms possess the characteristics which they have? More specifically, why do birds have wings and feathers? Why do whales have blubber? Why do plants have chlorophyll, photosynthesize, and grow toward the sun? Why do sharks have teeth? Why do lions hunt? Why do turtles have shells? Why do rose bushes have thorns? Why do jellyfish have poisonous tentacles? Why do bacteria and archaea have flagella, and why do they swim toward concentrations of glucose and away from concentrations of phenol? Why do coconuts have tough shells? Why do phytoplanktons swim toward light? Why do animals and humans feel sexual attraction and fall in love? Why do Club-winged Manakins, a bird species in the forests of the Andes, vibrate their feathered wings a hundred times a second, twice the rate of hummingbirds' wings? Why do flowers have bright colors? Why do crickets chirp? Why do animals learn and why do different species learn different things? Why do African wild dogs live in packs? Why do we have emotions, language, logical thought, and culture? Why do bees make hives? Why do dogs pant? Why do children talk so much? Why is it hard for them to sit still? Why do humans care about what others think about them? Why do we love our children? Questions about why species have the anatomical, physiological, behavioral, and mental traits they possess are almost limitless, yet there is one overriding reason that can explain them all.

The three categories of biological adaptation: solutions to biological problems

After the discussion in this chapter, it should be pretty clear that the particular traits which characterize any organism exist precisely because those specific features solve biological problems for the organism, and so promote its survival and reproduction, and thus the reproduction of the genes the organism carries inside. Biological problems such as the *energy problem*, the *water problem*, and the *temperature problem*, as noted above, are universal to all forms of life (even the extremophiles need energy and have limits to what they can withstand), and now we can add another, the *reproductive problem*—the problem of how to reproduce one's own kind, or, more accurately, at the molecular level, how to replicate one's genes. Using Dawkins' reasoning, we can see that this problem, like all biological problems for organisms, is really one for the genes. Through natural selection, "survival machines" have evolved splendid and varied solutions to the array of problems the "replicators," the genes, encountered in their journey over time to survive, and to thrive, from ancient beginnings to the present day.

There are countless other biological problems more or less general to all or most species (for example, how to deal with germs, how to expel waste products of metabolism, how to deal with predators, how to deal with gravity—i.e. with bony skeletons or by being suspended in water), and many others which are more idiosyncratic, at least in detail, to particular species or particular groups of species. But in all cases, biological problems arise in the environment, some features of which are general to all niches and others which are more specific to the particular environmental niches of particular species. These biological problems require solution by the evolving "survival machines" which encounter them. These *solutions* to biological problems are known as *adaptations*.

The astounding variety of life forms on earth display the wonderfully creative ways in which biological problems have been solved by natural selection. In fact, organisms can be thought of as specific collections of adaptations built by natural selection to solve their biological problems. Take any species. Think of its traits. Make a list of its characteristics and I am certain that your list will include not a single trait that is not, in one way or another, contributing to the solution of some biological problem, directly or indirectly, or a derivative of such adaptations. Organisms, whether plant, animal, bacteria, archaea, or virus, just don't have features which aren't explicable as solutions to problems of survival and reproduction or derivatives of these. Even human aesthetic and religious values may have adaptive usefulness and thus have roots deep in our evolutionary history.

Notice that when we examine the particular traits of species, we find that these solutions or adaptations to various biological problems, loosely fall into three general categories—*anatomical adaptations* or solutions, *physiological adaptations* or solutions, and *behavioral (psychological) adaptations* or solutions.

Anatomical adaptations are *structural features* that solve one, or more, biological problem for the organism. For example, thorns on rosebushes solve the problem for rosebush genes of how to protect their relatively stationary, photosynthesizing "survival machines" from being eaten by herbivorous "predators." Whale blubber helps whales solve the temperature problem, how to maintain temperatures within whale cells which facilitate efficient metabolism against entropy as whale-gene "survival machines" ply arctic waters. Sharks have teeth to catch and tear sources of concentrated protein-bound energy which, when digested, provide sustenance in the form of glucose molecules that power metabolism of the cells of shark-gene "survival machines." Turtle-gene "survival machines" have shells to protect against predators, and in Hawaiian Green Sea Turtles the shells protect the soft tissues from damage as the turtle is buffeted about by wave action against sharp algae covered lava rock on the shorelines where they feed. Flowers have bright colors because the coloration attracts insects which pollinate the parts of the plants necessary for these "survival machines" to replicate themselves and thus the genes they carry. The tough shell of a coconut, the shell of an Ostrich egg, or a human amniotic sac inside a womb are all structural features, anatomical adaptations, that protect reproductive cells and their supportive materials for the benefit of the genes to be replicated, whether by seeds falling from their genetic source in trees or by courtship and copulation.

Physiological adaptations are internal dynamic processes within an organism which solve one or more survival or reproductive problems. For example, jellyfish have poisonous tentacles because chemical production and delivery of neurotoxins to prey, paralyzing them, facilitates solution to the jellyfish energy problem, helping to preserve jellyfish genes. Plants photosynthesize as a means to solve their energy problem, permitting them to power their uphill chemical battle against entropy, preserving and replicating their genes. Dogs pant because the movement of large volumes of air over a wet surface, the tongue, increases evaporation of the fluids there, speeding removal of heat from the dog's body. This "heat of evaporation" works the same way that water evaporating from a hot patio cools the concrete. In this way, the dog solves one side of its temperature problem. Vertebrates have immune systems, another physiological adaptation or set of adaptations, to solve the biological problem of how to deal with germs—microbes whose own physiological adaptations require that they co-opt the cellular machinery of their "prey," causing illness in their victims as an unintentional by-product. We get a fever, a few notches up in our brain's regulation of body temperature, because higher body temperatures kill and inhibit the rates of reproduction of infectious bacteria. A plant species (Amorphophallus titanium) in Sumatra, Indonesia, so large that it produces flowers 5 feet tall, would make an outstanding food source for Asian elephants were it not for the fact that this plant species evolved chemical reactions within it that cause a bad smell so potent that it keeps even the hungriest herbivores at bay. The plant has evolved a protective shield of stink around it, since it is planted, and can't run away from predators, a physiological adaptation to the problem of hungry herbivorous predators. All these traits of organisms are examples of physiological solutions to various biological problems, solutions ultimately devised by genes, via natural selection, to protect and replicate themselves, by preserving the "survival machines" that carry them, nourish them, and reproduce them.

But behavioral adaptations are our greatest focus of interest in this book. *Behavior and minds are forms of adaptation, just like anatomy and physiology.*

Behavioral adaptations occur in an enormous variety of species in a stunning variety of forms, but are somewhat restricted in their distribution, because they didn't develop to any great extent in photosynthesizing organisms, the multicellular plants. Behavioral adaptation is found almost exclusively in the non-photosynthesizing organisms that we call animals. This makes good evolutionary sense. Because plants evolved photosynthesis, a physiological solution to the energy problem, in which their energy sources—sunlight, water, and carbon dioxide—*come to them,* plants could remain *planted,* and never had to develop sophisticated capacities for movement, nor the mechanisms for its control (brains and nerves). Because they rely almost exclusively on anatomical and physiological adaptation to solve their problems of survival and reproduction, with essentially no behavioral adaptation at all, they had no occasion to develop nervous systems. Brains and nervous systems are only necessary to creatures that rely extensively upon movement, behavioral adaptation, to solve their biological problems.

Because animals can't photosynthesize, they were forced to find energy to run their metabolism from other sources besides ubiquitous sunlight, carbon dioxide, and rainwater. Instead, animals had to rely upon energy sources found in compact energy-rich packets, plants and other animals, which are unevenly and often unpredictably distributed in the environment. Because their energy sources don't come to them, and in fact, may actively avoid them in the case of prey animals, most animals had to evolve ways to detect and move toward sometimes elusive sources of energy (plants and, especially elusive, other animals), and to capture and consume them. Sensory systems, muscles, and systems of muscular control, led to evolution of brains of ever increasing sophistication in both predator and prey, each locked in an evolutionary "arms race" of competition for survival and a chance to reproduce their genes. Predators, facing constant natural selection, evolved anatomy and physiology, as well as brain "designs," and the resulting psychological makeup, that made them better hunters. Prey animals, in turn, evolved better defenses, causing selection among the hunters for even better neural systems for more effective hunting behavior. Behavioral adaptations become more and more sophisticated as a result of natural selection for brains better matched to hunting prey animals, themselves evolving to become faster and smarter at predator evasion. The resulting escalation of behavioral solutions to the energy problem helped produce sophisticated, even "intelligent," brain "designs" for the stiff competition in these challenging hunting environments. Perhaps this is why carnivores tend to be smarter than herbivores, all other factors being equal. It takes more intelligence to catch an animal running or hiding or fighting for its life than it does to catch a clump of grass or a piece of fruit, neither of which runs at all. It should come as no surprise, then, that carnivorous ways were likely a part of the lives of human ancestral species and of pre-historic humans from our earliest days on earth. Meat is a very concentrated source of calories and other nutrients, and meat-eating may have made possible the development of bigger brained species, since large brains use a lot of energy (the human brain consumes 20% of the available metabolic energy, although it is only 2% of human body weight).

These same forces of predator-prey competition may even be a primary impetus for social living in many species. For example, lions live and hunt in groups called prides, a behavioral adaptation to the energy problem in this particular species of "survival machine." Field research by the animal behaviorist, George Schaller, showed that lions that hunt in groups, on average, have twice the hunting success as lions that hunt alone (mostly strong young males before they acquire a pride). Thus natural selection would have favored brain "designs" in lions which included circuitry in the emotional parts of the lion brain that produced affectionate ties, mutual social attraction, or at least mutual tolerance, disposition for cooperation as well as competition, especially in hunting situations, and other emotions that made living in groups and well coordinated hunting forays possible. Female lions (which, by the way do most of the hunting in a pride) even cooperatively nurse, making their milk available to the cubs of other females in the pride (their sisters, mothers, aunts, and female cousins) as well as to their own offspring. In the evolution of lion social behavior, we may find a good model of the evolution of human social behavior and evolution of a brain "designed" for life in social groups.

Directed movement to solve the energy problem is widely distributed in the animal kingdom—whether it is Hawaiian green sea turtles grazing on algae on volcanic rock coastlines, packs of killer whales hunting seals, pelicans diving for fish, or humans going to the supermarket (or to work) or walking to the refrigerator. Even microbes swim toward glucose dissolved in water for the same reason that lions, wolves, or sharks move toward and catch prey.

A wide range of movements occur in animals to solve other adaptive problems presented by the environment. Microbes not only swim toward glucose, they swim away from phenol to defend against poisoning—not only of themselves, but, ultimately, of their genes. Club-winged Manakin males, as well as crickets, vibrate their wings to make music to attract females, increasing the chances of reproduction by the genes they carry within them—the same reason that human's have sexual attraction and sex drive, which function to move individual humans distributed widely in physical space toward potential mates, and thereby closer to the eggs or sperm that carry DNA "waiting" to be replicated by the sexual behavior of the organisms that carry it. Phytoplankton, the foundation organism in the oceans' food chain, swim toward light to speed up their photosynthesis, helping them, without their knowledge or intention, to solve their energy problem more efficiently.

Animals show behavioral adaptations not only in their overt actions, but also in the organization of their information processing neural circuitry, creating *psychological adaptations* (features of the mind) such as emotions, logical thought, sex drive and romantic love, memory, mental images, sophisticated abilities for learning, language and the neurological foundations for culture. For example, humans not only have brain circuits that produce feelings of sexual and romantic attraction to draw reproductive partners into close physical proximity, but they also possess brain circuits which compute the *relative mate value* of various potential partners, leading to sexual selectiveness—that is, pickiness about who one will mate with, a choice that is dictated by *feelings* of lust and love, romantic attraction and passion, for the "desirable" partners, for the "good" choices (good for one's genes, that is) versus feelings of indifference, disinterest, or even disgust and revulsion for the "bad" choices (bad for one's genes), the "undesirable" partners. These guiding *feelings* are *psychological adaptations* built into our brain circuit "design" by eons of natural selection sifting through alternative brain "designs" over our evolutionary history to arrive at the computational configuration of circuitry that ultimately led to the highest rates of reproduction of genes. *Feelings are just the end product of computations by brain circuits "designed" to help guide the organism toward successful solution of one biological problem or another. Emotions are a form of psychological adaptation*, really an information processing adaptation, a form of behavioral adaptation in the scheme presented here. More about this will be presented in a later chapter.

All these traits, anatomical, physiological, and behavioral/psychological, are adaptations, solutions to biological problems faced daily by the "survival machines" we call organisms, and all originate from the same source, evolution by natural selection. Genes become better and better "replicators" of themselves by developing survival gadgets of enormous ingenuity, or they face extinction. And yet, there is no choice, no intention, and no awareness of the mechanisms involved at all, by genes or by the organisms that carry them. The genes act blindly, mere copying machines which make occasional errors in the hereditary information they encode, leading to variations in the adaptations that preserve and reproduce them. Then natural selection does the rest. To repeat the Darwinian logic, those genes that produce variations, in the anatomy, physiology, or minds and behavior of their "survival machines," which give them an edge over the competition, will survive and reproduce in greater numbers. Thus, new traits better matched to solve problems in the environment will spread throughout the species. Over time, genes which encode less successful alternative forms will disappear. This is evolution in action. And, as we have seen, it is not just well "designed" anatomy and physiology (bodies) that have emerged out of these creative processes, but so too have well adapted minds and behaviors.

In summary, the traits of organisms arise, by natural selection, as solutions to biological problems—some general, but others specific to specific environmental niches. These solutions to various problems of survival and reproduction fall into three general categories of biological adaptation: anatomical adaptations, physiological adaptations, and behavioral/psychological adaptations. Note that these categories overlap and are mutually interdependent (you can't have physiology without anatomy of some sort—digestion can't occur without a stomach—and you can't have mind and behavior without brain anatomy and neuron physiology), but these distinctions among types of adaptation are still useful, important, and often revealing.

One trend that seems to be apparent in the evolution of life on earth is an increasing dependence in more recent life forms on behavioral/psychological adaptations for solution to biological problems, rather than a more exclusive dependence upon anatomy and physiology alone. The most obvious case is evident in comparisons between plant and animal forms. Plants, by virtue of their capacity to photosynthesize chemical energy from sources that *come to them*, never had opportunity to evolve much capacity for movement (except slow tropisms such as growing toward sunlight or sources of water; similar to humans going to a drinking fountain or to the refrigerator, but much slower). As a consequence, plants have come to rely almost exclusively on anatomical and physiological adaptations. When plants are under "attack" from an herbivorous "predator" such as a horse or a wildebeest they don't run away screaming, or duck, or hide, or fight. Instead they evolved spikes or thorns or they exude chemicals with a bad smell, or ones that are toxic, to discourage herbivores from eating them—or sometimes, they just passively get eaten, and then rely upon anatomy and physiology to re-grow the lost parts, as long as the "injuries" to their bodies aren't too severe. Even in animals, there has come about increasing reliance upon behavioral adaptation in species more recently evolved. For example, think about how the wooly mammoth solved the problem of cold, or how a whale or seal or wolf deal with cold, compared to how a human does. All use anatomical adaptations, fur or a layer of fat, to insulate against cold, supplemented, in some species, by shivering, a physiological adaptation to cold. Contrast the adaptations to cold in these species with human adaptation to cold. Humans use shivering and a layer of insulating fat as well, but we rely much more upon making and wearing clothes, building a fire, inventing and using heating systems in our homes, all behavioral adaptations (to understand how much better our behavioral adaptations to cold are compared to our anatomical and physiological ones, just imagine a naked skier speeding down a snow-covered mountain. He's shivering all the way down, but how much better clothes or a warm fire would be at solving the problem of cold).

The reader may have noticed that making clothing, building a fire, and inventing heating systems are all learned behaviors, not exclusively genetically organized adaptations like a layer of blubber or fur. Though the processes of evolution are blind, the adaptations of organisms are far from random. Organisms, as discussed above, are collections of adaptations and these are not random, but highly organized, highly structured. Structuring things, whether buildings, machines, bodies, or behaviors, requires information—a lot of information (in Clyde Shannon's information theory, information is defined as constraints on randomness or uncertainty, which reduce it. The extent to which an event reduces uncertainty is a measure of the information the event holds). Where does all the information come from that produces the orderly structuring of organisms and their activities?

Anatomical and physiological adaptations are organized by information in DNA, but since phenotype is always the result of an interaction of genotype and environment, the environment in which the organism develops also plays a role in the final outcome.

Slow and fast information acquisition mechanisms for organisms

However, things are a bit different with regard to behavior. Behavioral adaptations can be organized by two major sources of information: 1) *information in the DNA (genetic),* just like anatomical and physiological adaptations, accumulated over the evolutionary history of the species by natural selection, and 2) by *information acquired from experience during the lifetime of the individual animal* (the definition of "*learned*" used in this book). Clearly, anatomical and physiological adaptations cannot be changed by learning. You can't learn to be taller, have a different eye color, change your digestion, or change your blood type. But behavioral adaptations *can* be modified by learning, by acquisition of information during the individual lifetime, at least in many animal species.

Behavioral adaptations in simpler animals with simpler brains are mostly, and in some species exclusively, genetically organized (genetic behavioral adaptation; reflexes, fixed action patterns, and some instincts are examples). For example, frogs stick out their tongues and catch any small, dark moving object which happens to pass through their field of view, usually a tasty bug of some kind. The behavior is not modifiable by experience. Experimenters threw metal BB's across the visual fields of frogs and the frogs predictably grabbed and swallowed them—again and again and again. Even frogs that became laden down with pounds of BB's didn't learn to modify their behavior at all. This frog behavior was organized by information in the genes that organized circuitry in the frog's brain in such a way that experience could play no role whatsoever in modifying the action.

By contrast, behavioral adaptations in many animal species are organized by both genetics and learning from experience (information acquired during the individual lifetime) in interaction together. In this regard, there seems to be another general trend in evolution—the more recently evolved species appear to depend to greater and greater degrees not only upon behavioral adaptation, but increasingly upon what I am inclined to call *learned behavioral adaptations.* However, for some, this terminology will be problematic because among biologists the term adaptation is generally reserved for traits which are genetically evolved, with little or no contribution of information acquired during the lifetime (i.e. learning). So, in an attempt to remain consistent with existing scientific terminology, we might call learned behaviors with adaptive consequences, organized by evolved learning mechanisms, *learned adaptive modifications of behavior*, or slightly less cumbersome, *learned adaptive behaviors*. Simply using the term "learned behavior" misses the adaptive nature of most learning, one of its most important and revealing features. But for sake of brevity, I will often use this simpler designation. Learning to build a fire or a house is *learned adaptive behavior*, so is making and wearing clothing, inventing and using modern agricultural practices, the domestication of animals, all those behaviors collectively known as modern medicine, and advances in human technology that help humans more efficiently solve problems of survival and reproduction, such as the energy problem (agricultural innovations like fertilizers and mechanical harvesters), the water problem (construction of reservoirs, aqueducts, water pipes, and water companies), the reproductive problem (finding dates on the internet) and so on. This sort of behavior is not only significantly dependent upon information acquired during the individual lifetime of an animal or a human, but it is generally adaptive because the learning itself is lawful and the learning mechanisms, upon which various forms of learning depend, are themselves the consequence of brain circuitry evolved by natural selection, ultimately serving the replication of genes.

At this point, it is extremely important to recognize that learned behaviors, the result of information acquired from the environment during the lifetime of the individual, are always still dependent upon genetic information in the DNA of the species. Even behaviors that are clearly learned, such as learning to do calculus or to build a light bulb, are still also dependent upon genetics, upon information in the DNA of the species that grows a brain that permits such learning in the first place. You can get your dog the very best calculus tutor that money will buy, even the inventor of calculus, Isaac Newton himself if he were still available, but your dog is never going to learn calculus. It just doesn't have the information in its dog DNA to make a brain with the requisite learning capabilities.

Thus, anatomical and physiological adaptations are genetically determined, structured by information in DNA, whereas behavioral adaptations, though also always dependent upon genetic information in the DNA, also can be organized, in part, by information from experience. Behavioral adaptations, are then, in a sense, of two types, those organized exclusively by genetic information, such as reflexes and fixed action patterns, and those organized by a mixture of genetic information and information acquired by experience, learned adaptive behaviors (learned behavioral "adaptations").

Because the information in DNA is so important to the formation of successful adaptations, we must ask how the "right" information (adaptive information) gets into the DNA. The answer of course, as we have seen in this chapter, is genetic evolution by natural selection. The "wrong" (maladaptive) information gets "weeded out" over generations because individuals (and the genes they carry) who possess maladaptive information die in higher numbers and do not leave offspring (or leave fewer offspring). Thus, over generations, the "right" information (adaptive information) gets preserved and species become better fit to their environments.

There are some interesting similarities between learning and genetic evolution. In fact, both are information acquisition mechanisms for animals. Just like learning, genetic evolution is an information acquisition mechanism, gathering and refining, generation after generation, the information stored in the molecular code of the DNA of each species. Though, both genetic evolution and learning are information acquisition mechanisms for animals, genetic evolution operates on the information stored in the species DNA, over long periods of time, over many, many generations. Genetic evolution can be thought of as *the slow information acquisition mechanism* for organisms. By contrast, learning is acquisition of information during the lifetime of the individual animal. It can occur in a matter of moments, rather than over generations, and thus it can be called *the fast information acquisition mechanism* for animals. This terminology reveals the adaptive function of learning—it permits successful adaptation to rapidly changing conditions in the environment, whereas genetic evolution can only organize adaptations to highly stable, long lasting conditions of the world. Learning permits the behavioral flexibility required for adaptation to rapidly fluctuating, local, and idiosyncratic conditions of the world that cannot be provided by anatomical, physiological, and behavioral adaptation organized by genetic evolution alone. More about these ideas will be discussed later in this book in the chapter on learning.

Psychology's First Fundamental Law

I define *psychology* as *the scientific study of the behavioral adaptations of organisms, behaviors derived from behavioral adaptations, pathological behaviors, and the information processing (mental) events that underlie behavior.* Historically, biology has typically tended to focus more upon study of anatomical and physiological adaptations (although ethologists, biologists who study animal behavior, have made important contributions to understanding behavior about which, unfortunately, many psychologists remain largely unaware). Psychology also studies by-products or derivatives of adaptation, and it also studies behavioral pathology, behaviors which are maladaptive—those which create problems of survival and reproduction rather than solving them (how many dates is someone going to get who is hallucinating bugs crawling under their skin, or who is experiencing paranoid delusions that everyone is trying to kill them, or who frequently starts crying uncontrollably for no apparent reason?—the chances of reproduction are severely reduced for persons with psycho- or behavioral pathology). Does the science of psychology have universal laws that apply to all species and all behaviors under a wide range of environmental conditions?

One of the questions posed earlier in this chapter was how movements of living organisms are different from the movements of non-living objects such as rocks rolling down a hill or planets moving in their orbits around the sun. To help answer this question and to seek psychology's first universal law, let's use another "thought experiment."

Imagine that you are in a pool hall playing a game of pool. Also imagine that somehow a dog has wandered inside. Now imagine that you strike the white cue ball with the cue stick sending the white cue ball on a trajectory toward another ball on the table. If you know the values of a few factors such as the masses of the two balls, the precise angle at which the cue ball strikes the second ball, the exact force with which it does so, and a friction factor for the friction between ball and the felt surface of the table, could you predict the movements of the ball struck by the cue ball? If you know any physics, you will know that not only can you predict the movement of the colored ball struck by the cue ball, but you can do so with exact mathematical precision. Simply plug in the numbers into the appropriate equation, do a few calculations, and the movements of the ball can be predicted perfectly. The laws of physics alone are sufficient to predict the movement of the inanimate object.

Now, imagine that the dog has come near your pool table and that, for some reason, you now poke the dog with exactly the same magnitude of force as you had used when you struck the cue ball. If you know the exact angle of the blow, as well as the magnitude of the force applied, the mass of the dog, and all relevant friction factors (like paws on pool hall floor), can you predict the movements of the dog? Well, no, you can't, at least not with anything like the precision you have when you predict the movements of pool balls. Instead of precise physical causal determinism like you have in the case of pool balls and other inanimate objects, the dog's response is much more variable; in short, there is a much larger set of possible outcomes, even though all the same values of force and friction are known just as well as they were when you predicted movements of the billiard balls. The dog might run out the door or to the other side of the room, it might bite the wooden pool cue, or it might attack and bite you, it might bark, yelp, whimper, or it could run under the table with its tail between its legs, it might roll over belly up, it may crouch in submission, or it might even show other possibilities that we can't easily imagine. The dog's behavior is much more variable, shows a much larger set of potential alternatives, than the behavior of inanimate objects like billiard balls. The laws of physics, which were so successful at predicting and explaining the movements of pool balls and other inanimate objects, are quite insufficient to explain and predict the movements of the dog (unless it were a dead dog). Additional laws are needed *on top of* the laws of physics to account for the behavior of the living organism. Laws of physics alone are insufficient. We need additional laws. We need laws governing living things. We need laws of biology.

There is a good reason for this. The reason the dog's behavior is so much more variable and difficult to predict is because the dog is not responding simply or primarily to the physical force applied to it (if it were, then the laws of physics would be sufficient as would also be the case if the dog were dead), but instead the dog is responding primarily, and most importantly, to *information*, biologically significant information contained in the event, in this case, a poke with a cue stick. And of course, to respond to information, the dog, or other organism must have some kind of mechanism to extract biologically significant information from the event and to organize a biologically appropriate movement in response. For the dog, the information processing mechanism, equipped to extract biologically significant information from events and to organize appropriate responses, is its brain. But, single-celled prokaryotes must also have information processing mechanisms guiding them toward glucose and away from phenol even though they don't have brains or even a nervous system. Still, in both cases, the event is evaluated on a fundamental dimension, "Is this good for me and my genes, or is this bad for me and my genes?" If good, then approach, close the distance between me and it; but if bad, avoid, create distance between me and it, or attack it to keep it away from me in the future, to discourage it from coming close to me again. In both cases, adaptation, the survival and chances of reproduction of genes, is served. But, none of this is conscious in the dog or in other animals experiencing such information processing by their brains—all that might be conscious would be emotion of one kind or another, the end result of such processing of biologically significant information.

Take another case. Even at the very basic levels of life we get a clue. Just look at the phytoplankton and the prokaryotes, bacteria, and archaea. Phytoplankton swim toward light, and the single-celled prokaryotes swim toward glucose and away from harmful phenol. Clearly, one of the differences between movement in living things compared to movement in non-living things is that movement in organisms is "goal-directed," it occurs to solve adaptive problems, in order to achieve states favorable to the survival and reproduction of the organism, although these reasons are completely unknown to the organism itself. Certainly single-celled organisms have no idea why they are behaving as they are. Neither do lions or elephants, rats or chimpanzees, birds or sharks, jellyfish or orangutans—or humans, for the most part. They just do what their respective genes have organized their brain circuits to make them do—organic robots guided by the "will," the information, encoded in the DNA of their species.

If we imagine many, many cases involving similar situations with a large variety of organisms, order begins to emerge, a lawfulness is recognizable.

What emerges is psychology's first and most fundamental universal law, what I call the *Law of Adaptation* (Koenigshofer, 1994b). This law (something like a general law in physics such as the law of gravitation) can be stated as follows: *organisms tend to behave in ways that promote the survival and reproduction of their genes* (Koenigshofer, 1994b). This law applies to the behavior of all organisms from single-celled prokaryotes and invertebrates like jellyfish, insects, arachnids, and sea anemones to the vertebrates including the bony fish, amphibians, reptiles, birds, and the mammals including jaguars, wild dogs, lions, tree shrews, monkeys, elephants, chimpanzees, rats, bearcats, snow leopards, whales, zebras, grizzly bears, panthers, marmosets, dolphins, buffalo, gorillas, human beings—in short to all animals. This law is truly universal.

Behavior, though variable by virtue of the fact that it is controlled primarily by biologically significant *information*, not primarily by force, mass, or other physical variables, is nevertheless lawful and predictable within a fairly narrow range of variability. Why haven't psychologists generally recognized this law long ago? Why aren't introductory psychology texts universally organized around this fundamental law of nature? The field of psychology is badly in need of an overarching universal law, an organizing principle to order the vast number of observations about behavior in nature and in the laboratory (Koenigshofer, 1994b). And here it is! A law that makes sense out of everything in psychology! And yet it has escaped notice (Koenigshofer, 1994b; however, see La Cerra, 2003). Is it perhaps because so few psychologists have been trained in anything biological? Is it because of the blinding biases of the Standard Social Science Model—the belief that human behavior is to be explained by culture and other influences of nurture to the exclusion of genetic and evolutionary causes? Perhaps it is the absence of the enlightening perspective provided by a comparative approach, across species, in psychologists who know little about the behavior of other species or about evolution and its profound implications for psychology. Is it because behavior is treated as if it exists in a vacuum, outside biology, the only meaningful context that will be able to make sense of it? We are social and cultural creatures, but social life itself is biological in origins and functions, and like other behavior, is the product of a biological organ with biological function and "purposes." Behavior is a property of organisms, where else but in biology should we look for psychology's overarching universal laws?

The reader might wonder why the Law of Adaptation, as I have stated it, focuses on genes, on DNA, rather than on individuals (organisms tend to behave in ways that promote survival and reproduction of their *genes*). First, consistent with the arguments above, organisms are "survival machines" which have evolved in service of the genes they carry within them. Natural selection works at the level of the gene, preserving genes that organize successful "survival machines," and discarding genes which have built organisms which are less effective in the competition to preserve and replicate the DNA that assembled them (Dawkins, 2006). But more importantly, by acting on genes, rather than on individuals, natural selection produces some surprising effects, particularly on behavior.

The original formulation of Darwin's evolution by natural selection saw nature as brutally competitive, "red in tooth and claw" as the poet Lord Tennyson put it. Darwin's theory of evolution seemed to imply that only self-interest could exist in animals and humans (basis for the objection, on moral or political principle, that some social scientists and humanities professors have to evolutionary approaches to human behavior—an objection, as we shall see, that is actually baseless).

If nature was all competition, it should always favor behavior that promoted one's own individual survival and reproduction, regardless of the costs to others. Certainly, natural selection, as it was originally formulated, supposedly acting on individual organisms, would seem to have "designed" selfish organisms with exclusively selfish brains. And further, they should become more and more selfish, over succeeding generations of evolution, under such supposed ruthless selection for self-interest. If you have a brain design that leads you to give your food, water, and other resources to others, to sacrifice yourself to predators so they won't eat your neighbor, to let your competitors in the mating game have first shot at desirable mates while you sit back with indifference and only mate after others have had their chance, then in Darwin's original formulation of how natural selection works, your genes would not survive into future generations. Thus, brain design that led to such behaviors would be weeded out in a hurry, leaving only the most self-interested brain "designs," those that produced extreme selfish behavior, to reproduce the genes for selfishness generation after generation. On this view, genes should produce "survival machines" characterized psychologically by extreme selfishness and ruthless competitiveness alone.

However, biologists observed that this did not seem to be the way things actually worked in nature. Biologists had long known that extreme selfishness was not the rule. Instead, humans and many animal species show behaviors that benefit others, even when such acts occur at a cost to the individual performing them. Perhaps the most familiar example of this is the behavior of parents toward their offspring. We have all heard stories of mothers, and sometimes fathers, risking their own safety to save their offspring, not only in humans, but in other animals as well. But perhaps the most striking examples of this kind of behavior, known among biologists as *altruistic behavior*, is seen in the social insects—bees, ants, and wasps (see chapter 9).

For example, bees collect honey and deposit most of it in the hive for the use of others in their colony, most especially the queen and her larvae. The substantial energy expended by the bee is not to feed itself, but to feed others. Bees also will sacrifice themselves to defend the hive, the queen, and her colony inside. When the hive is invaded by attack from wasps, soldier bees sting the invaders, but in the process rip out some of their own insides and thus die. How can Darwinian processes of natural selection explain such suicidal behavior? What does the altruist get, if anything, for its efforts and especially for the sacrifice of its own life? How could the genes responsible for self-sacrificing behavior continue into succeeding generations if the individuals performing such acts were dying as a result of such actions, thus seemingly eliminating their own chances to reproduce themselves?

In the wild, columns of army ants moving through the jungle navigate across puddles, streams, and other bodies of water in an ingenious way, using the sacrifices of the ants at the head of the column. These ants link their bodies together with their jaws forming a living bridge for the ants, further back in the column, to cross. The ants forming the living bridge drown; their altruism has the ultimate cost, their own death. Yet, there is no hesitation. The ants lay down their lives for the good of their group.

Male wolves regurgitate meat to their mates who are nursing their offspring in the wolf den, thus depriving themselves of the benefits of the food. Chimpanzees share meat with other members in their group after they have made a kill. Wildebeest come to the defense of a newly born wildebeest of their group threatened by a lion, putting themselves in danger of being killed and eaten in place of the newborn. And we all know stories of heroism and self-sacrifice in a wide selection of other species, including humans. As alluded to above, adults, especially mothers, of many species will often risk themselves to defend their offspring from predators and other dangers. This "maternal instinct" to protect one's young is very strong in most mothers, whether animal or human, at least in the mammals and birds. In animals that don't stay around after they lay their eggs to see the young hatch and to give the newly hatched or newly born sustenance and care (for example most fish, turtles, and lizards), as we would expect, such "motherly" behavior doesn't exist.

The existence of altruistic behavior in nature had puzzled biologists for quite some time because of its seeming inconsistency with Darwinian natural selection. How could altruism exist when natural selection seemed to favor "looking out for number 1" and to disfavor giving, sharing, cooperation, and other altruistic acts? Darwin's theory didn't seem capable of explaining a widely observed fact of natural behavior, altruism, ostensibly just exactly the opposite of the selfishness that Darwinian natural selection seemed to inevitably imply.

The solution came in 1964 when W. D. Hamilton published an article in the *Journal of Theoretical Biology* titled "The Genetical Evolution of Social Behavior." In this landmark paper, Hamilton argued for the gene-level operation of natural selection (natural selection acts on genes, not individual organisms) and that altruistic behavior could be explained as a result of what came to be known as *kin selection*. Kin selection takes into account a previously unrecognized fact of nature, that there are two ways to get your genes into the next generation: 1) act selfishly and survive to personally reproduce and thus pass on your genes through your own offspring, and 2) act altruistically toward your close genetic relatives, thus facilitating their chances of survival and reproduction. The latter option works genetically because close relatives share genes in common. For example, siblings share 50% of their genes. Thus, if I act altruistically toward my brother or sister, then I increase his or her chances of surviving to reproduce his or her genes, half of which are copies of my genes. By acting altruistically toward my brother or sister,

I get a genetic payoff, not consciously of course, but in a mechanistic way—genes for altruism, toward close genetic relatives, get preserved by the reproduction of the relatives who benefit from the altruism, and who also share some of these same altruistic genes. If we then apply Darwin's principle of natural selection, not to the individual, but to genes, so that we look at natural selection as operating on that molecular level, the level of DNA, then we see that there will be evolutionary "pressure" toward evolution of "survival machines" with brains "designed" for altruistic behaviors, such as sharing, giving, cooperation, and even self-sacrifice of the ultimate form, when the altruism is directed toward close genetic relatives (who share genes in common with the altruist). Hamilton showed that natural selection when conceived of as acting on the genetic level, rather than particularly and exclusively at the level of the individual animal, could predict both self-interested behavior and altruistic behavior, at least when directed toward close genetic relatives such as siblings, offspring, and even cousins, nieces, and nephews. However, the prediction was that the more distant the genetic relationship, the less likely altruistic behavior would be. This was expressed in an equation, *Hamilton's Rule*, which states that:

A personally costly action will occur if $C < R \times B$, where C is the cost to the actor, R is a measure of the degree of relatedness between the actor and the recipient, and B is a measure of the fitness benefit to the recipient.

Here is a good place to introduce the concept of *biological fitness* since fitness is one of the variables in this important equation. We have referred informally to this concept throughout this chapter. However, technically, biological fitness refers to the ability of a particular genotype (genetic makeup) to reproduce itself. It is measured in terms of the number of copies of one's genes that make it to the next generation and thus is typically equal to the proportion of the individual's genes present among all the genes of the next generation. Because it doesn't matter how one's genes get to the next generation, either through one's own personal reproduction or through the reproduction of one's close genetic relatives, biological fitness can be achieved in two ways: 1) by selfishly looking out for oneself increasing the chances of one's own personal reproduction and/or 2) by altruistically looking out for close genetic relatives, increasing their chances of successful reproduction. Thus, there are two ways to get one's genes to the next generation, and thus two forms of biological fitness, one's *personal or individual fitness*, measured by the number of offspring one personally leaves, and one's *inclusive fitness*, measured by the number of offspring left by one's close genetic relatives, plus the number of offspring left by one personally (one's individual fitness). Thus, it turns out that altruistic behavior toward close genetic relatives increases one's inclusive fitness and thus should be favored by natural selection, and should therefore result in animals with brains "designed" for both selfishness and for altruism (in religious terms, for "evil" and for "good").

To reiterate the first fundamental and universal law of psychology, the *Law of Adaptation* states that *organisms tend to behave in ways that promote the survival and reproduction of their genes.* Stated this way, in terms of genes, this universal law takes into account inclusive fitness, not just individual fitness, helping to explain altruistic behavior as well as "selfish" behavior. Out of the seemingly endless variety of behavior and mind "designs" in nature, order emerges. Minds and behavior suddenly make sense when the Law of Adaptation is recognized. Even what we mean by psychological disorders (a topic to be discussed again in more detail in a later chapter) becomes clarified in light of the Law of Adaptation. Sometimes animals, most notably humans, do not behave according to this law. After all, some people become addicted to drugs, kill their children, stay in abusive relationships, or even commit suicide. But exceptions to the Law of Adaptation only highlight its validity, because we intuitively recognize that behaviors that violate it are somehow pathological. In fact, on this view, the defining characteristic of psychopathology is behavior (and mental processing) which is counter to the Law of Adaptation. The more maladaptive a behavior is, the more it creates problems for the organism rather than solving them, and the greater the degree of pathology. Healthy organisms don't violate the Law of Adaptation. Healthy organisms behave in ways consistent with the Law of Adaptation—if they didn't, their genes would have been weeded out of the gene pool of their species long ago.

It is easy to see why this law emerges in nature. Behavior is a form of adaptation, one type of solution that organisms use to solve their biological problems. Look at the bodies of plants and animals. If bodies of all species are equipped with traits that promote survival and reproduction of their genes, specifically because these bodies have been "designed" by natural selection, then minds and behavior, also the products of evolution by natural selection, must likewise serve survival and reproduction of genes. Everything else in psychology follows from this. All other laws in psychology, as we will see in subsequent chapters, are corollaries of this foundational principle.

In the next chapter, we will see how the Law of Adaptation can explain why capacities for learning evolved in the mind "designs" of so many animal species, especially the mammals and birds, and how the laws of learning, even human learning, evolved to serve successful adaptation and the reproduction of genes.

CHAPTER SEVEN

Information, Learning, and the
Nature-Nurture Continuum

"Give me a dozen healthy infants, well-formed, and my own specified world to bring them up in and I'll guarantee to take any one at random and train him to become any type of specialist I might select—doctor, lawyer, artist, merchant-chief, and yes, even begger-man and thief, regardless of his talents, penchants, tendencies, abilities, vocations, and race of his ancestors."

John B. Watson,
Behaviorism, 1924

In much of the history of psychology, learning has been a catch-all explanation for almost everything. The quotation above, from the founder of Behaviorism in 1911, John B. Watson, illustrates the common belief that learning, and learning alone, is the source of human behavior. This view, as discussed in a previous chapter, is a left-over from philosophical assumptions originally formulated by the British Empiricist philosopher, John Locke, in the late 1600's (Locke, 1690/1947). On this view, the human mind at birth is a *tabula rasa*, a "blank slate," constructed entirely from information acquired from experience during the individual lifetime. Nothing, in mind or behavior, is built-in at birth, according to Locke. On this view, heredity (nothing was known about genes in 1690) contributed nothing to the organization of human minds and behavior.

The belief that experience and learning *are everything* in the determination of human behavior, guided by a brain that is little more than a general purpose learning machine, was so influential in the 19th century that the view was uncritically incorporated into the founding assumptions of early psychology and the social sciences (including sociology, political science, cultural anthropology, and economics). The same belief is inherent in Marxist philosophy and is popular with many in the humanities, including most historians. Its influence has been so great in psychology, the social sciences and humanities, that it has been termed the *Standard Social Science Model* (SSSM) by evolutionary psychologists, John Tooby and Leda Cosmides (Tooby and Cosmides, 1992). Psychology and the social sciences, and much of public policy, are grounded in the belief that experience is the only important factor in the determination of the human mind and behavior, and that genes, innate brain "design," and genetic evolution don't matter (or, from a political standpoint, that they *shouldn't* matter if we are to preserve ideals of equality and equal opportunity for all).

However, Cosmides and Tooby (1992) describe these views as "radically defective" and "biologically naïve." The idea of the *tabula rasa* is no more than 17th century superstition. But to be more kind, belief in the mind as a "blank slate" at birth, formed entirely by experience, is understandable, because these empiricist philosophical ideas were formulated and firmly accepted by the fledgling social sciences at least a century before people knew much of anything about the brain, evolution, or genes. And old ideas die hard. Even today, most people, even many academics, still believe that the claims of the SSSM are true (or want to defend them as true even though they may suspect, deep down, that they aren't actually the case; see Pinker, 2002). Sadly, most people still believe in the 17th century empiricist view of Locke that human behavior is mostly, if not exclusively, the result of learning, experience, and culture, with little, if any, contribution from innate brain structure, heredity, and genetic evolution (however, among those who do recognize the importance of genetics and evolution in human behavior, unfortunately there exists a small minority with racist agendas who have tried to use genetics and evolution to further their own racist views; any attempt to do so is completely without merit and should be rejected on ethical and empirical grounds without reservation). Far too many still believe that the human mind and behavior are primarily, if not exclusively, the consequence of learning and experience with little or no contribution from genes and genetic evolution.

But the SSSM has it exactly backwards. As we have seen, innate brain circuit "design" derived from eons of natural selection is the principal cause of the behavior and mental organization of each and every species, including humans. Learning does contribute important finishing touches to minds and behavior (at least the details of individual behavior, especially in the birds and mammals, but even in some invertebrates, such as bees or the octopus), but most people continue to exaggerate what learning can do. Learning does not provide all, or even most, of the information that organizes human behavior, neither is learning a single general process with unlimited potential, unrestrained at all by biological factors, as the SSSM would have us believe. Instead, *learning provides information that is secondary and supplementary* to the information for brain development which is coded in the DNA of each species. Furthermore, *learning is guided and restricted within a fairly narrow range of possibilities set by the DNA of* each species, including our own. There is not a single kind of learning, but many kinds. Learning does not fill in a "blank slate," as proposed by Locke and naively supposed in the SSSM, it just adds the "punctuation," a few "sentences" here and there, and modifies other "sentences" and "paragraphs" already in place at birth (and genetic potentials present prior to birth which interact with environmental inputs after birth) as a consequence of the evolution of specific brain circuit "design" in each particular species of creature. Learning takes place in brains, and brains, including the human brain, are not general purpose learning machines.

Brains, and their learning circuits, are formed during embryological development in very specific ways dictated by information originating from natural selection, and coded in genes, and DNA "switches" formed over the evolutionary history of each species (see discussion of the role of DNA in brain development in the last chapter), in interaction to a degree with environmental inputs. Among other things, this means that *learning itself is dependent upon genetically evolved learning mechanisms* in the brain of the animal (or human) that is doing the learning. *We can see this in the different learning capacities of different species.* Even adherents of the SSSM would probably agree that learning occurs in brains, but for believers in the "blank slate," the human brain is akin to a general purpose learning machine, producing learning unlimited in its scope by any innate factors of evolved brain circuit "design." Modern neuroscience has shown us that the brain, and most significantly the human brain, is far from a "blank slate," and that many of its learning circuits are specialized for quite particular forms of learning. Learning doesn't occur in "silly putty," but only in a brain genetically organized by evolution in very specific ways to do the learning (Pinker, 2002).

As was discussed in the previous chapter, *genetic evolution and learning are both information acquisition processes.* Each individual animal and its behavior results from a mix of these two information sources (just what proportion each contributes to that mix varies from species to species and from one behavior to another; see "the nature-nurture continuum" below). Natural selection weeds and prunes the information available in the gene pool of a species, discarding maladaptive information and retaining that which best serves the life and reproduction of the "survival machines" it shapes during embryological development—then, next, during the lifetime of each individual, learning mechanisms in the brain, themselves formed by DNA, extract, and put to adaptive use, additional information, acquired from the experience of the individual, to further improve the chances of survival and reproduction. Thus, learning is just another kind of adaptive mechanism, added on top of "instincts," evolved to serve the genes, to protect them, nurture them, and to reproduce them.

Contrary to dogma in the social sciences, as we shall see in coming chapters, humans have no shortage of instincts. In fact, the famous philosopher and psychologist, William James, founder of functionalism in the early days of psychology, argued that humans have *more* instincts than other animals, not less. One of these instincts is the instinct to learn, but to do so in ways specified and constrained by particular learning circuitry "designed" by natural selection to solve adaptive problems present over the evolutionary history of each species. Furthermore, our evolved emotional and motivational makeup as a species likewise dictate what interests us, what we attend to, and what features of the world we can perceive and understand, thus further constraining our learning, our minds, and our behavior.

When thinking about the "design" of minds, remember *the Law of Adaptation— organisms tend to behave in ways that promote the survival and reproduction of their genes.* Consistent with this principle, minds, like bodies, are "designed" by evolutionary processes to form a good fit with the conditions of the environment.

It is instructive to note that the world has two general categories of conditions in it distinguished by their duration: those that are relatively stable over long periods of evolutionary time, such as gravitational forces or the changing seasons, and those which change relatively rapidly, such as the location of a water source or a food source in the local environment of the individual. Some conditions of the world are very stable, and relatively unchanging for prolonged periods of time, others exist for short periods of time, or fluctuate rapidly, still others exist in specific environmental niches of specific species, or in the specific experience of specific individuals, and others exist universally, in every niche of the terrestrial environment. We should expect that different kinds of adaptive mechanism will develop to accommodate these different categories of condition found in the world. And this expectation matches the reality.

As pointed out in the last chapter, genetic evolution is the *slow information acquisition process* for organisms, taking place over many generations—on an evolutionary time scale. Thus, the adaptive information that results, stored in DNA, has been acquired over the evolutionary history of the species. As such, this slow information acquisition process can only accommodate long-term, stable conditions of the environment that are consistently present long enough for natural selection, to have the time it needs, to do its work.

By contrast, learning is the *fast information acquisition process* in humans and other animals. Depending upon the complexity of what is to be learned and other factors, such as the particulars of the learning circuitry of the brain of the species, *learning can occur in moments* (for example, learning not to touch a hot stove), or sometimes over *days or months* (for example, chimpanzees learning to "fish" for termites, or a lion or killer whale perfecting its hunting skills), but always, and only, within the lifetime of the individual animal. Learning is fast, genetic evolution is slow by comparison. Thus, the kinds of environmental conditions that each can "design" adaptive responses to is different. Genetic evolution can "respond" to long-term conditions of the environment and genetically accommodate them; learning can respond to short-term, local, and rapidly fluctuating conditions of the world.

What are the advantages of learning—how does the capacity to learn contribute to successful adaptation? Clearly, learning adds flexibility to behavior and flexibility in most circumstances will improve adaptation. For example, killer whales, formidable pack hunting animals, learn specific hunting skills that they apply depending upon the particular prey that they are hunting—seals, sting rays, or sharks. Learning permits adaptation to short-term, or rapidly fluctuating, and even novel conditions in the environment. When constrained in just the right ways by biology, learning also plays an essential role in cognition, particularly in concept formation, because it allows storage of information about events and objects which are similar on various dimensions permitting brains to form generalizations, make inferences and predictions, and to form concepts. We shall discuss more about how learning shapes cognition in a later chapter. For now, there is more to understand about ways in which learning and genetic evolution complement one another and why learning exists in the first place.

Genetic evolution is a means by which adaptive information about long-term, stable conditions of the world becomes incorporated into the DNA of a species, and thus, into the "design" features of its adaptations. For example, information about the regular effects and the intensity of gravity is genetically accommodated into the adaptive "design" of the bones and skeletal systems of land living vertebrates. Bones have just the required strength to accommodate the gravitational forces specific to the earth. Another example is found in the visual system. The long term, stable properties of light reflecting off objects in the terrestrial environment are genetically accommodated by the circuit "design" of the visual systems of primates. These "design" features of the visual cortex and thalamus produce *brightness and color constancies* (perception of stable brightness and color of an object regardless of changes in lighting), making visual perception of an object stable even though actual physical properties of reflected light change throughout the day with the angle of the sun, and in shadow (Carlson, 2011). This makes evolutionary sense. In order to respond in adaptive ways to objects we must be able to recognize them as stable distal objects in spite of changes in the properties of reflected light striking our retinas.

This later example is one illustration of an important general principle about "mind designs" in nature. Specific brain circuit "designs" have evolved by natural selection "as accommodations to pervasive and enduring properties of the world," not just to those properties of the particular niche currently occupied by a species but also to "the general circumstances common to all ecological niches" (Shepard, 1992). In other words, brain "design" evolves to match enduring properties of the world. Brain "designs" evolve in response to environmental regularities with adaptive significance and which reach sufficient degrees of stability over time to give natural selection the time it needs to work (more about the role of regularities in brain "design" in a later chapter).

Thus, characteristics of species, *including the brain "designs"* of animals and humans, should be expected to have evolved within them "genetic accommodations" to long-term, stable conditions of the world. For example, information about highly stable, long term changes in temperature, associated with annual changes in the seasons, are genetically accommodated by physiological adaptations in trees which go dormant in the winter, and by animals genetically "programmed" to hibernate, such as bears and squirrels, or to migrate, such as many species of birds. Brain circuit "designs" will evolve to match the adaptively important, long-term properties of the world. That is, the properties of our brain, and thus of our minds (our psychological makeup), will reflect the organization of the world. Natural selection makes this so, for us, and for each species. Any species which has brain "design" which is out of synchrony with the adaptively important features of the environment, in which it must live and compete, will end on the road of extinction. For the long-term, relatively stable conditions of the world, genetic evolution by the operation of natural selection can "create" properties of brain and body "design" which will successfully accommodate those long-term, stable conditions.

However, in other properties, the world is not so stable a place. In addition to long term, highly stable, regularities, the world also is characterized by rapidly fluctuating, short-term, local, and even individually idiosyncratic changes—for example, the location of local water sources or local food sources, such as a water hole frequented by prey animals, or the location of termite mounds full of juicy insects (a favorite of chimpanzees; Goodall, 1971), or in bees, the location of a field of flowers rich in nectar. One might learn, by specific experiences with local predators, important adaptive information about their specific behavior that might be useful in evading them, and, in social species, one must learn one's particular position in the social hierarchy of one's group, the fluctuating status of one's alliances in the group, past experiences with other members of the group, facilitating more effective future interactions with them, and so on. Specific information about these kinds of events in the world cannot be safely disregarded because their adaptive consequences are far too great. But neither can such short-term, variable information be acquired and stored by the *slow information acquisition process, genetic evolution*—genetic evolution just takes too long. Instead, to exploit the important adaptive information found in the environment in less stable, short-term, and local regularities, natural selection had to "design" much faster information acquisition processes—that collection of brain processes we call "learning"—the relatively rapid acquisition of information about short-term, less stable regularities, often specific to the local environment or experience of the individual, within the individual's own lifetime. Genetic evolution is just too slow. It can't form adaptations to short-term, rapidly fluctuating conditions of the world by itself, but it can "design" learning mechanisms, within the brains of animal species, to accommodate and to exploit the adaptively important information contained in these kinds of events in the world that are too brief, too idiosyncratic, too unstable to be adapted to, by genetic evolution alone. Seeing learning this way implies that there must be multiple learning mechanisms in the animal kingdom. There is not just a single form of learning, with uniform laws governing it, but there must be multiple and varied forms of learning, each often adapted to solution of particular biological problems faced by the organism.

Typically, most people think of learning in association with schools, books, and the study of subjects such as reading, writing, and arithmetic and then later, philosophy, business, history, mathematics, or science. But from this discussion we can see that this kind of learning, human verbal learning, is only one brand of learning, found only in a single species, and useful for acquisition of only particular kinds of information. In us, and in other species, there is a whole tool box of other categories of learning, each evolved to help animals find adaptive solutions to overcome specific environmental obstacles to survival and reproduction, particularly when adaptation to short-term, novel, local, and rapidly fluctuating conditions of the world are called for.

An example of learning in the bird species, Indigo Buntings, illustrates the complex interaction between genetic evolution, and learning, in the organization of behavior. It also will illuminate a general principle—part of the "mind design" of each species consists of innate "guides" about "what to learn and when to learn it" (Howard, 1997). These innate "guides" or *biological constraints on learning* are one of the important discoveries in modern psychology and neuroscience and expose the failed logic of the *tabula rasa* or "blank slate" assumption of the SSSM. The existence of built-in features of the mind, such as "guides" to learning, means that there must be specific circuit "design" in the learning circuitry of the brain, determining what can be learned, how it is to be learned, and when in the life cycle the learning will take place. This kind of specificity of learning is not possible in the kind of brain assumed by Locke and the adherents of the "tabula rasa" ("blank slate"). In that view of the brain and mind, there can be no innate structure of the mind and brain, *especially* in its learning mechanisms. But we find the opposite. If experience is everything in the organization of mind and behavior, then how does experience organize constraints on learning? How can learning create limits on its own processes? The constraints on learning must be the result of biology, the innate, evolved "design" of the brain that is doing the learning. The following example should help clarify.

Indigo Buntings migrate twice a year using the stars to find their way as they fly by night thousands of miles over land and across oceans. Behavioral biologist, Stephen Emlen of Cornell University showed that young Indigo Buntings learn patterns of stars while watching the night sky from the comfort of their nests. As the stars undergo apparent rotation throughout the night around the celestial pole (something you can observe yourself if you look at the stars early in the evening and then again several hours later), Indigo Buntings learn the location of the north star and other nearby stars by noting which star stays fixed. Later as adults, they orient during migration using learned information about star configurations (constellations) that they associate with the north-south axis of celestial rotation. They pick out and learn the location of the star that is stationary throughout the night (the north star) using a genetically organized learning program akin to *imprinting* (imprinting is an innate learning program in birds, such as geese, that causes them to follow the first moving object they see after hatching—usually, but not necessarily, their mother, as experiments by the great behavioral biologist, Konrad Lorenz, have shown,). Emlen also showed that the same star pattern can cause migration to the south or to the north, depending upon hormonal alterations within the bird's body, which change with the seasons (http://www.nbb.cornell.edu/neurobio/emlen/ Misc%20Info/research_accomp.html; http://elibrary.unm.edu/sora/Auk/v084n04/ p0463-p0489.pdf; retrieved, June 7, 2010).

Thus, learning is essential to successful migration in this species (a behavioral adaptation related to solution of the temperature and energy problems, i.e. dealing with cold and with scarcity of food in the winter). But how do the young Indigo Buntings know *what* to learn and *what* to pay attention to (specific patterns of stars and the star that doesn't show apparent motion during the night) in order to learn it? Why are they motivated to stare up at the night sky for prolonged periods of time and to pick out and learn the star that doesn't move? How do they know to do these things? Then, once they learn the star patterns, how do they know that they should use them to orient themselves when they are ready to migrate? They can't be thinking all this through. They haven't deliberated and then decided that this would be a good and reliable method for finding their way to warmer climates and better food sources. The first time they migrate, they have never done it before, and couldn't know what the environment would be like thousands of miles away prior to their first migration. Besides, they don't have the ability to understand astronomy, the seasons, or their own need to migrate. How do they know that as winter approaches they need to get "out of town"?

They "know" these things because it's in the genes. Thus, learning is not occurring in a vacuum. Much of what the bird needs to "know" is already programmed into its brain by evolution (we often call such innate knowledge "instinct"). All that learning does is to add the finishing touches. And the learning, itself, is highly organized to do just what needs to be done, to provide just the information that is needed to solve the adaptive problem. Genes organize the wiring of the learning circuits, guiding the bird's brain to learn just what it needs to know—the information about specific features of the night sky necessary to provide reliable directional cues that will guide migration in the adult bird.

You might think of it this way. In order to generate adaptive migratory behavior, the bird's brain has a kind of *computational problem.* The neural circuitry in the bird's brain must perform computations to make the bird fly great distances in the correct direction and at the right time of the year. How can it do these computations?

The neural computation by the bird's brain involves the movement of electrical signals (voltage shifts in neurons) through specific neuronal routes or pathways. The basic functional "design" of the neural circuits responsible for migratory behavior must already be in place as a result of Indigo Bunting evolution. All the bird's brain needs in order to complete the computations required for migration is specific information about the position and patterns of the stars that mark the celestial pole. Once this additional information is added by learning, then the neural computations in the bird's brain can be completed, finishing the guidance system needed for the bird's adaptive migratory behavior later in its life. *Learning just supplements and refines information already in the bird's brain, built into hard-wired circuitry assembled according to specifications in the bird's DNA.* This is an important general principle about the nature of learning.

But to really understand the nature of learning, we must ask, why is learning needed at all? Why couldn't all of the required information for successful migration simply be programmed into the bird's DNA at the outset? Why bother with learning mechanisms in the first place? In short, it's because some of the critical information needed is not stable enough over long enough periods of time for genetic evolution to accommodate it. The stars that guide migration change, and the change is too fast. The North Star and the stars near it change every few thousand years in a 26,000 year cycle of "axial precession," due to a wobble in the earth's axis. Currently, the North Star, which marks the north celestial pole, is Polaris located in the constellation, Ursa Minor, the "little bear," more commonly known as the "little dipper." But 3,000 years ago, the North Star was Thuban, in the constellation Draco. And 12,000 years from now, Vega, in the constellation Lyra, will be the North Star (http://en.wikipedia.org/wiki/Precession_of_ the_equinoxes, retrieved June 9, 2010). And herein lies an important lesson about the relationship between genetic evolution, DNA, and learning in the organization of behavior. *Learning mechanisms have to evolve, to supplement the information coded in DNA, when critical information required for successful adaptation is too rapidly fluctuating to be accommodated by the slow processes of genetic evolution.* Such rapidly fluctuating adaptive information, like the position of the stars marking the north celestial pole, requires the evolution of a specific learning mechanism causing the animal to attend to and to store the required information for later use. Thus, Indigo Buntings have evolved a *specific learning mechanism* (an *adaptive specialization of learning*) in their brains that causes them to sit up at night as nestlings, to watch the night sky, to pick out and to remember which star (the pole star) and star groups move the least during the night, as the sky appears to move about the north-south axis of celestial rotation. By doing so, these birds learn which star is the current north star, and thus where to orient when they begin migration later as adults.

To reiterate this important point, note that this crucial adaptive information about star patterns cannot be genetically programmed into the bird's brain, because position of the star that marks north changes too rapidly (every few thousand years) to be accommodated by the slow processes of genetic evolution. A faster information acquisition process, a specific learning mechanism, thus evolves to provide information from specific experiences (watching the night sky rotate) to supplement the innate, genetically evolved information in the bird's brain that makes it use stars, in the first place, as guideposts when it migrates.

A similar situation exists with another special form of learning known as *taste aversion learning*, discovered by psychologist, John Garcia, in the 1950s (Garcia, et. al., 1955). Omnivorous animals such as rats, coyotes, and humans, eat a wide range of foods. As part of an innate disposition for culinary exploration, such animals will often sample new potential food substances they encounter in their environments. In the natural environment, they have an innate "neophobia" or fear of new substances they haven't eaten before. But even with this innate "caution" built into their "mind design," testing out new foods involves risk of potential poisoning. So, all these omnivorous species are equipped with brain "design" which includes genetically evolved, specialized learning mechanisms ("learning organs," according to psychologist Randy Gallistel at Rutgers) that help them learn quickly and powerfully to avoid flavors previously associated with ingested substances which made them sick.

Humans are omnivores and thus this sort of learning is a fairly common human experience. You may recall a time when you ate something, and then later you felt sick, and, perhaps, to this day you are repulsed by that flavor, avoiding it at all costs. When I was a 7-year old boy, one afternoon I drank several Root Beer floats in about an hour. I got "sick to my stomach" a few hours later, and to this day I still can't stand even the smell, much less the taste, of Root Beer. As testimony to how effective taste aversion learning is as a way to modify behavior by specific experience, I have not had a single drop of Root Beer in over 50 years since, even though, before this unfortunate incident, it had been one of my favorites. (There was one exception, however, when a few years later in a dark theater I accepted a drink from a friend's paper cup, thinking it was Coke—then gagged on the taste of Root Beer, nearly spitting it out on the back of the head of the poor guy in front of me).

Experiments in rats and other animals have demonstrated that this kind of learning is genetically evolved since it is possible to selectively breed for it in animals, demonstrating that individual differences in this kind of learning are heritable, and therefore encoded in the genes (Koenigshofer and Nachman, 1974). In my case, the Root Beer, of course, was not toxic, but the learning circuits in my brain that made Root Beer so distasteful to me after a single experience, in which Root Beer flavor was followed a few hours later by sickness, evolved to protect omnivores, like me and you, and rats and coyotes, from poisoning (incidentally, vomiting is another protective mechanism, a physiological adaptation, but one that rats don't share with dogs, coyotes, and humans).

Garcia and researchers who followed recognized that the special features of this kind of learning were perfectly tuned by evolution to effectively handle an adaptive problem for omnivores, how to avoid being poisoned. Unlike most other forms of learning, taste aversion learning usually occurs in a single learning trial (a single experience) and it occurs robustly even though the offending flavor, formerly neutral or even initially preferred, is not followed by feelings of illness until much later, perhaps for several hours (that is, there is a long delay between ingestion of the flavored substance and its deleterious effects; technically this is referred to as a long CS-UCS interval—one of the distinguishing features of this kind of learning; the CS, conditioned stimulus, refers to the flavor stimulus and the UCS, unconditioned stimulus, in this case are the stimuli felt as "sickness," such as stomach cramps, nausea, etc.). This feature of this specialized from of learning makes evolutionary sense. If a substance is a dangerous poison you need a mechanism that can "teach" this essential fact to an organism in one trial. If you don't learn that a particular new flavor is a predictor of poisoning and illness the first time around, you may not get a second chance. And, since illness from poisoning usually follows only after an extended time (many minutes to hours) after ingestion of a poisonous substance has had time to move through the digestive tract, the long delays in taste aversion learning is a special adaptation (a "genetic accommodation") "designed" to accommodate this feature of the world and of one's own digestive physiology.

Here, once again, information in DNA and information acquired by experience interact, like cooperating partners in a kind of adaptive dance, in this case to produce adaptive modifications in feeding behavior in omnivores as a result of a specific type of experience. In cases of other kinds of learning, such as learning a predictive association between classes of stimuli that are not so biologically tied to one another, the learning takes much longer, that is, it requires many more learning trials, many more pairings of the stimuli before the animal "gets the idea" that one stimulus is a good predictor of the other (as in the *classical conditioning* of an unlikely stimulus like a bell to a stimulus such as the appearance of food—as in the famous experiment performed by Ivan Pavlov in dogs; more about this form of learning later). Typically, this is seen as a "weakness" of this later form of learning (classical conditioning) because it takes a long time to accomplish the learning, but in fact, this may, itself, be an *adaptation* "designed" by natural selection to prevent animals from learning incidental or accidental associations which are not reliable in the world, which would make such associations poor predictors of future events, and therefore adaptively disadvantageous.

Another informative example of learning occurs in the acquisition of bird song by white- crowned sparrows. These birds sing a distinctive species song, but research reveals that they sing different dialects of white-crowned sparrow song, depending on where they live (note the similarity to the human case where all humans speak a form of human language, the form of which varies according to the specific language(s) you are exposed to as you grow up). White- crowned sparrows in northern California, centered in the Berkeley area, sing a Berkeley dialect. A population living in southern California, centered around Santa Monica, sing the southern or Santa Monica dialect. Cross-rearing experiments (eggs from one group are hatched amidst the adults of the second group) show that the dialect is learned, but learning will occur only if exposure to the species-typical song takes place within 10 to 50 days after hatching, long before they start to sing. Exposure to the normal male song of the species before 10 days or after 100 days post-hatching has absolutely no effect. It is as if they had not been exposed to any song at all.

Furthermore, regardless of dialect, white-crowned sparrows will develop the ability to sing their species-typical song only if they are exposed to the song of their own species during the first summer after hatching. Hearing the song later has no effect, and they fail to develop normal song. There is another biological constraint on this form of learning as well. If white-crowned sparrows are exposed to the song of another species, such as canary song, contrary to what some might expect, they learn absolutely nothing, as if they had been exposed to no song at all. This makes evolutionary sense, considering that these birds are surrounded by other bird species and thus hear their songs as well as their own, so they must have something, "a guide," innately built into the song acquisition circuitry that prevents them from learning the song of other species. Regardless of environmental experience, *they can only learn the song of their own species, and only if they hear their own species song within a particular period of time after hatching* (Marler, 1970). This demonstrates that *what* can be learned and *when* it can be learned are genetically restricted by the evolved brain circuit "design" of the species. Recent research shows that killer whales, as well as birds, have dialects that differ from one group to another, suggesting that killer whales learn specific details of their species-typical communication from their social group, just as white-crowned sparrows, and humans do.

Animals can't learn just anything, at any time, as might be expected if the "blank slate" view of the brain were really true. But, of course, the "blank slate" is supposed to be a description of the human brain, not of animal brains. Are there genetically evolved constraints on human learning?

Constraints in human language acquisition such as a sensitive period, from about age two years to the beginning of adolescence, during which humans must be exposed to human language for normal language development to take place, suggest an important interaction between learning and genetics in the human brain, not just in animal brains. In addition, there is evidence for an innate, genetically organized set of learning circuits involved in language acquisition, the *Language Acquisition Device* (LAD), proposed by the linguist Noam Chomsky. As we saw in prior chapters, human language is dependent upon a number of specialized brain areas including Broca's and Wernicke's areas in the left cerebral cortex of most people. Confirming inborn brain structure in language learning, according to Chomsky and Pinker (Pinker, *The Language Instinct*), all human languages have grammatical structure based on the same innate properties of the human mind, a *universal grammar* that transcends the differences in detail among the grammars of different human languages around the world. Again, information in DNA provides innate knowledge, and then learning supplements and refines the innate information by adding needed details. Furthermore, in spite of the great complexity of human language, language acquisition takes place in all normal humans far too easily, without formal instruction or reinforcing rewards, to be explained unless there exist genetically organized brain circuits for language acquisition which contain innate knowledge about language (Pinker, 1994). This is technically known as the "poverty of the stimulus" argument in support of the hypothesis that humans must have innate knowledge about the basic structure of language—in the form of genetically evolved brain circuit design; once again, learning just fills in the details.

Other evidence that the human mind is not a "blank slate" includes experiments which show that human infants are genetically predisposed to learn about how objects behave in the physical world (physical reasoning) and that they have innate general principles about the continuity and solidity of objects built into their minds (Baillargeon, 2004). But it doesn't stop there. Over the past decade or so, cognitive scientists have uncovered evidence for innate brain organization in human infants for understanding objects, people, number, space (Spelke, 1994), faces, and tools (Gopnik, et. al., 1999).

Innate, genetically evolved circuit "design" characteristic of the human brain gives infants a set of inborn principles about how the world works that directs their later learning. This is even true for learning about human social relationships. Recall from a previous chapter evidence that human minds come equipped with "mirror neurons" and an innate "mind module" that permits us to understand the minds of other people, as we interact with them, and as we learn about our relationships with them. Recall from Chapter 4 my hypothesis that the human disposition to believe in "free will" as the cause of the behavior of other people may be an innate information processing shortcut built into the circuitry of the human brain to grease human social interactions. Some evolutionary psychologists and sociobiologists have argued that we even have an innate moral sense which we refine with learning and experience (Wilson, 1975; Barash, 1977; see Johnston, 1999; see chapter 9 of this book), and I believe that social anxiety (concern about what others think of us, including the pain of rejection) may be an evolved adaptation keeping us sensitive to our position in the social group, guiding our learning about how to stay in the good graces of those we identify as our social group (something essential to our physical survival in our evolutionary past when our brain circuitry was being shaped by natural selection in an environment filled with large predators and too little food). Differences in our personalities also affect what we learn about social relationships, other people, and about the world. And research shows that genetics plays a significant role in the different ways people process social information as a function of innate personality differences (differences that any parent with more than one child, excepting identical twins, can readily verify). About half of the variability in human personality, intelligence, and behavior is accounted for by genetic differences between humans (Pinker, 1994, p. 372–387). This means that, as is the case in animals, how humans learn, and what they learn, is influenced in important ways by information in our DNA. Even *humans* are far from being a "blank slate" at birth, far from just passively waiting for experience to transform them from a formless, blank being into just anything that experience, acting alone, can dictate (see the quote from John Watson at the opening of this chapter). Humans are, like other species, organized by the information accumulated in their DNA by eons of evolution by natural selection. Learning just fills in the details, adds the finishing touches, to each individual.

Specialized and general forms of learning: domain-specific and domain-general mechanisms

Among other things, these examples show that all learning is not the same. There is not just one kind of learning, but many kinds, each type "designed" over eons of evolution by natural selection for specific adaptive "purposes," not what one would expect if the mind were a *tabula rasa* equipped only with a general learning capacity unfettered by biological constraints and "learning guides" imposed by genetic evolution. Our brains and minds are not formless voids before experience shapes them, but instead, our brain/minds are highly and specifically organized prior to experience in ways that determine what experience can do to us and when.

As the examples above clearly show, learning in the animal kingdom is often *specialized* in the sense that learning mechanisms in brains are "designed" to provide supplemental information of a specific kind, and often at a specific time, needed to solve a *particular* adaptive problem, such as the location of stars for navigation during migration in Indigo Buntings, or what substances in the environment if ingested make an omnivore ill. Such specialized forms of learning including taste aversion learning, song acquisition in birds, and language acquisition in people are referred to as *adaptive specializations of learning*. Some evolutionary psychologists refer to such specialized learning mechanisms as *"domain-specific"* (see Barkow, Cosmides, and Tooby, 1992). That is, the learning that these *specialized learning modules* perform is restricted to a circumscribed set of adaptive problems and involves learning rules that are also specific to that class of adaptive problem or problem "domain"—a consequence of the genetic evolution of the properties of the specific brain circuitry for each form of domain-specific learning.

A fairly obvious example of such specialized learning rules is found in taste aversion learning, discussed above. As noted above, animals and humans can learn a powerful aversion to a specific flavor in a *single learning trial* even with *long intervals between the taste and sickness* (up to several hours or more) and this learning is *long-lasting* (in my lab while a graduate student at UC Riverside, when I tested a rat that had learned a strong taste aversion in a single trial, the aversion to the flavor was as strong a year later as it had been when originally learned even though the rat had not tasted that flavor at all in the interim). Other good examples of evolved *domain-specific learning mechanisms* discussed earlier are the learning of specific features of the night sky in Indigo Buntings and the acquisition of species-specific song in White-crowned sparrows. In each case, very specific, "domain-specific," information is learned and the rules governing the learning are also specific to the particular problem domain—how to navigate, how to avoid poisons if you are an omnivore, or how to acquire complex vocalizations. The learning circuits in the brain that do these specialized forms of learning can't do other kinds of learning, about other kinds of things. The learning circuitry is specifically "designed," genetically constrained, to learn just these very restricted forms of information to solve highly specific adaptive problems. As noted previously, this same domain-specificity of learning seems to be present in acquisition of human language and in many other forms of human learning.

In fact, specializations of learning are so abundant in nature that some evolutionary psychologists such as Randy Gallistel of Rutgers University have been inspired to make the claim that all learning, even in humans, is specialized, and, further, that there is "no such thing as a general purpose learning mechanism." According to Dr. Gallistel, existence of a general purpose learning mechanism makes about as much biological sense (none at all) as the existence of a general sensory organ that produces seeing, hearing, tasting, and touching. Gallistel argues that *adaptive specialization* of organs is the rule in nature, and that this same rule will apply to the design of learning mechanisms in the brain just as surely as it applies to the design of other organs of the body. The existence of adaptively specialized forms of learning challenges the view, proposed by adherents of the "blank slate," that the brain is an undifferentiated, general-purpose learning machine. According to Gallistel, "whenever learning occurs, it is made possible by an adaptively specialized learning mechanism—a learning module—whose structure is as specific to a particular learning problem as the structure of a sensory organ like the eye or the ear is specific to a particular modality" (Gallistel, 2000). Gallistel calls these specialized learning circuits in the brain *learning organs*, and, just like any other organ of the body, they must be specialized to perform the specific functions for which they were evolved. Gallistel believes that this *principle of specialization of cognitive and learning mechanisms* in the brain applies, not just to animals, but to humans as well. All learning is constrained in what it can do, by brain evolution. On this view, there is no such thing as a general learning mechanism, even in humans, says Gallistel (2000).

But not all psychologists agree. Even some *evolutionary psychologists* who typically emphasize adaptive specialization acknowledge that there may be one or a few *general forms of learning* (often referred to by cognitive psychologists and evolutionary psychologists as *domain-general or content-independent forms of learning*). It is in such *domain-general learning* capacities in humans that believers in the Standard Social Science Model may find some hope. Believers in the supreme importance of learning in the causation of human behavior typically assume that *human* learning is of a different order, and that it has much greater influence, than the learning found in other species. For them, arguments about innateness taken from examples of specialized forms of animal learning such as those discussed above would probably be viewed as having little relevance. But it is important to recall the evidence suggesting genetic constraints and evolved "learning guides" in some forms of human learning including human language acquisition, human social learning, human personality, and human learning about objects, tools, and number. Genetic constraints on learning, even in humans, may be far more extensive than even these pioneering studies suggest.

Still, there is no doubt that learning contributes substantially more to the determination of behavior in humans than it does in any other species. After all, humans learn to make and use tools of great "vision" and complexity, unprecedented in the animal world, and we have invented such things as philosophy, mathematics, science, medicine, agriculture, space travel, complex economies and abstractions such as money, legal systems, ideologies, and nation-states. Much of the learning involved in these wonders of human existence seems to lack the specific biological constraints that we find in many forms of animal learning. Is human learning a special case in the animal kingdom? If so, what might distinguish it from learning in other species? Are the differences which might be discovered between human and animal learning, differences in kind or just differences in degree? Is the bulk of learning in humans of some more general form, rather than any brand of adaptive specialization of learning? Is Gallistel correct when he says that there is no such thing as a general learning mechanism, even in humans? These are important questions. Accordingly, we now turn our attention to forms of learning which are more "general" than the adaptive specializations of learning discussed so far. Maybe there we will get clues about what makes human behavior so complex and so unique in the animal world.

Psychologists and other researchers in the early part of the last century, influenced by the founding assumptions of the SSSM, expected, and so looked for, "general" forms of learning, and that, according to some psychologists, is just what they found.

Ivan Pavlov, a Russian physiologist, discovered *classical conditioning* in the early part of the last century. Classical conditioning is a form of learning in which a previously "neutral" stimulus, that is, one without any initial adaptive significance, becomes paired close in time with a stimulus which, by its inherent nature, has *adaptive importance* for the organism. For example, in his classic experiment, Pavlov rang a bell, then, a few seconds later, he presented his dogs with food. After many repetitions of this pairing of stimuli, bell—then food, in close temporal contiguity (close in time), dogs began to salivate to the sound of the bell alone. Salivation to food in the mouth occurs without prior experience because it is a reflex genetically built into the circuitry of the brain stem. Over evolutionary time, it had always been advantageous for saliva to flow when food was in the mouth to facilitate swallowing and so that enzymes in the saliva could begin digestion even before the food reached the stomach.

Pavlov overturned the accepted view among physiologists of his time that reflexes were fixed, and impervious to experience. Reflexes (such as the salivation reflex, the eyeblink reflex, the knee-jerk reflex, the withdrawal reflex such as when you touch a hot stove and pull the hand away, postural reflexes that keep us upright, and so on) are built into the circuitry of the spinal cord and brainstem. Pavlov showed that reflexes could be changed, such that a stimulus in the environment without prior meaning to the animal (such as the bell in Pavlov's experiment) could come to elicit the reflex (salivation, for example) if that stimulus *consistently predicted* the natural stimulus (food, in this case) for the reflex.

Later, the American psychologist, John B. Watson, founder of behaviorism, used this same classical conditioning procedure to condition fear in a young child to the sight of a rat. When the child was first shown the rat, it showed no fear and even liked playing with the rat. Then, the next time Watson presented the rat to the child, he startled the child by banging metal pans together producing a sudden loud noise right behind the child's head, causing the child to cry. The next time Watson showed the rat to the child, the child immediately started to cry. Watson had classically conditioned a *learned fear* in the child, demonstrating that not only could reflexes in animals be classically conditioned, but so too could human *emotions*.

Pavlov invented terminology to identify the events in classical conditioning situations such as these. He called the stimulus that is initially biologically "neutral," without adaptive significance, the *conditional stimulus, the* CS (due to a translation error from Russian to English, this term has unfortunately come to be called the conditioned, rather than *conditional*, stimulus; conditional makes much more sense because it is a stimulus which can produce the target response, say salivation or fear, only as a result of, or *conditional upon, prior learning*—thus, *the conditional stimulus is the learned stimulus* because it can only elicit the target response *conditional upon prior learning*). The stimulus that reliably follows the CS, such as food or a loud noise, was called the *unconditional stimulus (UCS)* by Pavlov because it has *innate* adaptive significance, and therefore it can activate the target response (salivation or fear) *unconditional* upon (independent of) prior experience or learning. This term also suffered the same translation error and so is usually called the unconditioned stimulus (UCS or US), although, again "unconditional" makes more sense and is preferred in this book. The response to the CS is the *conditional response* (CR), the learned response; and the response to the UCS is the UCR, or UR, the *unconditional response (unlearned or innate; unconditional upon prior experience)* to an innately, adaptively meaningful stimulus, such as food or a sudden loud noise.

Traditionally, by influence of the ideas of early British associationist philosophers, classical conditioning was thought to be a form of *associative learning*. In classical conditioning, psychologists believed, animals and humans simply formed *associations* between stimuli that occurred close together in time. Temporal contiguity was seen as the primary, or even sole, requirement for classical conditioning to take place.

But, a deeper analysis reveals a different picture. What animals and humans are really learning in classical conditioning is not simple associations, but *predictive relationships* between stimuli or events in the environment. For animals and humans, classical conditioning is learning "what leads to what," in the environment or, as psychologist Randy Gallistel puts it, classical conditioning permits animals to learn "the causal texture of the world." In a way, what's learned is a predictive proposition of the form, "If *this* happens, then *that* will follow," or "If event A occurs, then event B will follow with some probability greater than zero" (Koenigshofer, 1990). For example, in Pavlov's experiment, dogs learned that if a bell "happens," then food will follow. The adaptive value of such learning is obvious. If an animal or human knows what is going to come next after the CS (a stimulus which is essentially acting like a signal of something adaptively important to follow), then the *prediction* or "hypothesis" can be used to make an adaptively appropriate response, in advance of the coming UCS. This response will be *preparatory* for the *anticipated* stimulus, improving adaptation to the coming event (the UCS) expected in the near future. If a chimpanzee observes that a specific facial grimace by a dominant male of its group is followed by an attack, then the next time the chimp observes this same grimace in this individual it can retreat to a safe distance or make gestures of appeasement to ward off an anticipated attack, which otherwise might result in serious injury. If a human suitor learns that a certain look in a potential partner indicates that a possible mating opportunity is imminent, then his body (well, especially a particular part of his body) responds in a way that increases his chances of reproduction as he anticipates what is likely to follow (an example of the classical conditioning of one of the sexual reflexes—with its circuitry in the spinal cord, just like other reflexes). As noted above, classical conditioning often involves modification of reflexes, something thought to be impossible before Pavlov's discoveries proved otherwise.

As John Watson's 1920 experiment demonstrated, *emotional responses* can also be modified by classical conditioning. Things in the world that are initially emotionally neutral (that are not associated with adaptively important information) can acquire emotional significance as a result of classical conditioning. If a man's mate puts on high heeled shoes each time before they have a sexual encounter, soon high heeled shoes will take on emotional significance because they have become predictive of an adaptively important event that regularly follows. If a boy hears a dog growling and then suffers a bite from the dog shortly thereafter, the sound of growling will in the future elicit the emotion of fear.

Classical conditioning often takes place beneath the level of conscious awareness even in humans. This suggests that it occurs in deep, more primitive parts of the brain, and is therefore, evolutionarily very old (evolved early in the evolution of animal life on earth). Psychologist Richard F. Thompson, formerly of the University of Southern California in Los Angeles, showed that conditioning of the eye blink reflex in rabbits takes place in the cerebellum, located in the older hindbrain, not in the more recently evolved cerebral cortex.

A personal experience of my own provides an example showing that classical conditioning of emotions can occur completely without awareness in humans. Many years ago, while I was walking to class, my head down reviewing my lecture notes, I unexpectedly had a powerful romantic response to a whiff of perfume, worn by a woman that I didn't even see, since she had already turned a corner to the other side of the classroom building by the time I "picked up the scent" and was able to look up to see who this wonderful woman was. After an hour or so of puzzlement about why I had experienced such strong emotions from such a brief olfactory stimulus coming from a woman whom I hadn't even seen, I then suddenly remembered that the perfume I had smelled was the same perfume worn by a former girl friend of mine whom I hadn't seen (or thought about) for over 10 years. One disembodied whiff of that perfume was enough to ignite in me all the intense passionate feeling I had for that girl friend (a Canadian, named "Vernaye") of so many years before—an example of a conditioned emotional response in me to an olfactory *conditional stimulus*, the perfume, which I associated with my former girl friend, even though I had no conscious awareness that such an association was forming ten years prior, or had been formed, until that day more than 10 years after the last time I had seen her, or smelled her perfume. The emotion was as intense and as fresh as it had been the last time I had smelled that perfume on my "mate" more than a decade earlier. I guess, in conventional language, many would say that I was obviously still "in love." And yet, we could argue that it was nothing more than classical conditioning, a classically conditioned emotional response (but maybe that's what much of passionate, sexual love is; more about what it is in a later chapter).

By the way, it is interesting to note that olfactory stimuli in humans (and many other species) are especially potent conditional stimuli for the conditioning of emotional responses. This is probably indicative of evolved circuit design in our limbic systems ("our emotional brain") reflecting the regular occurrence of emotionally salient events in conjunction with olfactory stimuli in our evolutionary past. Not only foods, feces, and rotting things have smells, but so do mates, and certainly each of these stimuli, and the olfactory stimuli they emit, have had important adaptive meanings to vertebrates like us since our evolutionary beginnings.

Some of you reading this book may have experienced classical conditioning of emotional responses by *visual* stimuli as well. Have you ever noticed how once you break up with a former lover that you start to see "his" or "her" car everywhere? You begin to have emotional responses to cars that you see that are similar to the car of the former lover, even though the former lover is never in them. The sight of cars that look like the car of the lover is enough to stimulate sometimes powerful emotional reactions—the heart races, your breathing rate increases, you look hard for the face of your former lover in the car, and then realize it isn't their car after all, just one that looks similar.

The Universal Law of Generalization and foundations of prediction and intelligence

This is an example of classical conditioning of emotion in humans, but it also illustrates an important phenomenon of conditioning, first discovered by Pavlov, known as *stimulus generalization*. What this means is that once you become classically conditioned to produce a conditional response (CR) to one particular stimulus (a particular CS, like the car of your ex-lover, in this case), you will then produce the same conditional (learned) response, although a bit weaker (in this case, an emotional response) to other *similar stimuli* (such as cars similar to the car of your ex-lover). This is the law of stimulus generalization. Furthermore, Pavlov discovered that the more similar a new stimulus is to the original conditional stimulus (CS), the stronger the conditional response to the new stimulus will be. Pavlov called this effect the *stimulus generalization gradient*.

Stimulus generalization is an exceedingly important functional property of brain circuit design because it permits an animal or human to form *categories* of stimuli (for example, those cars that might have the ex-lover in them, something adaptively important to you) and *to make predictions and inferences* about the likely adaptive significance of new things never directly experienced before (that is, inferences about new things similar to the original stimulus). For example, suppose a young seal is chased for the first time by a killer whale and is lucky enough to escape. The seal has learned to fear not only that particular killer whale but all similar stimuli—that is, all killer whales. This crucial information, and the circuit "design" for stimulus generalization which is built into the seal's brain and upon which this crucial information depends, is obviously of great adaptive significance for the seal. Based on a single experience with a single instance of the class of objects in the world that *we* know as killer whales, the seal has acquired *knowledge* about the whole category (called by philosophers, a "natural kind"), so that when the seal encounters another member of the category it *knows* what to do, even though it has never seen this *particular* killer whale before. Clearly then, stimulus generalization is an important component in intelligent behavior, involving the formation of inferences and their use to organize adaptive behavior about, and in anticipation of, future events or future states of the world. Brain circuit design that permits stimulus generalization must have been powerfully selected for in brain evolution.

Roger Shepard of Stanford argues that the requisite brain circuit design, which makes stimulus generalization an innate property of animal brains, evolved because of a fundamental and universal property of the natural world—in the world, *things that are similar tend to have similar adaptive consequences,* and so, for maximum adaptive benefit, similar things should be responded to in a similar way (Shepard, 1987b). The observation that things that are similar tend to have similar adaptive consequences is probably obvious to us when we think about it a little. We seem to know this *intuitively*—if the first apple we bite into tastes good, then probably other apples will generally also be good; if a bee stings us, then we are more cautious of all bees in the future; if we brush against a plant that is shiny with a particular characteristic shape and then later we break out in itchy red sores, we keep our distance from leaves with similar appearance in the future, and so on—but how do we know to generalize, *why* do we know to do this intuitively? What makes this understanding a part of our "common sense"? Well, this knowledge about how the world works (things that are similar tend to have similar adaptive consequences) is built into our brain circuit design by natural selection and is so deeply embedded into how our brains operate that we experience it as "common sense," we take it for granted. But brains didn't have to be organized this way. They might have entirely missed this general feature of the world. But they didn't. Brains are organized to maximally exploit this general feature of how the world works because of natural selection. Brain circuit designs that missed this important fact of the world would be weeded out, or more correctly, the DNA responsible for such inferior brain design would have been weeded out of the gene pool because animals which had such brains wouldn't survive and reproduce.

The *laws of stimulus generalization and stimulus generalization gradient* constitute not only general laws of learning, but also form general psychological principles governing the design of the *"cognitive architecture"* of brains—those aspects of brain design that produce cognition—perception, thought, and intelligence. The general rule is this: Things that are similar have similar adaptive consequences. This is a general, and rather abstract, feature of the world. And it is a feature of the world that has been persistently present for a very long time in the history of animal life on Earth. This sets up the conditions for genetic evolution to accommodate this feature of the world (the environment). Brain circuit "design" can be genetically evolved to exploit this adaptively significant feature of the world. That this has indeed happened is reflected in the fact that animal brains, in a stunningly wide range of species, are "designed" for generalization. And so, animals and humans recognize similarities among things in the world, form generalizations, and more or less automatically, often without intention or awareness, respond to things that are similar in similar ways. In other words, brain design reflects, and exploits, the general and rather abstract fact of the world, that things in the world that are similar in various critical features tend to have similar adaptive consequences. Again we see that *brain/mind design matches the adaptively significant features of the world.* This is the signature of natural selection at work.

One important source of the "knowledge" upon which intelligent behavior depends is *stimulus generalization* because it allows animals to make *adaptively useful predictions* about events and things in the world, more specifically about *categories* of things or events. For the seal, after one narrow escape from a predator it gains "knowledge" about the whole category of killer whales, permitting it to make the prediction when it sees its next killer whale that this one is likely to be as dangerous as the first one, and should be avoided at all costs. When the seal acts on this rule, this knowledge, about killer whales (a category), it is acting intelligently.

Note that these facts are perfectly consistent with the much broader law of psychological science that I discussed in the last chapter, the Law of Adaptation. The laws of *stimulus generalization* and *stimulus generalization gradient* follow this fundamental law (*organisms tend to behave in ways that promote the survival and reproduction of their genes*). Given natural selection as the origin of the extraordinary order in minds and behavior, the Law of Adaptation is an inevitability, and so are "design" features of the mind such as stimulus generalization and stimulus generalization gradient. Brain circuit "design" for stimulus generalization must have evolved early in brain evolution, and like other adaptive "design" features that work well, it has been extensively conserved over evolutionary time as species diverged, and so, as Shepard argues, it is essentially a universal in the animal kingdom. Because of this feature of mind "design," animal brains are programmed to form categories. Then from these categories, brain circuits make inferences, predictions, or expectations about these categories of things in the world. Such predictive generalizations act like rules in the mind guiding adaptive behavior. Brains extract countless such rules or principles about how the world works which can be drawn upon to deal with individual instances of events and objects as they are encountered in the future. Simply by correctly matching new things encountered in the world to one stored category or another, predictions about how best to respond are made without even having to think about it. Brain circuit "design" for stimulus generalization provides a mechanism whereby brains create a growing set of principles about how one's environment works. This set of predictive generalizations becomes the "knowledge" base of the animal or human used to form anticipatory, adaptive responses to the enormous number of things encountered, or which may be encountered, in the world. From these considerations, one begins to glimpse evolutionary origins of intelligence and begins to understand the way in which brains acquire knowledge—an ever expanding set of abstracted principles or generalizations about the adaptive meanings of things in the world and how best to respond to them. This is at the heart of what we mean by "intelligence."

General Forms of Learning vs. Specialized Forms of Learning in Nature

Classical conditioning is a form of learning found in a broad array of learning situations, and in a wide range of species, unlike the *adaptive specializations of learning* discussed earlier, which are each confined to a very specific learning situation, such as migration, requiring very specific information, such as where the celestial north is, and which occur in a single species, such as the Indigo Bunting. Classical conditioning, by contrast, is found in nearly every species ranging from insects and marine invertebrates all the way through the reptiles, birds, and mammals, including us. Stimulus generalization (and the stimulus generalization gradient) is also found broadly distributed throughout the animal kingdom. In this sense, classical conditioning and stimulus generalization are both "general" learning processes, both are "domain general" (present in many problem domains or learning situations), and species general.

Another form of learning that is "general" in this sense (across domains and across species), but simpler than classical conditioning, is *habituation*. Habituation means that when an animal or human is repeatedly exposed to an unchanging stimulus which has no adaptive significance for the animal, the response to the stimulus diminishes and eventually the animal *stops responding* to the repeated, adaptively insignificant stimulus all together (at least for a time). At that point, the animal is said to have *habituated* to the repeated stimulus. For example, if you gently poke a sea anemone it withdraws its tentacles. As you repeat this stimulus, it eventually stops responding to it completely, at least for a while. That's habituation. Or take a group of birds feeding along a roadside. At first, they fly away as a car approaches and then come back after the car has passed. As cars continue to periodically pass with no adverse consequence for the birds, they gradually learn that it is safe to ignore the passing traffic, and they no longer fly away when cars approach. They have habituated to passing traffic (note that this also involves stimulus generalization—if several cars can be safely ignored, then probably all cars can; note too that this is a "prediction" or tentative "hypothesis" by the birds, although it is very unlikely to be conscious; the birds act on the implicit prediction automatically). They have learned *not* to respond to an adaptively meaningless category of stimuli.

Habituation is feature of mind "design" which is highly adaptive. But one might wonder how can doing *nothing* be adaptive—how can doing nothing increase the chances of the survival and reproduction of one' genes (remember the Law of Adaptation)? Well, think of it this way. Organisms have limited resources, a finite amount of time, finite amounts of energy, and finite information processing capacities in their brains. Conserving these adaptively essential resources is exactly what habituation does. *Habituation* is so adaptive because it *is conservative*, it conserves or preserves the animal's limited resources; it prevents animals (and humans) from *wasting* time, energy, and limited information processing capacity of the brain on stimuli in the world that have been determined by experience to hold no adaptively significant information (that is, the thing habituated to has no import with regard to survival or reproduction). Think of the birds feeding at the roadside again. If they couldn't habituate, they would continue to fly off for no good (adaptive) reason indefinitely, endlessly wasting time and energy, unnecessarily flying away when they would be better off (adaptively speaking) not flying away, but instead continuing to use their limited time and energy to feed. We can readily see why habituation evolved. The bird that can habituate by virtue of its brain design is the one that is going to get the most food for the least amount of effort, compared to the bird that can't habituate. This is just the kind of situation that natural selection "thrives upon." Furthermore, once an animal (including the human kind) habituates to something, it becomes almost completely unaware of it, and since awareness is a kind of information processing that requires finite neural resources in the brain of the animal, habituation conserves this processing capacity too, freeing it up to process information about things with more adaptive significance. If the birds couldn't habituate to the adaptively meaningless passing traffic, they might easily miss more adaptively important information such as the sudden appearance of a predator such as a hawk, because they were unfortunately (from an adaptive standpoint) "distracted," that is, their finite reservoir of "attention" (the information processing capacity of their brains) had been "used up" on the non-adaptively significant stimuli associated with passing cars.

Boredom is a form of habituation of a higher order (with similar conservative functions). When you are bored, you have nothing available at the moment that is of sufficient adaptive significance to you to command your attention, your interest, your information processing resources. Significantly, this is frequently experienced as emotionally unpleasant, indicative of an innate exploratory instinct in us, an instinct to seek novelty and thus cognitive stimulation, to "exercise" our information processing resources, our "intellects," a testimony to how adaptively important information seeking and information processing is to an animal like us that depends so heavily upon behavioral adaptation, especially learned adaptive modifications of behavior. We are not only cognitively adapted to use acquired information, but we are emotionally designed for it as well. When you are bored, you "tune out" (that is, your brain "tunes out"); you are no longer responsive to the current set of stimuli; you have habituated. [This gives us some important clues about how to keep students interested in school. Subjects should be presented in ways that are adaptively significant to students in as immediate a way as possible. If you are trying to teach them math, make the math problems about sex, or dating, or being popular (if you assume X number of men and Y number of women in Hobokin County, how many combinations and permutations of sexual encounters can occur among them? If Fred is on a deserted island with 25 women with a mean age of 27 and a standard deviation of 1.8 years, what is the probability of him finding a woman on the island between the ages of 23 and 25?)].

One of the most important antidotes to habituation is *stimulus change* or *novelty*. A story from one of my students who had been in the submarine corps in the Navy illustrates. He said that when he was assigned to his first sub he had trouble sleeping because his bunk area was very close to the engine room. So, when he hit the sack, he was initially disturbed by the loud metallic clanging of the engines and couldn't sleep. However, after a few nights, yep, you guessed it, he habituated to the racket from the engines, to the point that he was barely even aware of the now familiar noise (which his brain had, without his awareness, determined to be without adaptive significance, and which thus could be safely ignored). He was able to sleep peacefully in spite of the loud clanging just on the other side of the bulkhead near his bunk. Now, what would wake him up was not the noise of the engines, but their *silence*. If the engines stopped, he immediately woke up, and became alert and "attentive" (the information processing resources of his brain became intensely focused) to the stimulus *change*. This is called *dishabituation*, the "undoing" of habituation, and it is also highly adaptive. The engines stopping could mean that something very important to survival and reproduction was happening or about to happen. Therefore, without even "thinking about it," the brain becomes alert, its information processing resources poised for action, to determine what if anything needs to be done (remember, brains are organized to produce adaptive action, goal-directed movement). After all, the engines might be stopping because something is wrong with them and the sub is on its way to the bottom and maybe there is something that can be done to prevent impending death. Or alternatively, the engines might be stopping because the sub has come into port, shore leave may be granted, and there might be a reproductive opportunity that most sailors wouldn't want to sleep through. Habituation to unchanging stimuli which have no adaptive significance, and *dishabituation* to stimulus change because it may signal adaptively significant events, are both *psychological adaptations* to long-term, persisting, general (and abstract) conditions of the world that impact survival and reproduction of one's genes (the Law of Adaptation again).

What are those long-term persisting conditions of the world that induced natural selection long ago for these features of mind design? Well, in a way, these are not so obvious, because they are abstract conditions, independent of most of the specific content of events. Here's what I mean. Habituation is a *psychological adaptation* that serves conservation of time, energy, and finite information processing capacities of the brain, put into action whenever an animal encounters objects or events in its environment that do not possess adaptive consequences for the animal. In the world of nature, in the details, this is a very diverse class of things, a category of things not specific to any particular set of *specific* features of stimuli, but rather to their general functional relationship to the animal, an adaptive one, or, in this case, lack thereof. Habituation occurs to things that do not have adaptive significance for the animal (or human)—a *relational* quality. Habituation is a form of learning, and it results in an adaptively useful *lack of response* to a whole class of stimuli in the world defined only by their lack of biological significance to an animal. This highly stable and long enduring, abstracted and general relational feature of an exceedingly large category of stimuli in the world sets the condition for natural selection to filter out brain circuit designs less fit to this condition, and to preserve those brain "designs" better fit, to adaptively exploit this abstracted "feature" of the world. This is very important, because what it shows is that natural selection can act not only on regularities or features of the world that have *specific* information content, such as the position of the north star, but natural selection can also act in response to *relational* features of the world that are regular over evolutionary periods of time at a more *abstracted level*, in the case of habituation, defined by the *abstract* category, "things that don't matter to my survival and reproduction and which therefore can be ignored without adverse adaptive consequence." And what is the adaptive response to stimuli of this abstracted category? "Tune out," cease responding, and therefore conserve valuable finite time, energy, and information processing capacity. An elegant design feature for any organism, and so it is no surprise that *habituation* should turn out to be *not only general, but universal*, in the animal kingdom, from sea anemones to President Obama. And, of course, similar arguments would apply to explain the evolution of brain circuit design that mediates dishabituation.

Notice that the arguments here are similar to Shepard's argument for a *universal law of generalization*—that generalization evolved ubiquitously throughout the brain designs of animals of diverse species because it is a genetic accommodation to a long-term, persisting, though abstracted ("content-independent" in the lingo of evolutionary psychologists) feature of the world, one which is common to all niches occupied by animals on the earth—-recall that this universal feature of the world is that things in the world that are similar on various dimensions or features tend to have similar adaptive consequences. "Things that go bump in the night" or make big noises of a particular growling quality, especially if they are bigger than we are, are likely to be dangerous, and have been throughout our evolutionary past. Things that smell "good" are probably like other things we have eaten before that smell "good" and which turned out in the past to be good sources of needed nutrients. If a particular vocalization by a monkey has signaled an approaching predator in the past, then it is likely that a similar call from another individual may also predict the approach of a predator. These examples show that stimulus generalization occurs across information processing domains in the brain, and so is a "domain-general" feature of mind design. For Pavlov's dog's, if one particular bell has reliably signaled the impending appearance of food, then similar sounding bells may have the same adaptive significance and therefore should be responded to similarly, that is, with a learned salivation response (the CR, conditional response, in Pavlov's terminology).

If additional information from the environment disconfirms the "hypothesis" or inference inherent in generalization (for example, if the new bell is *not* reliably followed by food), then *extinction*, or gradual disappearance of the learned salivation, the CR, to the new stimulus eventually follows. This leads to *stimulus discrimination*, learning to differentiate between similar stimuli which do not have the same adaptive consequences. In this case, one of the bells, the original CS, does reliably signal coming food, and so it makes adaptive sense for the animal to continue to salivate to this bell; but the new bell, a stimulus similar to the original CS, never does. Once the animal learns this, it stops responding, it stops salivating, to the new bell. Extinction is also highly adaptive because, *like habituation, extinction of a response to a stimulus that does not reliably predict a biologically significant event (such as occurrence of food) conserves the animal's finite time, energy, and information processing resources* by preventing an animal from continuing to respond uselessly to a stimulus which isn't going to lead to anything with adaptive significance. Again, as in habituation, time, energy, and the finite information processing capacities of the brain are conserved by extinction, and preventing such waste of valuable biological resources is going to promote survival and reproduction of the genes of the animal (or human) which is equipped with the requisite brain circuit "design."

In the case described here, stimulus discrimination leads to extinction of a response to a bell that doesn't reliably predict food, but stimulus discrimination in other conditions permits an animal to make adaptively crucial distinctions between similar stimuli which turn out to have different adaptive consequences. For example, one bell in Pavlov's lab might signal coming food, but Pavlov might set things up so that another similar bell, which initially would produce stimulus generalization and thus a salivation response, might be followed by a painful shock. In this case, rapid discrimination between these similar stimuli based on their very different adaptive significance would clearly be highly adaptive. Again, brain circuit design, and thus mind design, must accommodate such circumstances like these in the world. Brains must have circuit designs for stimulus generalization (probably as the initial default assumption or "hypothesis" built into their design), stimulus generalization gradient, stimulus discrimination, extinction, and habituation.

Evolution of Domain-general, content-independent learning, cognition, and intelligence ("g")

Here we can derive an exceedingly important principle about brain evolution and the evolution of "general" forms of learning, cognition (thinking processes), and intelligence. All of these terms refer to forms of biologically (i.e. genetically) constrained information processing operations "designed" to solve adaptive problems of greater or lesser generality and ubiquity, that is, to overcome obstacles to survival and reproduction that are more or less domain-general or domain-specific. The principle, which has yet to be widely recognized by psychologists and evolutionary biologists, is this: with regard to brain circuit design, *natural selection is "sensitive" to environmental regularities with adaptive importance even when those regularities only reach sufficient stability at levels of abstraction above the specific stimulus features of objects and events. Natural selection can select brain circuit design based on adaptively significant regularities of the world with varying degrees of statistical regularity (consistency) and at multiple levels of abstraction.* This is important because it permits natural selection to "design" cognitive and learning mechanisms of vary degrees of domain-specificity, from the highly domain-specific adaptive specializations of learning and cognition, such as the computations involved in bird migration or song acquisition in birds, to the abstracted domain-general psychological (information processing) mechanisms—such as habituation, dishabituation, classical conditioning, stimulus generalization, stimulus generalization gradient (based on the general and persisting feature of the world, across all ecological niches, that things that are more, or less, similar tend to have proportionately or probabilistically more, or less, similar adaptive consequences), extinction, stimulus discrimination (learning the adaptively significant differences between stimuli; roughly the opposite of stimulus generalization, and usually following it), general intelligence (often referred to by psychologists as the "g" factor), "improvisational intelligence" (Cosmides and Tooby, 2002) and others (see below).

This principle that natural selection is sensitive to regularities at multiple levels of abstraction, though perhaps difficult to grasp at first, is important because it gives us clues about how the more general (and more adaptively powerful) features of animal and human intelligence probably evolved. This principle recognizes that there are many regularities of the world that only achieve the required degree of regularity and stability for natural selection to operate upon them, to genetically accommodate them, when they are sufficiently abstracted away from the level of specific physical features toward the more abstract statistical and relational features of the world. At this more abstracted level of regularity, a more abstracted level of biologically significant information, in the world, emerges, sufficiently stable over long enough periods of time to permit natural selection the opportunity to pick out variations in brain circuit design progressively better suited to extraction and exploitation of the more abstracted informational features of the world. In short, using this principle we can understand the evolutionary origins of "general" intelligence (more detail about these arguments will follow in the final chapter of this book).

Suffice it to say here that evolutionary psychologists such as Cosmides and Tooby have found it difficult to understand how anything like "general" intelligence, or what they call "improvisational" intelligence, could have evolved (Cosmides and Tooby, 2002). They don't doubt that natural selection provides the answer but they can't see how selection could operate to produce such general cognitive capacities. However, the principle I state above, which I shall give the admittedly clumsy designation, the *Principle of Natural Selection at Multiple Levels of Abstraction and Degrees of Statistical Regularity, NS-MLASR*, can explain how circuitry evolved in brains that is "tuned" to detect and represent abstract relationships, such as causality, and relational features of the world such as occurs in classical conditioning, stimulus generalization, extinction, and habituation, independent of the specific stimuli in each kind of abstracted relationship (although in Chapter 8, we will discuss a "connectionist" model that may explain causality).

The principle above solves a mystery Cosmides and Tooby (2002) identify with regard to how "improvisational intelligence" evolved. It does so by hypothesizing that natural selection can operate on adaptively significant regularities of the world which emerge at multiple levels of abstraction. Thus, when variable events in the world have similar *relations* to one another, again and again in the environment, over very long periods of time, natural selection can select for brain circuit design that is responsive to the specific abstracted regular *relations* between events, independent of the specific stimuli involved, and in spite of their specific variability (irregularity). This occurs because the abstracted *relations* between variable stimuli reach sufficient levels of stability required for natural selection to fashion, over evolutionary time, the requisite circuit "design" sensitive to *relationships* between events without the circuitry being tied to specific events or event classes (Koenigshofer, 2002). This process of natural selection for mechanisms which accommodate abstracted properties of the world might explain how domain-general learning and cognitive mechanisms might have evolved in the form of PDP style networks (see discussion of vector coding and connectionism in the next chapter).

A Third General Form of Learning

A third form of learning that is "general" in the sense that it occurs in a broad range of learning situations ("domains") and in a broad range of species is *operant conditioning*, often described as the adaptive modification of voluntary behaviors by experience.

The most fundamental law of this "general" form of learning is called the *Law of Effect*. This law was first described by the American psychologist, Edward Thorndike, in 1911. The Law of Effect is simple—it states that the *effect of a voluntary response determines the likelihood (i.e. the probability) that the response will be repeated again in the future*. In short, if you do something and something pleasant follows, you tend to do it again. But, if you do something and something unpleasant follows, you tend not to do it again. In a nutshell, according to the *Law of Effect, the effect of a response determines its future probability*.

Operant conditioning and the Law of Effect are powerful adaptive mechanisms built by evolution into the "mind design" (and thus into the brain circuitry) of animals and humans. And, like classical conditioning, habituation, and their associated phenomena, operant conditioning is a "general" form of learning in the following ways: it is found in essentially all animal species, its laws are consistent across all instances of its occurrence regardless of species, and it occurs in a stunningly broad range of behavioral and learning situations involving a near universal set of non-reflexive ("voluntary") instrumental behaviors (behaviors which "accomplish" something for the animal, of course, in terms of its survival and the reproduction of its genes).

It is hard to overestimate how splendid this "design" feature of minds actually is. Operant conditioning permits animals and humans to generate behavioral adaptations to short-term, local, and even individually experienced events in the world, properties of the world that can't be accommodated by the slow processes of genetic evolution. And these adaptive responses organized by operant conditioning turn out to be adaptive *precisely because* they are guided by the principle that if you generate a "voluntary" behavior that is good for you and your genes, then, by virtue of the specifics of your brain circuit design, you will be rewarded by good *feelings*, subjective feelings of pleasure or happiness. A kind of contingency is set up by your brain/mind design that causes you to perform "voluntary" behaviors that lead to adaptive outcomes/effects (in more "primitive animals with much simpler brains consisting of many fewer neurons and much less complex circuitry, presumably no subjectively experienced feelings are involved, but innate circuit design, without feelings being involved, does the job—something like how the circuitry of a supermarket door makes it open when an approaching patron stimulates photo cells or puts pressure on sensors in a rubber pad immediately in front of the door; operant conditioning in bees or goldfish, for example, might be like this).

This happy consequence occurs because human brain design, and the brain design of other "higher" animals, evolved to contain, not just circuits for pain, but also circuitry for pleasure, located (as discussed in a previous chapter) in the *mesolimbic system* of the vertebrate brain, circuitry which includes neurons that originate in the *Ventral tegmental area (VTA)* of the midbrain and that terminate in the *Nucleus accumbens (NA)* and *amygdala*. Significantly, there exists, in addition, a *mesocortical circuit* which also originates in the VTA but projects connections to the *pre-frontal cortex which is known to be involved in "formation of short-term memories, planning, and strategy preparation for problem solving"* (Carlson, 2011, p. 102). Pleasure exists because it serves an essential biological function, not as a plot by the devil to test poor souls such as us. The brain (and thus life) not only has pain as part of its makeup, but also pleasure and happiness, because these emotions serve the biological purpose of telling us when we are engaging in voluntary behaviors that are good for us and our genes. And that feedback, the pleasant *feeling*, reinforces the adaptive behaviors, making them more likely to occur again in the future, thus driving "voluntary" behavior into adaptive directions. It is interesting to note here that both the *mesolimbic system* and the *mesocortical system* originate from the VTA and thus may be part of a larger circuit that is involved in the planning of future behavior and the preparation of strategies as part of what we experience as our own free will when we "voluntarily" select a plan of action from among various imaged ("imagined") alternatives as part of an IBOES information processing routine as described in Chapter 4. The mesolimbic reward system may participate in the evaluation of various response "choices" and help us select the best one, of course, "best" being measured in terms of adaptive consequences.

Of course, behaviors that we do that *aren't* good for us (and our genes), and our chances of survival and reproduction, generally result in some kind of pain, physical or emotional, with the consequence, if we are "psychologically healthy," that we reduce the frequency of such maladaptive behaviors in the future (remember the *Law of Adaptation* again; Koenigshofer, 1994b). The extent to which you, or any other animal, *doesn't* do this is a measure of your behavioral/psychological pathology. Psychologically healthy animals and humans behave according to the *Law of Adaptation*, that is, in ways that serve the survival and reproduction of one's genes (altruism— looking out for others over yourself—is not maladaptive or pathological when balanced with a healthy amount of self-interest; more about how *kin selection* evolved altruism and an adaptive balance between self-interest and altruism in a later chapter on our innate social nature and its accompanying "mind design"). The extent to which behavior violates the Law of Adaptation is a good measure or indicator of the extent to which the behavior in question is evidence for the presence of some form of psychopathology.

By these brain mechanisms of positive and negative feedback, experienced as good and bad *feelings*, our "voluntary" behavior is channeled into adaptive patterns, and yet doesn't have to be rigidly "programmed" beforehand by genetics, thus giving behavioral flexibility, while preserving the adaptive organization of behavior even without rigid, machine-like programming. As a result of this brain circuit design, reflected in the existence of the Law of Effect, we end up (if we are psychologically healthy) spending most of our time engaged in behaviors that are good for us and our genes, and relatively little time engaged in behaviors that are bad for us and our genes (to the extent that someone doesn't do this, they are demonstrating psychopathology). The Law of Effect thus drives adaptive responding to the environment while simultaneously maintaining the powerful adaptive advantages of response flexibility.

Notice that operant conditioning and the Law of Effect precisely follow the Law of Adaptation. The Law of Effect is just one instance of this more general law. Both operant conditioning and its Law of Effect are organized to produce behavior, in this case, learned "voluntary" behavior, which promotes survival and reproduction of one's genes. The "mind design" and behavior of "survival machines" like us, and other animals, serve the genes, as discussed in the previous chapter, but in an incredibly elegant way. Thus, these psychological principles, derived from the principles of evolution by natural selection, explain some of the deepest, even philosophical, questions about the nature of life—why does life inevitably involve both pleasure, happiness, and other "good" feelings, as well as pain, unhappiness, and other "bad" feelings. "That's life" because our "mind design," by biological necessity, must include circuitry for both types of *feeling* in order to provide animal (and human) brains a mechanism for the adaptive guidance of "voluntary" behavior which tunes it to the adaptive demands of the rapidly fluctuating and local conditions of the environment, including the social environment in the social species, like us.

Like phenomena of classical conditioning, the phenomena of operant conditioning follow the Law of Adaptation, and thus have evolved as specific adaptations to specific regularities of the world, and, as in the case of classical conditioning, the regularities are abstracted away from specific physical features of stimuli or events, but instead involve abstracted, *relational* regularities. *Operant conditioning, like classical conditioning, involves learning predictive relationships between events* in the world. It's just that the types of events in each case are different. In classical conditioning a probabilistic predictive relationship (a correlation, a co-variation, a predictive contingency, a conditional probability) is learned between two stimuli, a CS and a UCS, a signal and an innately adaptively significant stimulus. If event A occurs, then event B will follow with some probability greater than zero. Likewise, in operant conditioning, a predictive contingency, or conditional probability (if I *do* this, then *that* will follow with some probability greater than zero), is learned between a behavior and the outcome or effect of the behavior. In both cases, the animal is learning about "what leads to what" in the world. If event A occurs, then event B is likely to follow. In classical conditioning, if CS, then UCS is likely to follow. In operant conditioning, if I do behavior A, then effect or consequence B is likely to follow. These two types of conditioning permit animals and humans to learn, and thus to map, the "causal texture" of the world, including oneself, one's own actions, as causal agents within that causal texture of the environment.

For example, let's take a look at what psychologists refer to as *schedules of reinforcement*. As already discussed, when an animal or human does something beneficial to it and its genes, usually, by virtue of the brain's evolved circuit design, a pleasant feeling will follow. This is called *reinforcement* by psychologists because the pleasant feeling reinforces or strengthens the likelihood that this behavior will be repeated in the future under similar circumstances. Why?

First, because objects, events, and circumstances that are similar tend to have similar adaptive consequences—remember Shepard's *universal law of generalization*, itself a genetic accommodation evolved to an enduring, although abstract, property of the world—things that are similar, tend to have similar adaptive consequences and should therefore be responded to similarly. This principle is built-in as a default assumption in the "mind designs" of animals and humans because as a default information processing "assumption" it will maximize adaptive benefit (unless additional information from specific experience calls for stimulus discrimination).

Thus, we can derive a general principle about brain and mind "design." *Brain circuit design (and the resulting "mind design"), by virtue of natural selection, tracks and "maps" into neural representations in brain circuitry those enduring properties of the world that have adaptive significance.* In simpler terms, brain and mind design reflect the facts of the world because natural selection is the source of the design. In this case, the enduring property of the world is the fact that if a behavior in the past has led to pleasant consequences, then it is likely that the same behavior in the future will also lead to pleasant consequences, under similar environmental conditions. This specific example of a kind of order or regularity in the world is incorporated into the circuit design of the brain, by natural selection, and reflects this orderliness or regularity of the world.

Secondly, "good" feelings obviously are, by definition, desirable, and organisms, by their innate wiring, *by virtue of natural selection for that wiring*, "seek out" sources of pleasure, that is, they close the distance between themselves and sources of pleasure (those stimuli which activate the brain's pleasure circuitry because those stimuli are good for the genes which that brain "belongs" to). By virtue of this wiring "design," the following "program" is set in place: if something in the world, a stimulus, or my own behavior, is good for me and my genes, "good" or "positive" feelings (pleasure or happiness or joy, etc) will occur when, or shortly after, that stimulus or behavior occurs, and "good" feelings make me, by my wiring design, seek out that stimulus or repeat that behavior again in the future. The consequences for my genes (and for my behavior) are clearly adaptive. The genes are served by the fact that the brain and "mind design" of their "survival machine" *makes* the "survival machine" behave according to the Law of Adaptation, and the genes increase their chances of "survival" and reproduction as a result. *Genes and their evolution drive "mind design"toward adaptive organization, which drives adaptive behavior which, in turn, serves survival and reproduction of the genes carried by the organism.*

In schedules of reinforcement we have a situation that mimics the fact that in the world reinforcement may or may not follow an adaptive response every time the response is made. This is just the way the world works. For example, you might compliment your girlfriend. Sometimes she reinforces you with a kiss or a hug, but this kind of pleasant outcome doesn't follow every time you compliment her. This is an example of the fact that not all events and event-compounds (one event regularly followed by another) in the world occur with perfect regularity, but instead involve conditional *probabilities, rather than absolute certainties.* This leads us to the hypothesis that animals will accommodate this statistical fact of the world and will evolve mechanisms to assess and respond to probabilities.

A *conditional probability* exists when an event A increases the chances that another event, event B, will occur, but the probability is not 100%, but is still greater than zero. The natural world is full of conditional probabilities. This is just the way the world is structured as a few examples will illustrate. The presence of clouds increases the chances of rain but doesn't guarantee it. When a mouse sees a cat, the chances increase that the cat will chase the mouse, but the sight of the cat doesn't guarantee this outcome. If a chimpanzee threatens another chimp of lower status in the social group, the lower status chimp will likely show signs of submission and tactfully move away, but again, there is no absolute guarantee that it might not do something else. If a beautiful woman smiles and puts her hand in a man's, he may favorably assess his chances that a reproductive opportunity may be in the offing, but it may or may not follow in actual fact. Still, all other factors being equal, these behaviors by the woman increase the chances (the probability rises) that something leading to sexual behavior is going to follow, at least, at some point down the line. If a predator looks intently in your direction, the chances increase that it may be looking at you for dinner, but it may turn and walk away in search of other prey. If you say flattering things to an interviewer, who is considering you for a job, your chances of getting the job may be increased, but again, the chances are certainly less than 100% that you will get the job or even that the flattery will help much, if at all. The world is full of such situations involving conditional probabilities, and frequently the assessment of conditional probabilities is adaptively useful, and sometimes crucial. Brains are "designed" to assess and adaptively respond to such probabilities. (How brains might do this is still unknown, but understanding how the brain does this may involve larger issues of how the brain codes or represents the world in all of its subtle complexity. We will take this up in a later chapter when we discuss "vector coding" in detail).

Schedules of reinforcement, like any other schedule, tell you when something is going to happen. Schedules of reinforcement tell an animal when reinforcement is going to occur. In the simplest schedule of reinforcement, called *continuous reinforcement*, reinforcement or reward, and the pleasant feelings thereby activated, follows every time a target response is made (and is thus maximally *predictable*). For example, B. F. Skinner (1953), the Harvard psychologist who studied operant conditioning extensively in the laboratory, used a "Skinner Box" or operant conditioning chamber. In the box is a lever or button which an animal presses and then reinforcement, such as a small amount of food or water, may or may not be delivered into a small bowl in the box each time the animal responds correctly. In the case of a continuous reinforcement schedule, a rat in the Skinner box would be given a pellet of food every single time it presses the lever in the box.

In another class of reinforcement schedules called *partial reinforcement*, the rat would *not* receive food reward every time it lever presses but only part of the time following a lever press. If it received food reinforcement on a fixed ratio, such as one pellet of food every other lever press, we would say that it is on a *fixed ratio schedule of partial reinforcement* (designated FR 1:2, one food reinforcement for each two "correct" responses, i.e. lever presses, and we might have other variations such as FR 1:3, FR 1:7 and so on). In another variation on partial (or discontinuous) schedules of reinforcement, the ratio of food rewards to lever presses varies over time (called a *variable ratio schedule, VR*) and thus becomes much less predictable for the animal. Yet, animals continue to respond by making lever presses, and actually produce lever presses with just as great a frequency as rats (or other animals) on a fixed ratio schedule of reinforcement. In both cases, rats or other animals from pigeons to raccoons to cats, dogs, monkeys and apes, and even human children, in a broad range of operant conditioning situations, engage in continuous high rates of responding on these schedules of reinforcement (FR and VR). Clearly the laws of operant conditioning are "universal" across a wide range of species and a wide range of behaviors, and this suggests common brain design and thus common "mind design" across species, another example of Darwin's continuity of species manifested in laws of psychology.

Psychology is not only explained by Darwin's theory of evolution, but it offers support for Darwin's hypothesis of the continuity of species due to common ancestry. And something fascinating is revealed about brain evolution—many brain circuit designs which apparently evolved fairly early in more "primitive" species worked so well that these design features were conserved, or retained, in the brains of the more recently evolved animal species including the mammals such as rats, mice, dolphins, sea lions, killer whales, lions and tigers, elephants, monkeys, apes, and us. Evolution, including brain evolution, doesn't discard things that work, but conserves successful adaptive designs and builds upon them, and often overlays them with additional complexity where complexity pays off in terms of adaptation, while still retaining earlier design features that continue to work well (i.e. that increase successful adaptation). In brain design this is evident in the fact that old brain structures found in primitive vertebrates are not lost but are retained in the brain designs of newer, more recently evolved, and more complex species. We have many of the same brain structures that lizards and birds and rats possess. We just have a lot of new tissue on top of these older (in evolutionary terms) brain structures; mostly we have a lot of cerebral cortex overlaying these older, sub-cortical brain structures (sometimes called the "reptilian brain").

Another variation on partial reinforcement, which mimics some reinforcement contingencies found in the real world, are the *interval schedules of partial reinforcement* in which reinforcement is presented after a time interval has passed just as long as the animal has responded with a lever press (or other "correct" response) within the interval since the last reinforcement. A common example of an interval schedule of reinforcement in modern human life is a monthly paycheck (you get that reinforcement, your paycheck, as long as you show up and perform certain "correct" behaviors during that month—otherwise you get fired and so no paycheck).

Just as is the case with ratio schedules of partial reinforcement, there are two sub-varieties of interval schedules, fixed and variable (the pay check example illustrates a fixed interval schedule). Consider a rat in a Skinner box. In a *fixed interval schedule* of partial reinforcement (FI) of let's say 30 seconds (FI 30), a reinforcement such as food is presented every 30 seconds to the animal just as long as it has made at least one correct response, such as the lever press in the Skinner box, in the prior 30 second interval. In FI schedules, with enough training, we get an unusual pattern of responding called *scalloping*. In scalloping, the animal eventually learns to put off responding for as long as possible and to do the minimum required to get the maximum reward or reinforcement available in this particular environmental contingency, represented by the fixed interval schedule. The animal on an FI schedule of partial reinforcement learns to *procrastinate and to do the minimum required* because this is the most adaptive thing to do given the reinforcement contingencies in the environment in which the animal finds itself (that is, it is adaptive not to waste effort that will get you nothing in return, so there is a natural tendency to procrastinate and to do the minimum). Notice here that laziness is not a "personality trait" but a pattern of behavior that is actually adaptive, under certain circumstances of reinforcement. Doing *more* than the minimum has no adaptive payoff (i.e. won't result in any additional reward) and neither does responding early. But doing too little will result in loss of rewards. Even rats, given enough time, can learn this fact about their environment (in this case a laboratory environment) and adjust their response pattern accordingly, so that their behavior accurately tracks the reward contingencies in the environment, yielding the maximum reward available for the least amount of effort (an adaptive strategy because it conserves time and energy). It makes perfect adaptive sense to delay responding for as long as possible and to work (at lever pressing) just hard enough to maximize reward while conserving as much time and energy as the reinforcement contingencies in the environment permit.

It is as if the animal's brain has come equipped with behavioral control mechanisms that fine tune the timing and magnitude of effort that the organism expends, to the extent possible utilizing the information available from the environment. This can't be accidental, and most likely reflects the survival advantages of conserving the finite time and energy resources of the organism, while maximizing available reinforcement. Clearly, waste of such precious resources would be inefficient and thus maladaptive, and would be selected against as natural selection filtered through alternative brain circuit designs over eons of evolutionary time. It seems that brains and "mind designs" have incorporated an *efficiency principle* or a principle of conservation of biologically important resources, such as time, energy, and information processing capacity. In fact, stimulus generalization, category formation, and concept formation can be understood as manifestations of this same general principle of "mind design." Evolved brain circuit design has been refined by natural selection to an extraordinary degree to give animals (and humans) the capacity to precisely track the reinforcement contingencies in the world—an ability with obvious survival value in the struggle for existence. Such "mind design" seems almost inevitable as natural selection sifted through alternate circuit designs over the course of brain evolution in animals and humans.

We see this same *efficiency principle* operating in *variable interval schedules* of partial reinforcement. In VI schedules, the interval after which reinforcement is going to appear, and thus the interval that passes before at least one "correct" response is required for reward, varies unpredictably for the animal. Under these conditions, to maximize reward, the animal must maintain continuous high rates of responding (making lever presses without pausing) or miss many opportunities for reinforcement. As long as the rewards aren't too few and far between, such a response pattern, given a variable interval response contingency, maximizes reward and so maximizes fitness, since rewards are rewarding because they have biological value (such as food, water, or increase in one's status in the social group). And, as predicted, continuous high rates of responding is just what animals learn to do under *variable interval reinforcement schedules* (and *variable ratio schedules* as well, wherein appearance of reward following "correct" response is just as unpredictable for the animal).

The phenomenon of *operant extinction* is another case which illustrates this same *behavioral efficiency and conservation of the animal's time and energy resources. Operant extinction* refers to the observation that once reinforcement for a behavior is discontinued, the operant ("voluntary") behavior gradually decreases in frequency and eventually disappears altogether. For example, if a rat has learned to press a lever in a Skinner Box because the behavior is reliably followed by a pellet of food, then if the food reward is discontinued after lever presses, the rat soon stops pressing the lever. It is smart enough not to work for free. In other words, it has a brain design that makes it this way—that makes it "smart" in this regard. Continuing to engage in behavior that once led to reward, but which no longer does, is wasteful of time and energy, and prevents switching to new behaviors that might produce more adaptive outcomes. The fact that extinction is built into the "mind design" of animals as diverse as octopuses and people, and all the species in between, shows that natural selection can be very good at weeding out brain designs that are inefficient in conserving the finite time and energy of the organism, thus preserving brain designs characterized by greater efficiency, toward maximizing adaptive advantage.

Natural selection has designed behavioral control systems that produce surprising efficiency in the organization of behavior. Thus, even in these fine details of behavior observed when animals adjust their activity to meet specific schedules of reinforcement in the environment, including the disappearance of reinforcement altogether, the laws of operant conditioning shape patterns of behavior which accurately map the reward contingencies present in the environment, thus maximizing behavioral efficiency and adaptive benefit. This outcome contributes to the chances of survival and reproduction of genes, thus creating conditions for the evolution of the requisite brain circuit "design" that represents these laws of behavior.

One other phenomenon of operant conditioning brings the point home. When reinforcement for a behavior is stopped, and the behavior begins to go into extinction, the *rate* of extinction will vary depending upon the reinforcement schedule the animal was on. This involves the concept of *resistance to extinction*. The longer it takes the animal to stop responding, once reinforcement is discontinued completely, the greater the resistance to extinction. The general law is this: the less predictable the reinforcement the animal is exposed to during learning, the longer it will take the response to go into extinction once reinforcement for the response has ceased all together. Thus, partial schedules of reinforcement produce greater resistance to extinction, and the variable schedules of partial reinforcement (VR and VI), because of the unpredictability of the reinforcement they entail, produce the greatest resistance to extinction.

To understand this more easily, put yourself in the place of a rat in a Skinner Box. Assume a schedule of continuous reinforcement while you were learning to lever press for food. In this reward contingency, you press the bar, and you get the food, each and every time. Now, when, for some reason, in your "little Skinner Box world," lever presses are no longer followed by food—you are able to notice very quickly that things have changed. You used to get food every time you pressed the lever. You press now, and you don't get food. The rules have apparently changed. "Hey, what's going on here?" You (still the rat) make a few quick test lever presses, and still no food. "Damn" in rat talk. Rats in this situation are often observed to hit the lever with their paws with greater force, either to test the thing to see if it just needs a more vigorous and forceful whack, or they are just downright frustrated and express their frustration the same way we might. "Hey, I am playing by your rules, and now you do this!! How dare you, you damned cruel world!!" You whack the lever hard out of frustration—a natural adaptive response to a perceived obstacle preventing you from obtaining some adaptive outcome that you expect (itself an element of adaptive brain circuit design involved in emotion); sometimes more vigor of response motivated from the inner rage of frustration *does* work to get you what you want (that's why natural selection has designed brains that way), but not this time. Whacking the lever harder doesn't work, and so you (still the rat) stop responding very quickly.

Now, by contrast, assume that you (still the rat) were trained on a variable ratio schedule of partial reinforcement instead of continuous reinforcement. Because of your training on this partial schedule of reinforcement wherein reinforcement comes irregularly and unpredictably following correct responses (sometimes one or two lever presses are required to get reward, sometimes 10 or 15; you never know), once reinforcement stops all together, it takes you much longer to notice and to figure out that the rules have changed. You have become accustomed to lever pressing and often not being rewarded right away and you are accustomed to unpredictably. In this case, you continue to lever press longer after reinforcement (food following lever press) has been suspended all together. You are showing greater *persistence of responding* in the absence of any further reward, you are showing greater *resistance to extinction*.

This is similar to a salesman who never knows when his next sale (and therefore his next commission; reinforcement) is coming. On this variable ratio (VR) schedule of reinforcement (i.e. the salesman never knows how many sales pitches he will have to make before he gets rewarded with a sale and commission) the salesman will continue to respond (making sales pitches and sales calls) for a long time without reinforcement. That's *resistance to extinction*. Note that in rat or human, it is the schedule of reinforcement that determines the pattern of responding.

Note again, that your behavior (you are still the rat), persistence of responding in the Skinner Box in this case, is not due to your admirable character (after all you are a rat), but instead it is an effect produced by the schedule of reinforcement that you have been exposed to in your environment. Skinner was fond of pointing out that what looked like a personality trait or a character trait in someone (not just rats now), really could be more adequately explained by examination of the schedule of reinforcement that their environment was subjecting them to, rather than to any traits of personality (but remember, Skinner was a behaviorist, and favored *tabula rasa* ideas and would not have looked to genetic dispositions in personality, or of any sort, for causes of behavior).

Now the lesson from these examples involving resistance to extinction is that the brain and *mind design* of animals permits them to 1) use available information from the environment to *learn rules* about reward contingencies, 2) to effectively use these rules to organize behavior that is adaptively efficient, and then when conditions change, 3) animals can find the information, that is available to them in the environment, to *adaptively modify* their behavior to preserve its efficiency in light of the new conditions—i.e. the new "rules" governing the distribution of rewards in the environment. And Skinner showed that this happens in rats and pigeons and monkeys, not just in people. In short, animals have brain and mind "designs" that make them very good at *tracking the reward contingencies* in the world, an adaptively crucial requirement for a successful brain design.

This makes eminently good sense in terms of evolution. Rewards are things in the world that have biological value to an animal, such as food, water, access to mates, status in the group, and so on. Obviously, it is imperative to survival and reproduction that animals have brain and mind "designs" that make them acutely able to track availability of rewards and to understand what's required to get them. Life itself depends upon this sort of information processing by brains to guide the appropriate adaptive behavior required by the environment. We can expect that natural selection has precisely "designed" brain circuitry to be very good at this sort of thing and that the circuit designs that do this best would have been preserved, again and again, in the brain evolution of a great diversity of animal species—from octopus and goldfish, to the great variety of birds, to whales and dolphins, lions and elephants, and to the primates— prosimians, monkeys, apes, and humans. It should be noted (and the reader may have already figured this out) that brain and mind "design" are not only evolved to be very good at understanding reward contingencies in the environment (if I do this behavior, I will likely get that reward), but these brain and mind "designs" are also, by adaptive necessity, extremely good at understanding contingencies of pain and punishment in the world (if I do this behavior, I will receive that pain or punishment). As we shall see in a later chapter, as I have hinted earlier in several places, the information processing by brains involved in these kinds of computations results in what we experience as emotions.

Lest we fail to understand the universality of the laws of operant conditioning, think of the following example. From experiments with rats pressing levers in Skinner Boxes we learn that the *least predictable schedules of partial reinforcement (VR and VI) produce the greatest resistance to extinction.* But this is true not just for rats in Skinner Boxes. Think of slot machines in Las Vegas. Here, lever *pulling*, not lever pressing is the behavioral response of interest. Knowing what you know about schedules of reinforcement and resistance to extinction, what schedule of reinforcement would you program into slot machines in Vegas if you wanted to produce the greatest resistance to extinction in your human patrons (in order to make them keep gambling with as little pay out as possible, in order to increase casino profits)? Well, to maximize resistance to extinction of the lever *pulling* response in humans, who have planted themselves in front of slot machines in Vegas, you would use the same schedule of reinforcement as you used for rats lever *pressing* in Skinner Boxes—a variable ratio or variable interval schedule. And it works just as well on humans, for the creation of continuous high rates of responding and increased resistance to extinction, as it does in rats. A few small payoffs distributed unpredictably here and there (and of course make these payouts noisy and marked with flashing lights for the "benefit" of fellow gamblers) and you produce continuous high rates of responding (furiously dropping silver dollars into the slots and *pulling*) and if the rewards aren't coming for a period of time, well, then you get just what you want from these unpredictable schedules of reinforcement in order to boost your casino profits, great *resistance to extinction*. And it is not just in slot machines, it is the stock market, and romantic attraction to the lover who is less predictable in his or her distribution of the rewards of love, and in all sorts of other human (and animal) activities. The laws of operant conditioning appear to be universal.

The fact that the laws of operant conditioning are the same in an extraordinarily wide range of animal species, and across a wide range of operant ("voluntary") behaviors, demonstrates another general principle of brain/mind design: that *the basic features of the brains and "mind designs" of species, spanning an enormous range of the animal kingdom, must be strikingly similar.* How could the laws of operant conditioning be so universally similar across species unless the brain organization that makes operant conditioning possible in all of these animals was essentially the same? Once again, we see in the psychology (and underlying brain design) of animals and humans, extraordinary evidence for Darwin's profound hypothesis of the *continuity of species*, derived, as he astutely recognized, from their *common ancestry* (an idea also confirmed by modern molecular genetics and the mapping of the genomes of various species). The stunning beauty of Darwinian theory, that makes it capable of explaining, and bringing order, to so much in nature, is mind-boggling. As my six-year old son, Johnny says, it is a Darwinathon!

This kind of impressive accuracy and efficiency of animal brains in tracking the reward and punishment contingencies in operant conditioning situations in nature, across a wide range of species, is just what we might predict from psychology's first fundamental, and universal law, the *Law of Adaptation*—organisms tend to behave in ways that promote survival and reproduction of their genes. To do this, natural selection has weeded out brain designs over evolutionary time that failed to follow this overarching law—in this case, those designs that failed to accurately and efficiently track the contingencies of reward and punishment in the natural world and organize behavior accordingly. Successfully tracking such contingencies is one of the key features of what we call intelligence and is a key function of learning. And tracking and anticipating the contingencies of reward and punishment, further and further into one's own individual future, and organizing present behavior accordingly, is at the root of more advanced forms of intelligence involving planning, choice, and "free will." In fact, one way to view intelligence is to think of it as the capacity to mentally track, and plan behavior for, anticipated contingencies of reinforcement and punishment further and further into future time. As noted in an earlier chapter, lions hunting together have been observed in the wild to cooperate to set up ambushes of unsuspecting wildebeest. This high order of intelligence depends upon understanding the contingencies of reward on the plains of Africa and how best to plan and cooperate in order to successfully exploit them, and this must involve the anticipation of future, even in lions as they set up an organized ambush.

Content-independent learning and cognition

Adaptive patterns of behavior in response to various schedules of reinforcement and to complete cessation of reinforcement (in the case of operant extinction) are just a couple of examples which show that natural selection has been able to organize brain circuitry, and "mind design," to genetically accommodate some very abstract, "domain-general," regularities of the world. That is, the usefulness of regulating one's effort and distributing it to maximize adaptively significant rewards from the environment, over time, is a hallmark of intelligent and healthy behavior in an enormously broad range of environmental conditions and adaptive problems, and in a stunningly broad range of species.

This suggests that natural selection, acting over the course of evolution on brain circuit design, is also responsible for other abstract information processing ("mental") capacities of brains, such as the ability to detect cause and effect, to assess the predictability and conditional probability of events, and to readily recognize co-variation of events (i.e. circuit design that allows animal and human brains to understand that some things in the world predict other things; that is, things in the world "go together," they are correlated, they co-vary, and that some events *cause* other events in the world). These capacities are so readily performed by our brains that we take them for granted and don't bother to ask why we are so good at such abstractions. But it is precisely the fact that we are so good at such complex information processing feats that should stimulate our interest and lead us to suspect that natural selection has equipped brains with circuit designs that are precisely tuned for these capabilities. Things that are easy for us *are* easy because our brains were evolved to do such things efficiently. Brains, especially those characterized by high intelligence, show the capacity for readily finding correlation, covariance, and cause and effect in the world, and then using such "knowledge" to adaptively organize behavior. As mentioned earlier, Rutgers psychologist, Randy Gallistel, put it this way—conditioning (both classical and operant) allows animals to learn "the causal texture of the world." This capacity for learning predictive co-variation between events, that one event reliably predicts another, as in conditioning, is an essential ingredient in the mix of mental abilities that we call intelligence.

But note this. This ability to find and "understand" predictive relationships between things in the world is highly abstract. This ability is abstract in the sense that the brain has been "tuned" by natural selection, over the course of evolution, to find *"if-then" predictive relationships* (if *this* happens, then *that* will probably follow) between events of almost *any* type. This more "general" or "content-independent" form of learning contrasts with *adaptive specializations of learning* which are restricted to *specific* classes of events, such as taste and illness, as in *taste aversion learning* in omnivores, or the locations of stars in learning to find a reliable navigation beacon for migration.

In classical and operant conditioning the brain must be utilizing some *circuit design features* which are very general in their scope such that almost *any kind* of object or event (CS) or behavior (any voluntary behavior) can be recognized by the brain as predictably co-varying (correlated, or even causally related) with any other kind of object, event or operant ("voluntary") behavior. Stated in another way, in conditioning, animals are learning an *if-then predictive relationship* (if *this* happens then *that* will predictably follow) using brain learning mechanisms wherein the specific events themselves don't matter, what matters is the *relationship* between the events. In other words, the brain mechanism for this kind of learning is "tuned" by natural selection to find, in the world, and record in the brain, predictive *relationships* between events, but, in doing so, this learning mechanism is *not* selectively "tuned" to the specific events themselves that are involved, *but is open to a wide variety of stimuli and events as long as they are* in predictive *relationship with one another*. It is the abstract *relationship* between events that matters, not the events themselves (see chapter 10). The number and kinds of events that can be thus recognized as being in predictive relationship with one another, where one event reliably (but usually not perfectly) predicts the occurrence of the other, is, for all practical purposes, near limitless (however, even here there are some evolved genetic constraints—for example, animals don't learn taste-shock contingencies nearly as well as they learn external stimulus-shock contingencies, nor do they learn pairings of sound or color, "bright, noisy water," with illness).

Classical and operant conditioning are "general" in this sense, or more technically, these forms of learning are said to be "content-independent" or "domain-general" forms of learning, using the terminology of evolutionary psychologists. This sort of learning is called "content-independent" learning not because the animal or human is learning *nothing*. In fact, the animal *is* learning something, and something very important, in "content-independent" forms of learning. The animal is learning a specific kind of *relationship* of exceedingly important adaptive value, but the relationship being learned can exist between a very broad range of stimuli (notwithstanding the constraint against learning contingencies between taste and exteroceptive pain, such as shock, noted above).

In classical and operant conditioning, brains are constantly learning "rules" of the general form "if *this* happens, then *that* will likely follow"; they learn predictive relationships, contingencies or correlations between events in the world (between two stimulus events in classical conditioning, and between one's own "voluntary" behaviors and their effects in operant conditioning) (Koenigshofer, 1995b). In both types of conditioning, animals are learning "what predicts what" in the environment, and they can even learn something about the probability that such predictions hold true. It is this sort of information that builds what we call "knowledge" about the world, and from which "intelligent" behavior begins to emerge.

The mechanism in the brain for this kind of learning about "what predicts what" in the world may have some very general features and some very general, even abstract, principles governing it. Recall, from a prior chapter, that Canadian neuroscientist, Donald Hebb proposed, in his 1949 book *The Organization of Behavior* that "Neurons that fire together, wire together." This is a proposal about a mechanism for learning at the level of neurons in the brain that is very much alive today, with several lines of evidence in neuroscience supporting it, and it might be general enough to form a possible basis for learning predictive associations between objects, events, and behaviors in the natural environment.

However, as several psychologists have pointed out, conditioning is more than just simple *association*, governed by simple temporal contiguity (Rescorla, 1988; Koenigshofer, 1996c; Gallistel, 1995). Instead, animals learn predictive *contingencies* between events, or more technically, they learn *conditional probabilities* (if event A happens, what is the probability that event B will then occur?). According to evolutionary psychologist, Randy Gallistel, classical and operant conditioning are not general forms of learning at all, but "from a mathematical perspective, they are examples of problems in multivariate, non-stationary time series analysis. They are time series problems because what the animals are learning is the temporal dependence of one event on another" (Gallistel, 2000). Here, I agree with Gallistel that both classical and operant conditioning can be conceived as learning the "temporal dependence of one event on another." This is most certainly true and I have argued elsewhere that animals really are learning about temporal regularities between events when they become conditioned (Koenigshofer, 1995b). I also agree that conditioning may be conceived as a specific adaptive problem thus making conditioning, almost by definition, an adaptive specialization rather than a "general" (domain-general) form of learning, but the adaptive problem, is one whose content is about a relationship between events, not about specific events, and it is widely distributed throughout the animal kingdom and throughout a wide range of situations.

Thus, conditioning is clearly a form of learning much more general in nature than learning the night sky or song acquisition in birds, taste aversion learning, or human language acquisition. Conditioning is found across a far wider range of species, learning situations, and behaviors. Thus, all hinges on definition of terms, on what is meant by the term, "general." Perhaps domain-general and domain-specific should be viewed as two ends of a continuum not as absolute, all or none, distinctions. Certainly classical and operant conditioning are far more domain-general and content-independent than adaptive specializations of learning such as navigation by ants by landmarks, navigation by the night sky by Indigo Buntings, imprinting, and song acquisition by birds. Although by Gallistel's argument classical and operant conditioning both solve a problem in time series analysis, the problem being solved is only a *specific* problem if we conceptually "collapse" over the specific stimuli involved in each case of conditioning and focus instead on the abstracted relational aspects of the problem being solved by the animal in each instance of conditioning—the detection and representation of a conditional probability between events in the world. Just as Indigo Buntings learn by a highly domain-specific learning mechanism, unique to the Indigo Bunting brain, to navigate while plying three dimensional space during migration, animals learn by a more general learning mechanism found widely in the brains of animals throughout the animal kingdom to "navigate" the "causal space" of the world, piece by piece, conditioning experience by conditioning experience. And, using general mechanisms such as stimulus generalization, stimulus generalization gradient, habituation, extinction, and stimulus discrimination, knowledge of the world is built up, guiding adaptive behavior in service of the survival and reproduction of genes.

But how could natural selection work over the course of brain evolution to select for features of brain "design" which accomplish feats of information processing that appear to be so abstract and content-independent?

Cosmides and Tooby, whose 1987 article marked the birth of evolutionary psychology (Cosmides and Tooby, 1987), have puzzled over this question with regard to what they call "improvisational intelligence," the capacity to solve novel problems using general principles or rules of an abstract, content-independent *relational* nature (Cosmides and Tooby, 2002).

As one possible solution to this question, I propose that natural selection can evolve content-independent, domain-general learning and cognition because *natural selection can operate on environmental regularities at multiple levels of abstraction, whenever such regularities reach sufficient levels of stability over time*. It seems reasonable to hypothesize that in brain evolution, the more abstracted regularities such as causality detection, detection of conditional probabilities in operant and classical conditioning, and other similar content-independent capacities, will reach levels of stability required for natural selection to operate, when collapsing over specific content, while retaining the abstract relational qualities. It is then possible for natural selection to select for and to "design" mechanisms in the mind that can extract and represent relational features of the world (such as co-variation, causality, conditional probability, stimulus general-ization, habituation, and the like). In other words, the requisite enduring regularities, needed to make natural selection for such mechanisms possible, arise only when spe-cific events involved in the abstracted relations are "ignored" by natural selection when "collapsing" over specific instances to select for neural representation of the underlying abstracted, relational regularities. In this way, brain mechanisms can emerge which are capable of representing abstract relational features of the world such as particular kinds of conditional probabilities and co-variation of events, independent of the specific stimuli involved (Koenigshofer, 2002). When natural selection began to filter alterna-tive neural circuit designs based on how well they detect and represent the abstracted, relational features of the world, independent of the specific stimuli manifesting the par-ticular relation, mind designs with very great and very abstract information processing capacities began to emerge. Brain "designs" with these information processing proper-ties could discover and comprehend grand laws and use them to understand and pre-dict how the world works. The "improvisational intelligence" described by Tooby and Cosmides (2002) may be the result. This kind of domain-general encoding may help explain human capacity for the intellectual feats which distinguish our species from all others. We venture more deeply into these matters of intelligent "mind design" in a latter chapter, including an examination of brain circuit "designs" (parallel distrib-uted processing networks) which may accomplish abstract and general forms of learn-ing and intelligence. Suffice it to say at this point that the rudiments of such cognitive splendors are already present within the brain design that supports classical and oper-ant conditioning in simpler brains than our own.

Other forms of learning

In addition to habituation, classical conditioning, and operant conditioning, animals and humans are capable of more complex forms of information acquisition during their lifetimes. These more complex forms of learning have been termed learning sets, obser-vation learning, and perceptual learning.

Learning sets (Harlow, 1956) refers to the fact that when animals are trained to solve many cases of a particular kind of problem they begin to abstract out the common features of the problem set and then use this information to quickly solve new prob-lems of the same type. Even pigeons with their bird brains have been observed to learn learning sets given enough training. This may be an example of learning what, the con-nectionist philosopher, Paul Churchland, calls a prototype vector, wherein the animal learns the abstract pattern involved in the problem set and utilizes this information to solve similar problems (see discussion of vector coding and connectionism in next chapter).

Observation learning refers to learning to do something by watching another member of your species perform the behavior (Carlson, et.al., 2010). This kind of learning is not nearly as general in its distribution over species as conditioning or habituation. In fact, it seems to be restricted mostly to some mammal species, but might be possible to a lesser degree in the intelligent invertebrates such as the octopus. Humans and chimpanzees are particularly good at this form of learning. Humans readily pick up behaviors that they see others do, and the common phrase, "Monkey see, monkey do," although not particularly applicable to monkey species in general is applicable to the great apes, especially, it seems, to chimpanzees. Chimpanzees, like humans, are very good at learning by watching another member of their species do something. (The Human Spark, PBS video/DVD, 2009). The brain mechanisms involved in observation learning are still being worked out. But one discovery is especially relevant.

Recall that neuroscientists have discovered circuits of special neurons called "mirror neurons" in the motor association cortex (Carlson, et. al., 2010, p. 148). These neurons become active when we perform an action *or when we see someone else perform an action such as grasping, holding, or manipulating something* (Carlson, 2011, p. 385). These "mirror neuron" circuits might be critical for observation learning. The ability to learn by watching another member of one's species perform an action may occur not only in humans, chimps, and some other primate species, but also in mammals such as dolphins and killer whales.

Observation learning is especially important because of its role in *cultural transmission of learned behaviors* from one generation to the next, as well as within generations. Genetic information, that is, information stored in DNA, can be transmitted from one generation to the next by heredity (genetic transmission), when DNA from two parents is combined to create the information that will build their offspring. In short, parents transmit their DNA to future generations through reproduction of their DNA when they have offspring. However, learned information is not stored in DNA and therefore learned behaviors and learned information cannot be transmitted from one generation to the next by genetic transmission. Learned information must be transmitted across generation by non-genetic mechanisms of transmission, such as observation learning, or in us, in addition, teaching and instruction (school is a formalized method of cultural transmission of learned behaviors across generations), story-telling, books and journals, libraries, and, in more modern times, information storage technologies such as film, video, DVD, tape recordings, flash drives, and the internet. But first and foremost, observation learning is the minimum capability required of any species capable at all of any degree of cultural transmission. Japanese macaques have been observed to culturally transmit, via observation learning, learned methods of potato-washing and "rice-cleaning" on Koshima Island off the coast of Japan and to produce other culturally transmitted behaviors such as swimming and making snow balls, apparently for fun (see http://en.wikipedia.org/wiki/Japanese_macaque and http://www.bbc.co.uk/nature/life/Japanese_Macaque). And chimpanzees were observed by Jane Goodall (1971) in the jungles of Tanzania to culturally transmit, by observation learning, such learned skills as "termite-fishing" and crude tool-making, in the modification of branches and twigs to create "fishing poles" to stick into termite mounds. Human cultural transmission has undoubtedly played a key role in our success as a species. Our great capacity for observation learning, by virtue of our evolved brain circuit design, was central in our abilities for cultural transmission. Capacity for observation learning is not widespread in the animal kingdom. Rats, for example, learn nothing by watching another member of their species do something. Species of animal that don't have capacity for observation learning do not develop cultural transmission. Humans are so adept at cultural transmission, recall that in a prior chapter I made the claim that cultural transmission is our specialty as a species. It is the single mode of human adaptation that accounts for everything that we think of as uniquely human. Without our abilities for observation learning, and other mechanisms of cultural transmission, we would have no science or technology, no agriculture, no medicine, no literature, philosophy, or political systems. Without observational learning and cultural transmission, we would have to "reinvent the wheel" anew each generation. We would be much more like the other animals.

Perceptual learning involves ability to recognize things (Carlson, 2011, p. 349) and the context and meanings of them. This involves complex pattern coding by the brain.

To do justice to a discussion of perceptual learning we will have to await the introduction of ideas about how the brain encodes or represents complex stimuli, objects, events, concepts, and the multitude of things that occupy our minds. This discussion, in the later part of the next chapter about sensory systems and perception, will involve what Paul Churchland, of UC San Diego, refers to as "vector coding." Neural representations of complex, whole perceptual objects, experienced events stored in memory, and even representation of highly abstract concepts, all perhaps by neural coding "vectors," will set the stage for a discussion of perceptual learning in Chapter 8, on the nature of the senses and the perception of reality.

The Nature-Nurture Continuum

This chapter would not be complete unless we consider the "nature vs. nurture" issue. The ancient debate as to whether the human mind and behavior are innate (genetically determined), or the result of learning is best understood in a comparative context, wherein we consider not only the human mind and behavior but the minds and behavior of other species as well. When we ask whether mind and behavior are the result of genetics or learning, first of all, it is now obvious that all behavior is a mixture of both. For some, this is the resolution of the old problem. But there really is more that can be said. If we stipulate what is now obvious, that both nature (genes and genetic evolution) and nurture (learning, experience, and in some cases including the human case, culture) contribute to the development and causation of mind and behavior, still we must ask to what degree each contributes and in what ways. Far from being dead, the nature-nurture (no longer nature vs. nurture) issue is still alive and well, and is just as important as ever, but it is now redefined, not as one to the exclusion of the other, but as a mix of the two in which the relative mix is still at issue. How much each contributes to mind and behavior is a question that must be answered empirically for each species and for each mental and behavioral trait. This is because the mix of nature and nurture will vary from species to species and from behavioral trait to behavioral trait.

This idea is best illustrated by what I call the Nature-Nurture Continuum (see figure 7-1 below).

The Nature-Nurture Continuum

	Flying in flies	Navigation in Indigo Buntings	Bird song in White-crowned Sparrows	Tool making in chimpanzees	
Nature (genes and genetic evolution)	Web construction in spiders	Nest making in birds	Human Language Acquisition	Modern agricultural practices in humans	Nurture (environment during the individual's lifetime, learning, cultural evolution in some species)

Behavioral adaptations are organized by a mixture of information from genes and genetic evolution (nature) and from experience during the lifetime of the individual animal, that is, learning (nurture). But the mixture varies from species to species and from behavior to behavior. Generally, the simpler animals such as insects, fish, amphibians, and reptiles have behavioral adaptations organized more, and sometime exclusively, by information in their genes. Learning becomes an increasingly important source of information for the organization of behavior in the more advanced mammals, most notably, in us.

FIGURE 7-1. Behavioral adaptations are organized by a mixture of information from genes (acquired via genetic evolution of the species) and from learning (acquired from experience during the lifetime of the individual animal). This mix varies from species to species, and from behavior to behavior.

The Nature-Nurture Continuum explicitly recognizes that both genetic evolution (and the genes that have resulted from it) and learning determine mind and behavior but that the mix of these two sources of information varies across species and across behaviors and psychological traits. The figure above illustrates that in older species (species evolved earlier in evolutionary history and thus with less complex brain "design") behavior is organized more by genetic sources of information than by learned sources. In fact, in species such as flies, learning plays no role at all in the organization of behaviors such as flying. There isn't a little flight school for flies. They "know" how to fly without any learning or experience at all. Flying in flies is just built into the DNA of the species. That genetic information builds the neural circuitry for flying during embryonic development of the fly brain.

By contrast, in species more recently evolved, learning plays an increasingly larger part in providing information required for the adaptive organization of behavior, so that in very recently evolved species like us, learning plays a very large role in the life of the animal. However, this does not mean that genes and genetic evolution are any less important in species like us than in the older and less complex species such as insects, reptiles, or birds. In fact, it should be clear to the reader by now that learning mechanisms, even in humans, only exist, and exist in the forms that they do, strictly as a result of genes and the genetic evolution of the species doing the learning.

Even behaviors at the far right of the Nature-Nurture Continuum (see figure 7-1 above) such as learning calculus or learning how to make a light bulb or how to do agriculture, although clearly learned, are still highly dependent upon genetics and genetic evolution. Learning to do calculus is completely dependent upon having genetically evolved features of the cognitive and learning circuitry that make learning calculus possible. You can hire the best calculus tutor in the world, even Isaac Newton, the inventor of calculus, himself, to tutor your dog in calculus, but still, your dog will never learn calculus. Your dog just doesn't have the brains for it. That is, your dog does not have the proper information in its DNA necessary for the organization of its brain and its learning circuitry to make it capable of learning calculus no matter how good the tutor. This is obvious with regard to the dog, but typically we take for granted the genes and the genetic evolution that make such learning possible in humans. Genes make the learning possible or impossible, depending upon the genetic evolution of each species. Humans can invent and then learn calculus and other splendid things because information coded in the DNA of our species, as a result of its genetic evolution, creates a "mind design" in us that makes it possible for us to learn such things, just like the genetically evolved circuitry of the Indigo Bunting makes it capable of learning the night sky with ease. Learning never occurs in a vacuum or in a brain that is some random assemblage of formless matter but always in highly structured, genetically evolved learning circuitry. Thus, even behaviors like calculus, modern medical practices, agriculture, invention of the printing press, the manufacture of microchips, or creating rockets to the moon and the planets, which are all so clearly learned, still depend on the genetics and genetic evolution which built the brain mechanisms making such forms of learning possible. Every behavior and every mental trait involves a complex mix of information from genes, resulting from the evolution of the species, and information learned during the lifetime of the individual. There is no such thing as a behavior or a psychological trait that is purely learned without an equal or greater measure of information from genes and genetic evolution. All behavior is genetic, and some behavior is also dependent upon learning. Some behaviors like those at the far left of the Nature-Nurture Continuum, such as flying in flies, are purely genetic, organized independently of any information acquired from individual experience during the lifetime. But no behavior or mental trait is purely learned. Genes always play a role in every behavior and mental trait. Learning, even of things like calculus or how to make a light bulb, is first and foremost dependent upon genetically evolved learning capabilities. Some of these capabilities might be based on highly flexible circuit designs like those modeled in *artificial neural networks* (to be discussed in the next chapter), but even learning circuits such as these must get their formative properties from genes, and implementation of anything learned in the actual control of behavior will be influenced by genetic dispositions and temperaments in each individual. Surely, it is time for the myth of the *tabula rasa* to be buried forever in the obscurity it so richly deserves.

In sum, learning mechanisms are genetically evolved *adaptations*, the "designs" of which are encoded into the DNA of each species. Learning provides response flexibility while preserving adaptive constraints on behavior through evolved laws of learning, which are built into the brain circuit "designs" of animals, including humans. Many components of these learning circuit designs are conserved over evolutionary time, and thus show up repeatedly even as animal species have diverged again and again from common ancestry. Learning mechanisms can be highly specific adaptive specializations (domain-specific learning) to solve highly domain-specific adaptive problems (acquisition of bird song or learning the night sky) or they can be much more general in nature. Such general forms of learning utilize the same laws of learning over a wide range of species in the animal kingdom. Such general forms of learning, such as habituation and conditioning, are also "general" in the sense that they are found in an enormously broad range of learning domains (or adaptive problems) regardless of specific content (habituation, classical and operant conditioning).

Evolutionary psychologists have focused on adaptive problems with differing degrees of content-independence and differing degrees of domain-generality. Much of the controversy about domain-generality vs. domain-specificity of learning and cognitive mechanisms arises merely from this difference in focus. Both positions are correct. But each is correct under different conditions of the environment. All study adaptations to various kinds or levels of environmental regularity, a principle we will discuss again in a later chapter.

In addition to genetics and learning, there is a third source of information that organizes adaptive behavior—information from the immediate environment entering the brain via our sensory and perceptual systems. In the next chapter we consider the basic structure and functioning of sensory systems, and how they have evolved to provide workable neurological models of the adaptively significant features of the world for each species. As we shall see, natural selection has equipped each animal species with mechanisms to sense and perceive just what each needs to, in order to solve its biological problems, and thus to survive and reproduce in its particular environmental niche. Reality, it turns out, is thus species-specific, and furthermore, "reality" can't be known in any absolute, objective sense. Even in humans our sensory and perceptual mechanisms permit us to perceive just what we need to perceive in order to survive and reproduce, and little else directly. Cognitive mechanisms, some of which are relatively domain-general, in the human brain, then create, by informed conjecture, a vast interacting collection of information-structures commonly known as beliefs, which comprise our "knowledge," our "understanding," of our world—our "reality." It is this neurological model which we experience as our own subjective reality, as it guides our behavioral adaptations to our physical and social world. As we shall see, our realities are actually creations of our brains—and adaptive though they are, they are still *virtual* realities, far from reality with a capital R.

CHAPTER EIGHT

Sensory Systems, Virtual Reality Machines, and Worlds in the Mind

"What is real? How do you define real? If you're talking about what you can feel, what you can smell, what you can taste and see, then real is simply electrical signals interpreted by your brain."

Morpheus (Laurence Fishburne),
The Matrix (1999)

I live a block from the beach in San Clemente, California, a coastal town half way between Los Angeles and San Diego. It is the southern-most city in Orange County, just a few miles north of the sprawling, unspoiled coastal wilderness that makes up most of the Camp Pendleton Marine Base. The late President Richard Nixon's Western White House is still here, a white stucco, red tile roofed Spanish style rancho, hanging on a low cliff edge, known as Cotton's Point, overlooking the sea, a mere 45 minute walk from my front door, along the beach to the south. At the end of my block, when the air is clear of fog and haze, you can see Santa Catalina Island, roughly 26 miles across open ocean, jutting up as if a floating mountain on the watery horizon. Sometimes when I look at this view, as I did tonight, a few minutes after a pink sunset, I think about how the Spanish explorer Cabrillo, who discovered the island in 1542, must have had the same view of the island as I, as he sailed from its shores toward continental beaches and moored his ship in the natural bay here. He must have come ashore to these same beaches where I walk and watched similar sunsets. The clouds above the island, bathed in pink and orange, the mountainous figure on the sea silhouetted against the dimly lit sky at the horizon, and the jagged lines of waves forming and breaking again and again must have captured the soul of Cabrillo and his crew, just as this beauty still draws groups of locals to watch the sun set at this lovely spot every evening, even to this day. But though, I enjoy these thoughts of Cabrillo and his men, and of the beauty here, I am also a professor trained in biological psychology and because of this, I also have other thoughts about nature, perhaps a little less romantic to some.

Most people believe that the physical world of objects and events is characterized by colors, luminosity, sounds, heat and cold, tastes, and smells. The sunsets that Cabrillo and I and countless others over the centuries have enjoyed must be teaming with brilliant color, and the crashing sound of waves on the sand must unquestionably be in the world that surrounds us. In the minds of most people, the things in the world such as roses, automobiles, birds, the ocean, trees, beautiful sunsets at the ocean, and so on, have inherent in them properties such as color, shape, texture, and sometimes smells, temperature, and tastes. When looking at the pink and orange clouds of the sunset over Santa Catalina, when hearing the waves rumble on the shore, when smelling the salt in the air, most people believe that such things are properties of the world itself. Likewise, apples, we all know, are red and have a sweet tartness, and they make a thud when they fall from a tree. Cooking steak smells good, but uncooked meat left out without refrigeration for too long begins to smell bad. Your lover's skin and hair smell good, as do roses and orange blossoms. Most people accept such observations as no more than simple common sense. So why am I spending time on the obvious? Because, in this case, common sense is completely wrong; the obvious is really just a very convincing illusion. The world out there, that sunset with its radiant color, the sound of the crashing waves, the smell of salty air, all of that world outside of your head, is not what you imagine it to be, it is not what your senses tell you it is. The world of our experience is a creation of our brains.

Surprisingly, the world and the objects in it are not *really* luminous and colored, odiferous, and full of sound; in fact, even light itself is neither luminous nor colored, but as dark and colorless as radio waves, gamma rays, or X-rays. The sound of thunder or crashing waves isn't really out there in the world. Instead, there are only silent vibrations of the air created by these events. Roses and rotting meat really have no smell at all, but give off molecules of specific physical shapes which are in the real world, outside our heads, as odorless as a stone. The world, and even light itself, is really dark. There is no sound in the world, only profound silence. There are no smells, nor tastes. Chocolate cake isn't really dark rich brown and really has no taste at all. Apples aren't really red, they have no taste; they make no sound when they fall to the ground. And sugar isn't really sweet; it is really only a completely tasteless molecule. Color, luminosity, smells, tastes, and sounds don't really exist in the external physical world, but instead are properties of your brain and its physical activities—its information processing operations. Our brains create the rich, sensory texture of our subjective worlds. Our brains create the color, the sounds, tastes, and smells that we attribute to the external world.

Remember the old philosophical problem, "If a tree falls in the forest and there is no one there to hear it, was there a sound?" Common sense tells us that the sound would exist regardless of who was, or was not, there. But, because of insights from modern neuroscience we can now confidently answer with a resounding "No, there would be no sound." Pressure waves in the air, yes, sound, no. Sounds, smells, luminosity, color, and other such properties are known among philosophers and neuroscientists as *sensory qualia*, properties which exist only in the mind, in the specific information processing functions of the brain. The sensory qualia such as sound and color are just the brain's *code* for physical features of the world, such as silent pressure waves in the air or wavelengths of light, features which themselves are nothing like the sensory qualia (our sensory experiences) which represent them in our minds. The objective world "out there," in the space outside of our skulls, is really completely silent, dark, colorless, and without even the faintest smells or tastes. If a tree falls in the forest and there is no one (and no animal) there to hear it, *there is no sound*, only silent mechanical energy, vibrations in the air. The sound is created by the brain and exists only within it.

Now, this is not to say that the things out there in the world don't exist. They certainly do. Common sense is right about that. But the world is simply full of physical energies of different sorts—mechanical, electromagnetic, chemical—with differing physical properties that any physicist could measure, but all of that matter and energy outside our heads is actually without any of the qualities that we experience from it and ascribe to it. The sensory qualia such as smells, tastes, colors, luminosity, and sounds are *added* by the brain, and exist only within the brain/mind as codes for biologically significant features of the objective, quality-less, but real, physical world.

We see, hear, smell, taste, and feel because our brain converts physical energies of various sorts into these sensory experiences in order to guide our behavior toward successful survival and reproduction. This means that we never experience reality in any direct way, but always only through the filter of the biological "design" features of our sensory organs and our brain systems for sensation and perception. Reality is biologically formed in our "mind design" for *biological* purposes.

Now, I suspect that you are skeptical about such a surprising and radical proposition. And it is understandable that you should be (but see the quote from the film, The Matrix, at the opening of this chapter). I was myself until I learned enough about how sensory systems work to understand a deeper reality. Once I had acquired enough knowledge about how the sensory organs and the brain's sensory pathways function, this astounding claim became self-evident. We conjure up the properties such as color, luminosity, sound, smells, and tastes inside our own brain tissue as a consequence of the "design" of its circuitry. I am certain that the Spanish explorer, Cabrillo, would have scoffed at this seemingly absurd proposition. But in Cabrillo's day little was known about sensory physiology other than the belief that the eyes made you see, the ears were for hearing, and that you smelled with your nose. With only primitive knowledge about how sensory systems work, particularly the sensory circuitry of the brain, the common-sense view that our sensations were actually properties of the stuff in the external world made perfect sense, just as it still does to most people today. But today, we have much more knowledge about such biological processes, and this knowledge is producing astounding new insights about the nature of what we call, and *feel as*, "reality."

Information in DNA derived from the genetic evolution of each species, supplemented by information acquired and stored by each individual animal or human during its lifetime (learning and memory), interacts with information we gather through our senses to organize adaptive behavior. To do this there must be a constant interface between organism and the environment in which it finds itself. Animals have to navigate an environment of three-dimensional space, avoiding obstacles, dangerous precipices, and predators. They must find and recognize edible foods, drinkable water, and "desirable" (adaptively fit) mates. If they are members of a social species, they must discriminate and remember different individuals in the group, and all animals must discriminate safe, nutritious foods from rotting, germ infected, and otherwise toxic substances. In species with females that are cyclic breeders that are fertile and sexually receptive during limited periods of time, males must be able to tell when a female is fertile using cues from the body of the female such as the size and shape of her genitalia, her behavior, or the chemical composition of her secretions. To perform such functions, animal and human brains must have a particular "design," one tuned to biologically significant features of the world.

Imagine that your brain was somehow kept alive, confined in ceramic jar, without a body or sensory nerves, and thus completely isolated from the external world. Could you experience the world? Of course, the answer is "No." Even if this brain were equipped with a body and motor nerves connected to the muscles of its body, could you direct your behavior successfully (adaptively) in the world if your brain could not receive input about events and objects in the external world? Again, the answer is obviously, "No."

The brain, without sensory systems, is in fact isolated from the world, just as if it were isolated inside a ceramic jar. After all, the brain is inside your skull (very similar to being confined in a ceramic jar), hidden away from the external world in this dark, bony cavern. So, to interface with the world, brains must have systems that can somehow get information about the external world into the three pounds of neural tissue upon which consciousness of that world and of oneself, in the world, depends. Sensory systems provide the route by which the physical world, in coded form, can enter the otherwise isolated confines of your brain, tucked safely away inside a dark and silent cranial space.

What are these sensory systems really like? Sensory systems across the animal kingdom, from mites and mollusks to man, are very diverse, yet there is a surprising order in how they work. In fact, there is a set of general principles that apply to all sensory systems in all animals on our planet. These same general principles could conceivably be universal, and might one day be applied to help us understand the sensory systems of alien life forms on other planets, if such life forms turn out to exist. If extraterrestrial life does exist, several good working hypotheses about the their sensory systems will be derived from the general principles to be discussed below; wouldn't it be fascinating if sensory systems turn out to operate according to similar general principles, wherever complex life forms might be found in the universe? The laws of evolution, likely to be universal, might lead us to expect such continuity.

Of course, sensory systems are "input" systems to the brain, including not only vision, hearing, taste, the skin sensations, and olfaction, but the muscle and joint senses that inform us of the positions of our limbs, and, in some species, especially those that live in murky waters, we even find sensitivity to the electrical signals in the muscles of other fish, as they are stimulated to movement by their own nervous systems. But here is an extremely important fact to be clearly understood. The brain doesn't just receive the world, and the energies contained in it, directly, in their raw forms. It can't. It is completely insensitive to such energies in the world in their raw forms. The brain doesn't receive light (a form of electromagnetic energy), or mechanical energy (corresponding to sound and touch), or chemical energy (corresponding to tastes and smells) directly. In fact, peculiarly and quite unexpectedly from the standpoint of common sense, *the brain itself is completely insensitive to the external world and its energies in their raw forms.*

The brain uses neural code. It is entirely unresponsive to anything else. Before the brain can receive them, the energies in the external world must first be converted into neuron potentials, neural code, the only thing that brain is actually responsive to. In brief summary then, the brain is isolated inside the skull. Sensory systems bring "the world" into the brain, but not directly. The external world must be first converted into a code, neuron potentials, by the early stages of sensory operations. It is these *neuron potentials that enter the brain,* not light, color or luminosity, not sound waves, nor smells, or tastes, nor temperatures or any other features that we usually imagine to be part of the objective, external physical world. The brain has *never* experienced anything in the world directly because it never receives energies, objects, or events in the world directly. The brain is sensitive to *one* thing, neuron potentials (voltages), and nothing more. You, nor I, have never seen a single ray or photon of light, nor heard a single object fall, or smelled a single rose, felt a baby's skin, or tasted mashed potatoes or anything at all. How can I make such a bold and seemingly nonsensical claim, so counter to our every day experience? It sounds a like a touch of madness. But I assure you that it is not. Here's what I mean.

Imagine that you are a neurosurgeon. Like others of your profession, when you do brain surgery, one of the first steps is to open up the skull of your patient under a local anesthetic, which deadens the scalp and the skull, but leaves your patient conscious and alert. The reason this is possible is because there are no pain receptors in the brain itself, but only in the surrounding scalp, skull, and *meninges* (a three-layered membrane covering the brain and attached to the skull to help protect the brain; cerebral spinal fluid circulates between its layers providing a liquid shock absorber for the soft, jello-like tissue of the living brain).

Next imagine, that with the skull opened up and the brain exposed in a darkened surgery room, you direct a beam of bright light from a flashlight directly onto the visual area of the brain, the *occipital lobe*, a convoluted chunk of tissue located beneath the bone at the back of your head (this area is known as the *primary visual cortex*). To be sure that no light reaches your patient's eyes, imagine that your patient has been blindfolded. Now, with bright light illuminating the primary visual cortex, the site in the brain where "seeing" actually begins, would your patient "see" the light beam? I think that you will readily agree that your patient does *not* see the beam of light, even though bright light is flooding the brain's visual cortical tissue.

Why does the patient experience no visual sensation? After all, these brain cells flooded with light in the *primary visual cortex* are the neurons in the brain upon which visual experience depends. We know this because if this area of brain is destroyed (as sometimes happens with brain disease or injury), complete blindness is the result. This condition is known as *cortical blindness*. Why doesn't your patient see the intense light flooding his/her *visual* cortical tissue? The answer is that the brain itself is entirely insensitive to the world and its energies, in their raw forms. Light on the visual areas of the brain has absolutely no effect, because the brain areas for vision are not "designed" to be responsive to light. Brain tissue is sensitive only to the electrochemical messages known as neuron potentials (or to electrical stimulation from a surgeon's electrode), and nothing else.

We can illustrate this same principle using other senses. Imagine you plug the nose of your patient and then place a rose or some dirty socks right beside the exposed olfactory cortex (the cortex for smell). Will your patient smell the rose or dirty socks? Again, I think you can see the answer is clearly "No." Suppose you pour chocolate syrup over your patient's taste cortex, will the patient taste the chocolate? Again the answer is "No." Suppose you place a thin slice of lemon on the surface of the taste cortex. Will your patient taste the lemon? Again, "No."

Why not? Our common sense tells us that the sensory organs such as eyes, ears, and tongue are required. After all, even ancient peoples knew that you need eyes to see, ears to hear, etc. But these organs don't produce our sensory experiences. All they do is change energies in the world into a form that the brain can respond to. What's necessary then is the conversion of the energies from stimuli in the external world into a form that the brain can deal with, small voltages inside nerve cells, the neuron potentials. Neurons use electrochemical signals, neuron potentials, to code and process information. That's the only currency that the brain deals in.

This means, then, that the *first major step in any sensory system is the conversion of energy in the environment into neuron potentials*, the brain's code. This process is called *transduction,* the conversion of energy in the world from its raw forms into electrical signals in nerve cells. Transduction is accomplished within specialized neurons known as *sensory receptors.* Each of the senses has its own specific sensory receptors, which, by their particular structure, transduce only one specific type of energy—light, pressure waves in the air, pressure on the skin or in the joints, chemicals with specific molecular shape in the air, or in the mouth. Our patient didn't see the bright light shown on her/his visual cortex because the brain *never* sees light, it only sees neuron potentials! To help you understand what I mean, we must take a quick look at the steps involved in vision.

First, light in the world, reflected off objects, enters the eye through the *cornea* (the clear outer covering of the eyeball) and then the *pupil* (the small hole in the center of the iris, the brown, blue, or green colored muscle of your eye that controls the size of the pupil). After the light enters your eye, it strikes the light-sensitive inner surface at the back of your eye. This is the *retina.* The retina is light-sensitive because it has a layer of light-sensitive cells, the *visual receptors,* known as *rods and cones.* What we mean when we say that the rods and cones are light-sensitive is that these cells *transduce* or convert light into brain code, neuron potentials, the small voltages that act as electrical signals in brain circuits. Transduction of light into neuron potentials takes place in the eye, in the rods and cones. No vision is occurring yet. Vision takes place in the brain, not in the eye. After transduction, the resulting neuron potentials exit the back of the eyeball and travel along the optic nerve (actually composed of the axons of neurons in the retina, known as ganglion cells, that receive their input from bipolar cells, that receive, in turn, their input from the rods and cones) toward the brain. These neuron potentials are delivered to an area of the brain called the thalamus (specifically these potentials go to the visual part of the thalamus known as the LGN, the lateral geniculate nucleus), and then from there neuron potentials move along nerves to the primary visual cortex, where conscious seeing begins.

The utterly striking thing to be understood here is that *after transduction* of light into neuron potentials has been accomplished by the rods and cones in the eye (actually only the first step in seeing), *from that point on, light has absolutely nothing more at all to do with seeing.* This is a key point. Light never goes beyond the retina of the eye. Light comes into the eye, but *neuron potentials come out* and head for the brain, where seeing actually takes place. Light never reaches the brain; it never gets close. Only neuron potentials do. So, when we see, we aren't really seeing *light,* we are actually seeing our own *neuron potentials*! And it is those neuron potentials being pushed through a particular circuit design in our primary visual cortex that induces *visual qualia* such as the brightness and luminosity which we mistakenly attribute to light. It is neuron potentials coursing through the circuitry of the visual cortex that "look" colored and luminous. It is not light. Seeing occurs in the brain. Not in the eye. Yet, light never gets to the brain, ever, since it is immediately converted, at the very first step in the processes of vision, into electrical voltages, neuron potentials which leave the back of the eyeball to stimulate the visual circuitry of the brain. How do I know this? How do we know that seeing actually occurs in the brain, and not in the eye or in some ghostly, non-material mind? Because if you electrically stimulate the primary visual cortex in a conscious human patient in a completely dark operating room they will report "seeing" flashes of light and color. You can even do this in someone who has lost both eyes, due to accident, and they will report seeing luminosity and color too, even though they no longer have functioning eyes.

You can do a crude version of this experiment for yourself. Go into a completely dark room, and then into a completely dark closet in that dark room, being absolutely sure that no light at all is reaching your eyes. Then whack yourself hard on the back of the head, near the primary visual cortex beneath the back of your skull, and you will "see stars," flashes of luminosity and color, technically known as "phosphemes," *in the complete absence of any light*. The visual qualia that are produced are coming from the mechanical stimulation of visual neurons in your *primary visual cortex* as you whack yourself with a good solid blow to the back of your poor head. Since no light is in your dark closet, it is not light that is luminous and colored, it is the activation of visual circuitry in your brain that makes the color and luminosity appear. These properties aren't in light, and are not properties of light, but instead such visual qualia are properties of the activation of specific circuits in your brain. Light is not really luminous or colored (and neither are the objects in the world that it reflects off of, such as apples, lemons, or your car). Light is actually just as dark as radio waves, gamma rays, or other forms of electromagnetic energy. It may help make this point if I remind you that light is just one form of electromagnetic energy, like radio waves, X-rays, gamma, ultraviolet and infrared. All these forms of energy are the same "stuff," they just differ in *wavelength* (the distance between two adjacent wave peaks of the radiation). Thus, the world around us, even in "broad daylight" is actually completely dark; the brightness, luminosity, and color that we "see" are really just a construction by our brain, a kind of illusion, but one with adaptive information within it, an adaptive illusion. That is, the illusion, the model of the world created by our brain, has a functional correspondence with things in the external physical world, that is, with the features of things in the world that are adaptively significance to us as members of our particular species. But it is only a correlation; it is not the thing itself, or its objective properties.

Here's another example to help illustrate, and perhaps convince you—dreams. In our dreams we "see" images of objects, people, and events. The dream images are similar to images we experience while we are awake, and experiencing the world. For example, I remember dreaming once about a bull fight in Tijuana, Mexico. I was seated in the grandstands of a small tacky bull ring, and I distinctly remember "seeing" its cheap plywood walls, which "looked" about 10 feet high, and which were painted with a thick covering of very bright, orange paint. These bright and colored images were produced in my brain in the complete absence of light. But, of course, we all know this kind of "hallucination" happens regularly in our dreams, but what it shows us, if we think it through, is that visual qualia are in the brain, and don't "need" light.

Remember we can induce sensations of color and brightness even in the minds of people who have no eyes, if we electrically stimulate the circuits of their primary visual cortex with an electrode. You might object, however, and say that they are just seeing "sparks" or something similar from the electricity used to stimulate their brains. However, this objection is quickly dispensed with when we examine the effects of electrical stimulation in other parts of the cortex. For example, a neurosurgeon can use the same electrode with the same voltage as she/he used to stimulate visual qualia (such as luminosity or brightness and color) to induce taste qualia or smell sensations or sounds (auditory qualia) depending upon whether the electrode is applied to the taste cortex, the olfactory cortex, or the auditory cortex. The same electrical stimulus will produce these different sensations (sensory qualia) strictly dependent upon where in the cortex the stimulation is applied. This shows that not only visual qualia, but auditory qualia (sounds), smells, and tastes, are in the brain, not in the world or in the objects that are located in the world.

Let's briefly summarize. If the visual cortex is destroyed in humans, the person is blind (cortical blindness) showing that conscious seeing, visual sensation, requires activation of an intact visual cortex. This is confirmed by the fact that we can stimulate visual cortex electrically (just as occurs naturally when neuron potentials stimulate it) and produce visual sensations of brightness and color, even in the absence of light, and even in someone who has no eyes. In short, stimulate visual cortex and visual sensations are produced, even without eyes or light. Destroy visual cortex and no visual sensations, no seeing, is possible (cortical blindness) even with perfectly well functioning eyes. Finally, after transduction of light into neuron potentials in the eye, light has nothing more at all to do with seeing; light never reaches the brain where seeing takes place, therefore it can't be light that is luminous and colored, it must be the activation of visual circuits in the brain that "makes" luminosity and color out of patterns of neuron potential pushed through visual circuits in the brain; and all of this from a form of energy which is really just as dark and colorless as radio waves or other forms of electromagnetic energy. Light alone, no other wavelengths of electromagnetic energy, and the objects it reflects off of appear to be colored and luminous because visual receptors, by their structure, are only capable of transducing the range of wavelengths of electromagnetic energy that we label as "light." That transduction then results in the activation of visual cortical circuits producing the consequent sensations of brightness and color.

If we had visual receptors that transduced radio waves, then we would see radio waves! Different color sensations would be produced by different wavelengths of radio waves, just as different color sensations are produced, in us, by different wavelengths of light.

Now a question may have occurred to the reader which we haven't yet dealt with. Why are different sensations produced by different forms of energy? That is, why do silent pressure waves in the air produce "sound" sensations, auditory qualia? Why to chemicals dissolved in our mouths end up producing taste qualia? Why do molecules floating in the air produce olfactory qualia, "smells," when they strike olfactory receptors in our noses? The answer to these questions is in *the wiring*. Visual receptors connect to visual pathways that end in visual cortex in the occipital lobe. Auditory receptors, the "hair cells" in the cochlea of the inner ear, hook up with auditory pathways that lead to the auditory cortex of the temporal lobe. Taste receptors, via a few steps, send their neuron potentials to taste cortex, and olfactory receptors to the olfactory bulbs and then olfactory cortex. The subjective quality of the sensory experience, the nature of the *sensory qualia*, produced by any sensory system is dependent upon where in the cortex its pathways go. Thus, the particular area of *cortex* which ultimately ends up being activated, by the neuron potentials that result from the transduction of a particular form of energy, is the determining factor in the particular nature of the sensory qualia we experience from any particular type of energy—whether mechanical, electromagnetic, or chemical. In other words, the cortex determines the sensory experience.

This has some interesting implications. What if the visual receptors were somehow hooked up to the taste cortex? What would be the result? Well, think about it. Light would be transduced by the visual receptors. But the resulting neuron potentials would end up, not in visual cortex, but in taste cortex. So, with this rewiring job, you would get taste sensations from the transduction of light. *You would taste light.*

Different wavelengths of light, setting up different patterns of neuron potentials reaching different areas of the taste cortex, would produce different taste sensations, different taste qualia. Shorter wavelengths of light, transduced by one set of cones (cones are the visual receptors that are wavelength sensitive) in the retina, would produce neuron potentials that would go to one area of taste cortex, producing some particular taste (taste quale, singular of qualia). Longer wavelengths of light would be transduced by a different set of cones (there are 3 types of cones in the retina) setting up a different pattern of impulses to another region of taste cortex, producing a different taste sensation (see Figures 8-1 and 8-2, to be discussed in detail, later in this chapter). What these tastes would taste like, we can only speculate. Longer wavelengths of light, which in a normal visual system would produce visual sensations of "redness," might, in our altered visual system, generate a taste like that of apples or strawberries, but might just as well taste like mint, an onion, a lemon, or more probably something different from anything that that we had ever tasted before. There would be no way to predict, because at this point in the short history of the neurosciences, we don't yet know enough about how sensory qualia are coded within their respective regions of sensory cortex.

Now, you may object to this whole line of argument by saying that this is impossible because light just doesn't have taste. But, neither does it have luminosity or color. The subjective qualia produced by any form of energy in the external physical world is not in the energy itself, but in the particular configurations of the specific cortical circuits that get activated when that particular form of environmental energy is transduced by its specialized sensory receptors. But there is another problem. Why does activation of visual cortex make visual qualia such as brightness and color, while activation of auditory cortex makes auditory qualia such as loudness, pitch, and timbre, and activation of taste cortex makes taste qualia such as sweet, sour, or bitter? The answer is again, in the wiring, or more precisely, in the "wiring diagram" of each type of cortex, the specific pattern of connections of the neurons which make it up.

Along the lines of the "thought experiment" in which we considered what would happen if we rewired the brain so that the optic nerve went to taste cortex, let's consider a more realistic case in nature—the case of echolocation in bats. Several species of bats are noted for their astounding abilities to use echolocation to search out prey in dark caves or in pitch black nights. Bats are extremely accomplished in this regard. A bat, in complete darkness, can detect and locate a fluttering moth with astounding precision, and pick it off out of the air, effortlessly. Observing them do this in infrared light, invisible to them but visible to us via cameras designed for the purpose, makes it look as though they are "seeing" where they are going and where moths and other prey are to be found in the darkness. And it could very well be that this is exactly what they are doing—they are *seeing*, not with light waves, but with *sound waves*. They may be actually seeing brightly lit, luminous images in what to us is a completely dark cave. To a bat brain, the cave that looks completely dark to us may be brightly lit for them, not by light, but by "sound waves," no more than silent vibrations in the air. But how could this be? Sound waves aren't bright and luminous; common sense tells us that they have *sound* in them. But this isn't actually true either. So-called "sound" waves really are nothing more than *silent* mechanical vibrations in air. The sound is added by the human brain. If it is hard to imagine that sound waves could produce vision in a bat brain because sound waves aren't bright and luminous, consider this: neither is light! Light is just a form of electromagnetic energy in a specific range of wavelengths that we can transduce. In the actual physical world outside our heads, light is actually completely dark, just like radio waves or X-rays. Once light is transduced by rods and cones, the primary visual cortex of our brain does the rest. The specific sensory experiences (the particular sensory qualia—sound, luminosity, color, tastes, or smells) particular forms of environmental energy (light, chemicals, or vibrations in the air) generate is determined by the particular brain "design" of an animal or human. It all depends on the *circuit design* of the *cerebral cortex* that is activated by neuron potentials that are produced following transduction of energy by specific sensory receptors (rods and cones, auditory receptor "hair cells," taste receptors, etc). If auditory receptors in the bat transduce vibrations in the air from the beating wings of a moth and send their neuron potentials to an *auditory* cortex that has a circuit design something like our *visual* cortex, then visual-like images, with brightness, and perhaps even color, will be produced in the mind of the bat from reflected "sound" waves. The bat sees "sound" waves and can use them to illuminate a "dark" cave (dark to us) or a dark night. This is similar to research with rats showing that X-rays activate their olfactory cortex, showing that rats apparently can smell X-rays.

One thing that this analysis doesn't tell us is what features of circuit design in different areas of the cerebral cortex cause different sensory qualia. In other words, we need an answer to the question, what is it about the synaptic configuration of the circuitry of a visual cortex like ours that makes it produce *visual* qualia such as luminosity (brightness of light) and color, and what are the crucial differences in the circuitry of an auditory cortex like ours that make it produce experiences of sound. The same question exists for the taste and olfactory cortices that cause them to produce tastes and smells. Notice that these questions only arise when we realize that color, smells, tastes, and sounds are not really in "the world," or in the objects that fill the space outside of our heads, but are created by the brain. Energies "out there" in the physical world do exist, but they really don't have the sensory properties that we ascribe to them. We know this because neurosurgeons can stimulate all of these sensory qualia (luminosity, color, tastes, smells, feelings of touch on particular parts of one's body, and sounds) in a completely silent and darkened operating room just by electrical stimulation of the appropriate parts of the cerebral cortex (see Penfield, 1964, for example). This means that our brain circuit designs create these sensory qualia in our minds, and that they do not exist in the outside world as objective physical properties of that world. The production of sensory qualia must be a physical process in our material brains, so different sensory qualia in different areas of cortex means that there are different circuit configurations in different areas of sensory cortex (visual cortex vs. auditory cortex vs. taste cortex, etc) which when activated produce the qualitatively distinct qualia of the different sensory modalities (visual, auditory, olfactory, gustatory—taste, and somatosensory—touch). This is the principle in the *law of specific nerve energies* first proposed by Johannes Muller in 1835.

To discover what features of circuit design in different areas of the cerebral cortex produce the different sensory qualia requires that we consider what neuroscientists and psychologists call the problem of *representation*. How does the brain represent, in a physical neural code, the physical properties of the world and convert them into psychological experience? We will consider this complex question later in this chapter, but first, as background, we need to examine how the sensory systems work. We will explore this question by identifying general principles of the operation of sensory systems, and then we will consider some specifics of the visual system to illustrate.

Eight general principles in the organization and functioning of sensory systems

Given Darwin's proposition of the continuity of species we should expect to find general principles operating in the sensory systems of every animal species on this planet (and perhaps even in those of life forms elsewhere in the universe, if they exist). If you can understand these general principles it will be easier to learn the specific facts about each sensory system and to better understand how evolution has shaped the "design" of input systems to the brain.

We have already discussed the first general principle in the "design" of sensory systems. Recall from the discussion above, that the brain itself is completely insensitive to the external world in its raw forms. The brain uses neural code. It deals in neuron potentials. *The brain cannot deal with the world or its energies in their raw forms.* Energies in the external world must be converted into the only form that the brain can deal with, neuron potentials. Recall from above, that if a neurosurgeon shines a bright light directly onto the exposed visual cortex in a conscious human patient, particularly if the patient has been blindfolded, the patient doesn't see the light, even though the light is directly shining on the visual areas of the brain. What's missing here is the conversion of the energy coming from the external world (in this case, light from a flashlight) into a form that the brain can utilize. Therefore, *the first major step in any sensory system is the conversion of environmental energy into neuron potentials.* Recall that this process is called *transduction* and that the cells that perform transduction of environmental energy into neuron potentials are specialized neurons called *sensory receptors. The sensory organs themselves, such as eyes and ears, are accessory organs, which operate on the energies in the world preparing them in various ways for transduction by sensory receptors.* For example, the eyes focus an image on the surface of the retina where rods and cones then transduce the light from the projected image.

In the auditory system, the structures of the inner ear amplify the mechanical energy in the vibrations in the air before it reaches the hair cells for transduction. The ears collect and then magnify the silent pressure waves in the air via the mechanics of small bones in the inner ear, the hammer, anvil, and stapes, connecting the large membrane of the eardrum to the much smaller membrane at the oval window. The concentrated and thus amplified energy vibrates this smaller membrane setting up waves in a fluid inside a coiled tube, the cochlea, which pushes on cilia, tiny hairs, on the auditory receptor cells. This wave action on the cilia causes these cells to open their cell membranes to electrically charged atoms surrounding them. These ions then move into or out of the receptor cells. This movement of charged atoms (ions) through the cell membrane of the auditory receptors (the "hair cells" inside the cochlea) causes these cells to make an electrical potential, a receptor potential. Bingo! Silent pressure waves in the air have been *transduced* into neuron potentials. Soon a sensation of sound will be produced in the brain, as newly generated neuron potentials travel along an auditory nerve pathway to auditory parts of the brain, including the *primary auditory cortex*. Bingo again! Neuron potentials now conjure up the sensation of sound in the mind of the animal or human as these voltages are pushed through the specific circuit design of the primary auditory cortex in our brain's temporal lobes.

Note again, as in the case of vision, that once transduction takes place (the first step in sensory systems) then from that point on, the stimulus energy from the world has been converted to neuron potentials and therefore has nothing more to do with sensory processing or sensory experience. So, just as in the case of vision wherein we never really see light, but only our own neuron potentials as they reach and stimulate visual cortex, so too in hearing, we never really hear the silent pressure waves in the air that we call "sound waves," we only "hear" our own neuron potentials as they activate auditory cortex. We experience *auditory qualia*, sounds and their properties such as pitch and timbre, only as neuron potentials course through and stimulate a specific configuration of neuronal connections located in the primary auditory cortex. You may begin to see the picture that is emerging here. In vision and in hearing, we never really experience the world directly, because the energies coming from the external world outside our heads never get past the sensory receptors. All that ever reaches our brains is neuron potentials, and yet, from these, our brains create a model, a virtual reality, which we naively mistake for the real thing. But, that virtual reality is all we know, it's all we *can* know directly. And so naturally, it passes for the real thing. Should we be worried by this surprising revelation? Don't run any red lights in the belief that virtual reality is just imagination, because the virtual reality created by our brains, it turns out, is very good at duplicating or modeling the adaptively significant features of the physical world. It has to be, because alternative brain designs, those which did not happen to produce adaptively useful representations of the world, would have been "weeded out" long ago by natural selection. Our virtual realities are "tuned" by evolution to be extremely good models or representations of the world, or more accurately of the *adaptively significant* features of the world, those that bear on our ability to avoid danger, to find and recognize sources of nutrition, to find and select mates, and to solve our other biological problems. Reality is constructed in particular ways by our sensory systems and our brains to achieve biological purposes, the survival and reproduction of our genes (see chapter 6).

We shall see in chapter 9 that the same is true of emotions. Emotions are a kind of perception. Sensory systems such as the visual system and the auditory system focus on and create neural representations that give our minds information about things like wavelength of light, frequency of pressure wave, intensities of these energies, the locations of their sources in three-dimensional space, and so on, information that helps our brains locate and identify things in the world and their physical properties. Emotions focus upon and create "mental" (information processing) representations about the adaptive *value, or adaptive significance,* to us of specific things we encounter in the world, predisposing us to respond to them in ways that will facilitate the survival and reproduction of our genes. For example, my 9 year old daughter just screamed and then whined that a big black spider was on the wall beside her. She didn't consciously realize it, but her feelings of fear and disgust are the end product of rapid fire computations by her brain that assess the adaptive significance of this buggy thing, as her sensory and perceptual systems are identifying it and its location. Of course, the fear and disgust she experiences tell her that the spider is potentially dangerous. Her emotions tell her this thing is not good "for me and my genes" and therefore should be avoided or eliminated (she asked me to squash it). Remember in an earlier chapter, I described two basic behavioral dispositions in organisms, approach (close the distance between me and it) and avoid (increase the distance between me and it). Positive emotions predispose us to the first response, and negative emotions predispose us to the later response, whether the stimulus is a spider or a particular social relationship (ex-spouses usually put emotional and physical distance between themselves, although there are exceptions when there are enough positive emotions still left—for example, see the movie, "It's Complicated," with Alec Baldwin and Meryl Streep. The title indicates a situation, often faced by animals or humans, when there are conflicting emotions because there are both adaptive and maladaptive conditions associated with the person or other situation one is having emotions about—"it's complicated" and we feel conflicted because both adaptive and maladaptive consequences are part of the situation; by the way, this same situation is seen in other species as well. For example, rats that are first trained to press a lever for food reward and then later given a shock, as well as food, if they press the lever, show signs of emotional stress and conflict just as we would and they are even prone to develop ulcers and other psychosomatic illnesses as a consequence of the persisting conflict).

To better understand how and why the sensory systems work as they do, it is important to understand that there are different kinds of energy in the external world. Light is a form of electromagnetic energy. Sound and touch depend upon forms of mechanical energy, and taste and smell depend upon chemical energies. Sensory receptors have specialized "designs" so that they convert or transduce only one particular type of energy into neuron potentials. Therefore, each of the sensory systems must have its own specialized sensory receptors. The job of the sensory receptors in each of the sensory systems is to transduce or convert some specific form of environmental energy into the brain's code, neuron potentials. As already discussed, in the visual system, the visual receptors, located at the back inner surface of the eyeball, the retina, are of two major types— rods and cones—transduce electromagnetic energy. The auditory receptors, called "hair cells," located in the cochlea in the inner ear, transduce mechanical energy in the form of vibrations in the air into neuron potentials. The touch receptors, located throughout the skin's surface all over the body, convert mechanical energy from pressure on the skin into neuron potentials. Temperature receptors in the skin convert thermal energy into neuron potentials. And pain receptors transduce any very intense and potentially injurious stimulus into neuron potentials (temperature and pain receptors send their neuron potentials to a region of the thalamus known as the posterolateral thalamus; see Craig, et al., 1994). For the taste system, you can probably guess which structures contain the sensory receptors for this sensory system—the taste buds. The taste buds contain cells that transduce chemical energies in chemicals dissolved in saliva into neuron potentials.

The fact that each sensory receptor is best at transducing only one type of energy is the result of the specialized structure of each type of receptor. For example, the visual receptors, the rods and the cones, transduce light into neuron potentials because they contain chemicals, known as *photopigments* or visual pigments, which chemically break down into constituent molecules when struck by light. These photopigments are so sensitive they can respond to a single photon (a minute, fundamental particle of light). When photons of light strike *rhodopsin* (the photopigment in rods) or one of the three *iodopsins* (the photopigments in each of three types of cone, sensitive to a different range of wavelengths of the electromagnetic spectrum that we call "visible" light), the photopigment is broken down into smaller constituent chemicals, one of which, called opsin, acts on the cell membrane of the rod or the cone, causing changes that allow electrically charged atoms (ions) to move across the cell membrane of the rod or the cone, carrying with them their charges, modifying the voltage inside the rod or cone. And just like that, transduction of light into neuron potentials has been accomplished. As pointed out above, from this point onward, light has nothing else at all to do with "seeing."

In summary:

1. *The brain is completely insensitive to the external world in its raw forms.* The brain can deal with information only if it is in the form of brain code, neuron potentials.
2. *Because of this, the first major step in any sensory system is transduction,* the conversion of some specific form of environmental energy into neuron potentials.
3. *Each of the sensory systems has its own sensory receptors "designed" to transduce one specific type of environmental energy* (mechanical, chemical, or electromagnetic—light for example) into neuron potentials.

But these first three principles only take us to the point where transduction has occurred in sensory receptors in sensory organs. This alone is insufficient for us to have sensory experience of the world. Could eyes not connected to the brain see anything? Or ears not connected to the brain hear anything? No, of course not, even our common sense knows this couldn't be true. *Seeing, hearing, touch and other skin sensations, tastes and smells occur in specific regions of the brain.* After transduction, the resulting neuron potentials must go to the brain if they are to cause us to have psychological experiences, internal mental states, conscious sensations, which represent within our minds the external world, in the form of sensory qualia. How is this accomplished? How do neuron potentials in our brains become mental experiences representing the external world? Several additional general principles of sensory systems are involved.

4. *After transduction* of some specific form of environmental energy into neuron potentials, in most vertebrates including humans, *the resulting neuron potentials* go from the specific sensory organ (i.e. eye or ear, for example) along *specific sensory nerves* (for example, the optic nerve in the case of vision, the auditory nerve in the case of hearing) to the brain, specifically to a structure near the center of the brain, called the *thalamus.*

5. In mammals such as us, each of the senses, except the sense of smell, has its own area of thalamus, which receives neuron potentials from the respective sensory organ. For example, in the visual system, the part of the thalamus that receives neuron potentials from the optic nerve is called the LGN, *lateral geniculate nucleus.* In the auditory system, it is the MGN, the *medial geniculate nucleus,* which receives neuron potentials along the auditory nerve from the inner ear. As noted above, each of the senses, except the sense of smell, has its own specific area of thalamus. (Smell, the olfactory sense, probably the earliest to develop in evolution, has an anatomical organization that differs from the other more recently evolved senses. There is no area in the thalamus for the sense of smell, but the olfactory system has its own unique structure, the olfactory bulbs at the base of the frontal lobe). Information, coded in the form of neuron potentials, from the various senses (except smell) is processed in these sensory-specific regions of the thalamus (for example, see the discussion above about the specific area of thalamus for pain and temperature sensation).

6. *After this processing in the thalamus, in mammals like us, new neuron potentials generated there are sent on to the cerebral cortex for additional processing.* In mammals, *each area of thalamus* (i.e. LGN, MGN, etc.) "projects", *sends neural impulses* (action potentials) *to some specific area of cerebral cortex* for more processing. The specific area of cortex that receives neural impulses from a specific region of the thalamus is called the *primary sensory cortex* for that sense. Each of the

senses has its own primary sensory cortex. For example, the area of cerebral cortex that receives projections (nerve pathways carrying action potentials) from the LGN is the *primary visual cortex* (as noted earlier, the primary visual cortex is in the occipital lobe). The area of cortex that receives projections from the MGN of the thalamus is the *primary auditory cortex* (located in the temporal lobe). Interestingly, *there is an orderly mapping of the sensory surface of each sense onto the surface of the respective primary sensory cortex.* For example, the curved surface of the retina of the eye is mapped in an orderly way onto the surface of the primary visual cortex. For each point on the retina (which contains the visual receptors—rods and cones), there is a corresponding point on the primary visual cortex in the occipital lobe. Adjacent points on the retina have adjacent points on the surface of the primary visual cortex. *This point-for-point mapping or representation of the retina (the visual receptive surface) onto the primary visual cortex is called "retinotopic mapping." A similar arrangement exists for the other senses as well. There are topographic maps of each of the other sensory surfaces onto their respective primary sensory cortices.* For example, the skin surface of the body is laid out, point-for-point, on the surface of the primary somatosensory cortex (located in the *post-central gyrus of the parietal lobe*). However, this *"somatotopic" mapping* is upside down, and it is distorted due to the fact that more sensitive areas of the body have larger areas of cortex devoted to them, but nevertheless the mapping is orderly and precise. In the auditory system, the auditory receptors ("hair cells") are distributed over a membrane, called the *basilar membrane*, located inside the cochlea in the inner ear. The orderly distribution of these hair cells along the basilar membrane is systematically mapped onto the surface of primary auditory cortex in the temporal lobe. These mappings of the sensory surfaces onto their respective primary sensory cortex provides basis for the coding of various features of sensory stimuli, such as the location of objects and their parts in visual space, the locations of stimuli on the skin, and the frequencies of "sound" waves vibrating the eardrum. For example, the mapping in the auditory cortex reflects an orderly representation of the pitch or tone of "sounds" (dependent upon the frequency of the "sound" waves, the silent pressure waves in the air), and so the mapping in the auditory cortex is referred to as *tonotopic mapping*. These mapping functions from sensory surface (retina, basilar membrane, skin, etc.) to primary sensory cortex are "design" features which preserve much of the information in the sensory input from sensory surface, where transduction takes place, to the cortical level where the processing occurs that produces conscious sensory experience. Such topographic mapping between sensory surface and sensory cortex exemplifies what is called *anatomical coding*.

7. *After information processing in primary sensory cortex, additional information processing occurs in additional areas of cerebral cortex. These areas, in turn, are called secondary sensory cortex, third level (or tertiary) sensory cortex, fourth level sensory cortex, etc.* Each level of additional processing produces more abstract features in our perceptions of the world as if they are being built by more and more complex and specialized information processing systems at successively "higher" levels of the sensory pathways. For example, in the visual system, as noted earlier, the primary visual cortex (also known as striate cortex or V1) is located in the central area of the occipital lobe at the back of your head. Surrounding this area of cortex, like a donut, is secondary visual cortex (V2). In addition, there are visual areas 3, 4, 5 and 6 (V5, for example, processes information that allows you to see motion; in fact, in people with damage here, the ability to see motion is lost. Instead, when viewing a moving object, such persons with "motion blindness" see a series of still shots of the object in successively different stationary positions. Such persons have difficulty crossing a street because as cars approach instead of a moving car, they see a series of still shots of the car, frozen in space, but closer and closer in each succeeding view as the car approaches. When they try to pour liquid into a glass, they report that is appears as if the liquid were a frozen column, and they constantly overflow glasses or cups. There are areas of visual cortex that seem to be specialized for recognition of familiar faces, for color constancy, and for many other visual abilities. It is estimated that in us, and in other primates, there may be more than *thirty* different areas of cortex involved in the later stages of processing of visual information. One of these is *the inferotemporal (IT) cortex,* involved in our ability to recognize objects by sight alone. Damage here allows us to still see, but we can't recognize what it is we are seeing (this disorder is called *visual agnosia*). As is often the case with brain systems, the deficits that result from damage are quite specific. The inability in these patients to identify objects due to damage in the IT cortex is restricted to vision. If a dog is brought in, patients with visual agnosia can't identify it by sight, even though they can identify visual details, such as the observation that it has four legs, has fur, and a black wet nose, but as soon as they hear it bark, or smell it, they immediately identify it correctly as a dog. As noted in an earlier chapter, brain imaging experiments have shown that we even have specialized areas of the visual system for "visualizing" in our "mind's eye" ourselves engaged in various actions, basis for much of our perception of a separate self which has a "free will" (see chapters 4 and 5).

8. After these initial seven steps in information processing, somehow *the resulting patterns of electrical activity occurring in large populations of neurons (which make up complex circuits in the brain) produce mental experiences of the external world.*

This should remind the reader of earlier chapters in which we considered psychophysical monism. There I made the argument that mental experiences may arise as "emergent properties" of the structure and functioning of extremely complex circuits in the brain—entirely material in structure and function (see chapter 3). These conscious, psychological experiences arising from neural activity in our sensory systems are the "sensory qualia." For example, luminosity of light or colors of objects, both produced by neural activity in visual areas of the brain, are examples of visual qualia. Sounds, such as the sound of a cricket chirping or waves crashing on the beach, are auditory qualia. Tastes such as the taste of sugar or the taste of a lemon or chocolate (my favorite) are taste qualia. There are also somatosensory qualia (skin sensations) and olfactory qualia (smells). Notice that all of the sensory qualia are produced when patterns of neural impulses reach and activate the neurons in a particular sensory cortex. Neural impulses are *action potentials* and they are the same everywhere in the nervous systems of all animals. The thing that determines the nature of the sensory qualia, the type of sensory experience that one has from a particular sensory input, is *where* in the brain (which sensory cortex) the neural impulses, from the sensory organs, end up (Muller's 1835 *law of specific nerve energies*). So, for example, if we could somehow surgically redirect the optic nerves and connect them to taste cortex, as discussed earlier in this chapter, then sensations of taste, taste qualia, would result when light was transduced by rods and cones in the eyes. In other words, under these conditions, you would taste light, not see it. If our nervous systems were in fact actually wired this way, you would grow up thinking that light was tasty (just like you grow up thinking that light is luminous and colored) and that different wavelengths of light had different tastes. And you would be right to say that light tasted, well, at least as right as you are when you say, now, that light is luminous and colored—which is to say, you would not be right, at all. Light is neither tasty, nor luminous and colored. These different properties which we would ascribe to light are really properties of the activity of the neurons arranged in complex synaptic configurations that get activated in the presence of light when areas of visual cortex are activated.

These 8 general principles apply to all of our sensory systems and to the sensory systems of all the *mammals*, animals with cerebral cortex. The first four apply to the sensory systems of *all animals* in general. In species without cortex or others lacking even a thalamus, other brain structures characteristic of those species carry out additional processing of sensory information. Nevertheless, transduction of environmental energies by sensory receptors into neuron potentials which are then processed by additional neural structures in the brain of each species is universal to all animals, even invertebrates such as octopus and insects. Forms of life which we might discover elsewhere in the universe someday may be expected to follow a similar pattern of organization.

An extremely important thing to keep in mind is that *sensory qualia are entirely in your head (more accurately, in your brain)*. Although we grow up thinking that light is luminous and colored, in fact it is not. Light in fact is no more luminous or colored than X-rays or radio waves (both of which, like light, are forms of electromagnetic energy). Luminosity (the glowing quality that we attribute to light) and color are really properties of the brain's response to light, not properties of light itself. Light, in the external world, is really just as dark as other forms of electromagnetic energy (recall the forms of electromagnetic energy are gamma rays, X-rays, ultraviolet, visible light, infrared, T.V., radio, in order of increasing wavelength). The luminosity we associate with light is not *in* the light, but results from brain activity *in* the visual system of our brains. Luminosity and color are not in the world at all, but are creations of our brains' visual cortical circuit "design."

The experience of different colors is really a brain code for different wavelengths of light. (Light travels in waves through space; the distance between adjacent wave peaks is the wavelength of the light; the wavelength of light reflected from an object depends upon the chemical composition and other physical properties of the material out of which an object is composed). Within our eyes we have rods and cones (the visual receptors). There are three different types of cones (but just one type of rod). Each type of cone is maximally sensitive (maximally able to transduce) light waves within its own particular range of wavelengths. "Color vision" begins when a particular wavelength of reflected light gets transduced by a particular set of cones. These, in turn, send a particular pattern of neural impulses to specific neurons in the visual cortex (via the LGN of the thalamus), which when stimulated produce the mental experience of a particular color. None of this occurs in the brain of a dog or a cow or many other species which lack cones in their eyes (they have rods only). Is our perception of reality more complete or more accurate than that of the dog which lacks color vision? In one sense, the answer is yes—we have the capacity to code the wavelength of reflected light in the external world, the dog does not. But, nevertheless, the "color" we experience in our minds only exists there, not in the external world. So, in a way, we are somewhat misled by our color perception. There are different wavelengths of light, and it is adaptive for us to possess a mental code for these different wavelengths. (It makes it very easy to see ripened fruit against the leafy background of a tree, a real advantage to our tree-living primate ancestors who also had good "color" vision). But, the color in our minds is an illusion (recall the premise of The Matrix; see opening quote, this chapter). The light in the external world is not really colored; in fact, it is not even luminous (as noted earlier, it is as dark and non-luminous as X-rays or radio waves).

The luminosity of light, as we experience it, is dependent upon the fact that light (a particular range of wavelengths within the electromagnetic spectrum) gets transduced by rods and cones leading to activation of visual cortical neurons in our heads. If rods and cones were constructed differently, so that they transduced a different range of wavelengths within the electromagnetic spectrum, say, for example, that range known as radio waves, then we would experience radio waves as being luminous, and different wavelengths of radio waves as different colors. Regarding color specifically, here is something you can demonstrate to yourself that will show that the visual qualia, color, exists only inside brains. Imagine being outside around sunset. You will notice that objects in the environment still appear to have color. Trees still appear green. Their trunks still appear some shade of brown. You may see a red car parked nearby, and someone walks past you in blue jeans. But as the sun sets, and the daylight fades more and more, there comes a point at which the trees no longer are green, blue jeans are no longer blue, and other objects "lose" their colors, and all becomes blacks and shades of gray (if there are no artificial sources of light).

It is about 9 p.m. as I write this. A moment ago, I stepped outside. I saw a large tree. The shape of the tree including some of its leaves was clearly visible, but the tree was completely black and gray. There was no color at all. Now, think about this. Where did the color go? The answer is, it really wasn't there to begin with. What has happened, as the intensity of light drops off, is that color generating systems in the brain and nervous system shut down because the cones of the eye that transduce light according to wavelength require "bright", high intensity, light. When the color generating systems in the brain and nervous system shut down, the color disappears because the color was only in your head (your brain) in the first place, never really in the external world at all. The visual receptors that are involved in color perception, the cones, can only transduce the higher levels of light typical of daylight. At night, there is insufficient light to cause transduction in the cones, but still enough light for transduction by the rods, which are much more sensitive, capable of transduction of lower intensities of light. Cones activate parts of the visual system, at the level of the LGN and visual cortex, which generate color qualia, sensations of color. Without the activation of these brain systems, there is no color. You experience this absence of color firsthand at night (if there are no artificial light sources to raise levels of light to the threshold necessary to activate the cones and their associated color generating circuits in the brain). Color, just like luminosity, or sound, or tastes and smells or sensations on the skin, exists only inside living functioning brains.

During brain surgery, patients who have their primary somatosensory cortex stimulated report feeling things at various places on their skin. In one case which I witnessed (via a film of the surgery), the patient said with astonishment, when a point on his somatosensory cortex was stimulated, "I feel something on my teeth." When a nearby point on the same cortex was stimulated a moment later, he said with equal astonishment, "Now, it's on my tongue. I feel something on my tongue!" There was nothing on his teeth or on his tongue. The realistic feeling of something on the teeth or tongue was due to electrical stimulation of different, but nearby, regions of *primary somato-sensory cortex*. The fact that different points of stimulation produced skin sensations that seemed to be localized to different places on the skin surface reflects the system-atic mapping of the skin surface onto the surface of the primary somatosensory cortex (referred to earlier as "somatotopic mapping").

The lesson of these examples is that the world that we know and experience is really in our heads, in a virtual reality created by our brain activity. The color, the luminosity, the tastes, the smells and other sensory qualia are not properties of the external world or the things in it, but properties produced by the activity of nerve cells organized into complex circuits in the brain. I'm not denying that there is an external world out there, outside our heads, I'm just saying that it doesn't really look, sound, smell, feel, or taste the way we think it does. In the objective world outside our heads, none of these sub-jective properties actually exist. So what does the world outside our heads really look like? It doesn't really look like anything, independent of the properties of the "looker," the brain and nervous system that is doing the looking. What the world or anything else looks like is dependent as much upon the properties of the nervous system doing the looking as it is upon properties of the things being looked at. The world looks one way to a bee, another way to a snake, another way to a dog, another way to a bat, another way still to us. In each case, the nervous system creates a representation, a model, of the external world, the function of which is to guide adaptive behavior of the organism. Natural selection "designed" nervous systems for that adaptive "purpose", not to give the organism an objective model of absolute Reality with a capital R. *Reality is species-specific*. Each species' nervous system represents the aspects of the world important for the organization of successful behavioral adaptation for that species, within the envi-ronmental niche occupied by that species. Still, in spite of species differences in sensory systems and resulting differences in the representation of reality for each species, there are also likely to be aspects of the external world that are represented in similar ways across a broad range of species. These aspects of reality would be those which are more or less universal to the environmental niches of a broad range of species. For example, representation by the brain of gravitational forces and their direction is something that is probably universally found in a very broad range of species of animal life on earth. Gravitational pull identifies where "down" is for most species and all information pro-cessing about position of the body in space uses that same neurologically defined spa-tial reference.

To reiterate these points, let's consider once again the classic philosophical ques-tion: "If a tree falls in the forest, and there is no one (no brain, human or animal) to hear it, is there a sound?" Perhaps by now, the reader will already understand that in spite of the obvious contradiction with "common sense," the answer is "No, there is no sound". Without sensory receptors to transduce the mechanical pressure waves in the air into neuron potentials, which then stimulate the neurons in an auditory cortex, the only place where sound can occur, there can be no sound. Sure, there are "sound" waves out there in the external world regardless of whether anyone is present. But "sound" waves don't have sound in them. They are really no more than completely silent pressure waves in the air, which could deflect, say, a feather, as the pressure wave passed through the path of the falling feather. But those vibrations of air molecules, as real as they are, are still silent. Without a brain present, they cannot become *sound*.

You might say, well, I could put a tape recorder out there and record the sound of the falling tree and therefore prove that sound existed even though there was no person or no animal present. Well, all I can say is nice try, but still there's no sound, even if your tape recorder worked perfectly. Here's why. The tape recorder receives the vibrations in the air via a microphone which contains a membrane which simply vibrates along with the vibrations in the air that strike it. These silent physical vibrations are transduced by the tape recorder into blips on a magnetic tape because the vibrating membrane of the microphone of the tape recorder has a magnet attached to it, which in turn, vibrates inside a coil of electrified wire. When the tape is replayed the blips on magnetic tape are simply transduced back into mechanical vibrations of the membrane of the output speaker (using a similar magnet and coiled wire) causing vibrations in the air exactly like the vibrations in the air that were originally "recorded." Thus, all the tape recorder does is take mechanical vibrations in the air, transduce and store them as blips on magnetic tape, then when the tape is replayed, the machine simply reproduces the vibrations in the air that were there in the first place. So we are back where we started. There's no sound coming out of the tape recorder when we play the recording. All that comes out is silent, mechanical vibrations in the air, exactly like those produced originally by the falling tree. And once again, if there is no nervous system to transduce these silent vibrations coming out of the tape recorder into neuron potentials that are then sent to an auditory cortex (or similar neural structure) in some brain, then there will be *no sound*. Sound is a subjective psychological experience, an emergent property, resulting from specific neural events, and can exist, like luminosity and color, taste and smell, only in the neurological space inside of heads, that is, inside brains.

The Visual System

Now, with this background about sensory systems in general and the nature of sensory qualia, let's examine the visual system in more detail. This will allow us to not only learn some of the specifics about the visual system, but will provide an opportunity to illustrate the general principles above, using the visual system as an example. The fundamental question that we should keep in mind, as we proceed, is how does the visual system (or any of the sensory systems) do it—how might neural events (voltages moving through circuits made of neurons) produce our mental experiences?

A brief tour of the human eye

We begin with the eye. Its role is to function as an accessory organ that receives and operates, in various ways, on the energy that stimulates vision to make it possible for neurons, the receptors, to efficiently transduce light into a form that the brain can deal with, neuron potentials.

We will move through the basic anatomy of the eyeball quickly so we can move on to the brain and its visual mechanisms. The outer clear covering at the front of the eyeball is called the *cornea*. It does some preliminary focusing of light as it enters the eye. The *iris*, the colored part of your eye (usually brown, blue or hazel), is really a circular muscle that by contracting or relaxing controls the size of the pupil of your eye, regulating the amount of light that enters the eye. Behind the iris is the *lens* of the eye. It focuses light into a clear image onto the retina. Focus is accomplished not by moving the lens back and forth, as occurs in a camera, but by the lens of the eye changing shape. Changes in the thickness of the lens causes it to bend light more or less, thus changing focus, depending upon the distance to the object being viewed. Changes in the thickness of the lens of the eye are controlled by a set of muscles, *ciliary muscles*, attached around the perimeter of the lens. When the ciliary muscles contract (shorten), the lens is stretched (it's made of a clear, rubbery substance), making it thinner, so that it bends light less. This is the situation when you are looking at something farther away. When you are looking at something close, the light from the object must be bent more to achieve a clear focus on the retina. To accomplish this greater bending of light, the lens of the eye must be fatter, thicker. This occurs when the ciliary muscles are relaxed to the degree necessary, allowing the rubbery lens to pop back into its fatter, thicker shape. All of this machinery controlling the lens and the focusing of light is under the control of reflexes regulating the state of contraction of the ciliary muscles dependent upon the distance to the object at the focus of visual attention.

The *retina*, the "light-sensitive" surface at the back of the interior of the eyeball, contains the visual receptors, the rods and the cones. The retina actually consists of several cell layers. In order, from the deepest layer up to the more superficial layers, these cell layers are: the rods and the cones (the deepest cell layer, furthest from the light entering the eye), the *bipolar cells*, and then on top, the *retinal ganglion cells* (RG). The axons of the RG cells gather and leave the back of the eyeball (the "blind spot") to form the *optic nerve*. In addition to these 3 layers of cells stacked on top of one another, there are horizontal cells and amacrine cells which interconnect retinal neurons laterally within a layer.

The Dual Visual System

Human beings and many other primates have what's called a *"dual visual system"*—a cone system and a rod system. Each of these has different specialized visual functions. The *cone system* is specialized for "color" (more accurately, for *wavelength discrimination*; see discussion above about visual qualia) and for visual acuity (the ability to see detail). The *rod system* is specialized for vision in low levels of illumination ("night time vision"). The rods and cones are distributed differently over the surface of the retina. The cones are concentrated toward the center of the retina. This central area of retina is called the *fovea*. The central fovea has only cones in it, no rods at all. As we move outward from the fovea along the retinal surface, the concentration of cones drops off and the concentration of rods increases, so that the greatest concentration of rods (the visual receptors for night vision) is in the periphery of the retina. This is why when you are trying to see a very dim object at night (such as a distant ship on the night horizon or a very dim star), you should look just to the side of where you think it is. By doing so, you move the image from the fovea (where there are only cones, not sensitive to dim light) to the periphery of the retina where most of the rods are located. Notice that this takes an act of "will" since we are programmed with a natural disposition to position our eyeballs so that images of objects that we are interested in seeing are positioned automatically over the fovea of the retina where the greatest concentration of cones is located, because the cones are specialized for seeing detail.

In large part, the differences in function between the rod and cone visual systems in humans and other primates are due to differences in the wiring of the receptors to the retinal ganglion (RG) cells. The cones, concentrated in the fovea of the retina, specialized for "seeing" detail have this capacity because there are one-to-one connections between cones in the central fovea and their respective bipolars and RG cells. That is, each cone has its own bipolar cell and its own retinal ganglion (RG) cell and thus its own "private line" to the brain. This means that a very narrow beam of light will be transduced by a few cones, perhaps even a single cone, and the message sent to the brain via the RG cell that connects (via a bipolar cell) to that cone is very precise indeed, producing great visual acuity. If a particular RG cell connected to a single foveal cone sends a message to the brain, then the brain "knows" exactly where on the retinal surface the light source is. This precise message allows good visual acuity (ability to see detail). By contrast in the rod system of the human eye, the wiring is different. A large number of rods connect to each individual retinal ganglion cell. If a particular RG cell in the periphery of the retina sends a message to the brain, the brain doesn't "know" exactly where on the retina the light source is, because there are so many rods connected to any given RG cell in the periphery of the retina. Thus, the rod system is not good at detailed vision (visual acuity). To illustrate, imagine trying to read by moonlight. You can see the page, and even the letters, but you can't tell an "e" from a "c". Though the rod system is not very good at discriminating detail because so many rods connect to each retinal ganglion cell in the retina's periphery, it is good at getting a message to the brain, in the form of neuron potentials, even in dim light conditions. Dim light activates each rod only slightly, but because so many rods converge on the same retinal ganglion cell, the small activities of many rods summate in the RG cell, and it ends up sending a "strong" message to the brain, where seeing is actually occurring. This is why we can see at night at all. But remember, the rod system doesn't discriminate wavelengths of light, so no color sensations are produced by the rod system. So night time vision is "colorless." As noted above, this is because the *color-generation mechanisms* of the brain, associated with the cone system, are shut down in low levels of illumination. That's why the "green" trees are no longer "green" at night, but just shades of gray. What we see here is an elegant example of how neural circuit "design" can be highly specialized to accomplish specific information processing "goals," or adaptive functions. By one-to-one wiring in the cone system of the human eye, visual acuity is achieved, and by high degrees of convergent neural connections in the rod system, sensitivity in low levels of light is accomplished. Circuit "design" to accomplish specific adaptive "purposes" is evident even in the neural organization of the eye. This same principle will be found operating in the specific circuit configurations in brain systems "designed" by natural selection for specific information processing functions, which serve the adaptive organization of minds and behavior. For example, in the next chapter we will see this principle reflected in the specific features of circuit design in the parts of our brains that control emotion.

Recall that in the cone system, there are three types of cones (there's only one kind of rod). What makes them different from one another are three different types of *iodopsins* (cone photopigments that make each type of cone capable of transducing different ranges of wavelengths of light), one in each of the three different types of cones. One type of cone with its particular iodopsin transduces the *shorter* wavelengths of light best. In the presence of these shorter wavelengths of light, neural impulses are generated that go to particular visual cortical neurons (via the LGN), producing the visual quale (sensation), "blueness, " in the mind of the human, or other primate whose visual cortex is thus activated. A second kind of cone, containing a second kind of iodopsin, transduces *intermediate* wavelengths of light best, causing sensations of "greenness" in the mind, when neuron potentials originating from the transduction of light by these cones eventually end up activating particular sets of neurons in the visual cortex which somehow create the visual sensation (visual quale), "green." A third type of cone, containing the third type of iodopsin, transduces best the *longer wavelengths* of light, causing specific neurons in the visual cortex to be activated, producing the sensation of "redness" in the mind. In short, light of a specific wavelength will be transduced by a particular set of cones (because of the kind of iodopsin they contain). Those cones, via the LGN, connect to a specific set of visual cortical cells, which when activated by particular patterns of neuron potentials produce a particular "color" sensation or color quale. By these means, the *wavelength* of light is coded by the brain in a neurologically based psychological code for wavelength which we experience as "color."

Psychologists and sensory physiologists from the past had theorized about how color vision worked. Historically, there were two main theories of color vision. The *trichromatic theory* hypothesized that there were three primary colors and that these must be coded by the activity of three types of cells somewhere in the nervous system. William James formulated this theory just by observing that there seemed to be three primary colors in our conscious experience of the visual world. It turned out that his hunch was right. The three types of cell he hypothesized in his "trichromatic theory of color vision" turned out to be the three types of cone. The second theory was the *Opponent Process Theory* of Hering. Hering observed what are called color afterimages. If you stare at a red surface for a while, when you look away at a gray or white background you will "see" an afterimage of the object, but it will appear green, the "opponent" color. The reverse is also true. Additionally, if you stare at a blue object or surface for a while and look at the gray or white background, the afterimage is yellow. Again, the reverse is also true. A black surface produces a white afterimage. Again, the reverse is true—if you stare at a white image, then the afterimage appears black. Hering, on the basis of these psychological observations, concluded that there must be cells somewhere in the brain that coded pairs of "colors" by opposite or "opponent" neural events. In other words, an increase in the firing rate (the number of action potentials per second) of a particular neuron might code blueness, but a decrease in the firing rate of that same neuron would code for (and produce in the mind) the opponent color, yellowness. Hering's hunch also turned out to be correct. Subsequent neurophysiological research has revealed the existence of *opponent process cells* coding pairs of color sensations by increasing the firing rate to code one color and by decreasing the firing rate to code for the opponent color. Cells with these properties are found in RG cells of the retina, cells of the LGN of the thalamus, and in some regions of visual cortex. Thus, the trichromatic theory of color vision and the opponent-process theory of color vision (once thought to be contradictory) are actually both true, but true at different levels of the visual system— trichromatic theory is accurate at the level of the cones in the retina, the *opponent process theory* is accurate for retinal ganglion cells and certain cells in LGN and visual cortex.

In the primary visual cortex, V1, there are groups of neurons, called "CO blobs," that receive synaptic connections from "color"-sensitive LGN neurons (the neural pathway from LGN to striate cortex, V1, is called the *geniculo-striate pathway*, because it originates in the lateral geniculate and terminates in the striate cortex). The term comes from the fact that these "blobs" show up as cylindrical columns of neurons in the primary visual cortex of the occipital lobe when the cortical tissue here is stained with a dye for an enzyme called cytochrome oxidase (CO). The columns are oval in cross section, approximately 150×200 micrometers in diameter and are spaced at .5 millimeter intervals in the V1 cortex (Carlson, 2011, p. 161). But additional areas of the visual cortex, collectively known as *extrastriate cortex* (outside the striate or primary visual cortex, V1) are also involved in "color" processing. An adjacent area of visual cortex, V2, and another close by, V3, contain cells that are sensitive to "color" (wavelength of light). In addition, an area of human visual cortex located on the bottom side (ventral surface) of the occipital lobe, known as V4 in monkeys, is also involved in wavelength sensitivity ("color" perception). Brain damage in the *ventral posterior cortex* (lower surface of the occipital lobe) in the region of V4 often produces a perceptual disorder known as *achromatopsia* in which patients report that the world appears devoid of color, so that everything appears only in shades of gray (Banich and Compton, 2011).

"What" and "Where" Pathways

After additional processing in V2, V3, V4 and nearby areas, action potentials from the *striate* (primary visual cortex, V1) and *extrastriate* visual areas (outside V1) in the occipital lobe cortex travel into two forward-directed pathways: 1) from visual cortex, neuron potentials are sent forward to a *dorsal (upper) visual pathway* or "stream" leading to the parietal lobe (for visual localization) wherein information telling you *where* things are, in 3-D space, is processed; and 2) from visual cortex, neuron potentials go forward along a different, lower or *ventral visual pathway* or "stream" (for visual recognition and understanding) which terminates in the lower temporal lobe in an area called the *inferotemporal cortex* (IT cortex). Processing in this pathway tells you *what* things are, permitting you to identify and recognize what you are looking at. This is likely a region important in visual memories. As discussed earlier, damage to the *inferotemporal (IT) cortex* causes *visual agnosia*, the ability to see without understanding what it is that you are seeing, that is, without recognizing by sight even the most familiar of objects. People with visual agnosia would not recognize a kitten by sight, even though they could describe the details of what it looked like to them. This shows that they can still see clearly, they simply can't put the details together and recognize by sight what it is they are seeing. This demonstrates that a particular psychological function that we usually take for granted, the ability to recognize and understand what we see is actually dependent upon specific neurons located in a specific region of cerebral cortex. As explained a little earlier, the agnosia (literally, "not knowing") is confined to the affected sense. If the kitten meows, or if the person feels the size and texture of the kitten, the person immediately recognizes what the object is by using these other senses which rely upon brain areas that are undamaged. There is a variety of visual agnosia, called *prosopagnosia*, which is the inability to recognize familiar faces by sight, even when it is one's own face in a photo or in a mirror that is being viewed. Again the afflicted person can still describe in great detail the face they are looking at (even to the point of describing the pimples on the person's face or the person's hairstyle), but they still can't *recognize* the face (Carlson, 2011). In one case I observed, a woman patient made fun of the hair style of a woman she saw in a photo, unable to recognize that she was looking at a photograph of herself (if you find this a bit funny, think about the nature of humor, a response to something which appears contradictory, extreme or out of proportion in some unexpected or surprising way; Darwin suspected that laughter was a form of tension releaser in response to such stimuli. See *The Expression of the Emotions in Man and Animals* by Darwin, 1872).

With damage to the parietal lobe, or the *dorsal visual pathway*, which leads to the parietal lobe from the primary visual cortex, a person loses the ability to tell by sight *where* objects in the visual field are located. Such patients have trouble accurately pointing to objects in the visual field and they may get confused by words such as "behind," "forward," "in front of" or by commands such as, "Show me your *left* hand." In a sense they are "blind" to the location of objects.

The *dorsal visual pathway* or "stream" is often referred to as the "where" visual pathway and the *ventral visual pathway* or "stream" is frequently referred to as the "what" visual pathway. The existence of these two separate streams of information flow is not unique to vision. There is a similar arrangement in the auditory system—a dorsal pathway for spatial location of a "sound" source, and a ventral pathway that we use when we determine the identity of something just by hearing it. For example, I just heard the song of a bird outside my window. I can hear that the song is coming from a place outside my house in front of me at about 20 degrees left of center, and perhaps 30 yards away, a three dimensional specification of location. That's the *dorsal auditory pathway* working. The fact that I recognize the "sound" as bird song, including a visual image of a bird in my mind as I listen, is dependent upon my *ventral auditory pathway* specialized for auditory recognition and my ventral visual pathway for the visual image.

Let me summarize (and oversimplify) the basic anatomy of the visual system so far by listing in order the structures and events involved in the processing of information in humans and other primates, leading to vision: 1) Transduction of light into receptor potentials by the visual receptors, the rods and cones (*light, after this first step, has nothing more to do with seeing*)—2) bipolar neurons in the retina are activated by rods and cones—3) Retinal ganglion cells (RG) in the retina, activated by bipolars, generate action potentials—4) these action potentials ("nerve impulses") in RG cells are conducted along the axons of these RG cells (these axons bundle to make the *optic nerve*) to neurons in the LGN of the thalamus (more processing occurs here in LGN)—5) LGN neurons generate their own action potentials (nerve impulses) which are then transmitted to neurons in the *primary visual cortex* (also known as V1, striate cortex, Broadman area 17) via a neural pathway known as the *geniculo-striate pathway* and more processing occurs in primary visual cortex, then 6) primary visual cortical neurons generate their own action potentials which are then transmitted to additional visual cortical areas in the occipital lobe surrounding V1 for more information processing—7) after additional processing in V2, V3, V4 and nearby areas, action potentials from the occipital lobe go forward into two pathways: 1) forward to a *dorsal (upper) visual pathway* leading to the parietal lobe (for visual localization) wherein information telling you *where* things are in 3-D space is processed and 2) action potentials also go forward to a lower, *ventral visual pathway* (for visual recognition and understanding) in the inferotemporal cortex, (in the temporal lobe). Processing in this pathway tells you *what* things are, permitting you to identify and recognize what you are looking at. This whole sequence from rods and cones to the visual cortical areas is called the *visual pathway.*

Now, what is it in the properties of nerve cells and their circuits that might help us understand how the brain is processing information to accomplish these visual perceptual abilities? One way to study the functions performed by the brain is to ask what single neurons do to help accomplish some psychological or behavioral function. This question can be answered in part by the use of tiny recording electrodes placed directly into the cell bodies of individual visual neurons.

Single Cell Recording

With regard to the visual system, we already know what single *visual receptor cells* do. The rods and cones transduce light into neuron potentials. But what about the other cells in the visual pathway? What do these single cells do to contribute to "seeing"? To help find out, many vision researchers use a method called "single cell recording." This method involves recording the neuron potentials coming from selected single neurons along the visual pathway. The pioneering work in this area, in primate cortex, was done about 30 years ago by two Harvard neurophysiologists, David Hubel and Torsten Wiesel (Hubel and Wiesel, 1977). They ended up receiving the Nobel Prize for Medicine and Physiology for their work on the response characteristics of neurons in the visual cortex of the occipital lobe.

To do single cell recording, a brain researcher puts a microscopically thin piece of wire or electrically conducting glass pipette into the cell body of a single neuron inside the eye or brain of an animal such as a cat or a monkey. Then various visual stimuli are presented to the animal to which the cell belongs, on a screen in front of the anesthetized animal's face. Surprisingly, diffuse light will not activate visual cells. Instead, the visual stimuli must be more precise.

By carefully placing a microelectrode into single retinal ganglion (RG) cells in the retina, researchers have discovered that these cells will respond (fire action potentials) only if a point of light falls within a small circular region of the visual field, specific to that particular RG cell. This small circular region of the visual field within which a point of light will activate the RG cell is called the cell's *receptive field*. Research shows that each of the 100 million retinal ganglion cells in each human eye has a small circular receptive field unique to it. These 100 million small circular receptive fields overlap one another accounting for the entire visual field (the area of the world that can be seen at a single glance). The existence of these receptive fields permits a very precise coding by RG cells of the spatial location of points of light in the visual field of the animal. This probably forms part of the basis for our abilities to see shapes and to locate objects in space just by sight. Single cell recording methods in the LGN of the brain reveal that neurons in the LGN have similar small, circular receptive fields, perhaps serving the same functions as those associated with RG cells in the retina. It is believed by neuroscientists that the receptive fields of cells are "built" by the patterns of cells earlier in the visual pathway that connect or synapse with them. For example, a circular array of rods all connecting to a particular retinal ganglion (via the associated bipolar cells) would give that retinal ganglion cell its particular circular receptive field located in the same specific area of the visual field as the circular array of rods connecting to, or converging onto it. By similar processes very complex receptive fields could be built up, at each level of the visual pathway, just by the patterns of connections coming from cells earlier in the pathway. In other words, it is circuit "design" that determines many of the key functional properties of specific neurons. The circular receptive fields of RG cells and of LGN cells are just two examples.

But at the *visual cortex*, receptive field characteristics change drastically (although these characteristics are also created by the patterns of connections the cell receives). Hubel and Wiesel discovered that single visual cortical neurons in the occipital lobe have line-like receptive fields; that is, it is no longer spots of light in particular locations in the visual field that can cause visual cells to fire impulses, but at the cortex, lines and edges are required. Cells in the occipital lobe respond to lines or edges, but only to these linear stimuli if they are at the appropriate orientation in space. In other words, the receptive fields of single neurons in the visual cortex of the occipital lobe are linear, and orientation-specific. Each cell has a "favored" orientation of line or edge to which it will respond. These visual cortical cells are so finely "tuned" that lines or edges in the visual field which deviate from that optimal orientation by even a couple of degrees may be completely "ignored" by the cell. Furthermore, some of these cells are sensitive not only to the orientation of a line or an edge, but also to its direction of motion. Cells may respond vigorously (produce many action potentials per second) to a line at the "correct" orientation moving in one direction, but completely "ignore" the same line or edge if it is moving in the opposite direction. We say that cells in the visual cortex of the occipital lobe have linear, orientation-specific, (and sometimes) direction-of-movement-specific, receptive fields (areas of the visual field that will "fire" the cell if these features are present). Some, known as "hypercomplex" or "edge-stopped" cells are even sensitive to the length of the line or edge. They fire more electrical impulses per second (action potentials) as a line at the favored orientation is made longer, but at a certain point additional length reduces the rate of firing of such cells. What we have here in primary visual cortex are cortical cells that amount to visual *feature detectors*, which fire off action potentials (nerve impulses) only when they are presented with visual inputs with highly specific visual features, such as specific line, bar, or edge orientation, movement, and length.

This finding in the visual cortex of primates is similar to much earlier research in frogs showing that they possess "bug detectors" in their retinas, neurons that only fire to bug-like black dots moving rapidly across their visual fields. Indicative of the adaptive function of these "bug detectors" is the fact that these retinal neurons in the frog were connected to neural circuits that would cause the frog's tongue to shoot out of its mouth to pick off whatever was passing when a bug detector fired. From an evolutionary standpoint, it appears that these cells in the frog retina exist as a specific adaptation to help the frog solve its energy problem (see Chapter 6 for a discussion of biological problems and their adaptive solutions).

In primates, compared to the bug detectors of the frog, the visual *feature detectors* in primary visual cortex are much more general and abstract in the features that will fire them, lines and edges at specific orientations moving in a particular direction, rather than a much more specific (and thus restricted) feature, such as a flying bug. This is just one example of the kind of "mind design" in mammals that gives them much greater flexibility of response, and sophistication of neural representation for more complex "mental" (information processing) functions, compared to more rigid response characteristics typical of vertebrates such as frogs with older evolutionary origins.

What might be the function of visual cortical neurons with such precise, but general, receptive field characteristics? Well, just look around you and you will see that the objects in your visual world have borders or edges, at specific angles or orientations, and oft times they are in motion in a specific direction. Perception of shape and motion of objects is dependent in important ways upon the receptive field characteristics of visual cortical cells. Huge numbers of these neurons fire patterns of nerve impulses distributed over distinct areas of visual cortex to encode features of specific objects as they are viewed in the environment. Confirming this hypothesis, but also complicating things, is the finding by De Valois at UC Berkeley that visual cortical cells respond best to *spatial frequencies* in *sign-wave gratings* rather than to lines and edges (De Valois, Albrecht, and Thorell, 1978).

A sign-wave grating, if projected on an oscilloscope screen, looks like a series of fuzzy, unfocused parallel bands of alternating lighter and darker shades of gray. Along a line perpendicular to the alternating lighter and darker bands, the brightness varies according to a sine-wave mathematical function (Carlson, 2011, p. 159–160). Spatial frequency refers to how abruptly visual information changes from light to dark. Low spatial frequencies correspond to coarse visual patterns with less detail and broader bands. High spatial frequencies are found in fine-grained, detailed images and are associated with narrower bands in a sine-wave grating. Visual cortical neurons that receive input from the fovea of the retina, which provides the most detailed information about the visual world, tend to be sensitive to inputs with higher spatial frequencies than cortical cells that receive input from the periphery of the retina (populated by rods), which tend to be more sensitive to low spatial frequency inputs (Banich and Compton, 2011, p. 154–5).

Importantly, some research has shown that "interference patterns" created by interacting sine-wave gratings of light and dark can produce realistic, detailed, visual images of objects (video on *Vision* from the PBS *Brain* series). This suggests that the subtlety and variety of visual imagery, that the primate cerebral cortex is capable of, might be created from visual cortical neural activity which is coding such interference patterns. A kind of mathematically-based neural coding, taking place within large populations of visual cortical neurons, might generate visual images in the mind by using interference patterns, generated from interacting neural representations similar to sine-wave gratings with differing spatial frequencies.

The possibility that something akin to this might be taking place in our brain's visual system is consistent with some fascinating research exploring the receptive fields of neurons in the temporal lobe visual cortex. Mapping of the receptive fields of single neurons in the *inferotemporal (IT) cortex* shows neurons there have complex, specific, *whole-object receptive fields*. There are single neurons in *IT cortex* that will fire action potentials only if the animal to which the cell belongs is shown a picture of a *specific* whole object such as a tree or a monkey's face. A cell there that has a monkey face as its receptive field is so specific that it may fire only to the profile of the monkey face and not to the full-face frontal view. In that case, we can assume that there must be another cell, perhaps nearby, that responds to the full-face frontal view and other cells to other orientations. This kind of organization in the IT cortex is extraordinary. It suggests the idea of the "grandmother cell", the idea that the mental image of your grandmother (and each and every other recognizable whole object) is somehow coded within the responses of a single, specific IT cortical neuron whose receptive field is that specific image. Such a "grandmother cell" will only fire action potentials (nerve impulses) in the presence of your grandmother's face. Cells in the IT cortex may be storing visual memories. The fact that *damage to the IT cortex produces visual agnosia* (the ability to see, but not to recognize what is being seen) is consistent with this story. It is probable, however, that such cells *by themselves* are not encoding these specific mental images. It is much more likely that such cells are just one cellular component participating in much larger circuits which code specific visual images. When the image is presented to the person or animal, any neurons that are part of the circuit would show changes in their rates of firing in response to the image, since each such neuron would be a participating cell in the entire circuit (or interference pattern; see above) representing the image. So, rather than "grandmother cells" it is more likely that we have *"grandmother circuits"* in our brains, as well as other circuits, such as "apple circuits," "Volkswagen circuits," "tree circuits," and so on, that when activated (perhaps creating interference patterns) represent other specific visual images. In fact, there must be physical representations in the brain for every single *thing* that we have ever seen, or imagined. And the coding must involve huge populations of neurons, perhaps forming imagistic representations in the mind from interference patterns of interacting sine-wave grating-like representations in primary visual cortex or in areas of visual cortex beyond primary visual cortex. Such interference patterns may be processed in visual association cortex such as the IT cortex in the temporal lobe or in visual areas of parietal lobe.

Clearly, learning must be involved in the formation of these specific whole-object IT cortical circuits. That the IT cortex and other regions of visual association cortex may be involved in perceptual learning and visual memory is given support by a classic study published by Penfield and Perot in 1963. In experiments with conscious human patients during brain surgery (only local anesthesia was used), Penfield and Perot discovered that patients experienced memories of specific images or sounds, such as images of a specific street or the sound of the patient's mother's voice, when they used surface electrodes to electrically stimulate the visual and auditory association cortices (including the temporal lobe) of the patients. Even memories of specific musical pieces being play by an orchestra were elicited by stimulation of auditory association cortex (Penfield and Perot, 1963).

Other evidence that visual memories require visual association areas of the cortex comes from the observation that damage to brain areas that are involved in visual perception also impairs visual memories. Furthermore, thinking that involves visual images is also dependent upon specific regions of visual association cortex. When persons are asked questions that involved specific visual, auditory, tactile, or taste information, answering the questions activated regions of the association cortex involved in the actual perception of the relevant sensory information. For example, questions about visual and auditory information activated visual and auditory association cortex, respectively (Carlson, 2011, p. 350–351).

Multiple Maps in Sensory Association Cortex

The cerebral cortex beyond each primary sensory cortex is known among neuroscientists as *sensory association cortex*. In the visual system, *visual association cortex, also known as the extrastriate cortex*, includes all of the 30 or more cortical areas outside of the *striate cortex* (aka, the primary visual cortex). The extrastriate cortex includes all the visual areas in parietal, temporal, and occipital lobes outside the striate, including the IT cortex referred to above.

Recall that the primary visual cortex is retinotopically mapped—that is, there is a point for point map, or representation, of the surface of the retina onto the surface of the primary visual cortex (also recall that such mapping of receptive surfaces, such as the skin or basilar membrane, onto their respective primary sensory cortices characterizes other senses as well). It turns out that extrastriate cortical areas including V2, V3, and V4, have similar retinotopic maps. The purpose of these multiple retinotopic maps is not yet known (Banich and Compton, 2011). However, some interesting findings using functional magnetic resonance imaging (fMRI) suggest one possibility.

In one study, subjects were presented with a visual illusion created with distance cues that made one of two identical objects look bigger than the other. When subjects looked at the object that appeared larger, researchers found that a larger region of striate cortex was activated compared to when they looked at the object with the smaller apparent size. It is known from other research that perception of apparent distance cannot take place in the striate cortex but requires circuits found in visual association cortex. This means that computations made in association cortex must be acting back "down" onto circuits in the primary visual cortex modifying activity there, enlarging the region of striate cortex activated by the illusion (Carlson, 2011, p. 163) corresponding to the conscious experience of the larger object. Perhaps this kind of adjustment of activity in primary visual cortex requires, in part, interactions at a retinotopic level of analysis between various extrastriate regions and the striate cortex. Consider the fact that subjects consciously experienced the illusion that one object was larger than the other, even though both were exactly the same size, when a larger region of striate cortex was activated by the object that had the illusory appearance of being bigger. This suggests that the conscious visual experience of an object of a particular size was taking place in the striate cortex and that this conscious experience was under the influence of activity from extrastriate cortical regions. This helps us localize conscious visual experience to the visual cortex. This data is consistent with the finding that destruction of the striate cortex produces complete loss of conscious visual experience.

Another possible role of interactions between striate and extrastriate cortical areas, consistent with the existence of multiple cortical retinotopic maps, is to provide "reentrant circuits" that some researchers have suggested are an essential component in the neural "circuit design" needed for consciousness (see Edelman and Tononi, 2000).

Modular organization of the Striate Cortex

I often refer to "circuit design" in this book when speaking about minds and behavior. For the most part, the details of the microscopic circuit designs of various brain systems are still largely unknown in all but the simplest of animals. However, we can get a glimpse of what the organization of circuit designs might be like in the primate brain at large, at least in general principle, by examining some of what is known about the circuits of the striate cortex, one of the brain regions where some of these details are beginning to be worked out.

Most brain researchers believe that the brain is probably organized in "modules," composed of anywhere between a hundred thousand to a few million neurons. These modules are interconnected in incredibly complicated ways. Modules perform calculations, and then pass on the computational results to other modules that perform additional computations, and so on (Carlson, 2011, p. 161). The brain is thus composed of tens of thousands, perhaps hundreds of thousands (or more), of such modules. Any particular psychological function probably involves the computational activities of thousands of modules engaged in complex interactions with one another. In the primate visual cortex over 30 separate regions are interconnected by hundreds of known neural pathways that permit distributed, hierarchical processing of information with an order of complexity capable of producing conscious visual experience. Recall from an earlier chapter that *psychophysical monists* believe that all psychological events in minds are the *emergent properties* (see Chapter 2 and 3) of complex (physical) information processing events in entirely material brains.

The striate cortex is divided into approximately 2,500 "modules," each approximately 0.5×0.7 millimeters in size and containing roughly 150,000 neurons. Each module is dedicated to the analysis of various visual features confined to one small region of visual space within the entire visual field (the view of the world available in a single glance) of a human or other primate. Combined, these modules, acting like tiles in a mosaic, represent the entire visual field. The modules in striate cortex consist of two segments, each surrounding a "CO blob" (described earlier in the discussion about "color" vision). Each of the segments outside the "blob" receives input from one eye only, but this information is combined by circuitry within the module so that most cells in a module are binocular, responsive to inputs from both eyes (Carlson, 2011, p. 161).

The areas *outside* the CO blobs of striate modules are comprised of a systematic organization of cells that respond to all the various orientations of lines and edges (recall the orientation specific receptive fields of striate neurons). Cells that respond most strongly (that is, produce the greatest number of action potentials, i.e. nerve impulses, per second) to a particular line orientation are all grouped together into *orientation columns*. Neighboring columns contain cells with similar orientation preferences so that across a small chunk of cortex all possible orientations of line or edge are represented.

These orientation columns also contain cells that are "tuned" to respond optimally to specific directions of motion. Others are "tuned" to particular spatial frequencies (see discussion above about sine-wave gratings). Cells receiving input from one eye or the other are also arranged into columns, known as *ocular dominance columns*. Along with the CO blobs specialized for coding "color" (wavelength) information, all this together produces what are called *hypercolumns*. These hypercolumns collectively make up the entire retinotopic map found in the primary visual cortex.

The processed information provided by these splendid circuits of the striate cortex is then used by *visual association cortex* and other brain regions to produce adaptively useful psychological functions such as object recognition and navigation through three dimensional space (Banich and Compton, 2011, p. 154–6).

One of the most far-reaching implications of modern neuroscience is the idea that specific psychological experiences are actually specific physical states of the brain (see discussion of psychophysical monism in Chapters 2 and 3). Consistent with this hypothesis, studies in humans using functional magnetic resonance imaging (fMRI) reveal that *specific* regions of the visual association cortex are active during very specific psychological experiences.

For example, the inferior temporal lobe (IT cortex) and the *lateral occipital cortex* (LOC) are activated when subjects view *particular* object *categories* such as animals, tools, cars, flowers, faces, bodies, visual scenes, letters of the alphabet, and letter strings. This is significant because it suggests that highly abstracted features of visual stimuli are somehow being discriminated and represented by the brain's neural circuitry, and that the brain then utilizes such abstracted features to sort stimuli by category. Of course, we know that we can do this kind of thing in our minds. We form categories of things and use them continually in our everyday interactions with the world. What we don't know is how the brain represents such abstract forms of information; we don't know what the neural processes are that might be involved. Other examples of complex, abstract processing by the brain confirm that the brain areas involved are often highly localized.

Studies of brain damaged people, and studies using fMRI show that special face-recognizing circuits are apparently localized in an area of cortex known as the *fusiform face area* (FFA) on the ventral surface of the human brain, not far from the IT cortex. As mentioned previously, damage to the FFA produces prosopagnosia, the inability to recognize familiar faces, including one's own face in a photograph or in a mirror.

Another interesting localized, cortical processing module is the *extrastriate body area* (EBA), just posterior to the FFA. Studies using fMRI reveal that this area is activated best by photographs, silhouettes, or stick figures of human bodies and body parts but not other kinds of visual stimuli (recall that both the FFA and the EBA were discussed in Chapter 2).

Another specific area in the region of the IT cortex, the *parahippocampal place area* (PPA), located in a region of limbic cortex bordering the ventromedial temporal lobe, is selectively activated by the sight of scenes and visual backgrounds. Brain damage that causes *agnosia* for objects (inability to recognize them) surprisingly *spares* the patient's ability to recognize scenes, *even though objects in the scene can't be recognized.* This suggests that multiple brain areas are involved in the perception of complex visual inputs, and that apparently, different brain areas are organized to selectively process quite specific types of visual information. This sort of specificity of processing is not unique to the visual system. Other sensory systems show this same type of functional organization. The fact that quite specific regions of sensory cortex apparently process very specific components of a sensory input is particularly striking when one considers that the processing taking place in different parts of the cortex has to be somehow put all back together into a whole, unified perception at some level of processing. We know this because that's what we experience, whole, integrated perceptions of objects and events in the world, in spite of the findings in neuroscience that show us that the processing of sensory inputs is broken up into parts processed by diverse regions of sensory association cortex. This is known as the binding problem in neuroscience. How it is solved by the brain is still not known (see chapters 2 and 3).

Area V5 (also known as MT for medial temporal) and an adjacent area of visual association cortex, the MST (medial superior temporal) are involved in perception of motion and, as mentioned earlier, damage in these areas can cause "motion blindness" (Carlson, 2011, p. 166–70). In motion blindness the brain injured person can see normally except that they can no longer see movement. Objects in motion appear as a series of "still shots" of the object in a sequence of different locations, but no sensation of movement occurs in the minds of people with damage in these regions of the cortex. Once again, we see that a very specific aspect of a sensory input, in this case its motion, is processed by circuits apparently "designed" specifically to process a very specific type of information.

Evolution of information processing circuitry and modularity of the mind

This general observation about how sensory systems work is consistent with the hypothesis coming out of evolutionary psychology that the mind is really composed of a collection of specialized information processing modules, each of which is "designed" to carry out quite specific information processing functions (Cosmides and Tooby, 1992). This view of the mind and the brain is known as the *modular model* of the mind/brain. According to this view, the brain is best understood as a large collection of quite specialized information processing "organs." According to UC Santa Barbara evolutionary psychologist, Leda Cosmides, thinking of the brain this way is like seeing it as similar to a Swiss army knife, composed of a collection of specialized tools, rather than understanding it as a single general- purpose information processing machine, which in this analogy would be like the single blade of a "general-purpose" kitchen knife. The view of the brain as *modularized*, as comprised of a collection of very specialized information processing gadgets, is being confirmed again and again by findings in modern neuroscience.

This more enlightened view of the brain is consistent with an evolutionary story of the origins of the brain. It seems that as adaptive problems in the environment were encountered, natural selection "sifted" through various brain circuit "designs" that were available in any generation of a species and "picked" circuit designs that were better and better at solving some particular adaptive problem, and in the case of brains, the problem would have been an information processing problem. Of course, the "sifting" and "picking" occurred automatically, without any overall plan or purpose or intention. It was simply a fact of nature that when one individual was better able to meet the challenges presented by its environment than another individual, the one that was, by chance, better adapted would, all other factors being equal, have had a higher probability of surviving and reproducing, and thus passing on the information in its DNA that had happened to make it more successful. Success breeds success, or, perhaps more accurately, success breeds.

Whenever brain circuits were formed in the population of a particular species which permitted more adaptive processing of information needed to solve some survival or reproductive problem presented by the environment, such circuit "designs" would have produced a natural competitive advantage for the individuals possessing them, with the automatic outcome that such circuit "designs" would tend to be perpetuated over generations, and often times, built upon, by the same selection process, to produce even better, more adaptive designs over successive generations. It is important to recognize that evolutionary theory, at least as originally proposed by Darwin, sees such changes as taking place in small gradations, toward better and better design, over long periods of evolutionary time. It is also important to recognize that changes each generation are not starting from scratch but are building upon adaptive designs that already existed as a result of evolution by natural selection eons before. For example, the evolution of circuit design that permits neurons of the primary visual cortex (the striate cortex) to be "tuned" to features in visual inputs such as orientation, direction of movement, and spatial frequencies didn't develop from scratch in the mammals. There appears to have been a long history of similar neurons, and the circuit designs upon which their functional properties depended, already existing for millions of years in earlier vertebrate brains such as in fish, amphibians, and reptiles (recall the "bug detectors" in frogs). It also is worth noting that structures that might have evolved a long time ago in simpler forms in simpler species, such as cortical columns, also found in evolutionarily older mammals, appear in more advanced brains in more complex forms and in greater numbers. It appears that large leaps in information processing can occur in brain "design" just by adding more brain tissue, and at the same time, more processing units producing greater processing power, and more complex minds. This is not to say that further specializations of circuit design (not just increase in size or number of processing units) don't occur, they do. But further specialization of design is building on existing specialization. Furthermore, remember from Chapter 6 that relatively small mutations in segments of DNA that act as "DNA switches" or in the HOX genes that control these can sometimes produce sudden leaps of evolutionary change. Recall, for example, the fact that the human brain is 3 times the size of the chimpanzee brain (though the DNA of the two species is over 98% identical) may result from relatively few mutations in the DNA "letters" (nucleotide bases) of a DNA switch that controls the length of time that the cortex is growing during fetal development. Keeping that switch turned on longer may equip humans with more processing modules, more richly interconnected, accounting for some of the critical differences between chimp minds and human minds.

The complexity of the modular organization of the striate cortex shows that natural selection is capable of accomplishing quite a lot. The repetition of modules there suggests that during fetal development of the striate cortex there must be repeated iterations of some process that is organizing the basic circuit design, producing large numbers of processing modules in the striate that all have the same basic organization. Then, perhaps during later stages of fetal brain development, or more likely after birth, as visual inputs to the brand new visual cortex assert their effects on its development, specializations of the various modules occur, as the complex processing tasks involved in vision get parsed out to circuits still undergoing development, a process continually under genetic control but influenced by the patterns of input received by the developing visual system.

One of the problems for any sensory system, and for the brain in general, is how to encode information. Remember from the discussion at the beginning of this chapter that the energies from the environment never reach the brain, only neuron potentials do. So, the problem is, how can neuron potentials, no more than voltage shifts as the electrically charged atoms called ions move back and forth across cell membranes, *represent* environmental information? This is a problem in the coding of information.

Think of Morse Code. In Morse Code, two physical states, dots and dashes, arranged in patterns represent letters of the alphabet, and then, of course, strings of letters make up words. For the brain, the issue is how can voltage shifts in neurons, arranged into circuits with specific circuit designs, represent the adaptively important aspects of the world? For some of the simpler features of the world, we have a pretty good idea.

For example, intensity of stimulus energy in the world is represented in neural tissue in a pretty straightforward way. Take, for example, the intensity of light, represented in our minds as the sensation of brightness. In the visual pathway, brightness is represented by the frequency of action potentials (nerve impulses) per second plying their way along the optic nerve. The more intense the light stimulus striking the retina, the greater is the frequency of action potentials in the optic nerve, and the brighter the light is in our minds. A similar principle operates for the representation or coding of stimulus intensity in the other senses. What is interesting is that the mathematical function between stimulus intensity, its representation in frequency of impulses in sensory nerves, and perceived psychological intensity is not a linear one. Instead the function is such that it exaggerates the intensity differences in ranges of stimulus intensity that are most important to survival.

We also know something about how the location of stimuli in the environment is represented. For example, in the visual system it is the position of stimuli on the surface of the retina that codes their locations in two-dimensional space. This is dependent upon the retinotopic map between retina and the striate cortex, a kind of anatomical coding scheme. Similar anatomical coding exists in the somatotopic map found in the somatosensory cortex. To get the third dimension, depth, neural signals from the two eyes are compared in the striate cortex to compute the distance of a stimulus from the observer. Then, along with other cues such as linear perspective, shadows, the fact that nearer object often partially block the view of more distant objects, texture gradients, and size cues, the visual association cortex comprising the "where" pathway somehow puts together all of these diverse sources of information to create a 3-D image in our minds. But how does the brain encode or represent more complex and subtle information?

Representation of Complex Information in Brains and other Information Processing Machines

Research like that described above which shows that specific brain circuits in the cortex perform processing related to highly specific psychological functions provides some clues about how complex information is encoded in the brain. Detailed analysis of the responses of single neurons to specific receptive field characteristics such as orientation, spatial frequency, length, and motion, adds more to our understanding of how sensory input is encoded into neural activity. However, recordings from single neurons can't tell us how *groups* of neurons might work together to encode complex perceptual objects, such as the image of a Redwood tree, the taste of chocolate ice cream, or the sounds of a piece of music such as a Mozart masterpiece.

One of the most difficult problems yet to be solved by neuroscientists is a specification of the details of how the brain encodes and represents information, especially information which is complex, subtle, and abstract enough to encompass the range of subjective experience in our minds—from complex whole object and whole event perceptions, to abstract ideas, categories, and concepts. Clues about how the brain might accomplish such information processing feats come from a different quarter, from computer simulations of brain circuit designs by researchers in a relatively new field known as *connectionism*.

Connectionist Networks and Parallel Distributed Processing (PDP)

Connectionism originated in attempts to simulate some aspects of human and animal intelligence in computers, as a means of trying to understand how the brain might produce its perceptual and cognitive wonders.

The attempt to produce computing systems capable of simulating human or animal intelligence was not new. Traditional AI ("artificial intelligence") researchers, beginning in the 1960's and 70's, tried to duplicate human and animal cognitive performances using *serial processing*, the kind of processing performed by your home computer. However, despite decades of creating complex serial programs, these AI programs failed miserably. They lacked flexibility, and easily "broke down" if even minor changes were made in the problem they were programmed to solve. For example, attempts to create artificial vision in machines using serial processing programs failed because minor changes in the stimulus would prevent the machine from "recognizing it. A coffee cup could not be "recognized" by the serial system if it was presented to the machine at a slightly different angle or if it was missing a part such as its handle, computational achievements that present no problem at all for real biological brains.

But the new kind of AI (artificial intelligence) being developed by connectionist researchers beginning in the 80's was different. The connectionists, many at UC San Diego, used artificial computing systems, called *artificial neural networks*, which performed *parallel distributed processing (PDP)*, instead of serial processing. Artificial neural networks are composed of "artificial neurons" (known as "neurodes") arranged to form richly interconnected circuits, arranged in "layers," also richly interconnected. A typical network has an input layer, an output layer, and one or more layers of "hidden units" in between (see Figure 8-4; courtesy Paul M. Churchland, 1989; used with permission). These connectionist computing systems performed much better, and in fact showed surprising ability to produce "cognitive" performances with many features of flexibility, and even creativity, reminiscent of human cognition. For example, these PDP networks showed the ability to "learn" to solve problems presented to them by making modifications in the strengths ("weights") of their "synaptic" connections (thus, connectionism) among their "artificial neurons" (neurodes).

To understand the implications of connectionism, recall perceptual learning from the previous chapter. Artificial neural networks suggest a model of this form of learning, as well as a way in which the brain might code complex mental phenomena such as concepts and categories. From the connectionist perspective, as we have perceptual experiences, and as our perceptions are modified by new experiences, the attributes of the objects we subjectively experience in our minds may be represented as patterns of synaptic "strengths" or conductivities inside networks of brain cells. Learning, in this view, is just the modification of the "strengths" or "weights" (used here in a mathematical sense) of some of these connections, which would, in turn, modify the pathways that electrical signals would follow within the brain's cellular networks. The resulting modified neural activity would represent the newly learned perception. In this theoretical view, specific perceptions are stored in memory as particular sets of synaptic strengths (synaptic "weights") or conductivities in neural networks in the brain. Activation of a specific pattern of neural activity in the network, either by perception of the object or by retrieving it in memory, is equivalent to our mental experience of the perception. If we can learn how artificial neural networks operate, we may gain important new insights into how the brain works to form our perceptions and even our ideas and concepts.

One example of a very successful connectionist artificial neural network is NETtalk, created by David Rumelhart and his colleagues (1986). This PDP network composed of just 3 layers of richly interconnected *neurodes*, with "synaptic" connections modifiable by training, learned to "read" and pronounce (via a voice synthesizer) a 1,000 word text presented to the network via artificial "eyes" composed of an array of photocells. Of interest is that the network went through a "babbling" stage just like human children go through on their way to language competency. Starting from scratch, after sufficient numbers of inputs and feedback about error, NETalk adjusted its "synaptic" weights until it became accomplished at "reading" and pronouncing the 1,000 word text, and it achieved this after just 10 hours of training (such training is referred to as "training up the network"). Analysis showed that the network had computed a function between input and output that allowed it to successfully read aloud the written text. This rapid learning is possible because of the exceedingly rapid speed of computations by the computer that contained the connectionist network, making possible thousands of "iterations" each hour during the network's training. Now, here's where things get really interesting.

When Rumelhart and his colleagues decided to test the "trained-up" artificial neural network on arbitrary English text that it had never "seen" before, they found that the NETtalk network succeeded in pronouncing 95% of the new words correctly—that is, it *generalized* what it had learned on the first 1,000 word text, and was able to correctly pronounce the new written text with great accuracy without additional training (Churchland, 1988). Thus the artificial network not only was capable of learning, but it generalized to novel situations, one of the most essential elements in natural intelligence produced by biological brains. Finally, connectionist researchers examined how the network had succeeded in generalizing what it had learned from the original 1,000 word training text to the new text. And what they found was stunning. The network had discovered and encoded in its circuitry (neurodes with modifiable "synaptic" strengths or "connection weights") *rules* of pronunciation, including the *categorization* of letters into vowels vs. consonants as part of a hierarchy of categories "similar to those in standard English, demonstrating that the hidden units [of the network] had become sensitive to theoretically-relevant features of language (Bechtel and Abrahamsen, 1991, p. 96). And all of this was accomplished by the NETtalk network without it being explicitly programmed to do any of these things and without it being given any rules to follow. It *discovered* its own rules.

Similar to a natural brain with real synapses connecting real neurons (also modifiable by experience), the NETtalk connectionist network, given feedback about its performance on a complex cognitive task, was able to learn, to form abstract categories, and to successfully generalize to new, similar inputs. How did the artificial network do it? Although networks process information in somewhat different ways dependent upon the characteristics of the type of network, many networks seem to operate in part by extracting subtle *statistical regularities* inherent in the common characteristics and similarities, on various dimensions, to be found in large sets of inputs.

Such feats with a distinctive cognitive character are by no means unique to NETtalk, but are a regular feature of connectionist artificial neural networks. These networks discover common properties of individual cases (statistical regularities) and abstract them into the distinguishing features defining a category, represented in "connection weights" in a layer of hidden units (Koenigshofer, 1995). According to Clark (1993), with a threshold number of inputs, the network exhibits "a sudden dramatic leap in its generalization performance" to a form of representation which allows "the network to have knowledge of the principle or concept independent of the examples used in training."

In another case, a connectionist network was given the task of "learning" to discriminate between sonar signals from submerged rocks and sonar signals from metallic mines underwater. As the network experienced large numbers of sonar signals from both categories of object, its connection weights were modified, and the network learned the discrimination task by extracting out of the inputs presented to it, the key features that reliably distinguished between the sonar "fingerprints" of each type of object. The network gained expertise that rivaled and sometimes exceeded that of highly trained U.S. Navy sonar operators (Churchland, 1988).

Perhaps most extraordinary, one artificial neural network was given the task of discovering mathematical proofs of various, sometimes complex and obscure, mathematical theorems. This network succeeded in discovering a mathematical proof that had eluded human mathematicians for decades. When human mathematicians tested the solution discovered by the connectionist network they found that it was not only correct, but even "insightful." The artificial neural network did what highly trained human mathematicians could not do (see Churchland, 1988; and Churchland, 1989).

Vector Coding by Activation Vectors as a Model of Representation in Biological Brains

One connectionist theorist using ideas derived from PDP research has referred to the human brain as "the associative engine," an information processing machine capable of discovering statistical associations among events in the world, even at very high levels of abstraction, and then using these associations to create adaptively useful models or representations in neural code of how the world works—computational achievements that may characterize how the human mind works (Clark, 1993).

Inspired by connectionist thinking and research, philosopher, Paul Churchland, from the University of California at San Diego, has proposed an extraordinarily powerful theory of how the brain might code information. His theory is rich enough to account for how brains might encode information into complex perceptions, abstract concepts, and even ideas of great subtlety and complexity, suggesting a theory of how the brain works to create a human mind (Churchland, 1989). According to Churchland's theory, representation in the human brain may involve what he calls "vector coding" of features of the world, "placing" them in abstract, representational "state spaces" (Churchland and Sejnowski, 1992). Vector coding utilizes the mathematical concept of a vector, a string of numbers, each representing a quantity such as the firing rate of a neuron, as in this case. A simple vector might consist of 3 or 4 scalars, numbers composing the string that makes up the vector. In the case of vector coding, the numbers in a vector could represent firing rates of neurons coding different "dimensions" or features of a stimulus. A sensory quale, such as a particular taste sensation would be represented as the firing rates of a group of neurons, each scalar in the vector corresponding to the firing rate of each neuron in the group.

To illustrate "vector coding" I will use three examples from Paul Churchland (1989). What is meant by *vector coding* is illustrated nicely by Figure 8-1 (see pages 299–302; figures 8-1 through 8-5 courtesy of Paul M. Churchland; used with permission) which shows a geometrical rendering of an abstract "color qualia space" (Churchland, 1989). Shown are three types of wavelength-sensitive cells (like the three types of cones in the human retina). Cells of each type respond to a particular wavelength with a specific

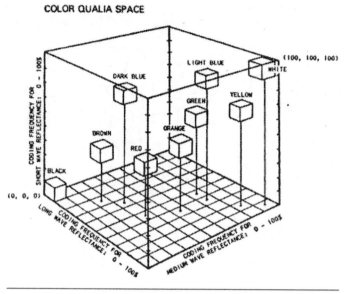

FIGURE 8-1.

level of neural activity that can be represented numerically. The set of numbers that results is known as an "activation vector" ("coding vector"), in this case, "a neural fingerprint uniquely characteristic" of a particular subjective color. There is a "unique vector, a pattern of spiking frequencies across the three neural channels, for every humanly possible" color sensation (here, spiking frequencies refer to the frequencies of action potentials, nerve impulses, in particular neurons in the three neural channels depicted). Note that any given color can be displayed graphically by an appropriate point in "a 3-D color-sensation space" and that "similarities in color turn out to be reflected in the similarities of their coding vectors, and [thus] by the closeness of their points" in the 3-D color qualia space. Thus, as Churchland states, "an activation space" defines "a similarity space" (Churchland, 1989).

Figure 8-2 depicts the same ideas using an abstract "taste space." Here there are four types of taste receptor. Each will be activated to a specific degree by any particular stimulus, say, a pineapple. Taken together, the activation levels of these four types of taste receptor compose a unique *activation vector* (neural coding vector) for "pineapple" flavor. Again note that any taste can be graphically displayed as a specific point in taste space and that similarity is reflected by closeness of points in that space (Churchland, 1988).

In Figure 8-3, a system for coding faces is shown using coding vectors along three dimensions of facial structure. One might imagine that in the brain, perhaps in the Fusiform Face Area, there are neurons that code these "dimensions" of facial structure.

TASTE SPACE

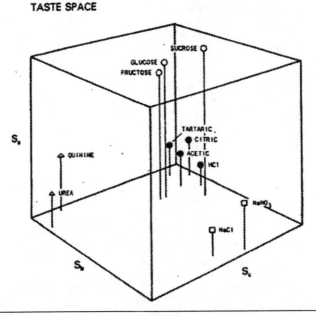

FIGURE 8-2.

In this scheme different faces would produce different firing rates in different face-component, or face-dimension neurons, such that each face would stimulate a unique pattern of firing of a hypothetical population of "face neurons." In this model of face representation, each human face would be represented by a specific activation vector. Again similarity is reflected in closeness of points (specific faces) in "face space."

These examples illustrate a scheme for representation in neural code that might have general applicability in many brain systems. Note that each of these examples illustrates a form of representation known as "distributed representation." In *distributed representations*, concepts or other semantic entities (such as color, taste, a visual image, or other unit of meaning) are represented by *a pattern of activation across a set of neural units*; thus no single unit can represent the concept on its own, and the same unit may participate in more than one activation vector, and thus in more than a single representation. In connectionist architectures (see Figure 8-4 showing a simple connectionist "architecture" or "circuit design"), networks which use distributed representations are referred to as *distributed networks* (in contrast to "localist" networks which represent concepts such that each concept has its own neural unit, and activation of that unit by itself represents the concept, perception, or other semantic entity; this is similar to the distinction, made above, between a "grandmother cell" and a "grandmother circuit").

To build *distributed representations* in an artificial neural network, or perhaps in a brain, requires identification of stimulus features that must be encoded. As artificial neural

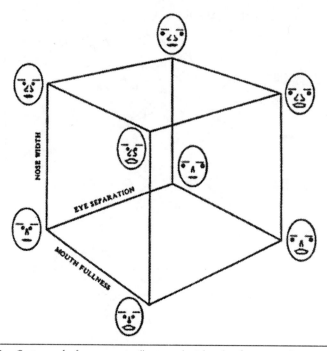

FIGURE 8-3.   Cartoon of a face space to illustrate the idea that faces vary along a number of dimensions, represented as axes of the state space, and that a system might code for faces using vectors whose elements represent such features as distance between eyes, fullness of mouth, and width of nose. Obviously faces have many features that are coded by mammals, and even three features included here are dubiously crude. (Courtesy P. M. Churchland.)

networks in computers work toward a solution to a computational problem (similar to computational problems which exist in actual biological brains), they use a process of *feature extraction* based on the sifting out of regularities in the inputs to the system. In a neural network that has been "trained up" (analogous to "getting sufficient experience"), the "hidden units" (the processing units located in a layer or layers between input and output layers; see Figure 8-4) become "sensitive to complex, often subtle, regularities that connectionists call *microfeatures*. Each layer of hidden units can be regarded as providing . . . an encoding in terms of a pattern of microfeatures" (Bechtel and Abrahamsen, 1991). Significantly, regularities in these microfeatures can then be the basis for representation of higher order representations, ultimately including whole object representations, and even the representation of much more abstract features in abstract concepts and categories. Networks can "discover" regularities in input patterns presented to them and use these to divide the input patterns into clusters based upon similarity, building categories and abstract concepts. It is important to note that adding additional layers of "hidden units" to a network can increase its computational potential enormously.

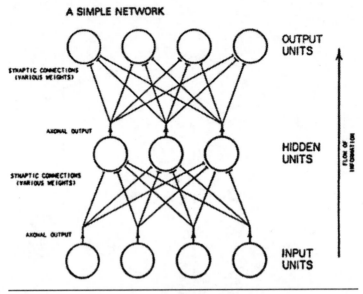

FIGURE 8-4.

Bechtel and Abrahamsen (1991) point out that one virtue of distributed representations is that they show "graceful degradation" of performance when damaged, just like real biological brains often do when they are damaged. That is, "part of the representation can be missing without substantially hurting performance . . . Once we distribute information as a pattern across [processing] units, we also distribute the resources used to process it. Thus, a distributed system becomes more resistant to damage." These authors also note that such systems are "well suited to producing . . . generalization . . . reflecting a general tendency of organisms to make generalizations." These observations are significant. Finding similarities in the functional properties of artificial networks and real biological brains suggests that parallel distributed processing in artificial networks may be a good model of how biological brains encode complex representations and process information about them. Here these authors suggest that the same kind of processing that occurs in artificial neural networks that predisposes them to generalize (i.e. like NETtalk discussed above] may be found in biological brains, and might also account *for the general tendency of biological brains to generalize,* one essential property of "mind design" that we recognize as intelligence. Recall that Roger Shepard at Stanford has proposed that a *universal* property of brains in the animal kingdom is a general disposition to form generalizations. What properties of the circuit "design" of biological brains might account for their disposition to generalize? Research with artificial neural networks, using vector coding and parallel distributed processing (PDP)

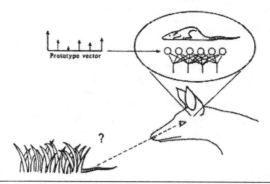

FIGURE 8-5.   A cartoon illustrating the idea of vector completion. The input to the retina with respect to the rat is limited to light reflected from only the rat's tail. But the coyote's visual system completes the vector, allowing the coyote to suspect that there is a rat in the grass. (From P. M. Churchland, 1989)

suggests an answer. This is another example of evidence that biological brains may have "circuit design" similar, in principle, to artificial PDP networks.

An example of how networks might create *categorical information* in a connectionist model of representation is the *prototype vector*. The idea of a prototype is the familiar one of a *general type* represented by an especially typical example. A robin may count as an especially typical bird whereas a penguin does not, because the robin shares more features with the prototypical bird than does the penguin. According to Clark (1993, *Associative Engines*), because of the structure of neural networks, they will "uncover which sets of features are most commonly present" in sets of inputs to the network, and they will discover "commonly occurring groupings of features . . ." In other words, statistical regularities in occurrence of particular features in the input to the network, and co-occurrence of sets of particular stimulus features, will be extracted and represented by PDP networks as a natural consequence of their architecture ("circuit design") and dynamics. Thus, for example, by having enough instances of "dog" inputs pushed through the network, say, ranging from dachshund to collies, the network will spontaneously generate a "dogginess" prototype representation (coded within its circuitry in patterns of synaptic "weights" among its processing units) which will abstract out the statistically typical features of "dogginess" and serve recognition of new cases of dog in the future. Connectionists point out that because such networks represent similar cases by means of overlapping hidden-unit vectors, such prototype representations are *automatically* extracted by the network. The theoretical significance of this property of PDP networks is that it suggests that PDP architectures ("circuit designs") probably exist in the brain, most notably in the cerebral cortex, and that these PDP "circuit designs" account for the natural disposition of our brains to create prototypes as a basis for our formulation of abstract concepts. And abstract concepts are one hallmark of human thought and intelligence.

In complicated networks with several layers of hidden units between input and output, this same process of similarity extraction might repeat at deeper and deeper layers of hidden units producing exceedingly complex representations. Thus, prototype representations need not be limited to those based upon statistical distributions of simple perceptual features, but may incorporate high order features of great subtlety and abstraction (Clark, 1993; Churchland, 1989).

In this regard, Churchland (1989, p. 214) proposes several varieties of higher order prototypes, including "etiological prototypes" which depict temporal sequences of event types, and "superordinate prototypes" which are formed out of instances of simpler, less inclusive "subordinate prototypes." Churchland sees *etiological prototypes* as encoding typical temporal sequences such as "the cooking of food upon exposure to heat, the deformation of a fragile object during impact with a tougher one, the escape of liquid from a titled container, and so on." He continues, "These sequences contain prototypical elements in a prototypical order, and they make possible our explanatory understanding of the temporally extended world." Churchland sees etiological prototypes as "what lie behind our causal explanations." Clearly such complex and subtle information as is to be found in Churchland's etiological prototypes must require very powerful representational resources. But Churchland handles this possible objection when he states that "the prototype vector embodies an enormous amount of information. Its many elements—perhaps as many as 10-to-the-eighth-power, . . . each constitute one dimension of a highly intricate portrait of the prototypical situation. That vector has structure, a great deal of structure, whose function is to represent an overall syndrome of objective features, relations, sequences, and uniformities." Churchland explains that when a complex vector such as this is activated by environmental input to the brain, usually there is "a dramatically ampliative" effect on the information that is made available. What he means by this is that typically a complex etiological prototype vector in the brain is activated by only partial information from the environment (for a simple example of this in a hypothetical coyote brain, see figure 8-5), but the partial information from the world is often sufficient to activate the entire vector providing information beyond what is in the current input, leading the creature to an "understanding" of what it is experiencing. Churchland explains further, "I am trying to provide a revealing and unifying characterization of the sorts of brain events that constitute explanatory understanding. Those events, I suggest, are prototype activations. An important subclass of activated prototypes represent typical temporal sequences or processes," basis for "what philosophers have called causal explanations." Many instances of such etiological prototypes represented in large, complex activation vectors, can be abstracted further by PDP style processing in neural networks to produce "superordinate prototypes." Churchland proposes that such *superordinate prototypes* form the basis for the representation of "general truths" such as those "typically found in science, logic, and mathematics" (such as atomic theory, the laws of motion, a sine wave function, and so on).

These ideas suggest that human brains may have microscopic circuits in many brain systems that have been "designed" by natural selection to perform parallel distributed processing using activation vectors which are capable of representing the kinds of high order abstractions that are characteristic of human "mind design," giving us "mental" powers (information processing capacities) beyond those of any other species.

Combined with the principles of vector coding, according to Churchland, PDP networks have enormous representational and computational potential, perhaps explaining how biological brains can accomplish complex perceptions, causal explanation, knowledge and understanding. Adding layers of "hidden units" (in biological systems "hidden" processing units are any of that enormous variety of neurons which lie between sensory transducers and primary motor neurons) rapidly increases the computational power of PDP circuits.

Patricia Churchland and Terry Sejnowski (1992) estimate that somewhere between 5 and 50 layers of such hidden units are to be found in biological brains, depending upon the neural system, and the species. Considering the computational power of networks with only 3 or 4 layers (recall NETtalk; see Figure 8-4), adding additional layers, perhaps *as many as 40 or 50*, as may exist in biological brains, expands computational power exponentially. Large numbers of layers of "hidden units" would provide biological brains with vast *computational* resources. Add to that the *representational* capability of large numbers of complex activation vectors, such as may exist in the human brain, and the result is a staggering magnitude of representational and computational potential. Paul Churchland (1989, p. 209) estimates that the human brain has "some $10\text{-}to\text{-}the\text{-}11^{th}$ power non-sensory neurons" and assuming that each neuron is capable of just "10 distinct levels of activation (a serious underestimation)," then "each brain subsystem" (he estimates perhaps a thousand of such systems) will typically possess a "specialized state space" with "$10\text{-}to\text{-}the\text{-}8^{th}$ power proprietary dimensions" and "at least $10\text{-}to\text{-}the\text{-}100\text{-}million\text{-}power$ functionally distinct positions within it. This is the number of distinct possible *activation vectors* [that each brain subsystem can generate]." Churchland continues, "To appreciate the magnitude of this number, recall that the total number of elementary particles in the entire universe, photons included, is only about 10-to-the-87th power." Thus, any single coding vector may conceivably have as many as $10\text{-}to\text{-}the\text{-}8^{th}$ power separate elements (scalars) within it. As noted above, a vector is a string of numbers, in this case, each number representing the firing rate of a neuron, coding some particular feature or dimension of an object, event, event sequence, idea, category, prototype, or abstract concept, within an abstract "state space." Note that the state spaces shown in the figures in this chapter have only 3 or 4 dimensions and so would be represented by activation vectors with only 3 or 4 numerical elements. Activation vectors with such an enormous number of numerical elements (10-to-the-8th power is Churchland's estimate), then each such vector would possess a "superastronomical" number of possible representational values. If we consider this enormous number of possible synaptic weights ("connection strengths" at the synapse between any two neurons) among the 10-to-the-8th power neurons in a brain subsystem, there is once again a "superastronomical range of possibilities." If each synapse is capable of only "10 distinct weights, then we have, *10-to-the-100-billion-power* distinct possible configurations of [connection] weights for that [brain] subsystem alone." According to Churchland, "this will allow for some stunningly complex and fine-grained representations [in the brain], since a single vector with 10-to-the-8th elements can code the contents of an entire book." Considering the number of synapses among the neurons of a single human brain, and the number of possible states of each of those synapses, the brain has capacity to represent for all practical purposes a near infinite number of possible "meanings." Therefore, he states, it should be considered "unproblematic that the brain should command intricate prototype representations of such things as stellar collapse, cell meiosis, redox reaction, gravitational lens, oceanic rift, harmonic oscillator, intentional action, and economic depression. Such phenomena, intricate though they are, are not beyond reach of the representational resources described" (Churchland, 1989).

But PDP networks utilizing vector coding are not only capable of prototype formation, representation of concepts of great complexity and abstraction, and generalization, but can in addition produce prediction and expectancy. Consider what connectionists term "vector completion," wherein a partial input is sufficient to activate a stored prototype or a stored memory. Figure 8-5 (Churchland, 1989), referred to earlier, illustrates the idea nicely. Here, the rat's tail is sufficient to activate a prototype-vector representation of "rat," allowing the coyote an expectancy, as well as recognition of the input, even when only a small portion of the stimulus is explicit (Note: I have argued previously— Koenigshofer, 1995b—that vector completion might provide the neural substrate for expectancy in conditioning). Surprisingly, network simulations have demonstrated that no more than 5% of a stimulus need be explicitly present to activate the appropriate prototype representation (Churchland and Sejnowski, 1992; see p. 20–23 in Clark, 1993; p. 204–213 in Churchland, 1989).

The enormous representational capacity of the vector coding scheme proposed by Paul Churchland, combined with the computational power of processing elements (neurodes or neurons) arranged in connectionist architectures with scores of layers of processing units, suggests a PDP model of the "circuit design" of the brain capable of explaining the richness of human mental experience. The detailed modular structure of the striate cortex with its profusion of functional columns and CO blobs may provide representations to PDP style networks located in visual association areas of the extrastriate cortex. These clearly also have their own specific structural and functional specializations which may incorporate PDP network organization, and along with other regions of association cortex may generate the activation vectors that represent *etiological prototype vectors* and *superordinate prototype vectors* that give human "mind design" its vast and intricate "mental" powers.

It is probable that complex brains use both serial and PDP processing in different brain systems engaged in performing different processing functions. In this PDP model of "circuit design," it becomes possible to see how the brain may actually accomplish such psychological adaptations such as *generalization, categorization, expectancy, rule-like performance in language and thought, anticipatory responding, inference (i.e. vector completion) and even co-variation detection* (one thing is reliably followed by another thing), *and causal explanation*—all hallmarks of intelligent action.

Furthermore, microfeature-level, distributed neuro-representations not only allow a mapping of statistical regularities in the world into "hidden unit" activation vectors, but permit the "discovery" of relationships (i.e. regularities) among microfeatures and higher order representations not explicitly present in the distal (outside) world, but "derived." Hidden units "can fractionate ideas into microfeatures and can achieve contiguity (joint activation) by means of the propagation of activity within the network, not just by occurring together in immediate experience (e.g. within the same sensory-level input pattern)" and thereby can achieve novel "microfeatures" (Bechtel and Abrahamsen, 1991, p. 102–3). What I am getting at here is how creativity and novelty might be introduced into the information processing operations of brains, making possible the kind of thinking responsible for the great human discoveries and innovations that we know the human brain is capable of inventing.

One activity characteristic of intelligence in brains might be centrifugally (coming from the "top" and acting down) originated weight space reconfigurations driving the formation of emergent representational wholes of new higher orders of statistical stability (Koenigshofer, 1995), an idea similar to Paul Churchland's concept of the "impulse toward unity" (Churchland, 1989, p. 242). What this means in simpler language is that "higher" brain regions such as some parts of the association cortex, probably frontal association cortex (known to be involved in the regulation of focused attention), may send neural impulses down (centrifugally) to other cortical regions causing them to reconfigure existing activation vectors to create novel "thoughts" which would be coded in the newly modified activation vectors. These "new ways of looking at the problem," represented in the newly modified activation vectors, might then act to facilitate a problem solution which had been eluding the computational system (one of the brain's subsystems, a part of the mind) working on the problem. "Focused thinking," then, according to this view, could consist in the generation of centrifugal activation vectors pushed through "weight spaces" (patterns of neuronal firing, representing ideas, concepts, categories, prototypes, etc) from "above," rather than through sensory pathways from sensory inputs. These centrifugal activation vectors might catalyze reconfigurations of weight space along a more abstracted similarity metric (corresponding to the experience of discovering a new general principle about the world) or to other reconfigured activation vectors better suited to the problem solution (Koenigshofer, 1995). In other words, what we have here is a model of "unconscious" brain processes involved in human creativity, intuition, "putting it all together," or "finding deeper truths."

Thus, novelty (creativity) is introduced into the active construction of neuro-representations of regularity not explicitly present in the inputs to the system. In this way, combinations and recombinations of "connection weight" configurations may allow production of novel similarity metrics, affording creation of novel concepts and the recognition of novel similarity relations, as in metaphorical and analogical reasoning, and in the generation of novel conceptual systems. In short, we have here a model of how creative and artistic thinking may take place in the brain. Statistical regularities in such cognitive and perceptual achievements, not surprisingly, would be based upon highly abstract similarity metrics, stored, in my view, in weight configurations (patterns of connection weights or strengths in large populations of neurons) in deep layers of hidden units within brain networks (recall that Churchland speculated there may be as many as 50 hidden layers in the human brain). The subtlety and complexity of representation and computation accomplished by artificial neural networks using PDP is impressive (i.e. NETtalk's discrimination of "theoretically-significant" aspects of language; see above), suggesting far greater representational and computational potential for real biological networks in brains using PDP style processing.

What we are dealing with here, in the later part of this chapter, which began with a discussion of sensory systems and how they might represent sensory information, is a theoretical model of how the "big stuff," the seemingly intangible stuff, in the human mind—ideas, concepts, beliefs, knowledge, understanding—might be encoded neurologically in the brain. According to this perspective, the things that seem so ethereal about the mind, like ideas and beliefs, may actually be more profitably understood by thinking of them as specific activation vectors, each one perhaps hundreds, thousands, or millions of numbers (scalars) long. Recall the "face space" in Figure 8-3. Any *activation vector* in that hypothetical abstract "face space" has only 3 scalars, it is only 3 numbers long. However, when it comes to the neural encoding of complex beliefs, ideas, and abstract principles in the mind, we are talking about *activation vectors* that might be hundreds or thousands of numbers (scalars) long, or longer. To fully appreciate what is being said here, remember that *activation vectors* are themselves a way of conceptualizing how many neurons acting together might code complex information "structures," such as perceptual wholes like the image of a recognizable object, ideas, categories, concepts and highly abstract principles constituting "knowledge" and "understanding." Activation vectors are a way of specifying a pattern of neural firings occurring in groups of neurons. Some of these activation vectors may be simple, like the 3 scalar vector specifying any "color." That vector is a way of specifying the magnitude of neural activity of 3 types of cones which determines where a "color" falls in an abstract three-dimensional "color space," and this point corresponds to a particular subjective experience of "color" in the person to whom this "color space" "belongs." Much longer activation vectors with many, many more scalars composing them would be needed to represent the "bigger stuff," the more intangible contents of our minds such as abstract concepts and beliefs, our "knowledge and understanding" of the world. These may involve "prototype vectors" which might themselves be further abstracted into "superordinate prototype vectors" of the kind that Churchland believes might represent very abstract ideas such as "scientific truths." Again, these very large vectors are also just a way to think about patterns of neural activity in groups of neurons in brain systems; it's just that the patterns of neural activity needed to represent the "big stuff" in the mind, such as abstract ideas, general principles, beliefs, knowledge, understanding and so on, involve much larger populations of neurons, sometimes billions of them, and superastronomical numbers of synapses and "connection weights." In this theoretical view, these would be neurons that are acting like units in very deep layers of "hidden units." Churchland (1989) even suggests that such abstract and very general pieces of knowledge such as "an individual's overall theory-of-the-world" may be "a specific point in that individual's synaptic weight space. It is a configuration of connection weights" (Churchland, 1989, p. 177).

Many evolutionary psychologists believe that the mind is a collection of highly specific information processing mechanisms or modules each designed by natural selection to do a specific kind of information processing to solve a specific set of adaptive problems. Such mechanisms are called *domain-specific psychological mechanisms*. In other words, these evolutionary psychologists see the mind as a collection of a specific set of specialized information processing adaptations (Cosmides and Tooby, 1987; Barkow, Cosmides and Tooby, 1992). Other evolutionary psychologists believe that in addition to *domain-specific* psychological mechanisms, the brains of many animals are also equipped with much more *general* information processing mechanisms, evolved for the solution of more ubiquitous and content-abstracted adaptive problems, such as classical and operant conditioning, habituation, and processes of logical reasoning. I favor the later interpretation which sees the mind as consisting of both domain-specific and domain-general learning and cognitive mechanisms.

Representational and computational processes such as described here could have evolved in both *domain-specific* (dealing with a specific and circumscribed set of adaptive problems) and *domain-general* (dealing with a large set of more ubiquitous adaptive problems) forms of learning and cognition. Parallel Distributed Processing (PDP) "circuit design," perhaps quite similar to multi-layered artificial neural networks, at least in functionality if not in micro-circuitry, could be common in domain-general brain systems for learning and cognition, and might also be found in domain-specific mechanisms. In other words, the features of PDP circuit "design" that permit neural networks to generalize, make inferences, and anticipate may appear in domain-specific circuits in the brain permitting these circuits to perform these functions but only within the specific domain wherein the domain-specific circuits operate. That is, in the course of brain evolution, some features of PDP circuit design may have "infiltrated" into domain-specific circuit "designs" giving them more cognitive power within their specific problem domains.

Connectionism usually starts with the working assumption of a "blank slate" in the form of a network that is *not* pre-loaded with any connection weights (synaptic weights; i.e. conductivities at specific synapses). All synaptic weights are initially set at the same "neutral" value. Then, on this view, the network acquires its "meaningful" synaptic weights, which encode information, from experience while it is being trained-up. However, this need not be the case. One can easily imagine that artificial neural networks could be pre-loaded with some specific, carefully selected (by the network creators) connection weights. This pre-loading could "bias" the network's operations in specific ways to more effectively achieve certain goals or types of problem solution. Pre-loaded connection weights would reduce flexibility but at the same time would presumably constrain problem solutions toward "time tested" paths (referring here to evolutionary time scales). Genetic evolution in real biological brains could do something similar by using naturally selected information in DNA to build PDP network architecture which included *genetic loading* of synaptic weights, which would thus be "biased" by genetic information. Genetic loading of specific connection weights into the synapses of an entire brain network with PDP "circuit design" could produce species-typical circuit designs, in which domain-specific design would be combined with PDP circuit organization. In my view, this later scenario is the more likely one in biological brains. In this way, *nature and nurture* could interact in the formation of brain circuits by the setting of connection weights (synaptic conductivities) in biological brains by both genetic evolution (nature) which operates over the long term, and by experience, including developmental inputs, during the individual lifetime (nurture; operating over a short time frame). If much of the "circuit design" of the brain has PDP architecture and utilizes "activation vectors" in large populations of neurons to encode perceptions, memories, and knowledge, this does not preclude a profound and deep influence of genetic evolution in brain and mind design. PDP style circuits in the brain could be genetically "loaded" to varying degrees by information in DNA—perhaps heavily loaded, creating profound evolutionary determinants of the human mind and behavior, but still allowing for the influence of learning (acquisition of information by experience during the individual lifetime). Such an arrangement would permit experience to supplement DNA in the "designing" of the momentary and dynamically changing "synaptic weights" in at least some of the circuitry of any individual. Evolutionary psychology and connectionism need not be in conflict. Both models of the mind and behavior could be correct, as both genetic and learned information interact together to form the specifics of "mind design" controlling the psychology of each species.

One final point about sensory systems is that they do not form representations of *all* of the energy around us, but only representations of energies and their features that are biologically and, thus adaptively, significant. For example, consider visual systems. Light is just a narrow band of wavelengths in the electromagnetic spectrum which includes, from shorter wavelengths to the very long—gamma rays, X-rays, ultraviolet, then light, infrared, radio and TV waves. If our rods and cones were constructed to transduce the band of wavelengths that we call radio waves, then we would see radio waves. Why are our visual systems "designed" so that we see light, rather than other wavelengths such as radio waves, ultraviolet, or gamma?

The answer lies in evolution. Most animals have visual systems that permit them to detect and discriminate "only a small range of electromagnetic frequencies centered around those reflected by the leaves of plants. This is not surprising since the survival of most animals depends on a food chain" that is based on plants (Johnston, 1999). The middle of our visible spectrum, which we perceive as "green," corresponds to the wavelengths of electromagnetic energy reflected by the chlorophyll molecules in the leaves of plants that permit plants to convert sunlight into sugar. Thus, it makes good adaptive sense that evolution should have selected for the construction of sensory receptors in animals that would convert *these particular wavelengths* into neuron potentials, to begin the process of vision.

But how can this argument account for the other wavelengths of light to which we are sensitive (our visible spectrum), those wavelengths on either side of "green"? To answer this question, we must consider how incident sunlight changes with changes in the weather and the time of day. Sunlight is made up of a wide range of wavelengths (sometimes referred to as frequencies, the inverse of wavelength) of electromagnetic radiation. That radiation reflected from the sky is in the shorter wavelengths ("blue" to us), but when passing through more dense concentrations of particles of dust and other matter suspended in the air, such as at sunset or in fog or haze, the wavelengths reflecting off of plants are in the longer ranges of the visible spectrum ("red" to us). Because of such fluctuations in the wavelengths of the incident light, animals had to evolve "blue" and "red" visual receptors, which transduce shorter and longer wavelengths respectively, in addition to the "green" receptors, in order to permit compensation for natural alterations in the wavelengths of reflected sunlight (Johnston, 1999).

But we don't see plants and other things in the world changing their colors throughout the day as the angle of the sun or the weather changes. If we did, identification of stable objects in the world would have been made more difficult, making adaptation to them less likely. Instead, we have evolved compensating mechanisms in our brain that produce what is known as *color constancy*, the ability to perceive a constant color in spite of changes in lighting at different times of day or under an overcast sky. A region of the extrastriate visual association cortex, designated area V4, contains circuits that compensate for lighting conditions by comparing the wavelengths of light of each point in the visual field with the average wavelength of light in the entire scene. For example, if the scene contains a high level of longer wavelengths (as would occur at sunset, for example), "then some long-wavelength light is 'subtracted out' of the perception of each point in the scene" (Carlson, 2011, p. 164–5), maintaining a constant color perception in our minds in spite of changes in the wavelength of incident light reflected from objects in the scene. Damage to V4 disrupts color constancy without interfering with the ability to discriminate different wavelengths (i.e. "colors"). A study by Conway and colleagues in 2007 using fMRI identified "color hotspots" in a large area of visual association cortex, including area V4. Next, they inserted microelectrodes into these "hotspots" and recorded the response characteristics of single cells inside and outside these spots, which they called "globs" similar to the wavelength-sensitive "blobs" in striate cortex. They found that neurons within the "globs" were, as expected, sensitive to wavelength, but responded only weakly to shapes. By contrast, interglob neurons, located outside the globs, responded strongly and selectively to shapes, but did not respond to the wavelength of stimuli (Carlson, 2011, p. 165).

Thus in the organization of sensory systems, we note a general principle (perhaps soon to be stored in a new *prototype activation vector* in your own brain) that sensory systems do not form representations of everything around us, but only representations of the properties of the world that are adaptively significant to us. If we broaden this principle a bit more, and generalize it beyond sensory systems to all systems of the brain, then we derive the most central idea of this book. Brains, and thus "mind designs," are organized to represent the features of the physical world that bear upon survival and reproduction of genes, and they will be composed of psychological mechanisms that most effectively serve these biological functions. This occurs as an inevitable consequence of the evolutionary origins of our brains. We can be "designed" in no other way. Brain evolution by natural selection drives our "mind design" toward adaptive organization. This means that the perceptions, feelings, and thoughts that our brains create are not only heavily constrained by this natural "design" process to serve survival and reproduction of our genes, but that our psychology creates a virtual reality in each member of our species that is highly species-specific and universal to all of us, and that our reality is tuned only to features of the world that have adaptive import.

Human minds and human nature are profoundly similar in all people, regardless of culture and experience, because the organization of our minds and our human nature is a consequence of the common genetic evolution shared by all members of our species. Though the human brain, as a result of evolution by natural selection, is equipped with almost unimaginable representational and computational resources which are subject to flexible modifications by experience, the learning that we can do is a consequence of our inherited brain circuitry, and can operate only within limits set by our adaptive brain "design." Brains create worlds in the mind, but these worlds are bounded by evolutionary limits. We can only get an occasional glimpse of other possible realities. Which reality is *more* real, one created by a bat brain, a lion brain, a bee brain, a dolphin brain, or a human brain? All are virtual realities created in the mind of each species in service of the survival and reproduction of its genes, and the reality which each animal brain creates will reflect the particular features of its environment that it must find ways to adapt to. Brain structure reflects the structure of the world in which the brain must exist. Brain evolution in each species creates a "match," an adaptive "fit," a dynamic synchrony, between adaptively significant properties of the world and the representations of the world which form an organism's own species-specific, genetically evolved virtual reality, fine tuned by experience, especially in the big-brained animals like us.

We have come a long way in this chapter from transduction processes in sensory systems all the way to higher-order representation and computation involved in mental processes such as perception and thinking. In the next chapter, we examine another kind of qualia, our "gut level" qualia, our subjective experience of emotions. In understanding the neural representation of our emotions, vector coding once again has applicability. Any particular feeling of emotion may be thought of as the activation of a specific configuration of synaptic weights in abstract *emotional weight spaces,* but this time much of the activation of neurons is in the *limbic system* of the brain, beneath the cerebral cortex. Another theme will apply once again too. Just like the operation of our sensory, perceptual, and cognitive systems, our emotions are psychological *adaptations* arising out of a long evolutionary history. Thus, our emotions, like our sensory systems and all other aspects of our "mind design," will show the distinctive "fingerprint" of evolutionary "design."

CHAPTER NINE

Emotions, Life as a Social Creature, and the Duality of Human Moral Nature

"Hume believed that moral behavior, though informed by understanding and reflection, is rooted in a deep, widespread, and enduring social motivation, which he referred to as 'the moral sentiment.' This is part of our biological nature. Hume, like Aristotle before him and Darwin after him, was every inch a naturalist."

Patricia Churchland
Braintrust: What Neuroscience Tells Us About Morality (2011)

"To us, these inner feelings are just part of the way we are. We don't question them, any more than we question why water comes out of our eyes when we are sad, or why we have eyebrows. We accept our feelings as part of our natural design, and we seldom question how they came to be or what function they play in our lives.

The fundamental requirements for reproductive success [in evolution] are the ability to survive to reproductive age, to reproduce, and to ensure that any off-spring also reach reproductive age. Any property of an individual that increases the effectiveness of any or all of these factors will increase the probability that the individual's genes will be represented in future generations. Qualitatively different feelings appear to be associated with these different aspects of reproductive success.

Victor S. Johnston
Why We Feel: The Science of Human Emotions (1999)

As was pointed out in an earlier chapter, perhaps the most fundamental discrimination all brains must make about things in the world is this: "is this thing good for me and my genes, or is this thing bad for me and my genes?" Our brains are constantly making these assessments because our very survival depends upon it. Even very simple organisms make this same fundamental discrimination, although in these simpler creatures certainly no feeling is involved. For example, single-celled organisms such as amoeba and paramecium approach food sources and flee objects or zones of the environment that are chemically or in other ways potentially harmful.

Our brains evaluate everything we encounter in the world in terms of likely adaptive effects, usually without our awareness of what's going on. If something we encounter in the world has potentially favorable implications for our genes, such as an attractive member of the opposite sex, (hmm . . . this looks like a good potential mate for me and my genes; or, at least so goes the unconscious evaluation underlying the feeling of attraction), then we get "good" feelings, and, as a result of our brain "design," we are drawn closer, both in physical space, *and emotionally* (particularly if we are in the reproductive phase of our life cycle and we haven't yet solved our reproductive problem to our satisfaction). On the other hand when we encounter something in the world such as a hungry, snarling mountain lion (or a "hungry," snarling lawyer for that matter) our brain computes the probable maladaptive consequences that are likely to follow for ourselves and our genes, and so we *feel* another emotion, fear, that drives us to put distance between ourselves and the "threat."

We are even capable of making sensory evaluations of the adaptive significance of potentially harmful microorganisms that we can't even see! For example, when we come upon a pile of animal feces filled with harmful bacteria, we stay clear; we put distance between ourselves and it, not because we know that the feces are filled with potential sources of infection, but because the feces smell "bad" and we *feel* feelings of disgust and aversion that "push" us away. Notice that we don't have to think in order to *do* the "right" thing, the *adaptive* thing; our feelings do the "thinking," the information processing, for us. The "bad" smell causes us to take defensive action, we move away, even without conscious understanding that our brain is organizing a protective movement. In this sense, feelings are similar to all cognitive mechanisms, brain operations that do information processing in order to organize adaptive behavior.

Likewise, we can recognize molecules that will benefit our chances of survival if we ingest them, because they are rich in nutrients, even though we can't see their chemical structures, and even if we know absolutely nothing about biology or biochemistry. The taste and olfactory systems analyze the chemical structures for us. Our "gut" feelings tell us all we need to know. How does this happen? How did our sensory systems get structured in ways that permit them to be sensitive to just the right adaptively critical information? How do we "know" what to do in response to adaptively significant things in the world? How did our feelings get the specific properties that equip them with such "wisdom"?

It is the evolution of our brain circuit "design" that provides the answer. Just as our bodies are the result of evolution, so are our brains and thus our human psychology. Bodies, brains, and our psychological nature are "designed" by natural selection to serve the "immortal genes." In the same way that a pelican "knows," by its innate brain circuitry, to tuck its wings and position its long beak at just the right angle as it dives headlong into the water to nail a fish, we have feelings innately built into our brain "design" to detect food substances or to recognize a favorable genetic makeup in a potential mate, and to *feel* pleasant *feelings* when we encounter such adaptively valuable things, drawing us to them, to ingest them, in the first case, or to mate with them, in the second. Our senses of smell and taste and our sexual instincts, by generating in us pleasant feelings or unpleasant feelings, inform us of the deeper *adaptive significance* of things in the environment—about how the specific things out there in the world will likely affect the survival and reproduction of our genes. Substances such as cooking meat on a fire, with chemical structures nutritious to us, smell "good" to us, and they taste "good" when we put them in our mouths. Certain features in a potential mate, signifying fertility and reproductive fitness "look good," and cause us to *feel* sexual attraction. These facts, and similar examples that we could easily imagine, provide further evidence of the *adaptive* organization of "mind design."

Our feelings are what Victor Johnston (1999) calls "the omens of fitness." Feelings exist for one reason only, because they inform us about the adaptive significance of the things we encounter in the world, about their likely impact on our genes, that is, on our biological fitness. Feelings evolved to tell us how the things we encounter in the world are likely to affect our survival, and the reproduction of our genes, and this evaluative function of feelings tells us how we should respond. "Good" feelings in general make us approach, and "bad" feelings make us withdraw, in blind service to the "interests" of our genes. Recall the argument from chapter 6 that we, and all organisms, are "survival machines" "designed" by natural selection to perpetuate genes. Feelings, and our human psychology in general, are part of that same gene-saving "design."

To fully appreciate this, consider once again our sensations of smell and taste. It is important to remember, as discussed in chapter 8, that neither the feces nor the cooking meat, nor anything else, really has any smell or taste at all. It is our brain "design," specifically evolved configurations of neuronal connections, that creates the smells and tastes *inside our heads* (see chapter 8) and gives them their subjective value. The fact that one thing smells "bad" and the other smells "good," that one thing feels "bad" and the other feels "good," is just a result of the adaptive "design" of our brain circuitry. And this adaptive "design" originates from natural selection acting over our evolutionary history as a species, weeding out "faulty mind designs" and retaining "mind designs" that work to preserve genes.

In our evolutionary past, when we led life as hunter-gathers, sugars, fats and salt were scarce commodities in our environment, so we evolved brain circuit "designs" that made these nutrients taste very good to us, so that we would be highly motivated to find and consume them. Today, humans have gotten so good at producing and distributing these nutrients that their ready availability (in fast foods, for example) threatens our health by increasing the risks of heart disease, high blood pressure, and diabetes. This is an example of how brain design, organized long ago, sometimes is not adaptive in the present day. Adaptive change via genetic evolution takes time, usually a lot of time. Evolution of the brain circuit "design" in the deeper parts of our brains, those regions of the limbic system and other parts of the sub-cortex that produce our pleasures and pains, takes place slowly. Too slowly to genetically accommodate rapid changes in our way of life such as the invention of methods for the efficient production and widespread distribution of fatty, sugary, salty "fast foods." We have to rely upon our knowledge, our self-discipline, our conscious, reasoned choice (other aspects of the adaptive "design" of our brains) to cut down on levels of these "tasty" nutrients that can harm us if we overindulge, as our more ancient brain circuitry urges. In this example, our "tastes" are outdated. Psychological adaptations, "designed" by natural selection in the Pleistocene, are no longer as good for our genes as they once were. Our deeper brain circuit "design" no longer fits well with our modern, culturally transmitted environment. We must rely on our cerebral cortex. The problem is that rational thought is often not as compelling as feeling is, in the control of behavior, especially when it comes to our appetites for food and sex. Emotions add the evaluative part of our experience and drive us either toward or away from things in the environment, too powerfully in the case of fats, sweets and salt, and sometimes even in the case of sex (i.e. risky behaviors that increase the chances of sexually transmitted disease).

However, most of our feelings *are* adaptive, even in our modern environment. So, as it turns out, our sensory systems not only encode and represent features of stimuli such as their chemical structure ("tastes" and "smells"), the wavelengths of light that they reflect ("color"), their shapes (interference patterns of sine wave functions), and motion, or the frequencies they generate when they vibrate in the air ("sound;" see chapter 8), but extensions of our sensory systems reach down deep into the emotional parts of our brains, and generate *evaluations* of the adaptive meanings of everything that we experience. These computations about the specific adaptive values of things we encounter in the world, yield subjective feelings in us which have a *hedonic tone*, that is, they feel "good" or "bad," because ultimately they are good or bad, adaptive or maladaptive, for our genes. Recall again from chapter 6 that bodies and brains are "survival machines" designed by natural selection to serve gene replication. Everything else in our psychology derives from that fact of biology. Positive and negative feelings are not ethereal, mysterious parts of the mind that need be beyond explanation. Feelings, and the configurations of neuronal connections that produce them, are mere psychological adaptations, evolved to serve the genes, by increasing the reproductive fitness of the organism that houses them.

Emotions are the consciously experienced end product of the information processing operations of the brain as it computes the adaptive significance, the consequences for reproductive fitness, of each thing (including persons) and each situation that one encounters in the world. In other words, emotions signal the probabilistic outcomes for reproductive fitness of things we experience in the world. Things (including people and animals) in the world that are harmful, or potentially so, elicit feelings that have a *negative hedonic tone* (unpleasantness). Things in the world that can provide *benefit or* present *opportunity for gain* produce feelings that have *positive hedonic tone* (pleasantness). The intensity of an emotion varies with the magnitude and the probability of any particular adaptive outcome. If I win $100 in the lottery I feel happy, but I feel much happier if I win $10,000. If I see a tiger a 1,000 yards away from me, I have less fear than if I see that same tiger 10 yards away, because the probability that the tiger will do me harm is much greater the closer it is.

Pains and pleasures exist for good biological reasons. Pain and other unpleasant feelings serve to protect the organism, while pleasure exists to make us do what's good for us and good for our genes. When we do something that is good for us and for our genes, typically a pleasurable feeling follows, and we tend to do it again. We are just wired that way, and that wiring has been the handiwork of evolution by natural selection. When we do something and something unpleasant follows we tend not to do it again (recall the Law of Effect from a prior chapter). The hedonic tone of emotions drives our voluntary and learned behaviors toward successful survival and reproduction, toward biological fitness, without need for rigid and inflexible reflexes to guarantee adaptive direction to behavior. Hedonic tone is a distinguishing feature of feelings. No feelings are neutral. They couldn't be if they are to fulfill their function as behavioral guidance systems.

To illustrate the importance of feelings, imagine a creature with a brain that, because of some mutation, was incapable of accurately assessing the adaptive value of things in the world. The behavior of such an unfortunate creature might produce maladaptive patterns such as eating feces or rocks, approaching predators instead of fleeing from them, preferring to mate with inanimate objects, or lacking any "desire" to mate at all (all these behavioral effects are seen in animals exhibiting the so-called "temporal lobe syndrome" after damage to emotion circuitry in temporal lobe limbic structures). Such a creature would not last long, and therefore it would fail to transmit the mutation, that caused its maladaptive behaviors, to the next generation. Thus, "faulty" (i.e. maladaptive) "designs" get weeded out in a hurry by natural selection, leaving only the better adapted "designs" for replication into future generations. Thus, feelings come to accurately reflect the adaptive significance of things in the world. The result is the adaptive organization of behavior. Feelings organized on any other basis would fail the organism and could not exist, if evolution is truly the source of our brain "design." The fact that feelings are adaptively organized lends support to the proposition that feelings, and minds in general, have evolutionary origins and serve biological functions.

Emotions, affects, and the circuits of hedonic tone

Notice that our feelings are of two types. First are those feelings we experience from *sensory qualia* (see chapter 8), especially from specific tastes or odors (things that taste or smell "bad," negative hedonic tone, and those that smell or taste "good," positive hedonic tone). Second are other feelings that we experience from much more complex stimuli such as perceptual whole objects (a desirable member of the opposite sex or a hungry lion) and situations (you have just gotten word that you are going to be audited by the IRS), including social situations and our social relationships. The former feelings are called *affects*, the later, *emotions*.

Victor Johnston (1999) notes that *affects* are caused by specific sensory inputs, such as sugar molecules or a mechanical stimulus on the skin, perhaps of a magnitude sufficient to cause tissue damage. By contrast, *emotions* are caused by specific "production rules," general contingencies in the world, often involving social situations, which produce particular emotions. These contingencies or *production rules* involve general conditions common to many different situations that produce a particular emotion. Johnston uses the emotion, fear, as an example. Fear is elicited by the expectation of events that elicit a negative hedonic tone, and thus a probable negative impact on *biological fitness* (our chances of surviving and reproducing). Note that a wide variety of events can cause the emotion of fear, for example the presence of a predator or a poisonous spider, a crash in the stock market, the loss of one's job, potential loss of one's mate, or losing one's footing at the edge of a steep cliff. In spite of the variety of situations, all elicit a negative hedonic tone, and all potentially involve some threat to fitness, to the chances of survival and reproduction of one's genes (loss of one's job or a crash in the stock market might lead to loss of one's home, one's status, or one's marriage, reducing future reproductive opportunities, or may threaten the well being of one's offspring; note that even very small probabilities of such calamities can elicit strong emotion, in this case, fear—see below).

Happiness, on the other hand, is elicited by events which lead to positive hedonic tone from the anticipation of some net gain or from positive and optimistic assessments of one's circumstances in the present or anticipated in the future. Happiness is produced by contingencies that signal a net gain in biological fitness, such as increase in one's status in the group, winning a desirable mate and sealing the deal in marriage, or avoiding some disaster at the last moment. A large range of events or circumstances can elicit happiness. The key is perception of a net gain of some kind for one's self or for one that we identify with or have affection for (that is, we can also feel happiness, and sometimes envy, at the gain of someone else, if we like them and identify with them; our happiness is vicarious). According to Johnston (1999, p. 80), "Such general production rules could evolve by natural selection if they offered adaptive solutions to a variety of circumstances that were commonly present and repeated encountered in ancestral environments." Notice that such general production rules, which elicit *emotions*, are different from the very specific sensory inputs that elicit positive and negative *affects*. Still, both affects and emotions have hedonic tone or direction, variation in intensity (degrees of pleasantness or unpleasantness), and are accompanied by physiological changes (such as changes in heart rate or blood pressure), and specific behaviors (such as crying or laughing or "making a face" in response to bitter tastes).

Both kinds of feelings are examples of psychological adaptations, features of the mind that exist to guide behavior to serve the survival and reproduction of genes. In fact, the existence of emotions and affects, and the fact that they are so closely related to the adaptive significance of stimuli that elicit them, gives strong evidence to the hypothesis that brain and "mind design" are the products of evolution by natural selection.

Here, in the properties of feelings, we have another example that demonstrates psychology's overreaching, universal law, The Law of Adaptation, which I proposed in an earlier chapter. The specific features of our emotions and affects are predictable from this universal law. Organisms tend to behave in ways that promote the survival and reproduction of their genes, and natural selection has built brain circuit "design" that assures this outcome. Feelings are not learned, they are *evolved* psychological adaptations. Although we can learn to associate feelings with new stimuli and circumstances, the feelings themselves are innate. It seems indisputable that the biological function of our feelings is to guide our behavior into adaptive patterns. Thus, the old wise saying, "Trust your gut feelings." Our gut feelings have behind them the accumulated "experience" of thousands upon thousands of generations of our animal ancestors struggling to survive and reproduce against the myriad environmental challenges to survival and reproduction. That "wisdom of the ages, that phylogenetic "experience" accumulated by our evolutionary ancestry, is encoded into our DNA, as natural selection weeded out less effective, less adaptive, brain circuit "designs" and preserved and replicated the better adapted circuit configurations.

But to profit most from our "gut" feelings, to know when we can trust them, and when we cannot trust them, we need to understand them. Evolution provides us the guiding principle for understanding our emotions and the brain mechanisms that mediate them. Why we have feelings at all, how we feel, and what we feel, whether the feelings are pleasant or unpleasant, intense or subtle, is just our brain's way of computing the survival and reproductive meaning of everything we come across in our environment. Things that induce positive feelings in us are usually good for us and our genes. Things that induce negative feelings in us signify the opposite. Things that induce no feelings in us at all have no survival or reproductive implications (no implications for biological fitness), and so are ignored by the emotional mechanisms in our brains. However, we can learn to associate stimuli that are initially neutral with stimuli that have natural survival and reproductive importance. This is one of the most important adaptive functions of classical conditioning, when a formerly neutral stimulus in the world becomes capable of eliciting emotion because the new stimulus, the learned or conditional stimulus, has been consistently followed by a stimulus that has innate biological significance (that is, for fitness).

The intensity of our feelings, whether pleasant or unpleasant, is usually an accurate, but magnified, indication of the extent to which something is beneficial or harmful. Johnston (1999, p. 83) proposes that feelings act like filters, or "discriminant hedonic amplifiers," that "define and exaggerate the reproductive consequences of environmental or social events associated with relatively minor fluctuations in reproductive potential. Each qualitatively different feeling arises from environmental contingencies that foreshadow fluctuations in the different aspects of reproductive success, while their hedonic tone—pleasantness or unpleasantness—reflects whether such changes represent a net gain or a net loss." What Johnson means by amplifiers is that feelings exaggerate small differences in the adaptive significance of events. So, for example, a pin prick to the skin, on average, has very small impact on one's survival and reproductive fitness, but the pain is significant nevertheless. Though the pin prick could get infected and ultimately lead to death, the chances of this happening are small, but still within the realm of possibility. The intensity of the sharp pain from the pinprick reflects the worst case scenario in terms of adaptive significance of the event. This makes us attend to the wound and decreases the chances of more deleterious effects on reproductive potential. Furthermore, the intensity of the negative hedonic tone makes it easier to learn from the experience, in this case, to be more careful the next time you are handling a needle. If the pain we experienced from the pin prick were exactly commensurate with the probable impact on reproductive fitness, instead of exaggerating it, the event is more likely to be ignored and a useful learning experience would have been missed, perhaps eventually leading to an accumulation of minor injuries that might ultimately mount to serious threat to reproductive fitness. That this possibility is not out of the question is demonstrated by cases of persons who have impaired ability to experience pain. Such persons die within a relatively short period of time from the accumulation of small injuries to which they fail to attend. As Johnson puts it, ". . . the tissue damage and reproductive consequences of a pinprick are, on average, very small. The immediate pain, however, is an evolved conscious experience that exaggerates the biological threat, because such instant amplification is required for learning to avoid such events. If this design underlies all human feelings, then we should expect them to be exquisitely sensitive to any environmental variables that have, or had, any direct impact on reproductive success in our ancestral environments." This same exaggeration effect in the organization of our "mind design" is found in our color vision. Very small differences in wavelength of light produce very different psychological experiences, the experiences of "redness" vs. the experience of "greenness." The qualitative differences we experience psychologically from physical energies in the world that involve only very minor physical differences serves our ability to discriminate biologically meaningful differences in the world. Small changes in reflected wavelength signal a ripe fruit from a "green" one, and thus cue large differences in sugar content, made much easier for us to detect when small differences in reflected wavelengths produce quite different qualities of visual sensation. These observations give additional evidence of the evolutionary origins of the circuit "designs" that create the properties of our minds.

To achieve useful computations of net gain or loss of reproductive fitness, the modern view is that specific positive and negative feelings are dependent upon *specific* evolved brain circuits, each with specific neural configuration or "design." But this was not always the predominant belief among psychologists. In the early 1900's famed American philosopher and psychologist, William James, proposed that the emotions were no more than sensory feedback from physiological changes in the body that occurred when the human or animal was in an "emotional situation." Thus, on this view, no specialized brain circuitry for each emotion was required. Sensory feedback to the brain via sensory nerves from the internal body organs was sufficient. For example, the perception of danger is known to stimulate increased heart rate, blood pressure, breathing rate, redistribution of blood from the digestive system and the genitals to the muscles, and other physiological changes as a result of activation of the *sympathetic nervous system* (also known as the "fight or flight" system). Among other things, this system releases adrenalin as well as directly stimulating several internal body organs—all physiological responses that make good adaptive sense in the preparation of the body to deal with a potential threat or emergency. James believed that when these internal physiological events took place, we *feel* these physiological changes, and it is these sensory feelings of changes in heart rate, blood pressure, breathing rate, etc. that *is* the feeling of emotion.

However, physiologist, Walter Cannon, showed that this theory, later known as the James-Lange theory of emotion, couldn't possibly be true because subjective feelings of emotion occur and can change much too rapidly, *before* the physiological changes in the body, and that the physiological changes that occur in "emotional situations" are much too uniform to account for the diversity of emotions that we are capable of feeling. Furthermore, Cannon observed that in persons with damage to their peripheral nervous systems, that prevented much of the feedback from their internal organs, normal emotions were still felt.

Walter Cannon emphasized the role of specific, *specialized* brain circuits, with quite specific circuit configurations, in generating the range of subjective emotions that we, and other animals, experience. Building on the work of Cannon and others, neuroanatomist, Paul McLean proposed three major evolutionary divisions of the brain, the so-called "triune brain," consisting of a lower and evolutionarily older "reptilian brain" made up of the brainstem and hypothalamus, an "old mammalian brain," associated with social emotions of love and loss, consisting of limbic structures (amygdala, insular cortex, and anterior cingulate cortex), and a "new mammalian brain," composed primarily of the more recently evolved cerebral cortex, involved in symbolic and abstract functions including ability to think about future and past. In this scheme, the frontal cortex integrates emotional information in the planning of goal-directed movements. Within the "reptilian" and "old mammalian" regions of the human brain is the "seat" of the emotions, and the frontal lobes are involved in their integration and regulation. Damage to the frontal lobes, particularly the *ventromedial prefrontal cortex*, leaves the emotions volatile and uninhibited.

Different circuits in the sub-cortex mediate different specific emotions, including their different *hedonic values* (pleasantness or unpleasantness). The *negative hedonic value* of affects and emotions involves a circuit composed of the *amygdala*, located in the limbic system beneath the temporal lobe cortex, parts of the brainstem, and the *insular cortex* located in the folds of the cerebral cortex about halfway between your ear and the center of your brain. The amydala is important not only in creation of emotions with negative hedonic tone, but also in the recognition of such emotions in others. Several studies show that persons with lesions in the amygdala have difficulty recognizing the facial expressions of emotion in others, especially expressions of fear. Brain imaging studies have found large increases in neural activity of the amygdala when people look at photos of faces expressing fear, but only small increases, or even decreases, in activity when they view photos of happy faces. One study recorded electrical activity from the amygdala and the visual cortex in response to photos of faces expressing several emotions including fear. Fearful faces produced the greatest response in the amygdala, and the response in the amygdala preceded the response in the visual cortex. The rapid response in the amygdala suggests that there is a direct neural pathway from the more primitive subcortical visual system to the amygdala (Carlson, 2011, p. 291) which permits very rapid assessment of the hedonic value of visual inputs, especially valuable to animals and humans when quick response to a predator or other immediate threat could make the difference between life and death.

The role of the amygdala in providing negative hedonic tone to perceptions can be quite subtle and is important in social interactions. Clinical studies of persons with amygdala damage by Antonio Damasio, now at the University of Southern California in Los Angeles, reveal a peculiar effect on responding in social situations. Persons with this brain damage show an inability to *mistrust* others. Consequently such persons have great difficulty functioning in the world outside the hospital because other people continually take advantage of them. This is interesting not only because it reveals the role of the amygdala in production of negative hedonic tone even in subtle social situations, but it shows that mistrust is a kind of fear, an emotion "designed" to protect the individual from social "dangers," or threats to one's resources, a feature of the environment that affects one's fitness in the social group. The amygdala plays a crucial role in the feelings and reactions generated by "objects and situations that warn of pain or other unpleasant consequences." The amygdala clearly has the capacity to act in response to social threats as well as physical dangers. Suspicion and mistrust are emotions that serve as adaptations to the possible threats posed by others in social situations. These emotions can be considered examples of social adaptations, providing protection against social threats. It has been described as the "sentry" of the brain, guarding the organism against threats ranging from predators and poisons to deceit and social manipulation. Confirming the importance of the amygdala in social behavior, Kevin Bickart of Boston University School of Medicine and colleagues (2011) found that amygdala volume is correlated with the size and complexity of social networks in adult humans.

The amygdala consists of three nuclei and it is the *central nucleus of the amygdala* that is most important in emotions generated by dangerous, harmful, or in other ways unpleasant stimuli (Carlson, 2011, p. 277–8), stimuli with negative consequences for fitness. The amygdala is also important for the learning of fear and other negative emotional responses to objects and situations. Fear learning is eliminated by destruction of the amygdala.

Closely related to the emotion of fear is anxiety, and a form of anxiety of particular interest is social anxiety. In one study when people were asked to make a list of their fears in order of intensity, they ranked speaking in front of a group of strangers as more threatening than dying! Why are we so distressed by social rejection or even the possibility of being judged negatively by others? Why should we care what others think of us, and, in particular, why should we care so much whether we are liked and valued by our group or not? Why are rejection or humiliation so "painful"? Being accepted and valued by the group seem to be extremely important to almost every human being. Being rejected, being an outcast can be devastating. Simply recall recent cases of suicide by teens or young adults who were humiliated or rejected by their peers, even on the internet. Recall mass murders committed at schools where the perpetrators acted out of revenge when others rejected them or denigrated them. Why do we care so much about how others feel about us, that is, about how they value us?

In a classic experiment on conformity by psychologist, Solomon Asch, people in a group were asked to report their judgments about the relative lengths of lines on pieces of paper. Unknown to the subjects in the experiment, everyone in the group except the subject had previously been paid by the experimenter to lie about the length of the line and to all agree on the incorrect judgment. Most subjects, rather than risking rejection and criticism, said they agreed with the judgments of the group of peers, even though the group's judgment was clearly wrong (Asch, 1951).

In another classic experiment, Stanley Milgram at Yale in the early 1960s showed that subjects were willing to follow orders to give, what they believed to be, painful and potentially dangerous electric shocks to a 50 year old man restrained in an adjacent room. An anonymous authority figure in a white coat commanded subjects to give the shocks at increasing voltage levels as they heard the man in the next room scream in agony as the shock level they believed they were administering increased. Over 50% of the subjects tested in this condition obeyed the commands of the authority figure completely eventually administering what they believed to be electric shock at the 450 volt level even as their victim fell silent after reporting that he had a heart problem (actually no shocks were given, and the victim was in the pay of Milgram, but subjects clearly believed they were giving the shocks). Why are human beings so afraid of being disobedient to authority, so fearful of non-conformity, so afraid of rejection and disapproval of others?

One approach to why we need the approval of other people is based in the idea that we are very social creatures by our genetic evolution as a species. In our evolutionary past, we lived in small groups (50–100 closely genetically related individuals, according to anthropologists) and we depended upon other members of our group for our physical survival, for protection against large predators (group defense) and for food (group hunting and sharing of food).

Under these conditions in our Pleistocene past, not being liked and valued by other members of the group might literally have meant an early death. When the saber tooth tiger came looking for dinner and picked you as a target, if you were not liked, not highly valued by the group, if you had been rejected by the group or even ostracized, then your cave-mates would be unlikely to put themselves at risk to save you. They would be more likely to let you be eaten. But, if on the other hand, you were liked or even loved, highly valued and respected, a high status individual in your group, then it is very likely that the group would have mounted a vigorous defense to protect you. Their emotions would rank your importance to the group, and high or low ranking would have meant life or death. We must have evolved very sensitive psychological mechanisms for keeping close tabs on how others felt about us, on our status within the group, and about the security of our alliances. If food were scarce, if you were not liked and valued by the group, if you had low status, the other members of your group would be unlikely to share what food they had with you. Not being liked could have led to starvation. Low status in the group would have also decreased your access to reproductive opportunities. Potential mates would not likely be attracted to low ranking individuals. Decades of animal research repeatedly shows that high ranking individuals do much more of the mating in the grop than low ranking individuals (for example, see Goodall, 1971). For species whose nature it is to live in groups, everything depends on one's position in the group. In our evolutionary Pleistocene past, survival and reproduction depended directly on how other members of the group felt about us, what emotions they had toward us, how they evaluated our worth within the group. Being liked and valued and having high ranking in the status hierarchy meant you would have the protection of the group, that they would share with you, and that you would have more reproductive opportunities. Not being liked, not being valued by others, having low status, would have literally meant death to you and your genes in our Pleistocene past. Though being rejected, having low status, being ostracized from the group no longer means death in a world of supermarkets without saber tooth tigers, because of our evolved brain circuit design, it can still *feel* like death to us.

Thus, as a social species, we likely evolved emotional circuitry in our brains that is keenly tuned to how others feel about us, how they evaluate us, and to calculate with surprising precision where we stand, our status, within the group hierarchy. Our "mind design," that of a highly social creature must also include circuits that readily fire off warnings of impending doom when our brains assess that our status in the group has fallen, that we have been devalued, that we are in social danger. The threat posed by an actual loss, or even the possibility of loss, of one's social standing makes most people feel very anxious, and outright rejection can be devastating. Being rejected or devalued by others, especially by others whom we value and whom we perceive as of high social value in the group (since it likely that they have greater control over the group's resources and over the group "will") is perhaps the most painful, because, in our Pleistocene past, it constituted such a large net loss of biological fitness.

In our evolutionary past, social anxiety may have served as a warning signal of the loss, or potential loss, of one of our most important resources as a member of a social species, our status in the group. These "instincts" for needing to be liked and respected are survival mechanisms built into our brains, powerful leftovers from our evolutionary roots, "designed" to make sure that we were highly motivated to maintain status in the group and to maintain alliances in the group, because being indifferent to whether we are liked and valued would have decreased the chances that the group would protect and feed us, increasing the chances of an early death. Could this be why we feel so upset when we sense we are not valued and liked by other people? Is this why it is so important for us to feel "included in the group"? Is social anxiety built into our brains as a survival mechanism from our deep and ancient evolutionary past, as members of a species highly social by our genetic nature? What else could explain why rejection can feel like death? Remember that our feelings, including feelings of social anxiety, are "discriminant hedonic amplifiers" which "define and exaggerate the reproductive consequences of environmental or social events associated with . . . fluctuations in reproductive potential." For a social animal such as we are, social variables such as status, affection from others, the state of our alliances, are as important to us as food, water, mates, and safety from predation, because in our ancestral social environments all of these depended on the former.

The emotion of social anxiety was part of an essential warning system in our evolutionary past signaling social danger, motivating us to action to reestablish our secure position within the group. What we call self-esteem is to a significant degree really a self-assessment of our "social value" within the group, as we perceive it. It is the stimulus which can trigger the warning mechanisms in our brains which signal "social danger," a threat so compelling because of its roots in our ancestral past when it was literally a matter of life and death. Freud coined the term "free-floating anxiety" to designate an all pervasive fearfulness without apparent object. Today it is recognized as one of the defining symptoms in *generalized anxiety disorder* (GAD), among the most common of the psychopathologies. I hypothesize that "free-floating anxiety" is actually not without object but that its object is a chronic self-perception of one's low "social value" in the generalized social group, in "society at large." It may be considered as a faulty calibration of the brain mechanisms of self-esteem as part of the evolved brain mechanisms for monitoring one's position in the social group relative to others, a *social evaluation module*. The "faulty calibration" of one's self-esteem or evaluative self-concept may come about as a consequence of negative evaluations from others perceived by the individual to be significant, or representative of the larger group. Because this brain module is conceived as an evolved mechanism for monitoring one's status and social valuation by "the group," it must be subject to genetic variation in the human population, and such variation may play a role in genetically based differences in social anxiety. However, "normal" social anxiety may not be pathological at all, but instead an adaptive signal indicating that one's position in a particular social group warrants closer monitoring and may require more careful attention to the nurturing or formation of adaptive alliances within the group. It is of interest that social anxiety and GAD involve activity in the amygdala, the primary brain structure in the circuit for the negative hedonic tone in emotions.

Another social emotion is anger. As expected it maintains the relationship between feelings and gene survival. Anger also involves the amygdala, as well as the hypothalamus. The production rule for anger assures that this emotion will occur in response to pain, to attack, to threat to resources, to loss or threat of loss, and in response to an obstacle to a goal (this later form of anger is usually referred to as frustration). In each instance of the production rule, a vigorous counter to the situation stimulating negative hedonic tone increases the chances that the situation may be "corrected" in favor of the animal or human feeling anger. In other words, the feeling of anger serves gene survival by motivating a high intensity defensive response which, all else being equal, increases the chances that the source of the potential threat, pain, loss, or other maladaptive outcome, will be removed. For example, we feel anger if someone takes or threatens to take something from us that we value, such as our money or other resources, our mate, our status within a group that we value. Anger may motivate strong enough resistance to prevent the loss, or may motivate revenge, which serves the adaptive purpose of putting the source of the threat "on notice" that "they can't get away with it." Creating a cost to those who threaten or create a loss discourages future attacks upon oneself or one's resources. It is worth noting that although we may feel anger at the loss of a loved one due to "natural causes," or to some natural calamity, we are less likely to feel anger as intense or as sustained if we feel anger at all; we are more likely to feel sadness and depression. Clearly, anger frequently elicits aggression. Aggressive behaviors are important to many animals in gaining "access to mates, defending territory needed to attract mates or to provide a site for building a nest, or defending offspring" and "all can be regarded as reproductive behaviors" (Carlson, 2011, p. 281–2). Anger and aggression also serve the adaptive function of self-defense. The more intense the emotions of anger, the more vigorous the defense or the more vigorous the attempt we may make to recover something taken from us, and the more likely the threat to biological fitness will be overcome. Variations in the intensity of this emotion range from mild irritation to seething rage.

The *positive hedonic value* of affects and emotions is dependent upon a mesolimbic circuit that includes the *nucleus accumbens* and the *lateral hypothalamus*, including a large fiber tract, the *medial forebrain bundle*. As pointed out in an earlier chapter, electrical stimulation of some regions of the hypothalamus causes rage and fear responses. Stimulation by electrodes of other sub-cortical regions, the nucleus accumbens and lateral hypothalamus, produces reward or pleasure and induces animals to vigorously press a lever wired to deliver electrical stimulation to these areas of their brains. As Cannon predicted, different sub-cortical circuits mediate different emotional responses including excitement, fear, anger, and sadness. Interestingly, neuroimaging studies show that when people view things that they like, and when they anticipate that they will acquire a desired gain, nucleus accumbens activity increases. So, not only receiving a reward activates the "pleasure circuitry" of the brain, but mere *anticipation* of a gain, even a symbolic gain such as money, causes increased neural activation in the *nucleus accumbens*. It is interesting that schizophrenics show a deficit in this brain response when anticipating a symbolic gain, perhaps offering a clue about the origin of one characteristic of people with the disease, lack of positive emotion in situations that in a normal person would elicit happiness or pleasure.

In psychology, historically there are two major theoretical approaches to emotion. The first, a *dimensional approach*, originated with the 19th century psychologist, Wilhelm Wundt. Wundt proposed that certain dimensions formed the basic elements that contributed to more specific emotions such as happiness and sadness. According to Wundt, the emotions could be thought of as existing on two dimensions, intensity or arousal, and valence or hedonic value (positive or negative). In this view, where any feeling lies, on these two dimensions, will give a pretty good description of almost any emotion. If we use a vector coding model of emotion to represent any emotion in this model, then a two-dimensional activation vector would be sufficient to code any emotion in the brain in an abstract two dimensional emotional space (see discussion of vector coding in the prior chapter). However, I suspect that many more dimensions actually exist in the variety of emotions that we experience and that a multi-dimensional vector representing neural coding involving multiple circuits is more likely to be closer to the truth.

A second theoretical approach to emotions relies upon distinct categories, rather than dimensions. According to this *categorical view of emotion*, originating with Charles Darwin, emotions are not just different combinations of arousal and valence, but are actually distinct categories of feeling, and emotional expression, that signal specific states that have survival value. Victor Johnston (1999) refers to emotions as "the omens of fitness," signals that tell us about the adaptive meaning of things that we encounter in the world, that is, what those things portend for our survival and chances of reproduction. Darwin argued that many emotional states show continuity across species, consistent with his theory that present-day species diverged from common, now extinct ancestors. According to Darwin, each emotion existed to help solve specific adaptive problems thereby increasing the chances of survival and reproduction of the genes of the species.

Psychologist Paul Eckman in the 1970's gave important support to the categorical view when he demonstrated that New Guinea tribesman recognized facial expressions of people from modern Western cultures, whom they had never been exposed to before, confirming that the discrete facial expressions, and the underlying feelings, for happiness, sadness, anger, fear, and disgust were not culturally learned, but universal to all human beings regardless of culture, and thus built into our genetically evolved brain "design." Adding evidence for this view, other research showed that these basic facial expressions were found in human babies that were born blind, indicating that these facial expressions could not have been learned, but must be dependent upon genetics and human evolution. This evolutionary view is strongly supported by Cannon's evidence, described above (and much more since), for the existence of specific sub-cortical circuits for specific emotions. It seemed that indeed, Darwin was right. Emotions exist as evolved adaptations that facilitate biological fitness, the survival and reproduction of genes.

Emotions lead to motion, goal-directed movement serving adaptation to biologically important stimuli in the environment. Think about one of our most powerful of human emotions, "falling in love." In evolution, survival is only part of the story. Survival without reproduction won't get your genes into the next generation. As Victor Johnston implies in the quote at the opening of this chapter, reproductive success is the driving force of evolution, not only of bodies, but of brains as well. As a consequence, our "mind design" is dominated by psychological mechanisms, emotional mechanisms, which drive us powerfully toward successful reproductive activity.

The famous 19th century Viennese neurologist, and founder of psychoanalysis, Sigmund Freud, recognized a central and determining role of sexual instincts in the human mind. His psychoanalytic theory of the structure of the human psyche places the sexual instinct, front and center, in his conception of the unconscious motives that control human life.

Sex dominates our thinking and our feeling. Some studies show that men, especially those in their prime reproductive years, think about sex dozens of times a day, much more frequently than anything else. Advertizing often utilizes sexual images to sell products. Teen pregnancies and abortions, violence motivated by sexual jealousy, the popularity of movies and books with sexual and romantic themes, erotic literature and pornography, prostitution and the sex trade, billions of dollars a year spent on cosmetics and beauty supplies, plastic surgery, sexually appealing clothing, steroids, and body building, 6,200 weddings a day and over 70 billion dollars a year spent on weddings in the United States alone, Viagra, and the recent fervor over the wedding of British royals, all testify to the central role of sex and sexual emotions in human psychology.

It is no accident that emotions related to mate selection, and sex, make up a very large part of our "mind design." Natural selection could have made us, and other animals, in no other way—sexual emotions and behavior are central to reproductive fitness. To emphasize this point, just imagine a thought experiment. Envision some hypothetical human ancestor that by some genetic mutation had brain circuit "design" that made him or her little interested in sex, devoid of emotions of passion, sexual attraction, and romantic yearnings. Then imagine another hypothetical human ancestor which due to a different mutation had brain circuit "design" that gave them strong sexual emotions, feelings that drove them to find the opposite sex of great interest, and that drove them to relentlessly pursue the opposite sex with strong feelings of attraction, passion, and amore. Who is likely to engage in more reproductive behavior? Who is more likely to get their genes into the next generation? Natural selection drives brain "design" powerfully toward the evolution of potent emotions that will motivate strong interest in the opposite sex and in reproductive behavior. It is not the devil that makes us so interested in sex, it is our genes, which, by action of *their* "designer," natural selection, "design" our brain/minds to unconsciously seek their perpetuation over generations by any means possible.

Of course, we are not aware of these evolutionary "goals," and neither are the genes or natural selection. We don't need to be aware of the reasons, for it all to work. The propagation of genes is an outcome that is simply built-in to how the mechanism of evolution works. Remember the discussion in chapter 6 about the self-replicators, the genes, who by evolving devices, whether in body or brain, that improve survival and reproduction of their "survival machines," assure their own continued existence. But again, none of this is conscious or intentional. It is just a fact of the evolutionary process that genetic variants that out-reproduce their competitors will come to dominate in sheer numbers, automatically, without intention, but just as a mechanical consequence of the dynamics of natural selection and evolutionary change. Brain "design" that makes animals, including us, highly interested in, and motivated by, sex is a winning brain design in the competition among genes for continued existence. Such brain "design" is just inevitable.

Notice that all of the emotion involved in romance and sexual attraction ultimately is for the single "purpose" of moving egg and sperm in the right direction. In sexual reproduction two separate individuals move about the environment independently of one another, until sexual *attraction* enters the picture. Sexual attraction takes two independent organisms and moves them, as if by a kind of magnetism, "animal magnetism," toward one another. The trajectory of behavior of one or both is modified. If the attraction is mutual the direction of movement of both closes the distance between them. Once close enough, the egg carrying animal and the sperm carrying animal make tactile contact, and this skin on skin contact triggers a whole new sequence of goal-directed movement that quickly results in sperm being placed in close proximity to the egg inside the body of the female, and this sequence of mental and behavioral events accomplishes "internal fertilization." In many aquatic species, external fertilization is enough, but still the male and female must be drawn close enough so that sperm will be able to find their way with sufficient probability to get the reproductive job done. For example, many species of fish deposit their sperm in the water near the female as she lays her eggs. This requires a synchronization of behavior between male and female. In one species, the female makes quivering movements as she is releasing her eggs into the water. The male is attracted by these movements (similar to human males who are reportedly attracted by the "quivering" bodies of women as they "shake that booty" or "belly dance" or wiggle this way and that in other forms of sensual dancing) and closes the distance between her quivering body and his; as he does so, he seeks to get as close to her body as possible, causing his body to rub against hers. That tactile stimulation of the male's body causes him to ejaculate his sperm into the water, in the same space in the water where the female is laying eggs, and at the same time. Two individual animals and their reproductive cells are thus put in the same space at the same time.

Whether any feelings are taking place in fish, we don't know, but we do know that feelings of attraction in humans function to draw male and female, and ultimately, sperm and egg, together. Sexual attraction, sexual passion, lust, infatuation, falling in love, all these feelings evolved because they serve this goal. The conventional wisdom in the social sciences that romantic love is a relatively recent invention by romantic Europeans is wrong. Cross cultural studies find romantic love in a wide range of cultures worldwide from the Zulus of Africa to Eskimos in the far north in Alaska (see Buss, 2008, p. 124–5). Studies using functional magnetic resonance imaging (fMRI) reveal that specific regions of the brain become active when one thinks about his or her lover. These regions are the caudate nucleus and the *ventral tegmental area* of the brainstem, the origin of the mesolimbic reward circuit which includes the nucleus accumbens. This brain system utilizes the neurotransmitter, dopamine, the happiness juice of the brain, which when released in the mesolimbic circuit produces a "rush" similar to that produced by the dopamine agonist, cocaine (see Buss, 2008, p. 125). No wonder the rush of falling in love can be addicting and when we lose that rush the withdrawal symptoms we feel can put us into a depression, as deep as that caused by cocaine withdrawal. The song "Addicted to Love" is recognizing the connection.

The "omens of fitness" and mate selection

However, things aren't as simple as getting just *any* sperm and any egg together. Selection is involved—what Darwin called *sexual selection*, a form of natural selection in which survival mechanisms are not selected for, but instead features which attract the opposite sex, even if such features might reduce survival chances. An example of one such trait is the beautiful but cumbersome tail of the peacock, which although attractive to pea hens, increases vulnerability to predators. Sexual selection occurs when an animal or a person shows preference for one mating partner over another. The result is that some genes get reproduced more frequently than others. Thus, sexual selection can drive evolution, as in the peacock's tail, and as we shall see, even in humans.

We don't want to mate with just anyone; our feelings make us discriminate among potential partners. Some potential partners are just more appealing than others. Our disposition to seek out some potential partners and to reject others produces *intraspecific competition* and this competition serves biological function. Males compete with other males of their own kind for females, and females compete with other females of their own kind for males. This intraspecific competition spurs the evolution of a host of traits for the specific purpose of eliciting strong emotions of attraction in the opposite sex, and humans, clever little creatures that we are, often use learned behavioral innovations, usually culturally transmitted, in the mating game. When women use cosmetics, get breast implants, wear jewelry, get botox injections, or when men buff up at the gym, get tattoos, flash their cash, or "dress to kill," and when either sex flirts, courts, gives gifts, songs, or poems to a member of the opposite sex, then *sexual selection* in human beings is at work. Courtship behavior on the part of both male and female is a way for each to advertise their good qualities in hopes of influencing the object of their romantic desire to commit themselves, and their reproductive potential. Genes are using evolved brain mechanisms to recognize and locate the best genes possible before committing to a match.

Sexual selection has been an important factor in the evolution of many traits that are not strictly for survival, but which arise to give advantage in the competition among members of the same sex for mates with high reproductive value. As mentioned above, the large tail of the peacock which is effective as a sexual attractant is also cumbersome and makes the male more vulnerable to predation. The evolution of traits that provide advantage in intrasexual competition, in spite of some disadvantages to survival, shows two important things about evolutionary processes. First, this is a clear indication that survival of the *individual* is not the primary outcome or "goal" of evolution, but instead that the reproduction of genes *is*. For example, the male sex hormone, testosterone, responsible for sex drive, reduces life span in human males. Males castrated in child-hood live an average of 5 years longer than non-castrated males. Male sex hormones and the sexual activity that follows reduce chances of personal survival. Sex drive in women is an even greater detriment to personal survival considering the perils of child-birth. If personal survival were the "goal" of evolution then we should have evolved brain circuitry to protect us from it; in that case, sex would feel very unpleasant. But the opposite is true, because reproduction of genes, not personal survival, is what is selected for in evolution (Johnston, 1999, p. 85). Whatever enhances the probability of successful reproduction of genes will be favored by natural selection, even if the favored traits sometimes reduce the survival chances of the individual. But the survival chances of the individual cannot be compromised too much, not to the degree that net repro-ductive potential is lost, but only when there is a net gain in reproductive success—for the peacock, having large tail feathers may reduce chances of survival, but the gain in reproductive success provided by this powerful sexual attractant outweighs the risks.

This leads to a second observation. Different kinds or circumstances of selection, *Darwinian natural selection* and *sexual selection* in this case, each selecting for different traits, can end up producing an optimal balance between competing selection processes in terms of fitness, and in terms of the actual traits (the phenotype) that an individual or species ends up with. Female chimpanzees develop a very large swelling of the genital area when they are sexually receptive and fertile. This enlarged reddened genital region attracts males, but it is cumbersome and must have made females, in this state, easier targets for predators such as leopards. However, the reproductive advantage in female-female intrasexual competition must have overcome the disadvantages to personal survival. The peacock's large tail feather display can get just big enough to maximize success in male-male competition for mates, but not so big that reduced chances of sur-vival exceed the reproductive advantages of the tail feathers. In other words, competing selection processes can reach an optimal cost/benefit ratio in the "design" of a trait. The reproductive *benefit* of the peacock's tail feathers in male-male competition exceeds the survival and reproductive *cost* to the peacock produced by increased vulnerability to predators (later in this chapter we examine another example of a compromise between opposing selection processes—Darwinian natural selection for individual survival and psychological self-interest and kin selection for kin altruism and selflessness).

An example of how evolution "designs" emotions in intraspecific competition is the disposition of males to fight over females in many animal species, including several species of primate. The emotion of anger is prominent in such encounters, at least in humans, and probably similar emotions occur in many of the non-human primates and perhaps in other mammal species. If males in competition over mates feel anger toward their rivals, especially in the midst of a fight, this emotion would likely be adaptive because it focuses and intensifies the fighting resources of the male onto the rival and increases the ferocity of the attack, boosting the chances that the attack will successfully deter the rival. But once the rival is soundly defeated, the anger quickly dissipates, and the attack ends. Continuing the attack on a rival that has already been defeated produces little additional gain and may put the victor at risk of unnecessary injury if the defeated animal fights back. In addition, continuing the attack on a defeated rival wastes time and energy, and may further disrupt group cohesion. Thus, fighting over mates might be considered an example of sexual selection, since fighting male rivals puts a male at risk of personal injury and constitutes a threat to personal survival, but this cost is "worth it" because such intraspecific fights over females win and preserve a male's access to the reproductive potential of females. Not fighting over mates would allow males to avoid injury or early death, but the gain in personal survival would be at the expense of mating opportunities. Such a "design" can't work in evolution, because genes responsible for such a psychology wouldn't be reproduced. Again, an illustration of the major principle of evolution, reproduction of genes, not personal survival is the inevitable outcome of natural selection. Furthermore, we see how natural selection for emotions that help secure reproductive opportunities is balanced by selection for other emotions that suspend attack when no additional gain is likely to result, thus reducing additional and unnecessary risk to personal survival. Many animal species have evolved brain circuit designs that detect signs of defeat in an opponent and lead to emotions of "compassion" which abruptly end an attack. Many species have evolved gestures of defeat and submission (such as crouching and exposing the neck to a rival) which tend to inhibit further attack.

Thus, our evolved sexually oriented "mind design" will include fine tuned emotional mechanisms for mate selection; but it will also include emotions such as jealousy and anger related to the keen competition for finding, winning, and keeping "desirable" mates. Just like our taste mechanisms include evaluative affects such as "good" taste associated with substances that will benefit the survival and reproduction of our genes, and "bad" tastes associated with substances that may reduce our fitness, our "tastes" in mates are also guided by feelings that involve evaluations of the "adaptive significance" of our choices from among a pool of potential mates.

The emotions that guide our mate selection involve feelings of attraction and desire for intimacy, for closeness, for physical proximity to "our heart's desire," as well as emotional closeness or proximity. If such feelings are really the end product of computations by our brains of the "mate value" of potential mating partners, then the quality and intensity of the sexual and romantic emotions should be systematically controlled by stimuli that are predictive of the fertility of potential partners. In other words, signs of fertility in the opposite sex should induce feelings of sexual attraction and romantic yearnings in our genetically evolved brains.

Our brains have been finely tuned by natural selection to be highly sensitive to cues of *biological fitness* as our emotions guide us toward selection of mates. Men's eyes and brains literally scan the faces and bodies of women in search of signs of fertility in potential (or imagined) sexual partners. The faces and bodies of women are full of cues indicative of their fertility. Women in their prime reproductive years enjoy a special status in human social groups because they are highly valued for their reproductive potential. For example, such prime reproductive females have access to resources, social power, and status within the group that others may not readily enjoy. Special status in the social group for females in their reproductive prime is found in other primate societies in addition to humans. Prime reproductive females have physical features which signal their high reproductive potential. These physical features engender strong emotions in males.

Fullness of lips and the length of the lower jaw are two important indicators of fertility found in the faces of women. In several studies, faces of women that were judged by men, across cultures, to be more beautiful are characterized by full lips, and by a lower jaw, a full standard deviation shorter than the lower jaw of the average man. And, consistent with an evolutionary hypothesis of "mind" design, fullness of lips and a shortened lower jaw are both features correlated with higher blood levels of the female sex hormone, estrogen, and consequently with greater fertility (Johnston, 1999). Thus, facial beauty of women is a display of *fertility cues*, which, men are tuned to respond to emotionally, as a result of the "design" of their evolved brain circuitry. The end result of this brain "design" in men is that they are drawn to women with optimal fertility, thus increasing the probability that their genes will be successfully reproduced. Emotion plays the key role here. However, as is common knowledge, just desiring the most desirable women is not enough. Women are involved in sexual selection too.

Women's brains are equipped with emotional tools as well which lead them to tune into cues of biological fitness in their potential sexual partners. For example, women, like men, are built (that is, their brains are built) to find facial and body symmetry strongly emotionally appealing. Facial and body symmetry is a good indicator of "good" genes and of resistance to parasites. Even slight deviations from body and facial symmetry are correlated with parasites during physical development.

Women also look for personality traits such as intelligence, willingness to share, and for signs that indicate the status of the man and whether he controls sufficient resources or has the potential to gain control of resources. A man who has resources and is willing to share them with his mate and his offspring would increase the chances of survival of both (Johnston, 1999, p. 147–153). An interesting study by La Cerra (1994) suggests that women prefer men as marriage partners who show a willingness to invest in children. After testing women's ratings of the attractiveness of men depicted in slides showing them caring for or neglecting children, the highest ratings of attractiveness were associated with men depicted interacting positively with children and the lowest ratings were given to men ignoring children in distress. La Cerra concluded "women's ratings of the attractiveness of men as potential mates are increased by cues of their affection toward a child and decreased by cues of their indifference toward a child in distress" (see Buss, 2008, p. 127).

Another cue indicative of reproductive potential that women find attractive in a potential mate is a deep voice. Reasons for this may be that a deep voice signals sexual maturity and the accompanying levels of the male sex hormone, testosterone, larger body size, and generally "good genes." Evidence that voice quality in men is important in women's choice of sexual partner is provided by the finding that men with attractive-sounding voices have sexual intercourse earlier, have a larger number of sexual partners, and are more often chosen by women for sexual affairs (see Buss, 2008, p. 128–9).

As suggested earlier, men use a woman's physical attractiveness as an indication of her "mate value," her overall desirability to men (Buss, 2008, p. 132), and *mate value* is closely tied to cues of fertility. One indication of fertility and sexual maturity in women is the hips filling out, leading to wider hips and a relatively smaller waist, that is, a reduction in the waist-to-hip ratio. Experiments by Singh (1993) have consistently found that men, regardless of their culture, universally prefer women of average weight, with wider hips and a thinner waist, in an optimal waist/hip ratio of 0.7. That is, a waist of 28 inches should be accompanied by hips of about 40 inches for maximum sexual attractiveness by this formula. Women with a higher ratio or women who are less than average weight or heavier than average weight are judged to be less sexually attractive by men across a wide range of cultures. Being too thin or being too heavy or having a waist/hip ratio greater than 0.7 are signs of reduced fertility, and these traits are *felt* by men, regardless of culture, to be less sexually attractive. Cultural and historical variations in "most attractive weights" do occur within a relatively narrow range, but the most attractive waist-to-hip ratio is a constant across cultures and historical periods.

However, Singh did not test lower ratios, and it has been suggested that lower ratios consistent with the classic 36-24-36 ideal woman's body (a waist-to-hip ratio of .67) may be judged even more attractive by men. It is significant that the biological mechanism that regulates the waist-to-hip ratio in women is estrogen levels. Estrogen is one of the female sex hormones. Estrogen reduces fat deposit in the belly and waist and increases fat deposits in the hips, thighs and bottom. Nice hips, thighs, and butt are universally judged to be irresistibly sexually attractive by men worldwide. The strongest feelings of attraction are produced by the strongest physical indicators of fertility (Bridgeman, 2003, p. 84 and 105–6). This suggests that men's emotions of sexual attraction and romantic interest are evolved *psychological adaptations* for the detection of reliable cues indicative of female fertility.

Another sign of fertility is derived from physiological changes in the body of a woman induced by changes in her hormones as she ovulates. Blood vessels in the skin enlarge, leading to a healthy "glow" in women who are ovulating, the time when women are maximally fertile. This glow is similar to the glow of the flushed reddish skin during sexual excitement. This glow is more apparent in younger women, with their smoother skin, and may also serve as a sign of youthfulness, another factor related to fertility (Bridgeman, 2003, p. 84). It is interesting that one of the standard uses of cosmetics, at least in Western cultures, is makeup that artificially reddens the cheeks. Perhaps, unconsciously, some time long ago it was discovered that a reddish "blush" simulated by cosmetics is an attractant to human males because of its association with ovulation and increased fertility. Perhaps male brains are tuned to pick up this unconscious cue of fertility even when it is only a simulation performed by women using makeup as a result of a cultural transmitted learned behavior. Here is an interesting case where cultural evolution has its roots in the biological evolution of our species-typical brain "design."

Of course, men are also attracted by facial beauty. Facial symmetry is a feature closely associated with judgments of facial beauty. This cue may be significantly related to biological fitness since asymmetry of body and face are associated with certain diseases, and the effects of parasites during development. A symmetrical body and face probably indicate better health, certainly a characteristic predictive of greater chances of reproductive success in a potential partner, and a sign of "good" genes to be passed on to any offspring. What our brain "design" has evolved to find beautiful may be reliable indicators of good health, and therefore high reproductive potential. The old saying that "beauty is in the eye of the beholder," may be better stated as beauty is in the *brain* of the beholder, as the brain computes estimates of reproductive value of potential mates based on cues of health and fertility.

Another key to feminine beauty is youth. All over the world, men prefer to marry women in their early 20s, regardless of their age and regardless of the social or economic status of the woman. Men seek beauty and youth and pay much less attention to social and economic factors. Interestingly, the age at which women can bear children with the fewest complications, that is, their age of peak fertility, is 23 years. Men as they age prefer partners progressively younger than they are. This evolved male strategy for mate selection may arise from the fact that males cannot produce offspring themselves and therefore must rely completely upon the fertility of their mate (Bridgeman, 2003, p. 100–104). Interestingly, the average age of Playboy centerfolds, ideals of feminine beauty, is 21.7 years (Johnston, 1993). It is easy to see how the relationship between youth and emotional judgments of sexual beauty would evolve. Brain "design" in males must evolve to put a premium on youthful female partners considering that women rapidly lose their fertility after age 30 and their maximum fertility is in their early 20s.

Another example of how biological factors in mate selection may determine cultural practices that enhance a biological marker is in the plucking and shaping of eyebrows by women. The male skull is characterized by a heavy, bony "brow ridge," which is much less pronounced in women and is one of the anatomical features that distinguishes the male face from the female face in humans. The large brow ridge of the male's skull gives the male face a characteristic heavy and prominent, low brow. Women's faces have a characteristically smaller brow. By plucking and shaping their eyebrows into a thin and arching shape, women unconsciously exaggerate this anatomical difference between their faces and men's faces enhancing a biological marker of their femininity. And it seems to work. Men's brains seem to be tuned to this biological marker and respond to its exaggeration by finding women's faces, with eyebrows artificially thinner and more arched, more sexually attractive.

A humorous example of the lengths to which women will go in the struggle to attract mates as part of intrasexual competition comes from Helen Fielding's novel *Bridget Jones's Diary* (Penguin Books, 1996). Bridget, 30-something unattached human female, sensing her prime years of fertility slipping away, writes in her diary: "Completely exhausted by entire day of date-preparation. Being a woman is worse than being a farmer—there is so much harvesting and crop spraying to be done: legs to be waxed, underarms shaved, eyebrows plucked, feet pumiced, skin exfoliated and moisturized, spots cleansed, roots dyed, eyelashes tinted, nails filed, cellulite massaged, stomach muscles exercised. The whole performance is so highly tuned you only need to neglect it for a few days for the whole thing to go to seed. Sometimes I wonder what I would be like if left to revert to nature. . ."

Emotions guide mate selection, and these feelings in men are responses, at least in substantial part, to physical cues of good health and fertility. Emotions of sexual attraction in men appear to be the end-product of computations by the brain of the fertility of women whom they might pursue as their potential sexual partners, those whose eggs may be fertilized by their sperm to produce offspring, the carriers of both their genes.

Women typically employ somewhat different criteria for determining the "mate value" of their potential mates. In our evolutionary past, the survival of the offspring of a woman would depend heavily upon the resources that her mate possessed. Though this situation has changed to varying degrees for modern women, the brain circuit "designs" that determine women's emotions as they select mates have not had time to change. "They continue to reflect the conditions that applied during the period of human evolution, the tough and hazardous life of nomads roaming the savanna, and young people still choose partners as though they were preparing for those conditions. Our genes tell us what is appropriate for the Paleolithic nomad" (Bridgeman, 2003, p. 99). In Paleolithic times (from the earliest known use of stone tools by Australopithecines, about 2.6 million years ago, through the advent of our species about 200,000 thousand years ago, to the end of the Pleistocene about 12,000 years ago), one important determinant of the survival of a female and her offspring was the resources controlled by her mate. Thus social status, resources already accumulated, and potential for acquiring and controlling additional resources, perhaps as indicated by signs of strength and intelligence, would be signs of a desirable mate for a woman in our hunter-gather past, and for many women today. Accumulating resources takes time. This may explain why women typically marry men a few years old than they are. Power, wealth, and status tend to be valued by women when they select their sexual partners. This is reflected in a quote attributed to former President Richard Nixon's Secretary of State, Henry Kissinger. Kissinger purportedly said that "Power is the ultimate aphrodisiac" for women (The New York Times, 28 October, 1973). Power, status and control of resources provide men greater access to young, attractive, and fertile partners.

One researcher found that high status men in six ancient cultures from Mesopotamia and Egypt to Aztec Mexico, Inca Peru, and imperial India and China, had much greater access to women with high reproductive potential, and the number of women corresponded closely with the status and rank of the man. In India, even until fairly recently, rich nobles had harems, the richer the man, the greater number of women he could afford. The Inca kings had "houses of virgins" of as many as 1,500 women available to them at any time they wished. One imperial Chinese emperor had a harem of over 10,000 young and presumably attractive women. These relationships between status and access to female sexual partners also hold in modern times. High status men report more affairs than lower status men and men who have higher incomes and who are higher in status tend to have more frequent sex and a larger number of children. Because increases in power and status provide greater access to reproductive women, Buss hypothesizes that men are more highly motivated to seek high status than are women. Consistent with this expectation and that the difference might be genetically evolved and not learned, sex differences in dominance motivation appear to emerge at a young age (Buss, 2008, p. 361–2). It is of interest that high status males in non-human primate species also have greater access to reproductive females than lower status males do (Goodall, 1971). Even in women in modern Western societies, who have achieved high status and their own resources through their own careers, male dominance, status, education, and wealth are still valued in their choice of sexual partners; "women's mate preferences show the hallmarks of adaptation: design features that are specialized for solving the complex adaptive problem of mate selection" (Buss, 2008, p. 133). Male college students take note: who would have thought that getting good grades might give you greater access to reproductive opportunities with higher "mate value" women? Well, the facts don't lie. If that doesn't motivate you to study harder, I don't know what will! And you nerdy guys, here's hope!

Although good looks are also important to women, probably as a marker of good health and good genes, as it is for men, women still find wealth, status, and power—in short, control of resources—much more important considerations in mate selection than men do. Men value signs of fertility as expressed in youth and beauty more than women do. However, both sexes value personality traits highly, regardless of culture. The traits most valued by both sexes in selection of a mate include being loving and kind, understanding, caring, and intelligent (Buss, 1989).

These personality characteristics also figure into the computations by the brain as emotions in mate selection develop toward a mate choice. Clearly such psychological traits as these are predictive not only of "good" genes, but also of other benefits to fitness, such as an increased probability that the mate can be counted upon during the long period of care required for the nurturing of human offspring. It is likely that, in our Pleistocene past, and to a significant degree in the modern world, a male that forms strong emotional ties with his mate is much more likely to stick around long enough to help care for his children, increasing their chances of survival and thus the survival and reproduction of his genes and the genes of his mate. Strong emotional ties are also likely to improve the chances of sexual fidelity. Propensity for caring and kindness are likely to be good predictors of a mate's willingness to share resources and to care for the other as well as for their offspring.

Recognizing cues likely to enhance reproductive fitness of a potential mate is one thing. But, the emotional mechanisms of the brain must also be tuned to read the emotions of one's partner and be able to recognize any signs of waning interest. Circuitry for detection of danger or threat to the stability of the mating relationship is likely to produce feelings of distress, anger, or jealousy in the other. And such feelings make perfect evolutionary sense, given that loss of a mate usually reduces opportunity for the reproduction of one's genes, at least in the short run and maybe longer term as well, and so threatens biological fitness.

Regarding jealousy, evolutionary psychologist, David Buss (Buss, 2008), at the University of Texas, Austin, has made the argument that men will experience stronger feelings of possessiveness and sexual jealousy than women because men, in contrast to women, never really know for sure whose baby is being carried by their mate. There is almost always the opportunity for a women to become impregnated by a man other than her partner so that a man never can be absolutely certain that the baby his partner is carrying is his, but the woman always knows it is hers. Therefore, in terms of evolutionary fitness, the male brain should be evolved to be more watchful of his mate to be sure she is not being unfaithful. If the male's partner is impregnated by a rival male he might end up expending his resources for the care of a child that is not his—not a good outcome for the man's genes. The strong emotions associated with sexual jealousy in human males is illustrated by a line from the John Lennon and Paul McCartney song "Run for Your Life," from the "Rubber Soul" album, in which is found the lyric, "I'd rather see you dead, little girl, than be with another man. Catch you with another man, that's the end, little girl . . . I'd rather see you dead" (Bridgeman, 2003, p. 88). One of the major motives for murder and domestic violence is sexual jealousy. Of course, women get jealous too, but, evolutionary psychologist, David Buss, predicted that women are more disturbed by *emotional* infidelity because weakening of emotional bonds may lead her partner to withdraw not only love but resources from her and provide them to a rival. Men, however, Buss predicted, will be more distressed by *sexual* infidelity because they are losing the reproductive potential of their partner. Furthermore, a man never really knows for certain whose child his mate is carrying, and thus it is more critical for men to be alert to advances of potential rivals. However, some research has called this prediction into question. Both men and women may be more equally threatened by emotional infidelity than sexual, but perhaps for different reasons; still both are equally concerned about protecting the relationship because the functioning sexual relationship is the key to reproductive success in both sexes (Bridgeman, 2003, p. 90). Buss has proposed that sexual jealousy is a psychological adaptation that provides enhanced fitness because it motivates behavior that makes infidelity less likely in one's partner. The adaptive functions served are similar to those served by "mate guarding" in some non-human primate species. As a means of reducing female promiscuity and discouraging rival males, male gorillas can guard up to eight estrus females simultaneously. Buss proposes that sexual jealousy in humans depends upon specifically evolved brain circuitry, a sexual jealousy module genetically built into human brain "design," evolved as a psychological adaptation to the adaptive problem of intrasexual competition for mates.

Other evidence that emotions and affects have evolutionary origins, as specific psychological adaptations for the solution of specific adaptive problems, comes from observations about the intensity of feelings. Although, the intensity of feelings must be related to the magnitude of the computed adaptive significance of an event, the relationship between these two variables is not linear. Recall that Johnston (1999, p. 83) proposes that feelings act like filters, or *discriminant hedonic amplifiers*, that "define and exaggerate the reproductive consequences of environmental or social events associated with relatively minor fluctuations in reproductive potential." This means that small differences in adaptive significance will be exaggerated in the production rules that produce emotions. For example, relatively small differences in the "mate value" of two potential mates may lead to big differences in the emotion that each mate choice elicits. This arrangement probably facilitates choice and decision-making toward better fitness. Consider two men, both of whom are very close in their biologically relevant attributes indicative of their respective genetic fitness and reproductive potential. Only slight differences between them in mate value can cause a woman to fall "madly in love" with one of them, and to be indifferent to the other. The large difference in emotion elicited in the woman by the two different men exaggerates the difference in their reproductive fitness. This exaggerated feeling assures that even small differences in reproductive value of potential mates will control behavior and guide it toward choices that optimize chances of reproductive success and biological fitness. Contrary to popular belief, love is not blind, it is just looking for cues of biological and reproductive fitness—cues which often times are not in complete accord with rational, conscious thought processes, processes that are much more subject to culturally transmitted values and beliefs ("memes," see Richard Dawkins, *The Selfish Gene*, 2006). Thus, because rational, culturally transmitted values don't always coincide with emotional computations of "mate value" by the more ancient emotional mechanisms in the brain, that is, with the wisdom of the "heart," conflict may arise between thought and emotion, reflection and feeling. Emotion usually wins out, in the choice of mates.

The disproportionate intensity of emotion with variations in the adaptive significance of things in the world is also exemplified in feelings of sexual revulsion. Many people, particularly young people in their reproductive prime, experience strong feelings of revulsion at the thought of having sex with persons of the opposite sex that are much older than they are or who are physically unattractive, that is, lacking in cues indicative of fertility and other cues of high "mate value." Teen aged girls or women in their early twenties when confronted with sexual advances from unattractive males, those with cues indicative of lesser "mate value," may actually make facial expressions of disgust and rejection similar to facial expressions made in response to "bad" tasting foods, such as spoiled milk or bacterial infected, rotting meat. In other cases, these facial expressions may be replaced by other acts indicative of rejection. Similar reactions of sexual revulsion are also found in young human males who may not only be strongly repulsed by the thought of sex with older, or otherwise unattractive women lacking in cues of high fertility, but who will ridicule and chide other males should they show interest in unattractive women or much older women. Again, the adaptive function may be to guard the reproductive fitness of young males with high "mate value," "saving" it for the best possible mate choice for their genes, just as emotions of sexual revulsion in young women may do.

An incident portrayed in a recent television series illustrates the idea. In an episode of the Showtime T.V. series "The Borgias," based on actual historical events, one young, beautiful, female character confesses to the Pope (Alexander VI) that she despises and abhors sex with her husband, whom she was forced to marry against her will, so much so that she purposely aborted her pregnancy because she couldn't "bear the thought of his [her husband's] vile presence" inside her body. Such strong emotions of sexual revulsion might actually be a form of psychological adaptation. Strong feelings of revulsion elicited by sexual encounters, potential or actual, with biologically less fit individuals may be a protective mechanism guarding the reproductive potential of highly biologically (i.e. reproductively) fit individuals. Though the attractive young woman in "The Borgias" killed her own offspring in the womb and suffers loss of reproductive success as a result, this act freed up her body for mating with more biologically suitable partners. Though such behavior is morally reprehensible, it may better serve the reproduction of the genes of the woman in the long run. In fact, in later episodes, as in real history, she ends up bearing several children with the Pope, Alexander VI, to whom she originally confessed her sin. This Pope, although substantially older than she, commanded extensive power, prestige, and substantial material resources, while she offered the Pope her youth and beauty, cues of fertility that even the Pope couldn't resist. This match ultimately led to several children by her that carried forward his genes, as well as hers, into future generations (in actual historical fact, Pope Alexander VI was not very good at resisting any of the temptations of the world; he became known for his infamous corruption and debauchery).

In lions in the wild, a similar strategy operates. When male lions from outside the pride move in and take over the pride by attacking and driving off the resident males, the newly victorious winners of the intraspecific male competition search out and systematically kill all the cubs in the pride. This grotesque display of infanticide is adaptive behavior on the part of the victorious males because it prevents the resident females from continuing to nurse and brings them back into estrus, making their reproductive potential quickly available to the new adult males. Such behavior also eliminates the genes of the resident males who were just defeated. In lions, females do most of the hunting. After killing all the offspring of their male rivals, the adult males new to the pride assure that the hunting efforts of the females will go toward the support of their genes, in their offspring, and not to the support of cubs carrying genes of rival males.

Consistent with these observations in male lions, who are apparently motivated (unconsciously, of course) by "gene selfishness," studies of child abuse in humans reveal that step children are more frequently the victims of parental abuse than are the biological children of parents. Recall the evil step mother in the story of Cinderella. Nothing was too good for her spoiled biological daughters, but poor Cinderella, the unlucky step-child, was treated badly no matter how good she was. Though only a story, such enduring culturally transmitted fables often reveal deeper truths about human nature. In this case, favoring one's biological children over step-children might be explained in terms of reproductive fitness. Behavior which tends to preserve some genes, those of genetic relatives, over those of non-relatives is a predictable effect of evolution by natural selection. Not to say that the outcome is good, or fair, or desirable, but only that it is consistent with a gene-centered view of evolution.

The emotions involved in the regulation of reproductive behavior provide examples of some of the adaptive properties of feelings in general. Happiness and pleasure when securing the reproductive potential of a mate with high mate value, or unhappiness, feelings of sadness, depression, anxiety, fear, and anger at the loss or anticipated loss of a mate are all part of the task of getting the reproductive problem solved. But there are many other adaptive problems for organisms to solve and, in animals and humans, emotions and affects evolved for these biological "purposes," as well. For example, the taste and olfactory systems guard the openings to the digestive tract and the lungs by causing an animal or human to repel potentially harmful substances (Johnston, 1999). Similarly, the emotions of sexual revulsion in women guard the entry to the vagina protecting it from the sperm of males computed by a woman's brain to be less biologically fit than those she might be able to attain in the marketplace of intrasexual competition.

However, observations of human behavior show us that what is sexually revolting to one woman may be valued by another woman. Often this difference is a consequence of a woman's assessments of her own biological fitness, although consciously it is unlikely that the woman understands this. For example, both women and men probably make assessments of what they have to offer to a mate and as a consequence of such assessments they may make adjustments in their expectations of what they can realistically expect in a mate. Women who are young and more attractive have more mating options and can afford to be pickier. Several studies show that women higher in *mate value* demand higher mate value in the men they select as partners (Buss, 2008, p. 132). One might predict that human males and females, all other factors being equal, tend to end up marrying and having children with mates with roughly the same mate value as they possess. This probably occurs as a consequence of some trial and error, and feedback that successes and rejections provide. A male that is frequently successful in attracting high "mate value" females, those displaying many of the cues of high fertility such as beautiful faces and bodies, gain confidence in their own mate value and may adjust their expectations upward. Studies show that sexually attractive people tend to have higher self-esteem on average than those less sexually attractive, all other factors being equal. Opposite experiences wherein a male suffers rejection by high "mate value" females, or even by those of lower "mate value," may lead to a lowering of expectations, and subsequent acceptance of mating partners with more modest mate value. This strategy is probably optimizing for the genes of such males (or females, since the argument applies to both sexes), who otherwise might not take advantage of the mating opportunities that are within their grasp. In other words, constantly trying for women (or men) who are "out of their league" may leave the low "mate value" male (or female) with many fewer mating opportunities than would be otherwise possible. Still, luck and persistence can sometimes pay off and the intrasexual competition can unexpectedly go the way of the man or woman who succeeds in landing an especially "good catch." However, in this case, we might expect the partner with lower "mate value" to be more alert, on average, for sexual rivals and to be more possessive and sexually jealous. All of these variables that operate in mate selection and the emotions that accompany their variations all involve computations carried out by our brains in service of optimal replication of genes. And most, if not all of the circuits involved, may be specifically evolved psychological adaptations for the successful solution to the complex problem of mate selection and reproduction.

However, the assessment of "mate value" is only one group of factors operating in the intraspecific competition for mates. Courtship behaviors used to woo potential mates also play a significant role in determining who ends up mating with whom. In animals, effective courtship displays, usually by males, play a significant role in the mate choices made by females. For example, the male grouse, a bird native to the Midwest, puffs up its chest and flaps its wings as it struts back and forth in front of a female. Good courtship displays can often win over a mate. This may be adaptive for the genes of the female since a good display requires good health and sufficient levels of male sex hormone, and thus may be a good predictor of reproductive potential in males. Research shows that up to 75% of the impregnations in the grouse are performed by a single dominant male and these males are the ones that attract the most females with their displays (Johnsgard, 1972, p. 63). The display of the male grouse is reminiscent of high school boys driving their fancy cars back and forth in front of the school, gunning their engines, mostly to attract the attention of beautiful girls. The message is, "Hey, look at me babe, I am a real stud, I can give you many strong, healthy babies." He is advertising not only his power, symbolically through the power of the machine that he commands, but he is advertising his material resources, and what wealth he has accumulated thus far, represented in the physical sign of his expensive car. Later on, it will be the size of his income, expensive gifts, and his career that he will add to his courtship display.

The courtship displays by males of a couple of species of fly are particularly instructive. In one species, the male fly kills an insect and then spins a cocoon around the kill and presents the "gift" to the female. While the female is distracted opening the package, the male hops on her back and deposits his sperm inside her. Before she finishes opening the food offering, he has finished the reproductive job and he is on his way. Is this very different from human courtship behavior? This behavior of the male fly of this species always reminds me of a human male taking a woman out to dinner; like the fly, the enamored man is making a food offering preliminary (if he's lucky) to mating. But, the behavior of the male of a closely related fly species is even more instructive. He doesn't even bother to kill an insect. The males of this species simply weave a cocoon with no dead insect inside. The courting male presents this empty cocoon to the female and while she is "unwrapping" the package, the male hops on and does his thing before she realizes that she has gotten an empty package. I can't help wondering how many human females have gotten "empty packages" from men who promised them everything just to "get into their pants" and then afterward nothing followed but "hot air." This mating strategy in the male fly shows that deception in courtship is not unique to humans.

Kin selection, altruism, and the social emotions

Altruism, in biology, refers to behavior that reduces one's personal fitness, one's personal chances of survival and reproduction, to provide benefit to another member of one's species. Some of the best examples of altruism in nature are found in the social insects—ants, bees, and wasps. Each species of social insect is comprised of individual members who are specialized in body and behavior for specific roles within the social group. For example, in honey bees there are fertile male "drones," a large number of sterile female workers, and the queen. For these insect species, the queen is the reproductive female. Worker bees do everything but lay eggs and mate. All reproduction in the colony is ultimately dependent upon successful reproduction by the queen. Most individuals in the group are sterile. Others, the male drones, are entirely derived from the queen, and mate only with her. Thus, ultimately the only way for most members of the group in these species to get their genes into the next generation is via the successful survival and reproduction of the queen. Personal survival of these individuals, without the queen, has no effect on reproductive success or biological fitness. The only way for sterile individuals in the group to assure the continuation of their genes into future generations is to slavishly serve the interests and needs of the group (sisters share 75% of their genes because of a haplodiploid system of sex determination in which unfertilized eggs become males and fertilized eggs become sisters of the queen) and particularly the needs and interests of the queen. This kind of social organization, found in the social insects, eusociality, produces extremes of altruism. Individual ants, bees, and wasps will readily sacrifice themselves for the good of the queen and the group upon which she depends. Bees, ants, and wasps labor tirelessly to construct hives and nests that protect and service the queen and her larvae. They work endlessly to supply queen and larvae with food. Bees fan the hive with their wings to maintain the hive at optimal temperature for queen and larvae. They fly long distances to find flowery sources of nectar, and then return to the hive and do a "waggle dance" that communicates to other bees in the hive the angle and distance to rich nectar sources using the sun as a navigational beacon. Worker bees readily sting invading wasps even though loss of their stinger results in their own certain personal death. Army ants foraging on the forest floor link their bodies together with their strong jaws making a living bridge of ants over which cross their fellows further back in the column when the group must cross a stream. The ants at the bottom drown. But no concern for personal safety or personal survival is built-in to the brain circuit "designs" of ants, bees, and wasps. They live for the group, for the queen, and her larvae, because this is ultimately the only means by which their genes can be transmitted to succeeding generations. Thus, in this kind of social structure, brain circuit "design" will evolve to extreme altruism. Animals like these have no individual self-interest built into their brain circuit design.

Humans are also a social species. That is, we depend upon regular interactions with other members of our species in order to accomplish solution to many of our adaptive problems. And, as I have emphasized in several places in this book, we are social by our genetic evolution as a species. We don't learn to be social. We and the other great apes must have evolved from much earlier ancestral social primate species. Being social is an evolved adaptive strategy which originated in our evolutionary past when, to beat the odds, living in groups that cooperated and shared to an adaptive degree was the only option. But humans and the other social mammals such as wolves, lions, chimpanzees, gorillas, bonobos, baboons, elephants, killer whales, and so on, reproduce individually, with each sex contributing half of the genes to their offspring, and therefore do not have to depend upon a single individual, a queen, that does their reproduction for them. This changes the conditions for the evolution of altruism. In social mammals, altruism also exists, but not in such extreme forms as we find in the social insects. In social mammals, *self-interest* is also built into the brain circuitry. For decades after altruism was first observed in animals, biologists were puzzled about how it could have ever evolved. Sharing, giving, cooperating, and self-sacrificing behaviors appeared to contradict what was thought to be the inviolable law of Darwinian evolution, brutal competition. But, the social insects gave the critical clue.

If animals, such as bees, ants, and wasps can increase the chances of their genes being reproduced in the next generation by behavior that served another individual, the queen (and her larvae), rather than themselves, then perhaps the same principle, operative in the evolution of their altruistic behavior, might also explain the altruism found in the social mammals. Altruism in the social insects reached such extreme proportions because members of these species got a genetic payoff for their altruism. The more they behaved in service of the queen and her larvae, the better the chances that their genes would be passed on in succeeding generations, via the successful survival and reproduction of their close genetic relative, the queen.

A similar principle might have operated in the evolution of the brain "design" for altruism in the social mammals. If a mammal behaved in service of another individual increasing the survival and reproduction of that individual, the altruist would receive a genetic payoff just as long as the individual benefiting from the altruistic act was a genetic relative of the altruist, just as in the social insects.

A good example of altruism is found in lions. Lions live in prides. The core of the pride is a group of closely related females, sisters, mothers and daughters, aunts and nieces, and female cousins. The males that dominate the pride, come and go, as new males periodically attempt a take-over of the pride. Most of the hunting is cooperative and is performed by the females. The females will also cooperatively nurse. If one lactating mother doesn't have enough milk for her cub, then other mothers in the group will nurse the cub of their genetic relative. All benefit from the cooperative hunting and from the cooperative nursing. This kind of altruistic behavior, one mother giving up her milk for the cub of another, is possible because all of the females in the pride are close genetic relatives.

Again, as in the social insects, the evolution of altruism occurs because relatives have some genes in common. The closer the relative, the more genes shared, and the greater the genetic payoff that altruism provides to the altruist. In lions, sisters are more likely than female cousins to behave altruistically toward one another by nursing one another's cubs. In other social mammals a similar formula would also apply. For example, in humans, brothers and sisters share 50% of their genes in common. In more technical terms, their *coefficient of relatedness* is .50; for human parents and offspring the COR is also .50; but for grandparent and grandchildren it is .25, and, all other factors being equal, the disposition for altruism will be greater in parents toward their children than toward their grandchildren.

To see how this works at the genetic level, let's use another example in humans. If a brother acts altruistically toward his sister by helping her in some way, the altruistic brother will gain a genetic benefit if his sister's chances of surviving and reproducing are increased by his helping, sharing, giving or other altruistic act toward his sister. If she reproduces, some of the genes that she passes to her offspring will be genes that she has in common with her brother. Assuming that some of the 50% of the genes that the siblings hold in common are responsible for a disposition for altruism toward close genetic relatives, then the genes for construction of brain circuits for altruistic emotions, such as affection and love, that motivated the brother, will be passed on by his sister to her offspring when she successfully reproduces. In this way, altruism, or more accurately, the brain circuit "design" for emotions that motivate altruism, can be naturally selected, even though the altruist is sacrificing some of his own resources, some of his own reproductive potential (see Hamilton's Rule, Chapter 6). That is, the altruist pays a price for his altruism. When a brother gives resources to his sister, those are resources that he no longer has to use for his own benefit, for his own survival and reproduction. Therein lies the altruism, the giving up of some of one's own survival and reproductive potential for the good of someone else. To balance the cost of this kind of behavior, there has to be some payout, otherwise, without genetic benefit to the altruist which exceeds the genetic cost to him, over the long run, the genes responsible for altruistic behavior will not be reproduced; these genes for altruism will be "weeded out" of the species gene pool, and thus the behavior itself, would cease to exist. But altruistic acts toward relatives do exist, not only in humans, lions, and the social insects but in many animal species. Therefore, there can be no doubt that altruistic acts such as giving, sharing, cooperation, and even self-sacrifice for close genetic relatives results in a net gain in reproductive success.

For example, imagine a hunter-gatherer in the Pleistocene era. Imagine that he has four brothers, each whom shares 50% of their genes with each of their siblings. Imagine that all five brothers, on a hunting foray, are cornered by a saber tooth tiger. If one of the brother sacrifices himself, out of love and affection for his brothers, and they escape as a result, then 50% of his genes times 4, that is, 200% of his genes survive to reproduce another day. By contrast if he had acted in his own personal self-interest and saved himself while his four brothers were killed, he would have saved only 100% of his genes, and thus, by acting selfishly, he would have received only half the gain in reproductive potential that he would have received had he acted instead to save his brothers. Almost paradoxically, by acting unselfishly on behalf of his close relatives, the altruist receives a net gain genetically. No one understood this logic before the biologist William Hamilton pointed it out in the 1960s.

The cost/benefit analysis that is implied here involves the technical definition of *biological fitness*. Biological fitness is measured by the proportion of one's genes that end up being transmitted to succeeding generations, that is, fitness is a measure of reproductive success. In its simplest form, fitness can be counted by the number of offspring that one produces which survive and reproduce themselves relative to that same number in other members of one's species. If I have three children that survive to reproductive age and you have only one, my biological fitness, my reproductive success, is three times greater than yours. If I have 10 children my biological fitness may seem quite high, but not if most everyone else is having 20 children. Fitness is relative to the reproductive rates of the other members of one's species.

To understand the evolution of altruism, it took Hamilton, in the early 1960s, to make the observation that there is more than one way to get your genes into the next generation (Hamilton, 1964). One way is the way that biologists of his time already recognized, by an individual's own personal reproduction. Act completely selfishly, motivated only by self-interest, and you can get your genes into the next generation by your own personal reproduction. This is the *individual fitness or personal fitness* of the animal or human that Darwin understood. But Hamilton realized that there was a second way to get one's genes into the next generation, by the successful reproduction of one's genetic relatives, as described above, because of the genes that close relatives share. Hamilton called this *inclusive fitness*, the combined fitness, or reproductive success, of an individual and the individual's relatives, in proportion to the genetic relatedness of the relatives (Bridgeman, 2003). Genetic relatedness is measured by the *coefficient of relatedness* (mentioned briefly in the example above), the percentage of genes that two individuals share by common descent. By acting altruistically toward genetic relatives, one increases the genetic relative's chances of survival and reproduction and, accordingly, increases reproduction of that portion of one's genes shared by the relative. These facts result in a kind of natural selection known as *kin selection*. That is, any trait, usually a behavioral trait or disposition, which increases *inclusive fitness*, will tend to be preserved and replicated over generations. Therefore, altruistic behavior toward close genetic relatives, *kin altruism*, will evolve in many social species as a result of kin selection because the altruistic behavior, by helping a relative to survive and reproduce, enhances one's inclusive fitness. Hamilton (1964) discovered an explanation for our positive social emotions, those that motivated our better side, our "good" side, our generosity, our sharing, giving, cooperation, and self-sacrifice. Darwin understood how natural selection could work to produce our self-interest, our anger, our aggressiveness, our competitiveness, and our killer instincts. Hamilton discovered how evolution could also explain our unselfish side, our better nature.

This reasoning can explain a lot about our emotions, especially those emotions that are part of our social existence. For example, it provides an answer to why we love our children. Of course, I know that each of us loves our children because they are cute, or because we are proud of them, or because we have lived with them since they were born, and, well, just because they are *our* children, they are a part of us. I know the common sense explanations. But why is this so? What underlies the common sense, and why is the common sense so common, so ubiquitous? After all, parents everywhere in the world love their children. Why are children so cute* to us, why are we proud of our

---

*All baby mammals have features that produce an urge to protect and give care. Disproportionately large eyes and/or heads (in baby humans, for example), limbs out of proportion to body (short and stumpy, in baby dogs, humans, lions, bears, tigers, etc), and flattened/non-threatening snouts and ears in the case of predatory mammals, or receding chins in baby humans, all feel "cute" to us. We evolved brain circuit "designs" that make these features "cute" just like we evolved circuits to make sugar "sweet."

kids, why does living with someone for a long period of time, especially our children, lead to affectionate tie⬤Why do we love our children just because they are ours? Why do we often feel that we would sacrifice anything for our children? Why is having children, loving them, caring for them, giving them the best we can, so important to human beings? *Kin selection* theory provides the answer.

Our children carry our genes. Our children are the means by which our genes will get transported to the next generation and beyond. Without our children, we are almost like ants, wasps, or bees without a queen, without larvae. We have no better means by which we can perpetuate our genes than through our children (although we can also receive genetic benefit through survival and reproduction of our siblings, this method is only half as effective for our genes; in other words the coefficient of relatedness between parent and child is .50, but between uncle or aunt and nephew or niece it is only .25). Kin selection theory states that whenever we care for our children, whenever we feel emotions for them that motivate us to give them everything that we can, whenever our love and affection for them leads us to sacrifice for them, to change their diapers, to feed them, to be sure they are warm and that they stay healthy and strong, we are acting altruistically toward them, and when we do so *we increase our inclusive fitness*. We enhance the reproductive success of ourselves and of our close relatives, *our* children, helping to assure the place of our genes in succeeding generations. Now, of course, I don't think about this in order to generate my feelings of love and affection and caring for my children and neither do you when you have similar emotions for your kids. We don't have to think about it, our emotions do the "thinking" for us. Our emotions are the psychological adaptations that cause us to do the right thing, the adaptive thing, for our *genes*.

Remember the first and most fundamental law of psychology, the Law of Adaptation, organisms tend to behave in ways that promote the survival and reproduction of their *genes* (Koenigshofer, 1994b). The emotions of love, protectiveness, affection, and so on, toward one's children serve one's genes. The genes they carry are the genes of their parents. So when we care for our children, we are also caring for our genes, we enhance our *inclusive fitness*. We love and cherish our children, and thereby are motivated to behave altruistically toward them, for the same reason that ants, bees, and wasps behave altruistically toward their queen and her larvae. Our altruistic behavior toward our children is engineered by kin selection which drives evolution of brain circuit "designs" that make us *feel* the emotions required to motivate altruistic behavior (also known as prosocial behavior) toward our offspring. But our altruism is not total; it is not absolute as it is in the social insects, because unlike these animals we reproduce individually, not through a queen. Though I have feelings that motivate me to take care of the reproductive "queen" of my household— my wife, mother of my children—that motivation is balanced by feelings that serve my own self-interest. Unlike the social insects that must rely upon a single queen of the entire colony for their reproduction, the social mammals like us reproduce individually in pairs. As a consequence of the kind of reproductive strategy that social mammals evolved, we undergo three varieties of natural selection: *sexual selection, individual Darwinian selection, and kin selection.* Each of these forms of natural selection has acted to shape different segments of our psychological makeup, our psychological or human nature.

As we have seen, sexual selection can "design" emotions arising from intraspecific competition for mates, such as sexual jealousy and strong emotional responses to signs of mate value such as youth and fertility. Individual Darwinian selection "designs" our emotional dispositions for self-interest, our self-protective "instincts," our self-centeredness, our "selfishness." But kin selection "designs" the altruistic dispositions in us, the emotions of love and affection that motivate our care-giving behavior toward our children, our emotions that lead us to sacrifice for them, to share with them, and to give them the best we can, especially when they are young and most dependent upon us (also as it happens, by natural selection, when they look cutest to us; see footnote above).

These altruistic instincts toward our children are not unique to the human species. Other animals will fight to the death to protect their offspring. Mother birds will put themselves at risk by "faking" a broken wing to draw a predator to them away from their nestlings. Birds and monkeys give warning calls that put them at potential risk from a predator but allow their fellows an edge to escape. Adult wildebeest have been observed in the wild to fall back out of a fleeing herd to encircle and protect a baby wildebeest being pursued by a hungry lion. The adults put themselves at risk of death to try to protect the baby as the lion attempted to penetrate their defensive circle to get at the more vulnerable prey. And certainly human mothers and fathers will risk their own lives to save their children's lives. Furthermore, indications of the emotions of sadness and depression follow the loss of one's offspring not only in humans. Jane Goodall observed a chimpanzee mother in the wild mourn the loss of one of her baby chimps for several weeks after it had died (Goodall, 1971).

Kin selection can also help explain our emotions toward other close relatives such as siblings, grandchildren, cousins, and nieces and nephews. Kin selection also explains these examples of *kin altruism.* (Of course altruistic emotions occur in other social mammals too. For an extraordinary film of Cape Buffalo trying to protect an injured member of their group from lions see: http://www.youtube.com/watch?v=m9fzXmcUgGI&NR=1; retrieved May 25, 2011). But how can we explain the altruistic acts that humans sometimes perform for non-relatives, for example, acts of heroism that sometimes occur among soldiers in combat situations? There are two possible explanations, which may not be mutually exclusive.

Prosocial behavior and altruism toward non-relatives

The first possible explanation is that the human disposition to help and to cooperate with non-relatives, and even to sacrifice one's life for someone unrelated, may be an evolutionary left-over from our days as hunter-gatherers in the Pleistocene. Anthropologists tell us that we lived in small groups of perhaps 50–150 closely related individuals. In social groups such as these, *anyone* we helped would have likely been a genetic relative and some genetic payoff, no matter how small, would have resulted from the altruism. Furthermore, cooperation and helping would help preserve a strong cohesive group, and a strong group would have benefited all group members, including oneself and one's close family members, even those distantly related. Today we live in much larger groups of individuals, most of whom are not related to us, except perhaps very, very remotely, perhaps thousands of generations removed. However, the emotional mechanisms in our Pleistocene brain "design" which predisposed us to help, and to act altruistically in other ways, toward genetic relatives, may not have had time to change much in the course of a mere 200,000 years of human evolution, 99% of which took place before agriculture and the end of small hunter-gatherer groups of genetically related individuals. It has been perhaps only 10,000 years since such groups were replaced by large concentrations of unrelated individuals in villages, towns, and eventually, modern mega-cities. Our genetically configured emotional makeup, originating from our Pleistocene past, under some circumstances may still make us respond to non-relatives as if they were genetic relatives in "our" hunter-gatherer group. This can be thought of as a kind of *vestigial psychological characteristic*. Because in our evolutionary history we lived in groups in which everyone was a relative, so that altruistic acts toward any member of the group would produce some increase in biological fitness, we may have evolved few, if any, strong cues indicative of relatedness, other than familiarity and close physical proximity (although for members of the same immediate family such cues do exist— i.e. "My goodness, she looks just like her father."). In other words, just being around someone for a protracted period of time may produce affectionate bonds, under some circumstances, that even today could be basis for motivation of altruism toward non-relatives. Furthermore, cultural practices and value systems could have developed, through cultural evolution, to reinforce this built-in genetically evolved component of our innate emotional brain "design." (Recall that cultural evolution occurs when some learned behaviors or memes that enhance net fitness are imitated or in other ways culturally transmitted, and thus are repeatedly practiced over generations, whereas other learned behaviors are abandoned). Religious values, culturally transmitted over generations, are one example of a group of moral tenets that put value on altruism and other acts of kindness toward one's fellows to the benefit of all. Think of the teachings of Jesus, for example.

However, in the Pleistocene, just as today, different human groups are in competition with one another for resources. Thus, other emotional dispositions in us to be suspicious of others whom we perceive to be from outside "our" group often act in opposition to dispositions for helping and cooperating with non-relatives, at least those who we perceive as outsiders. Our suspiciousness and wariness of perceived outsiders may be an evolved adaptation to this long-term condition of our social existence as a species.

In a military situation soldiers live and work and fight together for extended periods of time. This situation among non-relatives, where mutual survival is dependent upon cooperation and assistance among members of the group perhaps more closely approximates, in some ways, the kinds of close personal contact that may have been present in the social life of our Pleistocene ancestors. Emotional mechanisms leading to adaptations such as the formation of alliances and emotional bonding, as a result of close physical and social proximity for extended time frames among genetic relatives in human Pleistocene groups of hunter-gatherers, might still operate in modern human groups of non-relatives, perhaps especially in groups such as a platoon of combat soldiers.

This hypothesis is confirmed by observations made by the author and journalist, Sebastian Junger, who lived with a platoon of U.S. soldiers at a remote mountain outpost in eastern Afghanistan. He experienced firsthand the power of affiliation alone to produce strong emotional ties and a basis for altruism toward non-relatives. Junger states:

> "The affiliation that I experienced with these guys, the affection I had for them, frankly, the subjectivity that started to occur in my journalism really began to interest me, because I realized that my feelings for them roughly mirrored their feelings for each other. And what I was seeing in my inclusion in that group, what I was seeing was something very important about the group dynamics in a platoon. I was starting to understand why it is that soldiers will say, you know, the worst thing that can happen is that my buddy gets killed, and I would do anything to keep that from happening. And that just makes no sense to a civilian. But, if you're out there with those guys, and you start to feel the tug of that connection, it starts to make some sense."

Junger noted that when soldiers' tours of duty were over the soldiers missed being there in the war zone because they missed the human relationship, the sense of belonging and group purpose, and their reliance upon each other (see http://www.pbs.org/newshour/bb/military/jan-june10/junger_06-10.html, retrieved June 10, 2010). And emotions of anger and aggression unexpectedly surfaced when Junger was in a Humvee that was hit by enemy fire. He writes, "I was like, fuck you. You're not going to kill me. I had all these somewhat irrational anger responses and I started to understand how killing works. I don't want to kill anybody, but I felt that impulse come up in me. And I'm not even carrying a gun, I'm just carrying a camera, but still, there it was" (see Sebastian Junger's 2010 book, *War*, Hachette Book Group, New York). Even an anonymous attack directed at his group instinctively triggered the emotions that motivated a will to fight back not only in defense of himself but in defense of his group.

In our Pleistocene past, since everyone in the group was somehow genetically related to everyone else in the group, all that was necessary for kin recognition was the familiarity created by close physical and social proximity, over some period of time. Still today, as confirmed by the experiences of Junger in that platoon of U.S. soldiers, those same social cues alone may be more than sufficient to create emotional ties and group identification potent enough to motivate profound altruism even among non-relatives. If this explanation were true, then there should be a natural disposition as part of human "mind design" to readily form group identifications even with non-relatives, and to form emotional ties with members of the identified group simply as a result of close physical and social proximity (or psychological proximity or similarity), especially in situations where the group, as in a military situation, is composed of members that are mutually interdependent upon one another for survival. The observations of Sebastian Junger described above precisely confirm this hypothesis.

There should even be built-in to human "mind design" a genetically based predisposition to form group identifications, involving strong emotions, with other people with whom we simply have some things in common. And given our language abilities and consequent capacities for abstraction, the basis for group identification and the associated emotions can be quite abstract and even symbolic. Patriotic feelings, identification of oneself as American, Mexican, Filipino, Vietnamese, or French or other nationality, as Christian, Jewish, Hindu, Shinto, or Muslim, as a Harvard or Yale alumnus, and so on, and all the strong emotions and basis for emotional ties that exist as a result of these group identifications, give strong evidence of a genetically evolved disposition for such things in us.

In our evolutionary past, when humans were up against saber toothed tigers and other big, hungry predators, and when food was scarce and cooperative hunting and gathering was essential to survival, we had to evolve strong emotional dispositions that would promote group cohesion and altruism among group members. The genetically evolved part of human "mind design" that makes us form emotionally charged group identifications is so strong that I often see people driving around with Los Angeles Lakers flags flying on their SUVs or Oakland Raiders mascots painted on the back windows of their pickup trucks, and I have seen reports of rioting when one's sports team either wins or loses a championship (win or lose, it doesn't seem to matter much) as a result of the powerful emotions that we seem capable of generating when we identify with a group, even if that group entity, and the enthusiasm generated by its promoters, is just part of a money-making enterprise enriching its owners. As they say, "Go figure." Research even shows that when a man's sports team is victorious, his own testosterone levels rise temporarily. Would such things be possible were we not a species of animal highly specialized by our evolved brain circuit "design" to readily form groups and group identifications which engender such strong emotions? Not at all. Part of our evolution as a highly social species is a powerful disposition to identity with groups, to do so with intense emotion, and to draw lines in our minds between "us" and "them," in-group and out-group—and, in modern times with regard to groups of people that we identify only by abstractions such as nationality, political belief, or religious practices. Given these innate dispositions in our evolved emotional makeup, it is easy to see where war comes from and why it has been so persistent in human history.

A second explanation for altruism toward non-relatives is *reciprocal altruism*. This idea is expressed in the well known phrase, "You scratch my back and I'll scratch yours." Reciprocal altruism works regardless of whether the altruist (the donor) and the recipient of the altruistic act are genetically related. The mutual benefit for donor and recipient emerges from the social equation: if I help you now, you are likely to feel emotions that will make you more likely to help me in the future in the event that I should need help sometime. Thus, we both benefit and the fitness, the reproductive success, of both of us will be enhanced.

Configurations of our cognitive and emotional circuitry which facilitate the thinking and the emotions for reciprocal altruism will be naturally selected over time in a social species like us. The reader can see the role of emotion in reciprocal altruism just by remembering how one felt when someone did you an especially generous good turn, or when someone cared for you in time of need, especially if they appeared to be doing so without any expectation of reward. We have a strong disposition to feel affection and even love for such good people, even though they have no genetic relationship to us. These emotions of love and friendship can motivate us to want to give back to those who have given of themselves for us. Love and affection, friendships and alliances so formed may last a lifetime and may even live on in memory when such good people have died. In our evolutionary past, as well as in modern 21st century life, reciprocal altruism not only has adaptive advantage for those directly involved in the altruistic exchanges (those who forged such mutually beneficial alliances would have had selective advantage over those who could not) but there are group advantages too in terms of increased group cohesion, cooperation, and mutual care-giving, with less within-group conflict, presumably increasing the survival and reproductive success of all members of the group, perhaps with respect to other groups which happened to be less altruistic (group selection, another possible mechanism for the evolution of reciprocal altruism toward non-relatives is controversial among biologists, and is coun-ter to the gene-centric explanation for altruism favored in this book). Several social emotions in humans derive from reciprocal altruism including love and affection for non-relatives. However, protective mechanisms must evolve as well to detect "cheaters" who take benefits from such exchanges without giving back their fair share. Evolution-ary psychologists, John Tooby and Leda Cosmides (1992) at the University of Califor-nia, Santa Barbara, have provided evidence in several experiments of cheater detection mechanisms which they hypothesize involve a specialized set of brain circuits evolved as a cheater-detection module in humans to deal with the adaptive problem of cheaters in social exchanges including those involving reciprocal altruism.

Darwinian natural selection, kin selection, and the duality of human moral nature

There must be restraints on altruism built-in to human nature. If someone is too altruis-tic, their reproductive success would be too low and extreme altruism in a social mam-mal like us would be weeded out of the gene pool. For example, suppose I say to you that I know I have a great mate with high mate value, but I am so altruistic I am going to give her to you and let you have children with her, instead of me. In that case my genes, some of which are responsible for my extreme altruism, will not be reproduced, unless you are a close relative with genes that predispose the same degree of self-sacrifice in which case you would pass on my offer, but even if you take me up on my offer then only 25% of my genes will be replicated by your reproduction with my mate even if you are my same sex sibling, while, by contrast, if I mate with my mate, then 50% of my genes are replicated, including those genes which predispose me to altruism. Mutations in a social mammal which produced such extreme altruism would not be reproduced as frequently (if at all) as would competing genes which equipped me with an emotional makeup that made me more possessive of my mate and more motivated to mate with her myself.

The genetic cost of too much altruism in a *social mammal* puts limits on how much altruism can evolve, and how pure it can be. Take another example. Suppose times are hard and food is scarce, but I say to you, here take my food, not just some of it, but all of it, and not just today, but every day, I don't need it even though I am hungry and eventu-ally I will starve; you go ahead and eat all of my food. Take all of my water too, and all of my clothing, and if you need someone to work in your fields I will work for you for free as long as I am able. If I do this, as an extreme altruist without any constraints on my altruism, then clearly I will die and, as in the example above, my genes, including those responsible for my innate disposition for extreme altruism, won't get replicated. There must be sufficient levels of self-interest built-in to the "mind design" to balance any disposition for altruism in the social mammals like us (in bees, there are weaker constraints on altruism because many of the individuals in the colony are sterile and can only get genes into succeeding generations by altruism toward the queen, and this altruism can therefore evolve to much greater extremes).

Extreme altruism in social *mammals* can't work (the naked mole rat and the Damaraland mole rat are exceptions, but like the social insects they are eusocial species, all with reproductive queens and more or less sterile workers and/or soldiers). On the other hand, neither can extreme self-interest. For social life to evolve, there have to be reproductive benefits that outweigh the reproductive costs. Unless living in groups has sufficient adaptive advantage, then group life, and the emotional makeup to make social living possible, can't evolve. In order for social life to provide reproductive advantage there must be sufficient levels of cooperation, sharing, giving, and caring within the group. If not, social life as a form of adaptation will fail (see Hamilton's Rule, Chapter 6).

For example, if times are tough and food is in short supply and I hoard all the available food and then steal all of your food and the food of everyone else in my group, and if I then keep it all to myself, then my mate will likely die, my children will likely starve to death, all of my relatives in the group are more likely to perish, as will be all the members of my group. I would lose all the advantages of group living. Of course, fighting would eventually break out; the self-interests of others will drive them to prevent me from keeping all of the available food for myself. But fighting is costly, it wastes valuable energy that could be better used for other more constructive ends, it disrupts the group's stability and its ability to cooperatively hunt or to mount group defense against predators, and it can lead to injury and certain death if it is not restrained somehow to prevent "fighting to the death."

However, if dispositions of self-interest are constrained by emotions that inhibit excessive aggression within the group, and if at least some altruistic feelings toward at least some members of the group are present, then perhaps an optimal balance between self-interest and altruism can be found. Eons of evolution by natural selection, after millennia of trial and error, might hit upon just the right balance between the opposing emotional dispositions for self-interest and altruism. Evolution might achieve a psychological makeup in social mammals that finds the fulcrum that perfectly balances selfishness and unselfishness to achieve maximum reproductive fitness.

But where would the optimal balance be, between self-interest and altruism for any particular species and for any particular environment? The answer might vary, depending on the species and the specific environmental conditions. The optimal balance between self-interest and altruism may very well be determined by evolution in each social species and might reach a different balance within each species as environmental conditions changed over time. In fact, altruism might increase under conditions of relative plenty and decrease when times were tougher. How might this balance be achieved in the evolution of the "mind design" of our own species?

Recall two types of biological fitness, individual and inclusive. The form of natural selection that selects for personal or *individual (biological) fitness* I will call *Darwinian natural selection* because it was Darwin who first conceived of natural selection as acting on individuals and their individual reproductive success. This kind of natural selection selects for traits which enhance survival of the individual animal or human and the reproduction of that individual's genes via the individual's own direct, personal reproduction.

Thus Darwinian natural selection enhances individual fitness (keep in mind we are talking about biological fitness, not physical fitness!), the reproductive success of the *individual*. We can see how Darwinian natural selection "designs" the psychology of animals or humans for self-interest, for "selfishness."

Kin selection, on the other hand, is the form of natural selection that selects for traits that enhance the reproductive success, the biological fitness, of genetic relatives. Kin selection results in the evolution of kin altruism, emotions and behaviors that end up enhancing the survival and reproductive success of genetic relatives, such that the closer the relatedness between the altruist and the recipient of the altruism the greater the genetic benefit to the altruist (see above discussion). Kin selection enhances *inclusive fitness*, and promotes "unselfishness," behaviors which include giving, cooperation, helping, and self-sacrifice toward genetic relatives.

What this suggests is that human "mind design," and thus what we call our innate human nature, includes selfishness, our "bad" side, and "unselfishness," our good side, in a characteristic mix, as a result of two different, sometimes competing forms of natural selection that have acted to shape our particular species' psychology. Thus, the duality of our human moral nature may originate from these two different processes in natural selection acting on the formation of our "mind design." *Moral conflict (experienced psychologically) occurs when brain circuits evolved by Darwinian natural selection for "selfishness" or self-interest, one's individual reproductive fitness, are activated simultaneously with brain circuits "designed" for altruism, "unselfishness," by kin selection and selection for reciprocal altruism.*

Cultural traditions related to human moral conduct, via learning, cultural transmission and cultural evolution, may originate from these deeper biological causes, our evolved brain circuit "design" as a social mammal. These cultural proscriptions encoded into religious teachings and laws enhance the altruistic dispositions created by kin selection and extend them to non-relatives reinforcing the processes of reciprocal altruism. The benefit to social organization and human welfare of this cultural evolution is evidenced by the persistence of religious teachings which glorify and reward altruistic behavior and abhor selfishness, particularly in its extreme forms such as cheating, lying, stealing, infidelity, and doing physical harm to others, including murder. If constraints upon unbridled self-interest evolved to our adaptive benefit as a species that relied heavily upon group solutions to adaptive problems such as obtaining food and defending against predators, then culturally evolved constraints would help assure control of self-interest and facilitate unselfishness to facilitate adaptive harmony within social groups. Although note that this says nothing about conflicts between different human groups. During our tenure on this planet, intergroup conflict due to intergroup competition for resources, probably including mates, has not permitted the same evolutionary balance between self-interest and altruism as has arisen within the group. Evidence of less restrained conflicts *between* human groups, such as between nations and religious groups, is everywhere. Perhaps, evolution has been less efficient in "designing" mechanisms to restrain intergroup conflict and aggression than it has at restraining intergroup aggression.

Personal moral conflicts experienced by humans throughout history, and daily in the personal lives of every human being, may reflect these competing emotional and behavioral tendencies built simultaneously into our "mind design" by the competing forces of Darwinian individual selection, on the one hand, and kin selection and selection favoring reciprocal altruism, on the other hand. Whenever your own personal interests conflict with the interests of others and you feel a psychological conflict in your mind about whether to "look out for number one" or "to watch out for the other guy" and where to draw the balance, you are feeling, first hand, the effects of two sets of brain circuits in conflict, one evolved by Darwinian natural selection and the other by kin selection and reciprocal altruism. Human brain circuit "design and thus our "mind design," particularly those brain circuits that mediate social cognition and the social emotions of love, affection, happiness, hate, anger, sadness, and disgust, have evolved to maximize the adaptive advantages of living in groups. In other words, our dual moral nature, our "bad" selfish side and our "good" unselfish side, balanced against each other in an evolved equilibrium, arose in our brain circuit design as a central defining characteristic of what it is to be human, as a consequence of the often opposing forces of Darwinian selection and selection for altruism. We have "good" and "bad" within us as a result of natural processes of evolution.

One final ingredient must be added to this mix to fully understand that portion of evolved human "mind design" that includes our emotions and motivations. Sexual selection selects for personality traits which are reliable cues of high mate value, the indicators of the likelihood of high reproductive success. Some of these personality dispositions which arise from intrasexual competition are self-interested and aggressive and others are mate-interested and offspring-interested.

Thus, that large and highly influential part of our evolved human nature which we feel as our social emotions and social motivations, our social "instincts," is a consequence of a mix of Darwinian individual natural selection, kin selection, selection for reciprocal altruism, and sexual selection, each having evolved different components of our innate emotional and motivational nature. Because these properties of the mind are rooted in our genetic evolution as a species, there will be slight variations in the mix of these dispositions around a population average. These psychological traits will have their specific genes and gene combinations in the human genome. Inheritance of each cluster of social emotions and mechanisms of social cognition in particular combinations, dictated by specific variations in genotype for these psychological adaptations, will form slight variations in the phenotypic arrangement of "personality" traits in each individual, ultimately derived from evolution of brain circuitry by the different varieties of natural selection described above. A personality theory based on the inheritance of various mixes of these influences on social cognition and the social emotions in each individual is foreseeable. All things biological show individual variation in every biologically defined population, in this case the human population. Thus, we should expect individual variation in the inherited genetic mix of self-interest and altruism.

In a sense, what we have explained here is roughly equivalent to a more inclusive, more complete, and perhaps more sophisticated version of what Sigmund Freud attempted to describe when he invented the concepts of the Id, that segment of the human mind which he believed was characterized by simple instincts for sex and aggression, and the Superego, our moral and social inhibitions, which he apparently believed were strictly of cultural origin. But we can see that Freud only scratched the surface. He was a pioneer who only glimpsed a rough outline of deeper human nature revealed through a narrow crack he created in the Victorian thinking of his time. Furthermore, though he had an intuition that the deeper parts of human nature that include human emotion and motivation were "instincts," he had little idea of the processes, evolutionary processes, which had shaped them. Freud was 3 years old when Darwin published his book, *On the Origin of Species by Means of Natural Selection*, laying out the theory of evolution and a mass of evidence for it. Why Freud apparently didn't see the link between the theory of evolution and his own thinking was likely the same reason most people today still don't recognize the evolutionary roots of psychology. In Freud's day, like today, the full implications of evolutionary theory for human psychology are still unrecognized by most of the human population, to its tragic detriment. In evolution we find the key to understanding human "mind design." Perhaps 100 years more will be required before this becomes the commonly recognized truth at the core of our thinking about our own nature, minds, and behavior.

In summary, living in groups is one adaptive strategy evolved in some species, the social species, which only provides improved fitness, improved solution to adaptive problems in the "struggle for existence," when there has emerged optimal balance between the emotions of self-interest and the emotions that produce altruistic, prosocial behaviors. Social emotions are end products of information processing about adaptive problems solved within the context of interactions with other members of one's species. Just as the bees, ants, wasps, have evolved computational mechanisms in their neural circuitry dictating their social interactions, so have the social mammals, including human beings. Our human nature is to a large extent reflective of our social adaptations. Among other social variables, our social and emotional computational hardware must place value on our individual social interactions and relationships and compute the adaptive significance of other members of our group, including their relative "mate values," their potential as members of alliances with us, whether they are cheaters or fair players in reciprocal altruism, and so on. Several major points are:

1. Kin selection and reciprocal altruism are the sources of the evolution of altruism in the social mammals (unselfishness; sharing, giving, helping, cooperation, self-sacrifice)—inclusive fitness is enhanced by reciprocal altruism and kin selection for the psychological adaptations of altruism. However, individual fitness results from Darwinian natural selection that produces sufficient degrees of self-interest, ("selfishness") to protect individual reproductive fitness.

2. Our dual moral nature, selfishness and unselfishness, results from Darwinian selection for individual fitness, and kin selection for inclusive fitness; we have evolved emotional circuits that make us both selfish (self-interested) and unselfish (altruistic), mixed in the right (most adaptive) balance. Too much of either is not optimally adaptive—the right combination of selfishness and unselfishness in human nature resulted from the fine tuning of our emotional circuitry over evolutionary time in our Pleistocene social environment. The social/emotional psychological natures of humans and other social mammals thus ended up with just the right balances of selfish and unselfish emotions required to maximize reproductive fitness in social environments.

3. Social controls originating from learning, based in and guided by our innate, evolved dual moral nature, and transmitted culturally, have developed (via cultural evolution) to restrain individuals who don't have the "right" mix (due to genetic variability in the human population, and perhaps to non-optimal social experience particularly in childhood and adolescence) but instead have too much selfishness, too much self-interest: religious teachings, police, criminal law are all social institutions, culturally transmitted, "designed" to restrain individuals who are genetically afflicted (or developmentally impaired by maladaptive social experiences) with a balance between selfishness and unselfishness that is weighted too much toward self-interest. At the neurological level this may be due to genetic factors or a combination of genetic and environmental factors that impair normal, healthy development of inhibitory circuits in the frontal cortex.

4. "Pathogenic" environmental social conditions during brain development of children, as well as genetics, can lead to maladaptive emotional balances producing excess levels of self-interest (selfishness; as in psychopathic personality disorder, for example) or excess levels of altruistic dispositions (unselfishness), but almost always the former. Cases of the later are probably unfortunately exceedingly rare but when they do occur we duly admire and even worship such individuals who frequently are understood within a religious or spiritual context (saints and great religious teachers who understand and practice great kindness, moral wisdom, and self-sacrifice—morally, perhaps the highest and best expression of human nature).

5. Personality dispositions can be conceptualized as a specific collection (or relatively minor variations of) of operations of specific social information processing modules of the brain, expressed in particular social environments and interacting with individual social experiences, to produce an enduring psychological phenotype.

6. Social species, living in a social environment as well as a physical one, must have social adaptations (information processing adaptations) to do processing necessary for establishment and maintenance of successful social relationships. For social species, therefore, some of the most difficult biological problems that have to be solved include problems of social relationship such as social status monitoring and social status preservation each requiring emotions for calculating one's position in the social hierarchy (how we are valued by others; our value in the group; how much are we liked); knowing how to form and maintain alliances (friendships); social anxiety—warning signal that we must act to get back into the "good graces" of the group (because our life in the Pleistocene literally depended upon it).

7. Emotions evolved as adaptations to persisting conditions of the world over evolutionary time. Therefore, basic emotions that most likely evolved prior to the social emotions include innate fears of consistently dangerous things such as spiders, snakes, heights, and "things that go bump in the night." Fear and disgust are protective emotions that put safe, physical distance between us and harmful things. Likewise, anger and hate are defensive emotions which have elimination of a perceived threat to one's self, family or resources as the "adaptive logic" underlying their production rule. Landscape preferences for green open spaces indicative of reliable supplies of food and water may involve evolved emotions which guided choice of habitat in our Pleistocene past (Orians and Heerwagen, 1992).

8. An evolutionary theory of psychotherapy based in evolutionary logic utilizing the Law of Adaptation as a guiding principle should be possible. Successful adaptation to social life is equivalent to psychological health, but this does not

always mean adaptation to culturally transmitted social conditions or institutions, but rather to an underlying biologically based human nature, unless, and to the extent, that those social conditions and institutions support and foster actualization of evolved human nature, while protecting the same rights of others. And, if this sounds a bit political it is because the value implied provides an enlightened guiding principle for the evaluation of governments as well as evaluation of psychological therapies.

9. Humans and other social mammals progress through stages of physical development characterized by physical traits "designed" to induce specific adaptively important emotions from others in the social group: the "cuteness" of infants and children induces emotions of caring and affection toward them at a time when they are most dependent upon adult care-givers; this is followed by transition phase during childhood from less babyish features progressively toward facial and body appearance that will trigger sexual attraction in the opposite sex as the reproductive stage of life approaches; this appearance is maintained through the prime reproductive years but rapidly begins to wane thereafter, as sexual reproduction becomes less possible and the reproductive stage of life passes; after reproductive age and the stage of caring for offspring has passed, and one's genes have made it (or not) to the next generation, there is little "selection pressure" in evolution to maintain the body, so the "survival machine" "ages" and shows signs of aging, thus it becomes less and less "sexy" as signs of youth and fertility wane as the adaptive/evolutionary reasons for preserving such signs has passed with the end of the reproductive stage of life; thus we tend to get "uglified" with increasing age (or at least lose much of the sexual attractiveness, the beauty, we once had "in our prime," in the midst of our reproductive years). The different appearances we have at three different stages of life—cuteness during our period of dependency, sexual attractiveness during our period of reproductive function, and benign decline as we continue through our post-reproductive years, are predictable using evolutionary theory, as functionally related to our different biological stages of life.

10. Emotions are subject to modification by conditioning so that things in the world that are initially without adaptive significance, and therefore emotionally neutral, can become laden with emotion if they are predictive of things that do have adaptive significance already. The sound of your electric can opener initially induces no emotion in your cat until it occurs repeatedly just before it is fed. Thereafter, as long as food reliably follows the sound, the sound will elicit emotions of excitement and happiness in your feline (at least as long as it is hungry). In the few weeks after a break up, the sight of any car similar to that of your ex-lover's may trigger powerful emotions. If you are bitten by a dog, the sight of a dog nearby can now elicit fear, and so on.

11. In humans, with our great capacity for abstraction, we can learn emotional responses to abstract categories. As part of our long and ancient history as a social species, we probably evolved a strong predisposition to form "in-group" vs. "out-group" discriminations which, with our ability for abstract thought, also predispose us to the errors of racial, ethnic, and religious discrimination. Abstractions such as racial, national, ethnic, and religious stereotypes, and learned emotional responses to them, fail to take account of the fact that such categories are actually composed of real individuals, who possess individual characteristics which cannot be accurately reflected by the stereotypes—after all, they are only abstractions manufactured by our minds.

12. One of the major functions of subjective emotions, the conscious *feeling* of them, is that, as subjective experiences, they permit automatic evaluation of *imagined futures* (see chapters 4 and 5) with respect to likely effects on reproductive fitness. If emotions were no more than sensory feedback from physiological changes in the body's organs due to activation of the autonomic nervous system, as proposed by William James, or if they were non-experienced, unconscious states of the brain, that couldn't be felt, we couldn't manipulate them mentally as we assess the probable outcomes of various behavioral "choices" by imaging ourselves in future action (see discussion of intention and "free will" in chapters 4 and 5). From an adaptive perspective, feelings have to be felt subjectively to facilitate learning and adaptive decision-making.

13. Finally, understanding that "negative" emotions, such as fear and anger, are evolved, universal defensive adaptations to perceived threat to, or reduction in, reproductive fitness may help provide us greater control over them and perhaps insulate us from their destructive potential in the modern world. Understanding our fears and anger and the fears and anger of others, as just forms of adaptation evolved to serve genes, may permit us to depersonalize them to a degree, to take a step back from them to cool the passions, and perhaps more easily transcend them and their destructive influence in modern human relationships— from the personal level (our spouses, girlfriend/boyfriends, our children, our friends and enemies) to the international level and the conflict of nations and ideologies. We were all evolved by the same forces of natural selection. We all have strikingly similar "mind design." And we are all in this together.

Previewing the engines of thought

What I describe here is a model of human and animal "mind design," a model of just one aspect of the natural world. This modeling of how things work in nature involves a human mental activity often referred to as abstract thinking, the same mental faculty that Freud used when he derived his model of the mind, and the same used by Einstein or Steven Hawking or Isaac Newton to derive their mental models of how other aspects of the natural world work. How do humans do this? How has an adaptive curiosity-instinct, which we share with many animal species, been driven to such heights in the human case? What are the engines of abstract thought? In the next chapter we consider this question, and in doing so we will return to vector coding, connectionism, and genetically preloaded synaptic weights defining evolved production rules in the processes of abstract thinking.

One important point that must be kept in mind is that with regard to sensory pathways, all roads lead to the limbic system; all inputs with adaptive significance are evaluated and given hedonic tone. Therefore, all perceptions and thoughts are richly integrated with emotional or hedonic value and, at the same time, perceptions and thoughts are always constrained by feelings encoding the adaptive meanings of things in the world. Our brain and mind "design" create an adaptive illusion full of things rich in hedonic tone, and yet all of that feeling that gives the emotional tone to our world is, of course, all created by, and exists only in, the species-specific "design" of our minds. Can our abilities for abstract thought ever liberate us entirely from the limits of our adaptive illusion? After all, our "mind design" was evolved for solving biological problems that stand as obstacles to the continuation of genes. How could a set of information processing mechanisms evolved for survival and the reproduction of genetic material crack such mysteries as black holes, the molecular basis of life, gravitational lenses, atomic structure, or the "red shift"? Such feats are the product of what Cosmides and Tooby (2002) call "improvisational intelligence." We tackle it now in the next chapter.

CHAPTER   TEN

The Engines of Thought

"It remains a matter of keen debate whether human nature in general, and the human sciences in particular, will ever be brought under the explanatory umbrella of the natural sciences. The resources of the latter continue to expand, and their accumulated successes reach ever closer to the domain of the former. Yet certain salient features of the human condition continue to elude naturalistic explanation, and they present themselves, to some eyes, as forever beyond that form of understanding."

Paul M. Churchland, *A Neurocomputational Perspective:*
The Nature of Mind and the Structure of Science, 1989, p. 129

Human thought is as great a mystery as human consciousness itself. Its subtlety and complexity rival anything in the universe. Its ethereal properties have inspired philosophers and saints as well as ordinary souls to speculate about its origins since the very beginnings of recorded human history and before. But need it be one of those "features of the human condition . . . forever beyond [naturalistic] understanding"? Perhaps so, but remember from the start of this book I have reminded the reader that the goal of a scientific approach to the world is the attempt to explain as much of nature as possible by use of natural laws alone and thereby to bring all, even our understand of ourselves, "under the explanatory umbrella of the natural sciences." Whether this enterprise will ever ultimately succeed must, at this point, remain a judgment reserved for human beings yet to be conceived, those still to emerge upon this planet many generations hence. In times past, when our ancient ancestors looked into the dark night sky at the sparkling points of light scattered above, the sense of awe that was inspired must have convinced many that we would never understand the nature and origins of stars, comets, planets, and galaxies. But today, our knowledge of astronomy has revealed the answers to mysteries that could never have even been imagined before the invention of the first astronomical telescope by Galileo in early 17th century Italy. In a few hundred years, and with accelerating rapidity in this century, puzzles of the universe continue to be better and better understood in terms of the exquisite laws of nature. Will the same be true of the natural biological processes of human thought and consciousness a century from now? Of course, we don't know. But given the history of science in other arenas of the natural world, the odds are in our favor.

Let's begin with a review of the logic of evolution by natural selection with an eye to the aspects of the process that we will need to consider as we search for the engines of thought.

Chance variations in genes and thus in the individuals that carry them provide the alternative designs to be "screened" or "filtered" by natural selection for their relative fitness. Designs which just happen to be a better match or fit to the conditions of the environment, which affect survival and reproduction, are the designs more likely to survive, and so more likely to replicate the genes responsible for the better adapted design.

At the point of differential rates of reproduction of some genotypes over others in a population, evolutionary change has already begun. Some offspring receive the favorably mutated genes from their favorably mutated parents giving them reproductive advantage over other less well adapted competitors. However, for the *species* as a whole to change, the better fit mutated genes must multiply, spreading to increasing proportions of the population over generations, until most individuals of the population have the mutated trait. This means that the environmental conditions which made the mutation a favorable one in the first place must be present long enough to give the favorable mutation time to spread throughout the population. Genetic evolution of a trait can only take place if the environmental conditions that make that trait favorable are stable and long lasting enough to consistently provide the reproductive advantage that drives the increasing frequency of the trait in the population. In short, genetically encoded traits or adaptations can evolve in a species only to conditions which are long-term and widely experienced throughout a population over time. In some cases, at least, this also means that a genetically encoded trait will be perpetuated in a population only as long as the conditions of the environment that make the trait favorable continue to exist.

It is logically possible that each generation or each individual will face environmental conditions that are entirely novel and thus unique to that individual or to that generation, but if this were the case, then evolution could not take place at all. Genetic evolution takes time, generally a lot of time, because it must act over many, many generations in order for genes and traits that make an adaptive fit to environmental conditions to spread throughout the population. This means that genetic evolution can only fashion adaptive traits to environmental conditions if those conditions are present, and stable enough, over long enough periods of time, over sufficient numbers of generations. This is because evolution is a statistical process operating in part by chance (chance variations in genes) molded by the imperfect processes of natural selection which can be affected by other chance factors in the environment such as accidents, like being in the wrong place at the wrong time when a boulder falls from a cliff or a meteor falls from the heavens, or an infectious disease comes on your side of the mountain but not to the other side where your twin brother lives, etc.

All of this presents a big problem. If genetically encoded traits can only arise in response to conditions of the environment which are long-term and widely distributed in the experience of a population, then how do organisms adapt successfully to more rapidly fluctuating, temporary, or local conditions of the environment which may impact survival and probability of reproduction?

As we saw in an earlier chapter, evolution of learning mechanisms in the brain is the solution. But how general are the learning mechanisms that result? To what degree is the learning restricted to a specific domain or class of adaptive problems and thus to specific types of information?

Randy Gallistel (1995, 2000) has made the claim that all forms of learning are domain-specific and there cannot be any domain-general form of learning because no general adaptive problem exists to which the learning would apply. However, I think he is wrong about this. In part, the error comes from not recognizing that adaptive problems are domain-general or domain-specific in degrees, and further, that domain-general and domain-specific should be defined by the breadth of the range of species and conditions in which the particular kind of learning or cognition occurs. A type of learning or a cognitive mechanism can be more or less domain-general or domain-specific depending upon how widely it is distributed across species and learning situations.

As noted in chapter 7, Cosmides and Tooby (2002) have puzzled about how a general form of cognition applicable to novel and local conditions could ever even evolve. Recall that they refer to this form of cognition as "improvisational intelligence." The mystery arises precisely because this form of cognition permits adaptation to novel, local and even individually idiosyncratic environmental conditions, which by definition, have only been present for periods of time far too short for genetic evolution to accommodate. How could natural selection "design" a form of cognition that can deal with situations in the environment that are not long-lasting and stable, but just the opposite? This is an important question because it is precisely this kind of intelligence, this domain-general form of cognition, which may be at the root of human uniqueness.

In this concluding chapter I propose an analysis which will shed light on the role of environmental regularities, many statistical in structure, in shaping the evolution of domain-specific and domain-general learning and cognitive mechanisms, including that domain-general kind designated as "improvisational intelligence."

To this end, I will attempt a rough approximation to the human "cognitive architecture" and to what might take place in the human brain to produce abstract and creative thought. Is the model complete? No, it is not, but it is a starting point, perhaps on the order of some of the first systematic observations of the night sky even before the first rudimentary telescopes and the approximations to an understanding of one part of nature that they promised. At this point in the history of neuroscience and biological approaches to the mind, much is still speculative. It is hoped that the speculations in this chapter will be a step in the right direction, but even if they achieve that goal, the step will be only a very small one at best. Still, we have to begin somewhere.

One of the most contentious debates among contemporary psychologists and neuroscientists regarding the organization of the mind and brain concerns the degree to which the "architecture" of the human mind is domain-specific or domain-general. These concepts were introduced in an earlier chapter. We now examine the theoretical distinction between domain-specific and domain-general psychological mechanisms in more detail as background leading to a model of "mind design" that incorporates both views.

Evolutionary psychologists (EPs) such as Leda Cosmides and John Tooby, at the University of California, Santa Barbara, see the human mind as a large collection of adaptively specialized modules, or *domain-specific* information processing mechanisms, each specifically and rather precisely "designed" by natural selection to solve particular information processing problems that confronted ancestral humans in the evolutionary past (Cosmides and Tooby, 1987, 1992, 2000, 2002). Some of the problems which brains had to solve in our Pleistocene hunter-gatherer past included how to find nutritious foods, how to find and "secure" reproductively fit mates, how to navigate one's environment, how to avoid predators, how to distinguish friend from foe, how to successfully care for offspring, and so forth. This view of the mind stands in stark contrast to the human mind as general purpose information processor, as envisioned in the Standard Social Science Model (see chapter 1).

According to EPs, each module in the evolved "modular mind" was "designed" by natural selection to handle only a particular type of information unique to the module. For example, a language module processes linguistic inputs only, using processing rules unique to that module. A facial recognition module processes only those inputs that arise from face stimuli, again, using processing rules unique to that module, and so on. Gallistel (1995) has characterized each module as a specialized information processing organ. According to EPs, there may be hundreds or even thousands of such adaptively specialized organs, with highly specific circuit "designs," making up the human mind and brain (Cosmides and Tooby, 1992).

This model of the brain/mind is in distinct contrast to a general-purpose or domain-general view of the human mind and brain. On an extreme GP view, the brain uses similar brain areas with similar information processing rules for all information processing tasks. There are no specialized modules, all processing, all cognitive functioning, relies on the same general principles such as the use of logical rules. Much of what I have discussed in this book in prior chapters suggests that any conception of the human brain and mind which excludes domain-specific processing mechanisms can't be accurate. There is just too much evidence for the highly specialized nature of the structures and functions of different parts of the human brain. However, this does not necessarily mean that the human brain is without some domain-general processes. In fact, it is my view that the human brain is composed of a large number of domain-specific modules *combined with* some processing mechanisms that are much more domain-general. As will be discussed below, I hypothesize that the "general" process, accomplished by particular circuit "designs" in the brain, is the extraction and representation of statistical regularities in environmental features and their relations. But, before proceeding with an explanation of this rather abstract and esoteric hypothesis, some additional background will be beneficial for the reader.

Evolutionary psychologists have examined evolutionary factors in many psychological and behavioral characteristics in humans (Crawford & Krebs 1998; Simpson & Kenrick, 1997), including mating preferences (Buss, 1989, 1992), rape (Thornhill & Palmer, 2000), cheater detection mechanisms in social interactions (Cosmides and Tooby, 1992), parental investment and female inhibition mechanisms (Bjorklund & Kipp, 1996), judgments of attractiveness (Singh, 1993), pregnancy sickness (Profet, 1992), evolved constraints on visual perception (Shepard, 1994) and effects of family on pubertal timing (Ellis et al, 1999). They have also provided important theoretical insights about the modularity of mind and brain (Baron-Cohen, 1995; Buss, 1995; Cosmides and Tooby, 1987, 1992, 1994, 2001; Gallistel, 1995; Pinker, 1994, 1997; Symons, 1989).

However, by contrast, evolutionary psychologists typically deny any important role at all for domain-general (DG) processing mechanisms in cognition (thinking, perception, language) and learning (Koenigshofer, 1994, 2002; Zeiler, 2002, 2003). Cosmides and Tooby call GP models of the mind "biologically implausible" (Cosmides and Tooby, 1987, 1992, 1995; also see Gallistel, 1992). They claim that human information processing mechanisms "must be domain-specific" and any general processes which might exist in human mind design must be "weak," "inefficient," "inert" and "fatally flawed" unless combined with more computationally powerful and adaptively important *domain-specific* devices (Cosmides and Tooby, 1987, 1992; 1995, 2001). Many other EPs express similar views (Pinker, 1989, 1992; Symons, 1992; Gallistel, 1995) ascribing any general mechanisms in cognition and learning, which might exist, limited or uncertain adaptive significance. Psychologist, Randy Gallistel rejects the existence of general processes in cognition and learning, all together, based on the claim that such mechanisms contradict the *law of adaptive specialization* in biology (Gallistel, 1995, 2001). Thus, for many EPs, adaptively important general process mechanisms in cognition and learning have been squeezed out of the mind, replaced with domain-specific modules exclusively (Gallistel, 1995) or nearly so (Cosmides and Tooby, 1987, 1992, 2000, 2002; Symons, 1992).

Current EP models of mind and brain reject historically influential GP models

The view of the mind and brain as massively modular with no adaptively important, general processing mechanisms is of historical interest because it contradicts general process (GP) views that have a long and influential history in psychology. There is an enormous scientific literature over the past 100 years which assumed a central role for general processes in the organization of mind and behavior (Plotkin, 2002). For example, Skinner and Piaget believed that all learning, even human language acquisition was of the same general form (Plotkin, 2002). General learning processes such as conditioning or other general cognitive mechanisms such as logical rules, induction (Plotkin, 2002), or generalization (Wasserman, 1995) have been frequently proposed by psychologists as central in the organization of the human mind and brain, and as the essential source of the flexibility of behavior in humans and other species (for examples see: Couvillon and Bitterman, 1980; Flanagan, et.al., 2002; Glanzman, 1995; Gormezano and Tait, 1976; Plotkin, 2002; Rescorla and Solomon, 1967; Wasserman, 1993; Wolf and Heisenberg, 1991). But EP psychologists such as Cosmides and Tooby (1992), Gallistel (1995) and others, reject the view of the mind as any sort of general purpose information processing machine. According to Cosmides and Tooby this view of the mind simply reflects outdated "metatheoretical holdovers from the heyday of behaviorism." The behaviorists such as John Watson from the early 1900s and B. F. Skinner from the mid to late 1900s believed that almost all human and animal behavior resulted from the general laws of learning in classical and operant conditioning. According to the behaviorists, not only was all behavior determined by learning, but all learning in animals and humans was of these two general types. Modern evolutionary psychologists find such views to be "biologically naïve."

Contrasting Views on Origin of Behavioral and Cognitive Flexibility

Humans, especially, are noted for their ability to solve a wide range of adaptive problems by creative and inventive thinking that includes innovations ranging from modern agricultural practices to space travel. Where does this behavioral and cognitive flexibility come from if not from general learning processes such as conditioning or other general cognitive mechanisms such as logical rules, induction (Plotkin, 2002), or generalization (Wasserman, 1995)?

As noted above, EPs typically reject general processes in thinking and instead ascribe the flexibility of behavior to large numbers of domain-specific cognitive devices in interaction with one another (Cosmides and Tooby, 1992, 2000). Hundreds of specialized information processing modules interacting with one another would, on this view, produce all the flexibility needed to account for human cognitive and behavior flexibility, without any need of one or more general cognitive or learning processes. General process theorists counter that the specialization imagined by EPs in a completely modular mind cannot fully account for the extraordinary flexibility, creativity, and innovation characteristic of the human mind. We shall deal with this issue again a little later in this chapter.

The status of domain-general mechanisms is "one of the most contentious issues in psychology"

Proponents of GP (general process) views of mind and brain span a broad range of specialties, from traditional learning theory, and some varieties of cognitive science, to connectionism (see Pavlov, 1927; Spence, 1936; Skinner, 1938; Hebb, 1949; Bitterman, 1996, 2000; Donahoe & Palmer, 1994, 2002; Haier, et al 1988, 1992; Harris and Christenfeld, 1996; Luger, 1994; Thompson, et al 1998; Wasserman, 1995; and connectionists such as Clark, 1993; Holland, 1998; Rosenberg and Sejnowski, 1987; Rumelhart and McCleland, 1986).

Therefore, it is not surprising that EP conceptions of minds and brains as "massively modular" to the exclusion of important domain-general processes is quite controversial among psychologists, especially with regard to the human case. Many psychologists who accept evolution, nevertheless believe that some of the behaviors explained by EPs as products of domain-specialized mental modules are better explained by general processes such as logic and reasoning (DeSteno and Salovey, 1996, and Harris and Christenfeld, 1996). Furthermore, evidence from human neuropsychology usually interpreted in EP accounts as support for the modularity of the human mind and brain has been criticized and reinterpreted to support a non-modular model of human cortical organization (Goldberg, 1995; Finlay and Darlington, 1995). Even Fodor himself (1998, 2000), an early originator of the concept of modularity (Fodor, 1983), has been critical of EP on this issue and rejects a massively modular mind, insisting that there must be important general processes in cognition and learning. Many psychologists who do not reject evolution nevertheless do reject the notion held by many EPs that an evolutionary approach requires or even implies the exclusion of adaptively significant, computationally powerful, domain-general processing mechanisms in cognition and learning (Corballis, 2002; DeSteno and Salovey, 1996; Fodor, 1998, 2000; Goldberg, 1995; Harris and Christenfeld, 1996; Koenigshofer, 1994).

From this perspective, the central issue that separates many evolutionary psychologists (EPs) from their critics is not evolution, but how evolution "designed" the human brain. Did evolution produce a human mind and brain which includes adaptively important *domain-general* cognitive mechanisms or is the human mind made entirely of highly specialized, *domain-specific* processing mechanisms (Koenigshofer, 2002)? As Symons (1992) notes, "Historically, there have been two basic conceptions of human nature: the empiricist conception, in which the brain is thought to comprise only a few domain-general, unspecialized mechanisms; and the nativist conception, in which the brain is thought to comprise many, domain-specific, specialized mechanisms." According to Plotkin (2002), " . . . within the psychological community at large this is an unresolved and contentious matter, one of the most contentious in psychology."

Unraveling the "Enigma" of DG Mechanisms Will Unify Psychology

Because evolutionary analysis has contributed to our understanding of *domain-specific* cognitive modules, it would seem probable that the same analysis should be useful when applied to domain-general, "content-independent" (Cosmides and Tooby, 2002) cognitive and learning mechanisms of the kind referred to by Cosmides and Tooby (2002) as "improvisational intelligence." Yet, EPs have not aggressively pursued this course. Perhaps, this reluctance is a consequence of the theoretical problem that I discussed at the beginning of this chapter. For example, Cosmides and Tooby (2002) refer to the difficulties in understanding how, in principle, cognitive mechanisms seemingly content-general, "content-independent," (meaning without domain-specific content, but "general" in nature) or "content-free," responsive to short-term, local information, could have "even evolved." This unresolved question is also evident in much of their earlier work (Cosmides and Tooby, 1992, 2000), and explains why they are perplexed by what they call the "enigma of human intelligence" (Cosmides and Tooby, 2002).

In this chapter, as part of an exploration of that part of human "mind design" that makes creative and innovative abstract thinking possible, I attempt to fill this theoretical gap. I will present an analysis which shows how the same processes of natural selection which "designed" domain-specific (DS) cognitive modules (Cosmides and Tooby, 1992) could also have "designed" adaptively powerful, domain-general (DG), "content-independent" (CI) (see Cosmides and Tooby, 1992, 2000) mechanisms that can help explain the "enigma of human intelligence". It is important to note that the view that I will argue in this chapter sees DGCI (domain-general, content-independent) mechanisms as central to human adaptation and contradicts typical EP accounts of mind and brain which portray any DGCI mechanisms which might exist as "computationally weak," "fatally flawed," and of little adaptive significance (Cosmides and Tooby, 2001; Gallistel, 1995; Symons, 1992; Tooby and Cosmides, 1992). In my view, as I discuss below, both domain-general and domain-specific circuit "designs" are interwoven in human "mind design," explaining both our "instincts" and the origins of human capacities for creativity, innovation, and abstract thought.

In the coming pages, I attempt a unifying synthesis between current evolutionary psychology and the "general process" views of mind and brain which characterize traditional learning theory, cognitive science, and connectionism. In addition, I believe that the ideas I present below will provide the reader with a new way to understand the nature of human thought and its origins.

Regularities in the world at multiple levels of abstraction drive natural selection

I begin with a new way of looking at the dynamics that underlie evolutionary processes.

Psychologists and biologists often describe natural selection in terms of differential rates of reproduction in response to environmental conditions. But, not all environmental conditions become basis for evolution. What are the general properties of the environmental conditions which do become selection "forces" in the evolution of traits, particularly in the evolution of psychological traits? As preparation for arguments to follow, I list several propositions as part of a new way of thinking about natural selection, evolution, and particularly the evolution of brain and "mind design" : 1) the material world is constructed of systems of physical regularities (that is, physical structures, processes, properties, and events which regularly and predictably repeat); 2) redundancy inherent in repetitions of things in the world (objects, events, relations) provides basis for information in nature conceived as "uncertainty reduction," as described by classic information theorists (Shannon and Weaver, 1949); 3) uncertainty reduction (information) becomes genetically represented primarily by natural selection in the organization of organisms—in their structures and functioning (i.e. in their adaptations) whether anatomical, physiological, or neurobehavioral; 4) evolution by natural selection is thus recognized as an information-conserving system in that genetic evolution selects, represents, stores and transmits information (constraints on randomness which move organic "design" toward improved fitness) inherent in environmental regularities which have consequences for fitness; 5) different varieties and properties of regularities in the world generate different categories of adaptation corresponding to some of the common sense differentiations between anatomical, physiological, and psychological properties of animals; 6) the evolution of *information processing systems* in nature, which generate, store, and process *representations* of the world (which reduce "uncertainty" in the organization of behavior toward increased fitness) is a predictable, if not inevitable, consequence of the presence of repetition and regularity in nature; 7) cognitive mechanisms, like other adaptations, evolve to represent and exploit ("genetically accommodate," Shepard, 1992) the regularities of the world and thereby inform the adaptive organization of behavior; 8) different kinds of cognitive mechanism, including domain-specific (DS) *and* domain-general, content-independent (DGCI) processing mechanisms, evolve in response to the different properties of the environmental regularities accommodated by brain evolution, 9) *environmental regularities exist at multiple levels of abstraction* in a hierarchical, statistical structure of the physical world; 10) events in the world, which are highly variable at lower levels of organization, emerge, at more abstracted levels, into stable regularities which then act as enduring selection conditions sufficient to the "design" (no teleology implied) of cognitive architecture, including domain-general, content-independent mechanisms (Koenigshofer, 2002); 11) Cognitive mechanisms must evolve as responses to long-term regularities in the material and dynamic structure of the world, including those regularities which are statistical and abstracted from specific instances of objects and events with properties and relations in common; 12) in short, brain and mind "design" reflect the "design" or organization of the external world, particularly its statistical regularities, and their varieties.

The Universal Significance of Regularities in the World

For some readers with expertise in psychological science, my reference to the importance of regularities in the world will bring to mind Shepard's (1981, 1984, 1987a, 1992) hypothesis that "our perceptual/cognitive systems have in fact internalized, especially deeply, . . . pervasive and enduring regularities . . . in the terrestrial world" by "genetic accommodation to [such] regularities." Shepard argues that "natural selection must have favored genes not only on the basis of how well they propagated under the special circumstances peculiar to the ecological niche currently occupied, but also, . . . even more consistently in the long run, according to how well they propagate under the general circumstances common to all ecological niches." He notes that "all niches . . ., though differing in numerous details, share some general—perhaps even universal—properties" such as a three-dimensional, locally Euclidian space with a "gravitationally conferred unique upward direction," one-dimensional time with a "thermodynamically conferred unique forward direction," cycles of light and dark, and the fact that "objects having an important consequence are of a particular natural kind . . . however much those objects may vary in their sensible properties (of size, shape, color, odor, motion, and so on)" (Shepard, 1992). In short, there has evolved "a mesh between the principles of the mind and the regularities of the world" (Shepard, 1987a).

The universal regularities in the world which Shepard describes are content-*specific* (the information they contain is specific to particular situations) although common to all terrestrial niches and all terrestrial species. These regularities led to selection for "genetic internalization" of domain-specific (DS), species*g eneral* (SG) constraints on the organization of the perceptual/cognitive systems of terrestrial animals. As Shepard (1992) points out with regard to these universal regularities, they offer a way "to understand both the neurophysiological mechanisms and the cognitive and behavioral functions that those mechanisms mediate not as arbitrary design features of a particular species, but as accommodations to pervasive and enduring properties of the world." In other words, the "design" of organisms reflects the regularities, "the enduring properties," that exist in the physical world. This is an extremely powerful idea, because it helps us to understand why our bodies and brains are in synchrony with the environmental conditions in which we find ourselves. Bodies, brains, and minds must reflect the enduring conditions of the world or be eliminated by natural selection. Minds of animals and humans must be constructed to reflect and exploit the abstract informational structure of the world, not only the objects within it and their features, but their consistent relations to one another. The structure of thought, memory, emotion, motivation, the sensory systems and perception must be tied to the structure of the world just as closely as the structure of the stomach or the lungs is tied to chemical structure of food and air.

It is important to note that EPs such as Tooby and Cosmides (1992) also emphasize the significance of enduring environmental regularities in the evolution of the brain. However, they typically focus on environmental regularities which are more species-specific (SS), than those emphasized by Shepard, in order to explain the origins of more specialized cognitive (i.e. "information-processing") modules. As they put it, "However variable cultures and habitats may have been during human evolution, selection would have sifted human social and cultural life (as well as everything else) for obvious or subtle statistical and structural *regularities*, building psychological adaptations that exploited some subset of these regularities to solve adaptive problems."

Natural selection produces "representations" of environmental regularities

The repeated reference to environmental regularities in the literature concerning evolutionary origins of psychological mechanisms is not accidental, but, instead, it reflects a fundamental fact necessitated by the very structure and dynamics of natural selection (likely a property of many systems dependent upon feedback for their regulation). In fact, it could be said that all adaptations resulting from natural selection are, in one way or another, representations (neural representations, or representations in body/organ structure and functioning) of environmental regularities which impact reproductive fitness. Without enduring regularities of sufficient stability, conditions determining particular selective pressures are not present for periods of time sufficient for the operation of consistent selection over the many generations usually required for evolutionary change (see opening arguments in this chapter; for recent examples of very rapid microevolution of anatomical traits such as beak size, however, see Wiener, 1995). In other words, evolution takes time, and for something to evolve, the conditions in the environment that can be genetically accommodated by an evolved trait must be consistently present for extended periods of time. Inevitably, most genetically encoded adaptations are evolutionary responses—anatomical, physiological, or neurobehavioral—to enduring environmental regularities. For example, had eucalyptus leaves not regularly been present in the environment in which koalas found themselves generation after generation, a digestive physiology specific to that food source would not have evolved. If gravitational forces had not been consistently present and stable in their intensity over countless generations, bones of sufficient strength to withstand the downward pull of gravity would not have evolved. Had there not existed in human evolutionary history a multitude of conditions regularly present over many generations, domain-specific (DS) cognitive modules such as "a child-care module, a social-inference module, a sexual-attraction module, a semantic-inference module..." (Tooby and Cosmides, 1992) and so on could not have evolved as components of the human brain and mind.

Clearly, environmental regularities are the key to understanding evolution of adaptive mechanisms, whether anatomical, physiological, or behavioral and psychological, whether species-specific (Gallistel, 1995; Tooby and Cosmides, 1992) or species-general (Shepard, 1987a, 1987b). The evolution of organisms has not simply mapped their environments, but the adaptively significant *regularities* within those environments. A fundamental similarity among all types of adaptation—anatomical, physiological, or behavioral/psychological—is that all map those enduring environmental regularities which affect the chances of survival and reproduction of genes.

On this view, different categories of environmental regularities encountered by natural selection should generate different forms of adaptive response—some will be the strictly anatomical/physiological, while others will be neurological/behavioral. On this view, it is the more abstracted levels of statistical regularity in the world which form the physical basis in the world for "information" in the sense described by classical information theorists (Shannon and Weaver, 1949). The high adaptive value which accrues from exploitation of redundancy and predictive relationships inherent in abstracted regularity structures in the world likely set the stage, and became the driving force, for the evolution of sophisticated information processing systems in nature, i.e. brains.

The statistical structure of the world and principles for its incorporation into cognitive architectures

It is likely that a driving force present early in the evolution of information processing systems was selection for representational economy (RE) and consequent gains in processing efficiency (PE) (Koenigshofer, 1992, 1994a, 1995a, 1996a). One way information processing systems can accomplish representational economy and processing efficiency is by use of representational schemes which exploit the redundancy in inputs. For nervous systems this is made possible by the repetitive nature of features, properties, objects, events, relations, and other regularities of the world (reflecting the dictum, "there is nothing new under the sun"). Such regularities of the world may be perfectly consistent over time, but are often probabilistic and statistical. Furthermore, as discussed above, regularities may occur at multiple levels, from the "concrete" to the progressively abstract, and regularities at one level may themselves possess properties in common which can form the basis for higher-order regularities. This structure arises because features in the world and their spatial and temporal distributions regularly repeat over time frames of varying durations (Koenigshofer, 1994a).

To help clarify this point, and to suggest a basis for neural coding of this sort of information, imagine that "microfeatures" (Churchland, 1989) in the distal world are spatially and temporally distributed. In a multi-dimensional abstract grid, microfeatures can be located in abstract property spaces (Churchland, 1989) and in Euclidian space and time (see Figures 8-1, 8-2, and 8-3). Microfeatures and their distributions over space and time repeat, and they do so with varying degrees of regularity. Neural representations of the world include information about various physical attributes ("sensory qualia," one type of microfeature, Churchland, 1989) of sensory items, as well as their locations and extensions in space and time. Furthermore, these attributes co-vary. Statistical regularities in the distributions of microfeatures generate stimulus-driven perceptual object representations (Churchland's, 1989, "property-cluster prototypes," see chapter 8), stable (invariant) over various time frames, over various spatial locations and over various environmental contexts (for example, see Shepard, 1994). In this formulation, changes in perceptual objects may be imagined as redistributions in arrangements of microfeatures over time and space. Abrupt irregularities in the rate of such redistributions are detected as the boundaries of events, just as abrupt discontinuities in the distribution of material properties in space are interpreted as the boundaries of objects (Koenigshofer, 1992, 1994a).

An important feature of this formulation is that these dynamics can be represented by neural processes incorporating "vector coding" in which values of microfeatures in space and time are represented by "activation vectors" comprised of neuronal firing rates within specific neuronal populations (Churchland, 1989). Objects and events, so defined, and spatial and temporal relations among them, reoccur in the world with varying degrees of regularity. Many consistently co-vary, and they frequently have properties in common, properties which reoccur in different instances of the objects, events, or relations. All are varieties of statistical regularity in the world. This can even include regularities in temporal relations which may form basis for conditioning and perception of "causality" (Koenigshofer, 1995b, 1996c). Each instance of regularity offers an opportunity to enhance fitness by extraction, representation and exploitation of: (1) predictive relations among events, (2) similarity among events and objects forming basis for "expectancy" (Hull and others since) and for categorical relations (Feldman, 1997), respectively, and (3) for representational economy (RE) and consequent gains in processing efficiency (PE) by the use of representations which incorporate and exploit redundancy structures in inputs.

These gains are made even greater and more adaptively significant by the fact that repetitions at one level provide the basis for higher order, more abstracted regularities. Viewed in this way, it becomes apparent that brains represent not only regularities in simple features, what might be called first-order regularity representations, but also regularities in the spatial and temporal distributions of those features over various time frames, at multiple, often hierarchically organized levels of abstraction. Furthermore, regularities at one level of abstraction can form the basis for representations of regularities of even higher order, i.e. regularities in regularities (what might be termed meta-regularities). These must also be represented in abstracted "property" and relational spaces (see Figures 8-1, 8-2 and 8-3 and recall Churchland's superordinate prototype representations).

As discussed in chapter 8, Churchland (1989) has proposed "vector coding" as a possible representational scheme in neuronal systems which have the capability to neurally encode highly abstracted representational spaces such as those I propose here. On this view, a central feature of "information processing" in natural and artificial information processing systems is extraction and representation of regularity structures (redundancy exploitation and representation and thus "uncertainty reduction"—information in the classical sense of Shannon and Weaver (1949) and Attneave (1954). These regularity structures or representations can be transformed and manipulated in various ways, including representational projection to future states of the world by a kind of generalization of abstracted "representational skeletons" (see discussion below) across time frames of progressively longer duration, especially in humans (this is similar to what I proposed in chapters 4 and 5, the IBOES processing routine wherein a person images or imagines behavioral options, their probable outcomes, evaluates these in terms of adaptive significance, i.e. hedonic tone, and then selects the "best" behavior, in terms of biological fitness, to put into action—volition or the feeling of "free will" is the result).

As Shepard (1987a, 1994, 1995) has noted, the organization of the perceptual/cognitive systems of animals tends to evolve to accommodate the regularities of the world. Because, as I have proposed in this chapter, the world is comprised of ubiquitous, multilevel, hierarchical statistical regularity structures, cognitive architectures must have evolved as "genetic accommodations" to these regularity structures in the environment (Koenigshofer, 1994a, 2002). Natural selection encounters regularities of the world with adaptive significance and "designs" adaptive mechanisms to accommodate them whenever they attain sufficient stability over generations, *even when that requisite stability is attained only at abstracted levels of event regularity* (Koenigshofer, 1994a, 1996a, 2002).

The progressively abstract levels of the regularities which stimulated the evolution of complex information processing adaptations helps explain the observation by Sternberg (1990) that human and other sophisticated forms of animal "intelligence" are most often recognized by psychological scientists as having ability for abstraction and abstract reasoning as their central and most essential characteristic. The intuitive sense by lay persons and psychologists alike that a core component of intelligence is *abstraction* reflects the fact, revealed by arguments here, that it is the abstracted nature of certain regularities in the world that generates the bulk of that "information" in the biological world which is at the root of the evolution of information processing adaptations in terrestrial life forms, and thus at the root of the evolution of brains and "intelligent" life. It might even be argued that the "complexity" of life forms on earth can be roughly gauged by a "metric" incorporating the degree of abstraction of the regularities which natural selection has accommodated within the organization of the life form. More complex life forms accommodate more abstracted environmental regularities into their adaptive organizations by the evolution of brain circuit organizations which represent highly abstracted regularities of the world and which extract and represent regularities in those representations.

In sum, this *regularity hypothesis* of evolution proposes that natural selection encounters regularities of the world with adaptive significance and "designs" adaptive mechanisms (bodily features or features of mind and brain) to accommodate them whenever they attain sufficient stability over generations, even when that requisite stability is attained only at abstracted levels of event regularity. I ask that the reader be patient with the *abstract* and obscure meaning here. Such a difficult statement requires much more explanation. As the theoretical argument unfolds below I hope that the meaning of what I am saying will be clearer. At the moment just let me say that what I mean by "abstracted levels of event regularity" is the idea that although individual objects and events are variable in their details, they also have similarities which are stable across the individual instances. So, for example, birds differ from one another, but they also have distinguishing features that make them all recognizably members of the same abstracted class of thing, bird. This, of course, is what we mean by the concept of a cat-egory. Note that categories are abstractions that don't really exist in the world, but only in the mind. Similarities exist in the world that make things similar, but a concept, such as "bird" is a mental construction, a psychological adaptation that makes predictive knowledge about a group of things in the world possible. That is, when you form a cate-gory, such as "bird," then in the future when you encounter an animal that fits into your category, you then already know an entire set of facts about that new instance of "bird" which you have just encountered. And that information allows you to make useful pre-dictions about that thing, and about how you should respond to it. Such mental struc-tures in the mind, based on regularities that are characteristic of particular categories or concepts formed by abstracting out differences and retaining the constant features that characterize the category, form the basis for "knowledge" about, and "understand-ing" of, the world. The *regularity hypothesis of evolution* that I propose here is a general principle: things in the world repeat, and because of that fact of the world, information (in the classical sense of *information theory*) exists, that fact, in turn, provides evolution by natural selection an opportunity to "design" mechanisms to exploit that information for adaptive advantage. Minds were one result of this principle in nature.

A corollary of the regularity hypothesis of evolution explains distributions of adaptations

These considerations suggest a general principle which can guide classification of adap-tations and help explain their distribution over problem domains and over species: the distribution of any *regularity* in the world with adaptive consequences for organisms is a significant determining factor in the corresponding distribution of the *mechanisms* which will evolve to "genetically accommodate" it (see Figures 10-1 and 10-2). Regu-larities in the world which are widely distributed across a broad array of niches will tend to produce evolution of adaptations which are similarly widely distributed across spe-cies. Thus Shepard's "universal" regularities "common to all ecological niches" generate adaptations with features approximately "universal" across species. As an illustration, Shepard (1994) has pointed to the "universal regularities in the world" which account for universal "psychological principles of invariant color, optimum generalization, [and] simplest motion . . ." Traditional GP psychologists such as Skinner, on the other hand, have tended to focus upon components of the cognitive architecture "designed" by nat-ural selection as "genetic accommodations" to regularities (covariation of events) in the world widely distributed over problem domains, as well as species and niches, and so find "general" psychological processes (conditioning) perhaps as universal as Shepard's and certainly more ubiquitous than the DS mechanisms of most EPs (Shepard's "universal law of generalization" is reminiscent of references to generalization by some "general process" psychologists as a fundamental component of "general" cognition; see Wasserman, 1995). But while Shepard's regularities and the mechanisms to genetically accommodate them are "universal" and *content-specific* (his "universal law of generalization" being the exception with regard to the latter), traditionally conceived GP mechanisms are much more *content-general,* or "content-independent" as well as domain-general and "universal" (see Figures 10-1 and 10-2). By contrast, Cosmides and Tooby, and many other evolutionary psychologists, by focusing exclusively upon regularities more restricted in distribution in the world, look for and find domain-*specific*, content-*specific*, species-specific psychological adaptations. A form of "instinct-blindness" (Tooby and Cosmides, 1992) may be operating when traditional evolutionary psychologists neglect DGCI (GP) mechanisms in cognition and learning. As Shepard (1987) has pointed out, adaptations to very general features of the world may escape notice simply because the ubiquity of their presence makes them less "visible."

A major factor which has made domain-general cognitive mechanisms problematic for evolutionary psychologists is that domain-general mechanisms appear to be content-general or "content-independent" (Cosmides and Tooby, 1992, 2000, 2002). For a cognitive mechanism to be domain-general, it must be applicable across a wide range of problem spaces, and therefore it must process information from across a broad range of domains, to varying degrees independent of the specific content of the information (that is, the specific kind of information). Furthermore, the computational rules must be general enough, "content-independent," to process information from across the range of different contents (the different kinds of information and "problem spaces") over which the domain-general mechanism operates. Because evolutionary psychologists focus upon domain-specific problems, it has been difficult for them to see domain-general problems (for example, Symons, 1992, states "there is no such thing as a general problem"—instinct blindness again?).

Implied by the analysis I present here is the idea that, like *species-specific* and *species-general, domain-specific* and *domain-general* are better thought of as ends of a continuum in nature, rather than as absolutes (how this might be possible in terms of neural representation is discussed in a later section of this chapter). Psychological adaptations can be to varying degrees domain-general or domain-specific, depending upon the distribution in nature of the regularities to which the adaptation is genetically accommodated (see Figures 10-1 and 10-2). Furthermore, the degree of *abstraction* of any regularity in the world is correlated with the breadth of its distribution in the world and the ubiquity, content-independence, and domain-generality of the adaptive mechanisms which have evolved in response to it (Figures 10-1 and 10-2). How can this reasoning help explain the evolution of the particulars of human and animal "mind design"?

Abstracted regularity structures in the world drive evolution of "general-process" cognition

Many psychologists have proposed general processes involved in the organization of adaptive behavior. For Skinner and many other behaviorists, behavior was the result of learning and all learning could be reduced to conditioning (Plotkin, 2002). Wasserman has proposed *event covariation* and *generalization* as the basis for general-process cognition in a wide range of species (Wasserman, 1993). Shepard (1987b) also recognizes generalization as a universal property of intelligent creatures. Plotkin (2002) has proposed *induction* (a form of reasoning that makes generalizations based on individual instances) as the essential property of general and flexible cognition. However, there is an underlying pattern here. All of these general process mechanisms proposed as the key to general-process cognition or learning are derived from regularity of one sort or another. For example, classical and operant conditioning (forms of event covariation representation), event covariation, generalization, formation of categories and the representation of categorical relations and logical relations (derived from properties of categories), formation of learning sets, expectancy, and inference *are all derived* from the representation of kinds or instances of regularities in the world.

A central hypothesis in this chapter is that sets of *abstracted* regularities universal to all terrestrial environments provide sufficient opportunity, in a wide range of species, for evolution of DGCI (domain-general, content-independent), "general process," cognitive mechanisms. These domain-general mechanisms of "mind design" would be predisposed by genetic organization to "register" and represent commonly occurring relationships between things in the world such as event covariation (conditioning), categorical relations, and logical relations derived from categorical information.

Representational Skeletons

These neural representations of abstracted relations are "distilled" out of repeated instances of ubiquitous regularities in the event *relations* found in the world. These higher-order regularities are abstracted or "distilled" out of instances of objects and events in the world by collapsing over, or disregarding, the idiosyncratic content of individual cases, leaving an information-rich regularity structure which is content-abstracted and general in character. In a sense, the "meat" of individual instances, which are variable in detail, is cut away from the underlying relational invariants leaving only a "skeleton", a *representational skeleton*, rich in relational information, often domain-general in character. These representational skeletons are "content-free" with regard to specific objects or events, but provide content-abstracted representations of ubiquitous relational invariants in the world including causality, categorical relations,

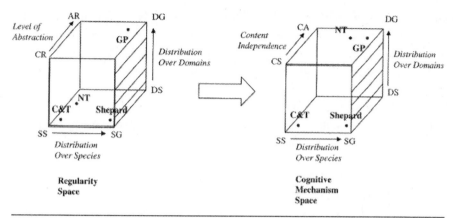

FIGURE 10-1. (Left) Three-dimensional regularity space showing properties of the environmental regularities focused upon in three approaches to the study of cognitive mechanisms. SS=species-specific regularity; SG=species-general regularity; DS=domain-specific regularity; DG=domain-general regularity; CR="concrete" regularity; AR=abstracted regularity. C&T=Cosmides and Tooby, 1987, 1992, 2000. Shepard=R.N. Shepard, 1987a, 1992, 1994. GP=general process approaches exemplified by Skinner and Piaget. NT=connectionist approach exemplified by NETtalk (Rosenfeld and Sejnowski, 19). Other connectionist networks depending upon the properties of the inputs and the problem spaces will appear at different "locations." (Right) By focusing on regularities with particular "locations" in regularity space, each approach discovers cognitive mechanisms differing from one another along similar dimensions, as shown in the three-dimensional cognitive mechanism space to the right. CA=content-abstracted cognitive mechanisms; CS=content-specific cognitive mechanisms. Note that in the space at the right, NETtalk is shown as dependent upon a "cognitive mechanism" which is domain-general and content-independent (content-abstracted) similar to GP mechanisms. It is shown in the center of the Distribution Over Species dimension to indicate "neutrality" in this property because circuit organization like that used in NETtalk mayor may not exist in natural brains. Thus, its species distribution is unknown.

Note Regarding Figure 10-1: Resolution of an apparent conflict between evolutionary psychologists and connectionists may lie in recognition of the differences in focus upon types of regularity among these researchers. Learning (and cognitive) mechanisms studied by evolutionary psychologists and connectionists can be placed in an abstract three dimensional space along dimensions of domain-specificity and content-independence (see Figure 10-1). This graphic representation reveals that when types or levels of abstraction of regularities in the world are recognized, order is brought to what appears, at first glance, to be diverse and even incompatible approaches to the study of learning and cognition. Each of the researchers shown in Figure 10-1 simply focuses on different types of adaptively significant regularities in the environment. The different focus leads to different conclusions depending upon which part of the "animal" they happen to investigate. The "animal" in this case is the system of environmental regularities which make up the world. Evolutionary psychologists investigate evolved psychological adaptations which "genetically accommodate" (Shepard, 1992) highly domain-specific regularities of the world. Connectionists model psychological adaptations evolved in response to much more domain-general, content-independent, or content-abstracted regularities of the world. The mind is actually comprised of both types of psychological adaptation (i.e. domain-specific and domain-general, content-abstracted or content-independent psychological mechanisms). See figure 10-1 showing an abstract regularity space depicting types of regularity *in the world* together with an abstract cognitive mechanisms space showing the *kinds of adaptive response to the different categories of regularities in the world* that have evolved. Various theoretical views about "mind design" are depicted as points within these abstract spaces.

logic and others inherent in and derived from the statistically regular properties of the world. Such *abstracted, domain-general* regularities are as "pervasive and enduring" as Euclidian space, the spectral properties of light, or cycles of light and dark (Shepard, 1987a) and it should be expected that these *representational skeletons* have been genetically "internalized" just as surely into the perceptual and cognitive systems of brains. Thus, by the account I present here, representations of the world by complex brains are expected to involve multiple, hierarchically structured levels of increasing abstraction, the organization of which is driven in large part by the hierarchical statistical structure of the world itself. Some of that structure is content-specific, and some is content-free or content-independent, but in all cases it must be consistently present over evolutionary time. These dynamics in nature produce cognitive mechanisms which are described as domain-specific (DS) or domain-general (DG) and content-independent (CI) or "content-free" (see Figure 10-2). The "content" of such DGCI *representational skeletons* is only "content-free" with regard to content of specific instances. However, such representational skeletons are content-rich in abstracted, relational structure, applicable over a wide range of situations and domains, often novel in *specific content* for the individual but *invariant (regular) in abstracted, relational structure.*

Thus, brains become equipped, over evolutionary time, with a collection of evolved domain-general, "content-independent" cognitive tools (representations) with which to confront the world—the world from which these cognitive tools are derived by natural selection. These "general" cognitive tools (representational skeletons) evolved as "genetic accommodations" to the regularities of the world, just as have the more domain-specific cognitive devices described by mainstream evolutionary psychologists (Buss, 1992, 1995, 1998; Cosmides and Tooby, 1992; Gallistel, 1995; Pinker, 1997). But the regularities represented in representational skeletons are truly independent of specific content while information-rich in the abstract relational regularities they incorporate.

Abstracted regularities of the world represented or encoded into what I have termed, *representational skeletons,* as well as more content-specific regularities, can simultaneously drive evolution of cognitive "design." This seems to have been missed by existing theoretical accounts of evolution by evolutionary psychologists (Koenigshofer, 2002). This omission leaves most evolutionary psychologists (EPs) without an explanation of how general process mechanisms could have evolved. From this theoretical gap, there follows in EPs a tendency to neglect "general" cognitive mechanisms such as logical relations, event covariation, causality, and categorization, because these theoreticians are puzzled about how such domain-general mechanisms "could have even evolved" (Cosmides and Tooby, 2002).

Beyond this, I hypothesize that brains have evolved a general disposition for extraction and representation of regularity. I discuss this later in this chapter as manifestation of a general principle in brain organization which I designate as NRSR,

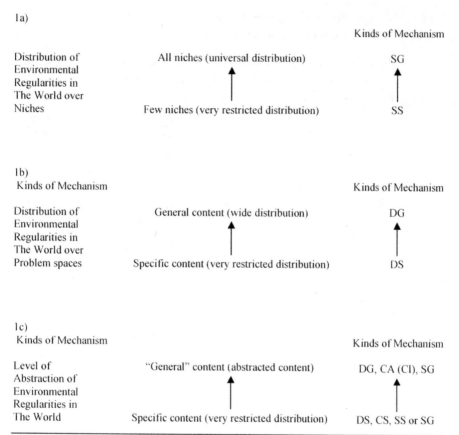

FIGURE 10-2. A general principle, as applied specifically to psychological mechanisms, for classification of adaptations explaining their distributions in the world. Distributions of regularities in the world and their levels of abstraction influence distributions of evolved mechanisms over niches, problem spaces, and species. DS=Domain specific. DG=Domain general. CS=Content specific. CG=Content general CA=Content Abstracted. CI="content-independent." SG=Species general. SS=Species specific. Each concept exists in the biological world as a continuum. Adaptations can be placed within a three-dimensional space defined by distributions over niches and problem spaces and levels of abstraction of the environmental regularity represented in the structure of the adaptation (Koenigshofer, 2002).

neuro-representation of statistical regularity. When this "design" feature of brains is applied to neural representations *themselves* inside the brain, the brain is then capable of generating the "invention" of "representational skeletons" of high levels of creativity and abstraction. This is significant because it suggests the nature of the *engines of thought* in complex animals, exemplified best by the exceptional abilities for abstract and creative thinking in humans.

The Problem of Short-term Regularities
and the "Enigma of Human Intelligence"

It is generally accepted that certain conditions are necessary for the operation of evolution by natural selection: 1) reproduction, 2) inheritance of traits, 3) variations within the population of reproducing entities, and 4) a selection process that eliminates alternatives which are less suited to some criterion (negative feedback) and preserves others better suited (positive feedback); in biological systems these criterion are provided by environmental demands (Tooby & Cosmides, 1995). However, as noted at the beginning of this chapter, there is a fifth component necessitated by the dynamics of the evolutionary process: there must be present, in the environment, enduring regularities which have "adaptive" consequences (that is, enduring regularities in the selection criterion), such that selection criterion are stable enough over long enough periods of time for evolution to operate. If some condition with adaptive significance is not present over sufficiently long periods of time in the environment of a species, there will not be sufficient time for selection to "design" a genetically encoded solution to that problem. Thus, one should expect that adaptive specializations will be "designed" by natural selection only for solutions to those problems present and stable over many generations. Conditions with adaptive significance, present for only a few generations or, especially, only within the lifetime of an individual, will seemingly have no "genetically internalized" (Shepard, 1987a) solutions to them.

As noted earlier, this generates a dilemma, because many events, which occur in the lifetime of an individual, are unique to the experience of that individual, or are examples of local events present for short periods of time, and in specific locales, and yet these events often hold important, sometimes even crucial, adaptive information. It is precisely the processing of this kind of short-term, local information which Cosmides and Tooby (2002) identify as central to their concept of flexible, "improvisational intelligence," and at the heart, they say, of what makes human cognition "so different" and simultaneously so problematic. For Cosmides and Tooby (2002), at the core of "the enigma of human intelligence" is the problem of how mechanisms for this type of information processing could "have even evolved," considering the short-term nature of the information and its local and restricted applicability in space and time. For them, the question is, if *content-specific*, adaptively specialized, information-processing mechanisms for such situations cannot have evolved because those situations are too variable over time, how is the adaptive information in immediate, short-term events, idiosyncratic to the individual, to be exploited?

It is certain that evolution did not evolve brain "design" that simply by-passed such adaptively rich information. Natural selection is very resourceful and opportunistic (e.g. see Mayr, 1974; Dawkins, 1987) and the adaptive significance of such information is simply too great to have been missed by evolutionary processes. This is evidenced by the fact that we see examples of the exploitation of this sort of adaptive information ubiquitously in human and animal behavior. Human beings and animals are simply very good at representing and exploiting general forms of regularity: at recognizing patterns, at deducing causal relations, at inferring to new instances on the basis of previous experiences with similar instances, at predicting outcomes from correlated cues and so on, *even when the specific events involved are idiosyncratic to the individual and evolutionarily short-term*. How could mechanisms evolve which exploit such information and which permitted human entry into what Tooby and DeVore call the "cognitive niche" (Tooby and DeVore, 1987)? The answer, again, is to be found in the abstracted relational regularities of the world encoded by the *representational skeletons* that I propose in this chapter.

Invariance of abstracted regularity structures (with variance in specific contents) explains evolution of domain-general, content-independent (DGCI) cognition

Symons (1992) has stated that "there is no such thing" as a general adaptive problem and that therefore there can be no general solution to adaptive problems. Use of the phrase "general problem" in this context can be construed to mean two different things. First, a problem may be general in the sense that it is shared by a wide range of species. Shepard (1987a, 1992, 1994), as already noted, sees several conditions (for example, the three-dimensional, Euclidian nature of physical space or the "terrestrially prevailing 24-hour oscillation in illumination and temperature") which constitute universal problems for terrestrial species, producing species-general design features which are "genetic accommodation to [such] universal regularities." Therefore, in this sense of the term, there are at least several general problems; in fact, on Shepard's account, there are several *universal* adaptive problems. The second meaning of "general problem" is a reference to problems that are domain-general and content-general or content-independent (Cosmides and Tooby, 1992, 2002) and which therefore might rely upon some general process for their solution. It is in this sense that Symons means to say "there is no such thing" as a general adaptive problem.

However, this claim misses the mark. Consistent with the arguments I present above, there *is a general adaptive problem* which is domain-general, content-general, and species-general. That problem, especially for complex animals such as humans, is how to exploit the vast amounts of adaptive information contained in events and conditions which are short-term, local, and often idiosyncratic within the individual lifetime of an animal or human.

According to Tooby and DeVore (1987), the essential event leading to hominid entry into the "cognitive niche" was evolution of cognitive mechanisms responsive to short-term, local, contingent information. But the question of just how brain "design" responsive to this kind of information might have evolved still presents an "enigma" for prominent evolutionary psychologists. As I have noted several times now, according to Cosmides and Tooby (2002), the central "enigma" in the evolution of human intelligence is to clarify how such cognitive mechanisms "could have even evolved."

Why does this pose such an "enigma" for Cosmides and Tooby and other prominent evolutionary psychologists? The answer again is variability, lack of stability of selection criteria. Because local, short-term conditions within the individual lifetime can be highly variable over time and from individual to individual, the information processing problem that arises cannot be solved by any content-*specific* cognitive adaptation. Thus, many EPs find themselves in a quandary because they generally only believe in such content-specific psychological mechanisms, and they reject, as noted earlier in this chapter, domain-general mechanisms as "biologically implausible." Yet, information contained in events which may be unique to the individual, in the content-specific sense, is far too rich in adaptive and predictive value to be "ignored" by natural selection. Because natural selection requires stable selection criteria, Cosmides and Tooby cannot see how natural selection could "design" the requisite cognitive adaptations to exploit this rich source of adaptive information.

However, as I have outlined above, the answer lies in understanding the nature of the environmental regularities involved in this type of adaptive problem. Identifying the regularities that can provide the requisite stability of selection criteria has been difficult perhaps because the regularities involved only become apparent when individual cases are abstracted to reveal underlying relational constants. Although regularities which occur locally and over short periods within the span of an individual lifetime are variable in *specific* content, *they are invariant in abstract statistical structure*, over generations. Natural selection could select brain "design," circuit configurations, that exploited this abstracted structure of the world.

The short-term and local character of such information has not only led Cosmides and Tooby (2002) to puzzle about how such mechanisms could have evolved, but has led other evolutionary psychologists to simply deny their existence (Symons, 1992; Gallistel, 1995). What seems to have been missed, perhaps leading to a fundamental misinterpretation of the design consequences of natural selection for brain "design," is that *variability of the specific contents of various short-term, idiosyncratically experienced regularities emerges into an enduring invariant—across situations, domains, and individuals, and over generations—when collapsing (abstracting) over specific contents.* The "abstracted" invariants which emerge can be the basis for selection of domain-general, *content-abstracted* (DGCA) cognitive structures such as the *representational skeletons* I propose in this chapter. Note that although Cosmides and Tooby (1992, 2002) call such processing mechanisms "content-free" or "content-independent," according to the formulation I present here, *"content-abstracted"* is a better term because it more accurately describes what is really going on. The "enigma" identified by Cosmides and Tooby (2002) of how evolution of cognitive mechanisms responsive to short-term, local information could have occurred is resolved by recognition that natural selection acts upon regularities at multiple levels of abstraction, "designing" responses to environmental regularities over evolutionary time, *even when they achieve sufficient stability and duration only at abstract levels of organization.*

Aside from trying to clear up a major theoretical issue in evolutionary psychology, what I am getting at here is an explanation for the reader of the evolution of the content-independent (more accurately, *content-abstracted*) processing mechanisms (such as *representational skeletons*) encoded into human "mind design" that make thought using abstract, logical principles possible, leading to the explosion of cognitive creativity and innovation found in modern humans. Logical and causal relations really do reflect how the world works, and these abstract, general principles became incorporated into "mind design" as natural selection "filtered" through alternate "brain designs" every generation, selecting those better at representation of abstract relations among things in the world, because such circuit "designs" could exploit the adaptively rich information in these abstract relations to better organize behavior. That is, our brain circuit "design" has built into it, by genetic evolution, innate representations of abstract, general principles (neurally encoded in representational skeletons) of how the world actually works, such as causality, covariation detection, generalization, categorization, and inference, because such circuit "design" enhanced reproductive fitness. This is how humans entered into "the cognitive niche."

Can natural selection operate on "abstracted" levels of regularity in the world to produce such domain-general, content-independent cognitive mechanisms? Though the selection criterion would be "abstract" for content-independent mechanisms charged with the representation of environmentally-based regularity structures regardless of their specific content, natural selection for such cognitive mechanisms could still proceed, as I have attempted to show above. More evidence is provided by Tooby and Cosmides. As Tooby and Cosmides (1992) themselves state (p. 69), "anything that is recurrently true (as a net statistical or structural matter) across large numbers of generations could potentially come to be exploited by an evolving adaptation to solve a problem or to improve performance. For this reason, a major part of adaptationist analysis involves sifting for these environmental or organismic regularities or invariances." Furthermore, what appears abstract may reflect properties of the beholder as much as properties of the world. As Tooby and Cosmides argue (1992, p. 88), "No instance of anything is intrinsically (much less exclusively) either 'general' or 'particular'—these are simply different levels at which any given system of categorization encounters the same world. . . . Selection operated across ancestral hominid populations according to

what were, in effect, systems of categorization, screening . . . variability for any recurrent relationships that were relevant to the solution of adaptive problems." It seems
clear that these evolutionary arguments by Tooby and Cosmides themselves, who have
made many important contributions to evolutionary psychology over the years, confirm the near inevitability of the evolution of domain-general, content-independent
(content-abstracted) processing mechanisms by natural selection for neural representation of abstracted regularities derived from the world. Our ability, and the ability
of some of the other primates, to form abstract concepts and general principles that
permit domain-general, content-abstracted processing, evolved as natural selection
favored brain circuit "designs" which could "find" and represent abstract statistical
regularities of the world in "content-free" representational skeletons (Koenigshofer,
2002). From these beginnings arose flexible, creative, and innovative human "improvisational intelligence."

The non-functionality of a completely modularized mind and the necessity for evolved DGCI cognition

Shepard (1992) notes "Adaptations to universal features of our world are apt to escape
our notice simply because we do not observe anything with which such adaptations
stand in contrast." To provide such a contrast, conduct a brief thought experiment, a
general method of inquiry favored by Shepard (1996).

Imagine an animal with hundreds of specialized mental modules, all of which might
be put to use for the solution of any specific adaptive problem, but imagine that the
brain of such an animal has no disposition to register similarity, patterns, or any other
forms of regularity, structural or statistical, among repeating events. Every event would
be recorded as entirely unique. No patterns would emerge, no generalization, no correlations, no causality, no prediction or inference. The mind of such an animal would
be useless, no matter how many adaptively specialized mental modules it possessed,
unless those modules were equipped by natural selection to represent regularities in
the inputs to them. In short, adaptively specialized modules must include, as part of
their "functional designs" (Cosmides and Tooby, 1987; Tooby and Cosmides, 1992),
"general" mechanisms for regularity representation. Generalization, inference, causality, inference and prediction are domain-general properties of brains evolved by natural
selection to accommodate abstracted regularity structures in the world. The resulting
"mind design" formed the basis for "general" intelligence.

The general disposition of brains to represent regularity is so widespread in
nature that even insects may show this disposition for representation of regularity in
their brains. For example, Lindauer (1961) studying habitat selection by honeybees
observed that when a swarm was offered two highly desirable hives on either side of a

field, scouts vacillated on their choice, depending upon wind direction. They made the final choice between the two sites only after several days of consistent westerly winds, picking the site that was more consistently sheltered from those winds. The bees were responding not only to wind direction, but they apparently were computing, and recognizing the overall pattern or *regularity* in wind direction—an amazing computational accomplishment for a bee brain. Imagine what a human brain must be capable of representing—presumably regularities much more abstract and complex. Recall from chapter 8, Paul Churchland's estimates of the representational power of the activation vectors possible in the human cerebral cortex, with perhaps 50 or more layers of "hidden units" arranged in a parallel distributed processing (PDP) architecture.

One underlying principle in the operation of the various forms of association cortex of complex mammals might be the extraction and representation of environmental regularities of increasing levels of abstraction to generate highly abstract representations of the world in the minds of human beings, including such things as gods, angels, demons, multiple universes, the germ theory of disease, or quantum physics.

What might such circuit design look like? Recall that connectionist networks, even with just 3 layers of processing units, and just one "hidden layer," were capable of extracting and representing quite abstract features out of data inputs. Recall for example that the network, NETtalk, learned to separate vowels from consonants by itself, without being programmed, and that this involved extraction of a general rule, an abstracted regularity, from data inputs fed into the network as it was "trained up" to read and pronounce written English text. Recall that extraction of statistical regularities in environmental inputs is a regular property of PDP neural networks (Clark, 1993). This suggests the possibility that PDP architecture might be a regular feature of processing modules in biological brains, either domain-specific modules as part of their information processing operations, or domain-general (content-independent, or content-abstracted, the term I suggest) "modules," evolved for the "purpose" of extracting abstracted statistical regularities from the environment and representing them in the form of concepts, categories, and so on.

Perhaps PDP connectionist-like neural configurations occur throughout brain systems permitting representation of abstracted regularity structures in the world. The resulting *representational skeletons* would be the source of several types of evolved, genetically encoded, domain-general, content-independent (DGCI) perceptual/cognitive "tools"—all arising out of representations of abstracted regularity structures in the world. Because of the wide distribution of the regularities which drove their evolution, we should expect that these cognitive tools will have very wide distribution throughout the animal kingdom. Therefore, these cognitive tools and the circuit "designs" which support them would appear to be "*general* process," but in another very real sense they are, in fact, evolved *adaptive specializations*, not in response to content-specific regularities, but, instead, to ubiquitous, abstracted regularities of the world. The fact that these "general process" circuit "designs" would be seen "everywhere," and therefore would have been more easily observed, may account for the early historic prominence of "general process" (GP) views of the mind that characterized British Empiricism and behaviorism. Thus, the DGCI perceptual/cognitive circuit mechanisms proposed in this chapter, although usually called "general process," are actually *adaptive specializations* to abstracted regularities of the world with "universal" distribution across niches and problem domains, and as such do not violate "the law of specialization in biology" which Gallistel has invoked as an argument against cognitive mechanisms such as logic or general learning rules emphasized by connectionists and behaviorists.

These DGCI circuit "designs" (perhaps PDP connectionist-like) form essential components of the cognitive architectures, the "mind designs," of a broad range of species because of the ubiquitous distribution of the regularities which "design" them (see Figure 10-1).

Examples of these DGCI circuit "designs" include those which produce:

1. representation/perception/recognition of "causality" among events in the world, derived from higher-order representations abstracted out of the consistent, relational regularities manifested in repeated event covariations in the world (regularities in the distribution of events in temporal "activation space," Koenigshofer, 1995b, 1996c; see discussion of vector coding in chapter 8); in other words, because things in the world that predict other things happen all the time and have been happening since the beginning of life on earth, our brains have evolved circuit "designs" tuned to find event covariations in the world and to interpret them as cause-effect relationships among things in the world, one of the most powerful features of "mind design" central to the production of intelligence; an early form of this same process in brain evolution was evolution of classical and operant conditioning in which animals represent "if-then" predictive relations between events in the environment (Koenigshofer, 1990, 1995b, 1996c);

2. representation of categories and categorical relations of increasing abstraction derived from regularities (similarities) in sensible properties of objects and events in the world at multiple levels of abstraction; these representations include associated representations of statistical regularities in the *consequences* for reproductive fitness of instances of each category (see Shepard, 1994); in other words, many things (objects and events) are similar in the world, that is, there are regularities in the features they display; brain circuits, "designed" for the "purpose," then abstract out the similarities, the regularities in observable (or abstracted) features of things in the world, and as a consequence, these

same circuits form higher order neural representations of the statistically regular properties of similar objects and events to form mental structures we refer to as categories; various categories of objects and events covary with one another and they are associated with specific adaptive consequences (i.e. this category of thing is good for me and my genes, or, alternatively, this category of thing is bad for me and my genes; for example, the category of big hungry bear is associated with the consequence "it is likely to attack me"); and,

3. representation of logical relations and logical operations, derived from operations on categorical relations (derived from abstracted regularities in the world); in other words, categories have logical relations with the individual instances that make up the category, so, for example, the logical statement, "Paul (an instance) is a man (category), all men (category) are mortal (property of a category), therefore (relation) Paul (an instance of the category men) is mortal (property of category to which Paul is an instance). Though this logic is stated in language, animals may still be capable of using similar logical rules even without language (see Kohler, 1927; Bittterman, 2000; Wasserman, 1993).

Observations of the cognitive and learning capacities of a wide range of species confirm that these capacities and the ability of animals to exploit short-term, idiosyncratic information confined to the individual lifetime, information of a seemingly domain-"general," content-independent" nature, is a property widely distributed in the animal kingdom over a broad range of problem domains (Byrne, 2002; Bitterman, 2000; Harlow,1956; Pepperberg, 2002; Savage-Rumbaugh, 1996; Skinner, 1938; Wasserman, 1993). Generalization, inference, expectancy, classical and operant conditioning and habituation as discussed in chapter 7 are also evolved general capacities of brains. In my view, these were derived from natural selection for brain circuit "designs" that accommodated the abstracted regularities of the world each of these involves (see chapter 7 and sections of chapter 8 on vector completion as a mechanism for inference and expectancy; see Figure 8-5).

Some readers may object and claim that this is simply "learning." But such a general characterization is uninformative. It can be mistaken for an explanation but it simply refers to the acquisition of information during the lifetime of the individual without specifying more about the phenomenon. It misses important components of the process, fails to specify what it is that is being represented by the "learning" process, fails to show the relationship between so-called "learning" and other mechanisms for incorporating environmental regularities into the information processing operations of brains, offers little insight about its nature that might help explain its evolutionary origins or about what circumstances in the world make it so ubiquitous yet so diversified in its manifestations, and offers no theoretical basis for understanding the relationships between this type of general process "learning" and more content-specific forms such as the acquisition of information about the location of the pole star in indigo buntings (Gallistel, 1995) or taste aversion learning in rats (Koenigshofer and Nachman, 1974). It is important to note that, in a vector coding representational scheme with PDP connectionist-like circuit "design," such specialized forms of learning are easily conceptualized as involving heavy "doses" of genetically loaded synaptic weights in the learning architecture as a result of natural selection for circuits optimal for these types of specialized learning situations.

The neurorepresentation of statistical regularities (NRSR) is a corollary of the regularity hypothesis of evolution

This line of reasoning derived from the *regularity hypothesis of evolution*, that evolutionary processes select traits in response to long-term *regularities* of the world that have adaptive significance, suggests an innate, general principle of brain organization: because of the significance of environmental regularities in evolution, there has evolved a general disposition of brains for the *neurorepresentation of statistical regularities (NRSR)* in the world at the multiple levels of abstraction at which they occur, whenever they reach sufficient degrees of stability. NRSR arises because of the persistent presence of statistical regularities inherent in the temporal, spatial and material structure of the world (Koenigshofer, 1992, 1994a, 1996a; see also Crosson and Sayre, 1967; Campbell, 1982) and this general feature of the world has been "genetically accommodated" (Shepard, 1987a) into the "design" of neural systems at multiple levels of organization. Churchland's (1989) property-cluster prototypes, social-interaction prototypes, and superordinate prototypes are examples, as are neural representations in a broad range of species of Shepard's (1992) universal environmental regularities such as a three-dimensional, locally Euclidian space with a "gravitationally conferred unique upward direction," one-dimensional time with a "thermodynamically conferred unique forward direction," and cycles of light and dark. But this general organizational principle is even seen at the details of the functional properties of individual neurons and neuronal circuits.

For example, the orientation selectivity of cortical neurons discovered by Hubel and Wiesel (1959) has been described as a manifestation of redundancy exploitation (Ohlshausen & Field, 1996; van Hateren & van der Schaaf, 1998), and redundancy is a form of regularity. Attick and Redlich (1992) argue that receptive field characteristics of visual neurons in V1 have been adapted to exploit regularities in natural images. Barlow (2001) argues that environmental regularities are exploited in sensory representations accounting for a variety of sensory phenomena such as lateral inhibition, the form of feature detectors, the organization of the extrastriate cortex and even aspects of the Gestalt laws of grouping, an idea I suggested several years before (Koenigshofer, 1992).

At more abstracted levels of functioning, Feldman (1997) describes the role of regularities in the formation of categorical representations. In addition, learning sets (Harlow, 1956) can be understood as exploitation by animals of the regularities in sets of similar problems. Monkey are capable of forming concepts as they acquire learning sets about oddity problems to the point where they can achieve one-trial solutions to a new problem similar to a set of problems they have solved before, showing that they have gained insight into the principle of the problem (Johnsgard, 1972, p. 48). That insight might be formed as the monkey extracts a representational skeleton abstracted from its repeated experiences with the problem set.

Classical and operant conditioning are each forms of representation of regularities in the temporal, and thus predictive, relations between events, stimulus events in the former, and an operant behavior and its outcome in the latter (Koenigshofer, 1995b, 1996c). Regarding complex cognitive functions, Nakisa and Plunkett (1998) demonstrate the importance of regularities in input in "open programs of development" crucial in human language acquisition. Additional examples discussed below provide even stronger empirical evidence of the importance of the representation of regularities as a key component in a wide range of sensory, perceptual, and cognitive phenomena as predicted by the ideas presented in this chapter. Note that, according to my formulation, both domain-specific (DS) and domain-general (DG) cognitive mechanisms have their origins in these hierarchical, statistical regularity structures of the world. Some of this regularity structure is domain-specific and some is domain-general or content-abstracted (see discussion above). The distribution over niches and degree of abstraction of the regularities driving natural selection determines whether, and the degree to which, cognitive mechanisms evolve as DS or DG and CI (see figures 10-1 and 10-2).

Early evolution of domain-general NRSR and the Law of the Unspecialized

As noted above, I hypothesize that the disposition of brains to: 1) extract and represent regularities in inputs derived from regularities in the environment (I call this general functional property of brains the *neurorepresentation of statistical regularities, NRSR*), and 2) to construct higher-order representations of regularities in the representations themselves (metaregularities) would have produced selective advantage during brain evolution: 1) by providing increases in representational economy and resultant increases in computational efficiency (Koenigshofer, 1992), and 2) exploiting the "predictiveness" inherent in the regularity structures in the physical environment

(Koenigshofer, 1992, 1994a, 1996a), that is, things regularly follow other things in the world, so representation of such contingencies, regularities, in event occurrences, leads to the possibility of predictions about future. These two factors would likely have been selection criteria very early in the evolution of nervous systems assuring that NRSR would have been an early and persistent feature of the organization of nervous systems generally, most likely heavily conserved to present-day forms (Koenigshofer, 1995a).

There are many reasons to believe that many domain-specific adaptive specializations in neural circuitry would have *followed* this initial, more general stage in evolution of neural organization. This was an early stage in the evolution of "mind design" which I refer to as proto-cognition (Koenigshofer, 1995a) which likely took place *before* the evolution of more domain-specific mechanisms. There is support for this view. For example, the late Harvard paleontologist, Steven J. Gould (Full House, p. 164) references an early and fundamental principle in biology, Cope's (1896) "law of the unspecialized" which states according to Gould "that founding members of highly successful lineages tend to be 'unspecialized' in the sense that they can tolerate a wide range of habitats and climates, and that they do not possess complex and highly specific adaptations to narrow behaviors or modes of life . . . [this] law of the unspecialized has held up well, and would be endorsed by evolutionary biologists today." Evolutionary specializations must have something to specialize from. On the view presented here, then, domain-specific (DS) cognitive devices such as those described by prominent evolutionary psychologists are likely to be adaptive specializations derived from evolutionary modifications of neural circuit "designs" initially more general and unspecialized which were "designed" according to selection criteria tending to favor NRSR. The significant adaptive advantages that NRSR provides with regard to increased representational economy and computational efficiency as well as exploitation of predictiveness of events by representations of their regularity makes it highly likely that "general" processing (derived from NRSR) must have been conserved during the subsequent evolution of adaptively specialized circuitry. Thus, on my view, we should expect that DS devices will show elements of a general disposition for NRSR embedded within DS processing operations. Additionally, whatever domain-general (DG) mechanisms may exist, they also will have design features consistent with the principle of NRSR proposed here. For example, it is well known that one of the features of conditioning is stimulus generalization, and this property of "mind design" can be understood as due to the extraction and representation of statistical regularities in stimuli in the environment and their associated implications for reproductive fitness (i.e. is this good for me and my genes or not). Stimulus generalization seems to be built into brain "design" as a default disposition, perhaps just one manifestation of a general disposition for NRSR in brains, as I hypothesize. Categorization and covariation detection, both domain-general processes (Wasserman, 1993) are also dependent upon NRSR. These observations confirm the hypothesis that evolution has favored a general disposition with brain "design" for NRSR, which by the way, is a known property of the operation of PDP connectionist-style processing architectures (Clark, 1993).

Considering these arguments, it is likely that for a wide range of species, whatever architectures exist mediating cognitive mechanisms, no matter how specialized the circuitry becomes, neural architectures must retain an organization that readily extracts and represents regularities in the world, of all sorts, of various durations and periodicity, at many levels of abstraction, and, in some species, even regularities in the representations themselves constructed by that architecture (representation of these meta-regularities is a possible source of some of the more abstract "higher cognitive functions" including components of Cosmides and Tooby's "improvisational intelligence" based in the formation and use of abstract propositions).

An example illustrative of representation of regularities (NRSR) as a general principle in information processing by neural systems at all levels, from sensory processing and up, is provided by Mackay (1986). He finds that, rather than features or images, the capture of covariation (a form of environment regularity to be discussed again later) forms the basis for representations in the visual system. Another is provided by Troyer et.al. (1998) who report the importance of input regularities in development of visual cortical organization by "correlation-based plasticity rules" and argue for Hebbian covariation-based intracortical circuitry in the mediation of the invariance of orientation tuning under changes in stimulus contrast, as well as a variety of other response properties of layer 4 visual cortical neurons. At other levels of neural functioning, the regular reoccurrence of features in different instances of objects and events can form basis for formation of categories even in animals (Pepperberg, 2002; Wasserman, 1993). In language acquisition, regularities in auditory features of spoken words experienced repeatedly within the differing contexts offered by a range of sentences in a range of circumstances may be one possible mechanism used by children to extract acoustic invariants which permit them to discover the boundaries of spoken words embedded within a continuous auditory stream (Koenigshofer, 1994a).

In master level chess players, it is the representation of regularities in the patterns of arrangements of chess pieces on the board that accounts for expertise in chess. Gobet and Simon (1996) note that "positions in chess games (with about 25 pieces on the board) can be stored in memory and reconstructed almost perfectly by masters after as little as a 5-s view of the board." By contrast, weak players can only recall some half dozen pieces. Significantly, this superiority of masters over weak players "nearly vanishes if the pieces are placed at random on the board" indicating that "the masters are recognizing and storing familiar patterns of pieces. . ." Experienced players become capable of higher order representations of regularity structures in spatial arrangements of pieces, facilitating the rapid assessment of the board, its efficient recall and efficient mental manipulation of patterns of pieces as wholes in the construction and planning of effective moves to come. Representation and storage of regularities in the spatial locations of pieces abstracted into higher order representations of these spatial regularities (something akin to spatial Gestalts or wholes) produces more economic and efficient spatial representations and consequent increases in efficiency of processing, accounting for much of the speed and superiority of chess masters.

There may be something like a module or set of modules related to spatial memory, planning ahead, anticipating outcomes of various spatial arrangements of objects, and even "a theory of mind module" (Tooby & Cosmides, 1992) which might be co-opted into sophisticated chess playing. The recruitment of groups of DS devices is often proposed by EPs as the source of human behavioral flexibility (Cosmides and Tooby, 1992, 2000; Symons, 1992). But even if such were the case, still a universal domain-general cognitive process involving the representation of regularity structures in inputs is also at work and is essential to the performance of good chess players. The representational economy provided by NRSR, and resultant gains in processing efficiency involved here, is as important as a spatial module, a theory of mind module or some other combination of DS cognitive devices, which traditional EPs might use to explain chess playing. This constitutes an interesting example because models of chess playing have been generalized by some cognitive psychologists to explanations of expertise in other cognitive domains including medical diagnosis, engineering and architectural design, as well as others (Charness, 1992; Ericsson & Staszewski, 1989, for complete references see Gobet & Simon, 1996).

Given the complexity of cognitive functioning in primates and other "advanced" mammals, it seems clear that representation of meta-regularities is not beyond the scope of what natural selection may have "designed" into information processing systems. One simple example is learning sets. A more complex example, as noted above, is the formation of complex categories and concepts, or the application of relational regularities abstracted from one domain to other problem domains to generate creativity and novel problem solutions.

Representational Skeletons, creativity, and "general process" cognition

Consistent with the principle of NRSR proposed in this chapter, once regularity structures are represented, then *abstracted* features common to the more specific lower-order regularity structures can be used to form an abstracted *representational skeleton*, incorporating an abstracted, "content-independent" or "content-free" relational structure, upon which can be hung content-specific instances of novel content in order to derive predictive projections about the novel content. That is, *creative thought* about novel instances is generated by substitution of new specific contents onto a representation of a statistically abstracted regularity structure (a "representational skeleton"), which because it is abstracted, representing abstracted relationships, is content-independent and so extremely flexible in the range of situations to which it can be applied. This formulation is reminiscent of what has been called metaphorical reasoning. In other words, meta-phorical thought utilizes higher order representations extracted, or *abstracted*, out of lower order regularities in the environment, and these higher order representations "ignore" content-specific details and retain content-independent relational information which can be applied to new problem spaces and novel content-specific situations. In the NRSR theory that I am presenting in this chapter, the "knowledge" that is applied to the novel situation is in the form of representations (perhaps in activation vectors using "vector" coding by neuronal populations) of abstracted, statistical, relational "features" of the world, which by virtue of the wide distribution of such constant relational "features" of the world, can be applied successfully over a wide range of problem domains to produce creative solutions to novel problems (novel in domain-specific or content-specific details, but regular and general, in abstracted, relational structure). Could this be basis for Cosmides and Tooby's "improvisational intelligence"? I believe that it is, and more. It can explain how creative thinking can occur and even offers a metaphori-cal model of the possible neural representations involved (abstracted representational skeletons upon which can be "hung" an enormous range of items of specific content). NRSR theory combined with representational skeletons can explain "improvisational intelligence" and its evolution and thus solves the "enigma" defined by Cosmides and Tooby in their 2002 article.

As noted earlier, economy of representation would have been favored by natural selection because it would have increased representational and processing efficiency in neural systems. Evidence from other quarters is consistent with this view. As pre-dicted by this hypothesis, evidence from PET studies shows that *increases in processing efficiency* in the brains of humans as measured by regional metabolic rates are associ-ated with learning, and with *increased levels of abstraction of representation* (Haier et al., 1988, 1992). The formulation presented here is consistent with efficiency models of differences in intelligence among people and results by Haier showing that higher IQ persons show less brain activity when performing cognitive tasks than lower IQ people. Such persons may possess circuit "designs" (microarchitectures) more efficient at formation of representations of environmental regularities and, more crucially, of meta-representations of regularities embedded within those regularity representations themselves.

Representational economy leads to processing efficiency and selection for DG cognitive mechanisms

NRSR of increasing levels of abstraction as a general principle in the organization of brains, favored by natural selection on grounds of representational and thus processing efficiency (as well as gains in predictive value of representations incorporating consis-tent environmental regularities), might well have provided evolutionary groundwork for development of "general" (DGCI) cognitive functions. Abstracted, more general, and more inclusive representations of adaptively significant attributes of the world would permit processing operations which would not have to be repeated anew for every instance of adaptively similar properties of situations, objects, relations and events. NRSR may well be the foundational organizational principle in the evolution of brains which naturally led to the processes of generalization and categorical operations in neural systems. These processes themselves were then presumably favored early on in evolution by gains in representational and computational efficiency as well as more specific adaptive advantages involving improved representation of the predictability and redundancy of events and event classes.

Categorization, generalization, and the formation of concepts of increasing levels of abstraction are "general" cognitive mechanisms (both domain-general and species-general) and these "general process" mechanisms involve representational strategies derived (at least in large part) from the general "bias" of brains toward extraction and representation of environmentally derived regularity structures (NRSR). Each of these DG, SG mechanisms would be expected to have wide distribution in the animal kingdom and across many problem domains because of selective advantages they provide by increasing representational economy (RE) and generating consequent gains in processing efficiency (PE). These cognitive abilities, as predicted, are found over a broad array of species across many problem domains, including humans, non-human primates (Sue-Savage Rumbaugh, 1996; Gardner and Gardner, 1975; Kohler, 1927), parrots (Pepperberg, 2002), rodents and pigeons (Wasserman, 1995), and insects (Bitterman, 2000). Work by Sue Savage-Rumbaugh with Bonobo chimpanzees, showing some interesting human language competencies, including an apparent comprehension of some aspects of syntax in these animals, suggests that, conservatively, at least some of what is required for competency in human language comprehension may be acquired without the benefit of evolved language-specific acquisition "devices" (work by Pepperberg, 2002, with Grey Parrots is also of interest here; contrast this view with Pinker and Chomsky) and suggests operation of computationally powerful, "general" cognitive and learning processes found in the Bonobo brain. Clearly there cannot be a Chomskian LAD in the brain of this non-human species (unless it is formed by experiential influences molding circuitry genetically organized for more general processes such as complex auditory analysis, or a general disposition for the neurorepresentation of statistical regularities experienced during the lifetime of the animal). Though never exceeding the level of competency of very young human children, apes such as the Bonobo, Konzi, can exhibit surprising sophistication in comprehension of grammatically complex spoken English sentences (Savage-Rumbaugh, 1996), suggesting that learning processes much more general in nature have substantial power to effectively process complex linguistic inputs, clearly without benefit of any domain-specific human language module in Konzi's Bonobo brain.

Among other things, Konzi's performance demonstrates that cognitive and learning processes (and the circuits which underlie them) which are *not* adaptively specialized to the solution of a particular problem at hand can produce some impressive results. That Konzi shows any competency at all in human language comprehension is itself theoretically important. If Konzi is utilizing some general cognitive and learning capacities present in the Bonobo, then it seems very difficult to characterize such processes as "weak" and "inefficient" and therefore adaptively unimportant (Cosmides and Tooby, 1987, 1992, 2000, 2001) or as non-existent (Gallistel, 1992, 1995). By contrast, these results suggest general mechanisms in cognition which are computationally powerful and efficient even for acquisition of a skill clearly not a part of the evolutionary heritage of the Bonobo. Human language acquisition clearly can't be a problem Bonobos consistently encountered in the evolutionary history of the species since no humans were around for most of their existence on this planet. Furthermore, where is the danger of combinatorial explosion (often cited by EPs as reason why effective, efficient, domain-general mechanisms couldn't exist, Cosmides and Tooby, 2000, 2002) manifested in the comprehension of spoken English by Konzi, if Konzi is using one or more domain-general cognitive mechanisms in this sophisticated performance?

If, as some EPs might argue, Konzi is utilizing some set of domain-specific cognitive mechanisms which have been recruited into the language comprehension task, then this weakens the concept of modularity itself which proposes domain-specific computational rules, which by definition are limited to specific problem spaces. If a domain-specific cognitive mechanism can be recruited into other functions, then it is to some degree general, more general, at least, than typically implied by EPs' definitions of adaptively specialized, domain-specific cognitive modules.

Though adaptively specialized domain-specific cognitive and learning mechanisms certainly exist, it seems clear that computationally powerful, domain-general mechanisms also exist, and these may well be operating in Konzi's ability for impressive comprehension of spoken human language.

Konzi's ability to understand spoken English sentences raises other issues about just how dependent upon domain-specific mechanisms language acquisition in humans might be, and about what roles more general learning capacities might play. Could early stages of language acquisition be dependent upon general conditioning processes, acting in concert perhaps with modules for "social intelligence" (Bloom, 2002) and a module for processing complexly patterned auditory inputs? Could such early experience with linguistic inputs "tweak" a "module" for processing complexly patterned auditory inputs, not necessarily linguistic in nature, into a language acquisition module? Karmiloff-Smith (1998) argued that specific language impairment (SLI), a developmental disorder in which children show a very specific deficit in grammar with otherwise normal intelligence (supporting existence of a grammar module), may actually result from a subtle deficit in acoustic processing in early childhood. Findings by

Muente (1997) show that ERP components (electrical activity of the brain associated with response to a specific discrete stimulus input) previously identified with specific aspects of language processing are actually elicited by a more general class of inputs, not specific to a particular stage of language processing (e.g. orthographic, syntactic, semantic) and, in some cases, not even specifically linguistic.

Along similar lines, other evidence implicates neural organization genetically more general than suggested by current EP models. Month-old infants can discriminate between *ba* and *pa*, an important distinction for later language comprehension. Similar studies have shown that infants who have habituated to hearing one language, such as Dutch, dishabituate when presented a different language, such as Japanese. This evidence was initially interpreted to indicate a genetic predisposition of children to pay special attention to language sounds. However, similar results were subsequently obtained with monkeys, so distinguishing Dutch from Japanese sounds apparently does not require a special language readiness of the brain (Ramus, Hauser, Miller, Morris & Mehler, 2000).

The development in childhood of what appear to be cortical modules for reading and writing, widespread only in recent history (Ellis & Young, 1988), is consistent with this idea that experience modifies circuits initially more general in nature into ones more functionally specific. Confirming this interpretation is the observation that ERP activity (electrical activity of the brain associated with response to a specific discrete stimulus input) associated with language comprehension of known words is bilateral and widely distributed over the cortical surface in normal 13 month old children, becoming lateralized and centralized around traditional language areas only after 20 months of age (Stiles, 1997). Similarily, in a discussion that I had with Sue Savage-Rumbaugh I suggested, and she agreed, that acquired experience with language stimuli may organize, for language, more general processing mechanisms in brains of chimpanzees and perhaps in the human brain as well (Savage-Rumbaugh, private communication, 1996). This raises the interesting possibility of culturally transmitted modifications in brain organization, generation after generation, perhaps obviating, or at least supplementing, the need for genetic transmission of all of the requisite circuit organization (Koenigshofer, 2002). This view is consistent with evidence that the human genome contains insufficient information to specify many details of brain organization and must be supplemented by information from environmental inputs during the lifetime (Deacon, 1996).

None of this is to say that important *domain-specific* cognitive mechanisms do not exist. I believe they do. The key point is that, in addition to DS mechanisms, there are also adaptively critical, computationally powerful, *domain-general*, content-general (content-abstracted) cognitive and learning mechanisms in the "mind designs" of animals and humans (Koenigshofer, 2002). And, as research with connectionist neural networks demonstrates, the kind of representation of *regularity structures* in the world that I have described above, can lead to cognitive functions in representational systems, whether natural (brains) or artificial (connectionist neural networks).

For example, as discussed in chapter 8, connectionist networks (see Figure 8-4) can perform tasks with a cognitive-like character with little initial structure. Categorization and generalization (as in NETtalk) occur as part of the dynamics of the network, as large sets of inputs are "pushed through" its layers (Koenigshofer, 1991, 1992,1994a, 1995a, 1996a; see Clark, 1993). As such, connectionist networks provide a model of learning, domain-general learning, and they suggest a model of some of the domain-general components of cognition such as categorization, generalization, and even inference and expectancy (see Figure 8-5). But connectionist networks suggest additional possibilities.

Recall from the discussion in chapter 8 that information is represented and stored in artificial neural networks by patterns of "connection weights," analogous to strengths of synaptic connections between specific neurons in a real biological brain. In a connectionist network which starts out with *neutral* connection weights (as is usually the case at the outset, prior to "training up" the network), as inputs are "pushed" through its layers, the weights then become adjusted by the network's "experiences" (the inputs that are "pushed through it"). This systematic change in connection weights with "experience" is how representations are formed and stored—and it is the means by which learning takes place in artificial neural networks. Significantly, this provides us a model of learning and representation in real biological brains. But it can also provide a model of the genetic evolution of brain circuit "design."

Genetic evolution of brain circuit "designs" could be largely a matter of natural selection for specific connection weights (in brains, synaptic strengths) within populations of neurons, thus forming functional circuit "designs" perhaps sculpted out of large populations of "uncommitted" neurons. This process of neural sculpting is known to take place during brain development, before birth, and after, as part of what is termed "programmed cell death." In genetic evolution, environmental regularities consistently present, over evolutionary time, could provide the conditions required for the natural selection of specific synaptic weights in specific populations of neurons that would produce representations in the brain of adaptively important regularities of the world present over sufficiently long periods of time (this bears similarity to what Gerald Edelman at UC Santa Cruz has called "neural Darwinism"). It is even possible that the parallel distributed processing (PDP) architecture characteristic of artificial neural networks might evolve in real biological brains as a long-term evolutionary response to the consistent presence of abstracted regularity structures in the world, consistent with the ideas I have presented earlier in this chapter. Natural selection may have "sifted" through countless alternative "circuit designs" over millions of years, "finding" and preserving, through higher rates of reproduction in each generation, the genes responsible for those "designs" which were better able to represent environmental regularities that had implication for survival and reproduction.

In a sense then, all cognition, and perhaps all brain "design," is "stimulus-driven" and yet ultimately genetic and evolutionary in origin. This is evident when brain development is conceived as occurring over a broad range of time frames, from the evolutionary down to the environmental fluctuations which occur within an individual lifetime.

Brain evolution may have begun in very simple ancestral creatures with very simple nerve nets, similar perhaps to those found in present-day jellyfish. The circuits that form among the relatively few neurons of such a simple nervous system would receive their specific information processing features from the natural selection of specific synaptic weights (represented in jellyfish DNA) within the nerve net of the species. By this process, the jellyfish evolves circuit "design" that organizes behavior which enhances its survival and reproduction. Remember circuit "designs" that don't enhance survival and reproduction as well as alternative "designs," available due to genetic variability within the species, get "weeded out" by natural selection. The better "designs" are thereby preserved because the individuals who happen to carry DNA that is responsible for the better "design" survive and reproduce with greater frequency, assuring that their favorable traits, in this case specific arrangements of synaptic strengths, are preserved into future generations.

Perhaps the reader is already anticipating where I am going with this. As species diverge from common ancestry, some evolve more neural tissue—larger numbers of neurons are produced during embryological brain development due to mutations, perhaps in DNA switches (see chapter 6). The additional numbers of neurons provide evolutionary opportunity for the development of new, more complex circuit "designs" capable of organizing more complex behavior. With more neurons, circuits with much greater structural and functional complexity become possible. The sheer volume and complexity of the information that can be represented and processed expands.

All the while, circuit "designs" are being tested and retested in the world by the animals that carry them, and those neuronal configurations that work best, those that best represent the adaptively significant regularities in the world, are preserved while those less well fit to the regularities of the world are discarded. Circuits organizing feeding and mating and simple defensive behaviors would have already evolved in the simplest of jellyfish-like ancestral creatures and these neuronal configurations, so critical to biological fitness, would be aggressively conserved as new species evolved.

As new species diverge, some of them undergo genetic mutations that produce even more neural tissue during their embryological development, providing more neurons, and thus the potential for neural circuitry with even greater capacity for representation of adaptively significant environmental regularities. By the way, representations of statistical regularities in the world include the representation of probabilities—probabilistic information about the likelihood of anticipated events (suggesting the existence in brains of something like *probability detectors* or *probability assessment operators*, perhaps derived as a component of PDP-style processing and represented as scalars quantifying probabilities in activation vectors). Evidence for some form of representation of probabilities of events is seen in the behavior of animals in some conditioning situations (Koenigshofer, 1995b, 1996c), and the use of probability information is certainly evident in our own decision-making and in our mental assessments about the likelihoods of possible future events (Koenigshofer, 1995b, 1996c).

If, as I suspect, neural network-like PDP circuit "designs" eventually did evolve in ancient creatures, then rudimentary proto-cognitive functions such as stimulus generalization and simple categorization would have emerged from the operations of these primitive nervous systems by virtue of the dynamics of PDP processing already described (Koenigshofer, 1995a). Once this innovation took place in the evolution of nervous systems, the advantages (described earlier in this chapter) would have driven the evolution of PDP connectionist-like architectures with increasing numbers of layers of "hidden units." Capacities for representation and processing of information about regularities in the world would have exploded. Sophisticated *prototype activation vectors* (recall Paul Churchland's vector coding) would become possible and, over time, as more and more layers of "hidden units" were added to evolving brains, the subtlety and complexity of the activation vectors possible within them would produce corresponding increases in cognitive power and an emerging "intelligence."

Recall Paul Churchland's speculations, discussed in chapter 8, about the number of layers of "hidden units" that may characterize the human brain. He suggested the possible existence of up to 50 such processing layers in our brains. Representation of regularities of high degrees of abstraction would become possible in brains like these, making possible, as I have argued above, the highly abstract, domain-general thinking that is so characteristic of the "improvisational intelligence" of human beings.

This story may appear to leave out the domain-specific processing mechanisms described throughout this book, but it doesn't. As natural selection "filtered" through competing circuit "designs" finding and preserving better and better PDP connectionist-like neuronal architectures, evolving domain-general cognitive capacities, it also was selecting for specific "loadings" on specific synapses within the evolving complexity of undifferentiated PDP circuitry to "tweak" that circuitry into particular domain-specific directions. For example, incorporation of the universal regularities in the world described by Shepard (see discussion about Shepard's universal regularities, above) would have likely taken place very early in brain evolution. Genetically evolved "loading" of synaptic strengths at particular synapses within an overall PDP neural "design" would give brains the adaptive advantages of both domain-general and domain-specific processing. Whenever mutations occurred which caused synaptic weights to take on values that benefited adaptive processing, by the formation of adaptively useful circuits, such mutations would be favored by natural selection and preserved over generations.

One can imagine a pallet of PDP circuits (in addition to content-specific circuits for feeding, mating, and so on) initially relatively undifferentiated in early evolution (remember Gould's reference to the law of the unspecialized), which becomes progressively more and more genetically "loaded" by genetically evolved synaptic strengths within the overall PDP brain "design." Thus, at birth, as a result of genetically controlled processes during embryological brain development, the animal or human comes equipped with an underlying PDP connectionist-like neural architecture capable of producing all of the domain-general cognitive capacities discussed throughout this chapter. Then, superimposed upon this PDP connectionist-like neural architecture is a large collection of particular domain-specific processing dispositions such as a fear module, a theory of mind module, a sexual jealousy module, and so on. These domain-specific mechanisms or modules are in the form of a huge number of genetically determined synaptic weights dispersed precisely throughout specific brain systems, as a consequence of millions of years of natural selection for specific configurations of such synaptic strengths. Now, add to this, the capacity for modification of many synapses by experience during the lifetime of the individual and we have a genetically evolved brain "design" that is capable of domain-general, content-independent processing, interacting with domain-specific processing, including capacity for modification during the individual lifetime through learning. We have a brain very much like the human brain. In fact, it is my view that, at least in general outline, this is pretty much how the human brain is organized, and the story outlined here is a plausible tale of how this particular "mind design" came about over the course of evolution.

Note that in this view, at one point, the brain is a kind of "blank slate" but the "blankness" isn't present at birth as the British empiricist John Locke proposed, it is far, far, back in the evolution of brain designs. The brain is "blank," relatively undifferentiated, only at its very beginnings in evolution, probably pre-jellyfish. Then, in some metaphorical sense, the "hand of experience writes upon it" (remember this quote from the British empiricist camp) but "the hand of experience" is not what Locke and his followers, including behaviorists and other proponents of the Standard Social Science Model, imagined. In my view "the hand of experience" refers to the effects of the environment on "mind design" and behavior, but not beginning at birth. Believers in Locke's "blank slate" imagine that "the hand of experience," the effects of the environment, act only on the animal or human during its own lifetime through learning. However, they got the timing wrong. Most of the effects of "experience" took place over the evolutionary history of each species as the accumulated "experiences," the effects of the environment, on the entire species over its evolutionary history directed natural selection toward adaptive brain "design." Experience, that is, the effects of the environment, have mostly taken place during the eons of evolution of brain "design" in each species, long, long before the birth of the individual. Brain "design," and thus "mind design" and the organization of behavior, is driven by the environment, it is thus "stimulus-driven," but the primary effect of the environment is on brain circuit design during brain evolution. By the time, an individual human being is born, the "hand of experience," the accumulated effects of the environment on the evolution of the species, has already written most of the book. There is no "blank slate" at birth. Far from it. There is *in place at birth*, an evolved PDP connectionist-like neural architecture along with a mass of *domain-specific synaptic loadings* all honed to processing "perfection" by millions of years of environmental influence directing natural selection of brain and mind "design."

Viewed in this way, many of the apparent inconsistencies between evolutionary and connectionist approaches to cognition disappear, and the rift between these two theoretical approaches to the mind (Gallistel, 1995) vanishes.

The Universal Significance of Regularities: Connectionist Neural Networks

To clarify some of these ideas, it will be useful to review the details of how connectionist networks operate. First, regarding the role of regularities in cognition, it should not escape the attention of the reader that regularities in the world play a central role in connectionist modeling of cognition, although, in this case, circuit organization develops as a result of "learning" by artificial neural networks (modification of "connection weights"), not as a "genetic accommodation" over the course of evolution. Recall the discussion of NETtalk (Rosenberg and Sejnowski, 1987) in chapter 8. This connectionist network was trained to transform printed text into audible speech. Cluster analysis revealed a hierarchy of partitions in weight space (Clark, 1993, p. 54) which captured and represented hierarchical systems of statistical regularities not explicitly expressed in the structure of the inputs (Churchland, 1989, p. 176). This is not a unique feature of NETtalk, but a regular feature of many connectionist networks. These networks discover common properties of individual cases and abstract them into the distinguishing features defining a category, represented in connection weights in a layer of hidden units within the network. Of interest is the observation by Clark (1993, p. 162) that with a threshold number of inputs, networks exhibit "a sudden dramatic leap in generalization performance" to a form of representation which allows "the net to have knowledge of the principle or concept independent of the examples used in training" (Clark, 1993). [Note the similarity between this description and a content-general, or content-independent cognitive mechanism. This is reminiscent of the performance of monkeys and human children in the acquisition of learning sets following repeated exposure to individual instances of a particular type of problem. Even monkeys gain knowledge of the underlying principle common to all instances of the problem type, so that eventually they solve complex cognitive tasks in a single-trial (Johnsgard, 1972)]. Thus, by virtue of the dynamics of the connectionist network, statistical regularities inherent in the inputs to the network can generate rule-governed behavior (based in a content-independent or content-abstracted representation) as a consequence of, but in some sense transcending, the statistical properties in the input data.

According to Clark (1993), because of the structure of neural networks, they will "uncover which sets of features are most commonly present" in sets of inputs and they will uncover "commonly occurring groupings of features. ." In short, statistical regularities in occurrence of features and co-occurrence of sets of features will be extracted by networks as a natural consequence of their architecture and dynamics. Because networks represent similar cases by means of overlapping hidden-unit vectors, prototype representations are automatically extracted, forming the basis for a machine form of categorization (for example, NETtalk extracted representations of consonants vs. vowels as it was "trained up" to pronounce written English text; other networks have extracted even more abstract prototype or categorical representations without being specifically programmed to do so, Clark, 1993; Churchland, 1989). Connectionist networks, like the domain-specific processing mechanisms of Shepard or Cosmides and Tooby, also represent regularities, but regularities represented in connectionist systems may be short-term and content-idiosyncratic (and thus variable). Connectionist systems can extract and represent content-independent regularity structures in inputs "pushed" through them, forming representational structures similar to what I have called representational skeletons. Keep in mind, that this is accomplished "automatically" by the structure and dynamics of the "circuit design" of the connectionist network. That information processing systems exist, albeit man-made, that can accomplish these feats of abstraction suggests that similar circuit "designs" might exist in organic brains. And they may even provide the basic hardware needed for the production of representational skeletons giving human beings our extraordinary capacities for flexible, creative, and innovative abstract thought.

Mind design, culture, and existential meaning

To fully understand our human nature, minds, and behavior we must explicitly recognize that we are biological entities first and foremost. Our brains and minds are products of, and subject to biological laws, all derived from the most fundamental of the biological laws—evolution. Our minds and behavior are shaped by culture and the experiences unique to each of us, but really only to a relatively minor degree, compared to the overwhelming influence on our "mind design" of the genetic evolution of our species. In fact, cultures themselves are really biological products—they arise from the universal, genetically evolved properties of the human brain, an organ with biological—evolutionary—origins. Cultures are a form of adaptation and they serve biological functions. Living in groups for us, as for the other social species, is also a specific evolved form of adaptation. We are social because of our evolved "mind design." Then, culture follows *after* the evolution of social existence as an adaptive "strategy." Being social and being cultural are forms of adaptation. We didn't learn to be social or learn to make cultures, although learning is needed for culture to emerge as a form of adaptation—being social and cultural creatures is part of our innate nature as a species; we reflect our social and cultural instincts. We are not social *because* of culture; we are cultural because we were first social. Learning can explain *differences* between cultures and their idiosyncratic features but it can't explain why we are social and cultural in the first place.

Being social requires a specific kind of brain "design" which includes genetically evolved emotional and cognitive adaptations that make social life possible, and which make it *work* as a means of solving our species-typical biological problems. Among other things we had to evolve brain circuit configurations that equipped us with just the right balance between self-interest and altruism, as part of our human nature. For social life to exist, there must be sufficient benefits for biological fitness to living in groups, but as we have seen in chapter 9, altruism cannot go too far; it must be balanced with sufficient degrees of self-interest. We have explored many of these social adaptations in this book, from the default assumption of free will, which "greases" our social interactions making them smooth and efficient (chapters 4 and 5), to our social emotions such as love for our children, our relatives, and our compassion for and attachments to non-relatives with whom we affiliate and identify (chapter 9), to specific brain "modules" such as the "theory of mind module" without which social interaction disintegrates, as in the case of severe autism.

Then, superimposed upon social life as an adaptation, there *follows* culture. Culture in us, just like in the several other social species known to have culture (though rudimentary, of course, compared to human cultures), depends upon additional brain adaptations—the genetically evolved capacity to learn by watching (chapter 7), the genetically evolved motives (emotions) to imitate, and to cooperate in specific ways, and then in us, the evolved capacity for language which adds power and efficiency to these other forms of *cultural transmission*.

Cultures stem from our underlying genetically evolved "human nature" which arises from our particular species-typical "mind design." Each culture depends upon the same set of universal human capacities for learning, thought and feeling characteristic of our species, no matter the ethnicity or culture—all biological products of our genetically evolved brain and mind "design." It is this set of evolved human "instincts" that makes cultural transmission our specialty as a species, and which is the ultimate source of the cultural products that separate us so much from other species—science and technology, complex political systems, religions, and complex economies. Even our most characteristic human trait that separates us most from other species, our ability for complex and abstract thought, is dependent upon specific evolved features of our brain "design."

We are not prisoners of genes, but we are products of them, and we are so to a much larger and determining degree than common sense and the "biologically naïve" standard model in the social sciences recognizes. Going back millions upon millions of years, from the first vertebrates that ventured out of the sea onto the land, the processes of evolution by natural selection shaped our "mind design" as surely as they shaped our bodies. Mind design like body design evolved in service of reproductive fitness. To truly understand ourselves, that fact must remain at the center of our awareness. We are "survival machines" and our bodies, brains, and minds serve the same master, the genes. Still, our emotions, our relationships with others of our kind, our ability to explore the wonders and beauty of this world that our brain's mind provides us, all lend wonderful meaning to the extraordinary journey we call "life."

NOTES

1. Many theorists assume that cognition is dependent upon linguistic operations performed on sentence-like representations. However, this view skirts the issue of cognition in animals and human infants and ignores the likelihood that fundamental properties of cognition evolved long before human language and that evolution of language itself must have been constrained by pre-linguistic cognitive structures. In a 1992 paper (Koenigshofer, 1992), I argued that many forms of cognition are not dependent upon language. Similarities among Gestalt principles of perceptual organization, conditioning, stimulus generalization, inductive reasoning, and organizational effects in memory suggest what I call a "generalized minimum principle" (a principle of representational economy) which constrains information processing in brains accounting for basic features of perception, conditioning, and cognition. Strategies of neural representation which exploit redundancy as a mean of increasing processing efficiency have been favored by natural selection, producing brains which have become increasingly efficient redundancy-extractors constructing increasingly higher-order "information-reduced" (in the classic sense explicated in the information theory of Shannon and Weaver, 1949), meaningfully-rich, efficient representations of the world. This *generalized minimum principle* acted as an early constraint in the evolution of perceptual processes accounting for many of the emergent properties of perception such as imagistic representation. Conditioning and cognition are seen as extensions of perceptual processes in which event relations are coded and represented in probabilistic, space/time Gestalts incorporating hierarchical systems of information-reduced, predictive rules about distal spatial and temporal regularities. Evolved, genetically encoded representation of such distal event relations present over evolutionary time frames might form basis for species-specific "theories" of event relations, an innate "syntax" of reality construction (Koenigshofer, 1992).

2. Historically, conditioning has been imagined to be dependent upon a simple physical "linking up" (via changes in synaptic connections perhaps via Hebbian rules) of neural representations of CS and UCS or operant behavior and effect

of the behavior. In this classic view, the psychological/behavioral link between "associated" events must be neurally encoded by a literal connection at synapses which fucntionally joins neural representations of the "associated" events. Thus, a conductive linkage of events is perceived to be the essence of conditioning at the behavioral and neural levels of analysis. However, behavioral data indicates that conditioning actually involves encoding of information about contingency or probabilistic predictive relations between events, rather than a simple association (Rescorla, 1992). This paradigmatic model of conditioning has limited the experimental questions asked about the neural mechanisms of conditioning and learning and has unduly constrained the possible answers forthcoming from such work. This is especially true about the role of time in conditioning. Within the traditional associationist view, the only role time plays is to assure that the connection forms. Time itself has no representation. Time is not conceptualized as a variable in its own right, requiring representation of its values and involving computations based upon those values. Evidence that the predictive value of a conditioned stimulus (CS) is a crucial factor in its conditionability (Rescorla, 1992) suggests that conditioning requires representation of the regularity with which one stimulus predicts the occurrence of another. I argued in a paper in 1996 (Koenigshofer, 1996c) that conditioning involves representation in the brain of the locations of events in a temporal map, and the computation of their covariations of occurrence , and thus the conditional probabilities inherent in those covariations. In that paper, I proposed that brains compute, represent, store, and retrieve temporal coordinates of events in a temporal representational "space" similar to abstract state spaces discussed by Paul Churchland (1989). Additionally, brains compute from this "temporal representational space" higher-order temporal representations for a variety of adaptive uses. Conditioning is one of these adaptive uses involving such derived representations, within temporal activation space. In this view, conditioning depends upon derived representations of event covariations with particular conditional probabilities (Koenigshofer, 1996c). Such representations are derived from extraction of temporal statistical regularities between the events of a covariant pair, as two events, such as CS and US, occur repeatedly in a consistent temporal sequence in the world. These representations include the magnitude of the regularity and thus its predictive utility. The representation of this statistical regularity, and its magnitude, in a temporal space, is stored in a connectionist-style weight vector (synaptic strengths) in a deep layer of "hidden units" whose weights define the temporal component of an abstract feature activation space, perhaps in frontal cortex, hippocampus, and/or cerebellum or other structures (see below). In this theoretical view, to accomplish an abstract feature/temporal activation space, recalling connectionist-style representation (Churchland, 1989), a temporal component (one or more scalars) forms a part of every activation vector representing an object/event. This process can be envisioned as a "temporal tagging" of activation vector representations of objects and events (and of the subsequent stored weight vectors), locating them in an activation space (Churchland, 1989) with at least one temporal dimension. This is analogous to the location of events and objects in connectionist-style neuronal spatial mappings of the distal world in sensory qualia spaces (see Figures 8-1, 8-2, and 8-3) and in abstract conceptual spaces (Churchland, 1989). Consistent with this hypothesis, Honig (1981) has suggested that animals may construct mental temporal maps of their experiences. Logan (1977) has argued that associations not only encode what has previously happened but when. I suggest that temporal tagging may form part of the "location" of objects and events in high-dimensional neuronal representational spaces, including at least one temporal dimension, producing something like space/time frames in a continuous representational and subjectively perceived life-long sequence (Koenigshofer, 1996c). Something like temporal tagging of neurorepresentations of objects and events, marking their "locations" in subjective time, seems necessary to account for our ability to discriminate before from after and to discriminate and remember sequences of objects and events (representations in which sequence is important have proved troublesome for connectionist models—see Bechtel and Abrahamsen, 1991, p. 236—however, I suggest that use of temporal tagging of representations in connectionist networks may provide a solution to this problem). Furthermore, there is ample experimental evidence that animals are very good at estimating the passage of time (Church, 1978; Church et al., 1976; Roberts, 1981) and Michon (1985), consistent with my hypothesis that a temporal dimension may be a component in activation vectors, has proposed that time has its own representational system distinct from that which encodes object and event attributes. Additionally, there is accumulating data suggestive of the existence of a subjective "internal clock" and of "subjective time quanta" (Dehaene, 1993; Treisman, et al., 1990). I suggest that this temporal tagging of neural representations might be accomplished by the presence in the brain of oscillating or rhythmic firing patterns in one or more networks of neurons continuously marking points in subjective time. Simulations with artificial neural networks have demonstrated that rhythmic firing patterns are easily generated by neural networks and there is evidence of such rhythmic activity in several parts of the brain, including the hippocampus (Churchland and Sejnowski, 1992). Conceivably, this sort of tagging of representations locating them in subjective time might be one function of the hippocampus in memory. Supporting this hypothesis is a report by Berz et.al. (1992) that pharmacological blockade of NMDA receptors, found in high concentrations in hippocampus (Squire, et.al., 1989; Churchland and Sejnowski, 1992), disrupts time discrimination performance, supporting a role for NMDA receptors and perhaps hippocampus in time representation functions. This suggests an alternative hypothesis about memory loss following damage to the hippocampus. Typically such losses are interpreted as lending support to a model of memory in which short-term memories are consolidated into permanent storage over some period of time lasting from minutes to years (Squire, et.al., 1989). However, I suggest that memory loss following hippocampal damage may be due, at least in part, to a failure to locate memories during retrieval due to a prior disruption of the proposed temporal tagging function of hippocampus rather than to a disruption of consolidation and failure of long term storage. Consistent with this interpretation is the observation that amnesic patients with damage to hippocampus can sometimes show long-term recall of events experienced after hippocampal damage if given aids to retrieval, a finding inconsistent with the hypothesis that loss of hippocampal function prevented long term storage and consolidation. Futhermore, Churchland and Sejnowski (1992, p. 282) suggest that one possible function of hippocampus is the "fixing of spatiotemporal tags" onto stored representations perhaps destined for cortex. They also speculate that hippocampus may "teach" the cerebral cortex less detailed, more categorical representations containing salient aspects of the hippocampal representation (see Gluck and Myers, 1993). This latter is surprisingly similar to my proposal in chapter 10 that there is a widespread disposition in brains (which I call NRSR; see chapter 10) to utilize statistical regularities in "lower level" representations to form more abstracted representations of meta-regularities and that this generates representational and computational efficiency and forms an important component of cognition (one function of dream sleep may be to reactivate representations of stored information, "memories," and then to reorganize them using NRSR, culling redundancy, thus conserving representational and computational efficiency). I believe that it is possible that one important function of the hippocampus is to deliver temporally tagged representations to the cortex, representations readied for future retrieval by the hippocampal temporal tagging. Consistent with this hypothesis, Gordon et al. (1985) have proposed that the order in which events occur is an effective cue for retrieval of an association. Other brain areas may also be involved in temporal tagging functions, such as frontal cortex. In my view, conditioning is not based on formation of a simple associative link, but is instead a derived representation of the magnitude of probabilistic event covariations computed from statistical regularities in the "distances" (magnitude and signs) between the temporal coordinates of events in multidimensional representational spaces. These are instantiated in patterns of neuronal firings in specific populations of neurons, conceived as large activation vectors. The computation of these regularities exploits a general computational feature of connectionist processing architectures for extraction and representation of regularities of all sorts. "Genetic loading" of synaptic weights interacting with this general learning mechanism could mediate adaptive specializations of conditioning such as taste aversion learning. This connectionist-like model of conditioning amounts to a fundamental reconceptualization of the engram. Instead of positing increased conductance between two neural representations (for CS and US), I propose that objects/events are encoded in distributed representations in multi-dimensional activation vectors which include a temporal component. If a temporal dimension were encoded into such representations then statistical regularities on the temporal dimension would be extracted and represented by connectioinist-style circuit configurations in the brain along with regularities in non-temporal features. Temporal relations between events in conditioning would be sculpted out of the statistically regular relative temporal locations of CS and US (or operant response and its outcome) in activation space with connectionist-like neural architectures. I believe that this conceptualization of the engram for event covariation detection in conditioning and "causality" gives a better accounting of the complex, predictive, informational coding which appears to mediate the more complex, higher-order phenomena in classical and operant conditioning. At the cellular level, patterns of LTP and LTD might perform the proposed "sculpting" function, wherein LTP is a covariation detector and LTD rids the representations of noise by acting as an "anti-correlation mechanism (see Churchland and Sejnowski, 1992). Current researchers investigating the neurophysiology of learning and memory search for simple increases or decreases in firing rates of neurons thought to demonstrate a strengthened or weakened synaptic connection between CS neurorepresentation and US neurorepresentation. However, in my view, no such simple correlations in firing rate will be found to be representationally meaningful. This is because representation of conditioning (and probably other learning) will be accomplished by modifications of synaptic weights within a synaptic weight distribution, in one or more layers of hidden units in a connectionist-like network brain architecture, which utilizes the extraction and representation of the statistical regularity of CS and US on a temporal dimension(s) in multidimensional activation space to sculpt a representation of the probabilistic covariation between these events. Thus, changes in synaptic weights will form a complex pattern of weights and neuronal firing, some increasing and some decreasing as the network produces an altered synaptic weight distribution to represent the complex informational "texture" extracted from regularities across learning trials. In my model, vector completion (see figure 8-5) provides the mechanism at the neural level for recall and expectancy of a US following presentation of CS (and for expectancy in operant conditioning and other event covariations as well). If a higher-order hidden unit representation of a covariation includes a CS-US compound (or other covariant pair, i.e. operant response and outcome in instrumental conditioning) and the probabilistic magnitude of the relation between them (computed from the history of covariation or lack thereof between events), then explicit presence of CS alone should be sufficient to induce vector completion generating an expectancy that the US is about to occur within some range of computable and representable probabilities. This model predicts that if a temporal tagging scalar is included as an element in the activation vectors representing CS and US in an artificial network, then, as the network is trained up with repeated CS-US covariations, the network will "discover" and represent the temporal regularity, just as networks discover and represent statistical regularities in other dimensions of activation space (Koenigshofer, 1996c).

3. NRSR theory, as I have proposed it in chapter 10, may help explain at least one basis for some human aesthetic values and may provide basis for a theory of art, music, and the aesthetics of scientific and other conceptual discovery. NRSR theory supposes that, as a result of the primary significance of regularities and their representation in evolutionary processes, the influence of the innate disposition to representation of regularities of all sorts should be evident throughout the brain and at multiple levels of organization. One implication is that human beings and at least some other animals should, at multiple psychological and neurophysiological levels, "seek out," be prone to discover, to prefer, and to feel rewarded by, manifestations of regularity in the world. One manifestation of "seeking out" and feeling rewarded by regularity, by pattern, is found in the "impulse toward unity" (Churchland, 1989) in our thinking as we construct an overall model of the world, and as scientists seek pattern in nature and feel powerfully rewarded when they discover it (what might be called an "instinct to order"). Another manifestation is in aesthetics. We tend to be attracted to and feel rewarded by visual patterns, as in artwork, architecture, patterns on clothing, and in interior design features such as wall paper with repetitive designs or uniformities such as wood molding or picture frames which help clearly define regular borders of walls or pictures. We also feel rewarded by, and take emotional satisfaction from auditory patterns in music whether in

melodies or in rhythmic beats. We also find reward in chanting, a regularity or repetition of the human voice and often times in movement especially in dancing. The visual appeal of looking out over a uniform landscape or view such as a uniform ocean or an open plain may be other examples of how we seem to be biologically prepared to seek and to feel rewarded by all sorts of patterns—visual, auditory, and conceptual (uniformity is likely just one factor in aesthetics, especially in the appeal to humans of certain landscapes; see Orians and Heerwagen, 1992). The underlying principle in the appeal of pattern, uniformity, order, and repetition may be *regularity*, and the brain's preference for it as a consequence of circuit design that gives it positive hedonic tone as a means to motivate the "search" for it. The underlying principle explaining these aesthetics may lie in our evolved disposition for NRSR, the general disposition in the brain for extraction and representation of statistical regularities of all sorts. For this disposition to be fully realized in an animal or human brain, the brain must be equipped with emotional circuitry that would make discovery, recognition, or perception of pattern, of regularity in general, have substantial positive hedonic value. At the behavioral and psychological level, such discovery and representation of regularity has deep adaptive significance because regularity means predictability and predictability of events permits projection of one's self into future to increase chances of successful adaptive organization of behavior, with the consequent positive effects on reproductive fitness. Additional gains, as discussed in chapter 10, include increases in representational and processing speed and efficiency. Thus some of our aesthetic feelings and values with regard to the emotional appeal of pattern in a broad array of human experience may be explained as a derived property in our brains of an innate disposition to prefer pattern and order because of an underlying adaptive organization of the brain which disposes it to NRSR (neurorepresentation of statistical regularities). These ideas might be designated as the NRSR hypothesis of human aesthetics. Note the similarity with accounts of brain processes inspired by classic information theory (Shannon and Weaver, 1949; Attneave, F., 1959; Crosson and Sayre, 1967; Campbell, 1982).

REFERENCES

Ammon K. and Gandevia, S.C. (1990). Transcranial magnetic stimulation can influence the selection of motor programmes. *Journal of Neurology, Neurosurgery, and Psychiatry;* 53:705–707. doi:10.1136/jnnp.53.8.705.

Asch, S. E. (1951). Effects of group pressure upon the modification and distortion of judgment. In H. Guetzkow (ed.) *Groups, leadership and men.* Pittsburgh, PA: Carnegie Press

Attneave, F. (1959). *Applications of Information Theory to Psychology; a summary of basic concepts, methods, and results.* Holt. New York.

Baillargeon, R. (2004). Infants' Physical World. *Current Directions in Psychological Science,* 13(3), 89–94.

Banich, Marie T. and Compton, Rebecca J. (2011). *Cognitive Neuroscience,* 3rd Edition, Wadsworth, Cengage Learning.

Barash, D. (1977). *Sociobiology and Behavior.* Elsevier. New York.

Barkow, J.H., Cosmides, L. & Tooby, J. Eds. (1992). *The Adapted Mind: Evolutionary Psychology and the Generation of Culture.* Oxford University Press. New York.

Barlow, H. (2001). The exploitation of regularities in the environment by the brain. *Behavioral and Brain Sciences,* 24, 602–607.

Baron-Cohen, S. (1994). The Mindreading System: new directions for research. *Current Psychology of Cognition,* 13, 724–750.

Baron-Cohen, S. (1995). *Mindblindness: An essay on autism and theory of mind.* MIT Press, Cambridge, Mass.

Baron-Cohen,S., Ring, H., Wheelwright, S., Bullmore, E, Brammer, M., Simmons, A. and Williams, S. (1998). Social intelligence in the normal and autistic brain: an fMRI study. *European J. of Neurosci.,* 1999, 11, 1891–1898.

Baron-Cohen, S., Ring, H., Bullmore, E., Wheelwright, S., Ashwin, C., & Williams, S. (2000). The amygdala theory of autism. *Neuroscience and Behavioural Reviews,* 24, 355–364.

Barth, John (1958). The End of the Road. Doubleday.

Baumeister, R., Masicampo, E. and DeWall, C. (2009). Prosocial Benefits of Feeling Free: Disbelief in Free Will Increases Aggression and Reduces Helpfulness. *Personality and Social Psychology Bulletin,* Vol. 35, No. 2, 260-268 (2009) DOI: 10.1177/0146167208327217

Becker, S. and Hinton, G.E. (1992). Self-organizing neural network that discovers surfaces in random-dot stereograms. *Nature* 355, 161–163.

Bechtel W. and Abrahamsen A. *Connectionism and the Mind.* Basil Blackwell, Oxford, 1991

Bermudez, J. L. (2001). Review of Jerry Fodor's The Mind Doesn't Work That Way: The Scope and Limits of Computational Psychology. *Philosophical Quarterly.*

Bickart, K., Wright, C., Dautoff, R., Dickerson, B., and Barrett, L. (2011). Amygdala volume and social network size in humans. *Nature Neuroscience 14*, 163–164 doi:10.1038/nn.2724

Bitterman, M. E. (1960). Toward a comparative psychology of learning. *American Psychologist,* Vol 15(11), Nov 1960, 704–712. doi: 10.1037/h0048359

Bitterman, M. E. (2000). Cognitive Evolution: A psychological perspective. In C. Heyes and L. Huber. *The Evolution of Cognition.* MIT Press. p. 61–79.

Bjorklund, D.F.and Kipp, K. (1996). Parental investment theory and sex differences in the evolution of inhibition mechanisms. Psychological Bulletin, 120, 163–188.

Boly, M. et. al. (2007). When thoughts become action: An fMRI paradigm to study volitional brain activity in non-communicative brain injured patients," *Neuroimage,* Volume 36, Issue 3, 1 July 2007, Pages 979–992.

Bradley, A. (2009). Expanding the Limits of Life, *Scientific American,* Dec.

Brass, M. and Haggard, P. (2007). To Do or Not to Do: The Neural Signature of Self-Control The Journal of Neuroscience, August 22, 2007, 27(34):9141-9145; doi:10.1523/JNEUROSCI.0924-07.2007

Bridgeman, B. (2003). *Psychology and Evolution: The Origins of Mind.* Sage Publications, Thousand Oaks, CA; London.

Buss, D. (1989). Sex differences in human mate preferences: Evolutionary hypotheses tested in 37 cultures. *Behavioral and Brain Sciences,* 12, 1–49.

Buss, D. (1992). Mate preference mechanisms: consequences for partner choice and intrasexual competition. In *The Adapted Mind: Evolutionary Psychology and the Generation of Culture.* Barkow, J.H., Cosmides, L. & Tooby, J. Eds. Oxford University Press. New York.

Buss, D. (1995). Evolutionary psychology: A new paradigm for psychological science. *Psychol. Inq.* 6:1–30.

Buss, D.M. et al (1998). Adaptations, Exaptations, and Spandrels. *American Psychologist, 53 (5),* 547.

Buss, D. (2008). *Evolutionary Psychology: The New Science of the Mind.* 3rd edition, Pearson.

Buunk, B., Angleitner, A. Oubaid, V. and Buss, D. (1996). Sex Differences in Jealousy in Evolutionary and Cultural Perspective: Tests from the Netherlands, Germany, and the United States. *Psychological Science* 7(6), 359–363. November.

Byrne, R.W. (2002). The Primate Origins of Human Intelligence. In *The Evolution of Intelligence.* R.J. Sternberg and J.C. Kaufmann, Eds. Lawrence Erlbaum Associates, New Jersey, London.

Campbell, J. (1982). *Grammatical Man: Information, Entropy, Language, and Life.* Simon & Schuster, Inc.

Cannon, T. (2009). Memory systems, brain plasticity, and susceptibility genes for schizophrenia. Invited address, May 24, 2009. Convention of the Association for Psychological Science, San Francisco.

Carlson, N., Miller, H., Heth, C., Donahoe, J, and Martin, G. (2010). *Psychology: The Science of Behavior,* 7th edition. Allyn and Bacon. Boston.

Carlson, Neil R. (2011). *Foundations of Behavioral Neuroscience,* Special Custom Edition for UMUC's Psychology 301, Pearson Learning Solutions.

Carr, C. (1993). Processing of temporal information in the brain. Annual *Review of Neuroscience, 16,* 223–43.

Chenn, A. and Walsh, C.A. Regulation of cerebral cortical size by control of cell cycle exit in neural precursors. *Science,* 2002, 297, 365–369.

Church, R.M., Getty, D.J., and Lerner, N.D. (1976). Duration discrimination by rats. Journal of Experimental Psychology: Animal Behavior Processes, 2, 303–312.

Church, R.M. (1978). The internal clock. In Cognitive Processes in Animal Behavior, S.H. Hulse, H. Fowler, and W.K. Honig, Eds. Erlbaum, Hillsdale, N.J.

Churchland, Patricia & Sejnowski, T. (1992). *The Computational Brain*. MIT Press, Cambridge, Massachusetts.

Churchland, Patricia. (2011). *Brain Trust: What Neuroscience Tells Us about Morality*. Princeton University Press.

Churchland, Paul. (1979). *Scientific Realism and the Plasticity of the Mind*. Cambridge University Press.

Churchland, Paul. (1989). *A Neurocomputational Perspective: The Nature of Mind and the Structure of Science*. MIT Press, Cambridge.

Churchland, Paul. (1988). *Matter and Consciousness*. Revised edition, MIT Press, Cambridge, Mass.

Clark, A. (1993). *Associative Engines*. MIT Press, Cambridge, Massachusetts.

Cole, Steve (2009). Social Regulation of Human Gene Expression. Invited Talk. May 22, 2009. Annual Convention of the Association for Psychological Science. San Francisco.

Colom, R, Jung, R.E., & Haier, RJ. Finding the g factor of intelligence in brain structure using the method of correlated vectors, *Intelligence*, 34, 561–570.

Colwill, R.M. (1993). An associative analysis of instrumental learning. Current Directions in Psychological Science 2(4), 111–116, August.

Corballis, (2002). Evolution of the Generative Mind. In *The Evolution of Intelligence*. R.J. Sternberg and J.C. Kaufmann, Eds. Lawrence Erlbaum Associates, New Jersey, London.

Cosmides, L. & Tooby, J. (1987). From evolution to behavior: evolutionary psychology as the missing link. In J. Dupre, Ed. *The latest and the best: essays on evolution and optimality*. MIT Press, Cambridge, Mass.

Cosmides, L. & Tooby, J. (1992). Cognitive Adaptation for Social Exchange. In *The Adapted Mind: Evolutionary Psychology and the Generation of Culture*. Barkow, J.H., Cosmides, L. & Tooby, J. Eds. Oxford University Press. New York.

Cosmides, L. & Tooby, J. (1996). The modular nature of human intelligence. *The Eighth Symposium of the Center for the Study of the Evolution of Life*, "The Origins and Evolution of Intelligence," March 15,1996, Univerisity of California at Los Angeles.

Cosmides, L. and Tooby, J. (2002). Unraveling the Enigma of Human Intelligence: Evolutionary Psychology and the Multimodular Mind. In *The Evolution of Intelligence*. R.J. Sternberg and J.C. Kaufmann, Eds. Lawrence Erlbaum Associates, New Jersey, London.

Craig A.D., et al. (1994). A thalamic nucleus specific for pain and temperature sensation. *Nature* 372, 770–773.

Crawford, C. and Krebs, D. (eds). (1998). Handbook of Evolutionary Psychology: Ideas, Issues, and Applications. Lawrence Erlbaum, Mahwah, NJ.

Crosson, F.J. and Sayre, K.M., Eds. (1967). *Philosophy and Cybernetics*. University of Notre Dame Press.

Crick, Francis (1994). *The Astonishing Hypothesis: The scientific search for the soul*. Touchstone. New York.

Dawkins, Richard. (1987). *The Blind Watchmaker*. Norton, New York.

Dawkins, Richard. (1989; 2006). *The Selfish Gene*. 2nd edition. Oxford University Press. New York. 30th Anniversary Edition, 2006, Oxford University Press. New York.

Dawkins, Richard (2009). *The Greatest Show on Earth: The Evidence for Evolution*. Free Press: Division of Simon and Shuster.

Deacon, Terrence (1996). Old genes, new tricks: Did evolution coax language from fly genes? *Eighth Symposium, Center for the Study of Evolution and the Origin of Life*, "The Origins and Evolution of Intelligence," March 15, 1996, UCLA.

Decety, J., Jeannerod, M., Durozard, D., & Baverel, G. (1993). Central activation of autonomic effectors during mental simulation of motor actions in man. *Journal of Physiology, 461*, 549–563.

Decety, J., Perani, D., Jeannerod, M., Bettinardi, V., Tadary, B., Woods, R., et al. (1994). Mapping motor representations with PET. *Nature, 371*, 600–602.

Decety, J., & Jeannerod, M. (1996). Fitts' law in mentally simulated movements. *Behavioral Brain Research, 72*, 127–134.

Dehaene, S. (1993). Temporal oscillations in human perception. Psychological Science, 4(4), 264–270, July.

Dennet, D. (1992). The Self as Center of Narrative Gravity. In F. Kessel, P. Cole and D. Johnson, eds, *Self and Consciousness: Multiple Perspectives*, Hillsdale, NJ: Erlbaum, 1992.

De Pinho, M., Mazza, M., Piqueira, J, and Roque, A. (2002). Shannon's entropy applied to the analysis of tonotopic reorganization in a computational model of classical conditioning. *Neurocomputing 44-46*, 359–364.

DeSteno, D. and Salovey, P. (1996). Genes, Jealousy, and the Replication of Misspecified Models. *Psychological Science* 7(6), 376–377. November.

Deutsch, J. and Deutsch, D. (1973). *Physiological Psychology*, Dorsey Press, Homewood, Illinois

De Valois, R.L., Albrecht, D.G., and Thorell, L. Cortical cells: Bar detectors or spatial frequency filters? In *Frontiers in Visual Science*, edited by S. J. Cool and E.L. Smith. Berlin: Springer-Verlanger, 1978.

di Pellegrino, G., Fadiga, L. Fogassi, L Gallese, V., and Rizzolatti, G. (1992). Understanding Motor Events: A neurophysiological study. Experimental Brain Research, 91, 176–180.

Donahoe, J.W. and Palmer, D.C. (1994). *Learning and Complex Behavior*. Allyn and Bacon, Needham Heights, MA

Downing, P.E., Jiang, Y., Shuman, M. and Kanwisher, N. (2001). A Cortical Area Selective for Visual Processing of the Human Body. *Science*, 28 September 2001: Vol. 293 no. 5539 pp. 2470–2473 DOI: 10.1126/science.1063414.

Edelman, Gerald. (1992). *Bright Air, Brilliant Fire*, Penguin Books.

Edelman, Gerald M. and Tononi, Giulio (2000). *A Universe of Consciousness: How Matter Becomes Imagination*, Basic Books, 2000

Ellis, A.W. and Young, A.W. (1988). *Human Cognitive Neuropsychology*. Lawrence Erlbaum Associates, London.

Ellis, B. (1992). The evolution of sexual attraction: evaluative mechanisms in women. In *The Adapted Mind: Evolutionary Psychology and the Generation of Culture*. Barkow, J.H., Cosmides, L. & Tooby, J. Eds. Oxford University Press. New York.

Fadiga, L., Craighero, L, and Olivier, E. (2005). Human motor cortex excitability during the perception of others' action. *Current Opinion in Neurobiology*, 15, 213–218.

Fanslow, M.S. (1993). Associations and memories: the role of NMDA receptors and long-term Potentiation. Current Directions in Psychological Science 2(5), 152–156. October.

Finlay, B. and Darlington, R.B. (1995). Linked regularities in the development and evolution of mammalian brains. *Science 268*, 1578–1584

Fodor, J. (1983). *The Modularity of Mind.*

Fodor, J. (1998). The trouble with psychological Darwinism. In *The London Review of Books 20(2)* January 15, 1998.

Fodor, J. (2000). *The Mind Doesn't Work That Way: The Scope and Limits of Computational Psychology.* MIT Press. Cambridge, MA

Feldman, Jacob (1997). The structure of perceptual categories. *Journal of Mathematical Psychology 41*(2):145–170.

Freeman, Derek. (1983). *Margaret Mead and Samoa: The Making and Unmaking of an Anthropological Myth*, Harvard University Press, ISBN 0-14-022555-2.

Gallistel, C.R. (2000). The Replacement of General-Purpose Learning Models with Adaptively Specialized Learning Modules. In M.S. Gazzaniga, Ed., *The Cognitive Neurosciences. 2nd ed.* (1179–1191) Cambridge, MA. MIT Press, 2000.

Gallistel, C.R. (1995). The replacement of general-purpose theories with adaptive specializations, In: *The Cognitive Neurosciences*, M. Gazzaniga (Ed.), MIT Press, 1995.

Gallistel, C.R. (1992). Classical conditioning as an adaptive specialization: a computational model. In *The Psychology of Learning and Motivation: Advances in Research and Theory*, D.L. Medin, ed. Academic Press, New York.

Gallistel, C.R. (1990). *The Organization of Learning.* MIT Press, Cambridge.

Garcia J., Kimeldorf, D.J., Koelling, R.A. (1955). Conditioned aversion to saccharin resulting from exposure to gamma radiation. *Science*; 122(3160): 157–158.

Gardner, B.T. and Gardner, R.A. (1975). Evidence for sentence constituents in the early utterances of child and chimpanzee. *Journal of Experimental Psychology: General*, 104, 244–267.

Gazzaniga, Michael S, Ivry, Richard B. and Mangun, George R., (1998). *Cognitive Neuroscience: The Biology of the Mind*, WW Norton and Company, New York.

Gluck, M. and Myers, C. (1993). Hippocampal mediation of stimulus representation: A computational theory. *Hippocampus 3*, 491–516.

Gobet, F. and Simon, H.A. (1996). The roles of recognition processes and look-ahead search in time-constrained expert problem solving: evidence from Grand-Master-level chess. *Psychological Science 7*(1), 52–55. January.

Goldberg, E. (1995). The Rise and Fall of Modular Orthodoxy: Special Issue Modularity and the Brain. *Journal of Clinical and Experimental Neuropsychology 17*(2), 193–208.

Goodale M.A, Milner A.D.(1992). Separate visual pathways for perception and action." *Trends Neurosci.* Jan;15(1):20–5

Goodall, J. (1971). *In the Shadow of Man.* Revised 1988, Houghton Mifflin Company, Boston.

Gopnik, A., Meltzoff, A. and Kuhl, P. (1999). *The scientist in the crib: What early learning tells us about the mind.* William Morrow and Company, New York.

Gordon, W.C., McGinnis, C.M. and Weaver, M.S. (1985). The effect of cuing after backward conditioning trials. Learning and Motivation 16, 444–463.

Gould, S.J., and Richard Lewontin (1979). "The spandrels of San Marco and the Panglossion paradigm: a critique of the adaptationist programme". *Proc R Soc Lond B* 205 (1161): 581–598. doi:10.1098/rspb.1979.0086

Gould, S.J. and Vrba (1982). Exaptation—a missing term in the science of form. *Paleobiology 8*, 4–15.

Gould, Stephen J. (1997). The New York Review of Books, Volume 44, Number 15, October 9, 1997.

Gould, S.J. (1997a). Evolutionary Psychology: An Exchange. *New York Review of Books 44* (10), 34–37.

Gould, S.J. (1997b). The exaptive excellence of spandrels as a term and prototype. *Proceedings of the National Academy of Sciences, USA, 94*: 10750–10755

Gross, C. G. Bender, D. B. and Rocha-Miranda, C. E. (1969). Visual receptive fields of neurons in inferotemporal cortex of the monkey. *Science 166*, 1303–1306, December 5, 1969.

Gross, C. G. Bender, D. B. and Rocha-Miranda, C. E. (1972). Visual properties of neurons in inferotemporal cortex of the macaque. *Journal of Neurophysiology, 35*, 96–111.

Haier, R.J. et al (1988). Cortical glucose metabolic rate correlates of abstract reasoning and attention studied with positron emission tomography. *Intelligence, 12*, 199–217.

Haier, R. J. et al (1992). Intelligence and changes in regional cerebral glucose metabolic rate following learning. *Intelligence, 16*, 415–426.

Haier R.J, Jung R., Yeo R., Head K., Alkire M.T. (2004). Structural brain variation and general, intelligence. *NeuroImage*, 23(1): 425–433.

Hamilton, W. (1964). The evolution of social behavior. *Journal of Theoretical Biology* 7:1–52

Harlow, H. F. (1956). Learning set and error factor theory. In S. Koch, ed., *Psychology: A study of a science*, Vol. 2, pp. 492-537. New York: McGraw-Hill.

Harris, C.R. and Christenfeld, N. (1996). Jealousy and Rational Responses to Infidelity across Gender and Culture. *Psychological Science* 7(6), 378–379. November.

Hebb, D.O. (1949). The Organization of Behavior. Wiley. New York.

Hesslow, G. (2002). Conscious thought as simulation of behavior and perception. *Trends in Cognitive Sciences, 6*, 242–247.

Hinton, G.E. (1989). Connectionist learning systems. *Artificial Intelligence 40*, 185-234.

Hirstein, W., and Ramachandran, V. S. (1997). "Capgras syndrome: a novel probe for understanding the neural representation of the identity and familiarity of persons." *Proc R Soc Lond B Biol Sci*, 264, 437–444.

Holland, J.H. (1998). *Emergence: From chaos to order*. Addison-Wesley. Reading, MA.

Honig, W.K. (1981). Working memory and the temporal map. In *Information Processing in Animals: Memory Mechanisms*. N.E. Spear & R.R. Miller, Eds. Erlbaum, Hillsdale, NJ.

Howard, R. W. (1997). The Guiding of Learning: an Overview, Analysis, and Classification of Guides. *Genetic, Social, and General Psychology Monographs*. Vol: 123, Issue: 2, 233.

Hubel, D.H. and Wiesel, T.N. (1977). Functional architecture of macaque monkey visual cortex. *Proceedings of the Royal Society of London, 198*, 1–59.

Inzlicht, M. (2009). Toward a Cognitive Science of Religion: Insights from Personality and Social Psychology. May 22, 2009. Annual Convention of the Association for Psychological Science. San Francisco.

Jacobson, M. (1993). *Foundations of Neuroscience*, 2nd Edition, Kluwer Academic Publishers Group.

Jeannerod, M. (2001). Neural simulation of action: A unifying mechanism for motor cognition. *NeuroImage, 14*, 103–109.

Johnsgard, P.A. (1972). *Animal Behavior*. W.C. Brown Publishers. Dubuque, Iowa.

Johnston, Victor, S. 1999. *Why We Feel: The Science of Human Emotions*. Perseus Books, Cambridge, Mass.

Jung, R. E. and Haier, R.J. (2007). The Parieto-Frontal Integration Theory (P-FIT) of Intelligence: Converging Neuroimaging Evidence. *Behavioral and Brain Sciences, 30*, 135–187.

Kanwisher, N. (2009). The Specialized Brain. Keynote address. May 22, 2009. Annual Convention of the Association for Psychological Science. San Francisco. http://thesituationist.wordpress.com/2009/08/25/aps-observer-sharpening-the-focus-on-brain-function/ (retrieved June 9, 2011).

Kaplan, S. (1992). Environmental preference in a knowledge-seeking, knowledge using organism. In *The Adapted Mind: Evolutionary Psychology and the Generation of Culture*. Barkow, J.H., Cosmides, L. & Tooby, J. Eds. Oxford University Press. New York.

Kenrick, DT. (1995). Evolutionary theory versus the confederacy of dunces. *Psychol. Inq.* 6:56–62

King, A.P. and Gallistel, C.R. (1996). Multiphasic neuronal transfer functions for representing temporal structure. *Behavior Research Methods, Instruments and Computers 28*(2), 217–223.

Knight, R.T. and Grabowecky, M. (1995). Escape from linear time: prefrontal cortex and conscious experience. In: The Cognitive Neurosciences. M. Gazzaniga, Ed. MIT Press.

Koenigshofer, K.A. (2002). A Ubiquitous Domain-General Problem and Evolved Content-Independent Processing. Paper presented at the annual convention of the Western Psychological Association, April 13, 2002, Irvine, CA

Koenigshofer, K.A. (1996a). Adaptive Response to Regularity: A General Biological Process in Learning and Cognition. Poster presented at the 1996 Convention of the Western Psychological Association, April, San Jose, CA.

Koenigshofer, K.A. (1996b). A Neural Network Predictor of Course Grade In Introductory Psychology. Poster presented at the 1996 Convention of the Western Psychological Association, April, San Jose, CA.

Koenigshofer, K.A. (1996c). Computation and Representation of Temporal Features: Reconceptualizing Conditioning. Poster presented at 1996 Convention of the American Psychological Society, June, San Francisco, CA.

Koenigshofer, K.A. (1995a). A Computational Theory of Protocognition: Network Representation of Distal Statistical Regularity. Poster presented at 1995 Convention of the American Psychological Society, June, New York, NY.

Koenigshofer, K.A. (1995b). Representation of Temporal Regularity in Activation Space: A New Engram for Conditioning. Poster presented at 1995, Convention of the American Psychological Society, June, New York, NY.

Koenigshofer, K.A. (1994a). Evolution of Intelligent Creatures: Neurorepresentation of Hierarchical Statistical Regularity. Paper presented at the annual convention of the Western Psychological Association, April, Kona, Hawaii.

Koenigshofer, K.A. (1994b). Evolution and Behavioral Adaptation as Organizing Concepts for Introductory Psychology. Poster presented at the annual convention of the Western Psychological Association, May, Kona, Hawaii.

Koenigshofer, K.A. (1992). A Nonsentential Theory of Cognition Based Upon a Generalized Minimum Principle. Paper presented at the annual convention of the Western Psychological Association, May, Portland, Oregon.

Koenigshofer, K.A. (1991). Information, Pattern, and Redundancy in Visual Perception, Conditioning, and Cognition. Paper presented at Western Psychological Association Convention, San Francisco.

Koenigshofer, K.A. (1990). Learning as Perceptual Registration of 'Real World' Event Relations. Paper presented at Western Psychological Association Convention, Los Angeles.

Koenigshofer, K.A. (1979). Cholinergic Manipulation of Amphetamine-Induced Learned Taste Aversion by Scopolamine, Physostigmine, and Neuroleptics. Paper presented at Western Psychological Association Convention, San Diego.

Koenigshofer, K.A. (1978). Dopaminergic Mediation of Amphetamine-Induced Learned Taste Aversion. Paper presented at Western Psychological Association Convention, San Francisco.

Koenigshofer, K.A. and Nachman, Marvin (1974). Selective Breeding for Taste Aversion Learning in Rats. Paper presented at Western Psychological Association Convention, San Francisco.

Kohler, W. (1927). *The Mentality of Apes*. Harcourt, Brace.

Kosslyn, S.M., Thompson, W.L., Kim, I.J. and Alpert, N.M. (1995). Topographic representations of mental images in primary visual cortex. *Nature* 378: 496–8.

La Cerra, M.M. (1994). Evolved mate preferences in women: Psychological adaptations for assessing a man's willingness to invest in offspring. Unpublished doctoral dissertation. Department of Psychology, University of California, Santa Barbara.

La Cerra, M.M. (2003). The first law of psychology is the second law of thermodynamics: The energetic evolutionary model of the mind and the generation of human psychological phenomena. *Human Nature Review*, 3: 440–447, 25 October.

Laughlin, W.S. (1968). Hunting: an integrating biobehavior system and its evolutionary importance. In R.B. Lee & I. DeVore (Eds.), *Man the Hunter*. Chicago: Aldine.

Levine, J., Gordon, N., Fields, H. (1978). The mechanism of placebo analgesia. *The Lancet*, Volume 312, Issue 8091, Pages 654–657, 23 September.

Libet, B.; Wright, E. W.; Gleason, C. A. (1983). Readiness potentials preceding unrestricted spontaneous pre-planned voluntary acts", 1983, Electroencephalographic and Clinical Neurophysiology 54: 322–325.

Lindauer, M. (1961). Communication Among Social Bees. Harvard University Press, Cambridge, Mass.Lloyd, EA. (1999). Evolutionary psychology: the burdens of proof. *Biol. Philos.* 14:211–33.

Locke, John (1690/1947). "An Essay Concerning Human Understanding," E.P. Dutton, New York

Logan, F.A. (1977). Hybrid theory of classical conditioning. In: *The Psychology of Learning and Motivation. Vol. 11.* G.H.Bower, Ed. Academic Press, New York.

Luria, A.R. (1966). Higher cortical functions in man. Oxford, England: Basic Books.

Marler, P., (1970). A comparative approach to vocal learning. Song development in white-crowned sparrows. *Journal of Comparative and Physiological Psychology*, 7, 1–25

Mayr, E. (1974). *Populations, Species, and Evolution*. Harvard University Press. Cambridge, Mass.

McCall, G. (2001). The Fateful Hoaxing of Margaret Mead: A Historical Analysis of her Samoan Research, book review by Grant McCall, *Australian Journal of Anthropology*, April.

McCloskey, M. (1991). Networks and theories: the place of connectionism in cognitive science. *Psychological Science 2(6)*, 387–395, November.

McDonald, P. et.al. (2009). Gene-Environment Interplay in Stress and Health: Network on Exposure to Psychosocial Stress and Addictive Substances. Symposium. May 22, 2009. Annual Convention of the Association for Psychological Science. San Francisco.

McGovern, K. (2007). Social cognition: Perceiving the mental states of others. In B.J. Baars & N.M. Gage (Eds.), *Cognition, brain, and consciousness*, pages 391–410, New York, Academic Press.

McGrew, W.C. & Feistner, A. (1992). Two nonhuman primate models for the evolution of human food sharing: chimpanzees and callitrichids. In *The Adapted Mind: Evolutionary Psychology and the Generation of Culture*. Barkow, J.H., Cosmides, L. & Tooby, J. Eds. Oxford University Press. New York.

Meister, I., Krings, T., Foltys, H., Boroojerdi, B., Muller, M., Topper, R., & Thron, A. (2004). Playing piano in the mind—an fMRI study on music imagery and performance in pianists. *Cognitive Brain Research, 19,* 219–228.

Michon, J.A. (1985). The complete time experiencer. In *Time, Mind, and Behavior*. J.A. Michon and J.L. Jackson, Eds. Springer-Verlag, Berlin.

Miller, K.D. (1990). Correlation-based models of neural development. In *Neurosciences And Connectionist Theory*. Gluck, M.A. and Rumelhart, D.E., Eds. Erlbaum Assoc. Hillsdale, N.J.

Miller, R.R. and Barnet, R.C. (1993). The role of time in elementary associations. *Current Directions in Psychological Science, 2(4)*, 106–111.

Miller, K.D., Erwin, E. and Kayser, A. (1999). "Is the Development of Orientation Selectivity Instructed by Activity?". *J. Neurobiol. 41,* 44–57.

Miller, Stanley L.; Harold C. Urey (July 1959). Organic Compound Synthesis on the Primitive Earth. *Science* 130 (3370): 245. doi:10.1126/science.130.3370.245. PMID 13668555.Mishkin M. and Ungerleider, L. (1982) "Contribution of striate inputs to the visuospatial functions of parieto-preoccipital cortex in monkeys." *Behav Brain Res.* 1982 Sep; 6 (1):57–77.

Muente, T. (1997). Neural substrates of language. Lecture in Cognitive Neuroscience 201G (J. Pineda), University of California, San Diego.

Nakisa, R.C. and Plunkett, K. (1998). Evolution of a Rapidly Learned Representation for Speech. *Language and Cognitive Processes 13* (2/3), 105–127.

Norenzayan, A. & Shariff, A.F. (2008) The Origin and Evolution of Religious Prosociality. *Science,* 322 (5898), 58–62.

Olds, J. and Milner, P. (1954). Positive Reinforcement Produced by Electrical Stimulation of Septal Area and Other Regions of Rat Brain." *Journal of Comparative and Physiological Psychology,* 47: 419.

Olton, D.S. (1989). Frontal cortex, timing, and memory. *Neuropsychologia 27(1)*, 121–130.

Orians, G. and Heerwagen, J. (1992). Evolved responses to landscapes. In: Barkow, J.H., Cosmides, L. & Tooby, J. Eds. (1992). *The Adapted Mind: Evolutionary Psychology and the Generation of Culture*. pp. 555–579. Oxford University Press. New York.

PBS (Public Broadcasting System). (2009). What Darwin Never Knew. NOVA 6188. DVD. WGBH Educational Foundation. Based on the books, *Endless Forms Most Beautiful* and *The Making of the Fittest* by Sean B. Carroll. Written by John Rubin.

PBS (Public Broadcasting System). (2011). Smartest Machine on Earth. NOVA 6221. DVD. WGBH Educational Foundation. Written by Julia Cort and Michael Bicks.

PBS (Public Broadcasting System). (2009). The Human Spark. HUSP 601. DVD series. WNET. ORG.

Penfield, W. Memory Mechanisms. *Archives of Neurology and Psychiatry*, 67: 178–198, 1952.

Penfield, W. and Perot, P. (1963). The brain's record of auditory and visual experience. A final summary and discussion. *Brain*: 86; 595–696.

Pepperberg, I.M. (2002). Evolution of Avian Intelligence, With an Emphasis on Grey Parrots (Psittacus erithacus). In *The Evolution of Intelligence*. R.J. Sternberg and J.C. Kaufmann, Eds. Lawrence Erlbaum Associates, New Jersey, London.

Pierson, L. and Trout, M. (2005). What is consciousness for? http://cogprints.org/4482/1/whatis-consciousnessfor.pdf, retrieved June 3, 2011.

Pinel, John J. (2009). *Biopsychology*, 7th Edition. Pearson, Boston.

Pinker, S. and Bloom, P. (1992). Natural language and natural selection. In *The Adapted Mind: Evolutionary Psychology and the Generation of Culture*. Barkow, J.H., Cosmides, L. & Tooby, J. Eds. Oxford University Press. New York.

Pinker, S. (1994). *The Language Instinct*. New York: Morrow.

Pinker, S. (1997a). Evolutionary Psychology: An Exchange. *New York Review of Books, 44*: 55–56. October 9, 1997.

Pinker, S. (1997b). *How the Mind Works*. W.W. Norton & Company. New York, London.

Pinker, S. (2002). *The Blank Slate: The Modern Denial of Human Nature*. Penguin Books. New York.

Polk, T.A., Park, J., Smith, M.R., & Park, D.C. (2007). Nature vs. nurture in ventral visual cortex: A functional magnetic resonance imaging study of twins. *Journal of Neuroscience*, 27(51): 13921–13925.

Pitcher, D., Walsh, V. and Duchaine, B. (2009). Transcranial magnetic stimulation studies of face processing. *Current Biology*. http://web.me.com/djpitcher/Site/ Welcome_files Pitcher_TMS_Chapter.pdf. Retrieved June 2, 2011.

Profet, M. (1992). Pregnancy sickness as Adaptation: A Deterrent to Maternal Ingestion of Teratogens. In *The Adapted Mind: Evolutionary Psychology and the Generation of Culture*. Barkow, J.H., Cosmides, L. & Tooby, J. Eds. Oxford University Press. New York.

Ramachandran, V.S. & Oberman, L.M. (2006). Broken mirrors, a theory of autism. Scientific American (November), 295, 63–69.

Ramus, Hauser, Miller, Morris & Mehler (2000). Language discrimination by human newborn and by cotton-top tamarin monkeys. *Science 288*, 349–351.

Rescorla, R.A. (1988). Pavlovian conditioning: it's not what you think it is. American Psychologist 43, 151–160.

Rescorla, R.A. (1992). Hierarchical associative relations in Pavlovian conditioning and Instrumental training. Current Directions in Psychological Science, 1(2), 66–70. April.

Rigoni, D., Kuhn, S., Sartori, G., & Brass, M. (2011). Inducing disbelief in free will alters brain correlates of preconscious motor preparation: The brain minds whether we believe in free will or not. *Psychological Science*, 22, 613–618. doi:10.1177/0956797611405680.

Roberts, S. (1981). Isolation of an internal clock. *Journal of Experimental Psychology: Animal Behavior Processes*, 7, 242–268.

Rose, H. & Rose, S. (2000). *Alas, Poor Darwin: Arguments Against Evolutionary Psychology*. New York: Harmony Books.

Rosenberg, C.R. and Sejnowski, T.J. (1987). Parallel networks that learn to pronounce English text. *Complex Systems, 1*, 145–168

Roth, M., Decety, J. et al. (1996). Possible involvement of primary motor cortex in mentally simulated movement: A functional magnetic resonance imaging study. *NeuroReport, 7*, 1280–1284.

Rumelhart, D.E. and McClelland, J.L. (1986). On learning the past tense of English verbs. In *Parallel Distributed Processing: Explorations in the Microstructure of Cognition*. McClelland, J.L., Rumelhart, D.E., and the PDP Research Group. MIT Press. London.

Rumelhart, D.E., Hinton, G.E. and Williams, R.J. (1986). Learning representations by back-propagating errors. *Nature, 323*, 533–536.

Savage-Rumbaugh (1996). *Eighth Symposium, Center for the Study of Evolution and the Origin of Life,* "The Origins and Evolution of Intelligence," March 15, 1996, UCLA.

Savage-Rumbaugh, S., Shanker, S., and Taylor, T. (1998). *Apes, Language, and the Human Mind*. Oxford University Press, New York.

Searle, John. (1992). The problem of consciousness. Claremont Conference on Consciousness and Cognition, Claremont, CA.

Shankman, P. (2000). Culture, Biology, and Evolution: The Mead–Freeman Controversy Revisited. *Journal of Youth and Adolescence*, Springer Netherlands, Volume 29, No. 5/October, 2000, ISSN 0047-2891: Pages 539–556.

Shannon, C. and Weaver, W. (1949). The Mathematical Theory of Communication. University of Illinois Press, Chicago.

Shariff, A.F., & Norenzayan, A. (2007). God is watching you: Supernatural agent concepts increase prosocial behavior in an anonymous economic game. *Psychological Science, 18*, 803–809.

Shariff, A.F., Cohen, A.B., & Norenzayan, A. (2008a) The Devil's Advocate: Secular Arguments Diminish both Implicit and Explicit Religious Belief. *Journal of Cognition and Culture, 8*, 417–423.

Shariff, A.F., Schooler, J.W. & Vohs, K.D. (2008b). The Hazards of Claiming to Have Solved the Hard Problem of Free Will. In (eds.) J. Baer, J. Kaufman and R.F. Baumeister, *Psychology and Free Will*. (pp. 181–204). Oxford University Press.

Shariff, A.F. (2008c). One Species under God? Sorting through the pieces of religion and coopera-tion. In (Bulbulia, J., R. Sosis, C. Genet, R. Genet, E. Harris, K. Wyman, eds.) The Evolution of Religion: Studies, Theories, and Critiques. (pp. 119–125) Collins Foundation Press.

Shariff, A.F., Norenzayan, A. & Henrich, J. (in press). The Birth of High Gods: How the cultural evo-lution of supernatural policing agents influenced the emergence of complex, cooperative human societies, paving the way for civilization. In (eds. M. Schaller, A. Norenzayan, S. Heine, T. Yamagi-shi, & T. Kameda) Evolution, culture and the human mind, Lawrence Erlbaum Associates.

Shema, R., Sacktor, T. and Dudai Y. (2007). Rapid Erasure of Long-Term Memory Associations in the Cortex by an Inhibitor of PKMζ. Science 17 August 2007: Vol. 317 no. 5840 pp. 951–953. DOI: 10.1126/science.1144334.

Shepard, R.N.and Metzler, J. (1971). Mental rotation of three-dimensional objects. *Science 171*: 701–703.

Shepard, R.N. (1987a). Evolution of a mesh between principles of the mind and regularities of the world. In J. Dupre, Ed. *The Latest and the Best: Essays on Evolution and Optimality*. MIT Press, Cambridge, Massachusetts.

Shepard, R.N. (1987b). Toward a universal law of generalization for psychological science. *Science,* 237, 1317–1323.

Shepard, R.N. (1992). The perceptual organization of colors: an adaptation to regularities of the terrestrial world? In *The Adapted Mind: Evolutionary Psychology and the Generation of Culture.* Barkow, J.H., Cosmides, L. & Tooby, J. Eds. Oxford University Press, New York.

Shepard, R.N. (1994). Perceptual-cognitive universals as reflections of the world. *Psychonomic Bulletin and Review* 1:2–28.

Shepard, R.N. (1996). Invited address presented at the annual convention of the American Psychological Society, June, San Francisco.

Simpson, J. & Kenrick, D. (eds). (1997). Evolutionary Social Psychology. Lawrence Erlbaum.

Singh D. (1993). Adaptive significance of waist-to-hip ratio and female physical attractiveness. *Journal of Personality and Social Psychology,* 65, 293-307.

Skinner, B.F. (1938). *The behavior of organisms; an experimental analysis.* Appleton-Century-Crofts. New York.

Skinner, B.F. (1953). Science and human behavior. Oxford, England: Macmillan.

Smith, B.H. (2000). Sewing up the mind: the claims of evolutionary psychology. In Rose, H & Rose, S. (2000). *Alas, Poor Darwin: Arguments Against Evolutionary Psychology.* New York: Harmony Books, pp. 129–43.

Spelke, E. (1994). Initial knowledge: Six suggestions. *Cognition, 50,* 431–445.

Squire, L. Shimamura, A. and Amaral, D. (1989). Memory and the hippocampus. In: *Neural Models of Plasticity,* Academic Press.

Sternberg, R.J. (1990). *Metaphors of mind: Conceptions of the nature of intelligence. New York.* Cambridge University Press.

Stiles, J. (1997). Development of spatial analytic processing. Lecture in Cognitive Neuroscience 201G (J. Pineda), University of California, San Diego.

Stone, V., Baron-cohen, S., Knight, R. (1998). Frontal Lobe Contributions to Theory of Mind. *Journal of Cognitive Neuroscience* Volume 10 Issue 5, September.

Sugita, Y. (2008). Face perception in monkeys reared with no exposure to faces. Proceedings of the National Academy of Sciences of the United States of America, 105(1), 394–398.

Symons, D. (1992). On the use and misuse of Darwinism in the study of human behavior. In *The Adapted Mind: Evolutionary Psychology and the Generation of Culture.* Barkow, J.H., Cosmides, L. & Tooby, J. Eds. Oxford University Press. NewYork.

Symons, D. (1987). If we're all Darwinians, what's the fuss about? In C. Crawford, M. Smith, & D. Krebs (Eds.). *Sociobiology and psychology: Ideas, issues, and applications.* Hillsdale, NJ: Erlbaum.

Tooby, J. & Cosmides, L. (1992). The psychological foundations of culture. In *The Adapted Mind: Evolutionary Psychology and the Generation of Culture.* Barkow, J.H., Cosmides, L. & Tooby, J. Eds. Oxford University Press. New York.

Tooby, J. & Cosmides, L. (1995). Mapping the evolved functional organization of mind and brain. In *The Cognitive Neurosciences.* M.S. Gazzaniga, Ed. MIT Press. Cambridge.

Tooby, J and Cosmides, L. (1995). Forward. In: (ed.), *Mindblindness: An Essay on Autism and the Theory of Mind.* MIT Press, Cambridge, MA pp xi–xviii.

Thompson, W., Slotnick, S., Burrage, M. and Kosslyn, S. (2009). Two Forms of Spatial Imagery: Neuroimaging Evidence, *Psychological Science,* September 29.

Thornhill, R. & Palmer, C. (2000). A natural history of rape: Biological bases of sexual coercion. Cambridge, MA: MIT Press.

Treisman, M. Faulkner, A. Naish, P.L.N. and Brogan, D. (1990). The internal clock: evidence for a temporal oscillator underlying time perception with some estimates of its characteristic frequency. Perception 19, 705–743.

Troyer, T.W., A.E. Krukowski, N.J. Priebe and K.D. Miller (1998). Contrast-Invariant Orientation Tuning in Visual Cortex: Thalamocortical Input Tuning and Correlation-Based Intracortical Connectivity. *Journal of Neuroscience 18*, 5908–5927.

Valenstein, Elliot, S., (1973). *Brain Stimulation and Motivation, Research and Commentary*, Scott, Foresman and Company, Glenview, Illinois.

Vohs, K. D., & Schooler, J. W. (2008). The value of believing in free will: Encouraging a belief in determinism increases cheating. *Psychological Science*, 19, 49–54.

Wada, Y. and Yamamoto, T. (2001). Selective impairment of facial recognition due to a haematoma restricted to the right fusiform and lateral occipital region. *J Neurol Neurosurg Psychiatry* 2001;**71**:254–257 doi:10.1136/jnnp.71.2.254.

Watson J.D. and Crick F.H.C. (1953). A Structure for Deoxyribose Nucleic Acid. *Nature* 171, 737–738.

Watson, James. (1968). *The Double Helix: A Personal Account of the Discovery of the Structure of DNA*. Republished 1980 by Atheneum Books.

Wasserman, Edward A. (1993). Comparative cognition: toward a general understanding of cognition in behavior. *Psychological Science 4*(3), 156. May.

Wasserman, Edward (2009). Personal communications, July 2009 through February 2010.

Wasserman, Edward (2009). Humans, animals and computers: Minding machines? *Revista de Psicología*, Vol. XVIII, Nº 2, received for publication consideration August 13, 2009.

Wiener, J. (1995). *The Beak of the Finch: A Story of Evolution in Our Time*. Vintage Books. New York.

Wilson, E.O. (1975). *Sociobiology: The New Synthesis*. The President and Fellows of Harvard College.

Winterer, G., et al. (2002). Volition to Action—An Event-Related fMRI Study. *Neuroimage 17*, issue 2, 851–858, Oct. 2002; doi:10.1016/S1053-8119(02)91232-2.

Woodhead, G.J., Mutch, C.A., Olson, E.C., Chenn, A. (2006). Cell-autonomous beta-catenin signaling regulates cortical precursor proliferation. *Journal of Neuroscience*, 26, 12620–12620.

Zeiler, M. D. (2002). The Function, Mechanism, and Evolution of Learning and Behavior: A Review of Sara J. Shettleworth's Cognition, Evolution and Behavior. *J. of the Experimental Analysis of Behavior, 78*, 225–235.

Zeiler, M.D. (2003). Personal communication.